THE
LIFE AND TIMES
OF
LAURENCE STERNE

Laurence Sterne
From a mezzotint engraving by Edward Fisher
after the first portrait by Sir Joshua Reynolds

THE
LIFE AND TIMES
OF
LAURENCE STERNE

BY

WILBUR L. CROSS

*Sterling Professor of English & Dean of the
Graduate School in Yale University*

THIRD EDITION
With Alterations and Additions

NEW YORK / RUSSELL & RUSSELL

PRINTED IN THE UNITED STATES OF AMERICA

THE
LIFE AND TIMES
OF
LAURENCE STERNE

THE PREFACE

M Y interest in Laurence Sterne, apart from his two main books, began in 1904 when I edited the Works of the humorist and his Life by Percy Fitzgerald. The publishers gave me a free hand to bring together all the letters and minor writings of Sterne, whether in print or in manuscript, that could be discovered within a reasonable period. This edition of Sterne's Works, though time has since proved it to be incomplete, contained many new letters and the unpublished "Journal to Eliza"—the emotional background to *A Sentimental Journey*.

Fitzgerald's *Life of Laurence Sterne*, which I edited with the permission of the author, was a pioneer book written by a young man midway in the Victorian age, and afterwards revised on the acquisition of important manuscripts by the British Museum. Subsequently Sir Sidney Lee contributed to the *Dictionary of National Biography* an admirable sketch of Sterne, to which I was greatly indebted at the beginning of my studies. It soon became clear, however, that many old errors about Sterne (some of them capital errors) still persisted; and there were also indications of letters and documents in existence which would enlighten the obscure places in Sterne's career and thus assist to a better understanding of the man and his works. I was curious to find out what I could. The book I then wrote (which was published by the Macmillan Company in 1909) was named *The Life and Times of Laurence Sterne*, after an old fashion for similar biographies that aim to give not only the personal history of a man but also some account of his friends, in accordance with the maxim that a man is known by the company he keeps.

The next year came Walter Sichel's *Sterne* bearing a London imprint. A second biography of Sterne within a few months led to a lively controversy in the London *Saturday Review* over where the second man got his materials on such short order. To describe the process, Percy Fitzgerald, who began the bloodless fray, invented the word "Sichelise." "This system of Sichelising," said Mr. Fitzgerald, "seems a simple and easy one. Find out the old and original biographies in which the spade work has been done, dates explored and fixed, original letters collected; take the materials and expatiate on them. Then take care to approach as from an entirely new point of view, as though you had made discoveries." At the same time Lewis Melville was writing a preface to still another biography of the humorist under the title of *The Life and Letters of Laurence Sterne*. This was a biography on a quite different pattern, wherein a large number of Sterne's letters were arranged in their chronological order, with preliminary essays and connecting links. It was the author's plan to let Sterne speak, whenever possible, in his own words, which, all must agree, are "infinitely better" than the words of anyone else. He owed "something," he said, to a recent "American biographer," but his chief reliance had been upon Sir Sidney Lee and others who had previously cultivated the Sterne domain.

Since my biography of Sterne, thus closely followed by two others, first appeared, many new facts about the humorist and his writings have been uncovered and many unpublished letters have escaped from the seclu-

sion of private collections. It was, for example, while
engaged upon Fielding that I met with Sterne's *Unknown World* in *The Gentleman's Magazine,* where
the poem was printed under the initials of his own
name. No one but a biographer can quite appreciate the
pleasure occasioned by a discovery, of minor importance
though it was, that settled the question of disputed authorship. And a similar pleasure was awakened by the
sight of numerous new letters in Sterne's own hand, un-
mutilated by editors. Moreover, there was published in
1923 *Mrs. Montagu, Queen of the Blues,* under the
editorship of Mr. Reginald Blunt, containing a number
of interesting letters that passed between the Bluestocking and Sterne, his wife (who was her cousin), and
Lydia (who was her godchild). In the light of all new
knowledge, I have gone through the first edition of my
Life of Sterne, which has been out of print for several
years, re-phrasing for accuracy of statement, and incor-
porating the fresh material. In the process, I have visu-
alized Sterne's career once more, as may be seen in the
"character" I have drawn of him. The result is the
present work.

The title should be sufficient warning to the reader
not to look for a series of essays on the different aspects
of Sterne's humor, or elaborate comparisons between
Sterne and the humorists before and since his time.
"Books do not live," Augustine Birrell has aptly remarked, "by comparisons, but by their pleasure-giving
qualities." On the temper of Sterne's art and style,
we have already ample disquisitions from Bagehot,
Traill, and Watts-Dunton, not to mention briefer critical opinions from Thackeray, Coleridge, and Carlyle.
Of his influence upon his own and other literatures I
once published a brief sketch; and others, before and

after, have written on various phases of that influence in France, Germany, and Italy, with less attention to England. It yet remains for some one to make, in justice to Sterne, a comprehensive study of this subject for the benefit of the world of letters. But such a study, were it at all adequate, would require of itself a volume. Though I have often quoted what was written of Sterne after his death, and have commented upon his rare qualities as literary artist, my main purpose has been biographical.

As the best way to depict a most singular character, I have employed "the direct method of scrupulous narration" rather than the "subtle strategy" that has come into vogue again since the Great War, of sudden and unexpected attack upon the flank or the rear, as if a biographer's attitude towards his victim should be altogether hostile. It seems quite unfair not to allow a dead man to speak for himself with such words as he may have left behind him in defence of the kind of life he once lived. Had I any motive to represent Sterne otherwise than he was, I should be disarmed by the humorist himself, who said famously: "If the characters of past ages and men are to be drawn at all, they should be drawn like themselves; that is, with their excellencies, and with their foibles." Nowhere have I intended to spare Sterne nor to idealize him. My endeavor has been, first and last, to tell the truth about him—to give him his chance among the immortals.

The questions ever before me have been: What sort of man was Sterne? How did he conduct himself in the days of his obscurity and after he had come into his fame? What did he do and what did he say? What books did he read? What were his pastimes? and what were his pleasures? Who were his friends? and who

were his enemies, if he had any? And what did they say
or think of him? In a word, wherein lay the secret of the
man whose speech and conduct filled the imaginations
of all who knew him intimately, whether in York, London, Paris, or Rome? These questions would be without
much interest, as Nepos once remarked in a similar case,
were not Sterne the author of two books which give him
a large place in modern literature, perhaps by the side
of Rabelais and Cervantes. Certainly the publication of
Tristram Shandy and *A Sentimental Journey* must
be kept in mind as the great events in Sterne's life.
Towards them and his other works must converge all
personal details. It is only because of these books that a
biographer can surely count upon a curiosity to know
something about the personality of him who wrote
them. And if the reader discovers, as he will, that *Tristram Shandy* and *A Sentimental Journey* are in part autobiography, and that their author was as strange a compound of whims as are they, then new points of vantage
may be gained for viewing and judging Sterne stage by
stage in his career, and for achieving a final portrait of
the man in relation to his works.

The materials for a Life of Sterne, though not abundant, are quite adequate at most points. For his childhood, we have the memoirs which he wrote out for his
daughter a few months before his death. For the period
covering his life as Prebendary of York and Vicar of
Sutton, we have a series of letters to a friend; a long
letter to his uncle, amounting almost to an autobiography; a body of anecdotes collected by one who, as a
boy, tagged at his heels and listened to his jests by the
fireside after supper; and a series of local pamphlets in
a lively warfare to which the Yorkshire parson contributed the chief merriment. For Sterne in his fame, we

have over two hundred letters to various friends; many references to him in the newspapers and in contemporary memoirs and correspondence; a journal of his uncensored emotions (sometimes recorded hour by hour) extending over four important months of the year before his death; and the observations of a young man of letters in Paris, who closely watched him in and out of the salons, conversed with him on various occasions, and wrote down his impressions of the Chevalier Sterne. Finally, there are the portraits of Sterne by the great painters of the age, who invited him to their tables, studied him there under the most favorable conditions, and asked him to sit to them the next morning.

Nevertheless a Life of Sterne proved no easy task for several reasons. In the first place, it was a slow process to collect materials which lie dispersed in many books, documents, and manuscripts. True, this work had been already performed to some extent by others; but what they had accomplished had to be verified and then extended in many directions. Again, it was necessary to keep always in mind the question how far *Tristram Shandy* and *A Sentimental Journey* were a rendering of actual incidents in Sterne's personal history. This question can never be quite answered; for all that a biographer can expect is corroborative evidence here and there from external sources. Whether he goes right or wrong in his inferences from such facts as are at his command, depends partly upon his judgment, and partly upon the conception he unconsciously forms of Sterne's character as he goes along. No one can ever feel quite sure of himself in dealing with these apparent correspondences. He knows that incidents in Sterne's life, all the way from boyhood down to near death, are in Sterne's books; but he knows also that they are entangled with much that belongs only to the realm of his art. The cautious and yet very large use I have made of *Tristram Shandy* and *A Sentimental Journey* will appear justified, I trust, in the course of the narrative.

Moreover, Sterne's letters, upon which a biographer must mainly depend, have survived in a wretched condition. Many of those that appeared in the years following his death are undated. Their sequence can be determined, if at all, only from internal evidence. The early collections sometimes contain forgeries which must be sifted out; and in letters for the most part genuine, passages have been suppressed and replaced by new ones. Names of correspondents and other persons are commonly indicated by an initial or two; and at times there is no clue to them at all, unless one may read a line of stars into a name. In a similar but not identical way, Sterne's correspondence as published in later times has been interpolated out of sheer dishonesty, or modified in phrasing so as to conform to the reticence of the Victorian era. Were there space here, it would be interesting to illustrate in detail how this has been done. A passage, for example, in one of the letters to the Rev. John Blake was deleted by the editor of the series, and compensation was made for the loss by inserting phrases which do not occur anywhere in the originals. In other cases, a letter in its published form may be at variance with the manuscript all the way through. Occasionally a letter has survived for comparison in three versions: as a preliminary draft, as it passed through the post, and as it was dressed up by an editor for the public.

At one time or another, I have examined all accessible manuscripts that have come to my notice. The largest single collection is in the British Museum, whose officers granted me the usual privileges for having them

copied or photographed. The story of Mrs. Draper's
life and of her friendship with Sterne was rendered
possible by the courtesy of the late Lord Basing, who
placed at my disposal Mrs. Draper's unpublished correspondence and other documents preserved at Hoddington, some of which have since appeared in print. A
part of the Letter Book in which Sterne kept letters
which he particularly liked, whether his own or from
his friends, was acquired by the late J. Pierpont Morgan, who generously gave me access to it. This old book,
besides containing a number of letters which had never
been published, proved the authenticity of several other
letters long supposed to be forgeries. Since the death of
Mr. Morgan, important additions have been made to
the Sterne correspondence by his son, J. Pierpont Morgan. These new letters of the Morgan Collection, now
rivalling the one in the British Museum, I have read
during the revision of my book. They are among the
liveliest that ever came from the gay pen of Laurence
Sterne. With the permission of Mr. Morgan and the
co-operation of Miss Belle da Costa Greene I am able
to print, with several photogravures, the entire Letter
Book, wherein may be read Sterne's letters as he first
wrote them or afterwards copied them out. When I began with Sterne twenty years ago, biographers still felt
the constraint of an era that had not quite passed. Fortunately they may now speak out and present manuscript letters without bowdlerizing them.

Copies of one or more letters were also once supplied
by Mr. Alfred Huth, of London, Mr. A. H. Joline, of
New York City, Mr. W. K. Bixby, of St. Louis, Messrs.
Charles Scribner's Sons and Messrs. Dodd, Mead & Co.,
of New York City, and Messrs. Robson and Co. and
Messrs. Henry Sotheran and Co., of London. Alas, sev-

eral of the men who in the first instance permitted me to examine their Sterne manuscripts are no longer living. A few months before his death, Mr. W. H. Arnold, of Nutley, N. J., sent me copies of three letters with the interesting "Memorandums" that Sterne left with Elizabeth Montagu on going abroad. These manuscripts were afterwards posthumously published. A copy of one of the "Hannah letters" I have just received from Mr. A. Edward Newton, of Philadelphia. Three other letters, though previously known to me, I have read again in the collection of Mr. R. B. Adam, of Buffalo; and Dr. A. S. W. Rosenbach, of Philadelphia, placed in my hands Sterne's own letters and the letters concerning him that have survived in the vast correspondence of Elizabeth Montagu.

In quoting from private manuscripts, I have aimed to keep well within the bounds set by their owners. All excerpts from original letters have been printed as Sterne and his friends wrote them, save that numerals and abbreviations have usually been written out in full, and occasional changes have been made in capitals and punctuation where the one or the other seemed very awkward or very obscure. In all this, I have remembered, though I could not always follow it to the letter, Sterne's injunction to his printer: "That, at your peril, you do not presume to alter or transpose one Word, nor rectify one false Spelling, nor so much as add or diminish one Comma or Tittle."

Underlying this account of the humorist's life, especially of his life in the north, is information derived from local records and newspapers. The Institutions of the Diocese of York and the Act Book of the Dean and Chapter not only shed light upon the details of Sterne's ecclesiastical appointments, but they also served to iden-

tify many of his friends at York. The parish book at
Sutton I found curious for its Shandean entries; and the
memorials of deeds in the Registry Office at Northallerton likewise revealed Sterne's dealings in land. In
this connection, I remember especially the Rev. Canon
Watson, of the Minster Library, by whose aid I discovered a copy of the first edition of Sterne's *Political Romance*. Subsequently I found two other copies of the
satire among volumes of anonymous pamphlets elsewhere. The Minster Library contains also many other
local pamphlets indispensable to the biographer, and a
file of *The York Courant*, covering a large part of
Sterne's active life. I should not forget, too, for their
assistance, Dr. George A. Auden, of Birmingham,
Mr. A. H. Hudson, Registrar of the Diocese of York,
the late T. B. Whytehead, Clerk of the Dean and
Chapter, and Mr. William Brown, F.S.A., of Thirsk,
with his exact knowledge of local conditions in the
eighteenth century. I was indebted to Mr. W. W. Smith,
of Lincoln, for Sterne's appointment to St. Ives, as recorded in the Act Book of the Bishop of Lincoln, and to
Mr. Edwin Abbott, Librarian of Jesus College, for all
entries relating to Sterne in the college register. Various
collectors in England and the United States have permitted me to inspect their first editions of Sterne's separate publications. Among them I wish to mention especially Mr. Harold Murdock of the Harvard University
Press.

By the courtesy of the owners, I have had by me pho-
tographs of the portraits for which Sterne sat in England, France, and Italy, many contemporary and later
engravings after these portraits, and a group of amusing
(sometimes coarse) caricatures. In various books nearly
all the great portraits of Sterne have been reproduced,

and several of the caricatures also, including his own cruel sketch of his wife. Naturally it has been rather difficult to choose among them for illustration here. Still, after all that may be said for the other portraits, the one by Sir Joshua Reynolds representing Sterne in the first flush of his fame is beyond question the best and most characteristic. This remarkable portrait, now at Lansdowne House, was photographed for me by permission of Lord Lansdowne. If the photograph may be trusted, time has wrought havoc with the original. The eyes, once wonderful, have grown dull and they will soon disappear altogether. So at last I decided to substitute for the original Reynolds portrait the very striking mezzotint engraving after it by Edward Fisher, which Miss Greene, the director of the Pierpont Morgan Library, placed at my disposal. In the text I have described a second and almost unknown portrait of Sterne by Reynolds, which is in no way comparable with the painter's masterpiece.

Sterne's face in repose was rather sober. No visitors, I daresay, were by to enliven it when he was painted by Gainsborough at Bath in ruffles and short wig. The Gainsborough now hangs in the Salford Art Galleries, where it is deteriorating as fast as the Reynolds portrait. The full face of youth is shown in the Ramsay portrait on the walls of the great hall at Jesus College. The prominent nose which was the occasion of many a jest dominates the portrait bust by Nollekens and is caricatured in Patch's sketch of Yorick confronted by Death. The Nollekens bust in terra-cotta, of which a marble replica was presented to the National Portrait Gallery a few years ago, somehow gives us Sterne as the twentieth century would like to have him.

With some hesitancy I have put aside several of the

portraits as less significant than others or because they may be easily seen elsewhere. Likewise all the third and fourth rate portraits belonging to the latter part of the eighteenth century, of which may be mentioned one by Thomas and another by Hopkins, neither of whom ever saw Sterne. Of the caricatures, some would give offence and others are very crude. There is one jolly little scene in Vauxhall Gardens where Yorick is pointed out to bystanders as he is walking with a lady on his arm. Is it Mrs. Vesey, the Bluestocking? I could not omit, of course "The Mountebank and his Macaroni," of which the second figure, by Thomas Bridges, shows Sterne not so much as a macaroni as a clown exhibiting himself on the streets of York in days long before he came into his fame.

Very interesting is Sterne as he appeared to a Frenchman in the water-color by Carmontelle, formerly in the collection of the Duc d'Aumale at Chantilly. A photogravure for this book has been made from a beautifully colored engraving by Messrs. Colnaghi and Company of London. When Sterne sat to Carmontelle, he was worn thin by disease and dinners. Did Sterne at that time really have the Voltairean features? Or did Carmontelle put them in by way of compliment? Through the courtesy of Mr. George A. Plimpton, of New York, who has recently added them to his collection of literary portraits, I am able to add the pastels of Sterne and his wife by Francis Cotes, dated 1759 and 1761 respectively. They are the "crayon-portraits" which Hawthorne once saw in the upper rooms of a bookseller in Old Boston. The novelist was rather hard, I think, on Sterne's wife, "looking," he remarked of her picture, "so haughty and unamiable, that the wonder is, not that he ultimately left her, but how he ever contrived to live a week with such an awful woman."

This last year an oil painting, said to be of Sterne, by an unknown hand, showing him wasted by disease, was purchased by the National Portrait Gallery. Where, one wonders, is the bust of Sterne that Roubiliac made for Garrick? . . .

April 10, 1925

A THIRD edition of this biography, now in a single volume, has given me an opportunity to revise certain statements on Sterne's life at York before he became famous, in the light of new material, such as the investigations of Mr. Lewis Perry Curtis, whose book entitled *The Politicks of Laurence Sterne* has partially restored a lost episode in the humorist's early career. Occasionally some rearrangement of paragraphs with emendations have been necessary or advisable in various other chapters for the proper sequence of incident. Several additions have also been made to the Bibliography, of which the most notable are Sterne's political writings and a complete manuscript of *A Sentimental Journey*, partly in Sterne's own hand, which has been acquired by the Pierpont Morgan Library. Again I have to thank collectors, readers, and critics for their assistance in the correction of minor errors.

The index has been prepared in collaboration with Miss Mary C. Withington, secretary to the Librarian of the University.

W. L. C.

Yale University,
    September, 1929.

THE CONTENTS

THE ILLUSTRATIONS

THE

LIFE and TIMES

OF

LAURENCE STERNE

CHAP. I.

Birth and Education. 1713-1736

I.

THE great humorist whose life I have undertaken to relate anew, would have been amused by a serious attempt
to discover him among his ancestors. Musty records preserved
religiously by his Yorkshire neighbors, that they might the
more readily boast the achievements of a great-grandfather,
interested him, it is true, greatly; but only because they furnished matter for jest. His *Tristram Shandy* is, as all readers
of it know, a burlesque history of a typical English family
(much like Sterne's own) that gained its rank in the time of
Henry the Eighth, and subsequently sank under the disgrace
of flat noses and inauspicious names. The Shandys could claim

in the sixteenth century, says Sterne with near reference to himself, "no less than a dozen alchymists," whose souls passed on, a century or two later, into an archbishop, a Welsh judge, "some three or four aldermen," and eventually into a mountebank. His more ideal self, which bears the name of Parson Yorick, the humorist aptly derived in direct line from Shakespeare's Yorick of Denmark, whose "flashes of merriment were wont to set the table on a roar" far back in the days of the good King Hamlet.

Despite this raillery of himself as akin to the old alchemists and court jesters, Sterne was glad enough to count among his ancestors an Archbishop of York and a succession of country gentlemen since the fifteenth century. Long annoyed by scribblers' tales about his early life and whence he came, he set down, some six months before his death, certain particulars of family history and of his boyhood for his daughter Lydia, "in case hereafter she should have a curiosity or a kinder motive to know them."

It may well be that Danish blood really flowed in Sterne's veins as well as in the imaginary Yorick's; for the family to which he belonged sprang from the yeomanry and minor gentry of old East Anglia—Norfolk and Suffolk—and the border shires where the Danes settled in great numbers. Thence various members of the family migrated to the north until Yorkshire became their chief home, while others settled in Ireland, establishing there a collateral branch, which included John Sterne (1624-1669), the founder of the Irish College of Physicians at Dublin, and his son, likewise named John (1660-1745), who became in turn Dean of St. Patrick's and Bishop of Clogher. The latter figures in literary history as an intimate friend of Swift and Stella, whom he entertained with profuse hospitality. The more learned of the family evidently associated their name with the old English word *stearn*, dialectical *starn* to this day, signifying a *starling*; for as soon as they rose to rank and wealth, their arms appeared, with some variation, as "gold, a chevron engrailed between three crosses flory sable, surmounted with a starling in proper colors for a crest." That starling, made captive, it will be remembered, was long afterwards brought into the *Sentimental Journey* as the motif for a pathetic discourse on the bitterness of slavery.

Laurence Sterne, the subject of this biography, was in direct descent from William Sterne, who was living towards the close of Elizabeth's reign at Cropwell-Butler, a village and manor to the south of Bingham in Nottinghamshire. William Sterne was in turn lineally descended, as his arms clearly indicate, from the Sternes that had been long seated near Cambridge, first at Stapleford and afterwards at Stow-cum-Quy, whence issued also the Sternes in Ireland. Remoter ancestry of the family points especially to the Sternes who by marriage with the Gambons came into possession of Whitwell Hall in Norfolk under the Lancastrian kings. A son of the William Sterne aforementioned, named Simon, settled at Mansfield, "a flourishing and genteel market town" some miles to the north of Cropwell-Butler, where he married Margery, daughter of Gregory Walker and widow of one Charles Cartwright. Of the marriage was born, in or near 1596, Richard Sterne, who, becoming Archbishop of York, was the first to give distinction to the family name.

This Richard Sterne, great-grandfather of the humorist, was a man who combined shrewd intelligence with that energy necessary for making one's way in the world. As a boy "two remarkable deliverances" were related of him by the old story-tellers. He fell into a sluice which carried him beneath a mill-wheel, and tumbled from a church-steeple where he was playing at see-saw with another boy; but in both cases he escaped unharmed under the guidance of "a gracious Providence." He attended the free school at Mansfield, whence he passed, at the age of fifteen, to Trinity College, Cambridge. After taking the usual degrees in arts, he was elected Fellow of Corpus Christi, and for ten years thereafter "engaged in the instruction of pupils with credit both to himself and to the college." In the meantime, both of the great universities honored him with degrees in divinity, and he became well known among ecclesiastics—the distinction seems rather grotesque—for a summary of "the 3600 faults in our printed Bibles," a feat in line with the labors of Scaliger and other learned classical scholars of the preceding generation who had awakened wonder by the multitude of errors which they were able to discover in ancient texts. Early in 1634, the Bishop of Ely, by direction of his Majesty, appointed him Master of Jesus College. To Sterne's prestige as teacher and scholar was now added that of an able administrator. By his efforts among the fellows and other friends, funds were raised for various purposes, but especially for building "the north side of the outer court" of Jesus College, which still stands "as a monument to his name."

The young Master of Jesus—not yet forty years old—was, as might be inferred from his position, a most ardent supporter of the existing order in church and state. Archbishop Laud summoned him to London and enrolled him among his chaplains, to say nothing of other substantial honors conferred upon him: all, doubtless, with a view to having at Cambridge an adherent who could be trusted to furnish full and accurate information concerning things ecclesiastical. To King Charles and his agents who came frequently to Cambridge, Sterne was also equally loyal. In the summer of 1642, the king set up his standard at Nottingham and made ready for battle. At that juncture, Sterne joined with two other Cambridge masters in collecting and sending moneys and plate to his Majesty. Cromwell was on the watch, and though the treasure reached the king, the masters were surrounded while at prayers in their several chapels, and taken up to London; led captive, says the contemporary account, "through Bartholomew Fair, and so far as Temple Bar, and back through the city to prison in the Tower, on purpose that they might be hooted at or stoned by the rabble rout." During three years of imprisonment in various places, Sterne was subjected at times to barbarous usage, barely escaping transportation; but these were among common incidents of the Revolution, as was likewise his ejection from the mastership of Jesus College.

During this dark period Richard Sterne once stepped forth to the light to take part in a memorable scene. The Revolution was moving on swiftly. The king had been defeated at Marston Moor, and Laud was about to go the way of Strafford. Scant four days were given the archbishop to prepare for death. On Laud's petition to Parliament that one of his ancient chaplains might be sent to him to administer spiritual comfort, if he must die, Dr. Sterne was selected. Sterne was with his friend and patron during the last three days of his life, and attended him to the scaffold. After reading his last sermon and last public prayer, Laud turned towards the block, and, as he did so, he placed the manuscript in the hands of his chaplain, that the world might have true and faithful copies thereof. Liberated soon after this terrible event, Sterne passed many subsequent years in seclusion at Stevenage in Hertfordshire, where, save for a small pension from one of Laud's friends, he earned a livelihood by taking pupils. When Charles the Second returned to his own, Sterne was among the first to win preferment. A few months in his Cambridge mastership once more and three years Bishop of Carlisle, he was translated in the spring of 1664 to the Archbishopric of York, where he sat until his death on June 18, 1683. His body lies buried in the chapel of St. Stephen in his own cathedral at York. To his memory his great-grandson Richard erected a marble monument with a canopy, beneath which half reclines a mitred figure with the head resting upon one of the hands. A fine portrait of the archbishop in his splendid robes, a mezzotint by Francis Place of York, hangs near Cranmer's over the dais in the hall of Jesus College. With eyes curiously askance, the dignified prelate looks down the hall, past Coleridge, upon the youthful portrait of his great-grandson, as if in question whether he should own him.

It would be impossible to imagine the archbishop sitting down to *Gargantua* or *Pantagruel*, the nearest approach to *Tristram Shandy* in those days. His face, with no trace of humor in it, looks too serious for that. As a young man, this Richard Sterne wrote Latin verses and commented upon the

Psalms. Later in life he bore a hand in Brian Walton's Polyglot Bible involving nine languages, and subsequently assisted in a revision of the Book of Common Prayer. After his death appeared a Latin treatise of his on logic, with illustrations drawn mostly from the Scriptures, as was the fashion in those days. While Archbishop of York, he made many friends and many enemies. To those who agreed with him "he was a man of eminent worth and abilities." "He was," says a letter from York just after his death, "greatly respected and generally lamented. All the clergy commemorate his sweet condescensions, his free communications, faithful counsels, exemplary temperance, cheerful hospitality and bountiful charity."* On the other hand, Burnet regarded him as only "a sour, ill-tempered" ecclesiastic, who, after gaining the see of York, "minded chiefly the enriching of his family." As a politician, it is said further, he was more than ordinarily compliant in his last years to the Court and to the Duke of York; wherefore came the suspicion that he was at heart a Papist. Baxter, who clashed with him in debate at the Savoy Conference over a reformed liturgy, was surprised to find deceit concealed by a face that "look'd so honestly and gravely and soberly."

Although these adverse opinions of two eminent divines were no doubt colored by political and religious dislike, they nevertheless point to a truth. Richard Sterne was a conspicuous example among the clergy of the Restoration whose ideals of church dignity and ecclesiastical polity had been derived from Archbishop Laud. To the new age they appeared narrow and bigoted. Like his famous descendant, the archbishop was also irritable and hasty in temper, and prone to provoke a quarrel. Edward Rainbowe, who succeeded him at Carlisle, found the episcopal palace barely habitable and brought suit against him for dilapidations. While he held the see of York, Sterne cer-

---

* Nicolson and Burn, *History of Antiquities of Westmoreland and Cumberland*, II, 290 (London, 1777). In contrast, see Burnet, *History of his own Times*, II, 208 (London, 1818); and *Reliquiæ Baxterianæ*, part II, 338 (London, 1696).

tainly amassed a fortune, but not, as Burnet charges, wholly for his own benefit or that of his family. The archbishop's benefactions were numerous and liberal. From his own purse he contributed, for example, £1800 towards the rebuilding of St. Paul's Cathedral after the great fire; and some years before his death he founded, by an annual rent charge of £60 on his manors in Yorkshire, six scholarships at Cambridge—four at Jesus College and two at Corpus Christi—for natives of Nottingham and Yorkshire. One of these scholarships was to come in the course of time to the author of *Tristram Shandy*.

The archbishop had married, sometime in middle life, a woman who was his junior by some years—Elizabeth, daughter of Edward Dickenson, lord of the manor of Farnborough, Hampshire, who bore him thirteen children. She died on March 6, 1673-4, at the age of fifty-eight, while on a visit to London, and was buried with her family at Farnborough. At his own death, ten years later, the archbishop divided his comfortable estates among his three surviving sons.* The eldest son Richard, to whom fell the largest share, married and took as his seat Kilvington Hall, near Thirsk and within the district where Laurence Sterne was eventually to hold several church livings. He was a justice of the peace and represented Ripon in one or more Parliaments under Charles the Second. Ralph Thoresby, the antiquary, who passed five days with him in the coach up to London, found him "very good company (not so hot as I feared, being the archbishop's son)."† William, the second son of the archbishop, besides inheriting "lands and tenements" at Ryther in the fertile valley of the Wharfe, was bequeathed five hundred pounds. He married Frances, daughter of William Cartwright of Normanton, and settled at Mansfield on the estate of his grandfather. The third son, known as Simon Sterne of Halifax, received by the terms of his father's will, in lieu of lands, five hundred pounds

* The will was signed and sealed on April 14, 1683.—Registry of Wills at York.

† Thoresby, *Diary*, I, 154 (London, 1830).

outright, three hundred pounds in East India stock, and a remission of his debts to the archbishop. This Simon Sterne of
Halifax, who seems to have been improvident in his youth,
was the grandfather of Laurence Sterne.

At this point another strain in the descent of the humorist
becomes of especial interest. Simon Sterne married, to his
great good fortune, Mary Jaques, heiress to a large estate at
Elvington, near York on the river Derwent. Her grandfather,
Sir Roger Jaques, was a prosperous merchant and alderman
of York back in the time of the first Stuarts. A staunch loyalist
in a city where the loyalists predominated, he rose, in 1639, to
the honorable post of Lord Mayor, and was knighted in that
year by King Charles while resting at York on his way north
against the Scots. Roger Jaques had been aided, no doubt, in
his career, gaining thereby social position as well as wealth, by
marrying into the Rawdons, one of the oldest and richest of
the northern families. The Mary Rawdon whose hand he succeeded in winning, was the daughter of a certain Laurence
Rawdon, who settled at York during the last years of Elizabeth, and made a fortune in trade. Her brother was the Marmaduke Rawdon who wrote an agreeable account of travels in
Britain and on the Continent.* In the glimpses given of her
by Marmaduke in his book, Lady Jaques, as she was always
called, appears as a charming, well-bred woman, who was
careful to live in accordance with her station. She goes up to
London with her husband to see the "rarities," including a
visit with a merry company to the *Royal Sovereign,* a big ship,
newly built and lying down the river; they have an audience
with the king and queen at Greenwich; and thoroughly tired
out with a month's feasting among relatives and friends, Lady
Jaques is glad to get back to Yorkshire once more. During her
last years—she survived her husband—she passed her time between Elvington and her house on the Pavement, then one of
the fashionable streets at York. She kept a coach and might be
seen on a fine day taking the air in it, accompanied by a blacka-

* *Life of Marmaduke Rawdon,* edited by Robert Davies for the
Camden Society (London, 1863).

moor running along by the side. It is altogether a delightful
picture such as one ought to find somewhere among the ancestors of Laurence Sterne.

The Mary Jaques whom Simon Sterne married was the
granddaughter of this genteel and vivacious Mary Rawdon.
Her brother Roger dying without issue, she succeeded as his
heir to the lordship of Elvington. With £1800 Simon Sterne
purchased Woodhouse, a large estate at Skircoat to the southwest of Halifax, with an Elizabethan mansion looking across
the beautiful valley of the Calder. Nothing very distinctive
has been discovered about him. He was a justice of the peace
and governor of a charity for the poor of Halifax. He died
at Woodhouse Hall, "having undergone a severe salivation
for a cancer in the mouth," and was buried at Halifax on
April 17, 1703.

Simon Sterne left three sons and three daughters. To Richard, the eldest son, born in 1680, descended the estates at
Elvington and Woodhouse. In the November following his
father's death, Richard married Dorothy, daughter of Thomas
Priestley of Halifax and widow of Samuel Lister of Shibden
Hall, two miles to the northeast of Halifax, where he resided
for several years. His first wife dying, he married in 1714
Esther, daughter and heiress of Mr. Timothy Booth of Halifax. Most fortunate in his marriages, he grew to be the
wealthiest of the Sternes, possessing, besides his inherited estates, lands at Ovenden and Hipperholme. He bore the chief
hand in reorganizing the grammar school at Skircoat, of
which the Archbishop of York appointed him one of the governors. He was also a governor of a similar foundation at
Hipperholme. Hot and litigious in temper, he became involved
in several law suits and in a bitter quarrel with the vicar of
his parish, who refused him the Sacrament. He died suddenly
at Bradford on October 9, 1732, while on his way to York,
and was buried at Halifax. He is the uncle who took in little
Laurence at Woodhouse and sent him to school. The third
son of Simon Sterne, named Jaques and born in 1695 or
1696, will enter these memoirs at a later stage, as the violent

Precentor of York who first helped his nephew and then turned against him in great bitterness. Between Richard and Jaques, was born, about 1692, Roger Sterne, the father of the humorist.*

To Roger Sterne, as a younger brother, there were open three obvious careers. He might have married, like so many of his ancestors, an heiress and settled in Yorkshire as a country gentleman. He might have gone like his brother Jaques to the university, and have easily secured a place in the Church within the patronage of some relative or friend of the family. Finally there was the army. He chose the army as in more accord, no doubt, with a roving disposition.

Among the crack regiments raised in 1702, on the outbreak of the war with France and Spain, known in history as the War of the Spanish Succession, was the Thirty-Fourth or the Cumberland Regiment of Foot. Its first colonel was Robert, Lord Lucas, and among the captains was Richard Steele, the wit and essayist. The men, as one may view them in old plates, made a smart appearance in their tri-cornered hats, long scarlet coats richly trimmed with yellow, and white gaiters reaching above the knees. Under their second colonel, Hans Hamilton, who succeeded Lord Lucas in 1705, they proved their mettle in Spain during and after the siege of Barcelona, where they were terribly cut up in a gallant charge against the French. With the prestige won in Spain, the regiment returned to England in 1707 to recruit; and the next year it was ordered north on the alarm of an invasion of Scotland by the French in favor of the Stuart Pretender. For several months the Thirty-Fourth was stationed at Leeds, and while there it

* The older pedigrees of the Sterne family have been corrected, revised, and enlarged in the *Publications of the Harleian Society*. See especially in this series *Familiæ Minorum Gentium*, II, 516-517; the *Visitations of Norfolk in 1563 and 1613*; and the *Visitations of Cambridge in 1575 and 1619*. Miscellaneous information is to be found in the *Northowram or Coley Register*, edited by J. Horsfall Turner (London, 1881). None of the pedigrees gives the date of birth for Roger Sterne; nor is it contained in the parish registers either at Halifax or Elvington.

may have gained, among its new recruits of 1708, Roger Sterne, then a mere stripling not more than sixteen years old.

In 1709, the regiment was sent over to the Netherlands, where it was engaged for some months in garrison duty, owing, says the chronicle,* to the fact that it was composed mostly of "young soldiers." The next year it joined the main army of Marlborough. At the siege of Douay, it was "employed on duty in the trenches, carrying on the approaches, repulsing the sallies of the garrison, and storming the outworks," in all of which it repeatedly distinguished itself. On the conclusion of peace at Utrecht in 1713, the Thirty-Fourth was withdrawn with other regiments to England and soon afterwards it was reduced. But on the uprising of the Scots in 1715 under the Earl of Mar, the regiment was re-formed with Thomas Chudleigh as colonel, who had in fact succeeded Hans Hamilton before the Peace of Utrecht. Among the new officers appears the name of Roger Sterne as one of nine ensigns. After varied service in Ireland, the restored regiment took part in the siege and capture of Vigo, in various operations in Flanders, and in the defence of Gibraltar. Under Chudleigh, as well as under Hamilton, the Thirty-Fourth was conspicuous for its bravery in the field and "its good conduct in quarters."

Notwithstanding his long service, Roger Sterne attained to no high place in the army. To the last he seems to have been only a poor ensign, improvident and good-natured. He was described by his son, it should be said in passing, as "Lieutenant in Handaside's regiment," which was the Twenty-Second. But the statement about his rank as well as his regiment was likely an error of memory. At the outset of his career the ensign made, in the view of his family, a most unfortunate marriage. Following the army in Flanders was "a noted sutler" named Nuttle, who was stepfather to Agnes Hebert, "widow of a captain of a good family," and clearly, as the name shows, of

* Richard Cannon, *Historical Record of the Thirty-Fourth, or The Cumberland Regiment of Foot* (London, 1844).

French descent on her father's side.* Roger Sterne was in debt to Nuttle, and, to quit the score, he relieved the sutler of further support of his wife's daughter, by marrying her on September 25, 1711. The story of Roger Sterne and his family subsequent to this whimsical marriage is related in the brief memoir that the humorist wrote out for his daughter Lydia the year before his death. The pathetic narrative is interwoven with the birth of Laurence and other children, and with those movements of the regiment which we have outlined in advance for the sake of clearness.

"This Nuttle," says the memoir, after telling why Roger Sterne married Agnes Hebert, "had a son by my grandmother —a fine person of a man but a graceless whelp—what became of him I know not.—The family (if any left), live now at Clonmel in the south of Ireland, at which town I was born November 24th, 1713, a few days after my mother arrived from Dunkirk.—My birth-day was ominous to my poor father, who was, the day after our arrival, with many other brave officers broke, and sent adrift into the wide world with a wife and two children—the elder of which was Mary; she was born in Lisle in French Flanders, July the tenth, one thousand seven hundred and twelve, New Stile.—This child was most unfortunate—she married one Weemans in Dublin —who used her most unmercifully—spent his substance, became a bankrupt, and left my poor sister to shift for herself, —which she was able to do but for a few months, for she went to a friend's house in the country, and died of a broken heart. She was a most beautiful woman—of a fine figure, and deserved a better fate.—The regiment, in which my father served, being broke, he left Ireland as soon as I was able to be carried, with the rest of his family, and came to the family seat at Elvington, near York, where his mother lived. She was daughter to Sir Roger Jaques, and an heiress. There we so-

---

* In *Notes and Queries* for Oct., 1910, R. M. Hutchinson-Low describes a Church of England Prayer Book, printed in French in 1706, over the preface of which appears the name of "Agnus [*sic*] Sterne." The book came to Mr. Hutchinson-Low's library from Halifax.

journed for about ten months, when the regiment was established, and our household decamped with bag and baggage for Dublin—within a month of our arrival, my father left us, being ordered to Exeter, where, in a sad winter, my mother and her two children followed him, travelling from Liverpool by land to Plymouth. (Melancholy description of this journey not necessary to be transmitted here.) In twelve months we were all sent back to Dublin.—My mother, with three of us, (for she laid in at Plymouth of a boy, Joram), took ship at Bristol, for Ireland, and had a narrow escape from being cast away by a leak springing up in the vessel.—At length, after many perils, and struggles, we got to Dublin.—There my father took a large house, furnished it, and in a year and a half's time spent a great deal of money.——

"In the year one thousand seven hundred and nineteen, all unhing'd again; the regiment was ordered, with many others, to the Isle of Wight, in order to embark for Spain in the Vigo expedition. We accompanied the regiment, and were driven into Milford Haven, but landed at Bristol, from thence by land to Plymouth again, and to the Isle of Wight—where I remember we stayed encamped some time before the embarkation of the troops—(in this expedition from Bristol to Hampshire we lost poor Joram—a pretty boy, four years old, of the small-pox), my mother, sister, and myself, remained at the Isle of Wight during the Vigo Expedition, and until the regiment had got back to Wicklow in Ireland, from whence my father sent for us.—We had poor Joram's loss supplied during our stay in the Isle of Wight, by the birth of a girl, Anne, born September the twenty-third, one thousand seven hundred and nineteen.—This pretty blossom fell at the age of three years, in the barracks of Dublin—she was, as I well remember, of a fine delicate frame, not made to last long, as were most of my father's babes.—We embarked for Dublin, and had all been cast away by a most violent storm; but through the intercessions of my mother, the captain was prevailed upon to turn back into Wales, where we stayed a month, and at length got into Dublin, and travelled by land to Wicklow,

where my father had for some weeks given us over for lost.——
We lived in the barracks at Wicklow, one year, (one thousand
seven hundred and twenty) when Devijeher (so called after
Colonel Devijeher,*) was born; from thence we decamped to
stay half a year with Mr. Fetherston, a clergyman, about seven
miles from Wicklow, who being a relation of my mother's,
invited us to his parsonage at Animo.——It was in this parish,
during our stay, that I had that wonderful escape in falling
through a mill-race whilst the mill was going, and of being
taken up unhurt——the story is incredible, but known for truth
in all that part of Ireland——where hundreds of the common
people flocked to see me.——

"From hence we followed the regiment to Dublin, where
we lay in the barracks a year.——In this year, one thousand
seven hundred and twenty-one, I learned to write, &c.——The
regiment, ordered in twenty-two, to Carrickfergus in the
north of Ireland; we all decamped, but got no further than
Drogheda, thence ordered to Mullengar, forty miles west,
where by Providence we stumbled upon a kind relation, a
collateral descendant from Archbishop Sterne, who took us all
to his castle and kindly entertained us for a year——and sent us
to the regiment at Carrickfergus, loaded with kindnesses, &c.
——a most rueful and tedious journey had we all, in March, to
Carrickfergus, where we arrived in six or seven days——little
Devijeher here died, he was three years old——He had been left
behind at nurse at a farmhouse near Wicklow, but was
fetch'd to us by my father the summer after——another child
sent to fill his place, Susan; this babe too left us behind in this
weary journey——The autumn of that year, or the spring afterwards, (I forget which) my father got leave of his colonel to
fix me at school——which he did near Halifax, with an able
master; with whom I staid some time, 'till by God's care of
me my cousin Sterne, of Elvington, became a father to me,
and sent me to the university, &c. &c. To pursue the thread of
our story, my father's regiment was the year after ordered to

* Should be Colonel Devischer——evidently a misreading of the manuscript.

Londonderry, where another sister was brought forth, Catherine, still living, but most unhappily estranged from me by my uncle's wickedness, and her own folly—from this station the regiment was sent to defend Gibraltar, at the siege, where my father was run through the body by Captain Phillips,* in a duel, (the quarrel begun about a goose) with much difficulty he survived—tho' with an impaired constitution, which was not able to withstand the hardships it was put to—for he was sent to Jamaica, [with his colonel and a part of his regiment] where he soon fell by the country fever, which took away his senses first, and made a child of him, and then, in a month or two, walking about continually without complaining, till the moment he sat down in an arm chair, and breathed his last—which was at Port Antonio, on the north of the island."†

Of the poor ensign, perhaps just advanced to lieutenant, who died under circumstances so distressing, far from home sometime in March, 1731, the son retained to the last most vivid recollections. "My father," the narrative goes on to say, "was a little smart man—active to the last degree, in all exercises—most patient of fatigue and disappointments, of which it pleased God to give him full measure—he was in his temper somewhat rapid, and hasty—but of a kindly, sweet disposition, void of all design; and so innocent in his own intentions, that he suspected no one; so that you might have cheated him ten times a day, if nine had not been sufficient for your purpose." At that time Laurence was still in school

* Christopher Philips. In the *Dublin University Magazine* for September, 1862 (Vol. LX. 285), are given details of the duel. "The affair took place," it is said there, "in a room; and Captain Philips put his rapier with such vigor through Captain Sterne's person, that he actually pinned him to the wall behind. Then, with infinite presence of mind, the little smart man begged Captain Philips, with much courtesy, that before withdrawing his instrument he would have the courtesy to brush off any plaster adherent to the point, which it would be disagreeable to him to have introduced into his system."

† A theatrical company that went out to Jamaica in 1733 to play the *Beggar's Opera*, buried, in the course of two months, "their third Polly and two of their men."—W. R. Chetwood, *General History of the Stage*, 41 (London, 1749).

at Halifax and his mother and sister Catherine were living with friends in Ireland. On the death of her husband, Mrs. Sterne received a pension of £20 a year, and to add to her income she afterwards opened an embroidery school. She proved to be, as will be duly related, an ill-bred woman, with whom none of her husband's family cared to associate. It is doubtless more agreeable to let the mind rest upon Roger Sterne, from whom passed to his son the volatile temperament of his race as we have seen it forming from the archbishop down through the Rawdons—vivacious, quick to take an affront, and yet withal most kindly. In the ensign who fought a duel over a goose surely lurked a humorist. But we should not forget the mother of Laurence Sterne. It is equally significant that there was probably French and Celtic as well as Danish and Saxon blood in the veins of the man who wrote *A Sentimental Journey through France and Italy.*

Clonmel, the place where Laurence Sterne was born, says the memoir, on November 24, 1713, is a small Irish town above Waterford, in the valley of the Suir. His mother had come there from Dunkirk that her child might be brought forth among her own people. He was named Laurence, it would seem, after that distant ancestor we have mentioned— Laurence Rawdon, sometime merchant and alderman at York and lord of the manor of Elvington. Hard as were the many long journeys and migrations upon the ensign and his wife during the subsequent ten years, the period must have been most agreeable to the boy himself. There were for him, who knew nothing of the tragedy of it, pleasant sojourns in Wales and in the Isle of Wight, and a whole year in an Irish castle with relatives and friends. When he fell through a mill-race, like his great-grandfather the archbishop, while the mill was running, and came out whole and sound, his mother was upset, to be sure, by the incident; but to Laurie, as the country folk crowded about him in wonder at his escape, it was a moment of triumph; for he was the hero of an incredible adventure.

He must have enjoyed, too, the large freedom of barrack life in England and in Ireland, however much it may have tested the endurance of his mother. There he met with new adventures and strange characters, the memory of which never left him. In after years, as he sat down in his Yorkshire parsonage to write his book, his childhood all came back to him— what he had seen with his own eyes and what his father had told him about the first serious engagement of the Thirty-Fourth Regiment of Foot in the battle of Wynendale, which Count de la Motte would have won, "had he not pressed too speedily into the wood," and about the Peace of Utrecht which broke my uncle Toby's heart as well as sent Roger Sterne adrift in the world. Out of those memories, fortified by much reading of Marlborough's campaigns and enriched by later observations, came my uncle Toby, Trim, and Le Fever. Of no one more than of Sterne is the saying of Wordsworth truer that the child is father to the man.

II.

HAVING learned to read and write while he lay in the barracks of Dublin, the boy was ready, by 1723 or 1724, for the rudiments of learning. His father then placed him in a grammar school near Halifax, that he might be under the eye of his uncle Richard at Woodhouse Hall. At that time Halifax took the lead in cloth-making among all the towns of north England. Defoe, who passed through the parish in his tour of Great Britain, was much struck by the thrift of the people living in long rows of houses on the hillsides, so thickly placed as to be within speaking distance of one another. All along in front of the houses were tenters on which were stretched pieces of cloth, which, says Defoe, "by their whiteness reflecting the bright rays of the sun that played upon them, formed, I thought, the most agreeable sight I ever saw."* Sterne is strangely silent in his books about this and other novel scenes to which he had been suddenly transferred. Thrift certainly made upon him no impression comparable with the gaiety of military life.

* *A Tour through Great Britain*, III, 78 (second edition, London, 1738).

Perhaps he chafed under the restraints of his new surroundings. It is a tradition, supported by an incident or two, that the
boy studied when he liked and got more whippings than lessons. It may be that he did not get along well with his uncle at
Woodhouse Hall, for he nowhere mentions this Richard
Sterne among the relatives that aided him. But his uncle surely
gave him shelter and helped pay the expenses of his schooling.
Though Sterne had nothing to say about his uncle, he spoke
with respect of the head of the school, describing him as "an
able master." Whoever he may have been, he saw in Sterne a
lad of unusual promise; being the first, as we say nowadays,
to discover him. It was not the master but the usher that did
the whipping to which reference has been made. Sterne himself related the incident, with some pride, for his daughter
Lydia. The master, says Sterne, "had had the cieling of the
school-room new whitewashed—the ladder remained there—I
one unlucky day mounted it, and wrote with a brush in large
capital letters, LAU. STERNE, for which the usher severely
whipped me. My master was very much hurt at this, and said,
before me, that never should that name be effaced, for I was
a boy of genius, and he was sure I should come to preferment
—this expression made me forget the stripes I had received."
   The name of the school where this escapade occurred,
Sterne failed to mention. The words of his memoir are simply
"My father got leave of his colonel to fix me at school—
which he did near Halifax, with an able master." At that time
there were, as there are now, two grammar schools near Halifax—the one at Heath, to the south of Halifax and within
easy walking distance from Woodhouse up over the moor; the
other at Hipperholme, to the east of Halifax and across the
valley from Shibden Hall. The former was an ancient foundation, with a stately building of freestone, dating from the
time of Queen Elizabeth. The latter, a smaller and less pretentious structure, was founded and endowed in 1661 by
Matthew Broadley, Esq., of London, formerly of Halifax.
Both were established for the instruction of youth in grammar
(Latin and Greek) and other literature and learning, and in

all those virtues and good manners which should be a part of a liberal education. By express statute, the masters of both schools were required to be able and sufficient persons, holding at least the degree of Bachelor of Arts from either Oxford or Cambridge. Of their scholars, such private records as may have been kept by the masters have all been lost or destroyed. In which school was educated the author of *Tristram Shandy?*

According to common tradition, at least a century old, Sterne prepared for the university at the Grammar School of Queen Elizabeth at Heath. A clergyman who attended the school between 1808 and 1820, said in a letter to a former master: "The legend during the time that I was at Heath respecting Sterne was that he was a scholar there, and the panel on the ceiling was pointed out, on which he was said to have daubed Lau: Sterne." An inscription similar to Sterne's, if not the very one, was actually seen and remembered by John Turney of Leek Wotton, in Warwickshire, who passed the year 1809-10 at Heath. Besides noting the fact in his copy of Sterne's works, he afterwards wrote of it more fully in a letter to a friend. "The name of Sterne," says the letter, "was marked on the ceiling of the school room in irregular characters, as if done by some one who knew he was doing wrongly and was fearful of being detected in the act. They were large letters, say (I speak from memory of course) about four and a half inches high, all capitals. They were black as if, as I thought, burnt in with a candle, the smoke from the candle causing them to be black.——LAU STERNE was inscribed about three yards from the Head Master's desk. It ran obliquely from S. W. with rather a turn to the East." The master of Heath in Sterne's time was a certain Thomas Lister, distantly related to the Listers of Shibden Hall. He graduated as Bachelor of Medicine at Jesus College, Cambridge, in 1688, and received his appointment to the school in the same year. After forty years of service, he died in April, 1728. On the supposition that Sterne was a Heath scholar, this, then, was the master who thought him winged for a higher flight than the rest of the boys. On the same supposition, the usher who flogged Laurence may perhaps be identified with one Abraham Milner, a young man eighteen or twenty years old, who never received a degree from either of the great universities, and afterwards opened a bookseller's shop at Halifax.

The case as thus worked out for Heath is a complete and very pretty tale which ought to be true. It really rests, however, upon nothing but vague tradition. It may all be a legend that has grown up round the mere fact that the school was at a convenient distance from the seat of Laurence's uncle. No one, of course, can be disposed to doubt the memory of the old scholar who could recall the Sterne inscription on the ceiling. It is, nevertheless, preposterous to suppose that the original inscription had survived eighty or more years of whitewash and plaster. What the Warwickshire gentleman saw and remembered was doubtless the freak of some boy of later date, who could not find "LAU. STERNE" on the ceiling, and so proceeded to put it there.

To strike more nearly at the heart of the story, the Heath Grammar School, so flourishing earlier and since, was, just in Sterne's time, in a wretched condition. It had for some years been neglected by its governors, who dropped out one by one until there was nobody qualified to receive rents or to fill up vacancies; and its statutes, very strict as one reads them, had all fallen into abeyance. The master, Thomas Lister (who had received a medical degree from Cambridge University), was described at his death by a Halifax lawyer as an "old little good for naught fellow," and by others as long "superannuated" and never efficient. For at least two years before his death, his "few petty scholars" were left to the usher, who was spoken of with equal contempt. Over this state of affairs Richard Sterne became hot as early as 1719, when he reported the mismanagement to the Archbishop of York, within whose jurisdiction the school lay. After years of trouble and expense, the squire succeeded in reorganizing the school under a revised charter bearing date July 31, 1729. A new master, one Christopher Jackson, was appointed in 1730, but he resigned the next year, either because he disliked his position or because he proved incompetent. By that time the school days of Laurence Sterne were nearly over. For two or three of the seven years that Sterne was at school, the master of Heath was superannuated, and for two more there was no master at all. It is difficult to imagine that Laurence could have been among the "few petty scholars" of this period or that he could have regarded as "an able master" the man whom another called a "good for naught." It is much more likely that Thomas Lister, whom, of course, Sterne saw, knew, and heard talked about at Woodhouse, sat for the burlesque portrait of that tutor whom Mr. Walter Shandy would by no means have for his son Tristram. "The governor," said Mr. Shandy, "I make choice of shall neither lisp, or squint, or wink, or talk loud, or look fierce, or foolish;—or bite his lips, or grind his teeth, or speak through his nose. . . . He shall neither walk fast,—or slow, or fold his arms,—for that is laziness;—or hang them down, —for that is folly; or hide them in his pocket, for that is nonsense.—He shall neither strike, or pinch, or tickle,—or bite, or cut his nails . . . or snift, or drum with his feet or fingers in company."

Around the Free Grammar School at Hipperholme has been elaborated no fanciful legend of Laurence Sterne, perhaps, as has been indicated, because the school was not so near to Woodhouse. But it is an unbroken tradition among the Listers of Shibden Hall that Hipperholme was Sterne's school. Miss Lister, who was living fifty years ago at an advanced age, distinctly remembered "her father telling her that Laurence Sterne used to walk to Hipperholme School from his uncle's house along an ancient foot-path which formerly ran through the yard of Shibden Hall." She said further that Sterne was "a frequent visitor" at the Hall, when her grandfather, born in the same year as Sterne, was a boy. It may be that the aged lady was mistaken. But a sober statement like hers, bearing none of the marks of fiction, must be accepted, unless there is evidence to the contrary. As a matter of fact, Hipperholme exactly fits into what Sterne said about his school. It was, said Sterne, "near Halifax." Hipperholme is near Halifax, though

not so near Woodhouse as is Heath. But Sterne did not say
"near Woodhouse"—that is an added phrase. It was possible
for him to have walked from his uncle's seat to Hipperholme;
for if he could find, as he says in *Shandy*, no short cut to learning, he found one to school through the park of Shibden Hall.
It seems, however, probable that Sterne stayed a good deal
with his friend and schoolmate at Shibden Hall, and he may
have lived in the earlier years—his own words would bear that
interpretation—with the master of Hipperholme, going to his
uncle for the week ends.

During the entire period of Sterne's schooling, the master
of Hipperholme was a Rev. Nathan Sharpe, connected through
the Priestleys with the Listers and with Richard Sterne, whose
first wife was a Priestley. He graduated Bachelor of Arts
at Jesus College, Cambridge, in 1695, and was appointed
to Hipperholme in 1703, where he remained till his death
thirty years later. A Mr. Sharpe, apparently this one, baptized
in 1704 the first child of Richard Sterne. Another member of
the family, Abraham Sharpe, also a Cambridge man, whom
Richard Sterne addressed as cousin, held the curacy of Sow-
erby Bridge near Woodhouse. Besides being a relative of the
master of Hipperholme, Richard Sterne was also a large landowner in the township and a governor of the school. Family
interests thus point directly to Hipperholme as the place where
Laurence Sterne acquired the rudiments of learning. When
Sterne came to Halifax, Nathan Sharpe was still in the prime
of life, not above forty-eight years of age. So far as can be
determined, he managed his school well, fulfilling that re-
quirement of the statutes which Sterne but repeated when he
referred to his teacher as "an able master." Just as Thomas
Lister may have been the original of that schoolmaster whom
the elder Shandy could not think of for his son, so Nathan
Sharpe may have furnished hints for the man he was in search
of. "I will have him, continued my father, chearful, facete,
jovial; at the same time, prudent, attentive to business, vigilant, acute, argute, inventive, quick in resolving doubts and
speculative questions;—he shall be wise, and judicious, and

learned:—And why not humble, and moderate, and gentle-tempered, . . . said *Yorick*." It was certainly a master of this character who rebuked his usher for whipping Laurence Sterne and by his praise made the boy forget his punishment.*

After all has been said, there still remains reasonable doubt as to where Sterne received his early education. The considerations here set forth in favor of Hipperholme establish conclusively that Sterne was for a time a scholar there, and render it highly probable that he was placed there from the first with the able master who was a friend and relative of his uncle. But it is possible, though not very probable, that he first attended Heath for a year or two, until its affairs reached a crisis, and that he was then transferred to Hipperholme. The question could be settled beyond all doubt only by the registry of the students of the period, but that, if it ever existed, has not survived.

The only document that gives us a glimpse of Sterne at school is an old exercise book that once came to the hands of Mr. Percy Fitzgerald, from what source he did not say, bearing the title, *Synopsis Communium Locorum ex Poetis Latinis Collecta*, written above the words "Lau. Sterne, September ye 6, 1725." As it bears in another place the date "1728," if there be no misprint, one must infer that Sterne remained in the same school through the period covered by the dates, for he would not likely be put to the same exercises under different masters. It also seems a fair inference that if Sterne was ever at Heath, he remained for only a short time, migrating to Hipperholme as early as 1725. The old "dogged eared volume," as described by Mr. Fitzgerald, shows that Laurence idled a good deal over his lessons, stopping to play, much like Shakespeare's schoolboy, over declensions which are made to include *Nickibus Nonkebus* and *rorum rarum*. Here and there

---

* Local traditions concerning Sterne's school are contained in Thomas Cox, *A Popular History of the Grammar School of Queen Elizabeth, at Heath, near Halifax* (Halifax, 1879). In 1906, I visited Halifax and the neighborhood that I might consider these traditions in the place of their origin. With my conclusion agreed the Master of the Heath School and the Listers of Shibden Hall.

occur the names of Sterne's schoolmates, as "John Turner," "Richard Carr, ejus liber," "Bill Copper," and "I owe Samuel Thorpe one halfpenny but I will pay him to-day." Elsewhere it is said that "labour takes panes." In one place appears a stave of notes with the names written below and signed "L. S." Most interesting as a clue to Sterne's taste then and in after life are the rude drawings scattered over many of the pages. Mingled with owls, cocks, and hens, are several heads of women, and curiously dressed soldiers with sugar-loaf caps, short-stock guns, and straps, such as he remembered from barrack life. There is "a drummer," "a piper," and over one "long-nosed, long chinned face" is written "This is Lorence."*

Notwithstanding the time spent in scribbling over his copybooks, Sterne then laid the foundation of a ready knowledge of the classical literatures. He learned to read and write Latin with great facility. Nearly all the authors in the usual curriculum of the period, he at some time quoted or referred to, evidently from memory. Horace came into his books perhaps more often than the rest. But Cicero, Pliny, Hesiod, and Isocrates are there also. Three other ancients touched his emotions deeply. It grieved him to think that "poor Ovid" died in exile. In *Shandy*, he related, as he remembered it from Vergil, the scene in the Elysian Fields where Aeneas meets "the pensive shade of his forsaken Dido," and added that she still awakened in him "those affections which were wont to make me mourn for her when I was at school." Uncle Toby's love for the *Iliad*, as well as for chapbooks in which there were soldiers and adventure and much fighting, is undoubtedly only a reminiscence of Sterne's own passion for them. If we may have it so, the boy purchased with his own pocket money "Guy of Warwick," "Valentine and Orson," "The Seven Champions of Christendom," and handed them round among his school companions. And of the *Iliad*, he says: "Was I not as much concerned for the destruction of the *Greeks* and *Trojans* as any boy of the whole school? Had I not three strokes of a ferula

* Fitzgerald, *Life of Sterne*, I, 9-10 (London, 1896).

given me, two on my right hand, and one on my left, for calling *Helena* a b * * * * for it? Did any one of you shed more
tears for *Hector?* And when king *Priam* came to the camp to
beg his body, and returned weeping back to *Troy* without it,
——you know, brother, I could not eat my dinner." In all
this Sterne doubtless carried back to his school days much of
his maturer sentiment; and yet it may be fairly inferred that
the characters in the books he read at school were real persons
to him in whose adventures he took an active and sympathetic
part beyond the habit of most boys. This love for ancient literature was quite sufficient for the master's prophecy, after the
whipping, that Laurence possessed talents that would bring
him to preferment.

Between school and university intervened for Sterne a period of uncertainty. By 1731 at the latest he should have been
ready for Cambridge. But just at this time news reached him
of his father's death in the West Indies; and the boy, then in
his eighteenth year, was left "without one shilling in the
world." His mother in much distress came over from Ireland;
and after scant courtesy from her husband's relatives, she returned to Clonmel with her pension of £20, barely sufficient
for the support of herself and Catherine, whom she kept with
her. Any aid to her son was out of the question. The next year
his uncle Richard, "being somewhat infirm in body," started
for York and fell dead at Bradford. By his will* made a few
weeks before his death, Richard Sterne bequeathed his royalty
and estate at Elvington and all his estates at Ovenden, Halifax, and Hipperholme to his eldest son Richard by Dorothy
Lister; and to a younger son Timothy by Esther Booth, were
bequeathed Woodhouse and all his lands within the parish of
Skircoat. Timothy, then only a boy, afterwards married and
settled at Woodhouse Hall, where, surrounded by horses and
dogs, he developed into a squire of the kind one may read
about in Addison and Fielding. Laurence never mentioned
Timothy, probably because he was under no obligation to him.

* Signed September 11, and proved October 25, 1732.—York Registry of Wills.

Richard, the eldest son and chief heir, barely twenty-five years old at his father's death, also soon married and took up his residence at Elvington. Between Richard and Laurence there must have been much in common, for the humorist, in spite of differences that sprang up later in life, always spoke with respect and affection of his cousin at Elvington. He became, said Sterne in reviewing his career, "a father to me"; to his protection "I chiefly owe what I now am"; and but for his aid, "I should have been driven out naked into the world, young as I was, and to have shifted for myself as well as I could."

The substantial service for which Sterne expressed this profound gratitude was an allowance of £30 a year towards his expenses at the university. After drifting about for several months, he went up to Cambridge, says the memoir, in 1732, but the date is clearly a slip in memory by a full year. He was enrolled, according to the record of it, as a sizar at Jesus College on July 6, 1733. The choice of this college out of all others at Cambridge was most natural, for his uncle Jaques and his master at Halifax, whether Mr. Sharpe or Mr. Lister, were both educated there; and his great-grandfather, Archbishop Sterne, had been one of its masters and generous benefactors. As in everything else connected with Sterne some fact or incident will appear out of the usual order, so it is with the official records of him at Cambridge. Fashioned himself unlike other men, it is as if all who had to do with him, whether closely or at a distance, were infected by his own strange courses. In his day sizars were admitted to Jesus College and elsewhere only after "being examined and approved." *Examinatus et approbatus* is the stereotyped formula. But no examination was required of Sterne. He was admitted "in his absence," reads the entry, "with the assent of Master and Fellows."

Moreover, the official who enrolled him put down his name as *Henricus* instead of *Laurentius*, and described him as a native of York, either by mistake or by the direction of the master. The next year—on July 30, 1734—Sterne, then in residence, was elected, after being duly sworn, to one of the scholarships founded by his great-grandfather "for natives of Yorkshire and Nottingham," though, as he was born in Ireland, he did not possess the necessary qualifications. Of these curious irregularities, the readiest explanation is that before Laurence was entered at Cambridge, his cousin Richard of Elvington had come to some agreement with the Master of Jesus, whereby all technicalities relative to birth-place and examination were to be waived in consideration of the young man's descent from Archbishop Sterne. The boy could not have been accorded greater favors had he been the son of a nobleman. For some reason—perhaps because of the fee— Sterne deferred matriculation in the university until March 29, 1735, nearly two years after he came into residence.

The Master of Jesus was Charles Ashton, a quiet scholar known for his studies in classical and patristic literature. Among the learned fellows Sterne had as his first tutor Charles Cannon, a young man about thirty years old. Cannon died in the winter of 1734-5 and Sterne was then transferred to Lynford Caryl, afterwards Master of Jesus, distinguished, said one who knew him, for affable manners, regular life, "unimpeachable integrity," and "a balanced precision and a sententious brevity of expression." Of Dr. Caryl, who guided him through the greater part of his studies, Sterne wrote thirty years later: "He was my tutor when I was at College, and a very good kind of man. He used to let me have my way, when I was under his direction, and that shewed his sense, for I was born to travel out of the common road, and to get aside from the highway path, and he had sense enough to see it, and not to trouble me with trammels." As a third tutor, Sterne had John Bradshaw, a fellow some six years his senior, who recommended him for his degree. Associated with Sterne under Bradshaw were a certain Thomas Mould, a Peter Tomiano, who failed to take a degree, and Frederick Keller, who became a distinguished fellow of his college and the literary executor of Dr. Ashton. Whether any unusual friendship existed between Sterne and Keller is not known; but it is interesting to observe in passing that the two men were prepared for their examinations by the same tutor.

Sterne, with his family pride, could not have been fully at ease in his position in the university. Sizars, to be sure, then performed no menial services at Cambridge; the time was past when they were required, as Eachard complains, to fetch water, sweep chambers, and make beds for their superiors; and the line was no longer fast drawn between them and the pensioners and fellow-commoners above them. There were nevertheless social and other distinctions which would be felt and resented by a sensitive nature. With no tassels to their caps, unlucky sizars wore in clear view the badge of poverty. Sterne's allowance from his cousin, with the £10 a year that he received from his scholarship, sufficed no more than for the essentials of maintenance and clothing. Gentleman then commonly spent thrice that sum. Without running into debt there could have been for Sterne no luxuries nor suppers and wine parties, such as were expected of youngsters from good families. Under the circumstances Sterne did exactly as one would expect of him: he borrowed money, from what source he does not say, and sought congenial companions here and there among the men who, in the university scale, ranked socially above him.

The names of but two of these friends have escaped oblivion. One was John Fountayne of Melton Manor, South Yorkshire, who was enrolled at St. Catharine's Hall. He was afterwards elected Dean of York and then he and Sterne were again placed in very intimate relations. Each, as will be duly related, came to the aid of the other in a noisy church quarrel which gave Sterne local reputation for a smart and witty pen. The other friend was John Hall, who some years later added Stevenson to his name and inherited Skelton Castle, over on the Yorkshire coast near Saltburn-by-the-Sea. He is the "dear cousin Antony" of numerous letters and the discreet Eugenius of *Tristram Shandy*, who warns Yorick against "unwary pleasantry," lest it bring him into "scrapes and difficulties" out of which no after-wit can extricate him. Five years younger than Sterne, Hall-Stevenson entered Jesus College as a fellow-commoner in 1735. Though the two men were together at Cambridge for only a year and a half, that time was long enough for a close friendship "which ever after . . . continued one and indivisible through life."

Hall-Stevenson was, as described by one who recollected him at college, "an ingenious young gentleman and in person very handsome." And so he appears in the fine portrait of him in velvet and lace that still hangs at Skelton. He was also an idler and decadent much given to the perusal of Rabelais and other facetious books in the French tongue. To Hall-Stevenson Sterne was undoubtedly indebted for his first acquaintance with the great master of French humor. The two young men used to sit together under the large walnut tree that shaded the inner court of Jesus College, not we may be sure "to study," as the York anecdotist relates it, but to read the common lounging-books, which in those days included, among others besides Rabelais, jest books, Aphra Behn's novels, Lord Rochester's poems, and the plays of Wycherley and Congreve. This old walnut tree they aptly called the Tree of Knowledge, inasmuch as they learned of good and evil while resting beneath its shadow.

Sterne's associations with Hall-Stevenson would seem to be ample warrant for the tradition that he "was careless and inattentive to his book," that is, to the prescribed studies; that "he laughed a great deal, and sometimes took the diversion of puzzling his tutors." But such a summary in a phrase or two is inexact and incomplete. Sterne's main quarrel with the learned society of fellows and tutors of Jesus College, as set forth in *Tristram Shandy*, was that they were mere men of reading, who with their slight knowledge of the world thought that "wisdom can speak in no other language than Greek and Latin." "There is a husk and shell," he said of pedagogues, preceptors, tutors and gerund-grinders, "which grows up with learning, which their unskilfulness knows not how to fling away." But among these unskilled scholars he did not include without reserve his own tutors, one of whom he took pains to describe not only as "a very good kind of man" but as "worthy." The ancient poets and historians that Sterne read while at Cambridge, he always mentioned and quoted with delight. Homer and Vergil, which were continued at college, he never tired of. Theocritus and Pindar charmed him for "the sweetness of the numbers" and "the musical placing of the words." Of the historians he liked best Thucydides, Herodotus, and Livy; while his praise of Tacitus was rather measured. The decisive style of Tacitus, he thought, overshot the mark, outwitting both author and reader. Eloquence, wherever found, always appealed to Sterne strongly. But when he came to the dry bones of literary theory, rhetoric, logic, and metaphysics, he was simply amused that intellect should employ itself in that way. All these studies, which entered largely into the curriculum, he turned in aftertime to banter and gay ridicule. The only rhetorician that he ever praised freely is Longinus, whom he declared "the best critic the eastern world ever produced." That admiration was based, it is quite clear, not so much upon the real worth of what Longinus wrote as upon his grand style. All the rest were his game. Near the opening of *Tristram Shandy* he begins his sport with those directions to writers which Horace laid down in the *Art of Poetry*. "I shall"—says Sterne there, shifting the figurative meaning of the phrase to the literal—"I shall start out, as Mr. Horace would have me, *ab ovo;* but beyond that I shall follow no rules of the ancients." Later on he has a fling at the Latin translation of Aristotle's *Poetics* which he read at college, explaining in lively banter the various parts of a drama—*protasis, epitasis, catastasis, catastrophe* or *peripetia*—which grow out of one another in the order the critic first planted them, and "without which a tale had better never be told at all."

Perhaps Sterne overflows most in ridicule when he turns to logic. In his day the students at Cambridge were supposed to read the Latin manual on logic written by Francis Burgersdicius, sometime professor at Leyden, and the Dutch commentators thereon. Formal logic also then pervaded the instruction not only in mathematics but also in physics and moral philosophy. Sterne evidently had great contempt for the exercises wherein he was required to defend or oppose according to the stiff and rigid rules of logic a thesis drawn from one of these subjects. The academical dispute seemed to him only an adroit manipulation of words and phrases. This attitude of his towards logic is summed up in the character and sayings of the elder Shandy, in whom nature blended her own rhetoric and logic without the aid of the schools. When the country squire —in an imaginary scene, which may have a faint counterpart in a visit of his own with his uncle or cousin Richard—went up to Cambridge to enter his son at Jesus College, the fellows and tutors whom he met there could not understand how a man that had never heard a single lecture on the Dutch logicians should be able to talk and reason as cleverly as themselves. The squire seemed to be aware, as well as the respondents and opponents whom they trained for the Public Acts, that a disputant should aim, not to convince, but to silence the man against him. It was known to him, as well as to Burgersdicius and his disciples, that "every thesis and hypothesis have an offspring of propositions; and each proposition has its own consequences and conclusions; every one of which leads the mind on again into fresh tracks of enquiries and doubtings." Mr. Shandy was also afflicted, just as were they, with "the commonplace infirmity of the greatest mathematicians," who work "with might and main at the demonstration, and so wasting all their strength upon it, . . . have none left in them to draw the corollary, to do good with."

It was the opinion of Mr. Shandy that the English schoolboy began his studies too late and was kept at them too long. Listen to the squire as he enumerates to a company gathered at Shandy Hall the stages that Sterne himself passed through from the cradle to the Bachelor's degree:

"Five years with a bib under his chin;

"Four years in travelling from Christ-cross-row to Malachi;

"A year and a half in learning to write his own name;

"Seven long years and more τυπτω-ing it, at Greek and Latin;

"Four years at his *probations* and his *negations*—the fine statue still lying in the middle of the marble block,—and nothing done, but his tools sharpened to hew it out!—'Tis a piteous delay!—Was not the great *Julius Scaliger* within an ace of never getting his tools sharpened at all?————Forty-four years old was he before he could manage his Greek;—and *Peter Damianus,* lord bishop of *Ostia,* as all the world knows, could not so much as read, when he was of man's estate.—And *Baldus* himself, as eminent as he turned out after, entered upon the law so late in life, that every body imagined he intended to be an advocate in the other world: no wonder, when *Eudamidas,* the son of *Archidamas,* heard *Xenocrates* at seventy-five disputing about *wisdom,* that he asked gravely, —*If the old man be yet disputing and enquiring concerning wisdom,—what time will he have to make use of it?*"

Mr. Shandy would have none of this delay in the education of his son Tristram, and so set about to discover "a North-west passage to the intellectual world." He found it in a running dance with the auxiliary verbs. By conjugating *have, do, shall, will,* etc., with a variety of nouns and pronouns, affirmatively, negatively, interrogatively, and hypothetically, it was shown conclusively that a young gentleman might be taught in a few lessons "to discourse with plausibility upon any subject, *pro* and *con,* and to say and write all that could be spoken or written concerning it, without blotting a word, to the admiration of all who beheld him." This is the key to all knowledge, the *ars magna,* says Sterne, that Raymond Lully and numerous scholastics have long sought for in vain. Once in the secret of it, a man may talk on forever about things and entities whereof he knows nothing. The great art was especially commended by Sterne to college tutors whose business it might be to provide topics in logic for the young gentlemen who come under their charge. He could assure them to a certainty that there was nothing like the use of the auxiliaries for setting "the soul a-going by herself upon the materials as they are brought to her." "By the versability of this great engine, round which they are twisted," may be opened, he declared, "new tracks of enquiry," and every idea be made to "engender millions."

The light of a new age in science and speculation was beginning to break upon Cambridge while Sterne was there. For some time Newton, Hobbes, Locke, and various modern historians and publicists had formed part of the usual course of reading.* To these writers Sterne took strong likes and dislikes. Pufendorf's immense work on the *Law of Nature* was not forgotten by the humorist when he came to describe in *Tristram Shandy* the incontestable rights of the Homunculus which the eminent jurist had forgotten to enumerate. Clüver, the German historian and geographer, he regarded as a pedant, who spent his time in trying to ascertain where the Goths and other Germanic tribes were first seated and so had nothing to say about their manners and customs. Why, asks Sterne in *Tristram Shandy*, did not "the learned Cluverius" mention in his *Germania Antiqua*, the wise custom among the Goths "of debating every thing of importance to their state, twice; that is,—once drunk, and once sober:—Drunk—that their councils might not want vigor;—and sober—that they might not want discretion." That story, Sterne would say, is more interesting than the geography of the country between the Vistula and the Oder. On the other hand Sterne admired Newton at a distance. Of Hobbes he knew enough to allude to that quaint title-page of the *Leviathan* whereon is depicted graphically the horns of a dilemma, upon which hang syllogisms of various sorts while masters and students stand about in their gowns. Finally, Sterne could never cease praising the author of the

* For the reading prescribed and recommended at Cambridge in Sterne's time, see Christopher Wordsworth, *Scholæ Academicæ* (Cambridge, 1877). Compare with Sterne, John Eachard's burlesque of the university curriculum in *The Grounds and Occasions of the Contempt of the Clergy* (London, 1670, reprinted in Arber's *English Garner*, VII).

Essay on the Human Understanding. After all his wanderings in logic and metaphysics, he discovered in the *great* Locke, the *sagacious* Locke, a writer who really knew what passes in a man's mind, and one whose search was ever after truth, not after adroit and dishonest means for defending propositions that every one knows must be false. The famous essay became Sterne's companion to the end of life and colored much of his own thinking.

Sterne received his degrees from Jesus College in due course, graduating B.A. in January, 1736-7, and M.A. at commencement in July, 1740. When he appeared for his first degree he could not have been included—needless to say perhaps—among "the hard reading men" of the type of Frederick Keller. But he had read, as we have seen, the books that he was expected to know; and they were tucked away in memory ready for his purposes when needed. An old anecdotist likely guessed the truth, if he had no authority for the statement, when he said that Sterne had a way of puzzling his tutors. But it was, we may be sure, only the good-natured banter of a man "who loved a jest in his heart." We miss greatly some authentic account of the impression that Sterne made upon his tutors and associates. On this point there is nothing beyond what was current thirty years after. It was then said that "Sterne left Cambridge with the character of an odd man, that had no harm in him; and who had parts if he would use them." A portrait of a beautiful youth by Allan Ramsay, believed to be Sterne at the age of twenty-seven, when he came up for his Master's degree, now hangs, as was said earlier, near Coleridge, in the hall of Jesus College. It is an oval face in the freshness of youth, such as Sterne himself admired, with full eyes and full lips, but hardly suggestive of the humor that was in him.

Sterne was destined for the Church, not because of deep and peculiar piety but because the Church was an obvious career to one who bore his name. On that path awaited him a livelihood and the preferment which his master had prophesied for him while at school. His immediate prospects, however, were far from bright. He began the world, as he often said, with "many difficulties and drawbacks." All along his family had looked upon him as the son of his mother rather than of his father. The annual stipend of £30 from his cousin Richard, inadequate at best, was paid irregularly, and not at all during his last year at Cambridge. So Sterne was compelled to borrow money elsewhere to settle his university debts. The expense of his food and clothing for the nine years at the Halifax grammar school was also charged up, he was now to discover, against him to be paid as soon as he should be able. From the first he had been a delicate boy like most of his father's children who had been left by the way one after another. In stature above middle height, he was slim and hollow-chested. A dread disease lurking in his blood became manifest near the close of his residence at Cambridge. One night he was startled out of sleep by a hemorrhage of the lungs, "bleeding," he says, "the bed full." Fortunately, Sterne possessed a buoyant nature which could win the race against debts and consumption.*

* The following are the original entries relative to Sterne in the register of Jesus College:

Under July 6, 1733:

Henricus Sterne Eboracensis absens admissus est in Ordinem Sizatorum cum consensu Magistri & Sociorum sub Tutore suo M^{ro} Cannon.

Under July 30, 1734:

Laurentius Sterne electus est et admissus, prius juratus, Exhibitionarius Episcopi Eboracensis in locum D^{ni} Hall.

Under January 14, 1736-7:

Eodem etiam die Fredericus Keller, Petrus Tomiano, Laurence Sterne & Thomas Mould habuerunt veniam sibi concessam petendi gratiam ab Academia ad respondendum Quæstioni, spondente M^{ro} Bradshaw.

Under August 4, 1737:

Literæ Testimoniales concessæ sunt D^{no} Sterne.

Henricus in the first entry was afterwards deleted for *Laurentius; Arch* was also written before *Episcopi* in the second entry. *Arch,* of course, should be *Archi.* M^{ro} is an abbreviation for *Magistro;* and D^{ni} an abbreviation for *Domini.*

"The Ramsay portrait," Mr. Arthur Gray, Vice-Master of Jesus College, informed me in 1908, "was presented to the college by one of the Fellows, Mr. Hugh Shield, K.C., a few years ago. It is traditionally and, I believe, correctly said to be a portrait of Sterne in his youth and is unquestionably by Allan Ramsay."

CHAP. II.

Marriage and Settlement at Sutton-in-the-Forest.
1737-1744

I.

AFTER obtaining his Bachelor's degree, Sterne immediately entered upon his career in the Church. On Sunday, March 6, he was duly admitted, among other candidates, to the order of deacons by Richard Reynolds, the Bishop of Lincoln, "being very well recommended," according to the customary formula, "for his exemplary life, good morals and virtuous qualities, and well instructed in the study and knowledge of sound learning." The scene of this general ordination was the chapel of Buckden Hall near Huntingdon, long since in ruins, but then the palatial residence of the diocese. On the same day, Sterne was licensed by the Bishop of Lincoln to the curacy of St. Ives, five miles to the east of Huntingdon.

St. Ives is an ancient market-town, which then consisted mainly of a single row of houses straggling along the north-eastern bank of the slow-moving Ouse. In the rear was a cattle market, and beyond were farms extending out into the fens, one of which, "a stagnant flat tract of land," was cultivated for five years by Oliver Cromwell. All Saints, where Sterne officiated, is a light and handsome church in the perpendicular style, overlooking the sleepy stream, with a lofty spire visible for miles out over the fens. Sterne came to the parish as curate to the vicar, one William Pigott, a graduate of Pembroke College, Cambridge. Perhaps the two men had been acquainted at the university, for the vicar did not receive his Master's degree until 1734. But of this we do not know. No memorials of the young curate of St. Ives longer exist; no entry of his in the parish registry; no tradition of him and his ways. Nothing remains but the bare record of his appointment in the Act Book of the Bishop of Lincoln. At most Sterne trod the flagstones of the ancient church at St. Ives for a scant year and then passed out to new scenes.

In the meantime, an important change had taken place in the attitude of the Sterne family towards the young man. His cousin Richard apparently broke with him over college debts and soon died before reaching middle life. His uncle Jaques, who had hitherto refused to aid him, now became his patron and gave him a good start in the world, as he well could from his position in the Church of York. This Jaques Sterne, before our memoir has finally done with him, will turn out to be a splendid example, equal to any in Trollope's novels, of the worldly-wise ecclesiastic who strives for high place mainly for his own comfort and aggrandisement. Without possessing the solid character of the old archbishop bearing the family name, he was proud, blustering, and bigoted, and withal totally devoid of humor.

Graduating at Jesus College, Bachelor of Arts in 1714, and Master of Arts in 1718, Jaques Sterne was ordained to the ministry in December, 1720, at Bishopthorpe, the palace of the Archbishop of York. On February 5, 1722, he was instituted Vicar of Rise, a small parish near the coast in the East Riding of Yorkshire, to which living was added on May 3, 1729, the neighboring vicarage of Hornsea-cum-Riston. A month before this last appointment he was installed Prebendary of Apesthorpe in York Minster, and was permitted the next year to exchange this prebend for Ulskelf. Accompanying his rise, in no way unusual up to this point, Jaques Sterne had received in 1725 the degree of Doctor of Laws from his college. He was henceforth to be known as Dr. Sterne, a title by which he liked to be called. Having once gained a foothold in the Church of York, Dr. Sterne added one dignity to another, never letting slip any that he already had except for something better. In April, 1734, the eager pluralist obtained the rich prebend for South Muskham in the Cathedral Church of Southwell, Nottinghamshire, which brought his annual income well above four hundred pounds. At the time of the appointment, he was too busy at York to appear in person at Southwell, and so the installation was by proxy. He was then in the midst of a fierce parliamentary contest, in which he won the day for the Whig candidate, Mr. Cholmley Turner, whose canvass he personally managed. After this brilliant success against the most stubborn and bitter opposition, Dr. Sterne easily took his place among those efficient church politicians of the period who were fighting the Whig battles for Walpole. Resigning the prebend of Ulskelf, he was appointed, on the seventeenth of November of the next year, Canon Residentiary and Precentor to York Minster, and Archdeacon of Cleveland. There was nothing further for him to ask for at present except a bishopric, but that could not be granted him.*

The motives that led Dr. Sterne to take up his nephew after years of neglect, one need not go far to seek. Laurence was no longer a helpless child whose education would be a drain upon the purse. He had made his way through the university, thereby displaying the Sterne energy and talents and proving himself the son of Roger Sterne rather than of a poor woman who followed the army in Flanders. No doubt Jaques Sterne thought it his duty to help along a member of his family who might come to something; but it is clear, in the light of subsequent events, that he mainly sought in his nephew a subservient tool for furthering his own ambitions. Clever politician as he was, he would first make him and then use him as an understrapper. What happened when the young man thoroughly understood this, would be, I daresay, interesting reading, if only we had the full details of the encounter. But all that, with the few details we have, is for another story. Peace reigned for some years. Pursuant to the plans agreed upon by uncle and nephew, Laurence Sterne left St. Ives, and came to York, where on February 18, 1737-38, he qualified as Assistant Curate in the parish of Catton, a few miles to the east of the city and near one of the seats of his family. This was but an interim appointment. On Sunday, August 20, 1738, he was

* For Jaques Sterne, see especially Le Neve and Hardy, *Fasti Ecclesiæ Anglicanæ* (Oxford, 1854); and G. Paulson, *History of Holderness* (Hull, 1890).

admitted to the priesthood by Samuel Peploe, Bishop of Chester, at a special ordination held in the Cathedral Church of Chester. Four days later he was collated by Lancelot Blackburne, the Archbishop of York, to the vicarage of Sutton-in-the-Forest, within the archdeaconry of Cleveland. The next day he was formally inducted into the living by Richard Musgrave, the curate of Marton, with Philip Harland, the squire of the parish, as one of the witnesses.*

Sutton-in-the-Forest is a small village eight miles or more to the north of the city of York. As one comes upon the hamlet from York, the road suddenly turns to the right, running almost due east. On the north side stood, as it now stands, the little stone church with square tower, dedicated to All Saints, and beyond was the parsonage hidden away among shrubbery. From his gate, Sterne looked directly across upon the grange of Squire Harland, while on either side of the road was a row of cottages with small enclosures; and in various directions lanes led away to scattered farmsteads. The vicarage, which included the entire township of Sutton and of Huby to the west, extended over an area of nearly eleven thousand acres. It had formerly been known as Sutton-in-Galtres, for it lay at the heart of the immense Forest of Galtres, which stretched north to the ancient Isurium and south to the very walls of York. For centuries a royal hunting ground wherein the old kings "pursued the wild boar, the wolf, and other beasts of prey with which it was infested," the ancient forest is now chiefly remembered, outside of local history, as the scene where Shakespeare's John of Lancaster met the northern rebels under Richard Scroop, Archbishop of York, and after persuading him to disband his power, treacherously broke faith with him, ordering his arrest and immediate

* All of Sterne's ordination papers with endorsements now repose in the British Museum (Additional Charters, 16158-16166). The information contained in these papers has been supplemented by an examination of the Institutions of the Diocese of York and the Acts of the Dean and Chapter. For the appointment to Catton, see L. P. Curtis, *The Politicks of Laurence Sterne*, 34 (London, 1929).

execution. "It was," says Thomas Gill's *Vallis Eboracensis*, "in many places thick and shady with lofty trees and under-wood, and in others wet and flat, full of bogs and moorish quagmires." In 1670 Parliament passed an Act for enclosing this wild waste; whereupon began those changes and improve-ments which have since converted Galtres into a rich and fruitful plain of meadows and pastures. In Sterne's time this transformation was not complete. Much of the forest had been levelled, meadows had been drained, and bogs had been filled up, but there yet remained many fields and large tracts of com-mon land that had not been brought under the plough. If no longer in the forest, the hamlet of Sutton still lay within one of its old clearings which ran off in all directions into barren moors and marshes with woods beyond.

The only attraction which this parish in the wilderness could have had for Sterne was the £40 a year that it put into his purse. He probably never expected to go into permanent residence. For the next three years he stayed mostly at York, it would seem, driving out to Sutton sometimes for Sunday service and the business of his parish. On one of these occa-sions, the vicar took down the parish registry, and, before en-tering a marriage or baptism, sprawled in large letters across the page LAU^RENCE STERNE, much as he had done on the ceiling of the Halifax grammar school. The first entry in his hand, it may be interesting to note, was the marriage of John Newstead of Huby and Mary Wilkinson of Stillington, on Easter Tuesday, Anno Domini 1739. But most of the records for this year, and all of them, I think, for 1740 are signed by Richard Wilkinson, a young man in deacon's orders, whom Sterne placed over the parish. Mr. Wilkinson was at Sutton on a slightly irregular appointment, merely as Sterne's assistant, for his license to the cure bears the date of December 17, 1740. His parish duties provided for, Sterne likely kept close to York, by the sources of pleasure and ecclesiastical preferment. Vacancies were then filled so promptly that candidates unless near at hand stood no chance of winning. On January 12, 1740-41, the prebend of Givendale in York Cathedral was re-

signed by the incumbent for the chancellorship, and five days
later Sterne was in possession of the stall. Thenceforth he became a member of the York Chapter and took his turns at
preaching in the great minster. "He sat down quietly," says
the contemporary account, "in the lap of the church; and if
it was not yet covered with a fringed cushion, 'twas not
naked."

At that time York was in truth as in name the metropolis
of the north. Many country gentlemen made it their residence
the year through, while others came in for the winter with
their families. Provisions of all sorts were cheap and plentiful
and hospitality abounded. Those who could not afford houses
of their own went into lodgings or put up at one of the inns,
of which the George in Coney Street was the meeting place of
gentlemen to talk politics, confer with their lawyers, make
and sign contracts, and nominate for mayor or member of
Parliament. Near by was Sunton's Coffee-House, one of several coffee-houses at York, and Sterne's favorite resort for
gossip or a convivial evening with the club to which he belonged. During the season, which began in November, there
were, says Defoe, who included York in one of his tours, "assemblies, music-meetings or some entertainment every night in
the week"; while for a week in May and August a concourse
of people, including the neighboring and distant nobility and
gentry, poured into the city from all sides for the amusements
of "the great races," held on the field of Knavesmire, then
one of the best courses in England. Chance visitors at the races
in Sterne's day were amazed at the prodigious sums lost and
won or left behind for lodgings, the theatre, and subscription
balls. For those who required greater excitement than watching Antelope and Grenadier* run for his Majesty's purse of a
hundred guineas, there was provided, twice a day during the
week of the races and frequently at other times, a main of
cocks with bye-battles,† between the gentlemen of York and

* *York Courant*, August 11, 1752.
† *Ibid.*, August 13, 1751.

the gentlemen of Halifax, Bradford, or some other respectable town of the north.

York had also her own company of players, chosen with a "particular care . . . to their private life that they might be as sociable off the stage, as entertaining upon it." They had long performed in one of the cockpits, but by the time Sterne came to York, they were moving into their theatre in the Mint Yard, modelled after those of London. There Sterne had an opportunity to see the whole range of the English drama from Shakespeare and Jonson down to a comic opera founded upon local scene and character.* And not far from the theatre were the Assembly Rooms, the very centre of fashion. The building, which was designed after Palladio by that Earl of Burlington to whom Pope and Gay paid generous compliment, was then regarded as very beautiful, though it now appears heavy and dingy enough. It contained a spacious and showy hall ornamented in the antique Egyptian manner, and six other rooms, all of which, writes Defoe, were "finely illuminated with lustres of an extraordinary size and magnificence."† To visitors of more sentiment than Defoe the overhanging lights on the evening of a concert or ball but revealed the brilliant scene below. "The ladies," said a correspondent of *St. James's Chronicle*,‡ "who vied in splendour with each other, I thought would never be tired of dancing, for some began on Monday and continued till Saturday night." And so it was at the theatre. Tate Wilkinson, the actor and mimic, who at a later date sometimes played at York, was dazzled, he says, when his eyes turned towards the boxes; "and no wonder," it is added in explanation, "for as London and Bath cull the choicest beauties from the three kingdoms, so does ancient York city at times allure them from Hull, Leeds, Doncaster, Wakefield, Pontefract, and every part of that noble, spacious and rich country."§ It is quite easy to see why a young bachelor should

* *York Courant* under various dates.
† *Tour of Great Britain*, III, 125-126 (London, 1738).
‡ August 26-28, 1766.
§ *Memoirs*, III, 144-145 (York, 1790).

have preferred York to a country parish tucked away in a forest clearing.

Among the young women with whom Sterne held senti-mental converse at the Assembly Rooms and elsewhere was Elizabeth Lumley, who was accustomed to come to York for the season. As Sterne eventually took Miss Lumley to wife, we should tell what is known of her and her kindred. When he first made her acquaintance, she was occupying gen-teel lodgings, with her waiting-maid, in Little Alice Lane, a narrow street which under another name still winds away from the south of the Minster Yard to an archway marking one of the old gates to the Cathedral Close. Most of the build-ings of the street were pulled down more than a half century ago; but the house where Miss Lumley was wont to take lodg-ings for the winter may perhaps be identified with St. Wil-liam's College, originally an ecclesiastical foundation for chantry priests, and afterwards converted into dwellings. It is an ancient and curious structure rambling around a court-yard; while in front a half-timbered upper story projects over one of stone into the street. The main entrance was by a door and wicket ornamented with beautiful tracery. It is a pleasing fancy, if nothing more, that Miss Lumley passed through that traceried doorway on the morning when she stepped over to the cathedral to become Mrs. Sterne. She could not boast, if casual references to her are to be believed, of the beauty that Tate Wilkinson and other visitors saw in the Yorkshire ladies. She was indeed "but a homely woman," yet possessing grace, vivacity, and a love for music and the diversions of society. She had been well bred, and "possessed," says the antiquary,* "a first rate understanding," which enabled her to help Laurie with his sermons. "She had many admirers," it is said further, "as she was reported to have a fortune." When Sterne began to pay court to her she was twenty-four or twenty-five years old —about a year younger than himself. It was altogether a fit-

* John Croft, whose anecdotes of Sterne, to be frequently quoted, have been published by W. A. S. Hewins, *Whitefoord Papers*, 223-235 (Oxford, 1898).

ting match, if a man so volatile as Sterne were ever to marry.

Miss Lumley belonged like himself to a good county family. Her father, the Rev. Robert Lumley, was the son of Robert Lumley, Gentleman, of Northallerton, a market-town in the North Riding, by Eleanor, daughter to John Hopton, Esq., of Armley, a suburb of Leeds. His grandmother, on the mother's side, was a sister of Thomas Rymer, the critic and historian. At the age of sixteen Robert Lumley, his father then deceased, entered Trinity College, Cambridge, as a pensioner, where he graduated, Bachelor of Arts in 1710-11, and Master of Arts four years later. Ordained deacon by the Archbishop of York on December 21, 1712, he seems to have obtained a curacy, though I have discovered no record of it, near Armley; most likely at Adel, a few miles to the northwest of the estate of his maternal grandfather. The little church at Adel, with its sculptured porch and chancel arch, is one of the loveliest survivals of Norman architecture in all England. Within the wide parish lay Cookridge Hall, the seat of Thomas Kirke, father and son, each of whom was known as "an ingenious gentleman, and virtuoso in all sorts of learning." They were both Fellows of the Royal Society. Cookridge was then famous in the district and beyond it for a "fine library and museum of antiquities" and for a park and wood laid out in "geometrical lines and centres." Thomas Kirke the younger married Lydia, daughter of Anthony Light of London, by his wife Elizabeth, daughter of William Clarke of Merivale Abbey, Warwickshire. Within a year and some months after the marriage, he died at the age of twenty-five; and two years later—on September 24, 1711—the young widow took as her second husband Robert Lumley. Of the marriage were born two daughters, Elizabeth and Lydia, of whom the former was christened in the beautiful Norman church at Adel, October 13, 1714. This is the Elizabeth Lumley who lived to become the wife of Laurence Sterne. By descent from Elizabeth Clarke, twice married, she was cousin to Elizabeth Montagu, the famous "Bluestocking."*

* By her first husband, Anthony Light, Elizabeth Clarke had one

On January 12, 1720-21, Robert Lumley was admitted to the priesthood, at an unusually advanced period in life, by the Archbishop of York, preparatory to his appointment on October 16 to the vicarage of Bedale, near Northallerton and the home of his childhood. In this old market-town, consisting of one long and wide street with the church of St. Gregory at the upper end of it, he remained until near his death in January or February, 1731-2. Bedale was one of the richest livings in Yorkshire—worth nearly £2000 a year—and so the Lumleys "lived in style," giving Lydia and Elizabeth "a superior education," as might be expected of a mother who had enjoyed the comforts and luxuries of Cookridge Hall. It is impossible to follow the migration of the family immediately after the death of the father. But Mrs. Lumley did not long survive her husband. On May 17, 1736, letters of administration of the father's estate were granted by the Prerogative Court of York to Elizabeth and Lydia Lumley, who are described in the preliminary application as spinsters living at Kendal, in Westmoreland. No inventory of the estate was returned. Soon after the loss of her mother, Lydia married the Reverend John Botham, a Trinity man and son of the vicar of the same name at Clifton-Campville in Staffordshire, where it may be the Lumleys also owned an estate. Mr. Botham, then rector of Yoxall in the same county, was afterwards appointed to the vicarage of Albury in Surrey. Lydia died on March 22, 1753, in her thirty-ninth year, and was buried in the ancient parish church within Albury Park. After the marriage of her sister, Elizabeth divided her time between Yoxall and the pleasures of York, settling at length, as said

daughter—the Lydia who married Thomas Kirke and afterwards Robert Lumley. After the death of Anthony Light she married Thomas Robinson, the grandfather of Elizabeth Robinson (who married Edward Montagu in 1742). Thus Elizabeth Lumley and Elizabeth Montagu had the same grandmother, but different grandfathers. Though they rarely met, they addressed each other as "cousin" in letters that passed between them. Sterne also, after his marriage, claimed the relationship for himself by courtesy.

above, for a part of the year under the shadow of the great minster.*

It took Sterne two years to win Miss Lumley. During the first months of the courtship, the lovers shared together the amusements of York and sat down to many a "sentimental repast" in the seclusion of Little Alice Lane, or with their confidante, "the good Miss S——," in a pretty cottage amid roses and jessamines, which from some odd fancy they called D'Estella, perhaps in memory of Stella, the name by which Swift addressed Esther Johnson.† It all reads like a little novel, could he have written anything so brief, by Samuel Richardson. Miss Lumley, though she owned she liked Sterne from the first, held him off with the excuse that she was not rich enough or that he was too poor to think of marriage just then. At this stage in the courtship, Miss Lumley went to her sister's in Staffordshire for a long visit extending into the winter, I should say, of 1740-41. Letters of course now passed to and fro. "I wrote to her often," says Sterne. Four of his letters Miss Lumley kept by her through life, doubtless as the ones that pleased her especially well. No one ever wrote love-letters

* Information concerning the Lumleys and the families into which they married lies scattered in *The Registers of the Parish Church of Adel* (volume V of *Thoresby Society Publications*, 1895); T. D. Whitaker, *Loidis and Elmete* (1816); Thoresby, *Ducatus Leodiensis*, edited by Whitaker (1816); *Register of Marriages in York Minster* (*Yorkshire Archæological and Topographical Journal*, II, 321); and Manning and Bray, *History . . . of Surrey*, II (1809). An etching of the church at Adel is given by H. T. Simpson, *Archæologia Adelensis* (London, 1879). Likewise of Bedale, by H. B. M'Call, *The Early History of Bedale* (London, 1907). I have also been furnished with the entries with reference to Robert Lumley in the Admission Book of Trinity College and the diocesan registries of York and Chester. New material on the Lumleys and Sterne may be found in E. J. Climenson, *Elizabeth Montagu*, two vols. (London, 1906), and R. Blunt, *Mrs. Montagu*, two vols. (London and New York, 1923).

† D'Estella had also another association for Sterne as the name of a village in Navarre. In *Tristram Shandy*, Bk. V, Ch. I, he refers to "the curate d'Estella," who wrote a book entitled, in its English translation, *The Contempt of the World and the Vanity Thereof* (1584).

much like them, except in imitation of them. They are studies in emotion, possessing the harmony and cadence of phrase and sentence that were to distinguish, a quarter-century later, the *Sentimental Journey* from all other English books.

In the first letter, Sterne, tired of the haunts of men, imagines for himself and Miss Lumley an earthly paradise where the polyanthus blooms in midwinter:

"Yes! I will steal from the world, and not a babbling tongue shall tell where I am—Echo shall not so much as whisper my hiding-place—suffer thy imagination to paint it as a little sun-gilt cottage, on the side of a romantic hill—dost thou think I will leave love and friendship behind me? No! they shall be my companions in solitude, for they will sit down and rise up with me in the amiable form of my L——. We will be as merry and as innocent as our first parents in Paradise, before the arch fiend entered that undescribable scene.

"The kindest affections will have room to shoot and expand in our retirement, and produce such fruit as madness, and envy, and ambition have always killed in the bud.—Let the human tempest and hurricane rage at a distance, the desolation is beyond the horizon of peace.—My L. has seen a polyanthus blow in December—some friendly wall has sheltered it from the biting wind.—No planetary influence shall reach us, but that which presides and cherishes the sweetest flowers. God preserve us! How delightful this prospect in idea! We will build, and we will plant, in our own way—simplicity shall not be tortured by art—we will learn of nature how to live— she shall be our alchymist, to mingle all the good of life into one salubrious draught.—The gloomy family of care and distrust shall be banished from our dwelling, guarded by thy hand and tutelar deity—we will sing our choral songs of gratitude, and rejoice to the end of our pilgrimage.

"Adieu, my L. Return to one who languishes for thy society."

The second letter strikes a more personal note in the account of Sterne's dreadful state after Miss Lumley's departure to her sister. Sterne fell into a fever, and the confidante, hearing of it, tried to console with him, with the result that they both broke down under the pressure of their emotions. Sterne took Miss Lumley's lodgings in Little Alice Lane during her absence, but he could neither eat nor sleep until Fanny, the house-maid, had braced his nerves with hartshorn:

"You bid me tell you, my dear L., how I bore your departure for S——, and whether the valley where D'Estella stands, retains still its looks—or, if I think the roses or jessamines smell as sweet, as when you left it—Alas! everything has now lost its relish and look! The hour you left D'Estella, I took to my bed.—I was worn out by fevers of all kinds, but most by that fever of the heart with which thou knowest well I have been wasting these two years—and shall continue wasting till you quit S——. The good Miss S——, from the forebodings of the best of hearts, thinking I was ill, insisted upon my going to her.—What can be the cause, my dear L., that I never have been able to see the face of this mutual friend, but I feel myself rent to pieces? She made me stay an hour with her, and in that short space I burst into tears a dozen different times—and in such affectionate gusts of passion, that she was constrained to leave the room, and sympathize in her dressing-room—I have been weeping for you both, said she, in a tone of the sweetest pity—for poor L.'s heart, I have long known it—her anguish is as sharp as yours—her heart as tender—her constancy as great—her virtue as heroic—Heaven brought you not together to be tormented. I could only answer her with a kind look, and a heavy sigh—and returned home to your lodgings (which I have hired till your return), to resign myself to misery—Fanny had prepared me a supper—she is all attention to me—but I sat over it with tears; a bitter sauce, my L., but I could eat it with no other—for the moment she began to spread my little table, my heart fainted within me.— One solitary plate, one knife, one fork, one glass!—I gave a thousand pensive, penetrating looks at the chair thou hadst so often graced, in those quiet and sentimental repasts—then laid down my knife and fork, and took out my handkerchief, and clapped it across my face, and wept like a child.—I do so this

very moment, my L.; for, as I take up my pen, my poor pulse
quickens, my pale face glows, and tears are trickling down
upon the paper, as I trace the word L———. O thou! blessed in
thyself, and in thy virtues—blessed to all that know thee—to
me most so, because more do I know of thee than all thy sex.—
This is the philtre, my L., by which thou hast charmed me, and
by which thou wilt hold me thine, whilst virtue and faith hold
this world together.—This, my friend, is the plain and simple
magic, by which I told Miss ——— I have won a place in that
heart of thine, on which I depend so satisfied, that time, or
distance, or change of everything which might alarm the
hearts of little men, create no uneasy suspense in mine—Wast
thou to stay in S——— these seven years, thy friend, though he
would grieve, scorns to doubt, or to be doubted—'tis the only
exception where security is not the parent of danger.—I told
you poor Fanny was all attention to me since your departure—
contrives every day bringing in the name of L. She told me
last night (upon giving me some hartshorn), she had observed
my illness began the very day of your departure for S———;
that I had never held up my head, had seldom, or scarce ever,
smiled, had fled from all society—that she verily believed I
was broken-hearted, for she had never entered the room, or
passed by the door, but she heard me sigh heavily—that I
neither eat, or slept, or took pleasure in anything as before—
judge then, my L., can the valley look so well—or the roses
and jessamines smell so sweet as heretofore? Ah me!—But
adieu!—the vesper bell calls me from thee to my God!"

During the correspondence, Miss Lumley entered complaint against her lover and their common friends at York
that they were neglecting her. Letters, no doubt, as was
Sterne's way, were not so frequent as they had been. In two
letters Sterne pleaded for mercy at "the amiable tribunal"
of pity, promising never to offend after. For her benefit he
moralized prettily on the art of the coquette, the family affections, and the death of his dear friends. As an index to his
reading at the time, we may observe, in addition to Eve's
bower in Milton's *Paradise Lost*, an apparent allusion to the

Beggar's Opera and a quotation from the *Essay on Man,* though not written out, as if Miss Lumley were thoroughly familiar with the moral essay of the great poet. Here and there, too, he played fancifully with phrases in Thomson's *Seasons,* making them more delicate and artificial. Winter was breaking, he finally told Miss Lumley, and she must come to York for the spring. "Return—return—" was the burden, "the birds of Yorkshire will tune their pipes, and sing as melodiously as those of Staffordshire."

The summons was heeded. What occurred afterwards Sterne himself related for his daughter Lydia. At her return, says the memoir, Miss Lumley "fell into a consumption—and one evening that I was sitting by her with an almost broken heart to see her so ill, she said, 'My dear Laurey, I can never be yours for I verily believe I have not long to live—but I have left you every shilling of my fortune';—upon that she shewed me her will—this generosity overpowered me. It pleased God that she recovered, and I married her in the year 1741." The fortune that could not be resisted had just come to Elizabeth and Lydia Lumley as heirs at law to the real estate of a distant and unknown relative who had recently died intestate at Leeds. Elizabeth's share in the income from the houses and lands amounted to thirty or forty pounds a year. When Eliza told Laurey about it, he took her and her fortune* on the impulse of the moment, just as his father before him had taken the widow of a brother officer. The pathetic scene we have described occurred, it is said, in the Assembly Rooms; "whence they went off directly . . . and were married." However that may be, the story closes with the terse record in the registry of York Minster that the Rev. Laurence Sterne and Miss Elizabeth Lumley of Little Alice Lane were married, under special license, on Easter Monday, March 30, 1741, by Richard Osbaldeston, Dean of the York Chapter. The romance which was thus quickly shuffled to a conclusion, like the last act of a play, had developed in Sterne a peculiar

* E. J. Climenson, *Elizabeth Montagu,* I, 84-85.

emotional state, to describe which he was the first of all writers to employ the epithet sentimental.* Had he then possessed the motive and matter for it, he might have written his *Sentimental Journey*.

Miss Lumley's marriage to a York prebendary rather amused Elizabeth Robinson (not yet Mrs. Montagu), who first heard of it from her brother Matthew, then drinking the waters at Bath. "Harry Goddard," he wrote to her, "is here, and informs me that our cousin Betty Lumley is married to a Parson who once delighted in debauchery, who is possessed of about £100 a year in preferment, and has a good prospect of more. What hopes our relation may have of settling the affections of a light and fickle man I know not, but I imagine she will set about it not by means of the beauty but of the arm of flesh. In other respects I see no fault in the match." Some days later, came a letter from Mrs. Sterne herself, telling her all about her illness, her marriage, and her love. Miss Robinson immediately passed the news on to her sister Sally, who was convalescing from a severe illness: "I never saw a more comical letter than my sweet cousin's, with her heart and head full of matrimony, pray do matrimonial thoughts come upon *your recovery?* for she seems to think it a symptom. . . . Mr. Sterne has a hundred a year living, with a good prospect of better preferment. He was a great rake, but being japanned† and married, has varnished his character. . . . What a wonderful occupation she made of courtship that it left her no leisure nor inclination to think of any thing else. I wish they may live well together."‡

* See, however, Boissy's *Le Français à Londres*, a one-act prose comedy first performed in 1727. The heroine says of love that it is in England *un commerce de sentimens* (Scene II). From this it is not a far step to Sterne's "sentimental commerce" or "sentimental repasts." In 1764, he "invented" the word *sentimentalize* for "Dr. Johnson's service."—*Original Letters*, 14 (London, 1788).

† Suggested by the color of his clerical dress.

‡ E. J. Climenson, *Elizabeth Montagu*, I, 73-74.

II.

STRAIGHTWAY after marriage, Sterne prepared to occupy his living at Sutton-in-the-Forest; by midsummer he was settled there with his bride. The "little sun-gilt cottage on a romantic hill" that he had dreamed of in his correspondence with Miss Lumley proved to be "a large ruinous house," which could be rendered habitable only after "great repairs." Under his predecessor, the late Rev. John Walker, it had been totally neglected and was ready to fall. Sterne's income at this time was hardly eighty pounds a year, Sutton being estimated at forty pounds and Givendale at some odd pounds short of that. Out of that sum Sterne was paying a curate. His wife, however, true to her promise, placed in her husband's hands—his honor laid as surety—her little fortune. This additional income enabled Sterne to renovate his parsonage; but like others who have made over old houses, he found the expense of it greater than had been anticipated. When he had done with the repairs, he recorded his emotions, along with the items of cost, in the following entry on the inside of one of the covers to his parish registry:

```
                              £   s  d
Laid out in Sashing the House,     12  0  0   A. Dom. 1741
In Stukoing And Bricking the Hall      4  16  0⎫
In Building the Chair House            5   0  0⎮ L. Sterne
In Building the Parlʳ Chimney          3   0  0⎬ Vicar
Little House                           2   3  0⎭
Spent in Shapeing the Rooms, Plastering, Underdrawing & Job-
     bery——
God knows what ————————————————————————————
```

It is curious that Sterne should first appear as a jester in this old dog-eared parish book. The dash he drew across the page on bringing the account to a close, leaving it to Omniscience to write in the long row of figures, is whimsical enough for *Tristram Shandy*. Mrs. Sterne's breeding also comes out here unexpectedly. She was to have her dwelling newly sashed after the latest style. The chair-house, too, was for her benefit, that she might keep a carriage for driving about the district or

Laurence Sterne   Elizabeth Sterne

From the pastels by Francis Cotes

taking a wheel into York to visit her friends. After repairing
and rebuilding, came "the entire furnishing" of the rectory at
an expense of which Sterne complained, though he gave no details. Their house in order, the vicar and his wife began to lay
out "pleasing walks," as they called them, "amid trees, shrubs,
and flowers." They were also as curious as Mr. Walter Shandy
"in wall-fruit and green gages especially." Their curate, the
Rev. Mr. Wilkinson, as it is faithfully recorded in the parish
registry, began the improvements by building an arbor, and
planting twenty or more elm trees in the large house garden
and the churchyard, a few of which may be still standing.
Then followed further planting with the necessary enclosures,
the details of which Sterne set down in his own hand. The
entries run:

Mem^d That the Cherry Trees & Espalier Apple Hedge were planted
in ye Garden October ye 9, 1742. The Nectarines and Peaches
planted the same Day. The Pails set up two months before

I Laid out in the Garden in ye year 1742, the sum of £8 15s. 6d.

L. Sterne

Laid out in Inclosing the Orchard, & in Apple Trees, &c——in y^e

£ sh d

Year 1743, 5 0 0

The Apple Trees, Pear & Plumb Trees, planted in ye Orchard y^e
28th day of October, 1743, by L. Sterne.

During this period of planting and repairing, Sutton was
visited by two hailstorms, the severity of which Sterne perhaps
playfully exaggerated, for we read in the parish book near the
end:

In the Year 1741

Hail fell in the midst of Summer as big as a Pidgeon's Egg, w^{ch}
unusual Occurrence I thought fit to attest under my hand

L. Sterne

In May 1745

A dismal Storm of Hail fell upon this Town & upon some other
adjacent ones, wch did considerable Damage both to the Windows
& Corn. Many of the Stones measured six Inches in Circumference.

It broke almost all the South & West Windows, both of this House and my Vicarage at Stillington.

L. Sterne

When Sterne finished his improvements he had made out of Sutton a comfortable retirement, which was to be his home for nearly twenty years. The old rectory, subsequently burned to the ground, lay back from the road to the north, in an orchard of shrubs, fruit, and flowers of his own planting. If his wife's income had been exhausted by the expense of coming into the living, two important preferments more than made up for the loss. On December 26, 1741, the prebend of North Newbald fell vacant by the death of the Rev. Robert Hitch, who had "overheated himself"* in the recent election for members of Parliament. At a meeting of the York Chapter held on the fifth of the following January, Sterne resigned Givendale for the wealthier stall of North Newbald. The formal installation took place on January 8. Besides being worth fully forty pounds a year, the new prebend carried with it a house in Stonegate near the minster, which could be let or used as a town residence.

Adjoining Sutton, two miles to the north, was the vicarage of Stillington, which fell to Sterne on the death of the incumbent, Richard Musgrave, formerly curate of Marton. The little church, set high over the hamlet, looks much as it did in Sterne's time. The old box pews remain and the old gallery in the rear is still used. Of the new appointment Sterne said, "By my wife's means I got the living of Stillington—a friend of her's in the south had promised her, that if she married a clergyman in Yorkshire, when the living became vacant, he would make her a compliment of it." The friend in the south who exerted his influence for Sterne was Thomas, Lord Fairfax, who soon afterwards settled in Virginia, where he became associated with the young George Washington.

The details of the appointment which enrolled Sterne

* Thomas Gent, the York printer, *Life*, 194-195 (London, 1832). Sterne is briefly described.

among the small pluralists of the period, may be discovered in
contemporary records. It is well to give them here. On February 27, 1743-4, the Dean and Chapter of York issued certificates to the Chancellor of England, the Archbishop of
Canterbury, and the Archbishop of York, praying that Sterne,
known for his "good life and conversation" be permitted to
hold Stillington along with Sutton. On March 3, the Archbishop of Canterbury signed the dispensation, "being moved
by your supplications" and the general considerations that "the
greater progress men make in sacred learning, the greater
encouragement they merit, and the more their necessities are
in daily life, the more necessary supports of life they require."
It was stipulated that Sterne should preach thirteen sermons at
Stillington every year, exercise hospitality for two months each
year, and in his absence provide a minister for the parish in
case the revenues were adequate for the purpose. The dispensation was confirmed by letters-patent of his Majesty on March
6. These preliminaries over, the Rev. Richard Levett, Prebendary of Stillington, who was the patron of the living, presented Sterne's name to Richard Osbaldeston, the Dean of
York, who made the appointment on the thirteenth. The next
day Sterne was formally inducted into the vicarage by Richard
Hanxwell, Vicar of Sheriff-Hutton.*

Stillington added to Sterne's resources another annual forty
pounds. He could now live comfortably and at ease. So near
was Stillington to Sutton that it was not necessary for him to
engage a curate for the new parish. At the same time Mr.
Wilkinson found another field of labor; and for several years
Sterne either performed alone the duties of two parishes or
employed curates who had not reached the dignity of a bishop's
license. He had, however, a trustworthy and obedient parish-
clerk, whom he facetiously called "my sinful Amen." It was

* The Richard Levett who nominated him to the living also held a
prebend at Southwell. He seems to have been the son of the vicar of
the same name at Wycombe in Buckinghamshire, who graduated at
Christ's College, Oxford, in 1697, and subsequently served as curate to
his father.

Sterne's custom to preach at Sutton on Sunday morning and to stroll over to Stillington for an afternoon service, using very likely the same sermon, for Sterne was not the man to expend unnecessary energy upon his parishioners. Once, said the brother of the squire of Stillington, as Sterne "was going over the fields on a Sunday to preach at Stillington, it happened that his pointer dog sprung a covey of partridges, when he went directly home for his gun and left his flock that was waiting for him in the church in the lurch."

In the dispensation granting him the right to hold Stillington as well as Sutton, Sterne was styled "Chaplain to the Right Honourable, Charles, Earl of Aboyn," that is, to Charles Gordon, fourth Earl of Aboyne, then a young man only sixteen or seventeen years old. When or under what circumstances Sterne first became connected with this ancient Scottish family there is, of course, no indication in the document itself.* But Sterne had ample opportunity for meeting the Gordons, for they frequently, if not regularly, attended the York races in August. Sir Sidney Lee suggested that Sterne may have made the grand tour soon after his marriage in company with the young earl or with some near relation of his.

The conjecture receives considerable support from *Tristram Shandy*. Before beginning that book, Sterne had probably travelled abroad. "Why are there so few palaces and gentlemen's seats," the elder Shandy is made to ask, "throughout so many delicious provinces in *France?* Whence is it that the few remaining *Chateaus* amongst them are so dismantled,—so unfurnished, and in so ruinous and desolate a condition?" In another passage of the first book, Sterne speaks of the muleteer who "drives on his mule,—straight forward;—for instance, from *Rome* all the way to *Loretto*, without ever once turning his head aside either to the right hand or to the left." With the Low Countries Sterne showed perhaps greater familiarity.

* In the *Champion* (April 12, 1740) Fielding remarks that chaplains to great men are entitled by statute to hold pluralities. This accounts for Sterne's seeking a chaplaincy in order to qualify for the living at Stillington.

Uncle Toby, in giving orders for his fortifications on the bowling green, insisted on having the town "built exactly in the style of those of which it was most likely to be the representative:—with grated windows, and the gable ends of the houses, facing the streets, &c. &c.—as those in *Ghent* and *Bruges*, and the rest of the towns in *Brabant* and *Flanders*." It was in Flanders, too, where Yorick got an asthma in skating against the wind. And finally Yorick says, in excuse for not looking into Saxo Grammaticus for his descent from Hamlet's jester, "I had just time, in my travels through *Denmark* with Mr. *Noddy's* eldest son, whom, in the year 1741, I accompanied as governor, riding along with him at a prodigious rate, thro' most parts of *Europe*, and of which original journey performed by us two, a most delectable narrative will be given in the progress of this work; I had just time, I say, and that was all, to prove the truth of an observation, made by a long sojourner in that country;—namely, 'That nature was neither very lavish, nor was she very stingy in her gifts of genius and capacity to its inhabitants.' " From all this it may be surmised at least that soon after his marriage in the spring of 1741, Sterne left his bride at home and took a flying trip to the Continent with a stripling from the house of Gordon, disguised as "Mr. Noddy's eldest son."* But if he then went abroad, it was for only a few months; for in September he was at York, playing a conspicuous rôle, to be described later, in a contested election.

Disgusted with politics, he was back at Sutton the next year, where we have had a glimpse of him cultivating his garden. At this time there began to crop up, in his mode of life, the ideals of the old squirearchy to which he belonged.

* The *Aberdeen Journal*, for January 6, 1795, said of the Earl of Aboyne at the time of his death: "His lordship received from nature a sound understanding, which was cultivated and improved by a liberal education. Having finished the usual course of study in the Scottish Universities, he went abroad, where mingling for several years with the higher ranks of life, his manners acquired a delicacy and gentleness which endeared him to all."—See *Notes and Queries*, eleventh series, VIII, 116.

Under different circumstances Sterne would have developed into another Simon or Richard of Halifax. The year of his marriage he was appointed a justice of the peace, and from enclosing and planting the garths about the rectory he branched out into miscellaneous farming for the increase of his winnings. Like most country parsons of his day, he looked after the collection and disposal of his tithes in kind, consisting of the corn and small tithes of Sutton and the hay of Huby, which belonged to his vicarage. He also cultivated the glebe of his benefice; and, not satisfied with this, he purchased a neighboring farm, described in legal phrase as "a messuage and certain lands." In this undertaking Mrs. Sterne joined with the zest of her husband. "They kept," said the local antiquary, who knew Sterne personally, "a dairy farm at Sutton, had seven milch cows, but they allways sold their butter cheaper than their neighbours, as they had not the least idea of œconomy, [so] that they were allways behind and in arrears with fortune." They also raised geese (which were regarded as Mrs. Sterne's perquisites) for the market and for presents to their friends.

Of Mrs. Sterne's "gooses," as he sometimes called them, that were permitted to run wild, Sterne occasionally wrote in pleasant humor. "My wife," runs a letter to a friend at York, "sends you and Mrs. Ash a couple of stubble geese—one for each; she would have sent you a couple, but thinks 'tis better to keep your other Goose in our Bean Stubble till another week. All we can say in their behalf is, that they are (if not very fat) at least in good health and in perfect *freedome*, for they have never been confined a moment." Just as Sterne here took his stubble geese as a theme for freedom, so in *Tristram Shandy* his experience in planting cabbages was turned to a defence of his digressive style. "I defy," it is said there, "the best cabbage planter that ever existed, whether he plants backwards or forwards, it makes little difference in the account (except that he will have more to answer for in the one case than in the other)—I defy him to go on coolly, critically, and canonically, planting his cabbages one by one, in straight lines, and stoical distances . . . without ever and anon straddling out, or sidling into some bastardly digression." As time went on, Sterne became occupied far more than he wished with his farming, as may be seen in the following extract from a letter to his York friend:

"I would have wrote on Saturday, but in Truth, tho' I had both Time and Inclination, my Servants had neither the one nor the other, to go a yard out of their Road to deliver it— They having set out with a Wagon Load of Barly at 12 o'clock, and had scarse day to see it measured to the Maltsman. I have four Thrashers every Day at work, and they mortify me with declarations, That there is so much Barly they cannot get thro' that speces before Xmas Day, and God knows I have (I hope) near eighty Quarters of Oats besides. How shall I manage matters to get to you, as we wish for three months!"

Sterne's dealings in land which made possible farming on so large a scale, may be uncovered in the office of the registry of deeds at Northallerton, where are kept the records for the North Riding. Conveyances to and from Sterne as there recorded, were mostly, after the custom of the time, in the form of lease and release. Unfortunately the original deeds were not engrossed in full, but only brief abstracts of them called memorials, which give merely such details as were necessary to identify the property in the conveyance. In no case is there, for example, an estimate of acreage; and whether a conveyance in a given case means an actual sale or a mortgage can only be conjectured, for there is never a statement to either effect. Besides all this, the record is evidently incomplete, as should be expected, for the conveyance by lease and release was originally a device to escape the expense and publicity of registration. Still, a shrewd guess, helped out by *Tristram Shandy* and a letter or two, leaves no doubt concerning Sterne's actual purchases. The dairy farm to which reference has been made, had formerly been in the tenure and occupation of one Richard Tindall, and consisted of a dwelling, other buildings, and various lands and closes. It was conveyed

to Sterne by William Dawson and his wife Mary, of Farling-
ton, a neighboring village and parish, by lease and release,
dated respectively the first and second days of November,
1744, the year after the planting of the rectory garden with
apples, pears, and plums. There is in the memorial no indication of its situation beyond the vague formula that it lay in
"the Town, Townfields, precincts, and Territorys of Sutton
in the Forrest." But the farm was situated, as is evident from
what will be said much later in the memoir, to the north of
the road leading through the hamlet, and it may have actually
adjoined the glebe of the parish.

The week following his purchase of the Tindall estate,
Sterne bought three pieces of land from Richard Harland,
Esq., the chief proprietor in the neighborhood. They are described in the indenture bearing date November 10, 1744, as
"one Stockiland lying in Murton Common field, . . . one
land called a Hespole and Clockil Ings at the end of it, and
another land called a Sankle Butt," all within the township of
Sutton. The character of these lands and the uses to which
they were to be put are sufficiently indicated by the local names
attached to them. Murton was one of the six common fields
of Sutton, which covered altogether thirteen hundred acres.
The "stockiland" within it Sterne evidently desired as additional pasturage for those seven kine we wot of. What the
word Hespole comes from I am not quite certain; but the alternative Clockil Ings is of course a corruption of Clockholm
Ings, meaning a low-lying, marshy meadow, covered with
flowered rushes, known locally as clocks or clockseaves. Sankle
Butt, short for Sancome or Sankholm Butt, was likewise "a
flat, spongy piece of ground," abutting upon some boundary.
It is a safe inference that Sterne was about to coöperate with
his neighbors in reclaiming the waste land of his parish, as
well as to compete with them in huge crops of oats and barley.

The Tindall farm, supplemented by these meadows and
pastures, comprised all the real estate that Sterne purchased at
Sutton, though land was to come to him in another way to be
related hereafter. In carrying through the purchases, Mrs.

Sterne's available fortune was strained to the utmost, and additional money was required, it would seem, for stocking the farm, for ditching, and for general improvements. At any rate, Sterne conveyed on the fifth and sixth of the following December the Tindall farm and perhaps the supplementary fields and meadows to William Shaw, a merchant of the city of York. This conveyance was clearly by way of mortgage. The high hopes with which Sterne, having once purchased the land, set out on his career as farmer, is reflected in *Tristram Shandy*—in the account of the elder Shandy's "paring and burning, and fencing in the Ox-moor," "a fine, large, whinny, undrained, unimproved common." "It was plain," as Mr. Shandy worked out the account, "he should reap a hundred lasts of rape, at twenty pounds a last, the very first year— besides an excellent crop of wheat the year following—and the year after that, to speak within bounds, a hundred—but in all likelihood, a hundred and fifty—if not two hundred quarters of pease and beans—besides potatoes without end." How Sterne's hopes were dashed to the ground and how he cursed himself for his folly must be kept for a later period.

Leaving his farming out of the account, Sterne drew himself, as Vicar of Sutton, in the character of Parson Yorick. Not only is this the tradition, but John Hall-Stevenson, who knew Sterne best of all men, looked upon the portrait as essentially true, quoting from it himself, as the newspapers had often done, the year after his friend's death. Yorick's parish, —"a small circle described upon the circle of the great world, of four *English* miles diameter, or thereabouts"—was Sutton laid by the side of Stillington. The "large grange-house," where "the good old body of a midwife" found hearty welcome, was the residence of the Harlands opposite the rectory. It was the parson's wife who established the notable woman in her profession, urging Yorick to procure the necessary license and recommending her to friends and acquaintances. Twice the midwife was summoned to the rectory. A daughter, named Lydia from Mrs. Sterne's mother and sister, was born and baptized on October 1, 1745, and was buried on the next day. Her place was taken by another Lydia, who was born and baptized on December 1, 1747. These records of the parish book, which touched Sterne so nearly, stand out prominently in his own hand, separated from the usual entries by the clerk and church wardens. Perhaps we should not take literally the account Sterne gives of the thin and lean Yorick riding about his parish and among the neighboring gentry on a broken winded pad as thin and lean as himself, drawing up, as he jogged along, "an argument in his sermon;—or a hole in his breeches." "He never could enter a village," says Sterne, "but he caught the attention of both old and young.—Labour stood still as he pass'd—the bucket hung suspended in the middle of the well—the spinning-wheel forgot its round,—even chuck-farthing and shuffle-cap themselves stood gaping till he had got out of sight; and as his movement was not of the quickest, he had generally time enough upon his hands to make his observations,—to hear the groans of the serious,—and the laughter of the light-hearted;—all of which he bore with excellent tranquillity."

This sketch, which furnished the subject for one of Stothard's graceful designs, is rather too elaborate and too much in the style of Cervantes for exact truth, to say nothing of its being an apparent imitation of a passage in Shakespeare's *King John*. Still, tradition points in the Vicar of Sutton to a man who, especially when older, cared little for decorum. "So slovenly was his dress and strange his gait," antiquary handed down to antiquary, "that the little boys used to flock around him and walk by his side."

Sterne and Yorick were certainly one in temperament. Both were compounded of whims and humors; both were light-hearted and outspoken. When Sterne described Yorick at the age of twenty-six, he described himself also at the time when he entered upon the living at Sutton. Of Yorick, it is said:

"His character was,—he loved a jest in his heart. . . . he was as mercurial and sublimated a composition,—as heteroclite a creature in all his declensions;—with as much life and whim, and *gaité de cœur* about him, as the kindliest climate could have engendered and put together. With all this sail, poor *Yorick* carried not one ounce of ballast; he was utterly unpractised in the world; and, at the age of twenty-six, knew just about as well how to steer his course in it, as a romping, unsuspicious girl of thirteen: So that upon his first setting out, the brisk gale of his spirits, as you will imagine, ran him foul ten times in a day of somebody's tackling; and as the grave and more slow-paced were oftenest in his way,—you may likewise imagine, 'twas with such he had generally the ill luck to get the most entangled. For aught I know there might be some mixture of unlucky wit at the bottom of such *Fracas:*—For, to speak the truth, *Yorick* had an invincible dislike and opposition in his nature to gravity;—not to gravity as such;—for where gravity was wanted, he would be the most grave or serious of mortal men for days and weeks together;—but he was an enemy to the affectation of it, and declared open war against it, only as it appeared a cloak for ignorance, or for folly; and then, whenever it fell in his way, however sheltered and protected, he seldom gave it much quarter.

"In plain truth, he . . . was altogether as indiscreet and foolish on every other subject of discourse where policy is wont to impress restraint. *Yorick* had no impression but one, and that was what arose from the nature of the deed spoken of; which impression he would usually translate into plain *English* without any periphrasis,—and too oft without much distinction of either person, time, or place;—so that when mention was made of a pitiful or an ungenerous proceeding,—he never gave himself a moment's time to reflect who was the hero of the piece,—what his station,—or how far he had power to hurt him hereafter;—but if it was a dirty action,—without more ado,—The man was a dirty fellow,—and so on:—And as his comments had usually the ill fate to be terminated either in a *bon mot*, or to be enliven'd throughout with some drollery or humour of expression, it gave wings to *Yorick's* indiscretion. In a word, tho' he never sought, yet, at the same time, as he seldom shunn'd occasions of saying what came uppermost, and without much ceremony;—he had but too many temptations in life, of scattering his wit and his humour,—his gibes and his jests about him.—They were not lost for want of gathering."

Yorick's good counsellor Eugenius—that is, John Hall-Stevenson—was wont to warn him against his indiscretions in words like these:

"Trust me, dear *Yorick*, this unwary pleasantry of thine will sooner or later bring thee into scrapes and difficulties, which no after-wit can extricate thee out of.—In these sallies, too oft, I see, it happens, that a person laugh'd at, considers himself in the light of a person injured, with all the rights of such a situation belonging to him; and when thou viewest him in that light too, and reckons up his friends, his family, his kindred and allies,—and musters up with them the many recruits which will list under him from a sense of common danger;—'tis no extravagant arithmetic to say, that for every ten jokes,—thou hast got an hundred enemies; and till thou has gone on, and raised a swarm of wasps about thine ears, and art half stung to death by them, thou wilt never be convinced it is so."

The only answer that Yorick would make to his friend's serious advice was "a pshaw!—and if the subject was started in the fields,—with a hop, skip, and a jump at the end of it; but if close pent up in the social chimney-corner, where the culprit was barricado'd in, with a table and a couple of arm-chairs, and could not so readily fly off in a tangent,—*Eugenius* would then go on with his lecture upon discretion." Yorick thought no ill could come of "mere jocundity of humour," of honest sallies in which there was no "spur from spleen or malevolence." But in this he was mistaken. As with Yorick so it was with Sterne in a less degree. Prudence, caution, discretion, the virtues that smooth one's way through life, were ever classed by him among the evil propensities of human nature; inasmuch as they check the spontaneous act and make one appear other than he really is. "I generally act," said Sterne, "upon first impulses," or "according as the fly stings." Delightful as he always was among friends who understood him, his jests and gibes were a source of annoyance to many people who were hard hit by them.

The clash came early with Philip Harland, his neighbor across the way, of whom Sterne wrote laconically just before his death: "As to the Squire of the parish, I cannot say we were upon a very friendly footing." The Harlands had emerged from the yeomanry in the seventeenth century. Of Richard Harland, Esq., who died in 1689, at the age of ninety-seven, a mural tablet in the parish church says: "He was a truly brave and honest man. He first engaged himself in that Troop of Noblemen and Gentlemen, associated to guard their Sovereign's Person at York, and had the Honour to serve as Lieutenant to that Body. The Civil Wars increasing, he adhered to the Royal Cause, in many Battles and Skirmishes, particularly with that fatal one of Marston Moor, he greatly distinguished himself; during the Usurpation, he with many other of the Unfortunate, suffered Fines and Imprisonment, untill the year 1660, when Monarchy, Religion, and Liberty were restored together." His grandson Richard, who had inherited the estate at Sutton and added largely to it, was among the most respected justices of the peace in the North Riding. It was of him that Sterne purchased several parcels of land already described. By the time Sterne came to Sutton, Richard Harland had settled at York as a counsellor at law, leaving the active management of his estate to his eldest son Philip, to whom it subsequently passed by will.*

Besides being in possession of the Grange, and another farm called Greenthwaite, and frontsteads and enclosures at Sutton, Philip Harland also held, under the Archbishop of York, a lease of the rectory and the greater tithes of the parish. Enough is known of him to warrant the statement that there was little or nothing in common between the squire and his vicar. First of all, they differed politically. Harland was a Tory who con-

* The will was signed July 31, 1747, and proved in the Prerogative Court at York, July 3, 1751. The *York Courant* (May 15) contained a glowing obituary notice.

tributed liberally to the county hospital at York,* founded by
Dr. John Burton, a violent leader of his party. Sterne was a
Whig who never subscribed a shilling to the foundation, but
ridiculed, as we shall see, the Tory physician and all that he
stood for. The one was a man of practical affairs, dull and
grave, while the other was a jester. The rubs and vexations
that necessarily accompanied them in the business of the parish, are darkly hinted at in *Tristram Shandy* along with raillery of the squire's showy activities. "A hundred-and-fifty odd
projects,"—says Sterne of Mr. Walter Shandy, while doubtless thinking of Philip Harland—"A hundred-and-fifty odd
projects took possession of his brains by turns—he would do
this, and that, and t'other—He would go to *Rome*—he would
go to law—he would buy stock—he would buy *John Hobson's*
farm—he would new forefront his house, and add a new
wing to make it even—There was a fine water-mill on this
side, and he would build a windmill on the other side of the
river in full view to answer it—But above all things in the
world, he would inclose the great *OX-moor.*" In heedless talk
like this Sterne was also ridiculing himself, but the stolid country squire would not understand that. Among other infirmities,
the squire was accustomed to boast of his ancestry. It was he
who erected in the parish church the monument to his great-
grandfather, Richard Harland. Sterne, we may be sure, heard
the high-sounding phrases of the inscription many times before
they were engraved in marble, and had them in memory when
he set up an altercation between Walter Shandy and my uncle
Toby over the jack-boots that Sir Roger, their great-grandfather, wore at Marston Moor.

Sterne's other parishioners, who lived in "the odd houses
and farms" about him, naturally took sides with the parson
or the squire. Perhaps they had some real grievance against
Sterne, inasmuch as the products of his dairy were sold below
the market price, then an offence for which one was liable to
fine and jail. There was a large car, or pond, over on Stillington Common, where, it is said, Sterne used to go for his skat-

* *York Courant*, September 5, 1749.

ing, when the fly stung him that way. On one occasion "the ice broke in with him in the middle of the pond, and none of the parishioners wou'd assist to extricate him, as they were at variance." Similar to this is the story which tells how Sterne narrowly escaped an attack from his parishioners: "Another time a flock of geese assembled in the church yard at Sutton, when his wife bawl'd out 'Laurie, powl 'em,' i.e. pluck the quills, on which they were ready to riot and mob Laurie."

It would be a mistake to infer from these stories and whatever else has been said, that Sterne lived in perpetual quarrel with the squire of Sutton and his other parishioners. He lacked tact and "good management" in dealing with them; and they —steady-going farmers, moving along in the paths of ancient habit and custom—could not understand the variable temper of their parson. The result was friction which sometimes grated aloud. At times their common affairs surely went on smoothly. Many of the trees that adorned Sterne's orchard came, says the parish registry, from the park of Philip Harland. The vicar and the squire on one occasion laid aside all differences and joined hands in enclosing the common fields and meadows of the parish. The anecdotist speaks of pleasant gatherings at the rectory and at neighboring houses, where Sterne performed on the bass-viol for his friends; and his wife, who "had a fine voice and a good taste in music," sometimes contributed to the entertainment by accompanying her husband on his favorite instrument.

This agreeable picture of Sterne among his parishioners has recently been confirmed by further documentary evidence discovered by Canon Ollard. In May, 1743, Archbishop Herring, in preparation for his first visitation after his appointment to the see of York, sent out a *questionnaire* to the clergy of the diocese, requesting information under twelve heads in regard to the affairs of their parishes. Among hundreds of returns, Sterne's, it is said, was unique for its completeness. There were, he informed the Archbishop, about a hundred and twenty families in his parish at Sutton, of whom five were Quakers who assembled in their Meeting House every Sunday to the number of thirty persons. Over the Quakers, whom he was trying to convert, he was greatly disturbed, though he had prevailed with one woman to come to church, and hoped to persuade her to be baptised. At that time he was holding two services on Sundays without the assistance of a curate, and was administering the Sacrament of the Lord's Supper five times a year. Of his two hundred and fifty parishioners rather more than a half had communicated at the previous Easter. During the six Sundays of Lent he regularly catechised in his church in the morning; and in the evening conducted a confirmation or instruction class at the parsonage from six to nine o'clock for children and servants. Over against gossip about Sterne should always be set the portrait of a faithful parish priest, solicitous for the spiritual welfare of the souls committed to his care in the midst of his farming and recreations. Except for occasional flares of temper, Sterne and his parishioners appear to have lived happily together.*

The vicar and his wife loved best to visit with the Crofts at Stillington Hall, whose friendship more than made up for any antipathies that existed between them and the Harlands. The Crofts, said Sterne in recollection of those days, "shewed us every kindness—'twas most truly agreeable to be within a mile and a half of an amiable family, who were ever cordial friends." The Crofts were an old Yorkshire family of merchants and aldermen that had been associated with Sterne's own kin for more than a century. One of Sterne's ancestors, Roger Jaques, Lord Mayor of York, was knighted, it will be remembered, by Charles the First in 1639. Two years later the king was again at York, where he was entertained by the new Lord Mayor, Christopher Croft, whom he also knighted before leaving the city. From this Sir Christopher, the founder of the family, was descended Sterne's friend, Stephen Croft. Born on December 8, 1712, less than a year before Sterne, Stephen Croft, as a young man, went out to Oporto, where he

* For a full account of Sterne's reply to the Archbishop's *questionnaire*, see S. L. Ollard in *The Times Literary Supplement*, March 18, 1926.

was engaged with others of his family in the wine-trade. (Croft's Port, now after two centuries, is still one of the best varieties of the wine.) On the death of his father in 1733, Stephen inherited the lordship of Stillington and a large estate —various lands and messuages—in the parish. He still kept up, after Sterne settled at Sutton, his connection with the factory at Oporto, but he then resided for the most part on his manor. His "amiable" wife, named Henrietta, was a daughter of Henry Thompson of Kirby Hall, Little Ouseburn, a few miles across the country on the way to Knaresborough.

There was also a younger brother, John Croft, who "grew up" at Stillington, and afterwards went to Portugal to make his fortune. He remembered Sterne well; and after coming back to York and turning antiquary, he wrote of him the anecdotes from which we have quoted liberally. Sterne was, he said, "a constant guest at my brother's table." The two men, Stephen Croft and Laurence Sterne, of the same age and of similar family connections, grew to be most congenial companions. The one brought to their common friendship jests innumerable; the other, the tales and adventures that come to a man of the world. Beyond this, Sterne took the Crofts into his confidence, telling them what books he read and studied most in forming his style; and there by the fireside of Stillington Hall, he read the first chapters of *Tristram Shandy* while it was in manuscript. But for Stephen Croft the sheets would have gone into the fire instead of to the printer.

CHAP. III.

Politics and Honors. 1741-1750

THE country parson was also a prebendary of York, who took an active part in the politics and intrigues within and without the Cathedral Close, at a time when the entire nation was stirred by civil and religious commotions. And yet, notwithstanding his activity, this is a rather obscure phase of Sterne's life after he reached man's estate, although light here and there is being thrown upon it. We know that he found time, in the midst of farming and parish business, to enter the thick of Yorkshire politics, but for following him in his courses the clues are often indirect and not quite trustworthy. General inference from his character and the position he occupied in the Church of York must be at times one's main guide. If the narrative, in consequence of this, now diverges in places from Sterne himself, it will at least bring into view the men with whom he touched elbow as friend and enemy; it will explain, too, some of his opinions and prejudices, and furnish the background to the inevitable breach with his uncle and mother.

On first coming to York, Sterne allied himself with the men whose voices were most potent in the diocese and chapter. The see was then occupied by Lancelot Blackburne, an old man above eighty years of age, "the jolly old Archbishop of York"—Horace Walpole called him—"who had all the manners of a man of quality." Like Sterne, the aged prelate was a wit and humorist whose career in the Church had been accompanied by ballads and anecdotes charging him with gay immoralities. It was he who collated Sterne to the vicarage of Sutton. The Dean of the Chapter was Richard Osbaldeston, then about fifty years old, a Cambridge man and sometime chaplain to George the Second. It was he who issued the mandate for Sterne's induction to Stillington. To him Sterne dedicated his first printed sermon "in testimony of the great respect which I owe to your character in general; and from a sense of what is due to it in particular from every member of the Church of York." But the man behind the throne, to whom Sterne really owed his first appointments, was of course his "rich and opulent uncle," Dr. Jaques Sterne, Precentor to the Cathedral and Archdeacon of Cleveland, to slip over his several other titles. The old archbishop dying in 1743, he was succeeded by Thomas Herring, a handsome and dignified ecclesiastic in the very prime of life. A graduate of Jesus College, the year before Dr. Sterne, he subsequently gained reputation as an eloquent preacher at Lincoln's Inn Chapel, especially for sermons on the corrupt state of contemporary manners and a denunciation of the *Beggar's Opera*, a kind of writing unknown to "the venerable sages of antiquity"! It was reserved for the moderns, said the preacher, to discover in "a gang of highwaymen and pickpockets a proper subject for laughter and merriment."* Afterwards Dean of Rochester and Bishop of Bangor, he proved an able administrator, and was duly elevated, as aforesaid, to the see of York. On Wednesday, the eighth of June, his Grace arrived at Bishopthorpe; and on the following Saturday, which was the seventeenth anniversary "of his Majesty's Accession to the Crown," he went to the cathedral, "accompanied by the Right Rev. Dr. Mawson, Lord Bishop of Chichester," where he listened to a sermon by the Rev. Laurence Sterne, "suitable to the Occasion."† That Sterne, not yet thirty years old, should be selected to preach the first sermon in St. Peter's before Archbishop Herring and other church dignitaries is an indication of the high esteem in which the young prebendary was held.

The new archbishop and Dr. Jaques Sterne were much alike in temper and opinion; and both were men of tremendous en-

* See appendix to *Letters from Dr. Thomas Herring to William Duncombe* (London, 1777), containing two letters to the *Whitehall Evening Post* on the *Beggar's Opera*, dated March 30 and April 20, 1728.

† L. P. Curtis, *The Politicks of Laurence Sterne*, 122 (London, 1929).

ergy. From the first they joined hands in support of Whig policies through thick and thin and against all Roman Catholics, real or imaginary. The year 1745, when Charles Edward Stuart returned to claim his own, was a strenuous period for them. On July 24, the young Pretender landed with a few friends in the Hebrides, and on August 19, unfurled his banner at Glenfinnan. After collecting a small army of Highlanders, he marched to Perth, where he rested for reinforcements and to discipline his troops. He then proceeded to Edinburgh, and met the English at Preston Pans on September 21, rushing upon them with a yell through the mists of morning and cutting them utterly to pieces. He subsequently crossed the English border, forced the capitulation of Carlisle, marched south through Penrith, Kendal, and Lancaster into Derbyshire, where he was checked and turned backwards into Scotland. The last scene of all was the terrible carnage of the Duke of Cumberland at Culloden on April 16, 1746, whence the prince fled, a fugitive among the mountains and islands to the west. At York, as at other towns in the north, the events of '45 threw the people into consternation. For a time shops were closed and all business was suspended.

Archbishop Herring sounded the alarm to the nation in a sermon preached in the cathedral on September 22, the day after the defeat at Preston Pans. This sermon was preparatory to a plan that the archbishop had been maturing for some weeks for uniting the people of Yorkshire into an association for "the security of his Majesty's Person and government and for the defence of the county of York." On September 24, the nobility, clergy, and gentry met at the ancient castle of York, where the archbishop presented the articles of association in an eloquent speech,* giving "the reasons of our present assembling." The commotions in Scotland, it was believed, were but a part of a general design concerted for the ruin of England by France and Spain, "our savage and bloodthirsty

* A Speech made by his Grace, the Lord Archbishop of York, at Presenting an Association enter'd into at the Castle of York (London, 1745).

enemies." The clergy of the diocese were especially commanded "to instruct and animate" their congregations "to stand up against Popery and Arbitrary Power under a French and Spanish government." By the archbishop's exertions a defence fund was collected amounting to £31,364, to which Jaques Sterne contributed £50. "Laurence Sterne, clerk," it is recorded, "subscribed and paid £10. 10s." and collected from his two parishes £15. 14s. 6d.*

Next to the archbishop, the church politician most active at York in 1745 and immediately thereafter was Dr. Jaques Sterne. When the Duke of Cumberland returned from the victory of Culloden, stopping on his way south at York, where he was granted the freedom of the city, he stayed, at his own request, with the precentor in the Minster Yard instead of with Archbishop Herring or the Lord Mayor. This compliment to Dr. Sterne is significant of the value that the government attached to his services. His sermons and addresses at the time, to say the truth, rather surpassed the archbishop's in fire and savage denunciation of the Pretender, Jacobites, and Roman Catholics. Especially notable is the charge that Dr. Sterne delivered to his clergy at Thirsk, a few miles from Sutton, and in other parishes of his archdeaconry, during his visitations of 1746. It was printed at York the next year under the title of *The Danger arising to our Civil and Religious Liberty from the Great Increase of Papists, and the Setting up Public Schools and Seminaries for the Teaching and Educating of Youth in the pernicious Tenets and Principles of Popery.* In this pamphlet, which was dedicated to the archbishop as the author of "that glorious Association . . . against the united Force of Popery and Rebellion," the archdeacon sought to revive the old laws of the time of Elizabeth and William the Third against saying or hearing Mass, proselyting, and Roman Catholic schools. After a brief account of the abominations of Popery, it was carefully and minutely explained to the clergy

* *An Exact List of the Voluntary Subscribers, with the sums each subscrib'd and paid for the Security of his Majesty's Person and Government* (York, 1747).

how they and the church wardens might bring all recusants in their parishes to the bar of justice for fine and imprisonment.

As if in further explanation of how it should be done, Dr. Sterne himself proceeded against the so-called "Popish Nunnery" at York. Many of the oldest and wealthiest families of Yorkshire were still Roman Catholics, and some of them had given either open or secret support to the House of Stuart, both in 1715 and in 1745. Several of these county families were accustomed to live on their estates in the country during the summer, and to come into York for the winter, living in large and fine houses with lavish hospitality in Micklegate, the muckle or great street of the city. In a narrow street branching off from Micklegate Bar, they established, in 1686, a boarding-school for their daughters, and placed in charge of it a Mrs. Paston. The little street outside Micklegate Bar soon got the name of Nunnery Lane, and the old brick house where the school was kept became known as the Nunnery. Over this institution the Church of York was at times very uneasy. In 1714, Mrs. Paston, like other Roman Catholics in Micklegate ward, refused to take the oath of allegiance to George the First, and in consequence her school was closely watched for some time. But everything became quiet in the course of a few years until the disturbances of 1745 and thereafter. Then Dr. Sterne made up his mind to put an end to this "Popish Seminary, set up for poisoning the minds of the King's Subjects." Two old women then in charge of the school, one of whom was styled "the Abbess," were summoned before an ecclesiastic court and convicted of recusancy. They were admonished and fined twelve pence a Sunday.* Not satisfied with this mild punishment, Dr. Sterne proceeded against them under the laws against saying or hearing Mass and against a Papist's engaging in the education or boarding of youth. The cause dragged on in the courts until 1751, when it was dropped. Throughout it all the "pious Doctor" was bantered a good deal on his "rough methods of making converts of the ladies"

* *York Courant*, October 3, 1749; and *St. James's Evening Post*, October 5-7.

and on "his stale ecclesiastical tricks." What he imagined, in
the blindness of his zeal, as a nunnery, was a quite harmless
boarding-school which flourished long afterwards without
molestation.

Until a quarrel broke out between them, Dr. Sterne's aide-
de-camp, so to speak, was his nephew, Laurence Sterne. The
young man had been initiated into York politics during the
summer of 1741, when occurred the general election that resulted in the retirement of Sir Robert Walpole. The adherents of Walpole, standing for things as they were in church
and state, were known as the Court Party, which was particularly strong among the clergy. The opposition, composed of
Tories and disaffected Whigs, was called the Country Party,
which, as the name implies, included a large body of country
gentlemen. Though the election was thus not a straight contest between Whig and Tory, these names, however, may be
used here for the sake of brevity to describe the parties in the
conflict. As was expected, a Whig and a Tory member for
the county and a Whig and a Tory member for the city of
York were elected to the new Parliament, to the general satisfaction of the moderates of both parties, who wished to preserve a balance of powers. Unfortunately for the peace of the
shire, the Whig member for the county died during the summer. For the vacant seat the Whigs nominated Cholmley
Turner of Kirkleatham, who had represented them in three
previous Parliaments. Against him the Tories put up George
Fox, of Bramham Park, who had large estates in Ireland also.
The battle that ensued was waged with extreme bitterness.
Each party accused the other of underhand and disgraceful
methods of securing votes, hinting, though not openly charging, bribery. What that fierce contest meant for the minor
clergy and the understrappers may be inferred from a brief
record to which reference has been already made. The Rev.
Robert Hitch, Canon and Prebendary of North Newbald, "a
fine tall personage," said Thomas Gent, a York printer and
bookseller, "overheated himself about obtaining votes for Par-

liament, that threw him into a mortal fever, which . . . conveyed his precious soul, I hope, into the regions of a blessed immortality."* That Laurence Sterne, then Prebendary of Givendale, likewise performed services deemed worthy of recognition, seems quite clear; for within ten days after the death of Mr. Hitch, he was appointed to the comfortable prebend so opportunely left vacant.

Though Sterne may have engaged in the open solicitation of votes as well as his predecessor who lost his life thereby, his main services to his church and party at this time and in succeeding years were performed by his facile pen. "In his younger years," so runs a letter of John Croft respecting Sterne, "he was a good deal employed by his uncle in writing political papers and pamphlets in favour of Sir Robert Walpole's Administration." "We have heard," said the *Monthly Review* for October, 1775, "of his writing a periodical electioneering paper at York in defence of the Whig interest." *St. James's Chronicle*, in its issue of April 10, 1788, had a longer version of the same story, which, the correspondent claimed, Sterne once told to a friend. "He wrote," it is said there, "a weekly paper in support of the Whigs during the long canvass for the great contested election, . . . and he owed his preferment to that paper—so acceptable was it to the then Archbishop." The essential truth of these traditions is confirmed by Sterne himself in his brief autobiography, wherein he says "my uncle . . . quarrelled with me . . . because I would not write paragraphs in the newspapers."

Beyond these statements, nothing was known about Sterne's political writings until Mr. Lewis P. Curtis† uncovered enough of them to show that Sterne played a conspicuous part in the by-election of 1741, as the chief writer for the Whigs in an acrimonious newspaper debate over the character and principles of Cholmley Turner and George Fox. At that time the leading newspaper published at York was *The York Courant*.

* Thomas Gent, *Life*, 194-195.
† For a full account of Sterne in relation to the elections of 1741-42, see L. P. Curtis, *The Politicks of Laurence Sterne* (London, 1929).

Though not violently partisan in ordinary times, it was owned and conducted in the Country interest by Cæsar Ward, the printer and bookseller in Coney Street, who tried to close the columns of his newspaper against the Whigs during excited canvasses. Only by browbeating and the consent to tone down scurrilous passages, could the Whigs then find admittance. In these circumstances, it was necessary for them to print and issue pamphlets and temporary sheets. This year they set up *The York Gazetteer*, with John Jackson, a young rival of Cæsar Ward, as printer. Though but one number of this newspaper for 1741 has yet come to light, it is reasonably certain that Dr. Jaques Sterne was behind the undertaking with his nephew serving for a time under him as the main contributor of articles and paragraphs in a warfare of political abuse. Very adroitly, too, the young prebendary found a means of breaking into the enemy's camp, where he carried on in *The York Courant* a lively controversy with a violent Tory. By piecing together some seven or eight of Sterne's letters, articles, and paragraphs in the two York newspapers one may see what he was doing for the Whigs, though the whole story cannot yet be told.

Sterne entered the fray as soon as it became apparent that the Tories would contest the return of a Whig for the county in place of the member who had died. By September he was in full swing. A master of mischief, he was by that time attacking George Fox in "villainous letters" to *The York Courant* under assumed names, as if the letters came from various country gentlemen. But Cæsar Ward detected Sterne's handwriting and requested "the Vicar" to come out of cover if he wished to have his letters printed. Sterne humorously accepted the challenge. Whereupon began a flow of vituperation in a political correspondence between Sterne and a certain "J.S.," who seems to have been the Rev. James Scott, Vicar of Bardsey, a parish to the north of Leeds. This give-and-take between two clergymen reveals many personal characteristics of Sterne, who really liked Cæsar Ward in spite of political antagonisms. There are indications that Sterne was writing "handbills" for distribution and that several of his articles in the York newspapers, which were quoted in London newspapers, were issued, with alterations, as pamphlets.

One of these pamphlets at least has survived. "J.S." had asked in *The York Courant* a number of questions concerning the political career of Cholmley Turner, and Sterne had replied with a series of similar questions about the political career of George Fox and his fitness to represent Yorkshire. Somewhat enlarged, Sterne's letter was reprinted as a brochure of eight pages under the title of *Query upon Query.* The war still went on with unmitigated personal abuse until the election of Cholmley Turner. Sterne's reward was the prebend of North Newbald.

Again there was peace in Yorkshire. But just as the Whig member for the county had died in 1741, so in the summer of the following year, Edward Thompson, the Whig member for the city of York, died. In the meantime Walpole had fallen from power. No longer could there be a party either for or against him. George Fox, who had been defeated in the county election, now stood for the city of York and was unanimously elected. The bells of the churches rang all day into the evening, when Mr. Fox gave a grand ball at the Assembly Rooms. Sterne, who shared in the enthusiasm over the election of a really fine man, immediately published his recantation in a characteristic letter to the printer of *The York Courant*:

Sir,

I find by some late Preferments, that it may not be improper to change Sides; therefore I beg the Favour of you to inform the Publick, that I sincerely beg Pardon for the abusive Gazetteers I wrote during the late contested Election for the County of York, and that I heartily wish Mr. Fox Joy of his Election for the City.

Tempora Mutantur, & nos mutemur in illis.
I am, Sir, your Penitent Friend and Servant.

L.S.

So ended humorously the first experiment in politics by the man who was to write *Tristram Shandy*.

It is safe to assume, though positive evidence is yet wanting, that Sterne again came to the assistance of his uncle as a journalist against the Jacobites of 1745. In that year *The York Gazetteer* came to an end, and was succeeded by *The York Journal or The Protestant Courant*, which its printer, John Gilfillan, announced would contain "the earliest, best and most authentic accounts of any in the North of England; and, being entirely calculated for the service of the King and country, he hoped it would meet with encouragement from all who wished well to the present happy establishment in Church and State."* To this newspaper, set up in November, 1745, under the patronage of the Church of York, Laurence Sterne was probably a contributor by direction of his uncle, whose archidiaconal charges were being printed by Gilfillan. But as no copy of *The York Journal* for 1745 has yet been discovered and only one copy for 1746, the question of Sterne's rôle in the undertaking must remain unsettled for the present.

It may be surmised, if nothing more, that the easy paragraph-writer was also the author of various letters to London newspapers, during the Jacobite alarm, descriptive of doings at York, of arrests, trials, and executions of those unfortunate gentlemen who joined the Pretender's army. "On Saturday last," to quote a sentence here and there from the York correspondent to the *London Evening Post* for November 6-8, 1746, "On Saturday last eleven of the rebels under sentence of death . . . were brought from the Castle in three sledges. . . . They walked up to the gallows without the least concern, where they prayed very devoutly. After which Capt. Hamilton mounted the ladder first, Frazier next, and the rest in order. . . . One of them said he died because his K—g was not upon the T—e. . . . Captain Hamilton was the first whose heart was cut out. . . . We hear that Sir David Murray, Bart. and

* Robert Davies, *Memoir of the York Press*, 323-324 (London, 1868).

fifty-two more have received notice of execution for next Saturday."

In this dreadful work of hunting out the Jacobites and bringing them to the bar of justice, no one was more zealous than Dr. Sterne. He was so ready, as a magistrate of the West Riding, to issue a warrant for commitment on vague and hearsay evidence, that the Secretary of State thought it necessary on one occasion to reprimand him. Two cases of his dealings with well-known Tory physicians of York are of especial interest here. One is that of Dr. Francis Drake, the distinguished antiquary and historian, who refused the oaths in 1745. Before and after his arrest and release, he assailed "Parson St—e" in paragraph after paragraph contributed to *The York Courant*, holding up to scathing ridicule the precentor's career in religion and politics. In reply Dr. Sterne, who was not permitted to employ the local newspaper, had recourse to "virulent advertisements," which circulated among the coffee-houses and passed on from hand to hand. Whether his nephew collaborated on these satirical pamphlets, we do not presume to know; all that can be said is that he was then probably writing for his uncle. The second case is that of Dr. John Burton, author and antiquary, who was also suspected of Jacobitism. In Dr. Sterne's long persecution of this able physician, Laurence was closely involved. His hatred and contempt for the high-flying Tory amounted to an obsession falling little short of insanity. Pilloried again and again in *Tristram Shandy*, Dr. Burton *alias* Dr. Slop is never dropped except to be pilloried a few pages on.

Three years younger than Laurence Sterne, Burton graduated, Bachelor of Medicine, at St. John's College, Cambridge, in 1733, and immediately began the practice of medicine at Heath, a Yorkshire village near Wakefield. The next year came on a contested election for the county, in which "the greatest exertions were made by the friends and opponents of Walpole." To the young physician, who espoused the Tory side with vehemence, was entrusted the entire charge of the electors of Wakefield, where "he was very active and vigilant in the discharge of his duties." "On the fourth day of the poll," it is said further, "he conducted a body of freeholders to York," saw to it that they voted, and then watched at a booth till the voting was over. The contest resulted in the return of one member on each side. But for the "pernicious activity" of the physician of Wakefield, it was claimed, the Whigs would have easily elected both their candidates.

The election over, Dr. Burton married a small heiress and went abroad to complete his medical education. He took the degree of M.D. at Rheims and attended the clinics of the great Boerhaave at Leyden. On his return he settled permanently at York "as physician and man-mid-wife," where he soon became very popular with the poorer classes, for he treated them free of charge, and founded, with the aid of wealthy friends, a hospital for the city and county of York, which was known among his political enemies as the Tory Infirmary. Meanwhile Dr. Burton had appeared in print. His first effort, which shows the way his studies were tending, was *An Account of a Monstrous Child,* a tract contributed to the *Edinburgh Medical Essays* for 1736. This was followed two years later by *A Treatise on the Non-naturals,* which excited the mirth of the author of *Tristram Shandy,* who enquired of the doctor "why the most natural actions of a man's life should be called his non-naturals."

Political animosities, which had long been smouldering, again broke out violently in the election of 1741. Dr. Burton again became conspicuous and repeated his success of 1734; whereupon he was subjected, according to his own narrative, to all sorts of abuse and calumny from the Whigs in general and from Dr. Sterne in especial. When, for example, Dr. Burton, who was living at that time in Coney Street, applied to the Corporation for a more respectable residence in the centre of the city, his political enemies interfered and tried to prevent the lease. He however obtained the large house that he desired, and went on with his profession, giving more and more attention to obstetrics, which, as a new science, exposed him to the ridicule of a large body of men and women who were content to have their children brought into the world after the old ways practised by the midwives.

The year 1745 was now at hand and Dr. Sterne had his revenge. On November 22, news reached York that the vanguard of the Highlanders was at Kendal. The inhabitants of York were alarmed lest the rebels should enter Yorkshire and march on to the city. Dr. Burton, who owned two farms near Settle, in the West Riding, not far from the borders of Lancashire, received permission from the Lord Mayor to post west to look after his estates, which seemed to be in danger. The rebels, however, took a route to the left of his property, leaving his tenants unharmed. After this discovery, the doctor went on to the village of Hornby in the North Riding, where he was taken prisoner, while being shaved at an inn, by a party of Highlanders, who entertained him at the castle and then conveyed him south to Lancaster. After a few days' detention, he was dismissed with a pass for his safety. On reaching York, he was met by his enemies, to whom had come rumors of his movements. He was immediately—it was November 30— brought before Thomas Place, the recorder, and Dr. Jaques Sterne, a magistrate for the West Riding, who issued a warrant for his commitment to York Castle as "a suspicious person to his Majesty's government." During the examination, Dr. Sterne, the unfortunate physician alleged, "made a great Blustering, and talked much, but it was *vox et praeterea nihil;* he was often in such a hurry with party fury, that he could not utter his words for *vox faucibus haesit,* and he presently foamed at the mouth especially when I laughed at him and told him, that I set him and all his party at defiance, unless false witnesses were to appear, which I own, I was not altogether without apprehensions about."*

Of what took place on that occasion and subsequently, Dr. Sterne published three brief accounts in a York newspaper,

* For the whole transaction, see Burton, *British Liberty Endangered* (London, 1749); and Robert Davies, *A Memoir of John Burton,* in the second volume of *The Yorkshire Archæological and Topographical Journal.*

presumably in *The York Journal, or Protestant Courant.*
These notices, it has been asserted, though without positive
evidence, were written by his nephew. The first of them was
sent up to the *London Evening Post,* where it appeared in the
issue of December 5-7. This paragraph, in the form of a letter from York, dated December 3, has great interest as very
likely from the pen of Laurence Sterne. It runs as follows:

"On Saturday last Dr. *Burton* was committed to the Castle,
by the Recorder and Dr. *Sterne,* as Justices for the West Riding of this county. It appearing from his own Confession, that
he went from Settle to *Hornby, knowing the Rebels were
there,* and upon a Supposition that the Duke of *Perth* was
there, wrote a Letter to him, which being opened by Lord
Elcho, he was sent for up by two *Highlanders* to the Castle,
and, as he says, carried along with them as a *Prisoner* to *Lancaster,* where he convers'd with Lord *George Murray,* and a
Person there call'd his *Royal Highness Prince Charles.* There
was the greatest Satisfaction expressed at his Commitment,
from the highest to the lowest Person in the City, that has been
known here upon any Occasion."

A few days later, Burton applied for release on bail. This
was refused by Dr. Sterne and three other magistrates, and a
further charge was brought against Burton on the information
of one John Nesbitt, a prisoner in the castle. A new warrant
of detainer was issued with an order to the jailer not to admit
the doctor to bail, as the new evidence amounted to a charge
of high treason. Dr. Burton lost his place on the hospital board
and it seemed as if he would be tried and hanged. But just before the assizes, the Secretary of State intervened with an order that the prisoner be conveyed up to London for examination before the Privy Council. He was detained for a full year
—till March 25, 1747—when he was summoned to the Cockpit and discharged. While in London, Dr. Burton conversed
with several gentleman who had fought on the Pretender's
side at Culloden, and afterwards wrote out what he learned
from them, in a little book entitled *A Genuine and True
Journal of the Most Miraculous Escape of the Young Cheva-*

lier (1749). By this time, too, he had begun, under the influence of Dr. Drake, his studies in archæology, which resulted in the *Monasticon Eboracense, or the Ecclesiastical History of Yorkshire* (1758), a monument to patient labor and research. After his release, Dr. Burton resumed his practice and professional studies at York, publishing in 1751 *An Essay toward a Complete New System of Midwifery*, and two years later *A Letter to William Smellie, M.D.*, of Glasgow, violently attacking the Scottish physician's theory and practice of midwifery. Thereafter he was known among his enemies as "Hippocrates Obstetricius."

Despite one's sympathy with the York physician in his long persecution, he was, to say the truth, very indiscreet in his conduct. Not a Jacobite and Papist surely, his extreme Toryism exposed him to a suspicion of being both, at a time when passions ran so high that little distinction could be made between a Tory and a Jacobite and none at all between a Jacobite and a Papist. It was then, to quote the doctor himself, "tantamount to downright Disaffection, to assert that the young Chevalier has not a cloven foot, or something monstrous about him." It must be said, in justice to the two Sternes, that the physician excited disgust among many others with whom he came into conflict, for he was obstinate, noisy, and meddlesome. An elaborate story got into print about a fracas that occurred at the inauguration dinner given by Henry Jubb, an apothecary, on being elected sheriff of York in the autumn of 1754. The dinner was held at the sheriff's house in Micklegate. There were present the Lord Mayor, who presided according to custom, several aldermen, and other leading citizens, including the York physician. Dr. Burton did not rise with the rest when the Lord Mayor proposed a toast "To the glorious and immortal memory of King William the Third"; and in consequence hot words passed across the table. Mr. George Thompson, a Whig wine-merchant, by that time "warmed with the convivial glass," just slightly filliped a cork towards the doctor in way of derision; and a few minutes afterwards tried to compel him to drink "Everlasting disap-

pointment [or "damnation" according to Dr. Burton] to the
Pretender and all his adherents." Burton said that he had religious scruples against drinking damnation to anybody. "A
most extraordinary scene of riot and disorder ensued." The
guests jumped upon the table; the doctor brandished his cane
right and left, levelling to the floor two gentlemen, one of
whom "collared him, tore his shirt and scratched his neck."
At length an attorney-at-law wrested the weapon from Burton and threw it into the fire. The scuffle ended with the for-
cible ejection of the infuriated physician.*

The name of Laurence Sterne does not appear in the list
of distinguished guests who attended this "entertainment,"
as it was mildly called, at Mr. Sheriff Jubb's. But whether
present or not, he shared in the extreme hostility of his party
towards Dr. Burton. We cannot say when and where Sterne
and Burton first came into conflict. We can only point to the
contested election of 1741 and the proceedings against the
physician in 1745-46, as the probable occasions, at a time when
the young prebendary was closely associated with his uncle in
electioneering and paragraph-writing. Burton's books on midwifery he read, and laughed at them. No sooner was *Tristram
Shandy* out than everybody at York knew that Dr. Slop and
Dr. Burton were one. As if to make the identification perfectly clear, Sterne paraphrased an amusing passage in Burton's attack on Dr. William Smellie of Glasgow; wherein
the Scottish physician was accused of converting the drawing
of a petrified child in an old medical treatise into a full-
fledged author, who of course had never existed.† Dr. Burton,
as he appears under the name of Dr. Slop, was the bungling
man-midwife to whom Tristram Shandy owed his broken
nose. In appearance the *accoucheur*, as he wished to be called,
was a "little squat, uncourtly figure . . . of about four feet

* See *An Account of What Passed between Mr. George Thompson
of York and Dr. John Burton . . . at Mr. Sheriff Jubb's Entertainment* (London, 1756).

† "If any thing can be added to shock human Faith, or prejudice
your Character as an Historian or Translator, it is your having con-

and a half perpendicular height, with a breadth of back, and a sesquipedality of belly, which might have done honour to a serjeant in the horse-guards." It was his custom to ride "a little diminutive pony, of a pretty colour—but of strength—alack!—scarce able to have made an amble of it, under such a fardel." Slung at the doctor's back might be seen a "green bays bag," in which jingled, as he rode along, his new-invented "instruments of salvation and deliverance." Dr. Slop runs through *Tristram Shandy* as an ill-tempered, ill-mannered, and vulgar Papist, the butt of all the current jests and prejudices against Roman Catholics.

Sterne's frightful caricature of an able physician and learned antiquary is unexplainable without reference to the fierce religious passions awakened by the events of 1745, when every church, from the Cathedral of St. Peter's to the remotest parish, rang with denunciations of Rome and all her ways. Archbishop Herring set the pace for his clergy when he announced from the pulpit that "no nation . . . can possibly be happy under Popery," for "it sinks the spirits of men and damps the vigour of life," and then went on to ascribe the dreadful state of society to contamination with "a Popish abjured Pretender." "Things every Day," declared the preacher, waxing eloquent in his rhetoric, "proceed from bad to worse: magistracy is contemned, dignity and order sunk to the common level, adultery and vagrant uncleanliness is become an epidemicall evil."* This cry was taken up by the archdeacons and carried to the country parsons.

Sterne, like the rest, heeded the call. He was at York Castle, we may count upon it, when the clergy and gentry entered into the association for the defence of Yorkshire, and at Thirsk when his uncle laid bare the abuses and horrors of the

verted *Lithopædii Senonensis Icon*, (which you call *Lithopedus Senonensis*) an inanimate, petrified Substance, into an Author, after you had been *six years cooking up your Book.*"—*Letter to Smellie*, p. 1 (London, 1753). Compare *Tristram Shandy*, footnote to ch. XIX, bk. II.

* *A Sermon Preached at Kensington on Wednesday, the Seventh of January* (London, 1747).

Church of Rome. His own sermons, such as without doubt belong to this period, might have been written, so far as their tone is concerned, either by the archbishop or by the archdeacon. The point of difference is but one of style. Neither of the men in higher place defined Popery, with reference to penances and indulgences, quite so neatly as Sterne when he called it "a pecuniary system, well contrived to operate upon men's passions and weakness, whilst their pockets are o'picking." He preached eloquently against the Mass and its mummeries, auricular confession, the arts of the Jesuits, and "the cruelties, murders, rapine, and bloodshed" that have ever accompanied Rome in her history. The long wars of his time, the high tax rate in consequence of them, and the pestilence that swept over the cattle after the insurrection of 1745, leaving "no herd in the stalls," he regarded as the last judgment of the Almighty upon a people who had forgotten the ways of righteousness, and were listening to the seductions of Jesuit missionaries.

It was a red-letter day in the life of the young prebendary when he rose into the pulpit of St. Peter's before a large and distinguished congregation, and drew for them the portrait of a victim of the Inquisition. "Behold," spoke the preacher as if out of a romance, "Behold *religion* with mercy and justice chain'd down under her feet,—there sitting ghastly upon a black tribunal, propp'd up with racks and instruments of torment.—Hark!—What a piteous groan!—See the melancholy wretch who utter'd it, just brought forth to undergo the anguish of a mock trial, and endure the utmost pains that a studied system of *religious cruelty* has been able to invent. Behold this helpless victim delivered up to the tormentors. His body so wasted with sorrow and long confinement, you'll see every nerve and muscle as it suffers.—Observe the last movement of that horrid engine.—What convulsions it has thrown him into. Consider the nature of the posture in which he now lies stretch'd.—What exquisite torture he endures by it.—'Tis all nature can bear.—Good God! see how it keeps his weary soul hanging on his trembling lips, willing to take its leave,—

but not suffered to depart. Behold the unhappy wretch led back to his cell,—dragg'd out of it again to meet the flames,—and the insults in his last agonies."*

Sterne's intense hatred of the Church of Rome, which carried him, with the rest of his party, to the verge of madness, was a phase of his early development that endured until he came to visit France and Italy and move freely among all classes in the two countries. Not till then was he aware that it was possible for Roman Catholics to be content and happy. In the meantime, his feelings against Rome naturally became less violent as his mind was drawn to other things. Immediately after the Jacobite crisis, various important changes affecting his own career took place in the Church of York. In the autumn of 1747, Archbishop Herring was translated to the see of Canterbury in recognition of "his tried loyalty and known zeal in the cause of Protestantism." His place was filled by Matthew Hutton, formerly Bishop of Bangor. Richard Osbaldeston, Dean since 1728 of the York Chapter, was likewise elevated to the bishopric of Carlisle. His successor was John Fountayne, Prebendary of Salisbury and Canon of Windsor. Dr. Sterne was disappointed of immediate reward, for he had lost favor at home because of his persecution of Dr. Burton and the "Popish Nunnery"; and his Majesty's ministers thought he ought to be satisfied with the various sinecures which he already enjoyed. At one time he offered £200 for the freedom of the city of York; but the Corporation, in spite of the inducement, refused him the honor. He tried for the deanery of York and for prebends at Westminster, Windsor, and Canterbury, in all of which he missed his aim. But in lieu of these places, he was transferred, in 1750, from the archdeaconry of Cleveland to that of the richer East Riding, and five years later he was appointed to the second prebendal stall in Durham Cathedral. There are extant several amusing letters† of his to the Duke of Newcastle, in which the plural-

* *The Abuses of Conscience*, July 29, 1750.
† British Museum, Additional MSS., 32719-32730.

ist pleads for these and other appointments, urging in his own behalf long and faithful services to church and state. The one asking for Durham is typical. It runs as follows:

"My Lord

"I hope Your Grace finds that it is not in my nature to be troublesome in my Solicitations; and indeed I am the less so, as I had the Honour of being taken in so kind a manner under Your immediate Protection. But hearing of the Bishop of Gloucester's Death, in my Passage thro' this Town to Bath, I am willing to hope that I shall not be thought impertinent in acquainting Your Grace that a Prebend in the Church of Durham, where there are two Vacant, as it lies near my other Preferments, will be equally agreeable to me, as either Westminster, Windsor, or Canterbury; but I submit it intirely to Your Grace's Judgment and Pleasure, only begging Leave to hope that as I have spent now upwards of Thirty five years in a faithful Service of the Crown, at an Expence that I believe no Clergyman else has done, that I shall, thro' Your Grace's Friendship and Goodness, receive a Mark of the King's Favour at this time, when there are so many Stalls vacant in different Churches:

"There will be no one with More Gratitude, as there has been none with greater zeal thro' life,

"My Lord,

"Your Grace's

"Most Dutiful and

"Westminster—September   "Devoted Servant
 the 19th 1752—   "Jaques Sterne"

In reply Newcastle asked Dr. Sterne for a list of his present holdings with their value, as preliminary to further grants. The list, which was duly written out and sent to the duke, contains these large items:

"A Prebend of Southwell. The reserv'd Rent of which is only £17—15s.—o, but there is a Corpse belonging to it at South-Muskham, of about £200 a year, and an House at Southwell.

"The Vicarage of Hornsea Cum Riston, in the East Riding of Yorkshire, worth £150—

"The Rectory of Rise something above £90.

"He has nothing else but the Arch-Deaconry, where he lives, worth about £60—and a Residentiaryship and Precentorship of York, which are inseparable in His Case, because if he parted with the Precentorship, he cou'd not continue Residentiary—worth betwixt three and four hundred pounds a year communibus annis."

Dr. Sterne's income, about £900 a year, as it appears from the memorandum, was really large for the eighteenth century, though the pluralist, with his lack of humor, could not see it that way.

His nephew undoubtedly expected promotion like the rest. If his services were less conspicuous than theirs, he was certainly still regarded as a young man of unusual ability, for since his sermon before Archbishop Herring, he had been invited to preach at York on two other extraordinary occasions. At that time the city supported two charities for maintaining and educating poor children—the Blue Coat School for boys, and the Grey Coat School for girls. On Good Friday, April 17, 1747, the young prebendary delivered in the parish church of St. Michael-le-Belfrey, by the great minster, the annual sermon for the benefit of these foundations. Besides the usual congregation of commoners, there were present the Lord Mayor, aldermen, and sheriffs, in full official capacity. The preacher most aptly chose for his theme "the miracle wrought in behalf of the widow of Zarephath, who had charitably taken Elijah under her roof, and administered unto him in a time of great scarcity and distress." Already a master of his art, Sterne rose, by one picturesque passage after another, to the pathetic climax where Elijah restores the widow's dead child to life, and, taking it in his arms, places it once more in the bosom of its mother. Finally came the direct appeal to the congregation, that the unfortunate children among them might not be sent out into a "vicious world" without friends and instruction. The appeal was heeded, for the collection amounted to more than sixty-four pounds.* A few weeks later the sermon appeared in print as a sixpenny pamphlet, bearing the title *The Case of Elijah and the Widow of Zarephath Consider'd,* and dedicated to "The Very Reverend Richard Osbaldeston," who had not yet received his appointment to Carlisle.

Eloquent as Sterne was on charity, he greatly surpassed that effort in the sermon preached in the cathedral at the close of the summer assizes, on July 29, 1750. The opportunity came to him as chaplain for that year to Sir William Pennyman, the high sheriff of the county of York. In the congregation were the judges for the summer session, "the Hon. Mr. Baron Clive and the Hon. Mr. Baron Smythe," the high sheriff and the gentlemen of the grand jury, the clergy of the cathedral, and commoners to the number of a thousand. For this official function the preacher selected as text a sentence from St. Paul's Epistle to the Hebrews: "For we trust we have a good conscience." Sterne began, as was henceforth to be his way on great occasions, by half denying the assertion of his text. In this instance was set up the claim against the Apostle that any man, if he thinks about it at all, ought to know whether he has a good conscience or not; it should be for him a matter of knowledge, not merely of trust, St. Paul to the contrary notwithstanding. After winning attention by this startling device, Sterne proceeded to draw from life admirable character-sketches of various types of men, ranging from the openly vicious to the casuist who permits conscience to be dethroned from the judgment-seat by passion, greed, self-interest, or false notions of honor. On the way he stopped for a gay thrust at his banker and physician, "neither of them men of much religion," to whom he trusted his fortune or life, simply because it was for their advantage to deal honestly with him: because, he said, "they cannot hurt me without hurting themselves more." But in case it should be to the interest of the one, added the preacher, "to secrete my fortune and turn me out naked in the world," or of the other to "send me out of it and

* *General Advertiser,* April 25, 1747.

enjoy an estate by my death without dishonour to himself or his art," then no dependence could be placed upon these men who make a jest of religion and treat its sanctions with contempt. Running all through the sermon, as an adroit compliment to the judges, were images and phrases taken from the procedure of law-courts, reaching their climax at the close, where Sterne likened conscience to "a British judge in this land of liberty, who makes no new law, but faithfully declares that glorious law which he finds already written."

At "the unanimous request" of "many Gentlemen of Worth and Character," the sermon was sent to the local press as another sixpenny pamphlet under the title of *The Abuses of Conscience*. On the title-page were the names of the two honorable judges; and the dedication was inscribed to "Sir William Pennyman, Bart.," and a long list of grand jurors. So well did Sterne himself like this clever sermon—the most closely reasoned discourse that ever came from his pen—that he afterwards slipped it into *Tristram Shandy*, where Dr. Slop, *alias* Dr. Burton, who surely was not present on its first delivery, was at length compelled to listen to it from the lips of Corporal Trim.

CHAP. IV.

Quarrel with His Uncle. 1747-1751

THESE unusual honors which Sterne was receiving were accompanied by no important advancement, owing, in the first place, to dissensions in the Church of York. During the crisis of 1745, the clergy suspended their petty differences and united against a common enemy in defence of the House of Hanover and the Church of England. But no sooner was the danger over, than they began once more to intrigue against one another, each seeking his own advantage without much regard to his associates. From the first there was friction between the new archbishop and the new dean, the one accusing the other of encroaching upon his rights and prerogatives, with the result that two more or less distinct parties were formed within the York Chapter.

On the one side were Archbishop Hutton and Dr. Jaques Sterne, with their followers, men of the same age and similar political and religious opinions. Against them were Dean Fountayne and several of the more liberal canons and prebendaries, including Laurence Sterne, who was an old college friend of the dean. These antagonisms hastened what was sure to come at some time, first an estrangement and then an open and bitter quarrel between the two Sternes, uncle and nephew. Apparently as early as 1742, there had occurred a hot scene between them, in the course of which Sterne told his uncle that he would write no more political paragraphs for him. "I . . . detested such dirty work," said Sterne long afterwards, "thinking it beneath me." The Jacobite insurrection, however, brought the two divines together again on a common footing destined to be of short duration. Wiseacres who gathered at the York coffee-houses said that the quarrel was really over "a favourite mistress of the Precentor's," who loved Laurie too well.

Soon Dr. Sterne was denouncing his nephew as "ungrateful and unworthy," and inveighing against him furiously in letters to mutual friends. The nephew, if we interpret aright a passage in *Tristram Shandy*, accused his uncle of being at the head of "a grand confederacy" against him; of playing the part, as it were, of Malice in a melodrama, who sets on "Cruelty and Cowardice, twin ruffians," to waylay a traveller in the dark. "The whole plan of the attack," says the passage, "was put in execution all at once,——with so little mercy on the side of the allies,——and so little suspicion in *Yorick*, of what was carrying on against him,——that when he thought, good easy man! full preferment was o'ripening,——they had smote his root, and then he fell, as many a worthy man had fallen before him." Yorick's head was so bruised and misshapen by these unhandsome blows that he declared, quoting Sancho Panza, that should he recover and "Mitres thereupon be suffered to rain down from heaven as thick as hail, not one of them would fit it."

Though the quarrel had been long brewing, the first serious blow, however, was struck, not at Sterne's head, but, highwayman-like, at his purse. As Prebendary of North Newbald, Laurence Sterne preached in the cathedral twice every year, on the sixth Sunday in Lent, and on the nineteenth Sunday after Trinity, when the harvesting of his crops was over.* Prebendaries and other officials who from sickness, distance, or disinclination found it impossible or inconvenient to take their turns at preaching, were accustomed to engage a brother living near by. Their agent in the negotiations was sometimes John Hildyard, a York bookseller, who knew everybody and whose shop in Stonegate was a gathering place for the minor clergy. Sterne liked to supply the places of others for the addition which it brought to his income. Writing to his archdeacon in 1750, he said: "My daughter will be Twenty Pounds a better Fortune by the favours I've received of this kind . . .

* A table of preachers containing Sterne's dates is given by Thomas Ellway in *Anthems . . . as they are now Perform'd in the Cathedral . . . of York . . . Durham . . . Lincoln* (York, 1753).

this Year; and as so much at least is annually and without much trouble to be picked up in our Pulpit, by any man who cares to make the Sermons, you who are a Father will easily excuse my motive."

It was no hard labor. The sermons were usually perfunctory, and Sterne could drive into York on a Sunday morning, breakfast with a friend, preach in the cathedral, and be back at Sutton or Stillington for the evening service. It meant a little physical exertion; nothing more. Dean Fountayne and various prebendaries, who were friends to Sterne, gave him their less important turns, and even his uncle down to 1750 permitted him to take his place on the twenty-ninth of May, a day of thanksgiving for the restoration of Charles the Second. All went on well until late in the autumn of 1750, when the quarrel between uncle and nephew came to a violent climax. On All Saints of that year Sterne came in and preached for the dean. It was a hollow and conventional sermon worked over from Tillotson on the text, "For our conversation is in heaven," and keyed to the tune: "Here we consider ourselves only as pilgrims and strangers.——Our home is in another country, where we are continually tending; there our hearts and affections are placed; and when the few days of our pilgrimage shall be over, there shall we return, where a quiet habitation and a perpetual rest is designed and prepared for us for ever." Just after the sermon Sterne strolled into Hildyard's shop to enquire about preaching a week or two later for Francis Blackburne, Archdeacon of Cleveland in succession to Dr. Sterne. Whereupon he discovered that his uncle was intervening against this source of his supply. There ensued a lively dialogue, which was broken off on the word *impudence* by the entrance of Dr. William Herring, the Chancellor of the diocese. Sterne related the whole story of the angry encounter in a letter to his archdeacon, dated at Sutton, November 3, 1750:

"I step'd," says Sterne, "into his [Hildyard's] shop just after Sermon on *All Saints*, when with an Air of much Gravity and Importance, he beckon'd me to follow him into an inner Room. No sooner had he shut the Dore, but with the awful Solemnity of a Premier who held a Lettre de Cachêt upon whose Contents my Life or Liberty depended——after a Minut's Pause——he thus opens his Commission: 'Sir—— My Friend the A. Deacon of Cleveland, not caring to preach his Turn, as I conjectured, has left me to provide a Preacher, ——but before I can take any Steps in it with Regard to you —I want first to know, Sir, upon what Footing you and Dr. Sterne are?'—'Upon what Footing!'——'Yes Sir, How your Quarel stands?'——'What's that to you—How our Quarel stands! What's that to you, you Puppy?' 'But Sir, Mr. Blackburn would know'——'What's that to him?'——'But Sir, don't be angry, I only want to know of you, whether Dr. Sterne will not be displeased in Case you should preach'—— 'Go Look; I've just now been preaching and you could not have fitter Opportunity to be satisfyed.'—'I hope, Mr. Sterne, you are not Angry.' 'Yes I am; But much more astonished at your *Impudence.*' I know not whether the Chancellor's stepping in at this Instant and flapping to the Dore, did not save his tender Soul the Pain of the last Word. However that be, he retreats upon this unexpected Rebuff, takes the Chancellor aside, asks his Advice, comes back Submissive, begs Quarter, tells me Dr. Hering had quite satisfyed him as to the Grounds of his Scruple (tho' not of his Folly) and therefore beseeches me to let the Matter pass, and to preach the Turn. When I ——as Percy complains in Harry 4

    ——All smarting with my Wounds
To be thus pestered by a Popinjay
Out of my Grief and my Impatience
Answered neglectingly, I know not what
——for he made me Mad
To see him shine so bright and smell so sweet
And talk so like a waiting Gentlewoman
—Bid him be Gone—and seek Another fitter for his *Turn.*

"But as I was too angry to have the perfect Faculty of recollecting Poetry, however pat to my Case, so I was forced to tell him in plain Prose tho' somewhat elevated——That I would not preach, and that he might get a Parson wh[erever he] could find one."

At this point, Hildyard produced his letter from the archdeacon with reference to the supply. After reading it and finding that it contained only "a cautious hint" against offending the precentor, Sterne cooled his angry humor and decided to take the turn. Three days later, as he was on his way to the postoffice with the letter from which we have quoted, Sterne met the bookseller, who pressed him not to let the matter transpire. Though Sterne "half promised" to hold back the letter, he finally sent it, after opening it and adding a strange postscript to the effect that it should do Mr. Hildyard no harm. The next week Sterne again wrote to the archdeacon, this time humbly apologizing for his heat. "It was my anger," he said finely, "and not me, so I beg this may go to sleep in peace with the rest." But it was too late for peace, though the archdeacon himself greatly wished it; for Dr. Sterne was soon informed of what had occurred in the bookseller's shop. On the sixth of the following December he signed the reprobation of his nephew in a letter to Archdeacon Blackburne, beginning: "Good Mr. Archdeacon,

"I will beg Leave to rely upon your Pardon for taking the Liberty I do with you in relation to your Turns of preaching in the Minster. What occasions it, is Mr. Hildyard's employing the last time the only person unacceptable to me in the whole Church, an ungrateful and unworthy Nephew of my own, the Vicar of Sutton; and I should be much obligd to you, if you woud please either to appoint any person yourself, or leave it to your Register to appoint one when you are not here. If any of my turns woud suit you better than your own, I woud change with you."

Despite this brand upon him, it seemed for the moment as if the Vicar of Sutton might win in the struggle with his uncle. Joined with Dr. Sterne against him were Archbishop Hutton and Dr. Francis Topham, the legal adviser to many of the clergy. For him were Dean Fountayne, Archdeacon

Blackburne, Chancellor Herring, and most of the active men in the York chapter, including the two resident canons— Charles Cowper and William Berdmore, a man, said Sterne, "of a gentle and pacific temper,"—and Jacob Custobadie, registrar and chamberlain to the dean and chapter. Besides all these sympathizers, a close friendship was forming between Sterne and Thomas, fourth Viscount Fauconberg of Newburgh Priory, in whose extensive manor lay Sutton-on-the-Forest and other townships in the York valley. The viscount (created earl in 1756) was then a lord of his Majesty's bedchamber and member of the Privy Council. His rank and his age—he was above fifty years old—perhaps precluded the easy intercourse that the Vicar of Sutton enjoyed with his fellow canons and prebendaries. He was rather a patron to whom Sterne looked for another and a better living. But under the circumstances, any signal preferment was impossible, for it would require the sanction of the Archbishop of York, with whom the Vicar of Sutton was out of favor. When, for example, the perpetual curacy of Coxwold, within the nomination of Lord Fauconberg, became vacant in 1753, Sterne had to be passed by for his former curate, Richard Wilkinson.

There were, however, within the sole gift of his friends several small offices that might be bestowed upon him as a mark of favor and confidence. In conjunction with Dean Fountayne, Lord Fauconberg led the way by appointing Sterne Commissary of the Peculiar and Spiritual Jurisdiction of Alne and Tollerton, which included also Skelton and Wigginton —parishes in the North Riding over which the Fauconbergs had exercised, under the Dean of York, important rights since the dissolution of the monasteries. On December 29, 1750, three weeks after he had been denounced by his uncle, Sterne appeared at the deanery, where he took the usual oaths and designated his surrogates who were to act in his stead in case of absence.* Six months later fell vacant the similar Commis-

* The record of the appointment in the Diocesan Registry of York is accompanied by memoranda of the annual visitations made by Sterne and his surrogates, beginning in 1751 and ending in 1767.

saryship of the Peculiar Court of Pickering and Pocklington, which formed a part of the dean's immediate jurisdiction, independent of the archbishop or the York chapter. For this office were pitted against each other Laurence Sterne and Dr. Topham, his uncle's candidate. After a noisy clash of arms, during which the lie was freely passed, Sterne received the appointment.

Behind Dean Fountayne's efforts in behalf of Sterne there was a piece of secret history, which may now be related. At Commencement in 1751, the dean went up to Cambridge for the degree of Doctor of Divinity. In order to qualify for this honor, it was necessary for him to preach a sermon in Latin—called *Concio ad Clerum*—before the university. Not being able to write it himself, he appealed to Sterne, who composed it for him. Ten years later, when the humor of the situation had faded, and Sterne was in a less generous mood towards the dean, he threatened to have the sermon printed over his own name, and remarked: "He got honour by it—what got I? Nothing . . . ."* That is, nothing but two lean commissaryships.

The two offices that Sterne thus obtained as a reward for his facility in writing Latin were as much civil as ecclesiastical. It was in both cases the incumbent's duty to make annual visitations of the clergy within his jurisdiction for proving wills and granting letters of administration, for swearing in church wardens and receiving their presentments of ecclesiastical offences, and for looking after the morals of the district generally. The fees from the two commissaryships both together amounted to but little. From the first Sterne received in no year more than two pounds and some odd shillings, and the second was estimated at only five or six guineas. But they were much coveted by cathedral officials, for they gave the incumbent an honorable position among the clergy of the diocese as a direct representative of the Dean of York and the Lord of the Manor.

* *Memorandums* in W. H. Arnold, *Ventures in Book Collecting,* 164 (New York, 1923). Reprinted in Chap. XXV of this biography.

It is not said how Dr. Sterne regarded these honors to his ungrateful nephew or his appointment the year before as chaplain to Sir William Pennyman, whereby he was enabled to preach an extraordinary sermon before an extraordinary congregation in the great cathedral. But that they set his wrath in a flame may be inferred from the brutal course which he was now taking to crush him forever. "When to justify a private appetite," says the author of *Tristram Shandy*, conveying a passage from Archbishop Tenison on Lord Bacon, "it is once resolved upon, that an innocent and helpless creature shall be sacrificed, 'tis an easy matter to pick up sticks enough from any thicket where it has strayed, to make a fire to offer it up with." So it was in this case. Sterne's ill treatment of his mother and sister Catherine—still a persisting legend—had long been given out by Dr. Sterne as the first cause of estrangement. After the death of Roger Sterne, his widow and daughter, as has been said in a previous chapter, settled on a government pension at Clonmel in Ireland. Sometime in 1742, they came over to England on hearing that Laurie had married an heiress. For a time they were persuaded to live in Chester, but by 1747 they had moved to York, near what they supposed was inexhaustible wealth. Thenceforth these unfortunate women were tossed to and fro in the quarrel, not as any real cause of it but as available weapons. At various times the nephew tried to patch up a friendship with his uncle, but all attempts were in vain. As early as 1747, he wrote to Dr. Sterne, requesting him to arrange a conference with his wife instead of himself, that there might be no explosion of temper. And late in 1750, Dean Fountayne sought to bring together mother, son, and uncle for a complete understanding. This friendly mediation also failed. Three months later Dr. Sterne struck his final blow. He placed Mrs. Sterne and her daughter Catherine in some charitable institution at York, perhaps the workhouse or "the common gaol," and then spread the report that they were there by neglect of the Vicar of Sutton. Stunned by the blow, Laurence Sterne at once sat down and wrote the following long letter, dated Sutton, April 5, 1751, to his uncle in defence of his conduct:

"Sir,—'Tis now three years since I troubled you with a letter in vindication of myself in regard to my Mother, in which that I might give you all imaginable conviction, how barbarously she had dealt by me, and at the same time how grossly she had deceived you by the misrepresentation which I found she had made of my behaviour towards her——I desired my wife might have leave to wait upon you to lay the state of our circumstances fairly before you, and with that the account of what we had done for my Mother, that from a view of both together you might be *convinced* how much my Mother had complained *without reason*.

"My motive for offering to send my wife rather than myself upon this particular business, being first merely to avoid the occasion of any heat which might arise betwixt you and me upon any thing foreign to the Errand, which might possibly disapoint the end of it——and secondly as I had reason to think your passions were pre-engaged in this affair and that the respect you owed my wife as a gentlewoman would be a check against their breaking out; and consequently that you would be more likely to give her a candid hearing, which was all I wished, and indeed all that a plain story to be told without Art or Management could possibly stand in want of. As you had thought proper to concern yourself in my Mother's complaints against me, I took it for granted you *could* not deny me so plain a piece of Justice. So that when you wrote me word back by my servant 'You desired to be excused from any conference with my wife, but that I might appear before you' ——As I foresaw such an Interview with the sense I had of such a treatment was likely to produce nothing but an angry expostulation (which could do no good, but might do hurt), I begged *in my turn* to be excused; and as you had already refused so unexceptionable an offer of hearing my defence, I supposed in course you would be silent for ever after upon that Head; and therefore I concluded with saying, 'as I was under no necessity of applying to you and wanted no man's direction

or advice in my own private concerns, I would make myself
as easy as I could, with the consciousness of having done my
Duty and of being able to prove I had whenever I thought fit,
and for the future that I was determined never to give you
any further trouble upon that subject.'

"In this resolution I have kept for three years and should
have continued to the end of my life—but being told of late
by some of my friends that this clamour has been kept up
against me, and by as singular a Stroke of Ill design as could
be levelled against a defenceless man, who lives retired in the
country and has few opportunities of disabusing the world;
that my Mother has moreover been fixed in that very place
where a hard report might do me (as a Clergyman) the most
real disservice*——I was roused by the advice of my friends
to think of some way of defending myself, which I own I
should have set about immediately by telling my story publickly to the world but for the following inconvenience, that
I could not do myself justice this way without doing myself
an injury at the same time by laying open the nakedness of my
circumstances, which for aught I knew was likely to make me
suffer more in the opinion of one half of the world than I
could possibly gain from the other part of it by the clearest
defence that could be made.

"Under the distress of this vexatious alternative I went directly to my old friend and college acquaintance, our worthy
Dean, and laid open the hardship of my situation, begging his
advice what I should best do to extricate myself. His opinion
was that there was nothing better than to have a Meeting, face
to face with you, and my Mother; and with his usual friendship and humanity he undertook to use his best offices to procure it for me.

"Accordingly about three months ago he took an opportunity of making you this request, which he told me you desired only to defer till the hurry of your Nunnery cause was
over.

"Since the determination of that affair he has put you in

* "The common gaol."

mind of what you gave me hopes of, but without success; you having (as he tells me) absolutely refused now to hear one word of what I have to say. The denying me this piece of common right is the hardest measure that a man in my situation could receive, and though the whole inconvenience of it may be thought to fall, as intended, directly upon me, yet I wish, Dr. Sterne, a great part of it may not rebound upon yourself. For why, may any one ask, why will you interest yourself in a complaint against your Nephew if you are determined against hearing what he has to say for himself?—and if you thus deny him every opportunity he seeks of doing himself justice? Is it not too plain you do not wish to find him justified, or that you do not care to lose the uses of such a handle against him? However it may seem to others, the case appearing in this light to me, it has determined me, contrary to my former promise 'of giving you no further trouble'—— to add this, which is not to solicit again what you have denied me to the Dean, (for after what I have felt from so hard a Treatment, I would not accept of it, should the Offer come now from yourself.)——But my intent is by a plain and honest narrative of my Behaviour, and my Mother's too, to disarm you for the future; being determined since you would not hear me face to face with my accusers, that you shall not go unconvinced or at least not uninformed of the true state of the Case.

    .   .   .   .

"From my Father's death to the time I settled in the world, which was eleven years, my Mother lived in Ireland, and as during all that time I was not in a condition to furnish her with money, I seldom heard from her; and when I did, the account I generally had was, that by the help of an Embroidery school which she kept, and by the punctual payment of her pension, which is £20 a year, she lived well, and would have done so to this hour had not the news that I had married a woman of fortune hastened her over to England.

    .   .   .

"The very hour I received notice of her landing at Liverpool I took post to prevent her coming nearer me, stayed three days with her, used all the arguments I could fairly to engage her to return to Ireland, and end her days with her own relations.

"I convinced her that besides the interest of my wife's fortune, I had then but a bare hundred pounds a year; out of which my ill health obliged me to keep a curate, that we had moreover ourselves to keep, and in that sort of decency which left it not in our power to give her much; that what we could spare she should as certainly receive in Ireland as here; that the place she had left was a cheap country—her native one, and where she was sensible £20 a year was more than equal to thirty here, besides the discount of having her pension paid in England where it was not due and the utter impossibility I was under of making up so many deficiencies.

"I concluded with representing to her the inhumanity of a Mother *able* to maintain herself, thus forcing herself as a burden upon a Son who was scarce able to support himself without breaking in upon the future support of another person whom she might imagine was much dearer to me.

"In short I summed up all those arguments with making her a present of twenty guineas, which with a present of Cloathes etc. which I had given her the day before, I doubted not would have the effect I wanted. But I was much mistaken, for though she heard me with attention, yet as soon as she had got the money into her pocket, she told me with an air of the utmost insolence 'That as for going back to live in Ireland, she was determined to show me no such sport, that she had found I had married a wife who had brought me a fortune, and she was resolved to enjoy her share of it, and live the rest of her days at her ease either at York or Chester.'

"I need not swell this letter with all I said upon the unreasonableness of such a determination; it is sufficient to inform you that, all I did say proving to no purpose, I was forced to leave her in her resolution; and notwithstanding so much provocation, I took my leave with assuring her 'That though my Income was strait I should not forget I was a son, though she had forgot she was a *mother.*'

"From Liverpool, as she had determined, she went with my sister to fix at Chester, where, though she had little just grounds for such an expectation, she found me better than my word, for we were kind to her above our power, and common justice to ourselves; and though it went hard enough down with us to reflect we were supporting both her and my sister in the pleasures and advantages of a town-life which for prudent reasons we denied ourselves, yet still we were weak enough to do it for five years together, though I own not without continual remonstrances on my side as well as perpetual clamours on theirs, which you will naturally imagine to have been the case when all that was given was thought as much above reason by the one, as it fell *below* the Expectations of the other.

"In this situation of things betwixt us, in the year '44 my sister was sent from Chester by order of my mother to York, that she might make her complaints to you, and engage you to second them in these unreasonable claims upon us.

"This was the intent of her coming, though the pretence of her journey (of which I bore the expences) was to *make* a month's visit to me, or rather a month's experiment of my further weakness.————She stayed her time or longer—was received by us with all kindness, was sent back at my own charge with my own servant and horses, with five guineas which I gave her in her pocket, and a six and thirty piece which my wife put into her hand as she took horse.

"In what light she represented so much affection and generosity I refer to your memory of the account she gave you of it in her return through York. But for very strong reasons I believe she concealed from you all that was necessary to make a proper handle of us both; which double Game by the bye, my Mother has played over again upon us, for the same purposes since she came to York, of which you will see a proof by and bye.

"But to return to my sister. As we were not able to give her a fortune, and were as little able to maintain her as she expected—therefore, as the truest mark of our friendship in such a situation, my wife and self took no small pains, the time she was with us to turn her thoughts to some way of depending upon her own industry, in which we offered her all imaginable assistance; first by proposing to her that, if she would set herself to learn the business of a Mantuamaker, as soon as she could get insight enough into it to make a Gown and set up for herself, '*That* we would give her £30 to begin the world and support her till business fell in; or, if she would go into a Milliner's shop in London, my wife engaged not only to get her into a shop where she should have £10 a year wages, but to equip her with cloathes etc. properly for the place; or lastly, if she liked it better, as my Wife had then an opportunity of recommending her to the family of one of the first of our Nobility—she undertook to get her a creditable place in it, where she would receive no less than eight or ten pounds a year wages with other advantages.' My sister showed no seeming opposition to either of the two last proposals till my wife had wrote and got a favourable answer to the one, and an immediate offer of the other. It will astonish you, Sir, when I tell you she rejected them with the utmost scorn, telling me I might send my own children to service when I had any, but for her part, as she was the daughter of a gentleman, *she would not disgrace* herself but would live as such. Notwithstanding so absurd an instance of her folly, which might have disengaged me from any further concern, yet I persisted in doing what I thought was right; and though after this the tokens of our kindness were neither so great nor so frequent as before, yet nevertheless we continued sending what we could conveniently spare.

"It is not usual to take receipts for presents made; so that as I have not many vouchers of that kind; and my Mother has more than once denyed the money I have sent her, even to my own face, I have little expectation of such acknowledgements as she ought to make. But this I solemnly declare upon the nearest computation we can make, that in money, cloathes, and other presents we are more than £90 poorer for what we have given and remitted to them. In one of these remittances (which was the summer [of] my sisters visit) and which as I remember was a small bill drawn for £3 by Mr. Ricard upon Mr. Boldero,* after my Mother had got the money in Chester for the bill, she peremptorily denied the receipt of it. I naturally supposed some mistake of Mr. Ricard in directing ——However that she might not be a sufferer by the disappointment, I immediately sent another bill for as much more; but withal said, as Mr. Ricard could prove his sending her the Bill, I was determined to trace out *who* had got my money; upon which she wrote word back that she had received it herself but had *forgot it.* You will the more readily believe this when I inform you, that in December, '47, when my Mother went to your house to complain she could not get a *farthing* from me, that she carried with her *ten guineas* in her pocket, which I had given her but two days before. If she could *forget* such a sum, I had reason to *remember* it, for when I gave it I did not leave myself one guinea in the house to befriend my wife, though then within one day of her labour, and under an apparent necessity of a man-midwife to attend her.

"What *uses* she made of this ungenerous concealment I refer again to yourself——But I suppose they were the same as in my sister's case, to make a penny of us both.

"When I gave her this sum, I desired she would go and acquaint you with it, and moreover took that occasion to tell her I would give her £8 every year whilst I lived. The week after she wrote me word she had been with you, and was determined not to accept that offer unless I would settle the £8 upon her out of my Wife's fortune, and chargeable upon it in case my wife should be left a widow. This she added was *your* particular advice, which without better evidence I am not yet willing to believe; because, though you do not yet know the particulars of my Wife's fortune—you must know so much of it, was such an event as my death to happen shortly, without such a burden as this upon my widow and my child, *that Mrs. Sterne would be as much distressed, and as undeservedly so as any widow in Great Britain:* and though I know as well as

* Arthur Ricard, Sr., and John Boldero, gentlemen of York.

you and my Mother that I have a *power in law* to lay her open
to all the terrors of such a melancholy situation——that I feel
I have *no power* in equity or in conscience to do so; and I will
add in her behalf, considering how much she has merited at
my hands as the best of wives, that was I capable of being wor-
ried into so cruel a measure as to give away hers, and her
child's bread upon the clamour which you and my Mother
have raised—that I should not only be the weakest but the
worst man that ever woman trusted with all she had.

. . . . .

"Was I, Sir, to die this night, I have not more than the very
Income of £20 a year (which my mother enjoys) to divide
equally betwixt my Wife, a helpless child, and perhaps a third
unhappy sharer, that might come into the world some months
after its father's death to claim its part. The false modesty
of not being able to declare this, has made me thus long a prey
to my Mother, and to this clamour raised against me; and
since I have made known thus much of my condition as an
honest man, it becomes me to add, *that I think I have no right*
to apply one shilling of my Income to any other purpose but
that of laying by a provision for my wife and child: and that
it will be time enough (if then) to add somewhat to my
Mother's pension of £20 a year when I have as much to leave
my Wife, who besides the duties I owe her of a Husband and
the father of a dear child, has this further claim:—that she
whose bread I am thus defending was the person who brought
it into the family, and whose birth and education would ill
enable her to struggle in the world without it——that the
other person who now claims it from her, and has raised us so
much sorrow upon that score brought not one sixpence into the
family——and though it would give me pain enough to report it upon any other occasion, that she was the daughter of
no other than a poor Suttler who followed the camp in Flanders, was neither born nor bred to the expectation of a fourth
part of what the government allows her; and therefore has
reason to be contented with such a provision, though double
the sum would be nakedness to my wife.

"I suppose this representation will be a sufficient answer to any one who expects no more from a man than what the difficulties under which he acts will enable him to perform. For those who expect more, I leave them to their expectations, and conclude this long and hasty wrote letter, with declaring that the relation in which I stand to you inclines me to exclude you from the number of the last. For notwithstanding the hardest measure that ever man received, continued on your side without any provocation on mine, without ever once being told my fault, or conscious of ever committing one which deserved an unkind look from you—notwithstanding this, and the bitterness of ten years' unwearied persecution, that I retain that sense of the service you did me at my first setting out in the world, which becomes a man inclined to be grateful, and that I am

"Sir,
"your once much obliged though now
"your much injured nephew,
"Laurence Sterne"

This "plain and honest narrative," exactly contemporary with the incidents described in it, gives the lie direct to the epigram of Horace Walpole's, so neatly expressed by Lord Byron, who said, with reference to a scene in the *Sentimental Journey*, that Sterne "preferred whining over a dead ass to relieving a living mother." It likewise explains the tradition, coming from John Croft, that Sterne left his mother to die in "the common gaol at York in a wretched condition, or soon after she was released."* If she was confined there as a vagrant, it was by order of Dr. Sterne that he might do his

* The story was told in its most complete form in a letter to George Whatley, treasurer of the London Foundling Hospital, from the Rev. Daniel Watson, Vicar of Leake, near Coxwold, in Sterne's time. Under date of January 10, 1776, Watson wrote:

"Shall I tell you what York scandal says? *viz.:* that Sterne, when possessed of preferment of £300 a year, would not pay £10 to release his mother out of Ousebridge prison, when poverty was her only fault, and her character so good that two of her neighbours clubbed to set

nephew, "as a clergyman, the most real disservice" in his
power. The letter is throughout a vindication of Sterne's conduct, so far as there can be any vindication of a son's break
with his mother. Whatever else may be said of Sterne he was
no niggard. He gave his mother and sister freely of his income
and would have made it an allowance. It was neither just nor
reasonable to ask him to settle upon them an annuity chargeable upon his wife's small estate. No one can have any patience
with his sister Catherine who refused the chance to earn an
honest living. His mother was no doubt vulgar, turbulent, and
untrustworthy, for Dr. Sterne himself, when he had no motive to the contrary, spoke of her temper as "clamourous and
rapacious."

And yet, to say the truth, Sterne's vindication of himself,
taken in the whole, does not leave the best impression of his
own character. It is difficult to think of a son's casting a slur
upon the birth of his mother, however humble it may have
been. For once Sterne's sense of humor, to say the least, deserted him. A man of finer grain would have taken in his
mother and sister and made the best of it. Mrs. Sterne and her
daughter, once fixed in York under the "protection" of Dr.
Sterne, certainly gave sufficient occasion for rumors, not
wholly without justification, of their neglect by the young
Vicar of Sutton. Dr. Sterne was thereby able to make the most
of the strained relations between mother and son, yet to continue a short period, for stirring up further enmities and
spreading the report of them where they would do the most
harm.

her at liberty, to gain a livelihood, as she had been accustomed to do,
by taking in washing. Yet this was the man whose fine feelings gave
the world the story of Le Fevre and the Sentimental Journey. Do you
not feel as if something hurt you more than a cut across your finger
at reading this? Talking on benevolence, or writing about it, in the
most pathetic manner, and doing all the good you can without shew
and parade, are very different things."

This letter, then in possession of John Towill Rutt, was published
in the *Monthly Repository of Theology and General Literature* for
January, 1808.

CHAP. V.

Pastimes and Friendships

STERNE had not won in the long warfare with his uncle.
Such at least is the intimation that he wished to convey in
the sketch of Parson Yorick. "Yorick," he says, "fought it out
with all imaginable gallantry for some time; till, overpowered
by numbers, and worn out at length by the calamities of the
war,—but more so, by the ungenerous manner in which it was
carried on,—he threw down the sword; and though he kept up
his spirits in appearance to the last, he died, nevertheless, as
was generally thought, quite broken-hearted." Though Sterne
did not literally die of a broken heart, he was bruised and
humbled to the dust. His friends, it is true, had stood by him
nobly through it all, but they were powerless to help him in
the way he most needed their help. Known as he was among
them as a gentleman of means, he could not in his pride go to
them and "lay open the nakedness" of his condition; to no one,
except perhaps Dean Fountayne, could he go and say that his
wife's fortune was in danger of being consumed, and that he
was scarce able to maintain himself on the livings he held.
Attempts, too, which at times were partially successful, were
made by his enemies to create misunderstandings between him
and his dean.

The damp and depressing climate of the York valley was
also working ruin to his delicate constitution, and he longed
for a parish among the hills; but that was denied him. Like
Yorick he was compelled to throw down his sword and retire
to Sutton to bide his time. During the next few years we are
to imagine him as still in touch with his friends at York and
their intrigues, but as entering more completely into the occu-
pations and pastimes of a country parson. "If you have three
or four last Yorks Courants," runs a letter written in the midst
of parish business, to a friend in the city, "pray send one to us,
for we are as much strangers to all that has pass'd amongst

you, as if we were in a mine in Siberia." Every summer he
drove through the beautiful Yorkshire country to Alne and
Pickering and other villages within the jurisdiction of his commissaryships, for he performed, as the records show, his visitations with scrupulous regularity. He made friends everywhere.
This is the period of his friendships, amusements, and farming. He was shuffling his cards anew for a last deal.

When Sterne, at the nadir of his fortunes, returned once
more to his farming, he felt again the gnawing of the old
land-hunger. He had, to be sure, no more money to invest in
land; and not even enough to carry through the projects that
he was forming; for he conveyed, by lease and release dated
the fifth and the sixth of April, 1753, his freehold to his
friends, Stephen Croft and Dr. Fountayne.* This conveyance,
considering his straitened circumstances, can mean only another mortgage on the Tindall farm. But there are sometimes,
as Sterne well knew, ways of obtaining land without purchase.
In the eighteenth century, the favorite way was an enclosure
or deforesting Act. What Sterne, unbiased by self-interest,
thought of these enclosures, which deprived poor parishioners
of fuel and pasturage, he has left on record in *Tristram
Shandy*. Mr. Walter Shandy, it is there related, rode out with
his son on a morning "to save if possible a beautiful wood,
which the dean and chapter were hewing down to give to the
poor"; that is, says Sterne's footnote, "to the *poor in spirit*,
inasmuch as they divided the money amongst themselves." But
in his own case, none the less for this opinion, Sterne could
waive all scruples against harming the poor of his parish. At
that time Sutton formed a part of the demesne of Lord
Fauconberg of Newburgh Priory. Besides being lord of the
manor, the earl was also "seized of several cottages, frontsteads, lands, and tenements" within the township. The second
large landowner was the squire, Philip Harland, who, in addition to his "divers freehold messuages," had inherited from
his father a lease of the rectory, including the greater tithes.

---

* The conveyance was registered at Northallerton on May 2, 1753.

Third in the list came Sterne as vicar of the parish and as owner of a "freehold messuage" in his own right. The three men, working together, easily obtained, through the influence of Lord Fauconberg, an Act of Parliament for enclosing most of those lands of Sutton which had long lain common.

The lands in question consisted, say the Articles of Agreement* bearing date January 15, 1756, of "six common Fields," containing "Thirteen Hundred Acres of Land, or upwards, and called or known by the Names of the North-field, Enhams, Murton-field, Thorp-field, South-field and West-field, . . . also certain common Meadow Grounds . . . called White-Car-Ings, Esk, and Sharoms, and also certain large and extensive Commons, called Brown Moor, Stockhill Sykes, Three Nook piece, Hinderlands, the Woods," and other pieces, the names of which were not well known. There were three thousand acres altogether. Commissioners, duly authorized by the Act, were appointed to make the allotments within three years after its passage. By the terms of the final instrument, which was enrolled in the registry office at Northallerton on March 23, 1759, Sterne received in his own right, exclusive of what was due to him as vicar of the parish, six parcels of land, comprising full sixty acres, with the buildings thereon. Sterne came out of the transaction as well as if he had been one of the commissioners himself. All of his allotments, as finally arranged, were close together in the North-field on the north side of the road through the village, not far from the rectory and, it would seem, near the Tindall farm, of which he had long been the owner. For Sterne's benefit Philip Harland exchanged with him three closes in the North-field for a more distant allotment; and Lord Fauconberg most generously resigned all right and title to two tenements separated from the parsonage only by the church and churchyard. By the favors of his friends, Sterne was thus lifted into a small country squire who cultivated his lands and had cottages for his laborers. In the meantime, he was growing, in rivalry

* The Articles of Agreement are recited in the preamble to the Sutton Enclosure Act.—*Private Acts of Parliament*, 29 George II, c. 10.

to the squire, huge crops of wheat, barley, oats, and potatoes, bringing under the plough new fields that had been used hitherto for pasturage.

As a relief to farming and the cure of souls, Sterne enjoyed many hours and days of careless relaxation. Common interest had brought together the parson and the squire on a better footing than formerly, though they may never have quite understood each other. It was but a few steps for either across the road for a chat over their crops and cattle. Between Sterne and the Crofts, nothing ever occurred to ruffle their friendship. The parson and his wife were ever familiar guests at Stillington Hall on an evening for supper and for jests and story-telling by the fireside. At this period, too, the Sternes were beginning to drive over to Newburgh Priory for dinners, choice wines, and Lady Catherine's parties at quadrille, a fashionable game of cards which had displaced the royal ombre of Pope's day. Earlier we caught just a glimpse of Sterne skating over the marshes of Stillington Common, and shooting partridges on a Sunday afternoon, while his congregation was already seated in church waiting for his appearance after the slaughter should be over. To these old-time amusements he now added painting.

That Sterne was a painter before he wrote *Tristram Shandy*, must have been surmised by every reader of the book; for he therein employs so easily the technical terms of the art for running up parallels on the mechanics of literary expression, or for describing the poise and movement of his characters—whether it be Corporal Trim standing in the kitchen, hat in hand, as he announces to Susannah and the scullions that "Bobby is dead and buried," or it be Mrs. Shandy listening at a keyhole to the conversation of her husband and my uncle Toby, in the attitude of "the Listening Slave with the Goddess of Silence at his back." On his famous mock dedication to any duke, marquis, or earl in his Majesty's dominions who may have fifty pounds to pay for it, Sterne remarks: "The design, your Lordship sees, is good,——the colouring transparent, ——the drawing not amiss;——or to speak more like a man of science,——and measure my piece in the painter's scale, divided into 20,——I believe, my Lord, the outlines will turn out as 12,—the composition as 9,—the colouring as 6,—the expression 13 and a half,—and the design—if I may be allowed, my Lord, to understand my own *design*, and supposing absolute perfection in designing, to be as 20,——I think it cannot well fall short of 19. Besides all this,——there is keeping in it, and the dark strokes in the HOBBY-HORSE, (which is a secondary figure, and a kind of back-ground to the whole) give great force to the principal lights in your own figure, and make it come off wonderfully;——and besides, there is an air of originality in the *tout ensemble.*" Some pages onward Sterne tells us that "good jolly noses" in "well proportioned faces, should comprehend a full third—that is, measured downwards from the setting on of the hair." He has a hit by the way at "the honourable devices which the Pentagraphic Brethren of the brush have shewn in taking copies." Their mechanical methods, he avers, have been stolen by "the great historians," who insist upon drawing full-length portraits "against the light": a method, it may be added, that "is illiberal,—dishonest,—and hard upon the character of the man who sits." He was out of patience with the cant about "the colouring of *Titian,* the expression of *Rubens,* the grace of *Raphael,* . . . the *corregiescity* of *Corregio,* . . . or the grand contour of *Angelo.*" Sterne nevertheless appreciated from afar the early masters and made a fine paragraph upon them in reference to the dash and the sudden silence of the author that comes with it at the moment the reader would have him go on:

"Just Heaven! how does the *Poco piu* and the *Poco meno* of the *Italian* artists;——the insensible MORE OR LESS, determine the precise line of beauty in the sentence, as well as in the statue! How do the slight touches of the chisel, the pencil, the pen, the fiddle-stick, *et cætera,—give the true swell,* which gives the true pleasure!——O my countrymen!—be nice;—be cautious of your language;—and never, O! never let it be forgotten upon what small particles your eloquence and your fame depend."

The amateur's first ideal was Hogarth, who could convey to the mind as much by three lines as others by three hundred. *The Analysis of Beauty*, out in 1753, Sterne recommended to his readers and, more to the point, carried over into *Tristram Shandy* its opinions and phrasing for praise and banter. He was particularly struck by Hogarth's pyramid and dark serpentine line on one of its faces, an ornament to the title-page, and by what was said of them thereafter as the beginning and end of all harmony, grace, and beauty. Beyond doubt Sterne had in mind Hogarth's distinction between the statue with its stiff lines and the living man who may conform to the line of beauty, when he placed Corporal Trim, with sermon in hand, before Dr. Slop and the Shandys:

"He stood,——for I repeat it, to take the picture of him in at one view, with his body swayed, and somewhat bent forwards,——his right leg from under him, sustaining seven-eighths of his whole weight,——the foot of his left leg, the defect of which was no disadvantage to his attitude, advanced a little,——not laterally, nor forwards, but in a line betwixt them;—his knee bent, but that not violently,—but so as to fall within the limits of the line of beauty;—and I add, of the line of science too;—for consider, it had one eighth part of his body to bear up;—so that in this case the position of the leg is determined,—because the foot could be no farther advanced, or the knee more bent, than what would allow him, mechanically to receive an eighth part of his whole weight under it,——and to carry it too.

"This I recommend to painters:——need I add,——to orators?——I think not; for unless they practise it,—— they must fall upon their noses."

Sterne's humor for painting, when he became tired of shooting partridges, greatly puzzled his parishioners. From their point of view, wrote John Croft thirty years after: "They generally considered him as crazy or crackbrained. At one time he wou'd take up the gun and follow shooting till he became a good shott, then he wou'd take up the pencil and paint pictures. He chiefly copied portraits. He had a good idea of drawing, but not the least of mixing his colours. There are severall pictures of his painting at York, such as they are." Among these portraits, most of which have disappeared, is a caricature of Mrs. Sterne, signed "Pigrich f[ecit]"—"in character of execution very like to Hogarth's Politician." It has the bust of a woman and the face of a man. A half century ago, this clever and cruel caricature was engraved for Paul Stapfer's *Laurence Sterne*, but on second thought it was suppressed. It has since been reproduced in Melville's biography of the humorist.

By driving into York, Sterne might pass an afternoon any day with a congenial fellow craftsman, a certain Thomas Bridges, who was a dry wit like himself. Each painted the other on the same canvas—Sterne as clown and Bridges as quack-doctor, standing upon a platform and humbugging a crowd at a fair. Bridges holds in his outstretched right hand a phial of his tincture, between thumb and forefinger, while gravely lauding its virtues as a panacea. Sterne, a youthful face in skull cap and ruff, hat in hand, seems ready to break into a jest at the expense of his serious companion. A medicine chest lies open between them; and in the background is a pretty street scene at York, terminating in the spire of one of the churches. This double caricature, called "The Mountebank and his Macaroni," Sterne once showed to an unknown "lady," who, on receiving it in her hands, "most cavalierly declared" that she would never part with it; and "from an excess of civility, or rather weakness," he let her keep it. Her name he wrote out and sealed in a billet so that the picture might be reclaimed after his death by his less sentimental heirs. The lady in question, I daresay, eventually changed her mind, and returned the enforced gift to Mrs. Sterne, as she was requested to do. When last heard of, the gay caricature was owned by Dr. James Atkinson (1759-1839), a York surgeon and bibliographer. He received it from his father, who was a friend of Sterne. Dr. Atkinson showed the portrait to Thomas Frognall Dibdin when at York in 1820, and permitted him to have it engraved for his *Bibliographical Tour,* whence it has come down to us in a good plate. Dibdin described the original as "a coarse production in oil" and yet *"a most singular original picture."**

For a year or more Sterne had the rare good fortune of associating with Christopher Steele and his apprentice, George Romney, who set up their joint studio at York in the autumn of 1756. Steele made a portrait of Sterne, and Romney afterwards "painted several scenes from *Tristram Shandy,"* among which one had as subject Dr. Slop's arrival at Shandy Hall, bespattered with mud—a caricature, it is thought, of Dr. Burton himself, whom Romney likely knew. These, said Richard Cumberland, were raffled off by Romney for what he could get for them in the days of his poverty.† The Dr. Slop, it is certain, was so disposed of at Kendal. No further details of the comradeship are surely known, though tradition has it that Sterne liked Romney better than Steele, and would have sat to him but for offending the elder colleague. Perhaps Sterne studied with them, for he learned from some source a new manner. Caricature in imitation of Hogarth, he continued to practise, it is true, down to the end of his life. A jolly tail-piece—two cocks fighting—to a pamphlet of 1759 may be Sterne's; and for the amusement of his friends, he illustrated a copy of the *Sentimental Journey.* But along with sketches of this kind, he tried his hand at ideal portraits in sylvan background, a few of which, though of later date, may have survived.

While at Rome in 1766, Sterne perhaps met Michael Wodhull of Thenford, the translator of Euripides, who was preparing for the press a collection of original poems, some of which had been issued as pamphlets. When the volume appeared in 1772, it contained three illustrations (not in the

---

* *Bibliographical, Antiquarian, and Picturesque Tour in the Northern Counties of England and Scotland,* I, 213 (London, 1838). Also *Memorandums* in Chap. XXV of this biography.

† *European Magazine,* June, 1803.

The Mountebank and his Macaroni

pamphlets) bearing on the left corner the name of "L. Stern del Romae," and on the right the name of I. A. Faldoni, evidently a misprint for G. A. Faldoni, a well-known engraver of the period. Over these designs of "L. Stern" hangs a mystery that has never been cleared up. It is rather more probable that they were made by a name-sake of Sterne's—one Lewis Stern (1708-77), who is said to have painted "game and other birds, flowers, fruit, and scriptural subjects in admirable style."* On the other hand, they were attributed to Laurence Sterne, without question, in the first collected edition of his works, brought out by his original publishers in 1780. If the curious designs are really Sterne's, they show the humor of the author who did not care to illustrate his own works for the public, but was quite willing to aid a friend. One of them represents a dryad reclining by a sedgy stream and gazing upon an Arcadian landscape. Another, adorning an ode to the Muses, has Pegasus in the foreground before the spring Hippocrene, which has just gushed from the solid rock in abundant streams, under the blow of his hoof, still uplifted; and above rises Mount Helicon, thickly wooded up to the temple of the Muses, whither travellers are climbing their way. Much in the same style is the third sketch for a stanza or two in an ode to Miss Sarah Fowler, the loveliest of all maids in the train of the Graces. Poesy stands erect, with lyre resting on her left arm, by a glassy pool that reflects her beauty; and above her head, encircled with a myrtle wreath, hover a group of cupids. With face turned towards Poesy, a deep-breasted nymph—is it Miss Sarah Fowler?—reclines on an urn, from the mouth of which she is pouring a libation of crystal waters into the stream beneath.

During these years of painting when Sterne frequently went into York for a day with Bridges or Steele and Romney, he formed a close friendship with "the Rev. Mr. Blake," a brother of the cloth with whom he had long been acquainted. The clergyman in question was the Rev. John Blake, a son of Zachary Blake, rector of Goldsborough and master of the

* _Notes and Queries_, third series, VII, 53.

Royal Grammar School in the Horse Fair near York. Ten years younger than Sterne, John Blake graduated at Christ Church, Oxford, Bachelor of Arts in 1743, and Master of Arts in 1746. While still a student at Oxford, he was ordained deacon by the Archbishop of York on June 9, 1745; ¬nd priest on June 14, 1747. His long residence at the university indicates that he was preparing himself for the instruction of youth. But in the meantime he served curacies at Wigginton, a small parish on the road midway between York and Sutton, and at St. Saviour's, an ancient church within the city. On December 2, 1756, he was collated by the Archbishop of York to the living of Catton, on the river Derwent, where Sterne had served as an Assistant Curate. His father becoming superannuated by this time, he succeeded him in the Royal Grammar School, under license of the dean and chapter, on May 13, 1757.* Blake was not only a scholar fully equipped for his post; he was also an active citizen whose name appears at intervals in *The York Courant,* as manager of the charity schools and contributor to the county hospital.

Through the summer and autumn of 1758, Sterne and Blake were engaged in a brisk correspondence, which was carried on by special messengers between York and Sutton. At that time the young master of the grammar school was in sore distress over the miscarriage of proposals for the hand of a "Miss Ash," a small heiress, living across the street with her widowed mother. The woman whom he wished to marry was perhaps Margaret, daughter of Elizabeth Ash, widow, who is described in her will as residing in the parish of St. John's, Micklegate, and possessing an estate at Tollerton. Sterne, who was called in for advice about the marriage settlement, warned his friend against a crafty grandmother, and an unscrupulous lawyer and justice of the peace, one John Stanhope, who was trying to enter the case. "The whole appears," wrote Sterne, remembering his Rabelais, "what I but too shrewdly suspected,

---

* With the exception of his appointment to the grammar school, all of Blake's ecclesiastical appointments, including his admission to holy orders, are recorded in the Institutions of the York Diocese.

a contexture of plots against your fortune and person, grand mama standing first in the *dramatis personæ*, the Loup Garou, or raw head and bloody bones, to frighten Master Jacky into silence, and make him go to bed with Missy, *supperless* and in peace——Stanhope, the lawyer, behind the scenes, ready to be call'd in to do his part, either to frighten or outwit you, in case the terror of grand mama should not do the business without him. Miss's part was to play them off upon your good nature in their turns, and give proper reports how the plot wrought. But more of this allegory another time. In the meanwhile, our stedfast council and opinion is, to treat with Stanhope upon no terms either in person or proxy. . . . Keep clear of him by all means, and for this additional reason, namely, that was he call'd in either at first or last, you lose the advantage as well as opportunity of an honorable retreat which is in your power the moment they reject your proposals, but will never be so again after you refer to him." Sterne's guiding hand seemed at times to be bringing the affair to a happy conclusion, but in the end he was unable to cope with the strategy of the astute lawyer; for Blake did not marry his "Miss Ash"; and the Margaret Ash, with whom we have identified her, became the wife of William Clark of Goodmanham, Yorkshire, where, according to the will of her mother,* which was drawn by Stanhope, Mrs. Elizabeth Ash held the right of presentation to the parish church and rectory.

"Mrs. Ash and Miss" were much annoyed, there are reasons for thinking, by the interference of the Vicar of Sutton. When Blake came out to Sutton to dine and confer with Sterne, it was his custom to make a secret of it to "the ladies over the way"; and when Sterne, obedient to his friend's "whistle," hurried off to York, he sometimes chose the evening, that he might not be discovered by those whom he would not fall in with for "fifty pounds." There were harmless secrets, too, which the vicar wished to keep from Mrs. Sterne. "I tore off," runs an exquisite passage in a letter to Blake, "I

* The will of Mrs. Elizabeth Ash was proved in the Prerogative Court of York, January 22, 1774.

tore off the bottom of yours before I let my wife see it, *to save a Lye.* However, she has since observed the curtailment, and seem'd very desirous of knowing what it contain'd— which I conceal, and only said 'twas something that no way concerned *her or me;* so say the same if she interrogates." Tell a lie to save a lie is a saying that would have done honor to Lord Bacon. The philosopher's *tell a lie to find a troth* lacks the color as well as the humor of the clergyman's mandate to his brother in the cure of souls.

Eventually Sterne found it inconvenient to have Blake's letters lying about the rectory, and so he burned them one by one as they arrived and were read. On the other hand, Blake kept those he received from Sterne. Fifty years ago they were owned by the late A. H. Hudson of York, who remembered them "as very long, written upon foolscap, and very amusing." From him they passed into a private collection, and thence to a dealer who disposed of them singly. Incomplete, mutilated, and out of chronological order, most of them were published by Percy Fitzgerald in his memoir of Sterne.

Despite their incompleteness, these letters to Blake are quite sufficient to let us into what Sterne was doing near the close of his residence at Sutton. Extracts from them have already been quoted for Sterne's ventures in farming. The life of a rural parson, one may see, was fast becoming irksome to him. Though the year brought large returns in oats and barley, the harvesting and threshing of his grain, which at one time seemed in danger of sprouting, kept him at home away from his friends at York. Once or twice he complained of bad roads and bad weather, of which he stood in mortal terror, for the damps of the York valley brought on his cough and asthma. One rainy night it was ten o'clock before the vicar and his wife reached Sutton after a visit to York "owing to vile accidents to which journiers are exposed."

Again on a morning when they were ready to take a wheel into the city to be with their friend on his birthday, they were prevented by a terrible downpour. So in the afternoon Sterne sent into York his "sinful Amen"—the facetious name for his clerk—to tell Blake how the matter stood and to say that he was considering the affair with Miss Ash "in all its shapes and circumstances." We really would have come in person, said Sterne, if we could. "We have waited dress'd and ready to set out ever since nine this morning, in hopes to snatch any intermission of one of the most heavy rains I ever knew,— but we are destined not to go,——for the day grows worse and worse upon our hands, and the sky gathering in on all sides leaves no prospect of any but a most dismal going and coming, and not without danger, as the roads are full of water—— What remains, but that we undress ourselves, and wish you absent, what we would most gladly have wish'd you present ——all happiness and many fair and less ominous birth days, than our prospect affords us." "I wish to God," to combine other letters, "you could some day ride out next week, and breakfast and dine with us. . . . However, I will come over at your desire, but it cannot be tomorrow, because all hands are to be employed in cutting my barley, which is now shaking with this vile wind——however, the next day (Friday) I will be with you by twelve and eat a portion of your own dinner and confer till three o'clock, in case the day is fair, if not the day after, &c., &c."

To free himself from local entanglements, Sterne was planning to lease his lands and tithes, in the expectation of peace and happiness for the next year and ever after. But that was not yet. His affairs, he complained, had been thrown into utter confusion by a parliamentary election that took place in the autumn of 1758. To add to Sterne's worries, the health of his daughter Lydia, now eleven years old, was causing him great anxiety. On rising one morning with the intention of an early start for York, he found Lydia so far relapsing that he sent a messenger instead with "two gooses" to say that he must "stay and wait 'till the afternoon to see if my poor girl can be left. She is very much out of all sorts; and our operator here, tho' a very penetrating man, seems puzzled about her case. If something favourable does not turn out to-day about her case, I will send for Dealtry," that is, Dr. John Dealtry, a Whig physician at York. His own health, too, was fast breaking under the strain.

Sterne nevertheless managed to ride into York every week or two except in the harvest season. He took his own turn in the cathedral on the nineteenth Sunday after Trinity, coming in early for breakfast with Blake; and he was again forced out of his "shell in Xmas week to preach Innocents" in place of Thomas Hurdis, Prebendary of Strensall. The sermon on the latter occasion seems to have been the one entitled *The Character of Herod*, as published in the usual collections. Sterne set out with "Rachel weeping for her children," but soon broke from his text and the scant Biblical narrative for a portrait of Herod on the lines of Josephus. Herod's complicated character—his generosity and munificence and cruelty—was "summed up in three words—That he was a man of unbounded ambition, who stuck at nothing to gratify it." The preacher closed with a story to the point out of Plutarch, followed by a wish that God in his mercy might "defend mankind from future experiments" in the slaughter of innocent people.

When Mrs. Sterne accompanied her husband into York for a day with their friends or "to make her last marketings for the year," one or both of them would dine with Thomas Bridges and his wife, or at the house of the Rev. Charles Cowper, Prebendary of Riccall. Sterne rather preferred to leave his wife with Mrs. Cowper on an afternoon, and to go by himself to the concert at the Assembly Rooms, not only for the music but for a chat with Marmaduke Fothergill the younger, or other friends that he was likely to fall in with there. In the round of visits he took in Dr. Fountayne, if the dean were in town, Jack Taylor, Mr. Blake, and "my poor mother," whose "affair," says a letter, "is by this time ended, to *our* comfort, and, I trust, hers." After a long period of misunderstanding and estrangement, a reconciliation between mother and son had evidently been brought about by her acceptance of the allowance that was offered to her many years before. Blake, it would seem, from a dark hint or two, had acted as mediator. For some purpose, at any rate, he was doling out money at York and sending accounts of it over to Sutton. If Sterne had time, it was his custom, though the letters say nothing about it, to stroll into the coffee-room of the George, a fine old hostelry in Coney Street, "where those who drank little wine and did not choose too much expence, might read the newspapers." To those who liked to sit there and gossip, he was well known for "a number of pleasant repartees," one of which has survived. The general drift of the story is probably true, for Sterne let it pass and Hall-Stevenson repeated an abridgement of it in the memoir of his friend.

"There was," according to the more elaborate version of the newspapers,* "a troop of horse in the town, and a gay young fellow, spoiled by the free education of the world, but with no real harm in him, was one of the officers. This gay boy, who loved all freedom in discourse, therefore hated a parson. Poor Yorick was obliged to hear healths he did not like; and would only shuffle about, or pretend deafness; but the hour was come, when these pretences were to pass no longer. The captain was in the middle of a Covent-garden story, loud, indecent, and profane in his expressions; when poor Yorick entered, he stopped on a sudden, and began, with all possible contempt and ill usage, to abuse the clergy, fixing his eye on Yorick, and pointing to him as an example on every occasion. Yorick pretended, as long as he could with any decency, not to hear his rudeness; but when that became impossible, he walked up and gravely said to him: 'Sir, I'll tell you a story. My father is an officer; and he's so brave himself, that he is fond of everything else that's brave, even to his dog; you must know we have at this time one of the finest creatures in the world, of this kind; he is the handsomest dog you ever saw, the most spirited in the world, and yet the best natured that can be imagined; so lively, that he charms everybody; but he has a cursed trick that spoils all; he never sees a clergyman, but he instantly flies at him.'———'Pray how long has he had that trick?' says the captain.———'Sir,' replies Yorick, 'ever

* For example, the *London Chronicle*, May 3-6, 1760.

since he was a PUPPY.' " According to Hall-Stevenson, "the young man felt the keenness of the satire, turned upon his heel, and left Sterne in triumph."

Whenever Sterne felt the need of more complete relaxation than was afforded by York and the neighboring squires, he had but to take a trip to Scarborough, or to drive over to Skelton for a week or a fortnight with his friend, John Hall-Stevenson. On these excursions his wife never went with him. Sterne and Hall-Stevenson, when we last saw them together, were reading Rabelais under the great walnut tree at Jesus College. John Hall—his friend always dropped the Stevenson —was a son of Joseph Hall of Durham by Catharine, sister to Lawson Trotter of Skelton Castle. In 1727, Trotter, who loved travel, sold the estate to his brother-in-law, on whose death six years later it passed to John Hall as the eldest surviving son, then only fifteen years old. After trifling away three or four years at Cambridge, the young man left the university without a degree, and made the usual tour of France and Italy. Returning home towards 1740, he married in that year Anne, daughter of Ambrose Stevenson, Esq., of the Manor House in the parish of Lanchester, Durham, and assumed his wife's surname along with his own. In after times he regarded the act as "premature," for his wife's property fell short of his expectations. A few months after his marriage his mother died; and his uncle, Lawson Trotter, was afterwards driven from the country, as a "noted Jacobite," for the part he took in the insurrection of 1745. In that eventful year, while Sterne was wielding a pen for the House of Hanover, Hall-Stevenson was brandishing a sword. After the battle of Preston Pans, he formed the neighboring bucks into a company of horsemen under General Oglethorpe, who was back from Georgia. They were all finely mounted, wrote a York merchant of the time, "with every man a horse and some two," and they acted as "a flying squadron, to harass the enemy on their march and to give intelligence." "They make more noise here," it is significantly added, "than they deserve,

their number being much magnified."* This appears to have
been the most exciting incident in Hall-Stevenson's career.
Once settled at Skelton, he continued to the end of his days in
the easy, self-indulgent life which he had begun at Cambridge, complaining now and then of his scant fortune and of
a mortgage of £2000 on his estate to a younger brother.

Hall-Stevenson possessed "a fine library," rich in old books
running back into the sixteenth century, among which he sat
and read on dull days and long winter evenings, now and then
scribbling a political satire, or loose verse-tale in imitation of
La Fontaine and other French fabulists, which were issued in
the form of anonymous pamphlets with notes and quotations
from Homer, Vergil, and Lucian. There was commonly a
facetious dedication to himself, as the man he most respected,
to the vacant reader, or to the macaronies of Medmenham
Abbey and Pall Mall. The author made no claim to finished
verse, writing, he said, like Grisset, only to save himself from
ennui. Horace Walpole discovered "a vast deal of original
humour and wit" in Mr. Hall's verses; but to Gray they
"seemed to be absolute madness." Here and there they contain
clever phrases, as in the opening lines of a reply to a savage
attack by Smollett in the *Critical Review*:

> "Ye judging Caledonian Pedlars,
>   That to a scribbling World give Law
> Laid up engarretted, like Medlars,
>   Ripening asperity in Straw."

* "Letter of Stephen Thompson, a merchant, to Vice-Admiral
[Henry] Medley" in *Report on Manuscripts of Lady du Cane presented
to Parliament by Command of his Majesty*, 77-78, (London, 1905).
A fine account of Hall-Stevenson is given by J. W. Ord, *History and
Antiquities of Cleveland* (London, 1846). See also Surtees, *Durham*,
II, 291-292; Nichols, *Literary Anecdotes*, III, 86-88; Alexander Carlyle, *Autobiography*, 453-454 (Edinburgh, 1860); Paver, *Supplement
to Consolidated Yorkshire Visitations* (British Museum, Additional MSS.
29651); and Lewis Melville, *Life and Letters of Laurence Sterne*, I,
97 (London, 1911). Sterne officiated at the marriage of John Hall and
Anne Stevenson on February 7, 1739-40.—See L. P. Curtis, *The Politicks of Laurence Sterne* (London, 1929).

In his humor, Hall-Stevenson re-named his seat Crazy Castle. It was a rambling pile of stone rising in a series of moss-covered terraces from a stagnant and melancholy moat, the abode of frogs and water-rats, and lying on the slope of a wooded ravine, two miles and a half inland from Saltburn-by-the-Sea. At one time, its master planned extensive restorations, but Sterne dissuaded him from them, saying, in remembrance of his own repairs at Sutton, that "the sweet visions of architraves, friezes and pedaments" were but the bait of the devil to lead one on into cares, curses and debts. Better follow, he admonished his friend, the advice of St. Paul to his disciples, that they should "sell both coat and waistcoat and go rather without shirt or sword, than leave no money in their scrip to go to Jerusalem with," that is, to London or Paris or Rome. For the amusement of his friends and Lawson Trotter, who was travelling abroad, Hall-Stevenson made a sketch of the castle, or had it made, as a frontispiece to a volume of *Crazy Tales*, which opened with a facetious verse-description of some of the details. Midway in the description, the verses hobble on—

> "A turrit also you may note,
> Its glory vanish'd like a dream,
> Transform'd into a pigeon-cote,
> Nodding beside the sleepy stream.

> "Over the Castle hangs a Tow'r,
> Threatening destruction ev'ry hour,
> Where owls, and bats, and the jackdaw,
> Their Vespers and their Sabbath keep,
> All night scream horribly, and caw,
> And snore all day, in horrid sleep.

> "Oft at the quarrels and the noise
> Of scolding maids or idle boys;
> Myriads of rooks rise up and fly,
> Like Legions of damn'd souls,
>   As black as coals,
> That foul and darken all the sky."

A very handsome and agreeable young man, Hall-Stevenson was thoroughly liked by friends and chance acquaintance, for whom "he kept a full-spread board and wore down the steps of his cellar." Alexander Carlyle, the Scottish divine, who crossed his path at the Dragon Inn, Harrogate, thought him "a highly accomplished and well-bred gentleman," and was drawn to him by a "mild and courteous manner." Mrs. Sterne, who saw him occasionally for a day at Sutton, had some misgivings about her husband's intimacy with him; but she readily admitted that he was "a fellow of wit, though humorous; a funny, jolly soul, though somewhat splenetic; and (bating the love of women) as honest as *gold*." It is a little strange at first sight that Sterne should have made out of him Eugenius, the discreet adviser of Yorick, for Hall-Stevenson was anything but discreet. And yet he was a man of the world who knew how to still a quarrel and keep his friends all good-natured towards one another. In spite of his idleness, he carried away from Cambridge a knowledge of the classics sufficient to quote from them freely, and from his travels on the Continent was brought back an interest in French and Italian literature. As in the case of Sterne, Locke's *Essay on the Human Understanding* was a book never to be forgotten.

Except for trips to London and the northern watering-places to meet friends, Hall-Stevenson shut himself up in Crazy Castle, where an inactive life brought on rheumatism and various disorders of the digestion, which were aggravated rather than helped by a free use of current nostrums. Some years of this treatment, attended with painful results, and he developed into a humorous hypochondriac of the family one may read of in *Peregrine Pickle* or *Humphry Clinker*. It was his whim to lay all his ailments to the damps of Yorkshire, especially to the cold and raw northeast wind, which was with him a synonym for death. His sleeping room, it is said, was in sight of the weather-cock—the cock was an arrow—over the old clock-tower shown in his drawing of the castle. On rising in the morning, the master looked first towards the arrow to see what the weather was to be; and if it pointed towards the northeast, he went back to bed, drew the curtains, and imagined himself *in extremis*. Sterne, who frequently bantered Hall-Stevenson on his nerves and the weather, in his letters as well as in *Tristram Shandy* and the *Sentimental Journey*, attempted a cure while on a visit to Crazy Castle. On a night, says the tale, he climbed the clock-tower, or engaged a boy to do so, and tied down the weather-cock in a westerly direction. After that all went well for some days until the cord broke and the arrow shot round to the northeast. Hall-Stevenson then took to his bed and Sterne went home.

The master of Skelton formed his merry Yorkshire friends into a convivial club, called the Demoniacs, in imitation of the Rabelaisian Monks of Medmenham Abbey, who were then creating great scandal in southern England. Medmenham Abbey was an ancient Cistercian monastery, beautifully situated, "by hanging woods and soft meadows," on the Thames, between Great Marlow and Henley. In this retired place, where once dwelt the old monks, a new and profane order was established by Sir Francis Dashwood, afterwards Baron Le Despenser, Lord Lieutenant of Buckinghamshire, Chancellor of the Exchequer, etc.,—a man seldom sober. With him were associated John Wilkes the politician, Paul Whitehead the poet, Sir William Stanhope, Lord Melcombe Regis, the Earl of Sandwich, and "other hands of the first water" up to twelve—the number of the Apostles. They called themselves Franciscans after their founder. Paul Whitehead, their secretary and steward, was known as St. Paul. Besides the first twelve, there was a lower order of twelve, who acted as servants to their superiors. Over the grand entrance was written for all who entered, *Fay ce que vouldras*, which was also the famous inscription on Rabelais's Abbey of Thélème. Every summer and at other favorable times, the Monks retired to their abbey for the worship of Satan and the Paphian Aphrodite in parody of the rites of the Church of Rome. On one occasion, it was a current story, when they were in the height of their mirth, invoking his Satanic majesty to come among them in person, Wilkes let loose a baboon decked in the conventional insignia of the devil. The consternation that followed, says the chronicler, was simply indescribable. The revellers were terrified nearly out of their senses, for they thought that the devil had really heeded their summons. The baboon, as frightened as they, leaped upon the shoulders of Lord Sandwich, who was celebrating the *messe noire;* whereupon the wicked nobleman fell upon his face, imploring first the devil and then heaven to have mercy upon his miserable soul. Soon after this incident, which could not be kept secret, the society was disbanded.*

The direct connection between this abandoned brotherhood and the Demoniacs who gathered under the roof of Crazy Castle is undeniable. Hall-Stevenson and Sterne afterwards numbered Wilkes, Dashwood, and other of the Monks among their intimate London friends. Hall-Stevenson may have visited Medmenham, and Dashwood, with little doubt, sometimes came down to Skelton, where he was known as "the Privy Counsellor." Sterne when away addressed the company at Skelton as "the household of faith" and sent them, in parody of the words of St. Paul, the apostolic benediction. In justice, however, to the Demoniacs, it must be said at once that they could have been only a faint reflection of the Monks of Medmenham. They were a company of noisy Yorkshire squires and parsons who assembled at Skelton for out-of-door sports during the day and for drinking and jesting through the night. To quote their host:

> "Some fell to fiddling, some to fluting,
> Some to shooting, some to fishing,
> Others to pishing and disputing."

As at Medmenham, everyone was expected to follow his own inclinations, doing whatsoever he pleased. "Why should

* For Medmenham Abbey, see Charles Johnstone, *Chrysal, or the History of a Guinea,* vol. III, bk. II, chs. XVII-XXIV (London, 1760-1765); *Letters to and from Mr. Wilkes,* I, 34-50 (London, 1769); and G. Lipscomb, *History of Buckinghamshire,* III, 615-616 (London, 1847).

a man," to paraphrase Rabelais, the originator of the idea,
"bring his life into subjection to rules and the hours? Why
should he not give full rein to will and instinct?—eat, drink,
sleep, or perhaps labour, because nature draws him that way
and not because custom calls or the bell rings?" Among the
Demoniacs, Hall-Stevenson was known as Antony, probably
because he was at the same time a recluse, and yet in the prime
essential wholly unlike the saint whose name he bore. Dislik-
ing field sports, he kept much within doors. But when Sterne
came over, squire and parson made excursions together to
Guisborough for sentimental visits with "Mrs. C——, Miss
C——, &c";, or they drove over to Saltburn, where they
amused themselves on an afternoon by racing chariots along
the sandy beach, "with one wheel in the sea." Of all pastimes
that took Sterne out of doors, none pleased him quite so much
as this; and none could be more exhilarating. Over sands hard
and firm enough for the modern automobile, the two Crazy-
ites might run their horses for five miles to the north, even to
Redcar, and then turn about for the exciting course homewards through the fresh spray of the ocean.

The fisherman of the group was the Rev. Robert Lascelles,
formerly of Durham. Graduating at Lincoln College, Oxford, in 1739, he joined Hall-Stevenson's "flying squadron"
against the Jacobite raiders, and subsequently obtained the
vicarage of Gilling, by Richmond in the West Riding. Late
in life he published a volume of merry verses on angling,
shooting, and coursing. This man of the cloth, whose fellowship Sterne especially enjoyed for his jesting, was nicknamed
Panty, cut short for familiar speech from Pantagruel, the
hero of Rabelais's romance. We read, too, of Andrew Irvine,
a Cambridge doctor of theology, and master of the grammar
school at Kirkleatham, a short distance away. Because of his
resemblance to an Irishman, he was renamed Paddy Andrew.

Among other Demoniacs, not so easily identified, were the
men whom Sterne affectionately addressed as "My dear Garland, Gilbert, and Cardinal Scroope." The first of the three
was Nathaniel Garland, a country gentleman; and the last

was likely a Yorkshire parson. An architect appears, too, under the Spanish disguise of Don Pringello, who was called over to rebuild Crazy Castle; but so great was his admiration for "the venerable remains," that he could only be prevailed upon "to add a few ornaments suitable to the stile and taste of the age it was built in." Could these men be uncovered they might prove as interesting as "Zachary," that is, Zachary Moore, whose name found its way into local history. He was the spendthrift of the company. Inheriting a rich and extensive manor at Lofthouse, some ten miles south of Skelton, he entered upon a career of riot and prodigality. "There is a tradition," says the historian of the district,* "that during his travels on the Continent his horses' shoes were made of silver; and so careless was he of money, that he would not turn his horses' head if they got loose or fell off, but replaced them with new ones." Among his strange caprices, apparently discordant with his character, was that of building a school at Lofthouse for the instruction of children in the Scriptures, the catechism, and the prayer-book. After thirty years of dissipation, he completed "the laborious work of getting to the far end of a great fortune"; and was then deserted "by the gay butterflies who had sported about him in his summer hour." By the aid of his London friends, among whom were men of "royal and ducal rank," he obtained an ensigncy in the British army and soon afterwards died at Gibraltar. Hall-Stevenson lamented his absence from Skelton in an ode beginning—

> "What sober heads hast thou made ake?
> How many hast thou kept from nodding?
> How many wise-ones, for thy sake,
> Have flown to thee, and left off plodding?"

Two colonels were sometimes with the company. One was "Colonel Hall"—George Lawson Hall, a brother of the master of Skelton, who married a daughter of Lord William Manners, and entered the army. The other colonel was probably Charles Lee, whom Alexander Carlyle met with

* J. W. Ord, *History and Antiquities of Cleveland*, 275-278.

Hall-Stevenson at Harrogate. At that time Lee was an officer on half pay. "Savage Lee," as people called him, fought in America throughout the French and Indian War, and settling afterwards in Virginia and obtaining a major-generalship in the Continental army, he sought to wrest the supreme command from Washington. The young officer, whoever he may have been, was a quarrelsome companion, whom Hall-Stevenson found hard to manage. More remotely connected with the Demoniacs was William Hewitt—"old Hewitt"—"a very sensible old gentleman but a very great humourist," who lived much abroad. Smollett, who met him at Scarborough and in Italy, told the story of his curious ending. Being attacked by a painful malady while at Florence in 1767, Hewitt resolved to take himself off, like Atticus, by starvation. "He saw company," says Smollett in a note to *Humphry Clinker*, "to the last, cracked his jokes, conversed freely, and entertained his guests with music. On the third day of his fast, he found himself entirely freed of his complaint, but refused taking sustenance. He said, the most disagreeable part of the voyage was past, and he should be a cursed fool indeed to put about ship when he was just entering the harbour." Persisting in this resolution, he soon finished his course.

The group of strange humorists that gyrated round Hall-Stevenson changed of course from year to year. One would fall out and another would be found to take his place. But Paddy and Panty, who lived near-by, might be counted upon at all times; and Sterne (sometimes called the Blackbird because of the color of his clerical dress) never missed, if he could help it, the great conclave of demons that assembled in October. "A jollier set," says the host, "never met, either before or since the flood." At night there were "joyous deliriums over the burgundy," when each contributed his share to the amusement and the jesting. Sterne fiddled, another piped, and Hall-Stevenson danced a saraband with a pair of bellows and tongs.

Sterne's love for the violin and cello and music in general, comes out again and again in *Tristram Shandy* and elsewhere.

Crazy Castle
From the frontispiece to "Crazy Tales"

The speech and movements of his characters, would one but observe it, are all deftly attuned to musical harmony. What, for example, would my uncle Toby be, as he lays his persuasive hand upon your heart, without "that soft and irresistible *piano* of voice, which the nature of the *argumentum ad hominem* absolutely requires"? It was a shepherd's pipe that gave the exquisite tone to the scene with Maria by the roadside in Bourbonnais: "Adieu, *Maria:*——adieu, poor hapless damsel!—— some time, but not *now*, I may hear thy sorrows from thy own lips——but I was deceived; for that moment she took her pipe and told me such a tale of woe with it, that I rose up, and with broken and irregular steps walk'd softly to my chaise." Yorick, it will be remembered from *Tristram Shandy*, quaintly characterized his sermons, as he marked and tied them up for future use, by an appropriate musical term. Most of them had *moderato* written across their backs, but here and there is an *adagio*, a *con strepito*, or *con l'arco*, or *senza l'arco*, etc. These are but examples. If they carry us a little away from Skelton, we certainly are brought back to an evening at the castle in that passage where Sterne tunes his *Cremona* and snaps a string:

"Ptr . . r . . r . . ing twing—twang—prut—trut—'tis a cursed bad fiddle.—Do you know whether my fiddle's in tune or no?—trut . . prut . .—They should be *fifths*.—'Tis wickedly strung—tr . . . a . e . i . o . u .—twang.—The bridge is a mile too high, and the sound post absolutely down,—else— trut . . prut——hark! 'tis not so bad a tone.—Diddle diddle, diddle diddle, diddle diddle, dum. . . . Twaddle diddle, tweddle diddle,—twiddle diddle,——twoddle diddle,—twuddle diddle,—prut trut—krish—krash—krush."

The jesting, hints here and there suggest, was racy and salacious, as one should expect from avowed Pantagruelists. There were running plays upon words, especially Latin words, for the facetious quibbles in fashion with Rabelais and the learned humorists of the Renaissance—varied by the retelling of old tales from collections in the French and Italian tongues. For their correspondence Sterne and Hall-Stevenson devised a Latin of their own after the style of the famous *Epistolæ Obscurorum Virorum*. The only one of these letters between Antonius and Laurentius ever published was written by Sterne in the midst of noisy companions at a York coffee-house, and sent over to Skelton on the eve of his setting out for London. As a Demoniac, Sterne defined for his friend in this letter the nature of the evil spirit that was driving him from home to the gaiety of the metropolis: *"Diabolus iste qui me intravit, non est diabolus vanus, aut consobrinus suus Lucifer—sed est diabolus amabundus, qui non vult sinere me esse solum . . . et tu es possessus cum eodem malo spiritu qui te tenet in deserto esse tentatum ancillis tuis, et perturbatum uxore tua."* If we had a sure key to the book, we should doubtless find that a large number of the jests and stories in *Tristram Shandy* had once been heard at Skelton. As if it were so, many are the glimpses of Yorick and Eugenius in conversation by the fireside and out in the fields. Especially graphic is the scene where Yorick, while telling a tawdry story "of a nun who fancied herself a shell-fish," is interrupted by his friend, who rises, walks around the table, and takes him by the hand. Then there is that smart repartee in parody of Alexander's reply to Parmenio, as given by Longinus *On the Sublime:*

"If I was you, quoth *Yorick*, I would drink more water, *Eugenius*—And, if I was you, *Yorick*, replied *Eugenius*, so would I."

Sterne's jests, commonly good-natured, could be at times sharp and bitter, for he went into wit-combats with the intention of winning, though he might come out of them, he says, "like a fool." On one occasion his host and Panty took him to task for his brutal treatment of a coxcomb, like "the puppy" at the George Inn, who had pushed his way into their society. "This man," said Sterne in memory of it, "lost temper with me for no reason upon earth but that I could not fall down and worship a brazen image of learning and eloquence, which he set up, to the persecution of all true believers—I sat down upon *his altar*, and whistled in the time of his divine service ——and broke down his carved work, and kicked his incense pot to the D——, so he retreated, *sed non sine felle in corde suo.*"

From this jesting and story-telling, Hall-Stevenson took the hint for his *Crazy Tales*, in which eleven of the Demoniacs relate gay intrigues "to promote good humour and cheerfulness" through a night at Skelton. Panty's tale of "The Cavalier Nun" was developed from an old monkish distich, which, slightly varied, Sterne long afterwards employed again to give point to *An Impromptu*, run off "in a few moments without stopping his pen," while the author was "thoroughly soused." Zachary chose his theme from Bandello, drawing a parallel between the Italian bishop and Sterne. The Privy Counsellor presented an imitation of Chaucer. Antony adjusted an old tale to the boarding-school; and Sterne, beginning with the great walnut tree and other reminiscences of Cambridge, wandered off into a cock-and-bull story, such as fitted his character, though not one of the best of its kind.

Like these Chaucerian tales of Hall-Stevenson's, *Tristram Shandy*, it is almost needless to add in conclusion, also had its living counterpart in Crazy Castle, but after a larger and different manner. Not that Sterne, so far as we can divine him, exactly transferred to his book living portraits of the men whom he met over the rich burgundy. But it was under the hospitable roof of Skelton that he associated, in jest, argument, and dispute, with those half-mad oddities of human nature which he knew how to transform, by the aid of other memories, into Eugenius, Mr. Walter Shandy, and my uncle Toby.

CHAP. VI.

The Parson in His Library

GOOD fellowship over bright burgundy was doubtless quite sufficient for drawing Sterne to Skelton for a week or two in October and oftener. But there was another attraction for him in the library of old books that had been long collecting by his host and the family before him. Indeed, writers on Sterne, repeating what was said a century ago, have given wide currency to the tradition that the humorist found and read at Skelton most of those strange volumes that go to the learning and adornment of *Tristram Shandy*. Though the tradition is far from the truth, Sterne's intimacy with Hall-Stevenson may have led him to reading curious books for one of his recreations in the long and obscure years at Sutton. We may fancy him on his visits to Skelton poring over his friend's big folios and taking three or four of them with him as he drove home. Nearer at hand was the library of his dean and chapter, rich in manuscripts, and old treatises on law, medicine, and divinity, wherein he could have met with his humorous instances of casuistry and misplaced learning.

But the books that became a part of Sterne's mental equipment must have been his daily companions at Sutton. When he emerges from obscurity, he appears at once as a book collector on his own account. If the first money from the sale of *Tristram Shandy* went to the purchase of a carriage and a pair of horses, the surplus from the second instalment was left with a bookseller for seven hundred books which were "set up in my best room." Before his fame and the competency that came with it, Sterne's purchases must have been more restricted, but even then his income was not so small as to leave nothing for his humor. In the eighteenth century, York was the centre of the northern book trade. From the surrounding district, libraries of country gentlemen were sent in to Cæsar Ward, John Todd, and other dealers to be disposed of at auc-

tion or private sale. Auctions were also held every few weeks
at inns and town-halls in the neighborhood. For a few shillings Sterne could have procured beautiful folios that would
now bring a handful of guineas, if they could be had at all.
To Sterne's reading in this formative period, we have a trustworthy, though incomplete, index in *Tristram Shandy*. He
there reflects of course himself and Hall-Stevenson in the
opposite tastes of the two Shandys, both of whom are collectors, one making a specialty of military architecture and the
other of the learned humorists.

Among the *facetiæ* that Mr. Walter Shandy most prized,
were Bouchet's *Serées*, and Bruscambille's *Pensées Facétieuses*,
including a prologue upon long noses, which was bought of a
London dealer for three half-crowns. The story of the purchase at the book-stall Sterne related with the passion of the
bibliophile: "There are not three Bruscambille's in Christendom—said the stall-man, except what are chain'd up in the
libraries of the curious. My father flung down the money as
quick as lightning——took Bruscambille into his bosom——
hied home from Piccadilly to Coleman-street with a treasure,
without taking his hand once off from Bruscambille all the
way." When in a confidential mood one day on a visit to Stillington Hall, Sterne told his friends there, as John Croft remembered it, what books he read and studied most. He placed
first the *Moyen de Parvenir* of Béroalde de Verville, and
added Montaigne, Rabelais, Marivaux, and Dr. Joseph Hall,
"Bishop of Exeter in King James the First's reign." But he
forgot, as was Sterne's way, to mention many an author that
ought to have been on the list. His fireside books were as odd
as the men with whom he associated at Crazy Castle. From
them he drew and then cast them aside, in just the same way
as he would take up his pencil for a caricature of his wife, or
his gun for an afternoon with the partridges.

First in the catalogue of books read by the Vicar of Sutton
were three of the world's greatest humorists—Lucian, "my
dear Rabelais, and dearer Cervantes." With Lucian, by whose
ashes he swore the "oath referential," Sterne was less familiar

than with the other two; but we must suppose that the *Dialogues*, read at Cambridge, were taken up again in the Sutton period, for he could, when in the mood for it, fall into Lucian's tone of gay mockery. The presence of Cervantes, whom he knew through Skelton's translation of *Don Quixote*, is felt in one place or another of every volume of *Tristram Shandy*, from the introductory sketches of Yorick and Dr. Slop on to the end, through scores of passages pervaded by this "gentle Spirit of sweetest humour." Rabelais, though Sterne sometimes ranked him after Cervantes, was really, I should say, first in his affections. A volume of *Gargantua* or of *Pantagruel*, Yorick was accustomed to carry in "his right-hand coat pocket," that it might be ready for the amusement of his friends, as they drew up to the fire after supper. On these occasions Yorick read to them, not from the original French— for Sterne then had little acquaintance with that, though he could pick it out by the help of Cotgrave's dictionary,—but from the current version of Ozell, a London scribbler, who spent his days in mutilating foreign classics for English readers. Ozell, text, notes, and all, Sterne had well-nigh by heart, and found them most serviceable in the act of composition. Without Rabelais, his jests, whims, anecdotes, and splendid extravagances, there would never have been a Sterne as we now know him.*

Rabelais, the most constant of his passions, drew Sterne on into the facetious tales and verses of the later Pantagruelists, both French and English, among whom he also luxuriated. The Guillaume Bouchet who delighted the heart of Mr. Walter Shandy, was a magistrate at Poitiers, where his *Serées*, or *Evening Conferences*, three volumes in the whole, began to appear in 1584. In this vivacious work, Bouchet and his friends meet at one another's house on appointed evenings for

---

* Sterne's immense obligations to Ozell's translation of Rabelais are indicated in the marginal notes to the Grenville copy of *Tristram Shandy* in the British Museum. For the humorist's borrowings from Rabelais and other French writers, see also John Ferriar, *Illustrations of Sterne*, two vols. (second edition, London, 1812).

a light supper and to relate incidents they have read of in books or heard of among their neighbors. Some one of them usually tells the main story, while the others break in with their contributions to the theme, be it of wine, water, or women, the fine arts, physicians, lawyers, or the clergy. The volumes of Bouchet are an epitome of the Gallic wit that lies scattered in the old *fabliaux* and innumerable *contes*, the aim of which is mirth and laughter.

Of books of this kind Sterne rightly gave his preference to the *Moyen de Parvenir* or *How to Succeed*, which made its appearance in 1610, without the author's name. It was written, the critics have established, by Béroalde de Verville, a canon of the Cathedral of Tours, otherwise known for several imitations of Rabelais. As in Bouchet, the plan is a symposium, where gather for conversation and story-telling Béroalde's friends under the names of famous men and women of antiquity, such as Cæsar, Socrates, and Sappho. Laughter, eating, drinking, and sleeping are proclaimed the four cardinal virtues. The conversations run from theme to theme without any apparent connection at first sight; but they are really all ordered with great skill, the last word of each discourse giving occasion for the one following. Next to Rabelais's profusion of wit, no other book has quite so many analogies with *Tristram Shandy*.

Bruscambille, another favorite with Sterne, was the *nom de théâtre* of a comedian named Deslauriers, whose *Fantaisies* or *Pensées Facétieuses* appeared in 1612. The author imagines himself on the stage addressing his audience in whimsical prologues, harangues, and paradoxes on cuckoldry, pedantry, long and short noses, or in defence of lying or of telling the truth, as whim may seize him. Bruscambille was a perfect master of what the French call *galimatias*, a mad flow of speech in which incongruity is piled upon incongruity for comic effect. "I met," says Bruscambille, to give an extreme example of his nonsense, "I met, gentlemen and ladies, last night a large, small man with red hair who had a beard as black as pepper; he had just come from a country where, except for the animals and the people, there was no living soul." How well Sterne learned the art of Bruscambille, everyone knows who has perused his books or letters, though, it should be observed, he never went quite so far as his original in a reckless topsy-turvy of ideas and phrases. Perhaps he went the farthest when he wrote "A cow broke in (to-morrow morning) to my uncle *Toby's* fortifications and eat up two rations and a half of dried grass, tearing up the sod with it, which faced his horn-work and covered way."

With these facetious writers Sterne classed Montaigne, who, though his work is of more serious import, wandered on whimsically, as everybody would have him, from one topic to another, so that the title of any one of his essays gives no clue to the content. Sterne knew his Montaigne well, not in the French but in the fine translation made by Cotton, the accomplished angler; and loved him with the affection of Thackeray, who took him, instead of an opiate, as a bedside book to prattle him to sleep when threatened by insomnia.* Nor should we forget Scarron's comic muse with skirts all bedrabbled, nor the tearful mistress of Marivaux and other French novelists with whom Sterne carried on frequent flirta· tions.

Last in the line (barring the sentimental Marivaux) were the English humorists—Swift and his group—who sought to fill the easy chair left vacant by Rabelais and his French descendants. To Sterne, Swift meant mainly *A Tale of a Tub*, a cock-and-bull story, with digressions upon criticism and madness, digressions upon digressions, and further digressions,

---

* When *Tristram Shandy* first appeared, a Mr. Brown, of Geneva, wrote out a fanciful sketch of the author as he imagined him from the book, and sent it on to Hall-Stevenson. Amused as well as flattered by the letter, Sterne replied, saying with reference to a conjecture that he was a reader of Montaigne: " 'For my conning Montaigne as much as my prayer book'—there you are right again,—but mark a second time, I have not said I admire him as much;—tho' had he been alive, I would certainly have gone twice as far [as you say] to have smoaked a pipe with him, as with Arch-Bishop Laud or his Chaplains (tho' one of 'em was my grandfather)."

which, says the author, serve a book in the way foreign troops serve a state, for they "either subdue the natives or drive them into the most unfruitful corners." Near Swift's *Tub*, doubtless lay, in Sterne's estimation, Dr. John Arbuthnot's *Memoirs of Martin Scriblerus*, long ago pointed out as having some resemblance to *Tristram Shandy*, in its humorous dissertations on science and mathematics, education, playthings, and the breeching of children. The genius of Pope, who bore a hand in the miscellanies of Scriblerus, Sterne took for granted, like the rest of his generation, easily quoting his proverbial lines. The friendship between the poet and his physician, as depicted in the *Epistle to Dr. Arbuthnot*—the one a satirist and man of letters pestered by friends and foes alike, and the other a faithful counsellor crying "Hold! for God's sake you'll offend"—struck Sterne's fancy especially, for he carried the situation over into *Tristram Shandy* for his Yorick and Eugenius. Finally, he never doubted the truth of Pope's doctrine of ruling passions, in accordance with which were constructed all of his own characters.

Sterne also dipped into the scribbling undercurrent of the Queen Anne wits for occasional refreshment. There he discovered Tom Brown "of facetious memory," one of whose anecdotes was turned to a new purpose in the opening paragraph of *Tristram Shandy*; and there he caught sight of two books as mad as any he himself was destined to write. One of them was *An Essay towards the Theory of the Intelligible World*, from the pen of "Gabriel John," the pseudonym, perhaps, of Tom D'Urfey, the profane wit and dramatist. It appeared, according to the humorous title-page, "in the Year One thousand Seven Hundred &c," and was to consist "of a Preface, a Postscript and a Little something between." On one page this "little something between" was reduced to a series of dashes in place of the usual text, with an explanatory note at the left saying, to quote half of it: "The Author very well understands that a good sizable *Hiatus* discovers a very great Genius, there being no Wit in the World more Ideal, and consequently more refined, than what is display'd in these

elaborate Pages, that have ne're a syllable written on them."
The other mad book, the work of John Dunton, a London
bookseller and adventurer, bears the title of *A Voyage Round
the World, . . . containing the Rare Adventures of Don
Kainophilus* (1691). To attract the reader, Dunton employed
every sort of type, including whole pages of capitals and black
letter, sprinkled with dashes and index-hands. He began his
tale with the prenatal history of his hero, and then ran off into
a series of cock-rambles which end nowhere, in order that
"people shou'd miss what they expected and find what they
never lookt for." When Sterne was charged with plagiarizing
from Dunton, he wrote to a friend to say that he once met
with the book in a London circulating library and took from
it "many of his ideas." The very copy of Dunton that Sterne
read now rests, it is probable, in the Boston Public Library.*

Not the least charm for Sterne about the old humorists
which fell in his way was the quaint erudition that went hand
in hand with their frank foolery. After the fashion of the
Renaissance, they took all knowledge for their province. Rabelais was a learned physician and Benedictine. Bouchet could
not discourse on the virtues of wine without giving first a history of the symposium from the Greeks down through the
amica convivia of the Romans to the drinking clubs of his own
day, embellished throughout with numerous quotations from
the ancient poets and historians. Béroalde passed in review the
arts and sciences of the time, ridiculing in his progress mathe-

---

* This copy was owned by the late James Crossley, an English antiquarian, and after the dispersion of his library in 1885, it found its
way into the Boston Public Library (February, 1886). On a fly-leaf,
Crossley wrote: "Rodd [Thomas Rodd, the London book-seller] once
showed me an original Letter of Sterne in which he mentions this Work,
from which he took many of his Ideas and which he had met with in a
London Circulating Library. As the present Copy came from Hookham's, whose Bookplate, which was on the original boards, I have pasted
opposite, there is little doubt that this was the identical copy read by
Sterne." As Hookham's Library was at 15 Old Bond Street, near
Sterne's London lodgings, there is good ground for the conjecture with
which Crossley closes his valuable note.

matics, metaphysics, casuistry, and current literature; and
setting up the claim that the *Moyen de Parvenir* was "the
centre of all books," wherein one might find clearly demon-
strated "the reason for all things that have been or ever shall
be."

Even Dunton's absurd book bore as sub-title *A Pocket Library*; and Arbuthnot—to pass by the better known Swift—
ran through, in burlesque, all the arts and sciences, back to
their origin among the monkeys of India and Ethiopia, who
were our first philosophers. Erudition like this, real or pretended, Sterne greatly enjoyed. It is sometimes said that our
classics, ancient and modern, are over-edited; that the author
is submerged in the annotations. Sterne, on the other hand,
never finding any fault with learning of this kind, disre-
garded, as we all well might, the author and bent his mind
upon understanding the editor. A good instance of this is his
apparent perusal of *Hudibras*, with "large annotations" by the
Rev. Zachary Grey, a Cambridge man, among the multitude
of which he may have found all that had ever been said about
the *homunculus*. A better instance is his use of *Philostratus
concerning the Life of Apollonius Tyaneus, with . . . Notes
upon Each Chapter*, by Charles Blount, the deist. One may
imagine Sterne's delight as his eye fell upon Blount's preface
to the reader: "Whether kind or unkind, I shall call you
neither, for fear lest I be mistaken. . . . As for my *Illustrations*: Notwithstanding they have some coherence with my
Text, yet I likewise design'd them as *Philological Essays* upon
several Subjects, such as the least hint might present me with."
True to his promise, Blount made the old spiritual romance of
Philostratus merely the occasion for learned essays, far exceeding in extent the original Greek, on dress, whiskers, swearing,
death, *et cetera*, themes which Sterne did not forget, as every
reader of him knows, when he came to write *Tristram
Shandy*. Nor did he then forget, when he arrived at Walter
Shandy's Tristra-pædia, an anonymous book of curious learning, entitled *Of Education, Especially of Young Gentlemen*
(1673), written by Obadiah Walker, an Oxford Fellow,

who became Master of University College. Probably not knowing who wrote the book, Sterne was sometime to burlesque delightfully Walker on precocious young men and old men of retarded intelligence, and on the manipulation of auxiliary verbs "by some of which all questions are made, and by which the *predicates* whether Verbe or Noun are joined to the Subject."*

Sterne spent some time on Erasmus—on the *Colloquia* and especially on the Μωρίας ἐγκώμιον, which had been done into English under the title of *Moriæ Encomium; or a Panegyrick upon Folly*. Erasmus, like Sterne after him, assumed the character of a jester, "playing at pushpin," or "riding astride on a hobby-horse," in his journey through a censure of men and morals. The *Encomium* was adorned "with above fifty curious cuts" by Holbein, of which two would attract Sterne above all others—one representing a fierce wrangle of disputants, and another depicting the instigation of the devil by means of grotesque imps hovering over the head and clawing the hair of their unfortunate victim. From Erasmus, Sterne passed on to the casuists and schoolmen, where he was amused by discourses on the space occupied by souls, the size of hell, debates on "the point of Martin Luther's damnation," "the pudder and racket in Councils about οὐσία and ὑπόστασις,—and in the Schools of the learned about power and about spirit,—about essences, and about quintessences,—about substances, and about space." In the course of this reading, he fell in with the *ars magna* of Raymond Lully; the terrible anathemas of Ernulf, Bishop of Rochester in the twelfth century; the *De Legibus Hebræorum Ritualibus* of Dr. John Spencer, Master of Corpus Christi College, Cambridge, wherein he stopped on the learned reasons for and against circumcision; and Sir Robert Brook's *Graunde Abridgement*, with other works in ecclesiastical law, which tried to explain to him that in certain nice cases, as in that of the Duchess of Suffolk, "the mother is not of kin to her child."

* See John M. Turnbull, "The Prototype of Walter Shandy's Tristra-pædia" in *The Review of English Studies*, April, 1926.

Beyond a doubt Sterne saw the *Utrius Cosmi, Maioris scilicet et Minoris Metaphysica, Physica atque Technica Historia* by Robert Flud, a Fellow of the College of Physicians at Oxford, and the first of the English Rosicrucians. The old folio had two dedications, one to the Almighty and the other to James the First. In the first chapter, Flud described, after Trismegistus and Moses, chaos—or the *ens primordiale infinitum, informe,* as his Latin has it,—under the form of a very black smoke or vapor; and for the assistance of the reader's imagination, he covered two thirds of a page with a black square, writing on each of its four sides *Et sic infinitum,* lest somebody might suppose that there were boundaries to the horrible shadow of undigested matter out of which the Almighty created his universe of worlds and stars. This square became of course Sterne's page dressed in mourning for the death of "poor Yorick."

Bacon's essays, we may be sure, were in Sterne's library, for he quoted from them and modified their phrasing with the greatest ease. He also possessed a copy of *Baconiana, or Genuine Remains of Francis Bacon,* a collection of posthumous miscellanies, which had been brought out anonymously by Thomas Tenison, Archbishop of Canterbury. One of the strange features of this book was the archbishop's "Discourse by way of Introduction," added as a tag at the end of the volume. Sterne was reading the misplaced introduction when he began *Tristram Shandy,* for he "conveyed" a passage from it to his twelfth chapter, and not unlikely derived from the archbishop the notion of inserting his prefaces and dedications midway in his own book. If an introduction may be put after the word *finis,* when all is supposed to be over, why, Sterne would argue, may it not be slipped in anywhere?

The scholar that most fascinated Sterne was Robert Burton, the Oxford recluse who wrote *The Anatomy of Melancholy,* "the only book," said Boswell of Dr. Johnson, "that ever took him out of bed two hours sooner than he wished to rise." Once under the spell of the *Anatomy,* there is no release for any man, whether he be of the staid character of Johnson or of the shifting temper of Sterne. "I have lived," wrote its author, to compress an autobiographic passage, "a silent, sedentary, solitary, private life in the university, penned up most part in my study. Though by my profession a Divine, yet out of a running wit, an unconstant, unsettled mind, I had a great desire to have some smattering in all learning, to be *aliquis in omnibus, nullus in singulis,* to roam abroad, to have an oar in every man's boat, to taste of every dish, sip of every cup." An earlier selfhood he discovered in Democritus, the ancient Greek sage of Abdera, "a little wearish old man, very melancholy by nature," who passed his time in his garden, writing under a shady bower, or cutting up divers creatures "to find out the seat of this *atra bilis,* or melancholy, whence it proceeds, and how it is engendered in men's bodies; . . . saving that he sometimes would walk down to the haven and laugh heartily at such variety of ridiculous objects, which there he saw." Since the treatise of the Greek philosopher, if ever written, was no longer in existence, Burton took up the subject anew to the intent that he might cure himself and the world of a dreadful malady. "I writ of melancholy," he said, "by being busy to avoid melancholy." Through "partitions, sections, members, and subsections," entangled with medicine, law, morals, and divinity, he cut out his theme, strewing his course with thousands of quotations, ancient and modern, sometimes inserted in the text, sometimes printed on the margin, neatly paraphrased, or left untranslated, *per accidens* or as it might happen.

The Anatomy of Melancholy, with its curious wit and learning, was the most useful volume in Sterne's library. If Sterne wished a Latin phrase to point a sentence, if he wished a good story, never stale if rightly retold, for an episode in *Tristram Shandy,* he had but to open Burton, and there it lay before him. Without scruple, he transferred to his own pages long stretches of the old book, with only such changes as genius cannot help making when it takes from others.

Besides the *Anatomy,* Sterne looked into all sorts of books on physiology and medicine. His list of physicians, from whom

he could quote directly or indirectly, begins with Hippocrates
and comes down through Coglionissimo Borri, who "discovered in the cellulæ of the occipital parts of the cerebellum
. . . the principal seat of the reasonable soul," to Dr. James
Mackenzie, who argued for the great effects "which the passions and affections of the mind have upon the digestion." An
extraordinary source of amusement to Sterne were treatises on
midwifery, which was then just becoming a part of the regular practice of physicians. In these books and pamphlets one
physician ridiculed and scolded another, holding up to contempt the instruments his opponent invented to bring children
safely into the world, and sometimes interspersing his narrative with noisy disputes between the doctor and the midwife
who was being displaced by the new science. Celebrated at the
time was the angry altercation between Dr. John Burton of
York and Dr. William Smellie of Glasgow. Burton's books,
now of great rarity, were worth owning even in Sterne's day
for their copperplates etched by George Stubbs, the horse-
painter. With local as well as distant controversies, Sterne thus
kept pace simply for the humor of it.

That Sterne should have also extracted humor out of mechanics and military engineering is the whim of his genius
most akin to madness. True, memories of childhood carried
him back to life in Irish barracks, but it is doubtful if he had
ever seen a town fortified against a siege. His knowledge of
the siege of Namur, for example, which plays so large a part
in *Tristram Shandy*, was derived mostly from *The Life of
William the Third, Late King of England*, an anonymous
military biography that appeared the year after his Majesty's
death. Treatises on the art of war such as Sterne perused, had
an immense run in the century before Sterne, when military
engineers brought to the construction of defences, and all that
pertains thereto, the assistance of the newer mathematics, like
Napier's *Logarithms* and Gunter's *Sines and Tangents*, which
performed wonderful feats merely by addition and subtrac-
tion, without the help of multiplication and division. Just as
with the old romances of chivalry, one Amadis begat another

in an endless progeny down through Esplandian, Florisando, and Palmerin; so it was with the books on military engineering, which in one language or another spread throughout western Europe. Inasmuch as their elaborate calculations fill and occupy the mind beyond all other studies, the author of the *Anatomy* recommended them among the best antidotes against melancholy.

The way in which Sterne entered upon their track, losing himself soon in the mazes, is reflected, I daresay, in what is said of my uncle Toby's reading in *Tristram Shandy*. Most of the first year my uncle Toby pored over "Gobesius's military architecture and pyroballogy, translated from the Flemish"—doubtfully identified as Leonhard Gorecius's *Descriptio Belli Ivoniæ* (1578),—that he might discourse learnedly on the uses of artillery. After this close preliminary study, he was able to read rapidly the next year ten or twelve other crabbed authors, just as the schoolboy, after going through his first book in Latin, is supposed to proceed easily with the rest. To take them chronologically, first came Girolamo Cataneo, whose *Libro di Fortificare, Offendere e Diffendere* (1564) contains "brief tables to know readily how many ranks of footmen etc. go to making a just battle"; Agostino Ramelli, with *Le Diverse ed Artificiose Machine* (1588), descriptive of various contrivances for lifting heavy loads, constructing bridges, and hurling ignited grenades and other artificial fires; and the Florentine Lorini, who published a book on fortifications in 1609, and served with honor under the kings of France and Spain. So much for Italy.

Then followed Marolois, whose *Fortification ou Architecture Militaire* (1615) told Sterne how to attack and how to defend, with many mathematical details and more than a hundred plates, including one of Ostend prepared to endure the most protracted siege; the *Nouvelle Manière de Fortification* (1618) by means of sluices, written by Stevinus, a distinguished Dutch mathematician and engineer of the dykes, within whose book Yorick's sermon on conscience long lay concealed; *Les Fortifications* (1629) of the Chevalier de

Ville, who attacked Artois under the eyes of Louis the Thirteenth, and was the first, it is said, to write upon the construction and effects of mines; the *Traité des Fortifications* (1645)
by the Comte de Pagan, who conducted the sieges of Caen,
Montauban, and Nancy, losing an eye and finally his sight
completely in the service of his king; and François Blondel,
who constructed great public buildings, arches of triumph, and
published among other books *L'Art de jetter les Bombes*
(1685). Nor should be overlooked one or more military books
in Latin, written by Johann Bernard von Scheither, an officer
in the Thirty Years' War. The long list for the second year
closes with the *Nouvelle Manière de Fortifier les Places*
(1702) by Baron Van Coehoorn, the great Dutch engineer
who fortified Namur—where my uncle Toby received his
grievous wound,—and gallantly defended the citadel until,
himself wounded and his regiment cut to pieces, he was
obliged to capitulate to his still greater rival, Prestre de
Vauban, afterwards Marshal of France. This was the Vauban
who designed new fortifications for most of the cities of
France and directed fifty sieges, winning town after town in
the Netherlands, with Louis the Fourteenth often standing
by, as at Namur, to witness the final blows that compelled
the surrender. The methods by which Vauban built and by
which he won, Sterne found explained in *De l'Attaque et de
la Défense des Places* (1737-42).

Notwithstanding his reading in all these books, Sterne—if
we may follow the hints from my uncle Toby—had not yet
learned much about projectiles. For this knowledge he went
to Tartaglia's *Quesiti ed Invenzioni Diverse* (1546), where
he was met with the demonstration that a cannon-ball does not
do its mischief by moving in a straight line. Having discovered
the road along which a cannon-ball cannot go, he set out to
discover next the road in which it must go. His search began
with the *Pratique de la Guerre* (1650) of François Malthus,
who gave precise directions for the use of artillery, bombs, and
mortars; and the search ended with Galileo and Torricelli,
whose infallible laws of the parabola he could not understand.

There Sterne stopped, hopelessly bewildered. In the strange journey he may have consulted now and then the *Acta Eruditorum*, a long and learned series of year-books in Latin, containing the latest discussions and discoveries in medicine, theology, and jurisprudence, as well as in mechanics and military architecture.

From this array of books, no one should infer that Sterne was a man of erudition. He probably could not follow a demonstration in mechanics involving the higher mathematics. It is, for example, noteworthy that he showed no interest in Stevinus's solution of the problem of the inclined plane, the achievement that gives the Dutch mathematician his place in the history of mechanics. As if ignorant of the brilliant discovery, Sterne referred to Stevinus as the inventor of "a sailing chariot . . . of wonderful contrivance and velocity," belonging to Prince Maurice, for a sight of which "the learned Peireskius . . . walked a matter of five-hundred miles." The truth seems to be that, while designing *Tristram Shandy* during the last years at Sutton, Sterne thumbed many old quartos and folios, amusing himself with maps, plates, and descriptions of sieges, to the end that my uncle Toby might be proficient in the phrases of military science. When in the act of composition, a short cut to knowledge seemed imperative, he had recourse to Chambers's *Universal Dictionary of Arts and Sciences*.* Somehow he learned to write, with the ease of an ex-

---

* Mr. Edward Bensly, in *The Times Literary Supplement* for November 1, 1928, first called attention to Sterne's indebtedness to military and other articles in Ephraim Chambers's *Cyclopaedia: or, An Universal Dictionary of Arts and Sciences*, first published in 1728. A copy of the second edition (1738) of this cyclopaedia was in Todd and Sotheran's *Catalogue* (1768), which included "The Entire Library of the Late Reverend and Learned Laurence Sterne." The *Catalogue* also contained many books on military history and engineering, such as Vauban's *New Method of Fortification* (1748). Accordingly, Mr. Bensly is not warranted in the conclusion that Sterne probably derived all his knowledge of military science from Chambers. The problem, however, is difficult; for of the 2,505 items in the *Catalogue*, there is no way of determining beyond doubt which ones came from Sterne's library. An examination of Chambers's *Cyclopaedia* shows that Sterne consulted it frequently on a variety of subjects.

pert, of scarp and counter-scarp, counter-guard and demi-bastion, covered-way, glacis, ravelin and half-moon, on through saps, mines, and palisadoes.

The books that have been enumerated by no means comprise all that Sterne read at Sutton. They are rather only the curiosities; but as such they are the most significant, for they show wherein Sterne fed his humor. He continued to quote from the ancient classics, which he had read at school and college, as if they were still his companions. To describe his impatient moods he cited Hotspur when "pestered with a popinjay"; and the name which he bears in letters was taken from the jester whom Hamlet once knew. He read Lord Rochester, Dryden, and others of the Restoration; and with the wits of the next half century he was still more familiar. Voltaire's *Candide*, Johnson's *Rasselas*, and other notable books he read as they came out, or saw them in the stalls of York dealers. But it is unnecessary to proceed with these miscellanies, since here is already, in Dryden's phrase, God's plenty. As a divine, Sterne knew well the religious literature that was expected of him. It is a pleasure to discover in him traces of Sir Thomas Browne's *Religio Medici* and of Jeremy Taylor's *Holy Living* and *Holy Dying*. For forming his style as a preacher he studied the sermons of Hall, Berkeley, Young, Tillotson, and other moralists and divines, from whom he drew liberally, sometimes merely paraphrasing the original when the harvest season, it may be, gave him scant time for independent composition. Nor should we forget the Scriptures which he read and re-read during the long winter evenings at Sutton, with the result that his style became saturated with the words and phrases of the English version. Many a clergyman since his time has run through indexes and concordances to the Bible in quest of "God tempers the wind to the shorn lamb"; but the labor has been in vain, for the sentence, possessing the beauty and melody of inspiration, is Sterne's own recoinage of a crude proverb.

Along with his reading, Sterne played with his pen occasionally as well as with his pencil and his gun. Between his political articles in the newspapers and the publication of *Tristram Shandy,* lay several whims in verse and prose, including a satirical pamphlet which was duly printed at York. One of these minor pieces—a very pretty fancy cast in the form of a letter to a Mr. Cook,—after remaining in manuscript for more than a century, was published in 1870 by Paul Stapfer in his study of Sterne.* How the French critic came by it we will leave to his own strange narrative:

"Two years ago, a friend of mine in England, an M.A. of the University of Oxford and then Vice-Principal of Elizabeth College in the island of Guernsey, was visiting a lady of his acquaintance at York. Among other things the conversation turned to autographs; whereupon the lady said she had an entire essay in the hand of Sterne, which had never been published; and she showed it to him. M. . . . , after examining it, said:

" 'I shall soon see a friend who is now at work on a study of Sterne; I am sure that he would be glad to have this piece; but I should not like to show it to him unless he may be permitted to copy and publish it.' '*You shall have it,*' replied the lady.

"I received the manuscript, copied and returned it. Some time afterwards I met the owner of it and naturally asked her how a precious manuscript like this came into her possession. The very vague information which she gave me in the course of the conversation left only the most confused impression on my mind. For this reason I intended later to ask her to write a short note upon the history of these sheets: but I learned that she was then so ill as to render impossible all correspondence. I was thus compelled to forego any exact knowledge of the matter, and even a second perusal of the manuscript which she had offered to place at my disposal again that I might make a facsimile of it."

"We have then," adds Stapfer in comment upon the story, "no external proof of the authenticity of the fragment. All we can say is that the hand, remarkably fair and firm, is iden-

* *Laurence Sterne, sa Personne et ses Ouvrages* (Paris, 1870).

tical with what we have already seen of Sterne's; but there is
no signature."

It would be quite easy to set up an argument against accepting as Sterne's this late discovery. Those who know Sterne
only from *Tristram Shandy* may say that it hardly resembles
anything in that book. Those who know Sterne a little better
may say that it is only one among the scores of imitations and
forgeries that followed in the wake of his popularity. And to
everybody the tale told by the lady of York, so far as there is
any, must seem a fabrication. But other manuscripts, Sterne's
beyond doubt, have drifted down in the same obscure ways;
and the content of the one in question is in perfect harmony
with an allegorical phase of mind through which Sterne was
passing in the first years with his books at Sutton. In this case
the allegory ends with a moral reflection, playfully supported
by a line from Pope's *Essay on Man*, occurring in the first
epistle near the passage which Sterne quoted in a letter to Miss
Lumley, back in 1740. The spelling and abbreviations, as
printed by Stapfer, correspond with Sterne's peculiar usage;
an apt phrase recalls now and then his fine sense for style; and
the background is Sutton without much doubt.

The interesting trifle—only half worked out—is a dream
or meditation. The Vicar of Sutton had spent, I should say,
an evening in his library over Fontenelle's *Entretiens sur la
Pluralité des Mondes*, in its day a famous book on the vast
number of new worlds discovered or made probable by modern science. "A leaf on a tree growing in the garden," said
Fontenelle, "is a little world inhabited by innumerable ani-
malcules invisible to the naked eye, to whom it appears as an
immense expanse with mountains and ravines. Those on one
side have no intercourse with those who live on the other, any
more than we have with men at the antipodes. Just so, it seems
to me, the great planets moving through the immensity of
space may be likewise inhabited with beings." The dwellers
upon earth, moralized Sterne with reference to this passage,
have commonly regarded themselves as the centre of the universe. "So considerable do they imagine themselves as doubtless

to hold that all these numerous stars (our sun among the rest) were created with the only view of twinkling upon such of them, as have occasion to follow their cattle late at night." Whereas the truth seems to be that "we are situate on a kind of isthmus, which separates two infinitys," one revealed by the telescope and the other by the microscope. "On one side infinite power and wisdom appear drawn at *full extent;* on the other, in *miniature.* The infinitely *strong and bold strokes there,* the infinitely *nice and delicate touches here,* shew equally in both the divine hand."

His mind under the sway of these speculations, the vicar laid aside his book, strolled out into his orchard, and stopped near one of those plum trees which he had planted on first coming to Sutton. It was a brilliant summer night without a cloud. As he stood there, Fontenelle's myriad worlds were all about him. Far above were the moon and the countless stars. By his side, on each green leaf of his plum trees were nations performing "actions as truly great as any we read of in the history of Alexander. Their courage, resolution, and patience of pain may be as great as that exhibited by the Macedonian army, nay and even the prize of the contest no way inferior to that which animated the brave Greeks. The possession or conquest of the leaf may gratify as many and as strong desires in them, as that of the earth in us."

Time and space, Sterne further reflected, are but relative notions depending upon the size and shape of the brain. To the beings that people the universe comprised within his plum tree, an hour or a minute may seem as long as four score and ten years to us. On the tricks that time and place may play with us, there came to Sterne's mind, "a very fine Spectator,"* wherein is related a story of Mahomet from the Koran. "The angel Gabriel," according to Addison, "took Mahomet out of his bed one morning to give him a sight of all things in the seven heavens, in paradise, and in hell, which the prophet took a distinct view of; and after having held ninety thousand conferences with God, was brought back again to his bed. All

* No. 94.

this, says the Alcoran, was transacted in so small a space of time, that Mahomet at his return found his bed still warm, and took up an earthern pitcher, which was thrown down at the very instant that the angel Gabriel carried him away, before the water was all spilt."

At this point in his reverie, Sterne returned to the rectory and went to bed. "From that time," runs the narrative, "I knew not what happen'd to me, till by degrees I found myself in a new state of being, without any remembrance or suspicion that I had ever existed before, growing up gradually to reason and manhood, as I had done here. The world I was in was vast and commodious. The heavens were enlighten'd with abundance of smaller luminarys resembling stars, and one glaring one resembling the moon; but with this difference that they seem'd fix'd in the heavens, and had no apparent motion. There were also a set of luminarys of a different nature, that gave a dimmer light. They were of various magnitudes, and appear'd in different forms. Some had the form of crescents; others, that shone opposite to the great light, appear'd round. We call'd them by a name, which in our language would sound like second stars. Besides these, there were several luminous streaks running across the heavens like our milky way; and many variable glimmerings like our north-lights." In his new world the dreamer passed several ages and then seemed to return to earth, where he was first rallied and then persecuted for his astronomical opinions. In process of time "began to be heard all over the world a huge noise and fragor in the skys, as if all nature was approaching to her dissolution. The stars seem'd to be torn from their orbits, and to wander at random thro' the heavens. . . . all was consternation, horrour, and amaze; no less was expected than an universal wreck of nature. What ensu'd I know not. All of a sudden, I knew not how, I found myself in bed, as just waking from a sound sleep. . . . I hurri'd into the orchard, and by a sort of natural instinct made to the plumb-tree under which pass'd my last night's reverie. I observ'd the face of the heavens was just the same as it had appear'd to me immediately before I left my former state; and that a brisk gale of wind, which is common about sun rising, was abroad. I recollected a hint I had read in *Fontenelle* who intimates that there is reason to suppose that the *Blue* on *Plumbs* is no other than an immense number of living creatures. I got into the tree, examin'd the clusters of plumbs; found that they hung in the same position, and made the same appearance with the constellations of second stars, I had been so familiarly acquainted with, excepting that some few were wanting, which I myself had seen fall. I cou'd then no longer doubt how the matter was."

The world to which the dreamer had been transported by the angel Gabriel for some thousands of years was, it would seem, none other than the blue surface of a luscious plum growing on his favorite tree. The luminaries that shone about him like "second stars" were other plums dangling above him. The "luminous streaks running across the heavens like our milky way" were branches of the plum tree, and "the many variable glimmerings like our north-lights" were the leaves playing in the moonbeams. The damage to Sterne's solar system had been caused by a wind that here and there sent a plum to the ground.

The dream is neatly rounded with a moral and a prophecy:

"O the vanity of worldly things, and even of worlds themselves! O world, wherein I have spent so many happy days! O the comforts, and enjoyments I am separated from; the acquaintance and friends I have left behind me there! O the mountains, rivers, rocks and plains, which ages had familiariz'd to my view! with you I seem'd at home; here I am like a banish'd man; every thing appears strange, wild and savage! O the projects I had form'd! the designs I had set on foot, the friendships I had cultivated! How has one blast of wind dash'd you to pieces! . . . But thus it is: *Plumbs* fall, and *Planets* shall perish. . . .

" 'And now a Bubble burst, and now a world.' The time will come when the powers of heaven shall be shaken, and the stars shall fall like the fruit of a tree, when it is shaken by a mighty wind!"

Akin to this fancy addressed to Mr. Cook is a meditation
in verse called *The Unknown World*, with the explanatory
title: "Verses occasion'd by hearing a Pass-Bell," that is, the
knell for the death of some parishioner at Sutton or some citizen of York. The poem, perhaps copied from a newspaper,
appeared in the *Gentleman's Magazine* for July, 1743, as
by "the Rev. Mr. St—n," and with a quotation for its motto
from John Hughes's *Siege of Damascus*: "But what's beyond
Death? Who shall draw that Veil?" Sterne liked the verses so
well that he took the manuscript with him to Coxwold, where
it was carefully guarded by his successors for a century; one
of whom—the Rev. George Scott—permitted Thomas Gill
of Easingwold to print it in his *Vallis Eboracensis* (1852), a
book on the history and antiquities of the York valley. Spirited
away from Coxwold, the manuscript is now possessed, it is
said, by a member of the Scott family. Though quite original
in its details, the poem bears some analogies to the Emperor
Hadrian's famous address to his departing soul as translated by
Pope and afterwards elaborated by the poet in *The Dying
Christian to his Soul*. The abbreviations of the manuscript
and the use of *y* for *th*, reproduced here, are a little puzzling
at first sight; and quaint obscurity is lent to the diction by astronomical and other symbols* which had come under Sterne's
eye in Burton's *Anatomy of Melancholy* and perhaps in one
of Pope's minor satires. Taken in order, the symbols ☉, ☽, ♉,
and ♃ stand for the world, God, heaven, and the soul:

> Hark^e my gay Fr^d y^t solemn Toll
> Speaks ye departure of a soul;
> 'Tis gone, y^{ts} all we know——not where
> Or how ye unbody'd soul do's fare——
> In that mysterious ☉ none knows,
> But ☽ alone to w^m it goes;
> To whom departed souls return

* The abbreviations and symbols of the manuscript, which do not
appear in the poem as originally printed in the *Gentleman's Magazine*
and elsewhere, were retained by Gill.

To take th^ir Doom to smile or mourn.
   Oh! by w^t glimm'ring light we view
The unknown ⊙ we're hast'ning to!
God has lock'd up ye mystic Page,
And curtain'd darkness round ye stage!
Wise ☿ to render search perplext
Has drawn 'twixt y^s ⊙ & ye next
A dark impenetrable screen
All behind wch is yet unseen!
We talk of ☿, we talk of Hell,
But w^t yy* mean no tongue can tell!
Heaven is ye realm where angels are
And Hell ye chaos of despair.
But w^t y^ese awful truths imply,
None of us know before we die!
Wheth^er we will or no, we must
Take ye succeeding ⊙ on trust.
   This hour perhaps o^r F^rd is well,
Death-struck, ye next he cries, Farewell!
I die! and y^et for ought we see,
Ceases at once to breath & be———
Thu^s launch'd f^m life's ambiguous shore
Ingulph'd in Death appears no more,
Then undirected to repair,
To distant ⊙^s we know not where.
Swift flies the ♃, perhaps 'tis gone
A thousand leagues beyond ye sun;
Or 2^ce 10 thousand more 3^ce told
Ere ye forsaken clay is cold!
And yet who knows if Fr^nds we lov'd
Tho' dead may be so far remov'd;
Only ye vail of flesh between,
Perhaps yy watch us though unseen.
Whilst we, y^ir loss lamenting, say,
They're out of hearing far away;
Guardians to us perhaps they're near

* They.

Concealed in Vehicles of air,
And yet no notices yy give
Nor tell us where, nor how yy live;
Tho' conscious whilst with us below,
How much y^{ms}* desired to know.
As if bound up by solemn Fate
To keep ye secret of y^{ir} state,
To tell y^{ir} joys or pains to none,
That man might live by Faith alone.
Well, let my sovereign, if he please,
Lock up his marvellous decrees;
Why sh^d I wish him to reveal
W^t he thinks proper to conceal?
It is enough y^t I believe
Heaven's bright^r y^n I can conceive;
And he y^t makes it all his care
To serve God here shall see him there!
But oh! w^t ⊙^{s} shall I survey
The moment y^t I leave y^s clay?
How sudden ye surprize, how new!
Let it, my God, be happy too.

The Unknown World is but one of many poems that Sterne
scribbled off for the entertainment of himself and his friends.
On his annual visits to Skelton, it was his custom to recite
cock-and-bull stories after the type of the one assigned to him
in *Crazy Tales*. In collaboration with his host, he composed,
it is said, on one of these occasions, the following classical inscription for the front of the reservoir which supplied Skelton
Castle with water:

"Leap from thy mossy cavern'd bed,
Hither thy prattling waters bring,
Bandusia's Muse shall crown thy head,
And make thee to a sacred spring."

In a quite different mood is the ode that Sterne inserted in
Tristram Shandy, beginning "Harsh and untuneful are the

* Themselves.

notes of Love," and suddenly breaking off in the second stanza with "O Julia!" But from these brief poems and numerous facetious and sentimental verses that once floated through newspapers and magazines as Sterne's, one quickly returns to *The Unknown World*. This clever meditation, with its warning to "my gay friend," and the flight of the soul to a region more than six times ten thousand leagues beyond the sun before the clay which it left became cold, is the best that the Muse could do for Laurence Sterne.

The Good Warm Watch-Coat. 1751-1759

STERNE'S meditations in verse and prose give us a glimpse of a very sober young man exercising his pen in the moral and devotional themes of a poet and dreamer, quite apart from his prevailing mood. They show wit rather than humor. It is clear that the Vicar of Sutton had not yet picked up the talent which lay nearest to him. Among his friends, as we have drawn his portrait at Stillington Hall and Skelton Castle, he was in no sense a moralist, but a parson who loved a jest above all else. During his last years at Sutton he belonged to a convivial club, composed of several clergymen and substantial citizens of York, who assembled o'nights at Sunton's Coffee-House in Coney Street, fast by the George Inn. Anecdotes were set afloat of what he said and did when chosen president of the evening, but they are too impalpable to find record here. As yet he had published nothing by which his humor could be judged. Now accident brought the occasion and he made the most of it.

Accident indeed brought out the humorist; but in the incidents of his life previous to the event, one may see working a half-conscious plan. As early as the date of the quarrel with his uncle over political articles in the newspapers, Sterne perhaps had a vague notion that he might some day become a writer on his own account; for he then told his friends that he was tired of employing his brains for other people's advantage. Much of his curious reading also looks like special preparation for a literary career; but his farming was for years an encumbrance that impeded him greatly. Fortunately for literature, his land projects had issued in miserable failure. Some months before the awards were made to him under the Sutton Enclosure Act, he resolved to rid himself of unnecessary parish business—land, tithes, and the botheration of all taxes. So he informed, late in the autumn of 1758, the Rev. John Blake in a letter concluding with the paragraph:

"I thank God, I have settled most of my affairs—let my freehold to a promising tenant——have likewise this week let him the most considerable part of my tyths, and shall clear my hands and head of all county entanglements, having at present only ten pounds a year in land and seven pounds a year in Corn Tyth left undisposed of, which shall be quitted with all prudent speed. This will bring me and mine into a narrow compass, and make us, I hope, both rich and happy."

And in memory of his sad experiences at Sutton, he wrote, six months before his death, to a certain Sir W—— who was planning to open marl beds upon his estate, to warn him against an undertaking sure to end in disaster. "I was once," Sterne told him, "such a puppy myself, as to pare, and burn, and had my labour for my pains, and two hundred pounds out of my pocket. Curse on farming (said I), I will try if the pen will not succeed better than the spade. The following up of that affair (I mean farming) made me lose my temper, and a cart load of turnips was (I thought) very dear at two hundred pounds."

While Sterne was interchanging letters with Blake about his farming, the weather, and parish business, it began to be noised about the coffee-houses that trouble was brewing among the clergy and officials of the cathedral; that the dean, to give a detail or two, had broken a solemn promise; that the dean and the archbishop were at the point of a complete breach, etc. At the heels of these rumors, which were spread far beyond York by country gentlemen who had come in for the election, the quarrel broke forth into a warfare of pamphlets. For the first time since his appointment to Sutton, Sterne was then at full leisure. The contested election of the year was over, his oats were threshed, his barley had been sold to the maltman, and his farm and tithes had been leased to a neighbor for a series of years. As friend and champion of the dean, Sterne entered the broil with rare zest, bringing it to a close in a burst of ridicule and laughter.

The story of this quarrel, which terminated in Sterne's
Political Romance—better known by its later title, *The History of a Good Warm Watch-Coat,*—may be pieced together
from the several pamphlets that were issued, *The York Courant,* and the local records of the time. Its beginnings go back
to intrigues and dissensions immediately after the coming of
Archbishop Hutton and Dean Fountayne. Some account of the
fracas has been given in an earlier chapter; it now remains to
add those details which concern Sterne and the first full display
of his humor in print. The story, were it allowable to infuse a
little imagination into it, might be made as good reading as
any one of Trollope's cathedral tales.

The archbishop, Sterne remarked, "might have had his virtues, but the leading part of his character was not *Humility.*"
The dean, an old college acquaintance of the humorist, was a
colorless, good-natured ecclesiastic, inclined however to insist
upon his prerogatives. Neither of these dignitaries resided in
York. The archbishop's palace was then, as now, at Bishopthorpe, two or three miles out of the city; and the dean
passed most of his time at Melton, his estate in South Yorkshire. Little differences that early sprang up between them
were fomented by Dr. Francis Topham, the leading ecclesiastical lawyer at York. Dr. Topham, a year or so older than
Sterne, "was descended from an ancient and honourable family of Yorkshire." Bred to the law, he graduated LL.B.
at Sidney Sussex College, Cambridge, in 1734, and received from the same university the degree of LL.D. in 1739.
Whether the two men met at Cambridge, it is nowhere said;
but they both settled at York at nearly the same time, where
Dr. Topham quickly established himself in the favor of those
high in the Church. Any office, however small, he was ready to
snap up for the increase of his income. He became in course
of time, though he did not yet enjoy all these positions, Commissary and Keeper-General of the Exchequer and Prerogative Courts of the Archbishop of York, "Official to the Archdeacon of York, Official to the Archdeacon of the East
Riding, Official to the Archdeacon of Cleveland, Official to

the Precentor, Official to the Chancellor, and Official to several of the prebendaries." He was thus able to lay by, needless to add, a handsome fortune, destined to be squandered by a spendthrift son.

Never satisfied with the offices that he held, Dr. Topham was always manœuvring for more. In the course of a few weeks after Dean Fountayne came to York in the winter of 1747-48, one or more friends of the hungry lawyer recommended him to the dean as a person eminently qualified for any legal position that might fall directly within the dean's patronage or might be secured for him through the dean's vote and interest in the chapter. It was well known that Dr. Topham had his eye at this time on two ecclesiastico-legal offices that were sure to become vacant very soon; to wit, the Commissaryship of the Peculiar Court of Pickering and Pocklington, which was in the dean's absolute gift, and the Commissaryship of the Dean and Chapter of York, in the disposition of which the dean's voice, as head of the chapter, was potent above all the rest.

The two offices, valued respectively at six and twenty pounds a year, were then held by Dr. William Ward, who was in feeble health and likely to die at any moment. Subsequent to the application of his friends, Dr. Topham had a formal interview with Dean Fountayne, which resulted in a general promise of the first office and of the dean's aid in obtaining the other. But Dr. Ward did not die so soon as was expected; and in the meantime the dean became less favorably impressed with Dr. Topham's character. A plan was devised whereby Dr. Ward should remain in nominal possession of the two commissaryships, while the fees should go to Dr. Mark Braithwaite, an advocate in the ecclesiastical court, a poor but estimable man, who felt unable to incur the legal expense incidental to the issue of new patents to the offices in question. To this arrangement Dr. Topham agreed with great reluctance and only, it was his claim, on the assurance that the positions should fall to himself on the death of Dr. Braithwaite, who, though in fairly good health, was of a delicate constitution as

well as somewhat advanced in age. The dean, however, did
not understand it that way; he thought himself rid of Dr.
Topham and all further solicitations from him or his friends.
But he was unacquainted with the resources of the man he had
to deal with. Dr. Topham, as the legal adviser to Archbishop
Hutton, watched closely the conduct of the dean, and on every
opportunity for creating friction between them, despatched
mischievous messages to his client when in London or wherever else his Grace might be. In the autumn of 1748, a dispute
arose over the appointment of preachers in the cathedral. The
dean, it was averred, ordered the pulpit locked against a prebendary chosen for the day by the chancellor. The dispute
lingered on through the following winter. As a reward for his
able defence of the archbishop's rights on this and other occasions, Dr. Topham was appointed, on June 28, 1751, Commissary and Keeper-General of the Exchequer and Prerogative Courts of the Archbishop of York, the most comfortable
office of all in the long list before enumerated.

In the meantime, so uncertain is human life, Dr. Braithwaite had died; and in June, 1751, the feeble Dr. Ward, who
had strangely outlived him by nearly a year,* followed in
his footsteps, leaving vacant the Commissaryship of the Dean
and Chapter and that of the Peculiar Court of Pickering and
Pocklington. Dr. Topham made a grasp for both of them,
notwithstanding the lucrative office he had just received. A
majority of the chapter, he thought, were for his appointment
to the first position. But the dean brought up the matter, it
was alleged, when the lawyer's friends were absent, and threw
his influence in favor of William Stables, Bachelor of Laws,
who was easily elected on the first of August. Dr. Topham's
charge that the chapter was made up against him was indeed
true, for there were present on that day only his enemies: the
dean, the canons residentiary—Charles Cowper and William
Berdmore—and Laurence Sterne. In spite of this rebuff, Dr.
Topham felt so certain of the second position that he had the
patent for it made out, with his name written in ready for the

* *York Courant,* August 21, 1750, and July 2, 1751.

dean's seal. The dean, however, gave the one legal office then in his sole gift to his friend Laurence Sterne, who had just written an eloquent sermon for him in Latin for the Cambridge Commencement. It was an amusing *quid pro quo*. The appointment, of which no record is discoverable, was probably made within a week or two after the election of William Stables to the other position.

Dr. Topham raised a loud clamor over this shameless betrayal of his hopes. It was everywhere given out by him and his friends that the dean had promised him two patents and had afterwards broken his word. This grave charge the dean let pass until he came to York again, a few months later, to preside over "a public Sessions Dinner" held at the residence of George Woodhouse, a wine-merchant of the parish of St. Michael-le-Belfrey. There were present the usual company of prebendaries and other officials of the chapter, Dr. Topham, and one or more country gentlemen. Knowing that an extraordinary scene might occur at the dinner, Sterne, always glad of a quarrel, rode in from Sutton. As soon as the plates were removed, the dean, turning to Sir Edmund Anderson of Kilnwick, openly accused Dr. Topham of spreading abroad false reports to the harm and discredit of the dean and chapter.

It is true, the dean admitted, that I once promised Dr. Topham my own Commissaryship of Pickering and Pocklington; but he subsequently renounced all claim to it in favor of Dr. Braithwaite. When it became vacant by the death of Dr. Braithwaite and Dr. Ward (in whose name the patent had remained), I looked upon myself as clearly and fully at liberty to dispose of it as I pleased, certainly without consulting Dr. Topham. As to the Commissaryship of the Dean and Chapter, it was not, as you all know, mine to give and I am not accustomed to promise what is not my own. Dr. Topham's affair is not with me but with the chapter in which my vote is only one among thirty.

After a general statement of facts in this tenor—though not in these words precisely, for we have only a few phrases to go by,—the dean faced Dr. Topham and demanded an explanation of his conduct. "Dr. Topham," to quote Sterne's attested account of what took place, "at first disowned his being the Author of such a Story to the Dean's Disadvantage; but being pressed by Mr. *Sterne*, then present, with an undeniable Proof, That he, Dr. *Topham*, did propagate the said Story, Dr. *Topham* did, at last, acknowledge it; adding, as his Reason or Excuse for so doing, That he apprehended (or words to that Effect) he had a Promise, under the Dean's own Hand, of the *Dean and Chapter's Commissaryship*." The dean then called upon "Dr. *Topham* to produce the Letter in which such pretended Promise was made." Dr. Topham replied that he had not brought the letter with him, or something like that. Whereupon the dean read to the company a letter that Dr. Topham had written to him while at Cambridge for his Doctor's degree in June, 1751, requesting the two commissaryships in succession to Dr. Ward. Then he took from his pocket and read a copy of his own curt reply, dated at Cambridge, July 2, 1751, in which the application was ignored or merely alluded to in the postscript: "I hope very soon to see you at York." Both letters were acknowledged as genuine by the crestfallen lawyer.

Only a little imagination is necessary on the part of the reader to construct out of this legal phraseology a hot encounter, as Mr. Sterne and the dean one after the other rise to their feet, shaking forefinger or fist over Dr. Topham and proving him a scoundrel. The way in which they silenced their enemy redounds, it must be admitted, not so much to their sense of justice as to their skill and adroitness. Three years before this, the dean had certainly promised the lawyer his own patent and his aid in obtaining the one in the joint gift of himself and the chapter. He had simply changed his mind. He had not foreseen his need of an oration in the style of Cicero from the pen of Laurence Sterne.

Dr. Topham, publicly set down a liar, kept quiet for several years, so far as there is any record of it; but he was only waiting for a good opportunity to return to the attack. In the spring of 1757, Archbishop Hutton was appointed to the see of Canterbury. His successor at York was Dr. John Gilbert, for some years Bishop of Salisbury. At best a man of mediocre talent and character, the new archbishop counted for little in the diocese of York, owing to the many physical infirmities that were coming upon him. He languished rather than lived at Bishopthorpe. Dr. Topham was a frequent visitor at the palace, making it his "Business to inquire after every Place and Remedy that might help his Grace in his Complaints." When the archbishop was too ill to see him, the interviews and correspondence were carried on between Dr. Topham and the archbishop's daughter,* who acted as secretary and adviser to her father in diocesan and other matters. On first meeting the new archbishop, Dr. Topham told him "That he would find it very difficult, if not impossible, to live upon good Terms with his Dean and Chapter," for they were "A Set of *strange* People." The archbishop was however assured by Dr. Topham that it was his policy on all questions of dispute to espouse "the Interests of the See of York, in Opposition to those of the Deanery." The foundations were thus carefully laid for a fresh quarrel, which first arose from a trivial incident.

In September, 1757, the archbishop issued, on the advice of Dr. Topham, a mandate for the *immediate* induction of the archbishop's brother into a prebend to which he had been appointed. This was an unusual proceeding, inasmuch as a delay of three days was customary between the reception of a mandate and an induction. But the case was urgent. The sick archbishop had just had a serious relapse when for the moment his life was despaired of; and should he die before the installation of his prebendary, the title, it was pointed out, would instantly accrue to the Crown. The chancellor of the diocese, after consulting with the residentiaries, decided to let the induction take the ordinary course. The dean, though he could have known nothing of the incident at the time, being absent at Melton, was nevertheless held responsible for "the dilatory *Capitular Forms* and Ceremonies of the Church of *York*." Another point of dispute was over leases. Dr. Topham set up the claim

---

* Emma Gilbert, afterwards the Countess of Edgcumbe.

that when the archbishop sends a lease to the dean and chapter, "the *Seal* of the *Corporation* ought to be put to it, upon its receiving the Assent and *Consent* of a *Majority* of the Body Corporate," by the general proxy which the dean was accustomed to leave with the chapter for unimportant matters. On the other hand, it was the dean's opinion that the seal ought not to be put to a lease without "a special proxy" from himself. Dr. Topham called the dean's attention to the statute of the thirty-third year of Henry the Eighth against this and other favorite negative powers of deans. The dean replied that he had never regarded a special proxy as quite essential in the case of leases, but that Dr. Topham had always insisted upon one whenever his own interests were involved.

It was not the intent of Dr. Topham, if we read him aright, to force these differences to a breach between the dean and the archbishop. He was simply ingratiating himself into special favor at the palace so that the archbishop might be kindly disposed to a new and questionable scheme on which his heart was now set. Back in 1751 the lawyer had been blessed by the birth of a son, that Edward Topham, playwright and libertine, who lived to bring into fashion short scarlet coats, short white waistcoats, and long leather breeches reaching well upwards to the chin, at a time when everybody had been wearing very long coats, very long waistcoats, but breeches very short in the waist, and thus very troublesome to aldermen and all other modest men of conspicuous rotundity. "Through life it was a feather in my friend Topham's cap," said Frederic Reynolds, a brother dramatist, "that when a boy, he was the unconscious founder of Sterne's literary career."* For his son, already at his accidence, the fond father wished to make handsome provision. On searching into the records of the dean and chapter, he discovered that the patent of the Commissary of the Exchequer and Prerogative Courts—his best paying office—had formerly been granted and enjoyed for two lives instead of for one life, as was then the custom. He

* *The Life and Times of Frederic Reynolds written by himself,* II, 190 *et seq.* (London, 1826).

naturally wished a revival of the good old times. So he went to the archbishop in the summer of 1758, and asked him for permission to open his patent of the office, which read for one life only, and "to add the Life of *another proper Person* to it," meaning thereby, as it quickly transpired, the name of his own son.

The archbishop at first readily assented to the plan, out of gratitude to the lawyer for his many services; but in the course of the next few weeks, he began to have doubts about the wisdom of the proposal. The transaction could not be completed, as Dr. Topham well knew, without the concurrence of the dean and chapter, which was, under the circumstances, quite difficult, if not impossible, to obtain, despite the archbishop's wishes. It is unnecessary to go far into the intrigues and flatteries now practised by Dr. Topham to win the friendship of the men whom he had grossly offended. Very amusing, indeed, is a letter that he sent over to Melton, by Mr. John Clough, registrar of the dean and chapter, to urge the dean, as friend and well-wisher, to act favorably in the matter of the patent at once before his elevation to a more exalted station. "As I have," said the message, "very lately had a *private Intimation* of the Bishop of *Winchester* having just had some very alarming Symptoms, I must expect to be *able soon* to *congratulate* you on your being added to the Bench of Bishops." The dean sent back the following cooling-card:*

"Melton, Aug. 14, 1758.

"Sir,

"I received your letter by Mr. *Clough,* and shall take the first opportunity to examine the Registers in our Office relating to the Patents of the Commissary, and also to consult my Brethren at *York,* upon the Affair you mention.

"I flatter myself that the Archbishop will not doubt of my Readiness to comply with any Request his Grace may make to me, being confident that he would not ask me to lend a

* This letter and all details of the sessions dinner are given in *An Answer to a Letter addressed to the Dean of York in the Name of Dr. Topham* (York, 1758).

helping Hand for the depriving his Successors of any of their customary Privileges of the Archbishoprick."

"I am, Sir,

"*Your most obedient*

"*humble Servant,*

"J. Fountayne."

That the question might be settled once for all, the dean, Dr. Topham, and several others were summoned to meet at Bishopthorpe on the seventh of November for a general conference. The two chief dignitaries, who had been misrepresented, each to each, by the intriguing lawyer, found themselves agreeably of one opinion; that it was inadvisable, notwithstanding ancient precedent, to grant the valuable patent for more than one life. The lawyer, enraged at this decision, says Sterne, "huffed and bounced most terribly," threatening everybody from the archbishop down to a timid surgeon, one Isaac Newton, who gave the story of the conference to the coffee-houses.

As nothing came of these angry violences, Dr. Topham decided to appeal to the public against the dean, whom he charged with working upon the sick man at Bishopthorpe. So during the second week in December was launched his anonymous pamphlet entitled *A LETTER Address'd to the Reverend the DEAN of York; In which is given A full Detail of some very extraordinary Behaviour of his, in relation to his Denial of a Promise made by him to Dr. TOPHAM.* Though the sixpenny pamphlet set about to deal principally with the commissaryship that fell to Sterne, it nevertheless touched upon all the bickerings of a dozen years. Two weeks later, the dean had ready his retort courteous, which bore the title: *An ANSWER To A LETTER Address'd to the DEAN of YORK, In the NAME of Dr. TOPHAM.* A feature of this very skilful reply was a formal declaration (from which we have quoted), signed by Laurence Sterne and other justices of the peace, as to what took place at the Sessions Dinner at Mr. Woodhouse's. Had he desired, the Vicar of Sutton could not well have kept out of the controversy, for, as Dr. Topham had put it, Sterne's appointment to the courts of Pickering and Pocklington first brought the quarrel to a head. In concluding his open letter, the dean announced that he had taken leave of Dr. Topham "once for all." Thus apparently sure of the last word, the lawyer poured forth the phials of his wrath in *A REPLY TO THE ANSWER TO A LETTER Lately addressed to the DEAN OF YORK*. With considerable humor "a late notable Performance," supposed to be the dean's, was described as "the Child and Offspring of many Parents." Mr. Sterne and some others, it was intimated, had been called in by the dean for "Correcting, Revising, Ornamenting, and Embellishing" his well-known faint and nerveless style.

The attestation and a phrase here and there in the dean's pamphlet were without doubt Sterne's; but they count for nothing in comparison with what Sterne now did. In his retreat at Sutton he had been at work during the last week on his own reply to Dr. Topham. Late in January, 1759, just after Dr. Topham's second pamphlet reached the coffee-houses, Sterne had printed, ready for distribution, *A Political Romance, Addressed TO ———, Esq; OF YORK. To which is subjoined a KEY:*—since re-named *The History of a Good Warm Watch-Coat*. As indicative of his aim, which was ridicule rather than satire or controversy, the title-page bore the motto from Horace:

"Ridiculum acri
Fortius et melius magnas plerumque secat Res."

The first edition of *A Political Romance* is so exceeding rare that most who have written on Sterne have doubted its being printed during the author's life-time. It was laid by in Sterne's desk, said Percy Fitzgerald and Sidney Lee, and at most circulated only in manuscript. It was "only posthumously printed," remarked Walter Sichel. This, we now know, was not the case. A copy indeed strayed up to London, where it was reprinted in part in 1769, the year after Sterne's death, by a bookseller in the Strand. The editor corrected the

A

Political Romance,

Addreſſed

To —— ————, *Eſq;*

O F

Y O R K.

To which is ſubjoined a

K E Y.

Ridiculum acri
Fortius et melius magnas plerumque ſecat Res.

Y O R K:
Printed in the Year MDCCLIX.

[Price ONE SHILLING.]

Facſmile of Title Page to "A Political Romance"

humorist's English, substituting elegant phrases for quaint and homely idioms, and cut away the *Key* and two long letters that go with it—in all, just one half of the romance as originally written and published at York early in 1759. It is this mutilated version only that has been known to readers and biographers of Sterne. Fortunately, however, a copy of the first edition found its way, a half century and more ago, into the splendid collection of Edward Hailstone, Esq., of Horton Hall, Bradford, England, who lent it to Robert Davies, the antiquary, while preparing his *Memoir of the York Press* (1868). On the death of Mr. Hailstone in 1890, it passed with many valuable books and manuscripts to the library of the dean and chapter at York, where it was uncovered in September, 1905. A few weeks afterwards another copy was found in a volume of pamphlets at the York Public Library. Still another copy, bound with the previous tracts in the controversy, has long rested, it now turns out, in the library of Trinity College, Cambridge. Nowhere was the pamphlet known by the library officials as Sterne's. There are probably a few other copies in existence.

Sterne cast his narrative into the form of an allegory, which becomes easy and delectable when we know the incidents underlying it. In order that things which seem great might appear as small as they really were, the diocese of York was cut down to a country parish, and the archbishop thereby reduced to the rank of a village parson. The dean, shorn of his surname, became merely John the parish clerk; and the cathedral chapter figured as the church wardens. Incidentally Mark Braithwaite appeared as Mark Slender, and William Stables as William Doe. Dr. Topham, renamed Trim, because he received so thorough a trimming at the last, was degraded to sexton and dog-whipper of the parish; and Sterne himself was slightly disguised under the name of Lorry Slim.

The late parson and John the parish clerk, says the tale, had just got snugly settled in the parish, when Trim "put it into the Parson's Head, 'That *John's* Desk in the Church was, at the least, four Inches higher than it should be:——That the

Thing gave Offence, and was indecorous, inasmuch as it approach'd too near upon a Level with the Parson's Desk itself.' This Hardship the Parson complained of loudly,——and told *John* one Day after Prayers,——'He could bear it no longer: ——And would have it alter'd and brought down as it should be.' *John* made no other Reply, but, 'That the Desk was not of his raising:——That 'twas not one Hair Breadth higher than he found it;——and that as he found it, so would he leave it.' "

This stiff dispute, shadowing forth in allegory the quarrel between Archbishop Hutton and Dr. Fountayne over the key to the cathedral pulpit, was "Trim's harvest." For a few days later John saw Trim emerging from the vicarage and "strutting across the Church-yard, y'clad in a good creditable cast Coat, large Hat and Wig, which the Parson had just given him.——'Ho! Ho! Hollo! *John!*' cries *Trim,* in an insolent Bravo, as loud as ever he could bawl——'See here, my Lad! how fine I am.'——'The more Shame for you,' answered *John,* seriously.—'Do you think, *Trim,*' says he, 'such Finery, gain'd by such Services, becomes you, or can wear well?' "

This was Sterne's way of saying that Dr. Topham had secured the patent of the Prerogative Courts of York.

"A snapper-up of unconsidered trifles" to deck himself out with, Trim had also been trying for some time to coax from John a pair of black plush breeches "not much the worse for wearing." He "begged for God's Sake to have them bestowed upon him when *John* should think fit to cast them." John told him that he ought to be ashamed of himself for creating such a racket in the village about "an old-worn-out-Pair-of-cast-Breeches, not worth Half a Crown." "In the first Place," said he in allusion to Dr. Topham's many comfortable places, "are you not Sexton and Dog-Whipper, worth Three Pounds a Year?——Then you begg'd the Church-Wardens to let your Wife have the Washing and Darning of the Surplice and Church-Linen, which brings you in Thirteen Shillings and Four pence.——Then you have Six Shillings and Eight Pence for oiling and winding up the Clock, both paid you at *Easter*.

——The Pindar's Place which is worth Forty-Shillings a Year,——you have got that too.——You are the Bailiff, which the late Parson got you, which brings you in Forty Shillings more.——Besides all this, you have Six Pounds a Year, paid you Quarterly for being Mole-Catcher to the Parish."

The cast-breeches—Pickering and Pocklington—after covering the thin legs of Mark Slender for a time, eventually fell to "*Lorry Slim*, an unlucky Wight, by whom they are still worn;——in Truth, as you will guess, they are very thin by this Time;—But *Lorry* has a light Heart; and what recommends them to him is this, that, as thin as they are, he knows that *Trim*, let him say what he will to the contrary, still envies the *Possessor* of them,——and with all his Pride, would be very glad to wear them after *him*."

Though Trim had thus missed the plush breeches, he yet "had an Eye to, and firmly expected in his own Mind, the great Green Pulpit-Cloth and old Velvet Cushion [the Commissaryship of the Dean and Chapter], which were that very Year to be taken down;——which, by the Bye, could he have wheedled *John* a second time out of 'em, as he hoped, he had made up the Loss of his Breeches Seven-fold. Now, you must know, this Pulpit-Cloth and Cushion were not in *John's* Gift, but in the Church-Wardens, &c.——However, as I said above, that *John* was a leading Man in the Parish, *Trim* knew he could help him to them if he would:——But *John* had got a Surfeit of him;——so, when the Pulpit-Cloth, &c. were taken down, they were immediately given (*John* having a great Say in it) to *William Doe*, who understood very well what Use to make of them."

After the old garments and worn pulpit decorations had been thus divided up—William Doe, Trim, and Lorry Slim each getting one or more pieces,—the parish fell back into its usual monotonous drone for seven or eight years, and would have droned on forever, had not the old parson left his flock for a better living and his place been supplied by a new incumbent, that is, by Dr. Gilbert. Then was struck up a lively tune. Trim at once hastened to the rectory, that is, to Bishopthorpe, to sell himself into servitude. Within a year, "he had," it was his boast, "black'd the Parson's Shoes without Count, and greased his Boots above fifty Times; . . . he had run for Eggs into the Town upon all Occasions;——whetted the Knives at all Hours:——catched his Horse and rubbed him down, . . . never came to the House, but ask'd his Man kindly how he did. . . . When his Reverence cut his finger in paring an Apple, he went half a Mile to ask a cunning Woman, what was good to stanch Blood, and actually returned with a Cobweb in his breeches Pocket."

For these services Trim demanded nothing but "an old *watch-coat* that had hung up many years in the church," apparently of use to nobody. But Trim had set his heart upon it, humbly asking for it: "Nothing would serve *Trim* but he must take it home, in order to have it converted into a *warm Under-Petticoat* for his Wife, and a *Jerkin* for himself, against Winter; which, in a plaintive Tone, he most humbly begg'd his Reverence would consent to. . . . No sooner did the distinct Words——*Petticoat*——*poor Wife*——*warm* ——*Winter* strike upon his [the parson's] Ear,—but his Heart warmed, and, before *Trim* had well got to the End of his Petition, (being a Gentleman of a frank and open Temper) he told him he was welcome to it, with all his Heart and Soul. 'But, *Trim*,' says he, 'as you see I am but just got down to my Living, and am an utter Stranger to all Parish-Matters . . . and therefore cannot be a Judge whether 'tis fit for such a Purpose; or, if it is, in Truth, know not whether 'tis mine to bestow upon you or not;——you must have a Week or ten Days Patience, till I can make some Inquiries about it;—— and, if I find it is in my Power, I tell you again, Man, your Wife is heartily welcome to an Under-Petticoat out of it, and you to a Jerkin, was the Thing as good again as you represent it.'"

Several days after this conversation, the parson, while turning the leaves of the parish registry in his study, came upon a memorandum about the watch-coat that opened his eyes as to its dignity and value. "The great Watch-Coat," he discovered, "was purchased and given above two hundred years ago, by the Lord of the Manor, to this Parish-Church, to the sole Use and Behoof of the poor Sextons thereof, and their Successors, for ever, to be worn by them respectively in winterly cold Nights, in ringing Complines, Passing-Bells, &c which the said Lord of the Manor had done in Piety, to keep the poor Wretches warm, and for the Good of his own Soul, for which they were directed to pray, &c &c &c. *'Just Heaven!'* said the Parson to himself, looking upwards, *'What an Escape have I had! Give this for an Under-Petticoat to Trim's Wife! I would not have consented to such a Desecration to be Primate of all* England; *nay, I would not have disturb'd a single Button of it for half my Tythes!'*

"Scarce were the Words out of his Mouth, when in pops *Trim* with the whole Subject of the Exclamation under both his Arms.——I say, under both his Arms;—for he had actually got it ripp'd and cut out ready, his own Jerkin under one Arm, and the Petticoat under the other, in order to be carried to the Taylor to be made up,—and had just stepp'd in, in high Spirits, to shew the Parson how cleverly it had held out." The parson, enraged at Trim's impudence, ordered him "in a stern Voice, to lay the Bundles down upon the Table,——to go about his Business, and wait upon him, at his Peril, the next Morning at Eleven precisely: Against this Hour like a wise Man, the Parson had sent to desire *John* the Parish-Clerk, who bore an exceeding good Character as a Man of Truth. . . . Him he sends for, with the Church-Wardens, and one of the Sides-Men, a grave, knowing, old Man, to be present: ——For as *Trim* had with-held the whole Truth from the Parson, touching the Watch-Coat, he thought it probable he would as certainly do the same Thing to others." The next morning at eleven, passions ran high at the rectory. Trim pleaded the Parson's promise, and, failing there, enumerated his humble services as the parson's man. But all in vain. The "pimping, pettifogging, ambidextrous Fellow . . . was kick'd out of Doors; and told, at his Peril, never to come there again."

To the allegory which thus relates how Dr. Topham finally met with signal disaster at Bishopthorpe, in his attempt to cut up and make over for his son the patent of the Prerogative Courts of York, Sterne subjoined an amusing postscript on the numerous hands, including his own, that the church-lawyer uncovered in the dean's pamphlet. They were all, said Sterne, as imaginary as the nineteen men in buckram with whom Jack Falstaff fought at Gad's Hill. Then came a gay tail-piece, which the printer wished to put on the title-page, representing two game cocks, in full trim, beak to beak, ready to strike.

Not able to stop here, though the story was really over, Sterne appended to his allegory a humorous *Key* and two letters, which cover, in the whole, as many pages as the entire previous narrative. The *Key*, it might be observed, was developed from Swift's "Grand Committee" that sat upon the meaning of *A Tale of a Tub*. Since this part of the romance, as aforesaid, has been seen by few men, it may be quite worth while to give some account of it, if for no other reason than this. But the continuation brings with it, as will be apparent at once, some interesting facts about its author.

"This *Romance*," says the *Key*, which is of course no key, "was, by some Mischance or other, dropp'd in the *Minster-Yard, York*, and pick'd up by a Member of a small Political Club in that City; where it was carried, and publickly read to the Members the last Club Night.

"It was instantly agreed to, by a great Majority, That it was a *Political Romance*; but concerning what State or Potentate, could not so easily be settled amongst them.

"The President of the Night, who is thought to be as clear and quick-sighted as any one of the whole Club in Things of this Nature, discovered plainly, That the Disturbances therein set forth, related to those on the *Continent:——*That *Trim* could be Nobody but the King of *France*, by whose shifting and intriguing Behaviour, all *Europe* was set together by the Ears:——That *Trim's* Wife was certainly the *Empress*, who are as kind together, says he, as any Man and Wife can be for their Lives.——The more Shame for 'em, says an Alderman, low to himself.——Agreeable to this Key, continues the President,——The *Parson*, who I think is a most excellent Character,——is His Most Excellent Majesty King *George*; ——*John*, the Parish-Clerk, is the King of *Prussia*; who, by the Manner of his first entering Saxony, shew'd the World most evidently,——That he did know how to lead out the Psalm, and in Tune and Time too, notwithstanding *Trim's* vile Insult upon him in that Particular. . . . The *Old-cast-Pair-of-Black-Plush-Breeches* must be *Saxony*, which the *Elector*, you see, *has left off wearing:*——And as for the *Great Watch-Coat*, which, you know, covers all, it signifies all *Europe;* comprehending, at least, so many of its different States and Dominions, as we have any Concern with in the present War.

"I protest, says a Gentleman who sat next but one to the President, and who, it seems, was the Parson of the Parish, a Member not only of the Political, but also of a Musical Club in the next Street;——I protest, says he, if this explanation is right, which I think it is,—That the whole makes a very fine Symbol.——You have always some Musical Instrument or other in your Head, I think, says the Alderman.——Musical Instrument! replies the Parson, in Astonishment,——Mr. Alderman, I mean an Allegory; and I think the greedy Disposition of *Trim* and his Wife, in ripping the *Great Watch-Coat*, to Pieces in order to convert it into a Petticoat for the one, and a Jerkin for the other, is one of the most beautiful of the Kind I ever met with; and will shew all the World what have been the true Views and Intentions of the Houses of *Bourbon* and *Austria* in this abominable Coalition."

This hypothesis of the president, so ably supported by the parson, met at first with a good deal of favor; but before the evening was far advanced, one hard-headed member after another began to ask questions, and then to suggest other explanations of the *Romance* until the president was made to tremble for his own hypothesis. "Every Man turn'd the Story to what was swimming uppermost in his Brain;——so that, before all was over, there were full as many Satyres spun out of it,——

and as great a Variety of Personages, Opinions, Transactions, and Truths, found to lay hid under the dark Veil of its Allegory, as ever were discovered in the thrice-renowned History of the Acts of *Gargantua* and *Pantagruel*."

A gentleman at the opposite side of the table, who knew nothing of the flirtations between France and Austria, but "had come piping-hot from reading the History of King *William's* and Queen *Anne's* Wars, . . . acquainted them, That the dividing the *Great Watch-Coat* did, and could allude to nothing else in the World but the *Partition Treaty;* which, by the Bye, he told them, was the most unhappy and scandalous Transaction in all King *William's Life:* It was that false Step, and that only, says he, rising from his Chair, and striking his Hand upon the Table with great Violence; it was that false Step, says he knitting his Brows and throwing his Pipe down upon the Ground, that has laid the Foundation of all the Disturbances and Sorrows we feel and lament at this very Hour."

The debate, after many a wild-goose chase, was concluded by a gentleman of the law who had been sitting quietly by the fire. "He got up,——and, advancing towards the Table, told them, That the Error they had all gone upon thus far, in making out the several Facts in the *Romance*,——was in looking too high. . . . He then took the *Romance* in his Left Hand, and pointing with the Fore-Finger of his Right towards the second Page, he humbly begg'd Leave to observe, (and, to do him Justice, he did it in somewhat of a *forensic Air*) That the *Parson, John,* and *Sexton,* shewed incontestably the Thing to be *Tripartite;* now, if you will take Notice, Gentlemen, says he, these several Persons, who are Parties to this Instrument, are merely Ecclesiastical. . . . It appears very plain to me, That the *Romance,* neither directly nor indirectly, goes upon Temporal, but altogether upon Church-Matters.——And do not you think, says he, softening his Voice a little, and addressing himself to the Parson with a forced Smile,——Do not you think Doctor, says he, That the Dispute in the *Romance* between the *Parson* of the Parish and *John,* about the

Height of *John's* Desk, is a very fine Panegyrick upon the *Humility* of *Church-Men?*"

The parson, nettled by this insult to the cloth, made a repartee on "the glorious Prolixity of the Law," which "highly tickled" an apothecary in the company, "who had paid the Attorney, the same Afternoon, a Demand of Three Pounds Six Shillings and Eight-Pence" for a lease and release. "He rubb'd his Hands together most fervently,——and laugh'd most triumphantly" at the parson's clever hit. The lawyer, understanding the real cause of the apothecary's jocular humor, turned to him, and "dropping his Voice a Third" said:

"You might well have spared this immoderate Mirth, since you and your Profession have the least Reason to triumph here of any of us.——I beg, quoth he, that you would reflect a Moment upon the *Cob-Web* which *Trim* went so far for, and brought back with an Air of so much Importance in his Breeches Pocket, to lay upon the Parson's cut Finger.—— This said Cob-Web, Sir, is a fine-spun Satyre, upon the flimsy Nature of one Half of the Shop-Medicines, with which you make a Property of the Sick, the Ignorant, and the Unsuspecting."

Stung by this discourteous retort, the apothecary, a surgeon, a chemist, an undertaker, and another apothecary, "were all five rising up together from their Chairs, with full Intent of Heart, as it was thought, to return the *Reproof Valiant* thereupon.——But the President, fearing it would end in a general Engagement, he instantly call'd out, *To Order*"; and thus saved a squabble. As soon as quiet was restored, it was ordered that the *Romance* and the minutes of the meeting likewise, as a key to the allegory, be printed at once and under one cover. A whitesmith, who had remained silent up to this time, objected to the publication of the *Key* on the ground that it was not one Key but "a whole Bunch of Keys." "Let me tell you, Mr. President, says he, That the *Right Key*, if it could but be found, would be worth the whole bunch put together."

The key that the whitesmith longed for has been placed in

the reader's hand bright and clean; but the key to the *Key*, so to speak, though it may be recovered, is now eaten out by the rust of time. The transactions of the "political club" by the Minster Yard, were, so far as we may surely go, a burlesque of the evenings Sterne passed with his convivial club that met at Sunton's Coffee-House in Coney Street. Under the disguise of a surgeon, lawyer, apothecary, undertaker, and the president who loved an hypothesis better than his life, he drew little portraits of the members—their mannerisms and favorite gestures, and their vehemence in canvassing local and larger politics of the day. What kind of men they were further than this or what names they bore, we may never know, except, to be sure, that the Vicar of Sutton is among them. He is the parson of the parish, smart in repartee and ready to defend by a counter-jest an attack upon the cloth that he wears, just as was related in the old story of the puppy. He, too, had paid lawyers for leases and releases in the purchase of lands. There is, besides, that apt reference to Rabelais, which shows what was running in Sterne's head; and finally there is the gentleman who, like my uncle Toby, spent his days and nights in reading of the wars of King William and Queen Anne.

According to the story, the *Romance* was read to the club, and, on the advice of the members, the manuscript was placed in the hands of Cæsar Ward, editor and publisher of *The York Courant*, who promised to see the facetious little book safely through the press. From Sutton Sterne sent in to the York printer precise directions, which were made a part of the pamphlet, following next after the *Key*. The letter to Cæsar Ward, which runs thus, is a curious piece of humor:

"Sir,

"You write me Word that the Letter I wrote to you, and now stiled *The Political Romance* is printing; and that, as it was drop'd by Carelessness, to make some Amends, you will overlook the Printing of it yourself, and take Care to see that it comes right into the World.

"I was just going to return you Thanks, and to beg, withal, you would take Care That the Child be not laid at my Door. ——But having, this Moment, perused the *Reply* to the *Dean of York's Answer*,——it has made me alter my Mind in that respect; so that, instead of making you the Request I intended, I do here desire That the Child be filiated upon me, *Laurence Sterne*, Prebendary of *York*, &c. &c. And I do, accordingly, own it for my own true and lawful Offspring.

"My Reason for this is plain;——for as, you see, the *Writer* of that *Reply*, has taken upon him to invade this *incontested Right* of another Man's in a Thing of this Kind, it is high Time for every Man to look to his own——Since, upon the *same Grounds*, and with half the Degree of Anger, that he affirms the Production of that very Reverend Gentleman's to be the Child of many Fathers, some one in his Spight (for I am not without my Friends of that Stamp) may run headlong into the other Extream, and swear, That mine had no Father at all:——And therefore, to make use of *Bay's* Plea in the *Rehearsal*, for *Prince Pretty-Man*; I merely do it, as he says, 'for fear it should be said to be no Body's Child at all.'

"I have only to add two Things:——First, That, at your Peril, you do not presume to alter or transpose one Word, nor rectify one false Spelling, nor so much as add or diminish one Comma or Tittle, in or to my *Romance:* For if you do,—— In case any of the Descendants of *Curl* should think fit to invade my Copy-Right, and print it over again in my Teeth, I may not be able, in a Court of Justice, to swear strictly to my own Child, after you had *so large a Share* in the begetting it.

"In the next Place, I do not approve of your *quaint Conceit* at the Foot of the Title Page of my *Romance*.——It would only set People on smiling a Page or two before I give them Leave;——and besides, all Attempts either at Wit or Humour, in that Place, are a Forestalling of what slender

Entertainment of those Kinds are prepared within: Therefore I would have it stand thus:

"YORK:

"Printed in the Year 1759.
"(Price One Shilling.)

"I know you will tell me, That it is set too high; and as a Proof, you will say, That this last *Reply* to the *Dean's Answer* does consist of near as many Pages as mine; and yet is all sold for Six-pence.——But mine, my dear Friend, is quite a *different Story:*——It is a Web wrought out of my own Brain, of twice the Fineness of this which he has spun out of his; and besides, I maintain it, it is of a more curious Pattern, and could not be afforded at the Price that his is sold at, by any *honest* Workman in *Great-Britain.*

"Moreover, Sir, you do not consider, That the writer is interested in his *Story*, and that it is his Business to set it a-going at *any Price:* And indeed, from the Information of Persons conversant in Paper and Print, I have very good Reason to believe, if he should sell every Pamphlet of them, he would inevitably be a *Great Loser* by it. This I believe verily, and am,

"Dear Sir,
"*Your obliged Friend*

"Sutton on the Forest,   "*and humble Servant,*
   Jan. 20, 1759.   "LAURENCE STERNE."

Having thus thrown off the mask of anonymity already worn thin, Sterne closed the whole performance with a signed letter to Dr. Topham, bearing the same date as the one just quoted. The lawyer, in his last pamphlet, had questioned the accuracy of Sterne's memory about the Sessions Dinner, and hinted that the Vicar of Sutton had had a good deal to do with the dean's previous pamphlet, as if Dr. Fountayne, without the aid of friends, were not quite equal to a controversy. Sterne took up in detail these and other points, assuring Dr. Topham that he had nothing to do with the dean's *Answer* beyond the attestation which he signed with others, and that his memory was still good. "As for the many coarse and unchristian Insinuations," said Sterne to Dr. Topham, "scatter'd throughout your *Reply*,——as it is my Duty to beg God to forgive you, so I do from my Heart: Believe me, Dr. *Topham*, they hurt yourself more than the Person they are aimed at; And when the *first Transport* of Rage is a little over, they will grieve you more too. And for the little that remains unanswered in yours, ——I believe I could, in another half Hour, set it right in the Eyes of the World:——But this is not my Business.——And if it is thought worth the while, which I hope it never will, I know no one more able to do it than the very Reverend and Worthy Gentleman whom you have so unhandsomely insulted upon that Score."

After this pretty compliment to the dean, Sterne added a postscript, which is, in conventional phrase, the best part of the letter:

"I beg Pardon for *clapping* this upon the *Back* of the *Romance*,——which is done out of no Disrespect to you.—— But the *Vehicle* stood ready at the Door,——and as I was to pay the whole Fare, and there was Room enough behind it, ——it was the cheapest and readiest Conveyance I could think of."

At the end of all came the Archangel Gabriel, as an appropriate design, resting upon a bank of clouds and blowing the last trumpet.

Altogether, the *Romance* was a clever elaboration of a phase of Swift's cruel and humorous philosophy. Reduce men to pygmies, and they at once become in character and conduct ludicrous and contemptible.

"Above five hundred copies" of the pamphlet, it was said, "were struck off"; and "what all the serious arguments in the world could not effect, this brought about." At once Sterne had at his feet both friends and enemies, begging that the *Romance* be suppressed. Dr. Topham sent word that he was ready, on this condition, to "quit his pretensions." Certain members of the York chapter told Sterne that this humorous recital of their disputes would never do. The archbishop and the dean were, to say truth, each handsomely complimented by the way; but the laugh was, after all, on them as well as on Dr. Topham; the publication, from any point of view was, they thought, offensive to the dignity of the Church. Apparently the man most active in the affair was Dr. Herring, the chancellor of the diocese, who tried to separate Sterne and Dean Fountayne, and almost succeeded in the attempt. Over the fracas Sterne became so hot that he privately expressed regrets for his encomium upon a "weak and ignorant" dean, and doubts whether Dr. Topham deserved to be hung up "in a ridiculous light." His heat, however, quickly subsided. Letters passed between Sterne and Dr. Fountayne which cemented anew their friendship "beyond the power of any future breach." And though with reluctance, Sterne heeded the advice of his clerical friends that the *Romance* be suppressed. Accordingly, with his assent, an official of the cathedral—probably the chancellor—bought up the copies remaining in the book-stalls, and burned them with those still at the printer's. That was the current story thirty years after. But several copies must have been sold beyond recovery; and Sterne himself managed in some way to keep from the flames "three or four" other copies which he guarded for the delight of his friends.*

* For statements in this paragraph, see *Whitefoord Papers*, 229; *London Chronicle*, May 3-6, 1760; and E. J. Climenson, *Elizabeth Montagu*, II, 175-176, 271.

CHAP. VIII.

The Publication of Tristram Shandy—Volumes I and II. January, 1759—May, 1760

I.

THE burning of the *Political Romance* was a dramatic incident that "contributed," according to the newspapers of the next year, "more to raise the reputation of Parson Yorick, than any thing he could have published. . . . Ten times more was said about this piece than it deserved, because it was burnt; and the general voice, which never reports without exaggeration, . . . cried it up as one of the most perfect and excellent things human invention ever had produced." To Sterne the miscarriage of his first literary effort was a keen disappointment, for "till he had finished his *Watchcoat*, he hardly knew that he could write at all, much less with humour so as to make his reader laugh."

Having once discovered his talent, the country parson, then in his forty-sixth year, gave himself up to the exercise and delight of it for the rest of his life. *Tristram Shandy* was begun —so the book itself says by indication—late in January, 1759, immediately after the mishap to the *Political Romance*. Sterne wrote as fast as he "possibly could," reaching the eighteenth chapter by the ninth of March, six weeks and some odd days after first setting out. By the twenty-sixth of the same month, he was well on in the twenty-first chapter; and by June, the first draft of two volumes was completed. His genius bore him on so easily and rapidly through the later stages that he felt it was in him to write two more volumes every year so long as he should live.

There were, however, times of doubt and depression. To say truth, *Tristram Shandy* came near going the way of the *Political Romance*. While the book was in making, Sterne took some of the loose sheets over to Stillington Hall, where he read them to Stephen Croft and a group of friends brought together for the purpose after dinner. Some of the company "fell asleep," said the brother of the squire, "at which Sterne was so nettled that he threw the manuscript into the fire, and had not luckily Mr. Croft rescued the scorched papers from the flames, the work wou'd have been consigned to oblivion." As soon as the copy was fully written out, Sterne consulted various friends at York about it. One of them, who may stand for several, said: "I took the Liberty to point out some gross Allusions which I apprehended would be Matter of just Offense, and especially when coming from a Clergyman, as they would betray a Forgetfulness of his Character." In reply Sterne "observed, that an Attention to his Character would damp his Fire and check the Flow of his Humour, and that if he went on, and hoped to be read, he must not look at his Band or his Cassock." Marmaduke Fothergill of York, the younger of that name, whom Sterne described as "my best of critics and well-wishers," kept iterating: "Get your preferment first, Lory, and then write and welcome." "But suppose," replied Sterne, "preferment is long o'coming——and, for aught I know, I may not be prefer'd till the resurrection of the just ——and am all that time in labour, how must I bear my pains." Against the cautions of another he cited later the name of a great predecessor, saying: "I . . . deny I have gone as far as Swift: he keeps a due distance from Rabelais; I keep a due distance from him. Swift has said five hundred things I durst not say—unless I was Dean of St. Patrick's." Finally, to ease his "mind of all trouble upon the topic of discretion," Sterne decided to appeal to Archbishop Gilbert, should his Grace come down to York in the autumn. Whether or not the archbishop read and approved, the author does not say.

When the book was ready for the press, as Sterne thought, in June, he offered it to the local booksellers; but "they wou'd not have anything to say to it, nor wou'd they offer any price for it." He then tried the Dodsleys, the great London publishers in Pall Mall. From the correspondence, of which only one letter is extant, it appears that in June Sterne wrote to one of the Dodsleys, Robert without doubt, offering him *Tristram Shandy* for fifty pounds. Dodsley wrote back "that it was too much to risk on a single volume, which, if it happened not to sell, would be hard upon his brother."* By this time Sterne was beginning to heed the strictures that were passed upon his manuscript. Besides the caution of his clerical brethren that he should consider the solemn color of his coat, to which a meditation upon death would be "a more suitable trimming," some objections were made to his style as too ornate, free, and unconsidered. "To sport too much with your wit, or the game that wit has pointed out," Sterne admitted to a nameless friend, "is surfeiting; like toying with a man's mistress, it may be very delightful solacement to the inamorato, but little to the by-stander." Though Sterne said further, "I have burnt more wit than I have published," he nevertheless promised to avoid the fault that was pointed out to him, so far as he could without spoiling his book, which, he insisted, must remain "a picture of myself." To the same critic the mischance that befell Dr. Slop while approaching Shandy Hall on a dark night seemed too minutely described. Sterne defended himself by an appeal to the manner of Cervantes, but finally brought himself to admit: "Perhaps this is overloaded, and I can ease it." All who saw the manuscript knew of course that Dr. Slop was a satire upon Dr. John Burton; and there are indications that several did not approve of the attack. As a result of these criticisms, Sterne carefully revised his manuscript during the summer, pruning and grafting. In June he had enough material, said one who claims to have passed a whole night with him over his papers, to fill "four volumes," instead of the two that were eventually published.

Besides cutting away many passages—a half may be an exaggeration—Sterne added, according to his own account, "about a hundred and fifty pages," and took "all locality" out of the book; that is, he removed here and there a sting from the local satire. Thus amended, *Tristram Shandy* met with

* Robert Dodsley had just turned over the management of his business to his brother James.

great favor. By October, "a strong interest [was] formed and forming in its behalf"; and the next month rumor among his friends as far away as London, had it that Mr. Sterne was "busy writing an extraordinary book." Among the gentlemen at York who liked *Tristram Shandy* because it made them laugh, was "a bachelor of a liberal turn of mind" named Lee, who came forward early in the autumn and promised Sterne "one hundred pounds towards the printing." Fortified by this substantial sum, Sterne submitted new proposals to Dodsley, asking for his aid in placing *Tristram Shandy* before the public. The letter to Dodsley, bearing no date but belonging to October or thereabouts, runs in part as follows:

"I propose . . . to print a lean edition, in two small volumes, of the size of Rasselas, and on the same type and paper, at my own expence, merely to feel the pulse of the world, and that I may know what price to set upon the remaining volumes from the reception of these. If my book sells and has the run our critics expect, I propose to free myself of all future troubles of the kind, and bargain with you, if possible, for the rest as they come out, which will be every six months. If my book fails of success, the loss falls where it ought to do. The same motives which inclined me first to offer you this trifle, incline me to give you the whole profits of the sale (except what Mr. Hinxman* sells here, which will be a great many), and to have them sold only at your shop upon the usual terms in these cases. The book shall be printed here, and the impression sent up to you; for as I live at York; and shall correct every proof myself, it shall go perfect into the world, and be printed in so creditable a way as to paper, type, &c., as to do no dishonour to you, who, I know, never chuse to print a book meanly. Will you patronize my book upon these terms, and be as kind a friend to it as if you had bought the copyright?"

In a postscript Sterne added at the end: "I had desired Mr.

---

* John Hinxman, a York bookseller. In 1757, Hinxman, who had served his apprenticeship with the Dodsleys, came to York and bought out the business of Mrs. Hildyard, the widow of John Hildyard (who had recently died). See R. Straus, *Robert Dodsley*, 260 (London, 1910).

Hinxman to write the purport of this to you by this post; but lest he should omit it, or not sufficiently explain my intention, I thought best to trouble you with a letter myself."

The arrangements for publication outlined in this letter were afterwards somewhat modified, but just how can not be determined beyond doubt, inasmuch as the succeeding correspondence between Sterne, Hinxman, and Dodsley is irretrievably lost. According to John Croft, Dodsley now offered Sterne forty pounds for the copyright* on conditions which the author was unwilling to accept. Be that as it may, by December, 1759, Sterne's perplexities over his book were at an end, and he was anxiously awaiting his fate, uncertain of what it might be. As the date of publication was approaching, he remarked: "I fear *Tristram Shandy* must go into the world with a hundred faults—if he is so happy as to have some striking beauties, merciful and good Judges will spare it as God did Sodom for the ten Righteous that are therein." The die had been cast. On January 1, 1760, the *London Chronicle* made the following announcement:

This Day was published,
Printed on a superfine Writing Paper, and a new
Letter, in two Volumes, Price 5s. neatly bound,

The LIFE and OPINIONS of
TRISTRAM SHANDY, Gent.

York, printed for and sold by John Hinxman
(Successor to the late Mr. Hildyard) Bookseller in
Stonegate: J. Dodsley in Pallmall and M. Cooper in
Pater-noster-row, London: and by all the Booksellers.

Whether this first instalment of *Tristram Shandy* was really printed at York or in London is a question in dispute among bibliographers. Sterne's design, as may be seen from the letter to Dodsley in October, was to place his book in the

---

* Neither this nor later instalments of *Tristram Shandy* were entered at Stationers' Hall, though we find Sterne subsequently disposing of his copyrights.

hands of a local printer, most likely Ann Ward, widow and successor of Cæsar Ward, at the Sign of the Bible in Coney Street, "with whose neat and accurate typography," says Robert Davies, the antiquary, "the author was well acquainted." Cæsar Ward, who died in April, 1759, had printed not only the *Political Romance,* but also two of Yorick's sermons. To the same press Sterne would naturally entrust *Tristram Shandy.* Without mentioning the name of the printer, John Croft remarked, in agreement with others, who ought to have known, that the first edition, running to "about two hundred copies," was "first printed at York," and adds that Sterne sent a set of them up to Dodsley, who "returned for an answer that they were not saleable." Against these assertions the bibliographical evidence, however, is nearly if not quite conclusive. All copies of the first edition in two volumes (so far as they have been inspected by the present writer or described by others at first hand) contain on the title-page the title: "The Life and Opinions of Tristram Shandy, Gentleman," a Greek quotation from the *Encheiridion** of Epictetus, the number of the volume, and the date "1760." There is nothing more; no place of issue, no name of publisher, no name of author. It is the same for all copies extant, so far as they are known: for those now in accessible private collections and for the copy—presumably an advance copy—which Sterne presented to his physician, Dr. John Dealtry of York.† The notion which still half obtains that there was an earlier private edition of *Tristram Shandy,* perhaps bearing on the title-page "York, 1759," is erroneous. The paper and the typography of the first edition of the first two volumes are essentially the same as those of the third and fourth volumes, which were printed in London the next year for R. and J. Dodsley. It is of course possible, though not probable, that Dodsley, in bringing out the second instalment of the book, matched the paper and the type of a York printer; but the natural inference is that Dodsley, on terms not now known, likewise had the first edition of the

* Ἐγχειρίδιον Cap. 5.

† This copy is described in the *Athenæum,* February 23, 1878.

T H E

L I F E

A N D

O P I N I O N S

O F

TRISTRAM SHANDY,
Gentleman.

Ταρασσει τὺς Ἀνϑρώπυς ὑ τὰ Πράγματα,
αλλα τὰ περι τῶν Πραγμάτων, Δογματα.

VOL. I.

1760.

*Facsimile of Title Page to the First Edition of
"Tristram Shandy"*

first instalment printed in London for Hinxman; that he kept with reluctance a bundle for the London market, and sent the rest down to York, to his former apprentice, who may be regarded as the real publisher of *Tristram Shandy*, in so far as it had any outside of the author and his friend Mr. Lee. The book was quietly placed on sale at York, without any advertisement in the local newspaper until February 12, 1760.

It was a current story that Sterne set about and continued *Tristram Shandy* as a relief to melancholy. "Every sentence," it was said, "had been conceived and written under the greatest heaviness of heart." Certain it is that the composition of his book was accompanied by domestic troubles that might have crushed a man of grave temperament, but they affected the light-hearted Yorick little if at all. The last reference in Sterne's correspondence to his mother occurs in a letter to John Blake in the autumn of 1758. He was coming in to York, he said, and wished to see his mother. A "Mrs. Sterne," perhaps this unfortunate woman, who may have been housed in "the common gaol at York" for a time before the reconciliation with her son, was buried from the church of St. Michael-le-Belfrey on May 5, 1759. It was the church where Sterne had preached a charity sermon many years before on the joy and rapture of the ancient Hebrew woman when the prophet Elijah placed in her arms her child, a moment before dead but now alive. His "proud and opulent" uncle Jaques Sterne, of many titles and many preferments, likewise died on the ninth of the following June, and was buried in the parish church at Rise. He left no children. Though the quarrel between uncle and nephew still remained abroach, Laurence yet expected a legacy. But just before death, Dr. Sterne, hitherto uncertain about the disposition of his property, willed all of his "real and personal estate whatsoever" to his housekeeper, Sarah Benson, widow, of the parish of St. Michael-le-Belfrey.* Disappointed of his reasonable expectations, Laurence "was so offended that he did not putt on mourning tho' he had

* The will was proved in the Prerogative Court of York on June 13, 1759.

it ready, and on the contrary shewed all possible marks of dis-respect to his uncle's memory."

The sentimental marriage with Miss Lumley had proved, as might have been foretold, uncomfortable to both parties. "Sterne and his Wife," said John Croft, in gathering up local anecdotes, " . . . did not *gee* well together, for she used to say herself, that the largest House in England cou'd not con-tain them both, on account of their Turmoils and Disputes." Both were very hot-tempered. Mrs. Montagu, who rather sided with Sterne, admitted that she could not imagine him "of a sort to make a good husband," and described Mrs. Sterne as a "fretful porcupine," with whom one could avoid a quarrel only by keeping at "a due distance." Mrs. Sterne was not in-terested in Yorick's efforts towards a literary career, and he reproached her as "the blaster of his fortunes." It was neces-sary for him to choose between his art and his wife. He chose his art. Perhaps it was after a quarrel with his wife that Sterne sent his Latin epistle, from which we have already quoted, over to Hall-Stevenson about a projected trip to London. He was sitting at the time in Sunton's Coffee-House on the eve of departure, undisturbed by the loud conversation around him, as he began recklessly: *"Nescio quid est materia cum me, sed sum fatigatus et ægrotus de meâ uxore plus quam unquam——et sum possessus cum diabolo qui pellet me in urbem."*

Over against this letter with its disagreeable inferences should be placed the rather pretty domestic scenes of 1758, when the parson and his wife, as described in the Blake cor-respondence, were frequently taking a wheel together into York for their winter purchases and visits to friends. But sometime in 1759, affairs reached a crisis, owing, rumor had it, to Sterne's misconduct. His wife, suddenly stricken with palsy, "went out of her senses," and "fancied herself the Queen of Bohemia." Her husband, falling in with the whim of her delusion, "treated her as such, with all the supposed respect due to a crowned head." "In order to induce her to take the air," it was said further, "he proposed coursing in the way practised in Bohemia. For that purpose he procured bladders and filled them with beans and tied them to the wheels of a single horse-chair, when he drove madam into a stubble field. With the motion of the carriage and the bladders' rattle it alarmed the hares and the greyhounds were ready to take them."* The sad condition of Mrs. Sterne affected the health of little Lydia, who had been ailing for some time, throwing the "poor child into a fever." On the approach of winter, Sterne took a small house in the Minster Yard at York for his wife and daughter, that the one might have the best medical attendance, and the other "begin dancing" and be put to school. Of Lydia he said: "If I cannot leave her a fortune, I will at least give her an education." And of his wife he wrote to Mrs. Montagu: "We have settled accounts to each other's satisfaction and honour, and I am persuaded shall end our days without one word of reproach or even incivility."

Regardful as was Sterne for the comfort of his family, the illness of his wife nevertheless sat lightly upon him. While she was living by the minster, perhaps under the care of "a lunatic doctor," the unsteady parson consoled himself by carrying on a flirtation with Miss Catherine Fourmantelle, a professional singer, then in lodgings with her mother at Mrs. Joliffe's, close by in Stonegate. The Fourmantelles belonged to a family of French Protestants who fled to England for refuge in the reign of Louis the Fourteenth. "They styled themselves," said John Murray, the London publisher, who informed himself in the matter, "Beranger de Fourmantel, and possessed estates in St. Domingo, of which they were deprived by the measures consequent on the Revocation of the Edict of Nantes. An elder sister, it appears, conformed to the Church of Rome, returned to Paris, and was reinstated in the family property."† The younger sister, Catherine, a woman of much beauty and good character as well as birth, endeavored to support herself and mother by her voice. She came

---

* John Croft, *Scrapeana*, 22 (second ed., York, 1792).

† Murray's preface to Sterne's letters to Miss Fourmantelle as originally published in *Miscellanies of the Philobiblon Society*, II (London, 1855-56).

down to York from London in the autumn of 1759, under an engagement to perform through the winter at the annual subscription concerts held in the Assembly Rooms. On the evening of November 29, for example, a day of thanksgiving throughout Great Britain for Admiral Hawke's victory over the French, the event was celebrated at York by a concert of vocal and instrumental music in which "Miss Fourmantel" took part with "the best voices in town." She sang again at the Assembly Rooms on the last day of the year and enjoyed during the ball that followed her performance a *tête-à-tête* with Yorick over his "witty smart book." At his dictation, she wrote of him the next day to Garrick: "You must understand he is a kind and generous friend of mine, whom Providence has attach'd to me in this part of the world, where I came a stranger." Near the close of her engagement, there was a concert for her benefit at the Assembly Rooms, for which she thanked "the ladies and gentlemen who honour'd her with their presence."* The progress of the sentimental intrigue is recorded in a series of brief notes that Sterne sent to Miss Fourmantelle during her stay at York. In the first of them, Sterne was not quite certain how his advances would be received, for he wrote on a Sunday:

"Miss, ——— I shall be out of all humour with you, and besides will not paint your Picture in black, which best becomes you, unless you accept of a few Bottles of Calcavillo, which I have order'd my Man to leave at the Dore in my Absence;——the Reason of this trifleing Present, you shall know on Tuesday night—and I half insist upon it, that you invent some plausible Excuse to be home by 7.——Yrs. Yorick."

Miss Fourmantelle was evidently glad of the delicious wine and the assurance that she should have her portrait, if all went well, on the next Tuesday evening. The sweet Calcavillo was succeeded by "a pot of sweetmeats" and "a pot of honey," though Miss Fourmantelle was "sweeter than all the flowers

* *York Courant*, February 5 and 19, 1760. The benefit was on February 15.

it came from," and, most strangely, by a copy of Sterne's first printed sermon, along with the following letter:

"My Dear Kitty,——I beg you will accept of the inclosed Sermon, which I do not make you a present of, merely because it was wrote by myself, but because there is a beautiful Character in it, of a tender and compassionate Mind in the Picture given of Elijah. Read it, my dear Kitty, and believe me when I assure you that I see something of the same kind and gentle disposition in your heart which I have painted in the Prophet's, which has attach'd me so much to you and your Interests that I shall live and dye your affectionate and faithful Laurence Sterne.

"P. S.—If possible I will see you this afternoon before I go to Mr. Fothirgils. Adieu, dear friend—I had the pleasure to drink your health last night."

The intimacy grew until it became at last "My dear, dear Kitty," and "I love you to distraction . . . and will love you to eternity."

This open flirtation—for the two met and conversed publicly at the Assembly Rooms and at the houses of mutual friends, and went shopping together at the mercer's—seems to have caused little or no scandal in easy-going York. Before *Tristram Shandy* went to press, Sterne touched upon the episode here and there in his book, wherein "dear, dear Kitty" becomes "dear, dear Jenny," wife, mistress, or child, whichever of the three the reader wills. The relation was, however, if Sterne's word is to be taken for it, "but that tender and delicious sentiment, which ever mixes in friendship, where there is a difference in sex."

Tristram Shandy, coming out at this time, made its way rapidly. Writing for Sterne from York to Garrick on January 1, 1760, in the letter from which I have already quoted, Miss Fourmantelle said: "There are two Volumes just published here, which have made a great noise and have had a prodigious run; for, in two days after they came out, the Bookseller sold two hundred, and continues selling them very fast." *Tristram Shandy* was for York, first of all, a local book, in a measure like the *Political Romance,* but moving through a larger and less perilous series of portraits than that afforded by religious controversy. The author had, to be sure, "altered and new dressed" the first draft for the removal of "all locality"; but it could not have been changed in its prime essentials. Indeed it is hinted in the book itself that a key might be prepared to certain passages and incidents which have "a private interpretation." As many times related, Sterne depicted himself as prebendary and rural parson in the indiscreet and outspoken Yorick who scattered his "gibes and his jests about him," never thinking that they would be remembered against him. Other characteristics of Sterne came out in Mr. Tristram Shandy, the name by which he first chose to be known in letters, and most appropriately, for *shan* or *shandy* is still a dialectical word in parts of Yorkshire for gay, unsteady, or crack-brained. It is of course really Sterne who speaks when Mr. Tristram Shandy says, after complaining of his asthma: "I have been the continual sport of what the world calls Fortune; and though I will not wrong her by saying, She has ever made me feel the weight of any great or signal evil;——yet with all the good temper in the world, I affirm it of her, that in every stage of my life, and at every turn and corner where she could get fairly at me, the ungracious duchess has pelted me with a set of as pitiful misadventures and cross accidents as ever small HERO sustained."

The elder Shandys, father and uncle, were obviously less specialized portraits, being the compound of many observations and memories reaching back to boyhood, when Laurie and his mother followed the poor ensign's regiment from barrack to barrack. A claim was put forward in *Macmillan's Magazine* for July, 1873, that my uncle Toby had an original in "a certain Captain Hinde" of Preston Castle, Berkshire. Sterne, it is said, made frequent visits to this "old soldier and country gentleman, . . . eccentric——full of military habits and recollections——simple-hearted, benevolent, and tenderly kind to the dumb creatures of the earth and air." There may be something in this persisting tradition, but the main hobby of my uncle Toby was evidently a hit at Sterne's friend—of uncertain name—in the *Key* to the *Political Romance*, who, with mind filled with the exploits of Marlborough, insisted on interpreting the incidents of the church quarrel in the terms of King William's wars. Mr. Walter Shandy also belongs, in one or more of his characteristics, to that convivial company which met at Sunton's Coffee-House. He was a further development of the president of the evening, who set forth his hypothesis as soon as the members were assembled, and fought for it stubbornly to the last ditch, preferring death to surrender. Yorkshire likewise knew that Eugenius, who plays the part of good counsellor to Yorick, meant John Hall-Stevenson, and people must have relished the absurdity.

To Dr. Topham, Sterne merely alluded by the way, under the name of Didius, the great church-lawyer, who had "a particular turn for taking to pieces, and new framing over again, all kinds of instruments" in order to insert his legal "wham-wham." Him he reserved for future instalments of his book, shifting his satire in the meantime to Dr. John Burton, re-named Dr. Slop, Papist and man-midwife. No one could doubt who was intended by "the little, squat, uncourtly figure . . . waddling thro' the dirt upon the vertebræ of a little diminutive pony" out to Shandy Hall to try his newly invented forceps upon the head of Mr. Tristram Shandy. To add to the gaiety of it all, Dr. Burton, woefully lacking in a sense of humor, solemnly disclaimed all resemblance to the caricature Sterne had drawn of him. Then another doctor of the neighborhood, thinking that Sterne might have meant him, called the parson up early one morning and entered vigorous protest against the "indecent liberties taken with him." After vain attempts to persuade the doctor of his error, Sterne, according to the story, lost patience, and remarked sharply as his visitor was going: "Sir, I have not hurt you; but take care: I am not born yet; but heaven knows what I may do in the two next volumes."

Amid the stir over *Tristram Shandy* at home, Sterne was looking towards London. "I wrote," he said, "not to be *fed*

but to be *famous.*" York might purchase the book for its local
allusions, jests, and ridicule of a well-known "scientific operator" seen on the streets every day; but in London it would be
judged on its wider merits, if it had any, quite apart from
personalities. Could *Tristram Shandy* stand that test? To all
appearance it was a mad performance not much like anything
that had ever come from the press. No wonder Dodsley hesitated and at first refused to become its sponsor. It is a novel,
people would say, in which nothing happens, in which everything is topsy-turvy, with a dedication, a mock epistle at that,
in the seventh chapter, and a sermon on conscience at the end,
—to pass over without comment an impossible marriage-settle-
ment, stars and long dashes, and an entire page smutched with
printer's ink. It is called *The Life and Opinions of Tristram
Shandy, Gentleman;* but the gentleman is only an embryo. It
turns out to be the life and opinions of the father and uncle
of Tristram Shandy; and why not call it so? That would be
the publisher's point of view; and in truth not much could be
said for the book on a cursory perusal.

But a reader at leisure could not fail to see that there might
be method in Sterne's madness: that every part of the book,
every episode, every digression, whim, aside, or innuendo, was
perhaps carefully premeditated, and the whole organized on
a plan which the author was keeping a half secret. As the
Greek motto on the title-page announced to all who could read
it, the book dealt not with adventures and men in action, but
with men and their opinions. Sterne knew that character may
be revealed quite as well by what men say as by what they do.
If you know what a man really thinks on a variety of subjects,
there is nothing left to know about him; for you have got his
heart and his brain. As if in burlesque of petty details of childhood prevalent in current fiction, Sterne set out with the conception and prenatal history of his hero, bringing to bear on
the ludicrous theme quaint and musty speculations of medical
writers over the animal spirits and the nature, endowments,
and rights of the *homunculus.* After merely stating *when*
Tristram was born, he proceeded to explain *how,* but stopping

to describe the preliminaries, he did not advance beyond them. Mention of the midwife of the parish led Sterne on to the parson's wife who set her up in business, and to parson Yorick himself, who could not be dropped without a full portrait, for he was most singular in his habits, humors, friendships, and death. That done, it was necessary to give some account of the hero's father and mother—of Mr. Walter Shandy, a Turkey merchant, who gained a competency in trade, and then retired from London to Shandy Hall to pass the rest of his days there with a dull and good-natured wife.

Naturally of an "acute and quick sensibility," the "little rubs and vexations" incident to the marriage state made the squire rather peevish towards others, though it was "a drollish and witty kind of peevishness." He was indeed so "frank and generous" in his heart that his friends never took offence at the "little ebullitions of this subacid humour." They rather enjoyed and relished it. Having nothing to do, Mr. Shandy spent his time on the old books that had been collected by his ancestors. In the course of his reading he fell in with the logicians and minute philosophers, from whom was derived the notion that there is something sacred about an hypothesis, as a means of arriving at truth, especially about a favorite one of his own making. "He was," says Sterne, "systematical, and, like all systematick reasoners, he would move both heaven and earth, and twist and torture every thing in nature, to support his hypothesis." It was his opinion "That there was a strange kind of magick bias, which good or bad names, as he called them, irresistibly impressed upon our characters and conduct. . . . How many CÆSARS and POMPEYS, he would say, by mere inspiration of the names, have been rendered worthy of them? And how many, he would add, are there, who might have done exceding well in the world, had not their characters and spirits been totally depressed and NICODEMUS'D into nothing?"

It was quite right that the Yorkshire squire should have a foil in his brother, my uncle Toby, unlike him in temperament and all else, save a crack in the brain that bespoke them of the same Shandy blood. As a boy, my uncle Toby read *Guy of Warwick*, *The Seven Champions of Christendom*, and all the romances of war and adventure he could find in his father's library or purchase with stray pence from the pedlar of chap-books. A young man, he enlisted in King William's army, and after years of honorable service, received an embarrassing wound in the groin at the siege of Namur. Sent home, he retired to a neat house of his own near Shandy Hall, and by the aid of Corporal Trim, set up on the bowling green in the rear of the house-garden, fortifications with "batteries, saps, ditches, and palisadoes," by means of which, with the assistance of maps and books on military science, he followed Marlborough's army on the Continent, demolishing town after town in imitation of the great captain. War, which brutalizes most men, developed in my uncle Toby all the finer instincts of human nature. He was of a peaceful, placid nature —"no jarring element in it,——all was mixed up so kindly within him; my uncle Toby had scarce a heart to retaliate upon a fly.

"——Go——says he, one day at dinner, to an over-grown one which had buzzed about his nose, and tormented him cruelly all dinner-time,——and which after infinite attempts, he had caught at last, as it flew by him;——I'll not hurt thee, says my uncle *Toby*, rising from his chair, and going across the room, with the fly in his hand.——I'll not hurt a hair of thy head:——Go, says he, lifting up the sash, and opening his hand as he spoke, to let it escape; go, poor devil, get thee gone, why should I hurt thee?——This world surely is wide enough to hold both thee and me."

These two brothers and the corporal, Sterne brought together in the back parlor of Shandy Hall on an evening while the parish midwife was above stairs with Mrs. Shandy. Then entered Dr. Slop, the celebrated *accoucheur*, fresh from disaster on the road, who was brain-cracked like the rest. At once began, to end only with Trim's recital of the sermon, the mad clash of opinions, accompanied by the most brilliant wit, irony, and mockery. There had been nothing comparable to the performance since the days of Sir Toby Belch and Sir Andrew Aguecheek. Not that Sterne really imitated Shakespeare anywhere; but he thoroughly understood Shakespeare's fools, and created anew a rare company of them. Then he set them at their wild play.

In describing *Tristram Shandy*, I have done not much more than paraphrase with free hand what was said of it within a few months of its publication. The honor of writing the first printed account of the book belongs to one of that company of literary hacks, who, with Ralph Griffiths at their head, presided over the *Monthly Review*, which issued at the end of every month from the sign of the Dunciad in the Strand. The men on this magazine were all so dull, said Dr. Johnson, that they were compelled to read the books they undertook to review. The scribbler to whom *Tristram Shandy* was assigned for December, 1759, prepared a long and faithful appreciation, patched with striking excerpts, and mild censure of the style as too much in the manner of Swift, and closing with a cordial recommendation of Mr. Tristram Shandy to the reader, "as a writer infinitely more ingenious and entertaining than any of the present race of novelists." Next came a paragraph of general praise in the *Critical Review* for January, 1760, managed by a society of smart gentlemen whom Smollett had brought together and trained, if I may quote the great lexicographer once more, to review books without ever reading them. The *London Magazine* followed in February with a high-flown apostrophe, beginning "Oh rare Tristram Shandy! ———Thou very sensible———humorous———pathetick———humane———unaccountable!———what shall we call thee? ———Rabelais, Cervantes, What? . . . If thou publishest fifty volumes, all abounding with the profitable and pleasant like these, we will venture to say thou wilt be read and admir'd." By this time the sketch of Parson Yorick, evidently the author himself, said the reviewers, was circulating through the newspapers, with blind conjecture as to who he might really be in the flesh.

During these months of suspense, Sterne was staying at

York that he might be near his wife and Miss Fourmantelle. Thus far he could have discovered nothing very unusual in the course his book was taking, though the reviews were rather more favorable than might have been anticipated of so wild a performance. Spice was now added to its reception by a letter from a London physician of his acquaintance, who took him to task for writing a book which could not "be put into the hands of any woman of character," and for alluding, under a gross Rabelaisian name, to a senile infirmity—"a droll foible," Sterne called it—of the late Dr. Richard Mead, one of the most distinguished physicians of the age. The unknown physician intimated that he was protesting not for himself alone, but with the assent of Dr. Mead's sons-in-law—Sir Edward Wilmot and Dr. Frank Nicholls, physician to his Majesty George the Second. After waiting four days for his humors to cool, Sterne sent back a gay reply in repudiation of the text that had been thrust upon him by his correspondent: *De mortuis nil nisi bonum.* "I declare," averred Sterne of the text, "I have considered the wisdom and foundation of it over and over again, as dispassionately and charitably as a good Christian can, and, after all, I can find nothing in it, or make more of it, than a nonsensical lullaby of some nurse, put into Latin by some pedant, to be chanted by some hypocrite to the end of the world, for the consolation of departing lechers." The letter further contained an adroit defence of his conduct on all points and a casual statement of his serious aim to do the world good by ridiculing what he thought "of disservice to sound learning," wherever it might be uncovered. His age certainly needed the correction which it received from him, but of that it is not here to speak.

Out of this hot correspondence, of which nothing is left save Sterne's one reply, came the news, just as Sterne would have it, that while *Tristram Shandy* was causing "a terrible fermentation" among London prudes and Sangrados, Garrick had read, admired, and passed the book on to his friends. It was a copy that the author had sent him from York. As soon as Sterne heard of Garrick's approbation, which he prized above any other's, he thanked him in a very fine letter for "the great Honour and Service your good word has done me," and in return offered to make a "Cervantic Comedy" out of *Tristram Shandy*. "Half a word of Encouragement," he said absurdly, "would be enough to make me conceive and bring forth something for the Stage (how good or how bad is another Story)." The great actor must have smiled when he read this proposal.

II.

WITH Garrick, the regulator of public taste, for its sponsor, the success of *Tristram Shandy* might well seem assured. Garrick's world, as Sterne knew, comprised the whole world of fashion. What cared Sterne for anybody else? Fine ladies and fine gentleman who were bored by books, would read, he was aware, anything to which Garrick gave the cue. London was as eager to see Sterne as Sterne was to see London. The story which I have now to tell, much of it in the words of John Croft's reminiscences and Sterne's own letters to friends at home, reads like romance rather than sober history. The visit to London came about by mere accident. On a morning of the first week in March, Stephen Croft, John's brother, rode in from Stillington for the York coach up to London. Meeting Sterne on the street, he offered to take him along as a companion and to pay all expenses, going and coming. Sterne at first demurred, saying that he had scarce time to prepare for the journey and that it would be wrong to leave his wife in her wretched illness. His hesitancy was, however, easily overcome, and within an hour after packing "his best breeches," he was on the way to London.

Reaching town, apparently on the evening of the fourth, the squire and parson lodged with Nathaniel Cholmley, Croft's son-in-law, living at that time in Chapel Street, Mayfair. To the surprise of the two other gentlemen, Sterne was missing the next morning at breakfast. He had gone out to Dodsley's at the sign of Tully's Head in Pall Mall to test the sale of his book. On enquiry of the shopman for the works of Mr.

Tristram Shandy, he was told that they "could not be had in London either for love or money." Later in the morning he saw James Dodsley himself, who readily closed with him for a second edition of *Tristram Shandy*, for two volumes more, which, it would appear, were already partially written, and for two volumes of sermons that Sterne had brought with him up to London and would be able to revise for the press within a few weeks. There was some haggling over the price by the country parson, who had had experience in buying and selling. Exclusive of the sermons, Dodsley agreed to pay the lucky author £630 on the score of *Tristram Shandy* besides the entire profit on the volumes already printed.* Sterne, who was not a man to hide his candle under a bushel, let it be known what a handsome bargain he had made. Gray, Walpole, and others were astonished. Some smiled, some were envious, as they saw a new dawn for the man of letters breaking over the head of Mr. Tristram Shandy. No time was wasted by Sterne and his publisher on preliminaries. In the *London Chronicle* for March 8-11, Dodsley announced that a new edition of *Tristram Shandy* would appear in a few days. Elated by his first success, Sterne further promised a fresh volume every

---

* The preliminary agreement between Sterne and Dodsley for the publication of *Tristram Shandy* is given by Melville (*Life and Letters of Laurence Sterne*, I, 205-206). It was as follows:

"It is hereby agreed between Mr. Dodsley and Mr. Sterne, that Mr. Sterne sells the Copy Right of the first and 2d Vols. of Tristram Shandy for the Summ of two hundred and fifty pounds—fifty pds. to be paid in hand—and that the remainder at the end of six months—Memd^m the Profits of the Books already printed to be all Mr. Sternes —the receipt of which fifty pounds I hereby acknowledge. And it is further agreed that the 3d and 4th Volumes, are to be sold and bought for the Summ of [four hundred Guineas erased] three hundred and eighty pounds.—

                                       L. Sterne
Mar. 8, 1760   Jas. Dodsley."
Witness, Richd. Berenger.

It is a fair inference from the inclusion in the agreement of a clause concerning "the Books already printed" that Dodsley had looked after the printing of the first edition of *Tristram Shandy*, as explained earlier in this chapter.

year. After placing this mortgage on his brains for the rest of his life, he "returned to Chapell Street and came skipping into the room and said that he was the richest man in Europe."

So swift ran the current of events during the next weeks that our narrative can hardly keep up with it. On the morning of March 6, Sterne called upon "dear Mr. Garrick," and in the evening of the same day attended Drury Lane, where he was "astonished" by the great actor's performance. The play for that night was Home's *Siege of Aquileia,* in which Garrick took the part of the stubborn old Roman general who preferred the welfare of his country to the life of his sons. What occurred within the next day or two, we leave to a letter, dated March 8, to Miss Fourmantelle, still at York. Sterne was sitting solitary and alone in his bedchamber after returning again from the theatre, as he wrote: "I have the greatest honours paid and most civilities shewn me, that were ever known from the Great; and am engaged all ready to ten Noble Men and Men of fashion to dine. Mr. Garrick pays me all and more honour than I could look for. I dined with him to-day, and he has promised Numbers of great People to carry me to dine with 'em. He has given me an Order for the Liberty of his Boxes, and of every part of his House for the whole Season; and indeed leaves nothing undone that can do me either Service or Credit; he has undertaken the management of the Booksellers, and will procure me a great price."*

On their first meeting, Garrick told Sterne of a wild rumor

---

* Sterne is reported to have told the story differently to his London friends. According to that version, Garrick at first presented him only with the freedom of the pit at Drury Lane. Meeting the actor some time later, Sterne remarked that Beard, though there was no acquaintance then between them, had offered him the freedom of the whole house over at Covent Garden. "I told him on the occasion," Sterne is made to say of Garrick, "that he *acted* great things and *did* little ones: —So he stammered and looked foolish, and performed, at length, with a bad grace, what his rival manager was so kind as to do with the best grace in the world—But no more of that—he is so complete on the stage, that I ought not to mention his patch-work off it."—*Original Letters of Laurence Sterne,* 60-61 (London, 1788).

in circulation that William Warburton, just elevated to the see
of Gloucester, was to be introduced into the next instalment
of *Tristram Shandy* as the tutor of Master Tristram. An
allegory, to give the story as elaborated by the clubs, had been
run up on the life of Job. Warburton was to appear as Satan,
who smote the ancient patriarch from head to foot, while
other well-known polemical divines—Zachary Grey, Charles
Peters, and Leonard Chappelow, who had been engaged in
angry disputes with Warburton, two of them on the Book of
Job—were to be brought in as Job's miserable comforters.
Through it all, my uncle Toby and Corporal Trim were to
operate on the distinguished tutor in the way they had already
done with Dr. Slop in compelling him to listen to the sermon
on conscience. Sterne had apparently come to London with a
half-formed plan similar to this whirling in his head. Had he
stayed at home and gone on as was intended, he might have
produced a burlesque, as rich as deserved, of the vain pedant-
ries of Warburton and his assailants. But once in London and
once aware of the position Warburton held among the bishops, nothing remained for Sterne but to lay the "vile story" to
the malice of his enemies. Unable to sleep because of it, Sterne
wrote off, near midnight of the sixth, a hurried letter to Garrick asking for an introduction to the author—"God bless
him!"—of the *Divine Legation*.

The next morning, Garrick sent a note to Warburton on
the "impertinent story," and received an immediate reply from
Grosvenor Square, in which the bishop expressed a desire to
have the distinction of Mr. Sterne's acquaintance. At their first
meeting, Sterne was pleased, one can well understand, to find
that Warburton had already recommended *Tristram Shandy*
to the best company in town, and defended the book in "a very
grave assembly" of bishops, apparently against the attacks of
Dr. Thomas Newton, the editor of Milton and soon the
Bishop of Bristol. Eager to become his patron, Warburton presented Sterne, on one of his visits to Grosvenor Square, with a
purse of guineas, and a bundle of books for the improvement
of his style. Sterne took the guineas and kept them. He took

the books also, but treated the advice that accompanied them with the contempt it deserved. No situation more humorous can easily be imagined than the dull and heavy Warburton instructing the light-hearted Yorick out of Aristotle and Longinus. So unusual was the gift of guineas that it led to a report, though there was nothing in it, that Warburton devised this way to escape becoming tutor to Mr. Tristram Shandy.

The patronage of Warburton, the friend and editor of the late Mr. Pope, as well as the champion of orthodoxy, made Sterne's brilliant reception doubly sure. Garrick could announce to the clubs that he had talked and dined with the author of *Tristram Shandy*, who was just arrived in town. He was a Yorkshire parson named Sterne, Garrick would say; the strangest sort of man he had ever met with; a bundle of contradictions, a jester and sentimentalist like the Yorick of the book, but withal a most agreeable gentleman, easy and affable in manners; in speech wild and reckless mostly, but at times uttering studied compliments in cleverly turned phrases, as if he had long been an adept in the art. It was Warburton's business to make enquiries of Yorkshire clergymen in London respecting Sterne's life in the north—how he was regarded by his brethren and how he had conducted himself as vicar and prebendary. The account Warburton received of Sterne was in all respects "very advantageous." The questionable jests in *Tristram Shandy* were clearly to be ascribed to an exuberance of wit and to the bad taste of a man who had lived out of the great world and its conventions; they were mere scratches, so to speak, upon Mr. Sterne's character, in no way penetrative of heart and brain. His conscience at ease on the score of Sterne's morals, Warburton took the author under his protection and recommended Mr. Tristram Shandy to the whole bench of bishops as "the English Rabelais." The bishops did not know, said Horace Walpole, in commenting on the incident, what was meant by Warburton's phrase, as they had never heard of the French humorist.

From his two friends, the news that the author of *Tristram Shandy* was really in London ran like a flame through society.

With a view to impending social demands, Sterne left Cholmley's on the eighth of March; and after looking over Piccadilly
and the Haymarket, moved into commodious lodgings at the
second house in St. Alban's Street, now no more, just off Pall
Mall. Stephen Croft, having finished his business, soon returned into Yorkshire, while Sterne remained to reap the personal delight of his fame. The new apartments, near Dodsley's shop and in the very heart of fashion, became the centre
of extraordinary scenes. "From Morning to night," Sterne
wrote to Miss Fourmantelle, "my Lodgings, which by the by,
are the genteelest in Town, are full of the greatest Company.
I dined these two days with two ladies of the Bedchamber;
then with Lord Rockingham, Lord Edgecomb, Lord Winchelsea, Lord Littleton, a Bishop, &c., &c. I assure you, my
Kitty, that Tristram is the Fashion." And again, with additional details, his head still topsy-turvy: "My Lodging is every
hour full of your Great People of the first Rank, who strive
who shall most honour me:——even all the Bishops have sent
their Compliments to me, and I set out on Monday Morning
to pay my Visits to them all. I am to dine with Lord Chesterfield this Week, &c. &c., and next Sunday Lord Rockingham
takes me to Court. I have snatch'd this single moment, tho'
there is company in my rooms, to tell my dear, dear, dear
Kitty this, and that I am hers for ever and ever."

And so it went on to the end of the season. Every morning
for two months Sterne's rooms were thronged with politicians,
courtiers, and men of fashion; and every evening Sterne was
hurried off his legs in going to these great people. It was most
fitting that Rockingham, the future Prime Minister, should
have led the way in honoring the Yorkshire author. At that
time Rockingham was Lord-Lieutenant of the North and East
Ridings and Vice-Admiral of Yorkshire, with a seat at Mal-
ton, not far from Sterne's livings. Since the Marquis and
Marchioness of Rockingham were regular subscribers to the
Assembly Rooms, where Miss Fourmantelle had sung, Sterne
must have been acquainted with both of them long before
coming to London. Winchelsea, related to Rockingham by

blood, was First Lord of the Admiralty. "Dick" Edgcumbe, wit and Privy Councillor, it may be conjectured, first brought together Sterne and Sir Joshua Reynolds. Two of the men of rank who overwhelmed the author with attentions were patrons of literature. Chesterfield, his political days long over, had retired to his luxurious house and garden in Mayfair, to devote himself to literature and the entertainment of his friends. Lyttelton had been the companion of Pope, Thomson, and Fielding, who dedicated to him *Tom Jones*, and never tired of praising his generosity, talents, and large fund of learning.

Of the associations that were linking Sterne through Lyttelton and Chesterfield to the great names of a past age, none pleased him quite so much as the singular manner in which Lord Bathurst sought him out at Carlton House a few weeks later. Sterne never forgot that distinction. "He came up to me," said Sterne long after, "one day, as I was at the Princess of Wales's court. 'I want to know you, Mr. Sterne; but it is fit you should know, also, who it is that wishes this pleasure. You have heard, continued he, of an old Lord Bathurst, of whom your Popes and Swifts have sung and spoken so much; I have lived my life with geniuses of that cast; but have survived them; and, despairing ever to find their equals, it is some years since I have closed my accounts, and shut up my books, with thoughts of never opening them again; but you have kindled a desire in me of opening them once more before I die; which I now do; so go home and dine with me.' "

It was in truth as fine a compliment as could be paid to genius. The aged peer, who had been the patron and protector of two generations of literary men, was dying in despair of ever meeting their equals again. He saw Sterne, ordered his table spread again, and resolved to live once more.

Amid these honors came that preferment in the Church which Sterne had missed ten years before. He had been disappointed, one may remember, when Coxwold went to his former curate, Richard Wilkinson, owing, it seemed quite clear, to the opposition of his uncle and the Archbishop of York.

Since then Dr. Sterne had died and a new archbishop was on the throne. On the tenth of March died also the incumbent of Coxwold, most unexpectedly, for he was still a young man. Within a few days after the news reached London, Lord Fauconberg, then at Court, nominated Sterne, on the solicitation of Stephen Croft, to the vacant living, then estimated at £160 a year above the customary dues; and on March 29, Archbishop Gilbert, who was passing the winter at his house in Grosvenor Square near Warburton's, completed the appointment. By this act all of Sterne's sorrows and tears were "wiped away." There was nothing more that he could "wish or want in this world."

Near the same time, Sterne was painted in his clerical gown by Sir Joshua Reynolds, at the request of Lord Ossory. The painting afterwards passed to Lord Holland, and at his death to the splendid gallery of the Marquis of Lansdowne. It is a marvellous portrait in pose and feature. As if already fatigued by three weeks of dinners, Sterne, say Reynolds's biographers, propped himself up while sitting to the great painter; and his wig contriving to get a little to one side, Sir Joshua, with the insight of genius, readily took advantage of the accident and painted it so, giving the head the true Shandean air upon which Sterne prided himself. The face, pale and thin, as one would have it, is all intelligence and humor. Reynolds, glad to confront the lion of the hour alone and face to face, would accept no fee. The portrait was at once placed in the hands of Ravenet, who made a mezzotint worthy of the original. With reference to it all, Sterne wrote, his thought on a full purse: "There is a fine print going to be done of me, so I shall make the most of myself and sell both inside and out."*

In the meantime, Dodsley was hastening forward the sec-

---

* The statement, many times repeated, that Reynolds painted Sterne at *one* sitting is quite erroneous. As shown by Reynolds's *Pocket Book* of appointments (MS. now in possession of the Royal Academy of Arts), there were *eight* sittings: the first on March 20 and the last on April 21.

The famous portrait is carefully described by Graves and Cronin in

ond edition of *Tristram Shandy*. At Garrick's table, Sterne had sat with Richard Berenger, gentleman of his Majesty's horse, a man of charming mind and manners conjoined with the gayer vices of the age; a sort of Hall-Stevenson bred to the city instead of to the country. To Dr. Johnson he was "the standard of ideal elegance," and Hannah More thought him "all chivalry, blank verse, and anecdote." He bade Garrick's guest tell him all his wants while in London, and he would fulfil them. Taking him at his word, Sterne addressed to him, as the day for the new edition of *Tristram Shandy* was approaching, a wild, profane letter beginning: "You bid me tell you all my Wants—What the Devil in Hell can the fellow want now? . . . The Vanity of [a] pretty Girl in the Heyday of her Roses and Lillies, is a fool to that of Author of my Stamp." This reckless outpour of speech was but preliminary to an urgent request that Mr. Berenger, "an impudent, honest dog," should sally out to Leicester Fields and demand of Mr. Hogarth "ten strokes" of his "witty Chisel to clap at the Front" of the coming *Tristram Shandy*. Hogarth sent back, free of charge, Trim reading the sermon on conscience in the back parlor of Shandy Hall before Dr. Slop and the two brothers. It was a scene that Sterne himself chose as the best for transmitting Hogarth and himself together, hand in hand, down to futurity.

It had been, according to John Croft, Sterne's idea, when first writing his book, to dedicate it to "Mr. Pitt, then Secretary of State, that it might lay in his parlour window, and amuse him after the fatigues of business as a lounging book." Thinking, doubtless, that a dedication from a humble clergyman to the Great Commoner might seem impertinent, Sterne abandoned the notion and satisfied himself with a mock epistle

A History of the Works of Sir Joshua Reynolds, III, 933-934 (London, 1899):
"Three-quarter length, canvas 50x40 in. . . . Sitting in a wig and gown; right elbow on a table, forefinger to forehead; left arm bent, hand to hip; knee breeches; on table are papers—on one, 'J. Reynolds, pinxt 1760'—and inkstand; a ring on the little finger of the left hand."

to "any one Duke, Marquis, Earl, Viscount, or Baron in these his Majesty's dominions," who would pay fifty guineas for the honor. Though still unacquainted with Pitt, Sterne could now have no hesitation, for he felt himself the equal of any minister of state. On the twenty-eighth of March, he sent his dedication over to Pitt with a brief note, not exactly asking his approval so much as taking it for granted that there could be no offence.

On the third of April, within a month after Sterne had set foot in London, appeared the new edition of *Tristram Shandy*, bearing the old title-page down through the sentence from Epictetus to the addition:

"The SECOND EDITION.
"London:
"Printed for R. and J. DODSLEY in Pall Mall.
"M.DCC.LX."

All copies had, I think, the frontispiece by Hogarth, which Ravenet engraved for Dodsley, and most, though not all, of them contained the handsome tribute "To the Right Honourable Mr. Pitt," preceded by a paragraph on the circumstances under which the book had been written in "a bye corner of the kingdom, and in a retired thatch'd house." There the author had lived, it was prettily said, "in a constant endeavour to fence against the infirmities of ill health, and other evils of life, by mirth; being firmly persuaded that every time a man smiles,—but much more so, when he laughs, it adds something to this Fragment of Life."

The second edition barely satisfied the market for the remnant of the season. Before the end of the year, Dodsley reprinted it twice again, making in all four editions within a twelvemonth, to say nothing of several piracies. As his book became more widely known, the adulation of Sterne went on at a quicker pace than ever. "Tristram Shandy," the poet Gray wrote to Thomas Wharton on April 22, "is still a greater object of admiration, the man as well as the book. One is invited to dinner, where he dines, a fortnight beforehand." "*Dinners for a month to come*" was John Croft's estimate, so that "it allmost amounted to a Parliamentary interest to have his company at any rate."

Giddy with these attentions, Sterne urged Miss Fourmantelle return to London and share with him the closing weeks of his triumph. Obedient to Yorick's call, she reached town by the middle of April and took lodgings in Meard's Court, Soho, within the district of balls, concerts, and masquerades. Sterne quickly saw that he had made a grave mistake in his thoughtlessness. He might hold in the abstract that prudence and discretion are only vices misnamed virtues; but the intimate friend of Garrick and Warburton could not take Kitty, in face of all the world, to the theatre or other places of amusement, however much she may have set her heart upon going with him; he could only send her tickets, with the hope that she would use them for herself and her friends. With great difficulty he contrived even to visit her for afternoon tea or for a sentimental evening; and before many days, numerous engagements to others so pressed upon him that he forgot all his appointed hours with her. On a Wednesday he sent her a note explaining why he had not called since Sunday and putting off an engagement until Friday. Five days without seeing the woman whom he had promised to make his wife, should God "open a dore," and to love forever and ever! "Dear Kitty" could not compete, I fear, with the ladies of her Majesty's bedchamber. So Sterne sent in his excuses for neglect and took his leave of her. His last letter, making a last appointment with her, runs as follows:

"Dear Kitty,——If it would have saved my Life, I have not had one hour or half hour in my power since I saw you on Sunday—else my dear Kitty may be sure I should not have been thus absent. Every minute of this day and to-morrow is pre-engaged, that I am as much a Prisoner as if I was in Jayl —I beg, dear girl, you will believe I do not spend an hour where I wish—for I wish to be with you always: but fate orders my steps, God knows how for the present.——Adieu! Adieu! On Friday at 2 o'clock, I will see you."

There was an epilogue to the sentimental comedy. On coming back to London, Miss Fourmantelle had tried to make an engagement at Ranelagh. But unaided she had failed. Then, towards the close of the season, Sterne persuaded John Beard, who was acting as manager of Covent Garden Theatre and also sang at Ranelagh, to take her into his company. The inducement was "a kind of Shandean sing-song, dramatic piece of rhyme," which Sterne, one day while at Garrick's house, wrote out for Beard and Kitty to sing together as "Swain" and "Nymph." Coming from Sterne, or, as rumor first had it, from Garrick, "the musical dialogue" awakened some curiosity. As Sterne's sole attempt, so far as is known, to write for the stage, the verses may be given in full here— not surely for any intrinsic merits, though they have the lilt of a song in the *Beggar's Opera*, of which it is an imitation:

Swain.

How imperfect the Joys of the Soul,
  How insipid Life's Journey must be,
How unsocial the Seasons must roll,
  To the Wretches who dare not be free.

Nymph.

Ev'ry Youth loyal Courage can fire,
  To the fair kind and constant must prove;
British Maids shall their Merit admire,
  And reward them with Beauty and Love.

Duetto.

Blooming Plenty shall Smile on our Fields,
  Sweet Contentment shall prompt us to sing:
And our own be what Industry yields,
  Long as George, gracious George is our King.

Swain.

Nought but Liberty Life can refine;
  'Tis the Wreath with which England is crown'd;
See we're bless'd with the Oak and the Vine,
  And we drain the Bowl all the Year round.

Nymph.

Oh, may Honor glow bright in each breast,
  And the faithless may Infamy brand,
To the Nation they always are best
  Who are true to the Nymphs of the Land.

Duetto: Blooming Plenty . . .

Swain.

Let us wake when our Genius inspires,
  Let no Follies our Virtue enslave;
Let us prove ourselves great as our Sires,
  And rise Britons as glorious as brave.

Nymph.

Let the Sons of Britannia proceed,
  Let them rouse up revenge if they dare;
Still we've Heroes enough that will bleed
  For their Country their King and the Fair.

Duetto: Blooming Plenty . . .*

Nothing more is heard of Miss Fourmantelle after her performance with Mr. Beard. She drifted away through concert halls nobody knows whither, but her image haunted Sterne's imagination down to the days when he felt death pressing upon him, and he then wondered how that face might look now that the beautiful singer was somewhere growing old.

How Sterne bore himself among the great people whither fate called him away from dear Kitty and what they thought

* *Dialogue. Sung by Mr. Beard and Miss Fromantel.* In *A Collection of New Songs sung by Mr. Beard, Miss Stevenson, and Miss Fromantel at Ranelagh,* 21 *et seq* (London, 1760?).

of him, were told in the April number of the *Royal Female Magazine*, issued on the first of May. The account was immediately copied into nearly all of the London newspapers. A notice so extended as this was rare in the press of the eighteenth century, even on the death of men conspicuous in church and state. Sterne was in truth our first writer about whom people cared much to know—how he lived, how he looked, and what he said and did when among his friends. The man who attempted to inform them was Dr. John Hill, a literary hack and quack-doctor, celebrated for an "elixir of Bardana" and various other nostrums, "excellent beyond parallel." To his purpose, the physician gathered up anecdotes running through the London clubs; and in addition to this, he must have had recourse to a friend of the author—perhaps Nathaniel Cholmley of Chapel Street—for details of Sterne's career in the north. There was in fact a hint abroad that Sterne himself furnished the material.

As is evident at a glance, the brief biography that Dr. Hill wrote for the *Royal Female Magazine* contains several inaccuracies, but its general truth is beyond contradiction. It would be a mistake to imagine Sterne as an awkward and unpolished country parson who had spent his time in the cultivation of his glebe, though he had indeed been engaged in that. He was a gentleman by birth who had been bred at the university; and he had been the associate of gentlemen all his life. His transition to London society was thus not so abrupt as it might seem, abrupt though it was. Notwithstanding many oddities, there was grace, native and acquired, in his manners, so that he adjusted himself to his new surroundings with the greatest ease. "I think," said Dr. Hill, "he is the only man, of whom many speak well, and of whom no body speaks ill. . . . Every body is curious to see the author; and, when they see him, every body loves the man. There is a pleasantry in his conversation that always pleases; and a goodness in his heart, which adds the greater tribute of esteem. Many have wit; but there is a peculiar merit in giving variety. This most agreeable joker can raise it from any subject; for he seems to have studied all;

and can suit it to his company; the depth of whose understandings he very quickly fathoms."

The humorist's ability to please by his smart jests and repartees, was slightly qualified by John Croft, who wrote of him: "Sterne was best and shewed himself to most advantage in a small company, for in a large one he was frequently at a loss and dumb-foundered. . . . He wou'd frequently come out with very silly things and expressions, which if they did not meet that share of approbation from the publick which he expected, he wou'd be very angry and even affrontive." Started by Dr. Hill, a story went through the newspapers of a sharp encounter between Sterne and Dr. Messenger Monsey, long chief physician to the Whig politicians; a learned and skilful man, but ostentatious and otherwise disagreeable in his behavior. The incident created so great a stir among Dr. Monsey's friends, including Garrick, that Sterne was compelled to soften some of the details, but he could not deny the main facts. In a letter to Stephen Croft, he claimed that Dr. Hill had made a mistake in the physician and in the place where the encounter occurred. Be this as it may, Sterne silenced the man across the table, to the delight of the other guests:

"At the last dinner," says the tale as originally told, "that the late lost amiable Charles Stanhope* gave to Genius, Yorick was present. The good old man was vexed to see a pedantic medicine monger take the lead, and prevent that pleasantry, which good wit and good wine might have occasioned, by a discourse in the unintelligible language of his profession, concerning the difference between the phrenitis, and the paraphrenitis, and the concommitant categories of the mediastinum and pleura.

"Good-humour'd Yorick saw the sense of the master of the feast, and fell into the cant and jargon of physic, as if he had been one of Radcliffe's travellers. 'The vulgar practice,' says he, 'savours too much of mechanical principles; the venerable ancients were all empirics, and the profession will never re-

* Charles Stanhope died at the age of eighty-seven, March 17, 1760.

gain its ancient credit, till practice falls into the old tract again. I am myself an instance; I caught cold by leaning on a damp cushion, and, after sneezing and sniveling a fortnight, it fell upon my breast: they blooded me, blistered me, and gave me robs and bobs, and lobocks, and eclegmeta; but I grew worse: for I was treated according to the exact rules of the college. In short, from an inflammation it came to an ADHESION, and all was over with me. They advised me to Bristol, that I might not do them the scandal of dying under their hands; and the Bristol people, for the same reason, consigned me over to Lisbon. But what do I? why, I considered an adhesion is, in plain English, only a sticking of two things together, and that force enough would pull them asunder. I bought a good ash-pole, and began leaping over all the walls and ditches in the country. From the height of the pole I used to come souce down upon my feet, like an ass when he tramples upon a bull-dog: but it did not do. At last, when I had raised myself perpendicularly over a wall, I used to fall exactly across the ridge of it, upon the side opposite to the adhesion. This tore it off at once, and I am as you see. Come fill a glass to the prosperity of the empiric medicine.' "

By the first of May, Sterne, all worn out and jaded, began to turn his thoughts towards home. In his absence, Stephen Croft had looked after the welfare of his wife and daughter, supplying them with guineas and charging them up to Sterne. Lydia was getting on well at school, though she had been annoyed by being called Miss Tristram and Miss Shandy. Mrs. Sterne was mending so that there could be on her husband's part no further serious thought of Miss Fourmantelle for a second wife. York had been kept posted of Sterne's extraordinary reception by letters from Cholmley to the Crofts at Stillington Hall. The anecdotes related by Dr. Hill also came down with the *Royal Female Magazine*, regularly taken at York, where they caused some hostile comment, since they touched on local affairs as well as on Sterne's courses in London. The behavior of Sterne at dinner with the London physicians was regarded as undignified; and the rumor that he was going to ridicule Warburton, after accepting a purse of guineas from him, disturbed the clergy, for they remembered the *Watch-Coat.* Sterne naturally wished to see his family, to set matters right, and to take up his preferment.

Several causes for delay, however, intervened. It was most difficult for Sterne to withstand the pressure of friends to stay on to the end of the month. At this time he was receiving "great notice" from Prince Edward, just created Duke of York. This royal scion, brother of the Prince of Wales, soon to become king, was a good-humored young man who gave himself up to pleasure and all manner of social functions. He had a tongue, says Walpole, that ran like a fiddlestick. Some years later he passed over to the south of France, and died there in consequence of cold and fever caught by dancing all night. Sterne supped with the Duke of York, and followed him to fashionable concerts where he was expected to perform. There yet remained, too, the final honor of all the honors that had been lavished on Sterne. He was invited to Windsor. On the sixth of May, Prince Ferdinand of Brunswick, who had won the battle of Minden the year before, was to be installed—in the proxy of Sir Charles Cottrell Dormer—Knight of the Garter, along with Earl Temple, then Lord Privy Seal, and the Marquis of Rockingham, who, as said once before, had taken the Yorkshire author under his especial protection. Nearly a week was consumed by the journey to Windsor, the installation, and miscellaneous festivities. The grand procession set out from London with Sterne in the suite of Lord Rockingham. It was a gorgeous scene in Saint George's Chapel on the next day when the investiture of surcoat, belt, and sword took place in accordance with the impressive rites peculiar to this ancient order of chivalry. From the chapel the knights with their retinues moved to the great guard-chamber, where a dinner was served, says Sterne, at a cost of fourteen hundred pounds. Before the second course, Garter King-at-Arms, attended by his knight-companions, entered the hall and proclaimed the styles of Earl Temple and the Marquis of Rockingham. At night there was "a magnificent ball and supper"; and on the next morning the men upon whom knighthood had been conferred and "the Right Hon. Mr. Secretary Pitt" were granted the freedom of the borough of Windsor. Sterne, then, if never before, met the great statesman to whom he had dedicated *Tristram Shandy*.

On returning to London with Lord Rockingham, Sterne had still many engagements to clear off his books, two volumes of sermons to watch in their last stage through the press, and the final contract to sign with Dodsley. In place of the single preliminary agreement of March 8, there were now two instruments, each dated May 19, 1760. According to the one, Sterne was to receive £450 for the sermons and the second edition of the first two volumes of *Tristram Shandy;* according to the other, Dodsley agreed, as in March, to pay him £380 for two more volumes of *Tristram Shandy* six months after publication.* In all £830! With a part of the money already paid in, Sterne purchased a carriage and a pair of horses that he might drive down into Yorkshire "in a superior style." He set out, if he followed his plans of a week before, on Monday, the twenty-sixth, that he might surely be in York on the next Sunday to preach in the minster before the judges of the summer session. Here in the great cathedral ended his triumph.

In beginning the story of how the Yorkshire parson came into his fame, I said that it would read like romance. To Sterne himself, it seemed all a dream; for writing to a friend of his sojourn in London, he said: "I was lost all the time I was there, and never found till I got to this Shandy-castle of mine." On that March morning when Stephen Croft by merest chance fell in with him at York, the author of *Tristram Shandy* was a poor and obscure country parson without the means of a journey to London. He was to be "franked" up and back by the squire of Stillington. Within three months he returned in his own carriage and driving his own horses, the best that could be procured. Six weeks at York and Sutton, and

---

* *Willis's Current Notes*, IV, 91 (November, 1854).

he was settled in his new parish. No man was better known in all England. A wager was laid in a company of London wits that a letter addressed "Tristram Shandy, Europe," would reach the popular author. The letter, says John Croft, duly reached York, and "the post boy, meeting Sterne on the road to Sutton, pulled off his hatt and gave it him."

A "curious cub" from Scotland, named James Boswell, who appears to have met Sterne in the Duke of York's company, thought Yorick "the best companion" he had ever known. The young Scot, who had not yet found his man in Dr. Johnson, looked on the scene of Sterne's progress, and as he looked, saw with wonder a country parson change—alter—and at length pass, by a perfect transformation, into a complete gentleman of the town.*

* F. A. Pottle, *Bozzy and Yorick*, in *Blackwood's Magazine*, March, 1925.

CHAP. IX.

The Sermons of Mr. Yorick. May and June, 1760

LOOKED at in other lights, the visit to London loses some of its brilliant hues. A successful author must expect many annoyances, alike from the friends and from the enemies that his books are sure to make; but Sterne perhaps encountered more than any other of his century, if we except Pope. The art, the jests, and the personal character of Mr. Tristram Shandy were all themes for censure as well as for praise. A persisting source of irritation to Sterne was the sketch which "Bardana" Hill drew of him for the newspapers. It had been written with kindly intentions merely for the sake of a guinea or two; but Sterne, unaccustomed as he was to anecdotes and chit-chat about himself, half-truths and half-lies, magnified the good-natured article into a malicious attack upon his honor as a gentleman. For a man so proud of his ancestry as was Sterne, it nettled him, first of all, to be told that he was "born of the barracks." Again, the incumbent of Coxwold had died, leaving, like Trollope's Rev. Mr. Quiverful, as his only estate a poor widow with unnumbered children. A report, coming into print with Dr. Hill, went current that Sterne had promised the destitute woman a hundred pounds outright and a liberal pension. Disclaim it as often as he would, the rumor pursued him through Yorkshire to his perpetual embarrassment; for had he wished to perform the charity, his means would not have allowed it.

Likewise the story that immunity from satire had cost Warburton a purse of guineas could not be laid for all his efforts. Sterne might set it down as a lie; but when it was again put into circulation by Dr. Hill, everybody had it and many believed it. Indeed, Warburton, despite the gift, was trembling for what might happen in the next instalment of *Tristram Shandy*. Add to this the indiscreet conduct of Hall-Stevenson. Sterne had been in London but a few weeks when his friend,

assuming the name of "Antony Shandy," greeted him with
Two Lyric Epistles; of which one was addressed "to my
Cousin Shandy on his Coming to Town"; while the other was
in honor of "the Grown Gentlewomen, the Misses of * * * *";
that is, the Misses of York. It was not a squeamish age. "Fine
ladies" as well as "fine gentlemen" repeated and laughed at
jests and stories coarser than any in the collection of Mr.
Tristram Shandy; but Hall-Stevenson went rather beyond the
relish of well-bred people of either sex; and Sterne was held
responsible for his cousin Antony's offence against this better
public taste. Though that was not quite just, he nevertheless had
read the epistles in manuscript, showing them to his acquaintance, and had permitted them to go to Dodsley's press, after
striking out a stanza here and there. Over these puerile verses,
discreditable alike to all who had a hand in them, the friendship between Sterne and Warburton was strained near to the
breaking-point. Sterne's full confession and penitence barely
saved him.

But Hall-Stevenson and Dr. Hill were only the beginning
of Sterne's troubles. Six weeks in London, and all Grub Street
broke loose at his heels. On its first appearance, the reviewers
for the leading monthlies had accepted, we have seen, *Tristram Shandy* as a book of unusual wit when compared with
the humorous trash then coming from the press. They did not
know at the time that the author was a clergyman, deserving
to be unfrocked for playing the part of a king's jester. Their
favorable opinion once delivered, they remained silent on the
reissue of *Tristram Shandy,* except for casual reference to it,
though they were but lying in wait for an opportune moment
to attack. For a time the newspapers, whose printers, or editors
as we should now call them, took no pains to form an independent estimate, merely reflected the magazines; but towards
the end of April, after the second edition of *Shandy* was out,
they opened fire. On April 28, the *Public Ledger,* to cite one
instance, published the first of a short series of imaginary letters from Mr. Tristram Shandy to his friend Bob Busby, in
which the young man claimed, in opposition to Sterne, that he

had been regularly born, and appealed to Dr. Slop in proof of it.

The merriment once begun, someone calling himself a Quaker by name Ebenezer Plain-Cloth, sent a letter to the editor in protest against the intrusion into public prints of "the frontless face" of Tristram Shandy. This is a specimen of what Sterne might see on taking up a newspaper at any time for the rest of his life. Scribblers who required larger scope for their wit resorted to shilling pamphlets running from forty to a hundred pages or more. Some of these pamphleteers adopted an abusive tone, wildly charging Sterne with various social and literary vices; while others imitated or burlesqued his book solely in the hope of making a few shillings out of its popularity. Of Sterne the man they knew nothing and cared nothing one way or the other. On reading the first of these lucubrations, Sterne remarked in a letter from London to Stephen Croft: "There is a shilling pamphlet wrote against Tristram——I wish they would write a hundred such." But as one mill after another took to grinding out *Shandys*, Sterne grew uneasy. "The scribblers," he began to complain, "use me ill, but they have used my betters much worse, for which may God forgive them." Finally, his nerves all shattered by three months of social dissipation, he fell into a semi-insane delusion, just as had occurred in the quarrel with his uncle, that a host of "profligate wretches" were setting upon him in the dark "with cuffs, kicks, and bastinadoes," that they might kill him with the public. In one of these moods he wrote to Warburton near the middle of June: "I wish from my heart I had never set pen to paper, but continued hid in the quiet obscurity in which I had so long lived; I was quiet, for I was below envy and yet above want."

Heaven forbid that we should go far into the pamphlets which so worked upon Sterne that he was on the point of renouncing authorship, though the narrative might not be without entertainment. "God forgive me," he wrote to Miss Macartney, afterwards Lady Lyttelton, "God forgive me for the volumes of ribaldry I've been the cause of."

The pamphlet which Sterne wished, on first perusal, multiplied a hundred-fold was *The Clockmaker's Outcry against the Author of the Life and Opinions of Tristram Shandy*. According to the fiction of the elaborate jest, a number of London clockmakers, meeting casually at their club, fall foul of the notorious clock scene at the opening of Sterne's first volume. One of the members, indignant beyond the rest at the humorist's treatment of an honorable trade, takes up *Tristram Shandy*, incident by incident, and denounces all, even the death of poor Yorick, which, though praised for its pathos, is declared to be "intirely borrowed." Some one of the company, if I remember correctly, ventured to put in a word in favor of the clever "scale of beauty" which Mr. Shandy applied to his mock dedication to any lord who would pay for it. Swift came the retort from the interrupted speaker to the effect that nobody should be so ignorant as not to know that the scale was stolen from the ingenious Mr. Spence's *Crito, or Dialogue on Beauty*.* As a whole, *Tristram Shandy* was pronounced to be nothing more than an imitation of *A Tale of a Tub*. Only there is this striking difference: Swift's wit is never without aim, while Sterne drifts on helplessly from one poor jest to another still poorer until he reaches inanity. In concluding his discourse, the angry clockmaker charged Sterne with the ruin of his business by degrading a harmless and necessary piece of furniture. "The directions," he complained, "that I had for making several clocks for the country, are now countermanded; because no modest lady dares to mention a word about winding up a clock, without exposing herself to the . . . jokes of the family. . . . Alas, reputable, hoary clocks, that have flourished for ages are ordered to be taken down by virtuous Matrons and disposed of as . . . lumber." The whimsical pamphlet bore an ironical dedication to "the humblest of Christian prelates," that is, to the ostentatious Warburton, who was taken to task for abetting Sterne's crime against society.

About this time issued from another press *Explanatory*

* So it was. See Spence, *Fugitive Pieces on Various Subjects*, I, 43-45 (third edition, London, 1771).

*Remarks upon the Life and Opinions of Tristram Shandy;
wherein the Morals and Politics of the Piece are clearly laid
open*, by one who claimed to be the son of the physician whom
Sterne had ridiculed in his seventh chapter. The brochure,
which need not be described here, closed with an "Advertisement to the Nobility and Gentry of all Europe," containing
some good raillery of Sterne's great reception. "As I expect,"
says the author, "in consequence of the foregoing work, to
receive invitations on every hand for parties of pleasure, re-
gales, dinners, and suppers——in order to prevent confusion
in my engagements, and that I may not make appointments
with persons I am intirely ignorant of, I beg the world, with
all convenient despatch, send their titles, names, and places of
abodes, with cards to my bookseller's, that I may pay compliments to them, according to their different ranks; or, where
upon a footing, according to their alphabetical succession. N. B.
Such noblemen, &c. as chuse to give me testimony of their
approbation of this book, by particular marks of their benefi-
cence, will please to take notice, that no *living*, however lucrative, can be accepted as I am not in orders."

After these two pamphlets came the deluge: *The Life and
Opinions of Miss Sukey Shandy*, which cost two shillings or
double the usual price; *Tristram Shandy at Ranelagh*, a miserable performance; *Tristram Shandy in a Reverie*, "printed on
the same Size as Tristram Shandy and very proper to be bound
with it," containing a *littera infernalis* from the departed
Yorick to his admirers on earth; *Letter from a Methodist
Preacher to Mr. Sterne; Letter from the Rev. George Whit-
field, B.A., to the Rev. Laurence Sterne, M.A.; The Cream
of Jest, or The Wits Outwitted . . . being an entire new
Collection of droll Wit and Humour, written and collected
by Corporal Trim during his Travels with Mr. Tobias
Shandy, etc. etc.* Something better than any in this list was
*Yorick's Meditations upon Various Interesting and Important
Subjects, . . . upon Nothing, upon Tobacco, upon Noses,
upon the Man in the Moon, etc.*, for several reviewers took it
to be really Yorick's, and the author of the tract received suffi-

cient encouragement from the public to proceed with *A Supplement to the Life and Opinions of Tristram Shandy*, "the best ape," said the *London Magazine*, "of the original Shandy we have yet seen."

A more elaborate continuation of *Tristram Shandy* appeared in September from the pen of one John Carr, the translator of Lucian, and then or afterwards head-master of the Hertford grammar school. It seemed to the schoolmaster that it was time for Tristram to be born, and so he brought him into the world. Carr attempted to pass off his book as a genuine third volume of *Tristram Shandy*, but the critics quickly detected the fraud. From these and similar burlesques, criticisms, and forgeries, with which the London booksellers flooded the town, Sterne could find no escape even in his Yorkshire retreat. If he looked into a London or a local newspaper, there they were all advertised; if he strolled into a bookstall at York, there they stared him full in the face. All this trash and abuse suggested, however, to an unknown wit a practical jest that diverted Yorick exceedingly when he heard of it some years later; and when it was related to Dr. Johnson, it brought forth a rhinoceros laugh. A certain gentleman, asking a friend to lend him an amusing book from his private library, was recommended to try *Hermes*, a dry and technical treatise on universal grammar by the learned James Harris. "The gentleman from the title," so the anecdote goes, "conceived it to be a novel, but turning it over and over, could make nothing out of it, and at last coldly returned it with thanks. His friend asked him how he had been entertained. 'Not much,' he replied, 'he thought that all these imitations of *Tristram Shandy* fell far short of the original.' "*

To have done with the scribblers who pestered Sterne with tags to his book, it is noticeable that he saw few men of letters while in London. The people who left their cards at the genteel rooms in St. Alban's Street and invited the popular author to

---

* Joseph Cradock, *Literary and Miscellaneous Memoirs*, I, 207-208 (London, 1826); and G. B. Hill, *Johnsonian Miscellanies*, II, 70-71 (London, 1897).

their tables, necessarily lay outside the realm of literature, except for a patronizing nobleman here and there, like Bathurst and Lyttelton. The men who were earning an honest living by their pens could afford of course no elaborate dinners; yet some of them might have made Sterne's acquaintance, had they so desired. A compliment to *Rasselas* in *Tristram Shandy* was an open bid for the friendship of Dr. Johnson; but Garrick never brought the two men together. And when they did meet more than a year later, it was with a clash of arms. Dr. Johnson and the rest were content to watch Sterne's progress through the mansions of the great and to make their comments thereon, occasionally in praise but more often in blame. For all the attentions lavished on him by rank and wealth, Sterne did not stand very well the test of the best critical opinion. Though he could not have known just what was being said of him in private companies and in the literary correspondence of the year, he was yet aware of a very hostile undercurrent. So in his sober moments, he was accustomed to liken himself, when complimented upon his prodigious run, to a fashionable mistress, whom everybody is courting because it is the fashion; but let a few weeks pass, and she will in vain "solicit Corporal Stare for a dinner."

It was not quite so bad as Sterne would make out. Thomas Wharton, then at Old Park, near Durham, wrote to the poet Gray in praise of *Tristram Shandy*, and the Cambridge recluse said in reply: "There is much good fun in it, and humour sometimes hit and sometimes missed. I agree with your opinion of it and shall see the future volumes with pleasure."* On the other hand, Horace Walpole, in giving Sir David Dalrymple of Edinburgh the literary news of the month, took occasion to say: "At present, nothing is talked of, nothing admired, but what I cannot help calling a very insipid and tedious performance: it is a kind of novel, called *The Life and Opinions of Tristram Shandy*; the great humour of which consists in the whole narration always going backwards. I can conceive a man

* Letter to Wharton, July, 1760, in *Works of Thomas Gray*, edited by E. Gosse, III, 53 (London, 1885)

saying that it would be droll to write a book in that manner, but have no notion of his persevering in executing it. It makes one smile two or three times at the beginning, but in recompense makes one yawn for two hours."* "A fashionable thing," Walpole called *Shandy* in sending a parcel of books to Horace Mann at Florence; and when he fell in with Sterne a few years later at Paris, he found the man's talk as tiresome as his writings. In neither, he said, was there anything to raise a laugh, though one were in a mood for laughter.

Of men of letters, Goldsmith almost alone spoke out in print against *Tristram Shandy*. Not yet author of the *Vicar of Wakefield*, he was then contributing to the *Public Ledger* his *Chinese Letters*, since known as the *Citizen of the World*. Between Sterne and Goldsmith as they appear to-day, one is impressed more by real similarities than by surface differences. Goethe, everybody knows, coupled the two names, in order to say that their genial humor and sane philosophy of life more than all else rescued him from Wertherian despair. But Goldsmith, all form, disliked the broken style of Sterne; and his imagination, immaculate as a maid's, could not endure Sterne's salacious wit. And so gathering up what gall there was in his white liver, he poured it forth on *Tristram Shandy* in his newspaper for June 30, and in subsequent issues.† From him came also the *Ledger's* imaginary letters to which we have previously referred. "I bought last season," said a London bookseller to Goldsmith's Chinaman, "a piece that had no other merit upon earth than nine hundred and ninety-five breaks, seventy-two ha ha's, three good things, and a garter. And yet it played off, and bounced, and cracked, and made more sport than a fire-work. . . . Ah, sir, that was a piece touched off by the hand of a master, filled with good things from one end to the other. The author had nothing but the jest in view; no dull moral lurking beneath, nor ill-natured satire to sour the reader's good-humour; he wisely considered, that moral and humour at the same time were quite overdoing

* Letter to Dalrymple, April 4, 1760, in *Letters of Horace Walpole*, edited by Mrs. Paget Toynbee, IV, 369 (Oxford, 1903).
† For example, the *Public Ledger*, September 17, 1760.

the business." At this point the visiting Oriental asked why such a book was published; and he quickly received the reply: "Sir, the book was published in order to be sold; and no book sold better, except the criticisms upon it, which came out soon after."

Sterne had revived, it was more directly alleged by Goldsmith, two obsolete forms of humor not much practised since Tom D'Urfey and his wretched crew. They may be called "bawdry and pertness," and "they are of such a nature, that the merest blockhead, by a proper use of them, shall have the reputation of a wit: they lie level to the meanest capacities, and address those passions which all have, or would be ashamed to disown." And finally of Sterne's vanity: "He must talk in riddles. . . . He must speak of himself, and his chapters, and his manner, and what he would be at, and his own importance, and his mother's importance, with the most unpitying prolixity; now and then testifying his contempt for all but himself, smiling without a jest, and without wit professing vivacity."

Dr. Johnson, much as he despised *Tristram Shandy*, thought Goldsmith went too far in writing the author down a blockhead, though he had himself called Fielding a blockhead. Not this year, but with reference to another and similar season, Johnson remarked to Goldsmith one day: "The man, Sterne, I have been told, has had engagements for three months." "And a very dull fellow," added Goldsmith. "Why, no, Sir," replied Johnson, and the conversation ended.*

Strict moralists of narrower outlook than Dr. Johnson were enraged at Sterne's performance. Richard Farmer, than classical tutor at Cambridge, spoke sharply to a company of students who in the very parlor of Emmanuel were expressing admiration of *Tristram Shandy*. "Mark my words," was his solemn prophecy, "and remember what I say to you; however much it may be talked about at present, yet, depend upon it, in the course of twenty years, should any one wish to refer to the

* Boswell's *Life of Dr. Johnson*, edited by Dobson, II, 44-45 (London, 1901).

book in question, he will be obliged to go to an antiquary to inquire for it."* Another storm centre was Delville House overlooking the harbor of Dublin, the residence of Mary Granville the Bluestocking, and her husband Patrick Delany, the Dean of Down and an old friend of Swift's. Faulkner, the Dublin bookseller, cried up *Tristram Shandy* to one of their clerical friends, and so they were on the brink of purchasing the book to read aloud by the fireside, when a note of warning arrived from Mrs. John Dewes, Mrs. Delany's sister in England. Whereupon the dean became "very angry" with Sterne, and declared that the book should never enter his house. Mrs. Delany, accepting her husband's decision, was terribly alarmed that *Tristram Shandy* should have been received in the household of Robert Clayton, Bishop of Cork and Ross, whom it diverted more than offended. "Mrs. Clayton and I," she wrote to her sister by the middle of May, "had a furious argument about reading books of a bad tendency; I stood up for preserving a purity of mind, and discouraging works of *that kind—she* for trusting to her *own strength and reason,* and bidding defiance to any injury such books could do her."†

Anxiety was felt in still other remote places for the influence of Sterne upon the morals of the kingdom. Mark Hildesley, for example, Bishop of Sodor and Man, and sometime chaplain to Lord Bolingbroke, enquired in the postscript of a letter to Samuel Richardson: "Pray, who is this Yorick? (a prebendary of York, I know he is). But what say you to his compositions, that have of late commanded so much of the attention and admiration of the wits of the present age. I am told, they have the countenance and recommendation of some ingenious Dutchess: is this true or not?" Richardson wrote back: "Who is this Yorick? you are pleased to ask me. You

---

* B. N. Turner's account of Dr. Johnson's visit to Cambridge in 1765, in the *New Monthly Magazine and Universal Register* for December, 1818; and *Johnsonian Miscellanies,* II, 429.

† Mrs. Delany to Mrs. Dewes, April 24 and May 14, 1760, in the *Autobiography and Correspondence of Mary Granville, Mrs. Delany,* first series, III, 588, 593 (London, 1861).

cannot, I imagine, have looked into his books: execrable I cannot but call them." And then, casting his more detailed opinion into the form of a letter from a young lady in London to her friend in the country, the novelist went on to say of *Tristram Shandy:* "It is, indeed, a little book, and little is its merit, though great has been the writer's reward! Unaccountable wildness; whimsical incoherencies; uncommon indecencies; all with an air of novelty, has catched the reader's attention, and applause has flown from one to another, till it is almost singular to disapprove: Yet . . . if forced by friends, or led by curiosity, you have read, and laughed, and almost cried at Tristram, I will agree with you that there is subject for mirth, and some affecting strokes, . . . and I most admire the author for his judgment in seeing the town's folly in the extravagant praises and favours heaped on him; for he says, he passed unnoticed by the world till he put on a fool's coat, and since that every body admires him!" After receiving Richardson's strictures "upon the indelicately witty Yorick," the Bishop of Sodor and Man "accidentally read" some passages in the book and re-named it "Shameless Shandy."*

Moralists and men of letters as far apart in temper as Richardson and Walpole, commonly excepted from their reprobation Yorick's "excellent sermon of a peculiar kind on conscience," which Sterne had introduced into his book, as one of a handsome volume at the service of the public. Criticism like that which we have repeated, only less violent, had been passed upon *Tristram Shandy,* from its inception, by Sterne's clerical brethren at York who saw the manuscript. Out of this criticism came no doubt the idea of balancing his character, so to speak, by following up the book with a collection of his sermons. With this end in view, he packed up a bundle of them along with his best clothes on that March morning when he set out for London with the squire of Stillington. The preliminary agreement made with Dodsley a few days later was, it will be recalled, not only for a second edition of *Tristram*

* Mrs. A. L. Barbauld, *Correspondence of Samuel Richardson*, V, 144-153 (London, 1804).

Shandy, but also for two volumes of sermons. After long delay and a continuous stream of advertisements in the newspapers, *The Sermons of Mr. Yorick* made their appearance on the twenty-second of May, the week before their author stepped into his carriage for the journey homewards. The two volumes, containing fifteen sermons in the whole, were brought out in the form and type of *Tristram Shandy,* with the Reynolds portrait as engraved by Ravenet for frontispiece. There was a curious preface, written partly as an apology for the author's pseudonym and for the haste with which the volumes had been put through the press, and partly to explain their character and to forestall a possible charge of plagiarism:

"The sermon which gave rise to the publication of these, having been offer'd to the world as a sermon of *Yorick's,* I hope the most serious reader will find nothing to offend him, in my continuing these two volumes under the same title: lest it should be otherwise, I have added a second title page with the real name of the author:——the first will serve the bookseller's purpose, as *Yorick's* name is possibly of the two the more known;——and the second will ease the minds of those who see a jest, and the danger which lurks under it, where no jest was meant. . . . I have little to say in their behalf, except this, that not one of them was composed with any thoughts of being printed,——they have been hastily wrote, and carry the marks of it along with them.——This may be no recommendation;——I mean it however as such; for as the sermons turn chiefly upon philanthropy, and those kindred virtues to it, upon which hang all the law and the prophets, I trust they will be no less felt, or worse received, for the evidence they bear, of proceeding more from the heart than the head. I have nothing to add, but that the reader, upon old and beaten subjects, must not look for many new thoughts,——'tis well if he has new language; in three or four passages, where he has neither the one or the other, I have quoted the author I made free with ——there are some other passages, where I suspect I may have taken the same liberty,——but 'tis only suspicion, for I do not remember it is so, otherwise I should have restored them to their proper owners, so that I put it in here more as a general saving, than from a consciousness of having much to answer for upon that score."

The second title-page, which was added for the comfort of the clergy and professional moralists, ran: "Sermons by Laurence Sterne, A.M. Prebendary of York, and Vicar of Sutton on the Forest, and of Stillington near York." Between the preface and the second title was printed a list of six hundred and sixty-one subscribers, which gathered in nearly everyone worth knowing in the kingdom—dukes, duchesses, earls, and countesses; bishops, deans, university fellows, canons, and prebendaries; statesmen, politicians, and physicians; long rows of men who could write esquire after their names, and Mr. Charles Burney, Mr. Garrick, Mr. Hogarth, Mr. Reynolds, William Whitehead the poet laureate, and Mr. Wilkes, Member for Aylesbury. In reading through the list, one wonders what use could be made of sermons by Wilkes, the profane politician, or by playwrights, actors, and wits, like Beard and Rich and Delaval. But taken as a whole, it was a handsome troop of titles and names which Sterne could show to his Yorkshire friends in proof of his great and sudden fame.

Sterne's sermons thus entered the world, guarded, as the author thought, with every precaution for their safety: no preface could be franker; no roll of patrons could be more impressive. But within a fortnight they were visited by a fierce assault from one of Griffiths's men in the *Monthly Review* for May. The point of attack was not the character of the sermons themselves, but their appearance under the assumed name of Mr. Yorick. This manner of publication, the angry reviewer considered "as the greatest outrage against sense and decency, that has been offered since the first establishment of Christianity—an outrage which would scarce have been tolerated even in the days of paganism. . . . For who is this *Yorick*? We have heard of one of that name who was a *Jester* —we have read of a *Yorick* likewise, in an obscene romance. ——But are the solemn dictates of religion fit to be conveyed from the mouths of buffoons and ludicrous romancers? Would

any man believe that a preacher was in earnest, who should
mount the pulpit in a Harlequin's coat?" Likewise a venerable
prelate remonstrated with Sterne for his unseemly conduct,
protesting that "he could not bear to look into sermons wrote
by the king of Denmark's jester." The conversation that ensued, ending with Yorick's witty retort to the troubled ecclesiastic, may be read in the *Sentimental Journey:*

"Good my lord! said I; but there are two Yoricks. The
Yorick your lordship thinks of has been dead and buried eight
hundred years ago; he flourish'd in Horwendillus's court——
the other Yorick is myself, who have flourish'd, my lord, in no
court——He shook his head——Good God! said I, you might
as well confound Alexander the Great with Alexander the
Coppersmith, my lord——'Twas all one, he replied.

"—— If Alexander king of Macedon could have translated your lordship, said I, I'm sure your lordship would not
have said so."

Aside from title and preface, the pretty volumes were
greeted with universal praise. Even Griffiths's man, bitter
though he was at the outset, went through the sermons one
by one in two issues of his magazine; and, carried away by
the preacher's eloquence, he was ready to avow after the first
volume: "We know of no compositions of this kind in the
English language, that are written with more ease, purity,
and elegance; and tho' there is not much of the pathetic or
devotional to be found in them, yet there are many fine and
delicate touches of the human heart and passions, which, ab-
stractedly considered, shew marks of great benevolence and
sensibility of mind. If we consider them as moral essays, they
are, indeed, highly commendable, and equally calculated for
the entertainment and instruction of the attentive reader."
Smollett's man in the *Critical Review* for May apprehended
that Yorick's name on the title-page might be an offence to
moralists and bigots; but for himself he beheld with pleasure
"this son of Comus descending from the chair of mirth and
frolick, to inspire sentiments of piety, and read lectures in
morality, to that very audience whose hearts he has captivated

with good-natured wit, and facetious humour. Let the narrow-minded bigot persuade himself that religion consists in a grave forbidding exterior and austere conversation; let him wear the garb of sorrow, rail at innocent festivity, and make himself disagreeable to become righteous; we, for our parts, will laugh and sing, and lighten the unavoidable cares of life by every harmless recreation: we will lay siege to Namur with uncle *Toby* and *Trim*, in the morning, and moralize at night with Sterne and Yorick; in one word, we will ever esteem religion when smoothed with good humour, and believe that piety alone to be genuine, which flows from a heart, warm, gay, and social." The long panegyric was broken by only one discordant note. The reviewer thought that Sterne had carried his familiar style, almost uniformly beautiful in its simplicity, to excess in the famous sermon which opens with a denial of the text. It was undignified, all must agree, for the preacher to set his own wisdom against the wisdom of Solomon.

The poet Gray, who understood the jest of the preacher exactly, enquired of his friend Thomas Wharton: "Have you read his sermons (with his own comic figure at the head of them)? they are in the style, I think, most proper for the pulpit, and shew a very strong imagination and a sensible heart: but you see him often tottering on the verge of laughter, and ready to throw his periwig in the face of his audience."* Even some of the Delany-Granville set who would not take in *Shandy*, were almost persuaded by the sermons that they had misjudged the author. "Pray read," Lady Cowper enjoined Mrs. Dewes, "Yorick's sermons, though you would not read *Tristram Shandy*. They are more like essays. I like them extremely, and I think he must be a good man."† Dr. Johnson was among the very few who were never won over. On a visit to Lichfield, an old friend placed a volume of the sermons in his hand for an opinion. Johnson asked him whether he ever read any others. "Yes, Doctor," replied his friend, "I read Sherlock, Tillotson, Beveridge, and others." "Ay, Sir," re-

* Letter to Wharton, July, 1760.
† *Autobiography and Correspondence*, first series, III, 593.

torted Johnson, "*there* you drink the cup of salvation to the bottom; here you have merely the froth from the surface." At another time Johnson nevertheless admitted that he had read Yorick's sermons while travelling in a stage coach; but he added "I should not have even deigned to look at them had I been at large."*

For some reason the notion has prevailed that Yorick's sermons were never really delivered; that they are only a bastard literary form, cast in a homiletic mould for the sake of publication. Sterne, however, made an explicit statement to the contrary. "Not one of them," said his preface, "was composed with any thoughts of being printed." Their publication, as I have remarked once before, was clearly an afterthought—a late device, as it were, on Sterne's part for averaging himself up with the public, and, I may add now, for laying a further tax upon the nobility and gentry of the realm. Besides his two parishes, Sterne had held for twenty years a prebend in York Cathedral. Twice every year—on the sixth Sunday in Lent and the nineteenth Sunday after Trinity—he drove in from Sutton to take his turns at the minster, and at various other times to supply the places of his brethren, especially of his friend Dean Fountayne, who, according to the usual arrangements, was appointed to preach the sermon for All Saints. The young prebendary, eager for preferment, liked this work, for it kept him before the public—and put every year twenty guineas into his purse. By 1760, he seems to have had by him thirty-odd sermons, carefully written out and laid aside, most of which had been prepared for the cathedral pulpit, and two of them for unusual occasions. From this convenient repertory were selected without doubt the fifteen that went into print.

In making up the volumes for the press, some caution was needed on Sterne's part, due to his habit of drawing freely from the great preachers of the past. His chief model, despite Dr. Johnson's contrast between them, was Archbishop Tillotson, whom Sterne had read at the university and kept by him

* *Johnsonian Miscellanies*, II, 429.

ever since. Next to Tillotson was Dr. Edward Young, Dean of Sarum and father of the poet, whose sermons were likewise a Cambridge book. Near them lay also, in Sterne's estimation, Dr. Joseph Hall, the unfortunate Bishop of Norwich back in the reign of Charles the First, whose *Decades* and *Contemplations* could be easily expanded into sermons. Besides these three, there rested on Sterne's shelf several other divines (including Dr. Samuel Clarke and Dr. Daniel Waterland) who were occasionally taken down and placed on his desk during the process of composition. From any one of them he might work out a sermon acceptable to his congregation, repeating and amplifying the original as much as he liked. But the issue under his own name of patchworks or paraphrases was a thing to be avoided.

For his future guidance it was the custom of the imaginary Yorick, says Mr. Tristram Shandy, "on the first leaf of every sermon which he composed, to chronicle down the time, the place, and the occasion of its being preached: to this, he was ever wont to add some short comment or stricture upon the sermon itself, seldom, indeed, much to its credit:—For instance, *This sermon upon the Jewish dispensation——I don't like it at all;——Though I own there is a world of* WA-TER-LANDISH *knowledge in it,——but 'tis all tritical, and most tritically put together.——This is but a flimsy kind of a composition; what was in my head when I made it?*

"N.B. *The excellency of this text is, that it will suit any sermon,——and of this sermon,——that it will suit any text.——*

"—— *For this sermon I shall be hanged,——for I have stolen the greatest part of it.* Doctor PAIDAGUNES *found me out.* ☞*Set a thief to catch a thief.——*"

This was also Sterne's custom as attested by Isaac Reed, the editor of Shakespeare, who saw the manuscript of two of Sterne's sermons and copied out the whimsical remarks sprawled across them. At the end of one bearing the title "Our Conversation in Heaven" was the endorsement: "Made for All Saints and preach'd on that Day 1750 for the Dean.

———Present: one Bellows Blower, three Singing Men, one Vicar and one Residentiary.———Memorandum: Dined with Duke Humphrey." At the end of the other, entitled "The Ways of Providence Justified to Man," Sterne wrote: "I have borowed most of the Reflections upon the Characters from Wollaston, or at least have enlarged from his hints, though the Sermon is truly mine such as it is."* And to the comment on the first of the two, the preacher might have added that the text and much else had been taken from Tillotson on "The Happiness of a Heavenly Conversation."

These two sermons Sterne cast aside for the present; but it was difficult for him to find fifteen which showed no traces of his borrowings. "Job's Account of the Shortness and Troubles of Life" went in with the original memorandum printed as a footnote: "N.B. Most of these reflections upon the Miseries of Life are taken from Wollaston," that is, from the widely read *Religion of Nature*. "Evil Speaking," though mainly a restatement of Tillotson's "Against Evil Speaking," passed muster after a casual reference to the witty archbishop. "Joseph's History" acknowledged a paraphrase from Steele's *Christian Hero*, but forgot Hall's "Contemplation on Joseph," out of which the sermon had been elaborated. It likewise seems to have slipped the preacher's mind that the charity sermon on "Elijah and the Widow of Zarephath" contained literal repetitions from Hall's "Elijah at Sarepta." To cover these and all other cases where notes or memory failed him, Sterne regarded as sufficient the general apology of his preface. It was of course not necessary for him to inform the public that the sermon on "Self-Knowledge" was merely a dilution of the one on "The Abuses of Conscience," which everybody had read in *Shandy;* for when a man has once said a good thing, there can be no harm in his repeating it. Doctor Paidagunes could find no fault with an author for doing that.

* These remarks were copied by Reed into a volume containing Sterne's first two sermons, published at York in 1747 and 1750 respectively. When the first edition of this book appeared, the volume was owned by Mr. W. A. White of New York City.

Quite as interesting as what Sterne said or omitted to say about the old divines who collaborated, as it were, with him on his sermons, are his notes on time and place of delivery. "The Case of Elijah and the Widow of Zarephath" was delivered, as we remember, at St. Michael-le-Belfrey before the charity schools of York on Good Friday, 1747, and published soon after. "Very few" read, said a new advertisement, this eloquent sermon, which the author placed among the best. The manuscript of the sermon on "Penances," now in the Pierpont Morgan Library, has the following memorandum at the end: "Preached April 8th, 1750. Present Dr. Herring, Dr. Wanly, Mr. Berdmore." "The Character of Herod," a footnote explained, was preached on Innocents' Day, presumably in the minster for the Dean of York. "The Pharisee and Publican in the Temple" was, in like manner, assigned to Lent, when the preacher came in to take his turn as Prebendary of North Newbald. To the same season belongs also, as the footnote again expressly declares, "The House of Feasting and the House of Mourning," one of Sterne's most brilliant studies in contrast. Many have believed that this sermon at least, whatever may be said of the rest, could never have been delivered. But the evidence all points to the contrary. It is almost a certainty that Sterne, rising into the cathedral pulpit on his Sunday in Lent, near the close of his residence at Sutton, and reading from Ecclesiastes, proceeded forthwith to attack the truth of his text with the startling phrase "That I deny." Except that it may be "fruitful in virtue," declared the preacher in conclusion, "Sorrow . . . has no use but to shorten a man's days——nor can gravity, with all its studied solemnity of look and carriage, serve any end but to make one half of the world merry, and impose upon the other."

Other notable sermons, like the one on happiness or its companion on philanthropy, were included without a note; perhaps because Sterne looked upon them as wholly his own and as suitable for any day in the church calendar. But if we had the full secret of these and the rest, we should doubtless find that they were published practically as they had been written at sundry times for his cathedral congregation and afterwards repeated at Sutton and Stillington. This is not to say that he did not make many minor changes in them as they were going through the press, adding or dropping out words, phrases, and clauses here and there to the advantage of his style. Such was his method, as we may see by comparing the three printed versions we have of the sermon on conscience. "That I deny," it may be, was an afterthought in place of a more general repudiation of Solomon. But that Sterne's revision of his sermons for Dodsley went beyond details is really impossible. Had he wished it, there was no time for rewriting them during the months he was in London marching from one great house to another.

Taking Sterne's first sermons as they stand, with all their faults and with all their commonplaces drawn out of Tillotson and others, they fully deserved the applause that attended their publication. Some of them could not have been very effective as spoken discourses. At times, we know, Sterne failed utterly as a preacher. When it was his turn to preach in the minster, "half of the congregation," says John Croft, "usually went out of the church as soon as he mounted the pulpit, as his delivery and voice were so very disagreeable." This we can well understand in the case of the more perfunctory sermons wherein the preacher made no effort to keep his congregation awake. But it was not always so. On special occasions, when he brought to bear upon his theme all the resources of an eloquent rhetoric, he filled church or cathedral and "gave great content to every hearer." According to a story which Sterne himself is reported to have related to a company of fellow clergymen, he was addressed one Sunday, as he was descending from the cathedral pulpit, by a poor widow sitting on the steps. She enquired of him where she might have the honor of hearing him preach on the next Sunday. After she had followed him about to his great discomfort for a succession of Sundays from one church to another, always taking the same position on the steps of the pulpit and always asking the same question, he finally chose as his text, modifying Holy Writ, the words:

"I will grant the request of this poor widow, lest by continual coming she weary me." "Why, Sterne," immediately retorted one of the company, "you omitted the most applicable part of the passage, which is,——Though I neither fear God nor regard man." "The unexpected retort," it was added, "silenced the wit for the whole evening."*

Uneven as they are for the pulpit, most of Sterne's sermons are admirable for the closet. In one of their aspects they were correctly described by contemporary reviewers as brief moral essays, any one of which may be easily read in fifteen minutes, or an entire volume at a sitting. After it is all over, a reader lays aside the book in a gentle frame of mind, having been soothed for two hours by a quiet and not too insistent optimism. He has been disturbed by nothing doctrinal, by no undue religious fervor, and by little religious cant—that jargon of the pulpit compounded of ill-understood and ill-related Biblical metaphors. If a passage becomes dull now and then, it is succeeded by a gay thrust at the Church of Rome, a flash of humor, or an apt quotation from Shakespeare, Epicurus, or Plutarch. Henry Venn, the evangelical divine, who read the sermons just after their publication, was grieved because there was nowhere in them "any mention of the Prince of Peace, in whom God was manifest." If we except a phrase or two, he wrote to a friend, "they might be preached in a synagogue or mosque without offence."† Likewise Walter Bagehot, unfortunately one of the last, I suppose, to look through Sterne's sermons, was disappointed to find that "there is not much of heaven and hell" in them. "Auguste Comte," he went on to say, "might have admitted most of these sermons; they are healthy statements of earthly truths, but they would be just as true if there was no religion at all; . . . if the 'valuable illusion' of a deity were omitted from the belief of man-

* Rev. John Adams, *Elegant Anecdotes and Bon Mots*, 267-268 (London, 1790).

† Letter dated June 20, 1760. In *Life and Letters of the late Rev. Henry Venn*, 71 (New York, 1855).

kind."* What the astute critic said is somewhere near the truth; and the statement is to their favor, though it was not meant to be so. Sterne could have given no offence to the deists of his age. In fact, he associated with them and prepared—as will be duly related—one sermon especially for a famous group of them. He preached a sort of common-sense philosophy, which, if it had little to do with Christian dogmas, never contradicted them. The evil and disorder in the world was as apparent to him as to the philosophers; he yet believed implicitly in the essential goodness of human nature and in the wise and just ways of Providence. The author of Yorick's sermons, said Lady Cowper, must be after all a good man; certainly a good man, if he followed his own instruction.

Apart from their excellent morality, Sterne aptly called his sermons "dramatic." Very likely he had in mind to some extent the breaks and pauses of the preacher and his direct addresses to Solomon, to St. Paul, or to God Himself in the course of the delivery; with all of whom he professed to disagree, though in the end he would come to the conclusion that the Scriptures, if properly interpreted, were always in the right. But Sterne was more than an actor. His best sermons are embryonic dramas, in which an effort is made to visualize scene and character, as though he were writing for the stage. Everywhere a lively imagination is at work on the Biblical narrative. If the preacher wishes to vindicate human nature against the charge of selfishness, he simply portrays the life of an average man, like scores in his congregation, from boyhood through youth, and through manhood on to old age, and lets the proof of his thesis rest with the portrait. No one who has heard or read the sermon is disposed to doubt the text that "none of us liveth to himself." If time and change be the theme, then again are brought on the imaginary stage the careers of two men—the one successful and the other unsuccessful, as the world views them—with a final justification, when the drama broadens, of God's dealings with His children. Human nature, the preacher may assert, is so inconstant that

* Bagehot, *Literary Studies*, II, 111 (London, 1879).

we can never know what a man will do. The statement may
be a commonplace to everyone in his congregation; but the
commonplace is forgotten in Sterne's illustration of it through
a whole series of portraits drawn with a few strokes from his
own experience and observation. Sometimes a sermon consists
of a single character-sketch rendered in full detail; it may be
Job or Herod. Again, for a study in contrast, two characters
run along parallel to each other, like Nathan and David, or
the Pharisee and the Publican in the Temple. Scenes of this
kind Sterne, avoiding all abstractions, realized completely and
triumphantly.

If Sterne's psychology was crude, so was all the psychology
of the age. Complex human nature can not be summed up in
Pope's neat doctrine of ruling passions, which was accepted
by Sterne. It does not explain Solomon to call him "a reformed
sensualist," nor Herod to conclude that ambition was the first
spring of his character, which, so to speak, put into motion all
the other wheels. But under Sterne's hands the method resulted
in most striking portraits. For setting forth the character of
these and other men in Scripture, Sterne frequently imper-
sonated them, spoke as he fancied they must have spoken, giving their points of view, their reasons for their conduct, in
conversation or in monologue. In this dramatic manner the
man of Jericho, for example, soliloquizes for a half page and
more after he had been passed by, "friendless and unpitied,"
by priest and Levite; and the Samaritan paused over the unfortunate traveller for a still longer meditation before deciding
to "soften his misfortunes by dropping a tear of pity over
them." Everywhere Sterne thus lets his imagination play upon
the few details furnished him by Scripture, building up scenes
and characters just as Shakespeare knew how to do from an
incident or two out of Holinshed. Sometimes, as in "The
House of Feasting and the House of Mourning," a beautiful
allegorical veil hangs over the drama, under which we pass
through scenes alternating with joy and sorrow, depicted with
perfect art. This dramatic discourse is Sterne's most complete
allegory of human life.

No more readable collection of sermons came from the press of the eighteenth century, and none with a clearer stamp of literature upon them. He is "the most taking composer of sermons that I ever read," the young James Boswell remarked of Mr. Tristram Shandy.

CHAP. X.

Shandy Hall. Tristram Shandy: Volumes III and IV.
June, 1760—May, 1761

TAKING several sets of sermons along with him for friends and subscribers in the north, Sterne left London for York—in his own carriage drawn by his own horses, as we have seen him—on Monday, the twenty-sixth of May. Driving leisurely, he should have made his smart entry through Micklegate before nightfall of the following Thursday, in ample time to appear in the pulpit of St. Peter's on Sunday. During his absence, his wife and daughter had occupied lodgings in the Minster Yard. Mrs. Sterne, he found on returning, had recovered from the delusion that she was the Queen of Bohemia, despite sore trouble with the daughter left in her charge. The schoolmates of Lydia, says John Croft, had plagued and taunted her, since her father's book came out, with the name of Miss Tristram and Miss Shandy. In revenge, she wrote love letters to the girls who thus annoyed her, under the signatures of the several players of the York company. As she had anticipated, many of the letters were intercepted by parents and guardians, with the result that the girls were flogged or shut up in dark closets or otherwise severely punished. But as she had not anticipated, the practical joke cast so great a slur on the theatre, that the players were compelled to take up the matter and ferret out the person who was playing fast and loose with their names. The discovery must have thoroughly humiliated Mrs. Sterne, who was always anxious for the good report of her daughter. It was, however, a piece of childish mischief that could not have greatly troubled the author of *Tristram Shandy*.

Before moving out to Coxwold, Sterne remained at York with his wife and daughter for three weeks for business and recreation. It was incumbent upon him, first of all, to make provision for the spiritual welfare of the parishes he was leaving. In the case of Sutton, with whose squire he was mostly at variance, he barely fulfilled his obligations. On coming into York for the previous winter, he had placed over that parish one Marmaduke Collier, who stayed on at a salary, as subsequently fixed, of £16 a year and the use of the parsonage house for residence. This cheap curate, who never attained to the dignity of a license, held his office solely on a private arrangement with Sterne as Vicar of Sutton. Much to the vicar's amusement, as well as to the loss of his library and some furniture, Collier eventually ran away, after accidentally setting fire to the parsonage and burning it to the ground. Stillington, the seat of Stephen Croft, naturally fared much better. In charge of this parish was entrusted another Marmaduke—Marmaduke Callis—who had served as minister in other churches in the diocese. On Sterne's formal presentation of his name to the Dean and Chapter of York, Callis received a license to the curacy—after some delay, to be sure—on September 26, 1761; and Sterne generously agreed to pay him an annual stipend of £40, or the entire income of the living.*

There was necessary also some readjustment of the mortgage on the Tindall farm at Sutton, previously held by William Shaw, who, it would appear, had recently died. For by lease and release,† dated the second and third days of June, 1760, Sterne, jointly with John and Timothy Place, linen drapers of the city of London, whose names occur in later records among heirs to William Shaw, conveyed this property to Elizabeth Thompson, widow, of Holtby, a neighboring parish. Though the transaction cannot be precisely cleared up, it was, without much doubt, a transfer of the Shaw mortgage to Mrs. Thompson. At this time or a little later, the two dwellings and half of the lands which had been allotted to Sterne under the Sutton Enclosure Act, were leased to one Benjamin Shepherd, who also, it is likely, was "the promising

* The appointments of Callis and Collier are recorded in the Institutions of the Diocese of York.

† Registered at Northallerton.

tenant" that Sterne found for the Tindall farm two years before. Several other fields from the same award were leased to one Robert Mozeen. All this and other business incident to a change of residence was quickly concluded, and by the middle of June, Sterne had assumed the duties of his new parish.

Coxwold, where Sterne soon brought his family, lies seven or eight miles to the north of Stillington on the edge of the moors. The village straggles up a long and rather steep hill and loses itself at the top as one travels westward towards Thirsk, eight miles away. Well up the hill on the left stands the pretty church of St. Michael, overlooking village and valley; and beyond the church, on the right, close to the roadside, is the house which Sterne used for residence and named Shandy Castle or Shandy Hall.* Though now made over into cottages for laborers, it is still, as in Sterne's time, a strange-looking gabled structure, as if it were once a cloister which someone far back turned into a dwelling—low, rambling, and dark, with a huge irregular stone chimney buttressing the eastern end. It is the very house, one would say, with its nooks and corners and surprises, from which should issue a book like *Tristram Shandy*. "A sweet retirement," Sterne called it, where a jaded clergyman might take up his rest. For years he had longed to leave the York valley, which aggravated his cough and asthma. Now he had but to step into the garden at the rear of Shandy Hall, and there lay before him a wide sweep of the Hambleton Hills. He doubtless missed the intimate society of the Crofts; but near-by lived the master of the Coxwold grammar school, and within a mile or two was the seat of Lord Fauconberg, his friend and patron.

Once settled in Shandy Hall, Sterne was ready to proceed rapidly with his book. The main lines that the story was to take had been designed the previous year, and several of the

* Shandy Hall belonged to Lord Fauconberg, to whom Sterne paid as rent twelve pounds a year. "The Original Manuscript of the Rent Book of the Yorkshire Estates of Thomas, Lord Fauconberg, from Lady Day 1755 to Lady Day 1771," is now in the collection of Mr. Lewis P. Curtis.

anecdotes, like the birth and the misnaming of the hero, there
are reasons for thinking, may have been then written out, but
afterwards cut away in order to bring the first two volumes
into a compass narrow enough to fit his purse or to please
Dodsley. But anything from Shandy Hall was now sure of a
market; and Sterne was so eager to lay a new tax on the public
that he sat down to his papers at York before moving over to
Coxwold. The new instalment of *Tristram Shandy* was resumed in earnest when he reached his parish; and we may, if
we like, easily obtain a few glimpses of him at work through
the summer and well on into the autumn.

His study, as a visitor enters the narrow hallway of Shandy
Castle, was a small room to the right, from the door of which
one still looks upon the yawning fireplace of the great stone
chimney. By the window stood in Sterne's day a plain deal-
table with pen and inkwell, before which the author, in loose
slippers and old dressing gown, took his seat in a cane chair,
having a back that ran up into ornamental knobs, symboliz-
ing, in Sterne's fancy, wit and discretion. Across the table
and along the chimney-piece were strewn books which he had
brought from his library at Sutton as most useful in composing the new *Shandys*. We can still read the titles of some
of them as clearly as if we now saw them. There lay, for
instance, *Rabelais* in Ozell's translation, Burton's *Anatomy*,
Locke on the *Human Understanding*, and the famous *Textus
Roffensis*, containing the solemn anathemas of the Church of
Rome. Before Sterne had long been at work, books, table, and
floor were spattered with ink, for he was a sloven with his pen,
thrusting it nervously into the inkhorn and then dropping it
upon himself or upon the floor on the way to his paper. The
act of composition was to him a sort of obsession, during the
strenuous period of which he imagined a host of quaint demons
grinning and clawing at his head and filling the room, just
as we see them in old prints. When the fit was on, he could
write almost continuously through the day—at will, he used to
claim, before meals or after meals, dressed or undressed, clean
shaven or in neglected beard. But he was unable to smoke

while composing and rarely at other times; "inasmuch as"—
he said in reply to a conjecture that humor so "refined" as his
must be hatched out by tobacco,—"inasmuch as the fumes
thereof do concoct my conceits too fast so that they would be
all torn to rags before they could be well served up." Sometimes, it is a local tradition, Sterne would issue forth from
Shandy Hall at a great rate, and half way down the hill would
come to a sudden stop, and then rush back to his study to note
down some fancy before it could escape him. And so it went
on for weeks, until his brains became "as dry as a squeezed
orange" and he had "no more conceit in him than a mallet."

Hardly had Sterne set pen to paper this summer, when there
began to arrive one disconcerting note after another from
Warburton, hinting at personal and literary indiscretions the
past winter and warning him to be on his guard in the future.
Incidentally Sterne was told not to worry about the "profligate
scribblers" who were hounding him, as such was "the common
lot of successful adventurers" in literature. This sort of hollow consolation, which may be akin to envy, disgusted Sterne,
who with a clever rhetorical twist remarked in a letter to Miss
Macartney a few weeks later, "that we bear the sufferings of
other people with great philosophy—I only wish one could
bear the excellencies of some people with the same indifference." Warburton, not exactly divining Sterne's talent, wished
him to compose a series of trifles, at once playful and moral,
such as could do no harm to their author and might instruct
as well as amuse the reader. On receiving that letter, Sterne
felt like throwing aside his manuscripts forever, and falling
back into the humdrum duties of a country parson. But that
was only a momentary impulse. Quickly regaining his emotional poise, he courteously thanked the bishop for his "kind
and most friendly advice," and added: "Be assured, my Lord,
that willingly and knowingly I will give no offence to any
mortal by anything which I think can look like the least viola-
tion either of decency or good manners, and yet, with all the
caution of a heart void of offence or intention of giving it,
I may find it very hard, in writing such a book as *Tristram*

Shandy, to mutilate everything in it down to the prudish humour of every particular. I will, however, do my best——though laugh, my Lord, I will, and as loud as I can too."

Warburton, elated by the reformation of Sterne, hastened to reply: "It gives me real pleasure (and I could not but trouble you with these two or three lines to tell you so) that you are resolved to do justice to your genius, and to borrow no aids to support it, but what are of the party of honour, virtue, and religion. You say you will continue to laugh aloud. In good time. But one who was no more than even a man of spirit would choose to laugh in good company; where priests and virgins may be present. . . . I would recommend a maxim to you which Bishop Sherlock formerly told me Dr. Bentley recommended to him, that a man was never writ out the reputation he had once fairly won, but by himself."

In the end, Sterne had only contempt for the literary advice with which Warburton was pestering him, and made a jest of it in conversation with his friends. No obstacle could stand in the way of his giving free utterance to what his attendant demons suggested to him, irrespective of the censures of the grave. Let his critics say what they might, he would write for that audience, be it great or small, who could be counted on to relish genuine humor. "I shall be attacked and pelted," he wrote to Stephen Croft, "either from cellars or garrets, write what I will——and besides, must expect to have a party against me of many hundreds——who either do not—or will not laugh.——'Tis enough if I divide the world;——at least I will rest contented with it." With his mind thus made up, Sterne placed at the head of his manuscript a Latin sentence which he had seen in Ozell's *Rabelais** from John of Salisbury, the great churchman and humanist of the twelfth century. "I have no fear," to paraphrase the Latin as Sterne adroitly modified it to his own purpose, "of the opinions of those unskilled in these matters; but pray none the less that

* *Works of Francis Rabelais*, revised by Ozell, I, cxx (London, 1737).

they spare my lucubrations, in the which it has ever been my aim to run from the gay to the serious and backwards from the serious to the gay."

The gay mood was to prevail mostly in the new volumes, which, among many things, tell of Mr. Walter Shandy's favorite hypotheses and how his expectations from them come to naught in the misfortunes that befall his son Tristram immediately after birth. Beginning where he had left off the year before, Sterne resumed the evening conversations between the two Shandys and Dr. Slop in the back parlor of the imaginary Shandy Hall, not to be confounded, as has been done so often, with Sterne's own habitation. In a bedroom upstairs lay Mrs. Shandy attended by the parish midwife and Susannah the housemaid. In the kitchen sat a group of idle servants, listening for the cry of a child from above. For some moments there had been a lull in the conversations of the back parlor. Walter Shandy had delivered a formal speech on the dangers that threaten a child's head at birth, and my uncle Toby was whistling Lillabullero in amazement at the alarming narrative, when a tramping was heard overhead near the bedside of Mrs. Shandy. Dr. Slop hurriedly took up his "green bays bag" containing his instruments of torture, but found, alas! that Obadiah had tied its mouth in a dozen hard knots for the safety of its precious contents. In vain he tried to unloose the intricate "roundabouts" and "cross turns" which Obadiah had drawn with all the might of his hands and teeth; and then calling in desperation for a penknife to cut them, he thereby cut also his thumb to the bone. Whereupon he began "stamping, cursing and damning at Obadiah at a dreadful rate."

My uncle Toby, who had not the heart to curse the devil himself with so much bitterness, suspended his whistling, and Mr. Shandy rebuked the profane doctor for unduly wasting his strength and soul's health by heavy cursing over small accidents. Instead of being so profane on trivial occasions, it would be much better, Mr. Shandy tried to persuade him, for a man who must curse to heed the example of a gentleman of his acquaintance, "who, in distrust of his own discretion, sat down and composed (that is at his leisure) forms of swearing suitable to all cases, from the lowest to the highest provocation that could happen to him, . . . and kept them ever by him on the chimney-piece, within his reach ready for use." Dr. Slop, who had never heard of the ingenious gentleman, became so interested in the anecdote that Mr. Shandy offered to show him a similar document, on condition that he should read it aloud before going upstairs. The doctor readily agreeing, Mr. Shandy forthwith reached up to the chimney-piece and gravely handed the Popish physician an authentic copy of the form of excommunication prepared for the English clergy by Ernulf, a learned Roman Bishop of Rochester in the old days. With wry face over an aching thumb tied up in the corner of his handkerchief, Dr. Slop was compelled to read through the terrible anathema, to the full discovery that it was not necessary to go outside his own church for an art and a gradation in cursing such as he had never dreamed of. Set beside the old bishop's copious profanity, the most violent oaths hitherto at his command, he was made to see, were tame and insipid, unworthy of the fine of five shillings which the government would inflict upon a gentleman for each petty offence.

His vocabulary of cursing enriched out of Ernulf's digest, Dr. Slop received an urgent summons above stairs from the frightened midwife; and the two Shandys, growing weary over a discourse on time and eternity, fell asleep as they sat in their easy armchairs by the fire. The two tired brothers would have slept on through the night, had they not been awakened by the creak of a rusty door-hinge, announcing the entrance of Trim to inform them that Dr. Slop had come down to the kitchen to make a pasteboard bridge for the poor child's broken nose. With a deep and agonizing sigh, the grief-stricken father staggered to his feet, extending a hand, as he did so, to my uncle Toby, who led him silently to his bed, where he might best digest his affliction, as everybody knows, by lying flat upon his face, with an arm and leg dangling upon the floor. To understand, says Sterne, why the sad mishap to the boy caused so great grief in his father, it must be explained that the elder Shandy had staked all on his son's nose. It had long been a settled conviction of his that a long nose, besides being a useful ornament to the face, was also a forecast of character and distinction in life; while a short or flat nose, like the ace of clubs that disfigured the countenance of his great-grandfather, meant as surely misfortunes and disgraces against which no man could ever bear up, whatever might be his other endowments of mind or body.

Mr. Shandy had derived his whimsical notion from wide observation on the rise and fall of the best county families and from a multitude of curious treatises that touched upon the theme. But the one that had been of most profit to him was a learned folio by the German Slawkenbergius, who devoted his life to the philosophy of the nose. Unlike all the other books, this one contained merry tales—a hundred of them—written out in the purest Latin, to illustrate and enforce the scholar's doctrine in its hundred-fold divisions. Of the two or three tales that Mr. Shandy always read with much delight, Sterne relates one that hinges upon the disorder and confusion caused among the inhabitants of Strassburg by the appearance one summer evening of a stranger who entered their gates, riding upon a mule and guarding with a drawn scimitar an immense nose which he had obtained (so he told the sentinel) at the Promontory of Noses. For some time, says Sterne, there had been no great and vital question in dispute between the Roman Catholic and Protestant universities at Strassburg, but now one of the finest was thrown at their heads. Taking sides, logicians and theologians proved and disproved through long and acrimonious debate, each faculty using its own appropriate jargon, that the stranger's nose was a real nose, that it was only a pasteboard nose, and that it was no nose at all, as if the affair were of as great moment as the altercation which divided the universities over the point in Martin Luther's damnation—whether the founder of Protestantism was damned to all eternity by the conjunction of the planets at his birth, and whether, the affirmative being proven, "his doctrines by direct corollary must be damned doctrines too." Slawkenbergius and his merry folio were, of course, pure fictions elaborated by Sterne for puzzling his learned public. The fanciful allegory of a land where one may purchase noses after his heart, was built up by Sterne mostly from a few hints out of Ozell's *Rabelais*, which lay at his elbow.*

The long digression on Slawkenbergius gave Mr. Shandy time to recover his grief in sufficient measure to converse and use his reason once more. No sooner had he reached that stage than he fell back upon another hypothesis whose aid might be yet invoked to save his son, disfigured and disgraced as he was by Dr. Slop's obstetric hand. For next to a man's nose, the squire held, with the old writers on his shelves, that a man's character and conduct all depend upon the name he happens to bear. Judas, do what he might, could have been only the traitor that he was; whereas Cæsar and Alexander conquered the world quite as much by the magic of their names as by their valor. *Jack, Dick,* and *Tom,* "like equal forces acting against each other in contrary directions," he also often affirmed, were neutral or indifferent names, numbering since the world began as many knaves and fools as wise and good men. It had been his intention to call his son *George* or *Edward,* which, though not the best names, stood rather high in his estimation as the titles of kings and princes. But to offset the broken nose, it was now necessary to choose the most potent name in his repertory, else his son would grow into a driveller and goose-cap. And so he resolved to christen him after Trismegistus, "the greatest of all earthly beings," whether considered as king, lawyer, philosopher, or priest, for he was all of them and more too.

But wisest fate said no. In the depth of night, while Mr. Shandy lay quietly sleeping, he was awakened by Susannah, who had come to tell him that his son was in convulsions near to the point of death, that Parson Yorick could nowhere be found to baptize him, but that his curate was already in the dressing-room, holding the child upon his arm, black as the ace of spades, and waiting for the name.

* See "the fair of noses" in Ozell's *Rabelais*, I, 317.

"TRISMEGISTUS, said Mr. Shandy, and Susannah ran along the gallery with the name to her mistress's room.

" 'Tis *Tris*——something, cried *Susannah*——There is no christian-name in the world, said the curate, beginning with *Tris*——but *Tristram*. Then 'tis *Tristram-gistus*, quoth *Susannah*.

"——There is no *gistus* to it noodle!——'tis my own name, replied the curate, dipping his hand, as he spoke, into the bason——*Tristram!* said he, &c. &c. &c. &c., so *Tristram* was I called, and *Tristram* shall I be to the day of my death."

"Of all names in the universe," Mr. Shandy "had the most unconquerable aversion for *Tristram*." It is a name, he would say, so low and contemptible that it "could possibly produce nothing *in rerum natura* but what was extremely mean and pitiful." Who, he used to ask (ignorant of the Tristram of romance), ever read or heard tell of "a man called *Tristram,* performing anything great or worth recording? No. . . . The thing is impossible." The next morning Mr. Shandy, as he was making tea with my uncle Toby, heard how Susannah and the curate lost *Trismegistus* between them; took down his hat from the peg, and walked away to meditate alone upon the final stroke of fortune.

There was, however, still one ray of hope, which Yorick, who was summoned for his advice, pointed out to the disconsolate father. Perhaps Tristram's name might be changed. At any rate they would all—Mr. Yorick and the two Shandys—attend the next Visitation Dinner at York and lay the matter before the eminent advocates and divines learned in ecclesiastical law. The dinner threatened to break up in hubbub before coming to the question at all; for by some accident a hot chestnut was dropped or poked into the breeches of Phutatorius, who accused Yorick of maliciously placing it there. The riot over the chestnut, however, soon subsided; and Didius, the great church-lawyer, brought forward Tristram's baptism for discussion. Mr. Shandy sat and listened to various amusing baptismal stories, learning, in the course of the evening, what made a baptism null and what made it valid in the period before the Reformation, and that in special cases, like the Duchess of Suffolk's, it had been adjudged by the highest courts that the mother may not be of kin to her child. The company at length broke up without determining the cause presented to them. Still, Mr. Shandy felt paid for his visit to the dinner, for never before had his brain been so tickled by the subtleties of dialectic wit. After the York dinner, the narrative quickly terminated with an account of the squire's project for enclosing the great Ox-moor, followed by the timely death of his eldest son Bobby, making Tristram thereby heir-apparent to the Shandy family.

The new instalment of *Tristram Shandy* had many correspondences with the performance of the previous year. In both were the same or similar freaks of structure and style. As before, real and fictitious documents were introduced so cleverly that it was hard for the reader to determine the character of the one or the other. Latin and English stared at each other on opposite pages, as in Pope's *Imitations of Horace*. In the fourth volume a chapter was dropped out and the pagination tampered with. The preface was again thrust in as an intermediate chapter; and a marbled page, which should have been the ornamental lining to a cover, was transferred to the body of the book, as an emblem of its motley character.

Local satire and allusion still abounded, though it has now become extremely difficult to uncover most of it. Philip Harland's experiments in farming were gently ridiculed in Mr. Shandy's trouble with the Ox-moor; and from first to last Dr. Burton was crucified to the delight of his enemies. The Visitation Dinner was clearly a reminiscence of that turbulent dinner of the York chapter back in 1751 at George Woodhouse's, when Sterne and the Dean of York confronted Dr. Topham of the prerogative court and silenced him. Doubtless the portraits of several officials and clergymen present on that occasion were once recognizable under the Rabelaisian names that Sterne gave them, like Agelastes, who never laughed at a joke, and Somnolentus, who always slept through one. Dr. Topham surely appeared as Didius and shifted into Phutatorius before the dinner was over; and the hot chestnut which Yorick picked up from the floor after it had traversed the breeches of Phutatorius, not as an insult, but because he thought "a good chestnut worth stooping for," was a ludicrous version of the old controversy over the commissaryship which Dr. Topham first resigned all right to, and afterwards claimed as his own when Sterne was willing to take it. And finally, the story of Tristram's christening may well have been a rendering of a local anecdote over the blunders of curates and sponsors at baptisms, with which the armory of clerical jest had long been filled. Perhaps something like it had occurred in one of Sterne's own parishes.——"Name this child," once said a clergyman at the critical point in a baptism. "Zulphur," responded the godfather. "That," said the clergyman, "is not a name." "Sulphur ——Sulphur"——was the only result of another trial to get at the name, and the priest smiled. "He means Zilpah, Leah's handmaid," suggested the clerk, and the child escaped a worse fate than Tristram's.*

It was Sterne's own opinion that the new volumes surpassed the old "in laughable humour," while they contained "an equal degree of Cervantic satire." And he was right, except that his inspiration was not Cervantes so much as Rabelais. His genius was yet to develop in other ways, but in satire he had now reached high water. Never since Rabelais had "the lumber rooms of learning" been so thoroughly overhauled and the learned blockheads dragged out and subjected to so keen a ridicule as in the wordy controversies over the stranger's nose and the points that nullify or make valid a baptism. It may be that some of the satire was misplaced and out of date; but, speaking generally, the old scholastic method of warfare still survived in philosophy and religion. Mr. Shandy was certainly not the last logician to employ the hypothesis as if it carried with it a sort of magic potency. Nor were the Shandy brothers the last men who, while invariably associating different ideas with the same words, have attempted to converse and reason together.

* P. H. Ditchfield, *The Parish Clerk*, 268 (London, 1907).

Coming nearer home, Sterne waylaid and pommelled deliciously the connoisseurs in art and criticism; one of whom measured the angles of *Tristram Shandy* with rule and compass, and pronounced it out of all plumb; and another timed Garrick's pauses in Hamlet's soliloquy, without observing the actor's wonderful manner of bridging chasms with eye, attitude, and gesture, for he could not look away from the stopwatch in his hand, he said, if he was to count seconds and their fractions. The gentlemen on the *Monthly Review* and other magazines who had belabored Sterne for publishing sermons under the name of Mr. Yorick, were singled out for good-natured ridicule. They rumpled, cut, and slashed at Yorick's jerkin unmercifully, he told them; but they did not reach the sarcenet lining, and he still remained unharmed. And as he laid aside his pen, he drank a health to the bigwigs and long-beards who had admitted Yorick's wit but lamented his lack of discretion, asking them to relax a little from their gravity and try him once more. "True *Shandeism*," he assured them, "think what you will against it, opens the heart and lungs, and like all those affections which partake of its nature, it forces the blood and other vital fluids of the body to run freely through its channels, makes the wheel of life run long and chearfully round."

The third volume of *Tristram Shandy* was completed on the third day of August, and the fourth in November, after George the Third had begun his "propitious reign." Leaving his parish in charge of an assistant curate, Sterne went up to London alone the week before Christmas to watch his book through the press, which in advance of his coming had been advertised by Dodsley through the autumn in order to hedge off the spurious *Shandys* which were threatening the market. For following Sterne this winter, we have only a few letters to Stephen Croft relative to business with which the squire from time to time entrusted him. Sterne had several pictures copied for his friend, and purchased two prints for him, which, after being lent to Miss Gilbert, daughter of the Archbishop of York, who was at Twickenham with her father, were duly posted to Stillington Hall. He also sounded the war-office several times on the chance of promotion for Mr. Croft's son Stephen, who held a commission in the army. Fortunately, Sterne could not write on business without writing about himself and his book; so that much may be read in and out of these letters, if we can interpret the allusions and will heed the silences.

On reaching London, Sterne was in high spirits and at once plunged into society with the old zest. Much as last year, he could write after a month of it: "I never dined at home once since I arrived——am fourteen dinners deep engaged just now, and fear matters will be worse with me in that point than better." But beyond the dinners, no two London seasons were ever alike for Sterne. Old friends and old enemies were absent from town or they no longer regarded him, and new ones appeared to applaud or to abuse him. This year he was struck by the great changes that had taken place in "the looks and political reasoning" of the coffee-houses and all the companies he attended. The nation, he found to his surprise, was divided over the German war (as it was called) into two hostile camps, which he humorously called "Prussians and Anti-Prussians, Butes and Anti-Butes," breaking up the old distinction between Whig and Tory. The winter before it was nothing but Pitt, and none dared question the conduct of the great war-minister. In the meantime the war in Germany had gone disastrously; the loss of life in the field had been terrible; Prince Ferdinand, the hero of a year ago, was calling for forty thousand more men, and for provisions, else his army would starve in a fortnight; officers who should have been with their regiments were loitering about St. James's Coffee-House and Hyde Park; corruption was rampant, and loud complaints were heard of Pitt's "making a trade of the war."

George the Second had died in October, and everybody, the visitor observed, was talking about the boy who had succeeded him. Sterne, like all the rest, closely watched the youth's habits and his policy of peace as it unfolded during the winter. It was a novel sight for him to see on the throne a young man

of energy, determined to be a king after the type set forth by
Lord Bolingbroke in his *Patriot King*. "The King seems resolved," Sterne wrote to his friends at Stillington, "to bring
all things back to their original principles, and to stop the tor-
rent of corruption and laziness. . . . The present system being to remove that phalanx of great people, which stood betwixt the throne and the subjects, and suffer them to have
immediate access without the intervention of a cabal——(this
is the language of others): however, the King gives everything
himself, knows everything, and weighs everything maturely,
and then is inflexible——this puts old stagers off their game
——how it will end we are all in the dark."

An admirer of Pitt, Sterne had come to London as a Prus-
sian, but he could not hold out against the strong sentiment
towards peace and a king who was fast winning the hearts of
his people by granting them free access to the palace, and by
appearing among them at the theatre and elsewhere. Sterne
on one occasion sat in the gallery of the House of Commons
through an entire day, waiting for the appearance of Pitt to
throw down the gauntlet in defence of the German war; but
"a political fit of the gout seized the great combatant and he
entered not the lists." Instead of the expected speech, Sterne
listened to a long and passionate debate, which began and ended
with incoherent abuse of all who were crying for peace. A
month later, he recorded the break-up of the ministry and the
humiliation of Pitt, though his fall was not yet. "The court is
turning topsy-turvy," he wrote to Croft, "Lord Bute, le premier——Lord Talbot, to be groom of the chambers in room
of the Duke of Rutland——Lord Halifax to Ireland——Sir
Francis Dashwood in Talbot's place——Pitt seems unmoved
——a peace inevitable——Stocks rise——the peers this moment kissing hands, &c. &c. (this week may be christened the
kiss-hands week) for a hundred changes will happen in consequence of these. . . . Pray, when you have read this, send the
news to Mrs. Sterne."

Just as the peers were kissing hands, an odd rumor was set
going by Sterne's enemies at York that George the Third had

forbidden him the Court. He wrote back that Charles Townshend and other friends were very merry over the report, and
assured him that he need fear "no accident of that kind." He
continued to attend, we may be sure, the king's levees, and in
February he was invited to the "grand assembly" of Lady
Northumberland, soon to be appointed to her Majesty's bed-
chamber. The only place where Sterne was not a welcome
guest seems to have been the house of Warburton in Grosvenor
Square. The bishop professed to have heard from Garrick and
Berenger certain stories about "our heteroclite parson" that
disabled him from appearing longer "as his friend and well-
wisher."* With many of the king's favorites who entered
the new ministry or were seen most about the Court, Sterne
claimed acquaintance, and with some of them he was in easy
social relations. Charles Townshend's appointment as Secretary
of War he announced to Stephen Croft a month in advance.
If he lost Warburton, he gained in his place John, Viscount
Spencer, one of the new peers. This most agreeable nobleman
sent him a silver standish, invited him to Wimbleton, and in
all ways befriended him as a patron should. It was a close
friendship that continued to the end. Lord Spencer, however,
was not a man to exert any restraint upon Sterne's conduct;
while Warburton, humbug as he was, did care for the conventions of the cloth and tried to keep Sterne within their
bounds.

Warburton's influence gone, Sterne soon drifted with the
tide of fashion and social dissipation. In running through the
list of the king's friends, one is amazed to find there, John
Wilkes excepted, the leading Monks of the disbanded Medmenham Abbey and other men whose lives were equally notorious. Sir Francis Dashwood, treasurer of the Chambers, and
subsequently Chancellor of the Exchequer, was the founder of
the profligate order; and a former member, George Bubb
Dodington, who still kept up a semblance of the brotherhood

* See Warburton's letters to Garrick dated June 16 and June 26,
1760, in *Private Correspondence of David Garrick*, 117-118 (London,
1831).

at his Hammersmith villa, was created Baron Melcombe of Melcombe Regis. Sterne made the acquaintance of Wilkes the year before, and now fell in with his compeers. One morning he breakfasted with Robert Vansittart, recorder of Monmouth,—the Monk who brought to the abbey the baboon to which Sir Francis was wont to adminster the eucharist. Sterne's name was also associated by John Croft with a pair of wits of the same general stamp—Samuel Foote, the clever actor and playwright, and Francis Blake Delaval, an amateur actor, then a member of Parliament for Andover. Foote, who had just produced the *Minor* at the Haymarket, was at the height of his popularity, and Delaval was soon to be created a Knight of the Bath. About the two men, who were inseparable, many scandalous stories were in circulation. With no danger of a break in their friendship, Delaval married Foote's mistress. Ten years after Sterne first knew them, Delaval was found one morning dead on the floor of his room, with an empty bottle of usquebaugh lying by his side. "It is therefore supposed," said the newspapers naïvely in recording the sudden death, "that he had got up in the night to get something to drink." No doubt it would have been better for Sterne and some aspects of his art, had he never known and associated with these men or their like; but it is just, as well as charitable, to suppose that he was drawn to them, not by their immorality, in which there is no evidence of his sharing, but by their extraordinary wit and good fellowship—qualities which attracted even Dr. Johnson to Vansittart. They were the fine gentlemen of the period.

Amid the earlier engagements of the season, Sterne had the proofs of his book to revise in the morning. It was his custom to make minor changes at the last moment, "pricking in the lights," so to speak, in modern phrase. This year there was some question about Slawkenbergius on noses, which, a reader will observe, is so placed that it could be cut out with a little readjustment of the text before or after the tale. Stephen Croft, who had acted as Sterne's adviser during the period of composition, objected to Slawkenbergius, probably on the ground that as a story it ran upon an equivocation too long drawn out to pass muster. Twice he remonstrated with Sterne by letter after the author had reached London. From Sterne's first reply, it seems quite likely that he met his friend's objection by shifting the emphasis of the episode from equivocation to a satire on misplaced and futile learning. Be this as it may, Sterne had decided to let Slawkenbergius stand, for his friends in London had read the manuscript and approved. In high spirits he then wrote to Stephen Croft: "As to the main points in view, at which you hint——all I can say is, that I see my way, and unless Old Nick throws the dice——shall, in due time, come off the winner,——Tristram will be out the twentieth——there is a great rout made about him before he enters the stage——whether this will be of use or no, I can't say——some wits of the first magnitude here, both as to wit and station, engage me success——time will shew."

Heralded by wits and coffee-houses, the second instalment of *The Life and Opinions of Tristram Shandy, Gentleman,* comprising the third and fourth volumes of the work, issued from Dodsley's press—a week later than the author had expected—on Wednesday the twenty-eighth of January, 1761, in company with a new edition of the first two volumes. It contained, as if to frighten away over-violent criticism, compliments to Reynolds as an easy and graceful painter, and to "my dear friend *Garrick,* whom I have so much cause to esteem and honour." Pitt was alluded to in the "statesman turning the political wheel . . . against the stream of corruption"; and Mr. Shandy spoke of the glory and honor surrounding the names of the young king and the Duke of York, of whom the latter had noticed Sterne the preceding May. On the other hand, Warburton was dealt a covert thrust in the reference to a bishop who complained of being splashed by Yorick's horse. Hogarth and Ravenet his engraver were again called in for a frontispiece, representing the scene in Mrs. Shandy's dressing-room the moment after Yorick's curate had christened Tristram by the wrong name. The *London Magazine,* then the semi-official organ of the ministry, very properly inserted a congratulatory note in its January issue, saying: "At length the *real*, the inimitable Shandy, again makes his appearance, and all the host of impotent cricticks and imitators look aghast, at his superior genius. Whoever of our readers have, with true relish read his former volumes, may be assured that their perusal of the third and fourth will not be attended with less delight."

But Sterne's friends among the great availed not with the professional critics, or with a large section of the public. Horace Walpole, writing to a Yorkshire parson early in March, observed by the way: "The second and third volumes of *Tristram Shandy*, the dregs of nonsense, have universally met the contempt they deserve: genius may be exhausted;——I see that folly's invention may be so too."* Outside the *London Magazine*, the author and his book were everywhere denounced in print. The *Monthly Review*, for example, in its March number, apologized for all that it had ever said in favor of the first volumes, and then proceeded to read Sterne a lecture on the proprieties and the art of writing one's self out. The publication of a book like *Tristram Shandy*, Sterne was told, might be only venial in a Foote, who professed to write nothing but farces, but no act could be more reprehensible in a dignitary of the Church. "Do for shame, Mr. Shandy, hide your jerkin, or, at least, send the lining to the scowerer's." "But your indiscretion, good Mr. Tristram," to go on with the address to Sterne, "is not all we complain of in the volumes now before us. We must tax you with what you will dread above the most terrible of all imputations—nothing less than DULLNESS. Yes, indeed, Mr. Tristram, you are dull, *very dull*. Your jaded fancy seems to have been exhausted by two pigmy octavos, which scarce contained the substance of a twelve-penny pamphlet. . . . Your characters are no longer striking and singular. We are sick of your uncle Toby's wound in his groin; we have had enough of his ravelines and breast-works: in short, we are quite tired with his *hobby horses;* and we can no longer bear with Corporal Trim's insipidity." Noth-

* *Letters*, edited by Toynbee, V, 32.

ing in the book entertained the reviewer, except Ernulf's "extraordinary anathema," which Sterne had purloined, it was charged, from some old newspaper or magazine.*

The *Critical Review* for April, though in the main milder in tone and appreciative here and there, likewise read Sterne a philosophical essay on the different kinds of humor, down to the bastard forms he was practising in imitation of Rabelais. Like his brother on the *Monthly Review*, this critic claimed that Sterne had lost his audience, but he explained it differently. There was really, in his view, no marked difference between Sterne's two performances. "One had merit," he said, "but was extolled above its value; the other has defects, but is too severely decried." Slawkenbergius's Tale, for instance, shows that Mr. Sterne can write Latin "with elegance and propriety," and in other places he displays "taste and erudition." The trouble has really been with the public, it was the reviewer's opinion, who, having once gorged itself with *Tristram Shandy*, could stand no more without "nausea and indigestion." "All novel readers," to quote him exactly, "from the stale maiden of quality to the snuff-taking chambermaid, devoured the first part with a most voracious swallow, and rejected the last with marks of loathing and aversion. We must not look for the reason of this difference in the medicine, but in the patient to which it was administered."

These outrageous attacks no one will take over-seriously, for their animus is too apparent for that. The offence that the reviewers took at the immoralities of *Tristram Shandy* was mere humbug, for their own magazines and newspapers spoke at times a more vulgar language than Sterne's at its worst. Sterne had chastised the reviewers because they censured him for publishing sermons under the name of Yorick, the king's

* The charge was unjust. The current translation of Ernulf's curse was the one, given with the Latin, in the *Harleian Miscellany*, VI, 493 *et seq* (London, 1745). The *Gentleman's Magazine* for September, 1745 (XV, 490), reprinted the translation. Sterne went to the *Harleian Miscellany* for the Latin and the translation, which he re-worked here and there for heightened phrase.

jester; and they were but repaying him in the same kind. There was not much more in it than this. If they had hitherto only rumpled his jerkin, they would show him that they could, when they wished, slash the lining. Sterne, as usual, professed indifference to them at first. Just as the storm was breaking over his head, he wrote to Stephen Croft: "One half of the town abuse my book as bitterly, as the other half cry it up to the skies——the best is, they abuse and buy it, and at such a rate, that we are going on with a second edition, as fast as possible." But when the storm rose to its fury, Sterne became excited also. "If my enemies knew," he then wrote again to Croft, "that by this rage of abuse and ill-will, they were effectually serving the interests both of myself, and works, they would be more quiet——but it has been the fate of my betters, who have found, that the way to fame, is like the way to heaven——through much tribulation——and till I shall have the honour to be as much maltreated as Rabelais and Swift were, I must continue humble; for I have not filled up the measure of half their persecutions."

For many readers Sterne's wit had no doubt lost its freshness, but so far as one can see, there was no immediate decline, as his enemies would have it, in the sale of *Shandy*, of which the second edition of the new instalment appeared on the twenty-first of May. Sterne was still the vogue as much as ever, only in a different set. "Where I had one friend," he said, "last year to do me honour, I have three now." And every new friend, it is implied, meant a new reader. In March his fine portrait by Reynolds was placed on public exhibition by the Society of Artists. As last year, the garreteers accompanied his progress with books and pamphlets, of which the most pretentious was *The Life and Opinions of Bertram Montfichet,* a faithful and humble copy of Sterne's first instalment down to the Greek motto, paper, print, size and number of volumes, with an uncle Dick for my uncle Toby. The author of *Explanatory Remarks upon Tristram Shandy* found an audience for a second part in continuation; and another wit outdid Sterne's oddities by publishing *A Book without a Title-page.*

Tristram Shandy also gave his name to a new country-dance, to a soup and a salad which could be had at the coffee-houses, and to a game of cards "in which the knave of hearts, if hearts are trumps, is supreme, and nothing can resist his power."

From the jests of scribblers, the transition is most abrupt to the last sight we get of Sterne in London for this year. *Lloyd's Evening Post* for Monday, the fourth of May, contained the following news-item:

"Yesterday morning a charity sermon was preached at the Chapel, belonging to the Foundling Hospital for the support of the children maintained and educated in the said hospital, by the Rev. Mr. Sterne, to a numerous audience, several of whom were persons of distinction, and a handsome collection was made for the further support of that charity."

This was Sterne's first and only appearance in a London pulpit. The Foundling Hospital, situated in Guilford street, was then a fashionable charity numbering among its numerous patrons many of the nobility. Peers, it is said, had stood as godfathers to deserted children in the Chapel of St. Andrew's, where Sterne officiated; Handel had frequently performed there, and on the walls hung portraits and other paintings by Hogarth, Reynolds, and their contemporaries, as gifts to the foundation. For several years the hospital had been scandalously mismanaged, and the last Parliament had revised its charter. It was a tribute to Sterne's popularity, if nothing more, for the new board of governors to turn to him as a preacher who would attract a large and generous congregation. It so happened that the new treasurer, George Whatley— known in America for his association and correspondence with Franklin—was acquainted with Yorick; and to him accordingly fell the duty of inviting "Dr. Sterne," as he was sometimes called, to take the annual charity sermon. After repeated promises, Sterne fixed the Sunday in a characteristic note, dated March 25, 1761, which he sent over to Whatley's lodgings in Lothbury:

"On April the fifth, 1761, and sure as the day comes, and as sure as the Foundling Hospital stands, will I——(that is, in case I stand myself) discharge my conscience of my promise in giving you, not a half hour (not a poor half hour), for I never could preach so long without fatiguing both myself and my flock to death——but I will give you a short sermon, and flap you in my turn:—preaching (you must know) is a theologic flap upon the heart, as the dunning for a promise is a political flap upon the memory:——both the one and the other is useless where men have *wit enough* to be honest. This makes for my hypothesis of wit and judgment. I believe you to have both in a great degree, and therefore I am, with great esteem and truth, your's,

"Laurence Sterne.

"P.S. I will take care to be walking under some colonnade, in or about the Hospital, about a quarter before eleven."*

But Sterne did not tread the round of the hospital colonnades on that Sunday morning in April, owing either to ill health or to social engagements. It took still another month to bring him up to the sticking-point; and then he appeared on the first Sunday of May, his coming announced by the newspapers. The politicians, wits, and men of fashion with whom Sterne had intimately associated for four months, one may be certain, came to see how the author of *Tristram Shandy* would conduct himself in his clerical gown. Yorick took for his theme the parable of the Rich Man and Lazarus, on the text "If they hear not Moses and the prophets, neither will they be persuaded, though one should rise from the dead." It was a sermon of attitudes, pauses, and paradoxes, which must have amused here and there his friends looking for Shandean eccentricity. The preacher put an imaginary speech into the mouth of a messenger from heaven calling upon his hearers to part with the vices that bring only death and misery to their doors, and addressed the Almighty directly on the distinctions be-

* This letter, from the original in possession of J. T. Rutt, was published in the *Monthly Repository of Theology and General Literature* for August, 1806. In the issue for the preceding March, Rutt gave an account of George Whatley.

tween the rich and the poor, asking Him what they all meant, and then answering the question himself in the assurance that each man's case shall sometime be reconsidered by a just God, as the Rich Man of the parable found out to his pain. By the way Sterne admonished his "dear auditers" against "the treachery of the senses," and exhorted them "to be temperate and chaste, and just and peaceable, and charitable and kind to one another." At times the orator rose to a degree of pathetic eloquence, as in his appeal for alms "in behalf of those who know not how to ask it for themselves." In closing, his voice became husky; and his audience should have wept in response to his final invitation for tears.

It was not a great sermon; indeed, it hardly equalled the one Sterne preached before the charity schools of York in the days of his obscurity; but it was in a measure successful. The treasurer of the hospital reported to the managers a contribution amounting to fifty-five pounds, nine shillings, and two pence.*

*The minutes of the Foundling Hospital contain two entries with reference to the sermon. On Wednesday, April 29, it was ordered:

"That a paragraph be inserted in the Daily Papers that a Charity Sermon will be preached in the Chapel of this Hospital on Sunday next by the Revd. Mr. Sterne."

The paragraph appeared in the *Public Advertiser* of Saturday, May 2. On Wednesday, May 6, the entry reads:

"The Treasurer reported that the Collection at the Anthem in the Chapel last Sunday, amounted to £55. 9. 2."

Shandy Hall Continued. Tristram Shandy: Volumes V and VI. June, 1761—January, 1762

IT was well on in June before Sterne took his seat in the coach for York. On the road between Stilton and Stamford, he got a fright, if we are to interpret *Shandy* literally, at the reckless driving of the postillion down a three-mile slope; and, thrusting his head out of the window, he vowed to "the great God of day" that he would lock up his study door the moment he reached home and throw the key into his draw-well at the back of Shandy Hall. Merely stopping at York, he hurried on to his family at Coxwold. During the first weeks after his arrival he was, in contrast with the summer before, ill at ease in his parish. "The transition from rapid motion to absolute rest," he complained in a letter to Hall-Stevenson, then in London, "was too violent.——I should have walked about the streets of York ten days, as a proper medium to have passed through, before I entered upon my rest.——I staid but a moment, and I have been here but a few, to satisfy me I have not managed my miseries like a wise man." The weather, too, was "cold and churlish" on the moors, as if it were "bleak December." His wife, piqued perhaps, as she had a right to be, at his long absence, received him coolly, declaring herself happier without him. "O Lord!" he cried out half-seriously in his desolation, "O Lord! now are you going to Ranelagh to-night, and I am sitting, sorrowful as the prophet was, when the voice cried out to him and said, 'What dost thou here, Elijah?'—— 'Tis well the spirit does not make the same at Coxwould—— for unless for the few sheep left me to take care of, in this wilderness, I might as well, nay better, be at Mecca."

The mood of discontent, not quite genuine, quickly passed. Husband and wife came to an understanding, and Sterne resumed his parish duties with unwonted zeal, preaching regularly every Sunday. This year or the preceding, the parson received, it used to be said at Coxwold, a summons to the death-bed of a poor widow on the outskirts of his parish; and after administering to her the last sacrament, he enquired what she intended to leave him in her will for his trouble. "Alas! Sir," answered the distressed woman, "I am too wretched to give a legacy even to my own relations." "That excuse," replied Yorick, "shall not serve me. I insist upon inheriting your two children, and, in grateful return for the bequest, I will take such care of them that they shall feel as little as possible the loss of an affectionate and worthy mother." "The expiring parent," concludes the anecdote, "at once comforted and surprised, assented; and Sterne religiously kept his promise." Whether the incident be true or not, it is interesting to get this traditional view of Sterne's kindness to his parishioners.*

Sometime during the summer, he drew up a plan for re-seating his church, in the manner of a cathedral, that there might be "better sound" and "better light." The plan was submitted to Richard Chapman, the steward of Newburgh Priory, who sent it, with detailed comments, to Lord Fauconberg, then in London, for approval. On the day of the king's coronation, the twenty-second of September, Sterne entertained his entire parish and all the countryside. The story of it was told by Mr. Chapman in his letter to the Earl of Fauconberg under date of September the twenty-fifth:

"I am extremely obliged to your lordship for the coronation news, and am glad your lordship got excused from attending, which might have been of bad consequence. Here a fine ox with his horns gilt was roasted whole in the middle of the town, after which the bells put in for church, where an excellent sermon was delivered extempory on the occasion by Mr. Sterne, and gave great content to every hearer. The church was quite full, both quire and aisle, to the very door. The text, &c., you will see both in the London and York pa-

* Yorkshire *Notes and Queries*, June, 1904. Sterne probably placed the children in one of the York schools for the maintenance and education of poor children.

pers. About three o'clock the ox was cut up and distributed amongst at least three thousand people, after which two barrels of ale was distributed amongst those that could get nearest to 'em. Ringing of bells, squibs and crackers, tar-barrels and bonfires, &c., and a ball in the evening, concluded the joyful day."*

Sterne paid for the ox and perhaps for the ale out of his own pocket. His extemporary sermon, which had been carefully written out, dealt historically with the Church in England under Divine Providence, from the time God sent the Romans into Britain to open a pathway for the Gospel, and *"then put his hook into their nostrils* and led these wild beasts of prey back again into their own land," down through the dark days of Popery to the Reformation, and on to the final deliverance of the kingdom from "the arts of Jesuitry" in the reign just ended. In conclusion the preacher exhorted his hearers to be loyal to King George the Third, and to live pure and sinless lives, that "the great and mighty God" might never have reason for withdrawing his mercies from the chosen people.

Earlier in the summer there had been some delay in beginning *Shandy* again. In July Sterne bought "seven hundred books at a purchase dog cheap," in consequence of which his study was topsy-turvy for a week before he could get them set up. He seems to have been thinking, too, of further preferment in the Church, for he wrote a *clerum,* or the Latin oration preliminary to the degree of Doctor of Divinity; but he went no further, owing, it may be surmised, to the death in August of the Archbishop of York. Dr. Gilbert and his daughter, who, it is said, really ruled the diocese, were both most friendly to Sterne. The new archbishop, Robert Hays Drummond, who was translated from Salisbury, also proved to be well disposed to him, but the election was not yet, and the favor of the new archbishop could not yet be counted on to assist him to a Cambridge degree. Once started, Sterne went

* *Report on Manuscripts in Various Collections . . . presented to Parliament by Command of his Majesty,* II, 188-189 (London, 1903).

on with *Shandy* with more than his usual pace. On the tenth of August he arrived at the story of Tristram's accident; by the first of September he was already in the fifth book; and by the close of October he may have been at the end. For nearly three months he worked steadily, amid the quiet of domestic scenes such as were never to return to him at Shandy Hall. Just as the conclusion was in sight, he wrote to a friend who had sent him belated congratulations on his appointment to Coxwold by the Earl of Fauconberg: "My new habitation . . . is within a mile of his Lordship's seat and park. 'Tis a very agreeable ride out in the chaise I purchased for my wife. ——Lyd has a pony which she delights in.——Whilst they take these diversions, I am scribbling away at my Tristram. These two volumes are, I think, the best.——I shall write as long as I live, 'tis, in fact, my hobby-horse; and so much am I delighted with my uncle Toby's imaginary character, that I am become an enthusiast.——My Lydia helps to copy for me——and my wife knits, and listens as I read her chapters."

At the outset of his work, Sterne was uncertain, any reader may see, as to the course his story was to run. Rabelais still rested at his elbow for hints, and Burton's *Anatomy*, I fear, lay wide open in front of him. Relying too much upon them and other books to awaken his fancy, he did not start out well in his first chapter, which opened with a riddle and closed with direct appropriations from Burton on "the relicks of learning" and on man as "the *miracle* of nature." The fragment on whiskers, which followed, was an elaborate *double entendre*, likewise pieced out of Burton, with the aid of the article on Margaret of Valois in Bayle's *Dictionary*, perhaps one of his seven hundred new books from London. The episode was skilfully stitched together, to be sure; but it was after all only a *double entendre*, without the brilliant satirical coloring of the chapter on noses, which it was intended to duplicate. From the old conversations in the parlor of Shandy Hall, Dr. Slop dropped out, except as he waddled through on his way to bind up Tristram's wound and to quarrel with Susannah. With Dr. Slop gone and Yorick put into his place, the butt of Sterne's satire went also. In consequence of this, the narrative moved on heavily for some pages through Mr. Shandy's philosophical lament over the death of Bobby, which came straight out of Burton.

Matters began to mend, however, when Sterne reached the story of Tristram's accident in the sashed window, which is one of Sterne's best anecdotes of that kind. All of Mr. Shandy's carefully laid plans for his son's physical welfare having now miscarried, through successive blunders of physician, curate, and housemaid, nothing remained for him but to try a new system of education upon Tristram, in the hope of making a prodigy of him. To this end he wrote a *Tristra-pædia* in rivalry with Xenophon's *Cyropædia*, descriptive of the training which Cyrus the Great was supposed to pass through to the rule of the East. With excellent ridicule, Sterne passed in review a young man's career at school and university, as exemplified in his own experience, out to the theory, in burlesque of Obadiah Walker on education, that a short cut to knowledge—a Northwest Passage, so to speak,— might be opened through skilful practice in manipulating the auxiliary verbs. That scheme for the quick multiplication of ideas pleased Corporal Trim and my uncle Toby also, for some of the bravest men, they said, that they had ever fought by the side of in the Low Countries, were auxiliaries.

Still, in spite of many good things, Sterne knew instinctively that he could not continue longer on the oddities of Mr. Shandy, and escape the danger of writing himself out, as his critics intimated that he had done already. He therefore passed to the kitchen of Shandy Hall and over to my uncle Toby's bowling green for a set of characters not yet so far exhausted. Sterne's wit was always whimsical, but he never rendered the supreme charm and delicacy possible to the whim until he placed my uncle Toby before his toy fortifications on the bowling green, gazette in hand, giving Corporal Trim directions for attacking and winning the last town that Marlborough had entered in triumph. "When the *chamade* was beat, and the corporal helped my uncle up it, and followed with

the colours in his hand, to fix them upon the ramparts——
Heaven! Earth! Sea!——but what avails apostrophes?——
with all your elements, wet or dry, ye never compounded so
intoxicating a draught."

Sterne had employed gesture, too, in the delineation of character, beyond the skill of most humorists; but he never attained
to the full scope and meaning of it until he let the corporal
discourse on life and death, standing amid a motley group in
the kitchen, who had just heard that Master Bobby would
never return from his travels:

" 'Are we not here now,' continued the corporal, (striking
the end of his stick perpendicularly upon the floor, so as to
give an idea of health and stability)——. . . 'and are we
not'——(dropping his hat plumb upon the ground—and paus-
ing, before he pronounced the word)——'gone! in a moment?' The descent of the hat was as if a heavy lump of clay
had been kneaded into the crown of it.——Nothing could
have expressed the sentiment of mortality, of which it was the
type and fore-runner, like it,——his hand seemed to vanish
from under it,——it fell dead,——the corporal's eye fixed
upon it, as upon a corps,——and *Susannah* burst into a flood
of tears."

Sterne was a sentimentalist, readers of this memoir need
hardly be told, from the time he took hartshorn to bear up
against the absence of Miss Lumley; but outside of some of
his sermons, his pathos had been kept well in abeyance except
for an occasional passage, like my uncle Toby's fly or the death
of poor Yorick. He was now reworking the old vein and refining it to pure gold. No humor could be gentler and more
winning than Trim's catechism, or my uncle Toby's lament
over the Peace of Utrecht, or the story of Le Fever, a poor
lieutenant, like Sterne's own father, who fell ill on the way
to join his regiment in Flanders and lay near death at the
village inn. My uncle Toby, though Le Fever was a stranger
to him, felt so keenly for the distress of a brother officer that
he could not sleep o'nights or bear for a moment the thought

of his dying. One evening, as Trim was putting his master to bed, he told him that it was all over with the poor soul, who would never march again, but must surely die. "He will march; said my uncle *Toby*, rising up from the side of the bed, with one shoe off: . . . marching the foot which had a shoe on, though without advancing an inch,——he shall march to his regiment. . . . He shall not die, by G——, cried my uncle *Toby*."

"The Accusing Spirit," Sterne commented famously, "which flew up to heaven's chancery with the oath, blush'd as he gave it in;——and the Recording Angel, as he wrote it down, dropp'd a tear upon the word, and blotted it out for ever."

The better part of these volumes was thus written under the clear and full inspiration of Sterne's genius. "Ask my pen," he says, why I write these details about Le Fever and my uncle Toby,——"it governs me——I govern not it." True, he has been accused of stealing my uncle Toby's oath, but I can not run down the theft, and think some mistake has been made about it. Certain parallels or analogies to it lie embedded in the so-called *exempla* of mediæval divines and moralists, but the search leads no further. Richard Rolle of Hampole, a hermit and author of the fourteenth century, for example, tells the story of a canon who was to be damned, it was supposed, because of imperfect repentance. A scholar wrote down his sins and gave the record of them to the abbot, who found them all blotted out, and the parchment as white and clean as if ink had never defiled it. Sterne's idea lay in this and other *exempla*, some of which he had met with in his reading; but he alone knew how to render it with humor and sentiment.

In the quiet and chastened humor that ruled Sterne while playing with pathos, his old enemies on the reviews escaped the usual long tirades. They were nevertheless not quite forgotten here and there. Sterne likened them, in beginning his sixth book, to a line of uncurried and forlorn jackasses, who viewed and *re*viewed him as he was passing over the rivulet of a little valley; "and when we climbed over that hill, and were just getting out of sight——good God! what a braying did they all set up together!" For the benefit of those who complained that they could not follow him through his digressions, he plotted the curves of his narrative, writing his own name beneath as the engraver. And for the moralists who feared contamination, he printed rows of stars in place of suppressed passages, and left one entire page blank, on which they might write what they pleased, to the end that his book should have at least one page "which MALICE will not blacken, and which IGNORANCE cannot misrepresent." Expressive of his general aim, he placed at the head of each volume, beneath the usual title, two Latin quotations (afterwards increased to three), one from Horace and one from Erasmus, taken not from the originals, but as he found them slightly changed in the *Anatomy of Melancholy*.* Speaking with Erasmus through Burton, he asked that his readers distinguish between his character as clergyman and his rôle as jester. "If any one," to paraphrase the Latin, "objects that my book is too light and fantastic for a divine or too satirical for a Christian, let him remember that 'tis not I but Democritus who has spoken." While the book was in making, Sterne sent a draft of the story of Le Fever (as far as the second paragraph of the thirteenth chapter) to Lady Spencer, with comments thereon in his own hand, as a step towards inscribing that part of his work to her Ladyship, and the two volumes as a whole to her husband, John, Lord Viscount Spencer.

In anticipation of Sterne's coming to London to superintend the publication of his book, the scribblers, expecting something of the old order, had been unusually busy. Not without wit—coarse, it is true—was a shilling pamphlet which appeared late in October under the title: *A Funeral Discourse occasioned by the much lamented Death of Mr. Yorick, Prebendary of Y * * k, . . . preached before a very mixed Society of Jemmies, Jessamies, Methodists and Christians, at a Nocturnal*

* *Anatomy of Melancholy*, edited by A. R. Shilleto, I, 138 (London, 1903).

Meeting in Petticoat Lane, on a text to be found in "the first chapter of the Gospel of the Jemmies, otherwise called the *Life and Opinions of Tristram Shandy*, at the words: Alas Poor Yorick!" The preacher told his congregation that the report current that Mr. Sterne was now living and writing the fifth and sixth volumes of *Shandy* was false. It is barely possible, he added in explanation of his jest, that the animal Sterne may still be alive, but the spiritual Sterne, all his wit and fancy, died with Slawkenbergius's Tale and passed into oblivion. The pamphlet was dedicated to "the Right Honourable, the Lord F——g and the very facetious Mr. Foote." In a footnote it was said with reference to Sterne's intimacy with Archbishop Gilbert, then dead a few months: "The late archbishop of York, Dr. G * * * * * t of leaden memory, used to say, that he was so delighted with the Life and Opinions of Tristram Shandy that he read them once every six weeks." At the heels of Yorick's *Funeral*, came *An Admonitory Letter addressed to the Rev. Mr. S——, . . . by a Layman*, in wild censure of Mr. Sterne's literary morals; and *The Life and Amours of Hafen Slawkenbergius*, purporting to be the tale which Yorick had half promised in his fourth volume but had left untold. It was intimated by the *Critical Review*, that Sterne bore a hand in some of these pamphlets, sending them forth, so to speak, as an advance guard to herald his approach.

Unaware of what awaited him, Sterne must have come up to London towards the end of November, a month before his custom; for the third instalment of *Tristram Shandy*—the fifth and sixth volumes—was advertised for Monday, December 21, 1761, though it bore the date of the new year. In this interval, while the author was correcting printers' blunders, occurred the only meeting, so far as is known, between Sterne and Dr. Johnson. "In a company where I lately was," the lexicographer is reported to have said to a group of friends, "Tristram Shandy introduced himself; and Tristram Shandy had scarcely sat down, when he informed us that he had been writing a Dedication to Lord Spencer; and *sponte suâ* he pulled it out of his pocket; and *sponte suâ*, for nobody desired him, he began to read it; and before he had read half a dozen lines, *sponte meâ,* sir, I told him it was not English, sir."* The scene of the encounter was at the house of Sir Joshua Reynolds. During the evening, it is said, Sterne displayed "a drawing too indecently gross to have delighted a brothel." Whereupon Dr. Johnson immediately left the room, and afterwards told Miss Reynolds that "he would rather give up the pleasure of her brother's society than meet such a contemptible priest as Sterne."† The lexicographer's criticism of Sterne's style, it has been supposed, was heeded; and thus by the irony of fate Dr. Johnson became, if not an actual corrector, at least a contributor to the good English of a man whom he despised. But Sterne, I fancy, let the dedication stand as it had been written, loose and ungrammatical as it was in structure from the Johnsonian point of view, and yet clear and beautiful to one who reads for the meaning and not to parse the sentences.

Sterne's early arrival in London was made imperative by the loss of his publisher. During the summer some misunderstanding had arisen between him and James Dodsley, the cause of which one can only conjecture, as no scrap of their correspondence over it is known to be extant. The last instalment of *Tristram Shandy,* after its first great run was over, had not sold well, for there had been no edition since the one in May. Perhaps Sterne, in his disappointment, laid the blame upon his publisher rather than upon the public. Moreover, Robert Dodsley, with whom Sterne had begun negotiations for the publication of the first volumes of his book, was now thoroughly out of the business, and was devoting himself to literature. His brother James was quite another man. Whatever may have been the reason, author and publisher parted company in October, when Sterne took the unusual course of advertising his fifth and sixth volumes in the London newspapers without a

* The *New Monthly Magazine and Universal Register,* December, 1818 (vol. X, p. 389).

† A note by Lady Phillipina Knight on the margin of a copy of the first edition of *Boswell's Life of Dr. Johnson* in the Library of Princeton University.

publisher's name. Not till well on in December did any of
these announcements bear the name of "T. Becket and P. A.
Dehondt," at the sign of Tully's Head in the Strand, to whom
Sterne transferred his patronage and remained faithful to the
last. Becket, however, did not immediately purchase the copyright. Four thousand sets were printed at Sterne's expense, and
the publisher was to sell them on commission.

Under the new management, the price of the set was reduced from five to four shillings, and advance copies were
widely distributed to the press without much direct advertising.
No great difficulty could have been encountered in matching
exactly Dodsley's paper and type, so that the new volumes
should present to the eye the same look as the old; indeed, they
appear to have had the same printer. But the change of publisher was attended with one inconvenience. Every season spurious works in danger of being thought Sterne's were placed
on the market by unscrupulous booksellers. Last January it was
The Life and Opinions of Bertram Montfichet. Now it was
another *Slawkenbergius,* which was timed to appear on the
same day with *Tristram Shandy,* as a sort of supplement to be
bound with it. Equally impudent was *The Life and Adventures of Christopher Wagstaffe, Gentleman,*—"a lively and
facetious imitation of Mr. Sterne's famous performance,"—
the hero of which claimed to be, in allusion to Sterne's plagiarisms from John Dunton, a grandfather of *Tristram Shandy.*
So long as Sterne's books carried the imprint of Dodsley, there
was no good reason for anybody's being deceived by the imitators and forgers; but the case was quite different when Becket
became his publisher. As a natural, though perhaps not quite
necessary, precaution, Sterne went through the labor of inscribing his name in each set, usually near the top of the first
page to the right, after the dedication to Lord Spencer. The
signature caused here and there a smile or jest, for the last author to make use of this device, it so happened, was "the ingenious Mrs. Constantia Phillips" of scandalous memory.

Critics and moralists who had been lying in wait to pounce
upon Sterne once more, were taken aback when they saw him

step forth in a new and unsuspected character. Some of them, to be sure, who did not read the volumes, fell into the old abusive tone. A week after their appearance, Warburton, for example, who could scarcely have seen them, fired his parting shot at Sterne in a letter from Prior-Park to his friend Richard Hurd, afterwards Bishop of Worcester:

"Sterne has published his fifth and sixth Volumes of Tristram. They are wrote pretty much like the first and second; but whether they will restore his reputation as a writer with the publick, is another question.——The fellow himself is an irrecoverable scoundrel."*

No one who read agreed with Warburton. Garrick and other friends told Sterne that his "thought of the accusing spirit flying up to heaven's chancery with the oath" was sublime. The *Admonitory Letter* to which I have referred was declared by Sterne's old enemy on the *Critical Review* to be "founded on misapprehension." The critic was compelled, as a matter of business, to point out Mr. Sterne's gross faults and obligations to Rabelais; but my uncle Toby's oath, though a conceit, must be pronounced "a conceit of genius." Even the *Monthly Review*,† so bitter last year and still bitter enough, found the new instalment superior to all the rest, and printed entire the death of Le Fever as showing wherein lay Mr. Sterne's great excellence. Indeed, the story of Le Fever, it has been said, was copied into all the magazines and newspapers of the kingdom. Though the statement is not quite true, it nevertheless circulated very widely in this way. The *London Chronicle* set the ball rolling in its issue of December 19-22, and subsequently gave the passage describing "Corporal Trim's Manner of Saying his Catechism." *St. James's Chronicle* for December 22-24 included quotations from it in an appreciation covering nearly three columns. And so we might go on to the *London Magazine* and the *Gentleman's Magazine* for

* *Letters from a Late Eminent Prelate to one of his Friends*, 335 (London, 1809).

† *Monthly Review*, February, 1762; *Critical Review*, April, 1762.

January, and to other periodicals of the winter which helped
to spread Sterne's good fame farther than it had yet gone.

Sterne had come to London, says his dedication to Lord
Spencer, in "bad health," which he attributed to hard writing,
combined with preaching through the summer. He was hardly
strong enough to carry on a flirtation whose incipient stages
seem to date from the preceding May or June. The object of
his sentimental regard was Mrs. Elizabeth Vesey, who lived
at Lucan near Dublin, but passed her winters in London without her husband. The time came, though it was not yet, when
everybody knew Mrs. Vesey, the famous Bluestocking, who
brought her husband over from Ireland, got him into Dr.
Johnson's club, and established for herself a coterie in rivalry
with Mrs. Montagu's. Her "spirit, wit, and vivacity" quickly
won Sterne's heart. To Mrs. Montagu, who introduced them,
he wrote: "In my life did I never see any thing—so truly
graceful as she is, nor had I an idea, 'till I saw her—that grace
could be so perfect in all its parts, and so suited to all the
higher ordinances of . . . life, from the superintending impulse of the mind." And to the "fair lady" who was known
to her friends as "The Sylph" because of her perfect grace
Sterne was writing a few weeks after he had first met her:
"Let me ask you, my dearest Mrs. V., what business you had
to come here from Ireland—or rather, what business you have
to go back again—the deuce take you with your musical and
other powers—could nothing serve you but you must turn
T. Shandy's head, as if it was not turn'd enough already: as
for turning my heart, I forgive you, as you have been so good
as to turn it towards so excellent and heavenly an object . . ."
He would give, he told her, the last rag of his priesthood for
a touch of her divine hand.

Sterne took Mrs. Vesey to Ranelagh, where they sauntered
alone through the rooms while the crowd was in the gardens;
and when too ill for that, he summoned a chair to convey him
to her "warm cabinet," that he might listen alone to her "gentle, amiable, elegant sentiments," delivered "in a tone of voice
that was originally intended for a Cherub." With Mrs. Mon-

tagu, they visited together the studio of Sir Joshua Reynolds, to whom Lord Bath was then sitting for his last portrait. Sir Joshua was having some trouble with the old man, who at first wanted to be painted "half standing." But Sterne persuaded him to sit down in his chair, and then with the ladies began to amuse him so as to take the pain out of his face.*

Over-exertion brought on the most severe hemorrhage Sterne had ever had. His friends advised him to take a long rest. For some time indeed he had been thinking of going abroad; but he could not quite see his way to it on account of the expense—unless he could find a bear to lead round Europe. His serious illness now settled the question for him. As France and England were still nominally at war, though the fighting had ended, Sterne could obtain no passport for his safety. Somewhat concerned, he appealed to Pitt, who gave him letters to members of the French ministry, behaving, says Sterne, "in every respect to me like a man of good breeding and good nature." The Archbishop of York "most humanely" granted him a leave of absence; Garrick lent him twenty pounds for "some unforeseen expenses," and towards the end of the second week in January, Sterne started across the Channel in a race with Death.

Uncertain who would win, Sterne made a will in favor of his wife and daughter, and placed in the hands of Mrs. Montagu for Mrs. Sterne's benefit a sort of advisory testament dated December 28, 1761. In these "Memorandums left with Mrs. Montagu, In case I should die abroad," Sterne tells his wife where she may find his manuscript sermons, letters, and *Political Romance* (in his bureau and trunk at Coxwold, in his garrets at York, and with Hall-Stevenson), how much Becket owes him, how much is due him on his livings, and in fine how much his estate is worth. She is advised to sell his library and have Garrick invest everything for her, as he has already promised to do, in Government securities. His real estate he valued at £1800. Had Sterne died then there would have been altogether for Mrs. Sterne about £3,000. While writing out

* Blunt, *Mrs. Montagu*, I, 14.

Dec: 25: 76. Memorandums left with Mrs. Mon-
=tague, In Case I should die abroad. L. Sterne

my Sermons in a Trunk at my friend
Mr. Halls St. John Street. — 2 Vols, to be picked
out of them — N.B. There are enough for 3
Vols. —

My Letters, in my Bureau at Coxwould
& a Bundle in the Trunk with my Sermons —

Note. The large piles of Letters in the Garrets
at York, to be sifted over, for in search for some
either of Wit, or Humor — or what is better
than both — of Humanity & good nature — these
will make a couple of Vols! more — and as not one
of 'em was ever wrote, like Popes or Voitures
to be printed, they are more likely to be
read — if there wants aught to serve the
Completion of a 3d Volume, — the Political Romance
I wrote wch was never publish'd — may be
added to the fag end of the Vols! . . Tho
I have 2 Reasons why I wish it may not
be wanted — first, an undeserved compli=
=ment to One, whom I have since found to
be a very corrupt man. — I never knew
him weak & ignorant — but thought him ho-
=nest .   The other reason is

Reduced facsimile of a page of the Memorandums
left with Mrs. Elizabeth Montagu

what might be his last words to his wife, he dropped two tears on the paper and, with his mind on another world, assured her that "we shall meet again."

Nobody expected that Sterne would live through the winter. The first intelligence of him that came back from France was the following item in the *London Chronicle* under date of February 2-4:

"Private Letters from Paris bring an account of the death of the Rev. Mr. Sterne, author of Tristram Shandy."

The sad news passed on from one newspaper to another, with occasional comment by correspondents. No sooner was Sterne supposed to be dead than all his faults were forgotten against him in the vivid impression left by his last beautiful volumes. An old soldier, for example, signing himself *A Plebeian*, who had been captivated by my uncle Toby, sent a letter to *St. James's Chronicle* for February 16-18, saying:

"I see there are letters in town mentioning the death of Mr. S——: I hope it is not true; but whether true or false, it is to be hoped no man, but one who can boast of a better heart and greater knowledge, will, for the future, ever employ his pen to sully the reputation of a man, who has given the world the greatest character that human nature can attain to."

Subsequently another *Plebeian*, who had read his namesake's communication, but did not know that the newspaper had already printed the episode of Le Fever, remonstrated with the editor in these words:

"I am surprised that you, who are capable of distinguishing what is worthy of the public notice, should have omitted thus long the inserting in your Chronicle the affecting story of Lieut. Le Fevre, from the last volume of Tristram Shandy. As a friend to society, as one who feels for the woes of another, and knows the force of example, I beseech you to insert it, when you have room for so long, but inimitable performance. Till I saw this letter, I was not so great an admirer of the author of Tristram Shandy, as to be displeased to see some of the dirt thrown at him stick to his coat; but this letter has made me a penitent convert, believing it impossible, that a man so capable of painting the lively impressions on his Uncle Toby's heart, on hearing an affecting story, can himself wear a heart that is not made of the best materials."

A few weeks later, "the report" of Mr. Sterne's death was announced as "premature"; and a wit discoursed in verse upon it in *St. James's Chronicle* for March 6-9. The lines, catching the tone and movement of Sir John Suckling's "What! no more favours? Not a ribbon more?," ran on fluently:

> "How! *Shandy* dead! (a well-bred lady cries)
> With him each grace, each social virtue dies!
> No more, alas! shall that instructive sage
> Expose to light the follies of the age;
> No more dear Satire through the nation reign,
> With *Shandy* fled to *Pluto's* drear domain.
>
> *   *   *   *   *
>
> Madame your sad solicitude dispell,
> Illustrious *Yorick's* still alive, and well!
> Th' ingenious writer yet again shall soar,
> On fancy's wing, to heights unknown before.
> The dire report which filled our minds with woe,
> Was, doubtless, raised by some illiterate foe."

In the meantime the rumor of Sterne's death had reached York and Coxwold before any of Sterne's letters to his wife or to Lord Fauconberg. Whereupon his parishioners, wrote the steward of Newburgh Priory, all went into mourning out of respect to his memory.*

* *Report on Manuscripts in Various Collections*, II, xvii (London, 1903).

CHAP. XII.

Reception in Paris. January—June, 1762

THOUGH still alive, Sterne had barely escaped the fate
that was beginning to press upon him. The dread disease
of his youth, which had been held in check since his college
days, had broken out again to his alarm. The last hemorrhage
left him so weak that, in his way of saying it, his "spider legs"
could no longer support him; his voice was gone to a whisper,
and his face was as pale as a dishclout. But hope at no time deserted him. "When DEATH," he said, addressing his buoyant
spirits in memory of the crisis, "knocked at my door—ye bad
him come again; and in so gay a tone of careless indifference,
did ye do it, that he doubted of his commission." The unwel-
come guest, nonplussed by his reception, turned from Sterne's
lodgings, saying as he went in apology for his intrusion,
"There must certainly be some mistake in this matter." "By
heaven!" vowed Sterne, in a hoarse whisper across the table to
Eugenius, as soon as death was gone from his door, "By
heaven! I will lead him a dance he little thinks of——for I
will gallop . . . without looking once behind me, to the banks
of the *Garonne;* and if I hear him clattering at my heels——
I'll scamper away to mount *Vesuvius.*" Eugenius, one of
Sterne's names for Hall-Stevenson, who was with him in London, "led me to my chaise——*Allons!* said I; the postboy
gave a crack with his whip——off I went like a cannon, and
in a half dozen bounds got into *Dover.*"

At Dover awaited him a rough mid-winter passage across
the Channel. While the sea chopped about with the wind in
wild sport, Sterne lay in his cabin, "sick, sick, sick," sure that
death had him by the throat this time. He landed at Calais in
the evening, and left early the next morning by post for Paris
via Boulogne, Montreuil, Abbeville, Amiens, and Chantilly.
He was too ill on the route to observe much, though "passing
through the finest country," and he seems to have slept or

dozed most of the journey, except when aroused by some accident to the chaise or by the postboy's demand for his fare at the successive stages. We should not forget, however, Janatone, the beautiful daughter of the innkeeper at Montreuil, who greeted him as he stepped from his chaise on a fine evening, and whom he stood watching after supper, as she sat knitting "a white thread stocking, . . . long and taper," pinned to her knee, as if to say it was her own.

All the way, save for brief intervals like this, his imagination was haunted by Death, that "long-striding scoundrel of a scare-sinner" ever posting at his heels. If he were to be overtaken, he prayed that the encounter might take place at some "decent inn," away from the concern of friends. The inn must have been very bad at Abbeville, where he lay a night, for he ordered his chaise at four o'clock the next morning, that he might not meet the scoundrel there, of all inns in the universe. Thus travelling in haste from post to post, "a pale man clad in black" was driven into Paris on the evening of January 16 or 17, 1762, completely exhausted by the journey. The physicians whom he consulted told him plainly that he "could not live a month." At best the only hope they were able to hold out to him was a sojourn in the south of France for the winter. The man who sent the notice of Sterne's death to the London newspapers was only anticipating, as every good news-writer should do, an event certain to occur by the time his letter reached its destination.

But it was ordered quite otherwise. To the surprise of his physicians, Sterne mended so rapidly that by the time he was able to go south they all advised him to stay on in Paris for the present. His quick recovery he attributed not to their medicines, but to nature, who was allowed to work her cure in the clear elastic air of Paris, aided by novel sights and the attentions of a host of new friends. When first heard from directly, he formed one of a company of "fifteen or sixteen English of distinction" living with or near one another in the Faubourg St. Germain, a quarter of the city to which strangers usually resorted. They dined and supped together, occasionally attended the theatre *en masse,* and in smaller groups made excursions in and about the city. Among these gentlemen was George Macartney,—not yet Sir George,—"a handsome and dashing young Irishman," who was to have a long and honorable career as diplomatist and colonial governor. He had come abroad as companion to one of Lord Holland's sons—Stephen Fox, a brother of Charles James Fox, the future statesman. Both of Lord Holland's sons were mere striplings. Stephen, though known as "the eldest cub of the Fox," was only seventeen years old; while Charles James, still a student at Eton, was four years his junior. It is almost incredible that Lord Holland should have wished to initiate his son into social dissipation so early; but such was his premeditated plan, and Macartney was chosen as his agent. With Macartney and Stephen Fox, Sterne made his first visit to Versailles; and the next morning Macartney introduced him to Monsieur Titon, an aged patron of art and literature, to whom Sterne had letters from Garrick. Mr. Fox took him for a week down the Seine to St. Germain-en-Laye for change and rest, and they often went together to the theatre. They usually attended the Comédie Française, close at hand, near the Boulevard St. Germain. The other theatre, the Comédie Italienne, which had just united with the Opéra Comique, was further away in the Mauconseil quarter. At the Comédie Française, Sterne saw and admired Clairon, Dumesnil, and Préville.

Préville, whom he saw in Boissy's *Le Français à Londres,* he declared to be "Mercury himself," so light was he in appearance and manners. Clairon he thought "extremely great," especially in *Iphigénie;* and Dumesnil "in some places still greater than her." He was invited to Clairon's receptions on Thursday, when the actress "gives to eat (as they say here) to all that are hungry and dry"; and before the winter was over he was admitted to the shrines of all "the best goddesses" of the theatre. For Garrick's sake, as well as for his own, he interested himself in all things dramatic, purchasing and sending to his friend comic operas and pamphlets on the stage, and trying to persuade him to bring out in London an adaptation of

Diderot's *Natural Son* which had been made by "a lady of talents." But as time wore on, the French theatre and all matters pertaining to it lost their attraction for him. He was bored by the conversations heard everywhere over the comic opera, then at the height of fashion, and by passionate disputes over what should be done with the Jesuits—whether they should be tolerated or expelled from the kingdom and their property be confiscated. "O God!" he cries out in a letter to Garrick, "they have nothing here, which gives the nerves so smart a blow, as those great characters in the hands of Garrick!——but I forgot I am writing to the man himself. . . . The whole city of Paris is *bewitch'd* with the comic opera, and if it was not for the affair of the Jesuits, which takes up one half of our talk, the comic opera would have it all——It is a tragical nuisance in all companies as it is, and was it not for some sudden starts and dashes—of Shandeism, which now and then either break the thread, or entangle it so, that the devil himself would be puzzled in winding it off—I should die a martyr——this by the way I never will."

Of the Comédie Française, where they performed mostly tragedies, Sterne soon grew tired because of the long moralizing speeches of the actors, saying he got enough preaching in his youth. "A tragedy," he tells Garrick, "is to be damn'd to-night——peace be with it, and the gentle brain which made it!" When he wanted to hear a sermon, he preferred to go and listen to Père Clement, preacher to the King of Poland, whom one of the parishes—St. Roche probably—had engaged to give "a dozen sermons" through Lent at a cost of 600 livres. A fine sketch of the dramatic orator he drew for Mrs. Sterne: "He is King Stanislas's preacher——most excellent indeed! his matter solid, and to the purpose; his manner, more than theatrical, and greater, both in his action and delivery, than Madame Clairon, who, you must know, is the Garrick of the stage here; he has infinite variety, and keeps up the attention by it wonderfully; his pulpit, oblong, with three seats in it, into which he occasionally casts himself; goes on, then rises, by a gradation of four steps, each of which he profits by, as his discourse inclines him; in short 'tis a stage, and the variety of his tones would make you imagine there were no less than five or six actors on it together."

Always keeping in touch with the English colony and its amusements, Sterne was drawn, within a fortnight, into the whirl of French society, where he reigned as the lion of the hour. It was his first London reception all over again, under clear Parisian skies. At the moment English newspapers were announcing his death, he was writing to Garrick in the elated tone of his letters from London to Miss Fourmantelle two years before:

"Well! here I am, my friend, as much improved in my health, for the time, as ever your friendship could wish, or at least your faith give credit to——by the bye I am somewhat worse in my intellectuals; for my head is turned round with what I see, and the unexpected honours I have met with here. Tristram was almost as much known here as in London, at least among your men of condition and learning, and has got me introduced into so many circles ('tis *comme à Londres*). I have just now a fortnight's dinners and suppers upon my hands—my application to the Count de Choiseul goes on swimmingly, for not only M. Pelletière (who, by the bye, sends ten thousand civilities to you and Mrs. Garrick) has undertaken my affair, but the Count de Limbourgh——the Baron d'Holbach, has offered any security for the inoffensiveness of my behaviour in France—'tis more, you rogue! than you will do——This Baron is one of the most learned noblemen here, the great protector of wits, and the Sçavans who are no wits—keeps open house three days a week—his house is now, as yours was to me, my own—he lives at great expence.
——'Twas an odd incident when I was introduced to the Count de Bissie, which I was at his desire——I found him reading Tristram——this grandee does me great honours, and gives me leave to go a private way through his apartments into the Palais Royal, to view the Duke of Orleans' collections, every day I have time——I have been at the doctors of Sorbonne——I hope in a fortnight to break through, or rather

from, the delights of this place, which, in the *sçavoir vivre,* exceeds all the places, I believe, in this section of the globe."

It should not be inferred that everybody in the French capital was reading *Tristram Shandy.* New to Paris, Sterne was yet to learn to make due allowance for French politeness in the many compliments paid to him as the author of a "famous book." *Tristram* was not translated until years after Sterne's death, and it was never very well understood in France. Still, the book was already known in a way. Anglo-maniacs here and there certainly had copies, which they tried to read—Voltaire with most success. For the rest, dependence was placed upon those French journals devoted largely to European literature, which did not fail to give *résumés* of *Tristram,* prefaced with anecdotes of the Anglican clergyman who had written it to the dismay of his clerical brethren. The attention of literary Paris was first called to Sterne's book by the *Journal Encyclopédique* in the number for April, 1760, issued on the first of May. *"C'est ici,"* declared the London correspondent, *"le monstre d'Horace. Des pensées morales, fines, délicates, saillantes, solides, fortes, impies, hazardées, téméraires; voilà ce que l'on trouve dans cet ouvrage. . . . L'Auteur n'a ni plan, ni principes, ni système: il ne veut que parler, et malheureusement on l'écoute avec plaisir. La vivacité de son imagination, le feu de ses portraits, le caractère de ses réflexions, tout plait, tout intéresse et tout séduit."* Garrick, it was added, had given the ecclesiastic the freedom of his theatre and a lord had presented him with a benefice. The same periodical also noticed the second instalment of *Tristram Shandy* in its issue for May, 1761, saying *"Toute le monde convient, après avoir lû cette brochure, qu'elle n'a pas le sens commun, et cependent on se l'arrache des mains; quelle inconsequence!"*

Sterne was likewise taken up by Suard, the journalist and man of letters, in the *Gazette Littéraire;* and Voltaire, who was then at Ferney writing his *Dictionnaire Philosophique* (1764), quoted from Trim's sermon a passage containing the most subtle analysis within his reading of the

insidious ways in which gain and lust may deceive the conscience. The portraits of Dr. Slop and the two Shandys, Voltaire thought "superior to the paintings of Rembrandt and the
sketches of Callot"; while the "comic book" as a whole might
be best compared with "those little satires of antiquity which
contained qualities piquant and fascinating."* Finally, Voltaire gave Sterne the title by which he was to be henceforth
known in France; he called him, with Swift in mind, "the
second Rabelais of England." The information about Sterne
that accompanied him through the salons was thus of that
vague kind most apt to excite curiosity to see and converse with
the famous author. He bore withal the credentials of Pitt and
Garrick.

Sterne entered Parisian society, his letter to Garrick shows,
through the salon of Baron d'Holbach, the Encyclopedist, who
became his personal surety until a passport could be obtained
from the ministry. D'Holbach, or the Baron, as his friends
addressed him, was a cosmopolitan of large wealth, most simple and affable in bearing, and altogether the best type of gentleman under the old régime. He divided his year between his
house in the Rue Royal, the very heart of aristocratic Paris,
and Grandval, a beautiful château a few miles up the Seine,
where he entertained favorite guests for days and weeks.
Because of his hospitality towards all persons of distinction,
whether French or foreign, he was known facetiously as "the
host of Europe." When in Paris, he invited to his table, every
Sunday and every Thursday, a company of philosophers and
men of letters, numbering from ten to twenty. A lavish dinner, served at two o'clock, was prolonged by conversation until
the hour for the theatre. The Baron's salon was aptly called
by one who frequented it "the Institute of France before there
was one"; for at his table were canvassed all questions in science, art, literature, politics, and religion. It was there, says the
Abbé Morellet, who often dined at d'Holbach's with Sterne,
that Roux and Darcet explained their theory of the earth;
Marmontel set forth the principles of his *Elements of Litera-*

* *Œuvres de Voltaire*, VII, 369 (Paris, 1876).

ture; and the host expounded his system of dogmatic atheism so clearly and persuasively as almost to win the assent of men who in their hearts could not accept his theories. On the other hand, Horace Walpole found the "Holbachian club" very dull. "I forgot to tell you," he wrote from Paris to George Selwyn in 1765, "that I sometimes go to Baron d'Olbach's; but I have left off his dinners, as there was no bearing the authors, and philosophers, and *savants*, of which he has a pigeon-house full. They soon turned my head with a new system of antediluvian deluges, which they have invented to prove the eternity of matter. The Baron is persuaded that Pall Mall is paved with lava or deluge stones. In short, nonsense for nonsense, I like the Jesuits better than the philosophers."* Sterne, too, with his imperfect knowledge of French, was at first restless under the long discourses of the savants, whom he was careful not to include among the wits; but, we may be certain, he never betrayed his impatience. He caught the Holbachian manner and was soon able to discourse in rivalry with the best of the circle.

At times four great intelligences shone in upon the Holbachian group. With the two greatest of them—Voltaire and Rousseau,—Sterne had no personal acquaintance; he may or may not have known the shy d'Alembert; but he formed an intimate friendship with Diderot, who was then, like himself, almost a member of the Baron's household. It was a delightful family as Diderot himself described it in letters to Mademoiselle Volland. Madame d'Holbach was a most agreeable woman, *douce et honnête*, with an aversion for her husband's and all other philosophy. There were several pretty children and a sprightly mother-in-law, Madame d'Aine, who knew and repeated all the current gossip and scandal. Diderot, when Sterne knew him, was midway in the *Encyclopédie*, a work which helped on immensely the emancipation of France from outworn dogmas and philosophies. Far apart as the two men were in their attitude towards existing institutions, the one a conservative and the other an iconoclast, they were neverthe-

* *Letters*, edited by Toynbee, VI, 370.

less closely bound by intellect and temperament. Both were sentimentalists; both admired Locke, though they read the master differently; and both easily fell into buffoonery over their burgundy, to the delight, one may fancy, of old Madame d'Aine, who matched them jest for jest, while the modest Madame d'Holbach, "exquisitely dressed," sat and listened complacently to the wild and reckless warfare. It is a bit amusing to find the English sentimentalist complaining that Diderot's *Natural Son*, as he read it in translation, contained too much sentiment for his own taste, and so probably for Garrick's also. In memory of their friendship, the details of which have mostly slipped into obscurity, Sterne sent over to Becket for a box of books as a present to Monsieur Diderot. The box must contain, said the motley memorandum, the six volumes of *Shandy*, Chaucer, Locke complete, the drumstick edition of Colley Cibber, together with Cibber's *Apology*, Tillotson's *Sermons* in small volumes, and "all the *Works* of Pope—the neatest and cheapest edition—(therefore I suppose not Warburton's)." Poor Warburton! In return, Diderot honored Sterne some years after his death, by imitating and paraphrasing *Shandy* in a novel called *Jacques le Fataliste*.

At d'Holbach's, Sterne met, in the person of Jean Baptiste Suard, a young man who played about him as a sort of Boswell. Suard was born and educated at Besançon—the birthplace of Victor Hugo,—where his father held the post of secretary to the university. An incident of Suard's youth, as bearing upon his character, is worth telling. A mere boy just out of the university, he was summoned before the governor of Besançon as a witness against a companion who, after fighting a duel with an officer of the garrison, immediately went into hiding to escape punishment. Suard refused to betray his friend. He was himself consequently arrested and imprisoned for a period on the island of Sainte-Marguerite off the coast of Cannes, where, in want of other books, his time was passed in reading the Bible and Bayle's *Dictionary*. After the death of his father, the youth drifted to Paris, with a view to literature. He was befriended by Buffon and Madame Geoffrin,

and more substantially by Panckoucke, the well-known publisher, whose gifted daughter he married. During these years,
he learned English and acquired a very good knowledge of
contemporary English literature. For a time he was associated
with the Abbé François Arnaud on the *Journal Etranger;* and
when Sterne came to Paris, Suard and his former colleague
were projecting the *Gazette Littéraire,* a similar periodical under the auspices of the foreign ministry. At the same time
Suard was also preparing for the press a *Supplément aux Lettres de Clarisse Harlowe.* Ten or twelve years later, he was
elected to the Academy, largely through the influence of
Mademoiselle de Lespinasse. Suard lived on through the Revolution and the Consulate, translating many English books, and
taking an active part in scientific and literary societies, especially in the reorganization of the Institute of France.

Suard, only twenty-eight years old when he first saw Sterne,
was an impressionable young man, extremely polished in manner and very facile with his pen. Under the mask of his excessive politeness, however, was a keen intelligence and an independent judgment which could assert itself when necessary, as
Madame Geoffrin found when she tried to check and direct
his tastes. Boswell-like, he watched Sterne closely in and out
of the salons, noting the peculiarities of his "comic figure," his
gestures, and the turn of his phrases, whether English or
French; and for further observation invited him often to his
house, where he was equally welcomed by Madame Suard.
After Sterne had come and gone, Madame Suard wrote a most
just and delicate appreciation of the *Sentimental Journey;*
while Sterne's "habitual gestures and words were so engraven
in the memory and imagination of her husband that he could
never hear Sterne's name mentioned without believing that he
really saw him and was listening to him."

Suard often said that he had never seen a man at all like
Sterne—always courteous to a degree and yet perfectly frank
in his criticism of the French and their ways, always in a sense
the same and yet always at the mercy of momentary impressions. The Court went into mourning, and Sterne at once as-

sumed the badge. He came into France with only a reading knowledge of French; but as soon as Fox and Macartney left Paris, he took lodgings in a French family, that he might honor his hosts by speaking their language, if not accurately, at least fluently. One night the whole fair of St. Germain— "a town in miniature"—burned to the ground, and "hundreds of unhappy people," who had lost their all, were driven from their booths to the streets in tears. The next morning, Sterne's barber, as he was shaving him, wept over the terrible misfortune to the poor creatures, and Sterne wept with him. Stopping one day before the statue of Henry the Fourth, on the Pont-Neuf, a crowd gathered about him, attracted by his peculiar movements. Turning round, Sterne called out: "Why are you all staring at me? Follow my example, all of you!" And they all fell on their knees with him before the King of France. A slave, says Garat, Suard's biographer, would never have rendered, unbidden, such homage to Henry the Fourth.

On one occasion, Suard asked Sterne to explain his extraordinary personality—a temperament really stable and yet volatile to all appearance. Sterne, in an unusually serious mood, readily complied with his friend's request, in a formal statement, which almost startles by its truth and relative completeness; for genius, it is supposed, never understands itself, and Sterne has said equivocally elsewhere that he could give a better account of any other man in the world than of himself. Whether the self-revelation took place over the wine at Baron d'Holbach's or when the two men were alone together, the narrative does not specify. His so-called originality, Sterne declared, should be attributed "to one of those delicate organizations in which predominates the sacred informing principle of the soul, that immortal flame which nourishes life and devours it at the same time, and which exalts and varies, in sudden and unexpected ways, all sensations." This creative faculty, said Sterne, "we call imagination or sensibility, according as it expresses itself, under the pen of a writer, in depicting scenes or in portraying the passions." But beyond his natural endowment, must be considered, Sterne added, certain acquired traits affecting mind and style, which had come from "the daily reading of the Old and New Testaments, books which were to his liking as well as necessary to his profession"; and from a prolonged study of Locke, "which he had begun in youth and continued through life." Anyone, he told Suard, who was acquainted with Locke might discover the philosopher's directing hand "in all his pages, in all his lines, in all his expressions." In conclusion, he said of Locke's philosophy, which had thus tempered everywhere his thought and manner of procedure, in his *Sermons* as well as in *Tristram Shandy:* "It is a philosophy which never attempts to explain the miracle of sensation; but reverently leaving that miracle in the hands of God, it unfolds all the secrets of the mind; and shunning the errors to which other theories of knowledge are exposed, it arrives at all truths accessible to the understanding." Finally, it is "a sacred philosophy, which the world must heed if it is to have a true universal religion, a true science of morals, and which man must heed also if he is to gain real command over nature."* Sterne, of course, never talked quite like this, but this is the way he was understood by his French admirer.

Sterne's singular and piquant personality, together with his *bonhomie,* made him a welcome visitor everywhere. He edified philosophers by his clear and enthusiastic exposition of Locke; he entertained wits by his jests and droll stories; and awakened, says Suard's biographer, "new emotions in tender hearts by his naïve and touching sensibility." Among these tender hearts, may we include Suard's friends, Madame Geoffrin and Mademoiselle de Lespinasse, whose salons ranked first for intellectual brilliancy? We may, I think, and must. True, Sterne nowhere mentions these fascinating women, but for that matter he nowhere mentions his Boswell. A few years later, when the *Sentimental Journey* came out, Mademoiselle de Lespinasse wrote two short pieces in Sterne's style, one of which recites a signal act of charity on the part of Madame Geoffrin. Sterne is represented as listening to the pathetic tale

* D. J. Garat, *Mémoires Historiques sur la Vie de M. Suard,* II, 147-152 (Paris, 1820).

and as being so overcome by it that he "clasped Madame Geoffrin in his arms and embraced her with ecstasy."*

As in this imaginary scene, Sterne always let his emotions run forward while he scampered on after them, whithersoever they might lead. "I laugh till I cry," he wrote to Garrick, "and in the same tender moments, *cry till I laugh*. I Shandy it more than ever, and verily do believe, that by mere Shandeism, sublimated by a laughter-loving people, I fence as much against infirmities, as I do by the benefit of air and climate." In a similar vein ran a letter to Hall-Stevenson from his friend Monsieur Tollot, a gentleman of Geneva and an admirer of Rousseau, then travelling in France after a nervous breakdown. Falling in with Sterne at Paris, he was struck by the buoyancy of the pale and sick Yorick, in contrast with his own miserable temperament, which never let him forget his headaches and vertigoes. On a rainy day in April, when wind and rain were so violent that he was compelled to stay in and betake himself to divers glasses of Bordeaux in order to keep off the blue devils, Monsieur Tollot sat down and wrote to the master of Skelton, saying by the way: "I sometimes envy," to translate the Genevan's French, "the happy disposition of our friend Mr. Sterne. Everything assumes the color of the rose for that happy mortal; and what appears to others dark and gloomy, presents to him only a blithe and merry aspect. His only pursuit is pleasure; but he is not like most others who do not know how to enjoy pleasure when it is within their grasp; for he drinks the bowl to the last drop and still his thirst is unquenched."†

Perhaps Sterne enjoyed himself most in the society of Claude de Thiard, the Comte de Bissy, and in the coteries to which "this grandee" introduced him. The count, then forty years old, had behind him a conspicuous military career, in which he reached the rank of lieutenant-general. In peace he

---

* *Œuvres Posthumes d'Alembert*, II, 22-42 (Paris, 1799); and Garat, as cited above.

† W. Durrant Cooper. *Seven Letters written by Sterne and his Friends*, 21-22 (London, printed for private circulation, 1844).

had devoted himself to English studies, translating Bolingbroke's *Patriot King*, which gained him admission to the
Academy. Called in from the field, as the Seven Years' War
was now really over, he was living at Court, with apartments
in the Palais Royal. It was a graceful compliment that he paid
Sterne when the humorist first called, by appointment, for aid
in securing a passport from the Duc de Choiseul, the prime
minister. *Tristram Shandy* lay open upon the count's table.
Sterne afterwards played with the scene fancifully in the *Sentimental Journey*, substituting *Hamlet* for *Shandy*. But we
may, I think, safely reconstruct certain parts of the conversation from Sterne's imaginative account of it. They talked of
Shakespeare and of *Shandy*. The count was puzzled by Sterne's
assumption of the name of Yorick, for which he could divine
no reason. Sterne, reading the count's perplexed face, led him
on into the notion that he was really jester to his Majesty
George the Third, and at length disillusioned him humorously:

"*Pardonnez moi*, Mons. le Count, said I——I am not the
king's jester.——But you are Yorick?——Yes.——*Et vous
plaisantez?*——I answered, indeed I did jest——but was not
paid for it——'twas entirely at my own expence.

"We have no jester at court, Mons. le Count, said I; the
last was in the licentious reign of Charles II.——since which
time our manners have been so gradually refining, that our
court at present is so full of patriots, who wish for *nothing* but
the honours and wealth of their country——and our ladies are
all so chaste, so spotless, so good, so devout——there is nothing
for a jester to make a jest of——

"*Voilà un persiflage!* cried the Count."

The interview was followed by the first of many invitations
to dinner. One day the count enquired how he liked the
French, and whether he had found them as urbane as the
world gave them credit of being. Sterne replied that they were
indeed polished "to an excess." His host, noting the word *excesse*, asked him to explain frankly what he meant by the implied criticism. Sterne went on to say adroitly and politely that
courtesy, though in and of itself a commendable virtue, might

lead to a loss of "variety and originality of character." To illustrate his hypothesis, Sterne took out of his pocket "a few of King William's shillings as smooth as glass" and proceeded:

"See, Mons. le Count, said I, rising up, and laying them before him upon the table——by jingling and rubbing one against another for seventy years together in one body's pocket or another's, they are become so much alike, you can scarce distinguish one shilling from another.

"The English, like ancient medals, kept more apart, and passing but few people's hands, preserve the first sharpnesses which the fine hand of Nature has given them——they are not so pleasant to feel——but, in return, the legend is so visible, that at the first look you see whose image and superscription they bear. But the French, Mons. le Count, added I (wishing to soften what I had said), have so many excellencies, they can the better spare this——they are a loyal, a gallant, a generous, an ingenious, and good-temper'd people as is under heaven——if they have a fault, they are too *serious*.

"*Mon Dieu!* cried the Count, rising out of his chair.

"*Mais vous plaisantez,* said he, correcting his exclamation. ——I laid my hand upon my breast, and with earnest gravity assured him it was my most settled opinion."*

Having once mastered the art of courtesy, the humorist easily outdid the French as he passed through the great houses to which his friendship with the count recommended him. Sterne and Choiseul met in one of the fashionable salons. The duke observing a group about an odd-looking Englishman and overhearing scraps of the conversation, turned to a friend and enquired, "Who the deuce is that man over there, that Chevalier Shandy?" On being told that it was the author of the bizarre book which he had heard of if not read, he stepped up

* The essential truth of this anecdote is confirmed in an article which appeared in the *London Chronicle* for April 16-18, 1765, or nearly two years before the publication of the *Sentimental Journey*. Under the heading, "Foreign Literature," the newspaper gave an abstract of Suard on Sterne, from the *Gazette Littéraire de l'Europe*, in which the incident is related somewhat differently.

to Monsieur Sterne, and a dialogue ensued which made Sterne "as vain as a devil." The duke subsequently signed a passport for Chevalier Sterne, remarking pleasantly, as he handed it to the Comte de Bissy, that *un homme qui rit ne peut être dangereux*. In return, Sterne begged that the prime minister be assured that he had not come into France to spy out the nakedness of the land.

On being introduced by the Comte de Bissy to the Duc de Biron, Maréchal de France, who, says Sterne, had formerly "signaliz'd himself by some small feats of chivalry in the *Cour d'amour*, and had dress'd himself out to the idea of tilts and tournaments ever since," the duke expressed a wish to cross the Channel to see the English ladies. "Stay where you are, I beseech you, Mons. le Marquis," broke in Sterne, forgetting the duke's title, "——Les Messrs Anglois can scarce get a kind look from them as it is." The duke invited Sterne home to a ten o'clock supper. In like manner, Sterne made the acquaintance of La Popelinière, the richest of the farmers-general, who, as described in a letter to Mrs. Sterne, "lives here like a sovereign prince; keeps a company of musicians always in his house, and a full set of players; and gives concerts and plays alternately to the grandees of this metropolis." Instead of the English ladies, the farmer-general enquired about the English taxes, saying "They were very considerable, he heard." Sterne admitted that the taxes of his country were considerable enough, "if we knew but how to collect them," and made the gentleman a low bow. That evening Sterne received an invitation "to his music and table" for the season.

La Popelinière had a musical rival in Baron de Bagge, chamberlain to the King of Prussia. The baron was a melomaniac of large wealth, who fancied that he possessed great musical talent, though he could scarce play the violin. He came to Paris and opened a salon with an array of musicians, whom he paid to take imaginary lessons from him. It was not Sterne but another who once remarked to the baron that he had never heard anyone play the violin like him. Sterne found the baron's concerts "very fine, both music and company." The next night after attending one of them, he supped at the Temple, with the Prince de Conti, who lived there in great state, with a court of his own.

With much amusement Sterne studied the various feminine types seen in the salons, a summary of which he gave in a sketch of Madame de Vence, said to have been a descendant of Madame de Sévigné. "There are three epochas," he observed in speaking of her, "in the empire of a French woman—She is coquette—then deist—then *dévote*. . . . When thirty-five years and more have unpeopled her dominions of the slaves of love, she re-peoples them with slaves of infidelity——and then with the slaves of the church. Madame de V[ence] was vibrating betwixt the first of these epochas." Seated upon the sofa together "for the sake of disputing the point of religion more closely," Sterne told her that, whereas it might be her principle to believe nothing, it was nevertheless a most dangerous thing for a beauty to turn deist, and thereby remove all those checks and restraints which religion cast about the passions. "I declare," says Sterne, "I had the credit all over Paris of unperverting Madame de V[ence]——She affirmed to Mons. D[iderot] and the Abbé M[orellet], that in one half-hour I had said more for revealed religion than all their Encyclopedia had said against it." Madame de Vence put off, as it turned out, the epoch of deism for two years.

"I remember," says Sterne further, "it was in this *Coterie*, in the middle of a discourse, in which I was shewing the necessity of a *first cause*, that the young Count de Fainéant took me by the hand to the farthest corner of the room to tell me my *solitaire* was pinn'd too strait about my neck——It should be *plus badinant*, said the Count, looking down upon his own—— but a word, Mons. Yorick, *to the wise*——

"——And *from the wise*, Mons. le Count, replied I making him a bow——*is enough.*

"The Count de Fainéant embraced me with more ardour than ever I was embraced by mortal man."

Anecdotes must always be accepted with a grain of allowance. "I do a thousand things," Sterne wrote to Garrick, "which cut no figure, *but in the doing*—and as in London, I have the honour of having done and said a thousand things I never did or dream'd of—and yet I dream abundantly." The anecdotes that are here mingled with the narrative, however, are very much better authenticated than is the usual case,— some by Suard through his biographer Garat, and most by Sterne himself, who, of course, ornamented them after his own fashion. In paying the French in their own polite coin, Sterne came at times, as he felt himself, perilously near sycophancy. "For three weeks together," he said, shortening the period for artistic purposes, "I was of every man's opinion I met.——*Pardi! ce Mons. Yorick a autant d'esprit que nous autres.*——*Il raisonne bien,* said another——*C'est un bon enfant,* said a third,——And at this price I could have eaten and drank and been merry all the days of my life at Paris; but 'twas a dishonest *reckoning*——I grew ashamed of it.——It was the gain of a slave——every sentiment of honour revolted against it——the higher I got, the more was I forced upon my *beggarly system.*" But to go on. In one of the salons Sterne encountered Crébillon the younger, wit and novelist, author of *Les Egaremens de Cœur et de l'Esprit.* Before they separated, they entered into a comic convention. Crébillon agreed to write Sterne "an expostulatory letter upon the indecorums of Tristram Shandy" and Sterne was to reply with "a recrimination upon the liberties" in Crébillon's works. The two pamphlets were "to be printed together—Crébillon against Sterne —Sterne against Crébillon—the copy to be sold, and the money equally divided." The scheme miscarried, either because, as Sterne predicted, Crébillon was too indolent to perform his part of the jest, or because—and more likely—he was unable to read and understand *Tristram Shandy.*

Of all the prizes Sterne drew in the French capital, none pleased him quite so much as his winning the attention of Louis Philippe, Duc d'Orléans. Though only thirty-seven years old, the duke had already had a brilliant career in the army. At Dettingen a horse was shot under him. The war with England over, he had come in from the field, and was

Laurence Sterne
From a reproduction of the watercolor
by Louis Carmontelle

giving himself up, like other officers of rank, to pleasure and friendships, alternating his residence, with a strolling court, between the Palais Royal and his seat at Bagnolet. For his entertainment he kept in his household Carmontelle, to write novels and farces and to paint his friends at Court. Struck by Sterne's eccentric character, the duke requested the pleasure of adding, from Carmontelle's hand, the humorist's portrait to a favorite collection of small water-colors. Carmontelle drew Sterne in profile at full length, as he stood on the terrace of the Palais Royal, with the city and the dome of the Invalides in the background. Sterne turned his face towards the palace gardens, and bent slightly forward as he laid his right arm across the back of a chair, half closing the hand. His left hand he thrust into a pocket, and threw one leg gracefully across the other. His spare figure was dressed faultlessly for the occasion in complete black, with ruffled lace-sleeves and lace-cravat tied loose, just as the Count de Fainéant had told him it ought to be. One misses the fine eyes of the front view chosen by Reynolds, but about the mouth are the same lines of mirth and good nature, with a trace of the full lips so conspicuous in the Ramsay portrait of Sterne's youth. It is the portrait of a man growing old in his labors and pleasures, taken, Sterne thought, "most expressively."

Sterne's original design of going south had been upset by the improvement of his health, and "the great civilities" of his new friends, from whom he found it hard to break away. So he decided to trail on in Paris until the end of May and then return home through Holland. But early in April came disturbing news from York. His daughter Lydia, who had suffered from asthma for several years, was declining so rapidly that her mother feared she could not survive another English winter. On receiving the alarming message, Sterne reconsidered his plans. For himself, his cheeks now rosy, he was ready to go back to his desk. And yet perhaps it would be better, after all, for him to summon his wife and daughter over to Paris and pass a winter with them at Toulouse, "free from coughs and colds." The faculty strongly advised this course

for the complete restoration of his own health beyond likelihood of relapse. Sterne at once wrote to Lord Fauconberg and
the Archbishop of York, explaining the situation, and thereby
gaining their assent to an extension of his leave of absence
from Coxwold. He was going, he told them, to the south of
France, not so much on his own account as his daughter's,
whom he was anxious to save if possible. But Sterne, as well as
his physicians, had misread his condition. Near the middle of
April, he went out to Versailles to solicit the necessary pass-
ports from the Duke of Choiseul. On his return, he was attacked with a fever, "which ended," Sterne says, "the worst
way it could for me, in a *défluxion poitrine*, as the French
physicians call it. It is generally fatal to weak lungs, so that I
have lost in ten days all I have gain'd since I came here; and,
from a relaxation of my lungs, have lost my voice entirely,
that 'twill be much if I ever quite recover it."

As usual, Sterne was soon out of bed as if nothing serious
had occurred. But the season was passing and there were
fewer engagements. When the curtain falls upon his five
months of dinners, he was, as first seen, among his countrymen, doing honor to his Majesty George the Third. This was
the last scene in the Shandy drama for the present. The story
is told by the other chief performer, by Louis Dutens, the
diplomatist, in his *Memoirs*. Dutens, though a Frenchman, had
been at the Court of Turin for some time as *chargé d'affaires*
for the King of England. On the appointment of George Pitt,
first Baron Rivers, as Envoy and Minister to Turin, Dutens
was ordered to Paris to take part in the preliminary negotiations for peace between France and England. He set out from
Turin on the tenth of May, travelling in company with the
Marquis of Tavistock, son of the Duke of Bedford—a young
man only twenty-three years old,—and John Turberville
Needham, the Roman Catholic scientist who had a hot tilt with
Voltaire over the question of miracles. Needham was on the
journey homewards, after making the grand tour as tutor to
John Talbot Dillon, a young Irishman about Lord Tavistock's
age, who will figure later as one of Sterne's close associates.

Dillon, it may be said immediately for his further identification, spent most of his life in foreign travel and in writing about Spain and other lands he visited. Emperor Joseph the Second of Austria bestowed upon him the title of Free Baron of the Holy Roman Empire. On the anniversary of George the Third's birthday, the fourth of June, Lord Tavistock invited Sterne and a few other English gentlemen who were still in Paris to meet his Turin friends at dinner. Without formal introduction, as was the Continental way, the guests sat down to table. What occurred I may leave to the pen of Dutens himself, a queer character, who had done queer things at the Court of the King of Sardinia, vague rumors of which had doubtless reached Sterne:

"I sat," says Dutens,* "between Lord Berkeley, who was going to Turin, and the famous Sterne, author of Tristram Shandy, who was considered as the Rabelais of England. We were very jovial during dinner; and drank, in the English manner, the toasts of the day. The conversation turned upon Turin, which several of the company were on the point of visiting: upon which Mr. Sterne, addressing himself to me, asked me if I knew Mr. Dutens, naming me. I replied, 'Yes, very intimately.' The whole company began to laugh; and Sterne, who did not suppose me so near him, imagined that this Mr. Dutens must be a very singular character, since the mention of the name alone excited merriment. 'Is he not a rather strange fellow?' added he, immediately. 'Yes,' replied I, 'an original.'——'I thought so,' continued he; 'I have heard him spoken of': and then he began to draw a picture of me, the truth of which I pretended to acknowledge; while Sterne, seeing that the subject amused the company, invented from his fertile imagination many stories, which he related in his way, to the great diversion of us all."

"I was the first," Dutens goes on to say, "who withdrew; and I had scarcely left the house, when they told him who I was: they persuaded him that I had restrained myself at the

* *Memoirs of a Traveller*, II, 5-8 (London, 1806).

time from respect to Lord Tavistock; but that I was not to
be offended with impunity, and that he might expect to see
me on the next day, to demand satisfaction for the improper
language which he had used concerning me. Indeed he thought
he had carried his raillery too far, for he was a little merry:
he therefore came the following morning to see me, and to
beg pardon for anything that he might have said to offend me;
excusing himself . . . by the great desire he had to amuse the
company, who had appeared so merrily disposed from the moment he first mentioned my name. I stopped him short at once,
by assuring him that I was as much amused at his mistake as
any of the party; that he had said nothing which could offend
me; and that, if he had known the man he had spoken of as
well as I did, he might have said much worse things of him.
He was delighted with my answer, requested my friendship,
and went away highly pleased with me."*

* This merry jest was strangely employed by Thackeray to prove
that Sterne was not a true gentleman, although he may be regarded as
one by "my Superfine friend." It is perhaps worth while to quote the
novelist's paragraph (afterwards suppressed), as an example of the way
in which Sterne has been often misinterpreted. After re-telling the story,
Thackeray remarked:

"Ah, dear Laurence! You are lucky in having such a true gentleman as my friend to appreciate you! You see he was lying, but then
he was amusing the whole company. When Laurence found they were
amused, he told more lies. Your true gentlemen always do. Even to
get the laugh of the company at a strange table, perhaps you and I
would not tell lies: but then we are not true gentlemen. And see in
what a true gentlemanlike way Laurence carries off the lies! A man
who wasn't accustomed to lying might be a little disconcerted at meeting with a person to whose face he had been uttering abuse and false-
hood. Not so Laurence. He goes to Dutens; . . . embraces him, and
asks for his friendship! Heaven bless him! Who would not be honoured
by the friendship of a true gentleman, who had just told lies about you
to your face?"—*Cornhill Magazine*, II, 633.

CHAP. XIII.

Journey to Toulouse. July and August, 1762

AMID the merriments of the English colony, Sterne was playing admirably the part of paterfamilias. His wife and daughter had come into York for the previous winter, and were living in a house in the Minster Yard, under the protection of Hall-Stevenson. "My family, my Lord," he wrote to the Earl of Fauconberg, "is a very small machine, but it has many wheels in it, and I am forced too often to turn them about—not as I would—but as I can." No sooner, however, had Sterne regained his emotional poise, after the first exciting weeks in Paris, than he got into touch with the complicated machine at home, and guided its movements as well as he could at long distance. He related in letters to Mrs. Sterne such incidents in his great reception as he thought would interest her most, and gave her instructions in the care and management of Lydia, who should be kept by all means to her French. As presents to his wife, he sent home two snuff-boxes, in charge of a friend, one filled with garnets and the other containing an etching of Carmontelle's water-color. When it was decided that Mrs. Sterne and Lydia should come over and go south with him, he posted off letter after letter, describing in minute detail all arrangements for the journey. As he stated it in one of the letters, "I have almost drain'd my brains dry on the subject."

It was not an easy thing for an English parson with only a moderate income to establish his household in another country; but Sterne took up the practical problem with the method and good sense that he had applied in earlier years to numerous parish questions. Toulouse was chosen for several reasons. Provisions he found, on enquiry, were cheap there; several English friends, including "old Hewitt" and his family, were to be there for the winter, and the town was recommended to him by the faculty. While his plans were forming, he was referred for practical help to an "Abbé Mackarty"—a member of the Irish MacCarthy Reagh family, then settled at Toulouse. The Abbé, who had previously rendered similar aid to Hall-Stevenson and the Skelton set, was commissioned to take a pleasant house for the Sternes, near or within the city, at his discretion.

A house engaged and the cost of living reckoned up, Sterne next adjusted his affairs at home to the new arrangements. James Kilner, master of the grammar school at Coxwold and assistant curate of the parish, was recommended to the Archbishop of York for the priesthood. Richard Chapman, steward of Newburgh Priory, was to look after the affairs of the parish in Sterne's interest. In like manner, Stephen Croft was to represent Sterne at Sutton and Stillington, where important parish matters needed attention, for some of the landowners wished to enclose Rascal Common. Sterne wrote back that he would not stand in the way of the project, provided he received his share. A bureau had to be broken open for Sterne's deeds, and Croft was given a power of attorney to act for the vicar. The squire was also delegated to provide for the commissary's visitations of Pickering and Pocklington. All moneys received were to be sent up to London by Sterne's agents, to Selwin, banker and correspondent of Panchaud and Foley, in Rue St. Sauveur, Paris. In turn, the banking firm at Paris was to remit to Messrs. Brousse et Fils of Toulouse. Besides all this, Mrs. Sterne was enjoined to bring over at least three hundred pounds in her pocket, for that amount would be immediately necessary. There were still other little preparations incident to a long journey, to which Sterne did not fail to call her attention:

"Bring your silver coffee-pot, 'twill serve both to give water, lemonade, and orjead—to say nothing of coffee and chocolate. . . . Do not say I forgot you, or whatever can be conducive to your ease of mind, in this journey——I wish I was with you, to do these offices myself, and to strew roses on your way—but I shall have time and occasion to shew you I am not wanting——Now, my dears, once more pluck up your spirits—trust in God—in me—and in yourselves—with this, was you put to it, you would encounter all these difficulties ten times told——Write instantly, and tell me you triumph over all fears; tell me Lydia is better, and a helpmate to you ——You say she grows like me——let her shew me she does so in her contempt of small dangers, and fighting against the apprehensions of them, which is better still. . . . Give my love to Mr. Fothergill, and to those true friends which envy has spared me—and for the rest, *laissez passer*. . . . Dear Bess, I have a thousand wishes, but have a hope for every one of them——You shall chant the same *jubilate*, my dears, so God bless you. My duty to Lydia, which implies my love too. Adieu, believe me   Your affectionate,   L. Sterne."

Owing to many delays, it was the twenty-first of June, or a day or two after, when Mrs. Sterne and Lydia set out from York for London, under the most precise directions from the head of the family. "I would advise you," he wrote to them, "to take three days in coming up, for fear of heating your-selves.——See that they do not give you a bad vehicle, when a better is in the yard, but you will look sharp——drink small Rhenish to keep you cool, (that is if you like it). Live well, and deny yourselves nothing your hearts wish. So God in heaven prosper and go along with you." On arriving in Lon-don, they put up with their friends Mr. and Mrs. Edmunds,* who showed them many "marks of kindness," to the satisfac-tion of Sterne. Into the scant week they stayed in town was crowded much business and shopping, if they followed the in-structions of letters that had been coming every post from Paris. Most important of all, Mrs. Sterne was to go with Mr. Edmunds to Becket's and collect what might be due on the *Shandys*. Becket had sold 2824 copies, which should have yielded the author £300 or more. How far Sterne had already drawn on his publisher for expenses in Paris is not known; but there was probably a comfortable sum still to his credit.

* Sterne usually gives the name as Edmundson. Edmunds, who was a stationer in the Poultry, acted as a sort of agent for Sterne in dealing with Becket.

Next, Mrs. Sterne and her adviser must, if possible, induce Becket to purchase the remainder of the edition, numbering in the whole 4000 sets, by the offer of "a handsome allowance for the chances and drawbacks" on his side. Should they succeed to this extent, then they might try him on the copyright, holding out as a bait the promise of the nay-say on the next instalment of *Shandy*. Becket gave Mrs. Sterne a bill addressed to his Paris correspondent in settlement of the account to date, but did not touch the bait set for the unsold copies and the copyright.

After this business with Becket, Mrs. Sterne should make additions to her wardrobe. "If you consider," wrote her husband, "Lydia must have two slight negligees——you will want a new gown or two——as for painted linens, buy them in town, they will be more admired because English than French. ——Mrs. H[ewitt] writes me word that I am mistaken about buying silk cheaper at Toulouse than Paris, that she advises you to buy what you want here——where they are very beautiful and cheap, as well as blonds, gauzes, &c.——these I say will all cost you sixty guineas—and you must have them—for in this country nothing must be spared for the back——and if you dine on an onion, and lie in a garret seven stories high, you must not betray it in your cloaths, according to which you are well or ill look'd on."

Then came numerous small purchases conducive to the peace of the household, which Sterne huddled together in his letters:

"Do not forget the watch-chains——bring a couple for a gentleman's watch likewise; we shall lie under great obligations to the Abbé M[ackarty] and must make him such a small acknowledgement; according to my way of flourishing, 'twill be a present worth a kingdom to him.——They have bad pins, and vile needles here——bring for yourself, and some for presents——as also a strong bottle-skrew, for whatever Scrub we may hire as butler, coachman, &c., to uncork us our Frontiniac. . . . I had like to have forgot a most necessary thing, there are no copper tea-kettles to be had in

France, and we shall find such a thing the most comfortable utensil in the house——buy a good strong one, which will hold two quarts—a dish of tea will be a comfort to us in our journey south——I have a bronze tea-pot, which we will carry also—as china cannot be brought over from England, we must make up a villainous party-coloured tea equipage, to regale ourselves, and our English friends, whilst we are at Toulouse." In the list were also knives and cookery-books, with three sets of *Shandy* and three sets of *Sermons* for presents to Parisian friends. And finally to the comfort of a wife who had the amiable habit of snuff-taking: "Give the Custom-House officers what I told you——at Calais give more, if you have much Scotch snuff——but as tobacco is good here, you had best bring a Scotch mill and make it yourself, that is, order your valet to manufacture it——'twill keep him out of mischief."

If Sterne's plans did not miscarry, a good-natured horse-trader, who had brought over a sister of Panchaud's, conducted Mrs. Sterne and Lydia to Dover, put them up at the Cross Keys, and saw them across the Channel on a cartel ship. At Calais they were to lodge at the Lyon d'Argent, the master of which they must look out for, as he was "a Turk in grain." With the inn-keeper they would find a letter giving final directions, with an enclosure from "Mr. Colebrooks, the minister of Swisserland's secretary," addressed to the custom-house officer. "You must be cautious," Mrs. Sterne was warned again, "about Scotch snuff——take half a pound in your pocket, and make Lyd do the same." Otherwise you may be detected and have to pay a duty, was the implication.

At that time it was almost impossible for travellers to get from Calais to Paris, since all the chaises of France had been sent to the army to bring in the officers. By good luck, however, Sterne obtained a fine one from his friend Thomas Thornhill of London, who was returning from a Continental tour. "You will be in raptures," wrote Sterne, "with your chariot.—Mr. R. a gentleman of fortune, who is going to Italy, and has seen it, has offered me thirty guineas for my bargain.——You will wonder all the way, how I am to find room in it for a third——to ease you of this wonder, 'tis by what the coachmakers here call a cave, which is a second bottom added to that you set your feet upon, which lets the person (who sits over against you) down with his knees to your ancles, and by which you have all more room——and what is more, less heat,——because his head does not intercept the fore-glass——little or nothing——Lyd and I will enjoy this by turns; sometimes I will take a *bidet*——(a little post-horse) and scamper before——at other times I shall sit in *fresco* upon the arm-chair without doors, and one way or other will do very well.——I am under infinite obligations to Mr. Thornhill, for accommodating me thus, and so genteelly, for 'tis like making a present of it." The chaise was to be left at Calais with a written order for its delivery to Mrs. Sterne. "Send for your chaise," was the last caution, "into the court-yard, and see all is tight——Buy a chain at Calais, strong enough not to be cut off, and let your portmanteau be tied on the fore part of your chaise for fear of a dog's trick——so God bless you both, and remember me to my Lydia."

Travelling *toute doucement*, owing to the heat, and refreshed by the tea they brought with them, Mrs. Sterne and Lydia arrived in Paris on Thursday, the eighth of July. It had been for Sterne a long and anxious period of waiting, varied by some amusements. The summer had set in hot about the first of May, and the heat increased every day, until Paris became "as hot as Nebuchadnezzar's oven." Sterne nevertheless undertook to go about as if he were in cool Yorkshire. One good story of his excursions he himself told at the expense of his facility with French. True, he had quickly attuned his ear to understanding the language, and he learned to speak it easily, but only after an Englishman's fashion, that is, with a disregard of the idioms and the auxiliary verbs. "I have had a droll adventure here," as Sterne described it for the entertainment of Lady D——, "in which my Latin was of some service to me——I had hired a chaise and a horse to go about seven miles into the country, but, *Shandean-like*, did not take

notice that the horse was almost dead when I took him——
Before I got half-way, the poor animal dropp'd down dead
——so I was forced to appear before the police, and began to
tell my story in French, which was, that the poor beast had to
do with a worse beast than himself, namely *his master*, who
had driven him all the day before (Jehu-like) and that he had
neither had corn, or hay, therefore I was not to pay for the
horse——but I might as well have whistled, as have spoke
French, and I believe my Latin was equal to my uncle Toby's
Lilabulero—being not understood because of it's purity, but
by dint of words I forced my judge to do me justice——no
common thing by the way in France."

His imprudence, together with attention to his wife's journey and the approaching settlement at Toulouse, brought on,
towards the end of June, another severe hemorrhage. "It happen'd in the night," he wrote to Hall-Stevenson, "and I bled
the bed full, and finding in the morning I was likely to bleed
to death, I sent immediately for a surgeon to bleed me at both
arms——this saved me, and with lying speechless three days,
I recovered upon my back in bed; the breach healed, and in a
week after I got out." Sterne at once gave up a design of taking his wife and daughter to Spa through the hot summer,
convinced now that he must hasten to Toulouse for rest
and quiet. They remained in Paris for a week or ten days,
time enough for sight-seeing and necessary purchases of silks,
blonds, and gauzes. As a present to Mrs. Edmunds, they sent
over to London by "Mr. Stanhope, the Consul of Algiers (I
mean his lady)" an India taffety, in memory of recent hospitality and kindness. Lydia, said her father, did nothing at first
but sit by the window of their apartments and "complain of
the torment of being frizzled." He expressed the wish that she
might ever remain thus the "child of nature," for he hated
the "children of art."

The day before leaving Paris, the Sternes received a pleasant visit from Lawson Trotter, an uncle of Hall-Stevenson
and once the master of Skelton. The old Jacobite, who feared
to return to England after the year forty-five, came on busi-

ness wherein Sterne acted as agent for Hall-Stevenson. He stayed to dinner, after which Sterne showed him a copy of the *Crazy Tales* just out; and was "made happy beyond expression" by the book and "more so with its frontispiece," the humorous sketch of Skelton Castle. But for Sterne himself, the visit awakened homesickness for Yorkshire. " 'Tis now," he wrote a few weeks afterwards to Hall-Stevenson, "I wish all warmer climates, countries, and everything else, at ———, that separates me from our paternal seat——*ce sera là où reposera ma cendre—et ce sera là où mon cousin viendra repandre les pleurs dues à notre amitié.*"

On Monday, the nineteenth of July, as near as can be made out, the Sternes began the long and expensive journey to Toulouse by way of Lyons, Avignon, and Montpellier, travelling by post most of the way, as was Sterne's custom. Their chaise, which was narrow and cramped, despite the cave for Lydia's feet, they piled with luggage, before and aft, mountains high. For such a load were necessary at least four horses with two postillions, which would be exchanged for fresh ones at the successive stages. As the posts were then farmed out by the king, the exactions were most oppressive, especially at royal posts like Lyons, where one paid double. It is certain that the three hundred pounds which Mrs. Sterne brought over in her pocket shrunk more than half by the time the party arrived in Toulouse. The serious details of the journey Sterne never cared to recall, but the humorous side of it he touched upon in a letter or two, and made it the main subject of the next volume of *Tristram Shandy*. By abating his extravagances here and there, perhaps we may tell the story somewhat as it was, though the narrative will be scant and never quite trustworthy.

Sterne chose the longest route to Toulouse with the manifest intent of sight-seeing. He took with him the *Nouveau Voyage en France* by Piganiol de la Force, the Baedeker of the period, who mapped out all the post roads and described all the things which a traveller should observe by the way and at the halting places. In the pocket of the chaise were placed also note-books or loose sheets, on which Sterne was to record his own impressions. But owing to the extreme heat, and the many annoyances at the different posts, Sterne implies that he paid little attention to the guide-book's list of *videnda*. None of the first places on the route—Fontainebleau, Sens, and Joigny—interested him much, until he reached Auxerre, about which he could "go on forever"; though he had in fact little to say of the town, where he may have strolled about for a day or two. On a visit to the ruined Abbey of St. Germain, the sacristan pointed out the tomb of St. Maxima, in life "one of the fairest and most beautiful ladies, either of Italy or France," who four centuries ago came to Auxerre to touch the bones of St. Germain, and, after lying in her coffin two hundred years or more, was enrolled among the saints. Sterne thought that her rise, like the rest of the army of martyrs, was "a desperate slow one"; and asked, as he walked on to the next tomb, "Who the deuce has got lain down here, besides her?" The sacristan, starting to reply that it was St. Optat, a bishop—was cut short by his visitor, who remarked that the bones of St. Optat were most fortunate in their resting place, as Mr. Shandy could have foretold from his name, the most auspicious that a bishop might bear. This may have been a sly hit at the Archbishop of York, who still enjoyed the old option of appointing a favorite to a benefice in the diocese of a newly consecrated bishop. So ended Auxerre.

All the way from Paris there had been more than the usual stops and hindrances from broken ropes, slipping knots, and loosened staples. Still, the family had travelled thus far with a degree of comfort; but as they proceeded farther south, vexations were turned to downright suffering. Their conveyance proved hopelessly inadequate; the inns grew more and more intolerable; the roads were dusty; and the southern sun beat upon them with deadly rays. After it was all over, Sterne wrote to his friend Foley, the banker, with special reference to the journey from this point southwards: "I never saw a cloud from Paris to Nismes half as broad as a twenty-four sols piece.——Good God! we were toasted, roasted, grill'd, stew'd and carbonaded on one side or other all the way——and being all done enough (*assez cuits*) in the day, we were ate up at night by bugs, and other unswept out vermin, the legal inhabitants (if length of possession gives right) of every inn we lay at." On one of these fierce days, just as Lyons was in sight, the chaise overturned and broke "into a thousand pieces." Chaise and luggage were thrown "higgledy-piggledy" into a cart, behind which the pilgrims walked demurely into the town.

As they were passing through the streets to the inn of Monsieur Le Blanc, in the western quarter of the town, a pert chaise-vamper stepped nimbly up to Sterne and asked if he would have his chaise refitted. "No, no, said I, shaking my head sideways——Would Monsieur chuse to sell it? rejoin'd the undertaker——With all my soul, said I——the iron work is worth forty livres—and the glasses worth forty more—and the leather you may take to live on." Thornhill's beautiful chariot, which cost Sterne ten guineas, accordingly went for four louis d'ors. To make good the loss as well as to avoid further misfortunes on the road, Sterne decided to take the boat to Avignon, which left the next day at noon. By changing to this mode of travel, his purse would be the better, as he reckoned it, by four hundred livres. The next morning he was up early, breakfasting on "milk-coffee," and ready to start out by eight o'clock to see those curiosities of Lyons which Piganiol de la Force made so much of. Whereupon a series of cross-accidents intervened to bring all to naught.

As he was about to pass from the *basse cour* of his inn to the street, he was met at the gate by an ass munching the stem of an artichoke. He had to stop and watch Old Honesty drop and pick up the bitter morsel half a dozen times, and then to try, out of pleasantry, the effect of a macaroon upon him in place of the artichoke. So much of the famous communion with the ass at Lyons may possibly be fact. Once outside the gate, Sterne was stopped by a commissary from the post-office "with a re-script in his hand for the payment of some six livres odd sous, . . . for the next post from hence to St. Fons" in the route to Avignon. Puzzled at the demand, Sterne explained to the commissary that he did not intend to take post, but was going by water down the Rhone. *"C'est tout égal,"* replied the commissary, and handed Monsieur the rescript to read for himself. From the curious document, Sterne learned why Monsieur La Popelinière, the rich farmer-general, was able to keep open house and a band of musicians for the entertainment of all Paris; more specifically he learned, by the help of the officer, "that if you set out with an intention of running post from *Paris* to *Avignon,* &c., you shall not change that intention or mode of travelling, without first satisfying the *fermiers* for two posts further than the place you repent at." After a vigorous protest, Sterne paid the six livres in order that the revenues of the kingdom might not fall short through the fickleness of an English gentleman.

Determined, however, to make an immediate record of the imposition, Sterne put his hand into his coat-pocket for the note-book he had brought with him; but, to his consternation, the note-book, containing all his clever observations, was gone —lost or stolen. As soon as his head cleared up a little, it occurred to him that he had left his notes in the pocket of his chaise, and in selling the vehicle, had sold his notes along with it. So he hastened off to the chaise-vamper, where they were discovered and returned to him. As Sterne pointed the story for his comic history, the sheets had been torn up the night before by the wife of the chaise-maker, and used as papillotes in frizzling her hair. She untwisted the papers from her curls and placed them gravely one by one in his hat.

The morning was now so far advanced that only an hour was left for seeing the objects for which Lyons was renowned. With François, his *valet de place,* he ran over to the Cathedral of St. Jean for just a look at the mechanism of the wonderful clock set up in the choir by Lippius of Bâle. He got no farther than the west door of the cathedral, where a minor canon told him that the "great clock was all out of joints and had not gone for some years"; so he hurried away to the Jesuits' library, where reposed, among the treasures, a general history of China in thirty volumes, all in the Chinese language and Chinese characters. That curiosity he was destined not to peruse, for the library was closed, all the Jesuits being ill, Sterne opined, of a colic. This was Sterne's way of saying that the Jesuits were out of favor with the ministry.

Nothing remained on his schedule of *videnda* except the Tomb of the two Lovers, outside the gate, in the Faubourg de Vaise. The origin of that tomb or little temple and what it meant, Sterne knew from his guide-book, had been for a long time a question in dispute among the savants. Adopting the sentimental explanation, he felt sure that it was a monument erected to the constancy of Amandus and Amanda, who, after long separation and captivity, met at Lyons, and, flying into each other's arms, dropped down dead for joy. That spot of all others in the world must not be missed. The site of the tomb was easily found, but no monument was visible, for it had been razed to the ground many years before, as was indeed the fact, by the *consulat de Lyon*.

Sterne re-crossed the city barely in time for the noon boat, aboard which his family and luggage awaited him. He is strangely reticent on the voyage down the Rhone, except to intimate that he was pleased with the rush of the stream while his boat shot merrily along between "banks advancing and returning," and by the foot of the vine-covered Hermitage and Côte-Rôtie. On the evening he landed at Avignon, the wind was blowing violently, though it had not reached the fury of the mistral; and Sterne lost his hat. He wished to enquire of some learned man about the proverb that "Avignon is more subject to high winds than any town in all France," but he could find no one to converse with except his landlord, for everybody else was either duke, marquis, or count. To escape for the future the discomforts of the journey from Paris to Lyons, he sent his wife and daughter on by post, while he engaged for himself a mule and servant with horse.

As he was setting out from his inn, a ludicrous adventure befell him much like one that happened to Smollett at Joigny a year later. The irritable novelist, sitting in his chaise before the post-office, waiting for a change of horses, was politely addressed by a man who stepped up to the chaise-window. Supposing the stranger to be the inn-keeper of the place, Smollett turned to him savagely and ordered him to help a servant in adjusting the displaced trunks. A few minutes later he learned to his chagrin that he had insulted a gentleman. Under similar circumstances Yorick's conduct was more urbane:

"Prithee, friend, said I, take hold of my mule for a moment——for I wanted to pull off one of my jack-boots, which hurt my heel——the man was standing quite idle at the door of the inn, and as I had taken it into my head, he was someway concerned about the house or stable, I put the bridle into his hand——so begun with the boot:——when I had finished the affair, I turned about to take the mule from the man, and thank him——

"——But *Monsieur le Marquis* had walked in——"

On the morning of the start, Sterne was in buoyant mood, in anticipation of the rare journey through the rich plain of Languedoc to the banks of the Garonne. He was also in excellent health. "I had left Death," he said playfully, "the Lord knows—and He only—how far behind me. . . . Still he pursued——but like one who pursued his prey without hope—— as he lagg'd, every step he lost, soften'd his looks." One may fancy the scene as the travellers crossed the bridge at Avignon. Ahead was the chaise with Mrs. Sterne and Lydia, followed by the owner of the outfit striding along on foot, with a gun thrown across his shoulder to frighten off robbers; next came Sterne riding a mule; and a servant on horseback brought up the rear, bearing his master's luggage, in case the company should get separated at night. If Sterne tells the truth, he loitered behind terribly, stopping and talking to everyone on the way—peasants at their work, strolling beggars, pilgrims, fiddlers, and friars. "I was always in company, and with great variety too; . . . I am confident we could have passed through *Pall-Mall* or *St. James's*-Street for a month together, with fewer adventures——and seen less of human nature."

With Sterne time counted for nothing. Meeting a couple of Franciscans, who were more straitened for it than himself, he even walked back with them half a mile in order to complete an interesting conversation. He watched a drum-maker, who was making drums for the fairs of Beaucaire and Tarascon, enquiring of him the principles that underlay the instruments, not because he wished to know them, but because he wished to see the working of a peasant's mind in an attempt to explain them. Of a gossip he bought a hand-basket of Provence figs for five sous. Though a very small trade, it gave him another and finer opportunity to study the peasant in a case of abstract reasoning; for, on lifting the vine-leaves, he discovered beneath the figs two dozen of eggs, which the old woman had forgotten. Thereupon arose a nice question of property: To whom belonged the eggs? It might be said that the eggs were Sterne's, inasmuch as he had paid for the space they occupied. Against this position it might be said with equal justice that he had not purchased eggs, and so they could not be his. Sterne was quite willing to resign all claim to the eggs; but then arose a still nicer question: To whom belonged the basket? The question puzzled alike the philosopher and the peasant; for without the basket to carry them in, neither the eggs nor the figs had any value.

Sauntering along in this delightful fashion, Sterne made a spurt somewhere between Avignon and Beaucaire, and caught up with the chaise in time to share in the second serious mishap since leaving Paris. It was towards the end of July, the gala week at the fair of Beaucaire. "Can you conceive," he wrote in his amusing way to Foley, "a worse accident than that in such a journey, in the hottest day and hour of it, four miles from either tree or shrub which could cast a shade of the size of one of Eve's fig leaves—that we should break a hind wheel into ten thousand pieces, and be obliged in consequence to sit five hours on a gravelly road, without one drop of water, or possibility of getting any——To mend the matter, my two postillions were two dough-hearted fools, and fell a crying. ——Nothing was to be done! By heaven, quoth I, pulling off my coat and waistcoat, something shall be done, for I'll thrash you both within an inch of your lives——and then make you take each of you a horse, and ride like two devils to the next

post for a cart to carry my baggage, and a wheel to carry ourselves——Our luggage weighed ten quintals——'twas the
fair of Baucaire——all the world was going, or returning
——we were ask'd by every soul who pass'd by us, if we were
going to the fair of Baucaire——no wonder, quoth I, we have
goods enough! *vous avez raison, mes amis.*"

The next post, whither the postillions were sent for cart
and chaise, was indeed Beaucaire. Thence the unfortunate
travellers proceeded to Nîmes and Lunel, where Sterne closed
his narrative in the exquisite idyl of Nannette and the village dance which he took part in at the end of a sultry day.
Under the inspiration of the roundelay which he heard that
evening—

"Viva la joia!
Fidon la tristessa!"—

he danced all the way, he would have us understand, from
Lunel to Montpellier, "where there is the best Muscatto wine
in all France"—and thence on through Narbonne and Car-
cassonne to his habitation at Toulouse.

CHAP. XIV.

A Gentleman of France. August, 1762—*May,* 1764

THE ancient capital of Languedoc stretches along the right bank of the Garonne, crossed by the noble Pont-Neuf. The centre of the town was then, as it is now, the Place du Capitole, the seat of the municipal government. Close by were the University founded by Pope Gregory the Ninth, and the Museum of Fine Arts, with the academies of science and belles-lettres. From the Capitole, streets ran off in all directions, terminating at the north in the beautiful church of St. Sernin, the pride of Toulouse, and at the south in the Parliament buildings, stately mansions, and extensive gardens and suburbs. To the southwest was the Cathedral of St. Etienne, over which presided Loménie de Brienne, to become Minister of Finance under Louis the Sixteenth. On his arrival early in the second week of August, 1762, Sterne was pleased with the town beyond anticipation. The Abbé Mackarty had rented for him a large and well-furnished house from Monsieur Sligniac, apparently on the outer edge of the southern quarter, and had attended to all those little details necessary to a stranger's comfort. As soon as he had unpacked and looked about him, Sterne wrote to Hall-Stevenson on the twelfth of August:

"Here I am in my own house, quite settled by M[ackarty]'s aid, and good-natured offices, for which I owe him more than I can express or know how to pay at present.———'Tis in the prettiest situation in Toulouse, with near two acres of garden. . . . I have got a good cook———my wife a decent *femme de chambre*, and a good-looking *laquais*.———The Abbé has planned our expences, and set us in such a train, we cannot easily go wrong———tho' by the bye, the d———l is seldom found sleeping under a hedge."

And two days later he gave Foley other details:

"Well! here we are after all, my dear friend———and most deliciously placed at the extremity of the town, in an excellent house well furnish'd and elegant beyond anything I look'd for——'Tis built in the form of a hôtel, with a pretty court towards the town——and behind, the best gardens in Toulouse, laid out in serpentine walks, and so large that the company in our quarter usually come to walk there in the evenings, for which they have my consent——'the more the merrier.' ——The house consists of a good *salle à manger* above stairs joining to the very great *salle à compagnie* as large as the Baron d'Holbach's; three handsome bed-chambers with dressing rooms to them——below stairs two very good rooms for myself, one to study in, the other to see company.——I have moreover cellars round the court, and all other offices—— Of the same landlord I have bargained to have the use of a country-house which he has two miles out of town, so that myself and all my family have nothing more to do than take our hats and remove from the one to the other.——My landlord is moreover to keep the gardens in order——and what do you think I am to pay for all this? neither more or less than thirty pounds a year."

Alternating between his *hôtel* and country-house, Sterne entered upon the life of a French gentleman, at the small expense, as his wife estimated, of two hundred and fifty pounds a year. Connected with his country-house was "a handsome pavillion," which he re-named Pringello's Pavilion in honor of Don Pringello, the fanciful title of an architect whom Hall-Stevenson had recently celebrated in *Crazy Tales*, as one of the Demoniacs. Within easy distance was similarly established the eccentric William Hewitt, whom Sterne had met at Skelton and Scarborough. The two families were constantly passing to and fro for dinner or supper. Between meals Sterne took to drinking ass's milk in the morning and cow's milk in the evening, a diet which was recommended to him in this way by the physicians. In the heat of summer there was little society at Toulouse, for the French gentlemen were away in the country, and the usual English colony was scattered at various resorts and in travel. With nothing thus to distract him, Sterne sat down in his study or his pavilion to *Tristram Shandy*, in the hope that another instalment might be completed for the next London season. He did not begin, as is quite evident, with the seventh volume, which describes the tour through France from Calais. Notes he had made for the journey, but it had not occurred to him that his travels could be grafted into *Tristram Shandy*. They were to form, as first designed, a work separate and distinct. His imagination was away in Shandy Hall and Yorkshire, with my uncle Toby, Corporal Trim, and the widow Wadman, on a day in mid-August when he unscrewed his inkhorn under the "genial sun" of Toulouse, in the "clear climate of fantasy and perspiration." Hall-Stevenson's *Crazy Tales* lay before him. Ten times a day he looked at the curious frontispiece of Skelton Castle; and with his face turned towards its turret, so near as the direction could be made out, he plunged into my uncle Toby's amours, comprising the eighth book of *Tristram Shandy*.

He advanced only a short distance, hardly beyond the opening "crazy" chapters, containing a mad address to his readers in imitation of Rabelais, and a claim that his method of composition was "the most religious," if not the best in the world; "for I begin with writing the first sentence——and trusting to Almighty God for the second." While in this exultant mood, he "fell ill of an epidemic vile fever, which killed hundreds" about him. For six weeks he lay between life and death, attended by the local physicians, whom he declared "the errantest charlatans in Europe." "I withdrew," he wrote to Hall-Stevenson in October, "what was left of me out of their hands, and recommended my affairs entirely to Dame Nature ——She (dear goddess) has saved me in fifty different pinching bouts, and I begin to have a kind of enthusiasm now in her favour, and in my own, That one or two more escapes will make me believe I shall leave you all at last by translation, and not by fair death."

Sterne soon became as "stout and foolish" as ever, and resumed my uncle Toby's amours, while the Abbé Mackarty was out vintaging, and Lydia was "hard at it with music, dancing, and French speaking." As he sat at his table with a bottle of

Frontiniac and glass at his side for a pledge to Hall-Stevenson, he thought that he had as good reason for being contented as the rest of his household. But Toulouse somehow, he could not quite explain it, was no longer to his taste. Had it not run counter to one of his hypotheses, he would have laid his weariness to the climate, for the hot summer was being followed by a bitter cold autumn, which obliged him and his family "to sit with whole pagells of wood lighted up to our noses." In searching for a cause of his discontent, he finally attributed it to "the eternal platitude of the French character." Everybody was civil to him, but civility with no variety in it wearied and "boddered" him to death. To put him into spirits once more, he longed for a visit from Tollot—who was again in Paris with Sir Charles Danvers,—in order that he might die, not of ennui, but of laughter.

On the approach of winter, Sterne's gaiety returned without the aid of Sir Charles. French society doubtless improved as soon as families of rank left their châteaux and came in for the season and the local parliament. The Comtesse de Fumel and Monsieur Bonrepos received on several days every week; and the Baron d'Orbessan, President of the Assembly, kept open house to which all were welcome, whether French or foreigners.* Of these and other fashionable salons Sterne must have been an *habitué*, as were Tollot and Hall-Stevenson when they visited Toulouse. They particularly liked the Baron d'Orbessan, who was himself something of a Demoniac. Many English travellers, who had been running about Europe, fixed upon Toulouse for the whole or a part of the winter. There was a happy society of them distributed about in lodgings, and gyrating around the *hôtels* of the Sternes and the Hewitts. Among them, as they came and went through the winter, was a shadowy Mrs. M—— (Meadows, perhaps), with whom the Sternes sometimes dined; a family named Hodges; and a Mr. Woodhouse, "a most amiable worthy man," who stopped on his way to Italy, and whom Sterne took into his own house.

* W. Durrant Cooper, *Seven Letters written by Sterne and his Friends*, 6 (London, 1844).

Every night they were all together at one place or another, "fiddling, laughing and singing, and cracking jokes."

Early in December they went to the Hodges', "living together like brothers and sisters," and practising a play for the Christmas holidays, a diversion which had been suggested by Sterne as a *soulagement*. Towards the middle of the month, as luck would have it, a company of English strollers arrived in Toulouse to act comedies, if an audience could be found. On Sterne's initiative, the two groups of amateurs united forces and shifted their scene of action over to his great *salle à compagnie*. After a fortnight in making costumes and in learning their parts, they presented there Mrs. Centlivre's *Busy Body*, with a grand orchestra improvised for the occasion. The next week they played Vanbrugh and Cibber's *Journey to London*, which Sterne, if he carried out his design, re-wrote in part, turning it into *A Journey to Toulouse*. It is all very pretty to see Yorick in the rôle of playwright and stage-manager and possibly actor.

The rest of the winter passed in interchange of visits; and when the English colony began to break up in the spring, the Sternes were invited to the Hewitts' country house for a week or fortnight. But we have no further festivities to relate, for Yorick was becoming depressed again. His purse was empty. Since settling with Mrs. Sterne, Becket had sold up to April, 1763, only 182 copies of the last *Shandys*, and after that the sale came to a stand-still. "Ten cart-loads" of the volumes, Sterne said, still remained on their hands. That estimate was an exaggeration for 991 sets, enough, none the less, to disappoint him of a hundred pounds which he had expected at this time. So Sterne had to depend upon remittances out of Yorkshire, which were obviously inadequate for his mode of life. He was spending more than twice the clear income from his farms and parishes. By December he was reduced to "half a dozen guineas"; and in March he had only "five Louis to vapour with in this land of coxcombs." Foley, his banker, though very kind and considerate, naturally hesitated to advance the small sums which Sterne succeeded, however, in coaxing from him month after month. To poverty of purse was added poverty of spirit. During the winter, Sterne worked intermittently at *Tristram*, and revised more of his old sermons, perhaps writing new ones, with a view to publication; but his progress had been slow. April came and nothing was ready for the press; nothing could be sent over to Becket for further revenue.

Behind this double bankruptcy, financial and intellectual, which threatened Sterne, lay the wretched state of his health. Toulouse, ill-drained and subject to cold and damp winds in winter, had not agreed with him at all. True, there were days extending into weeks when he felt well, and imagined that the dread disease had been arrested, for there were as yet no returns of the hemorrhages of last summer. In these periods he went on with his literary work, and wrote "long nonsensical" letters to Hall-Stevenson, as if completely re-instated in health and spirits; but such was really not the case. Over against the joyous letters to the master of Skelton should be set one to Archbishop Drummond in May, 1763, dismal in its forebodings and yet flashing with humor:

"I have been fixed here with my family these ten months, and by God's blessing it has answered all I wished for, with regard to my daughter; I cannot say so much for myself, having since the first day of my arrival here been in a continual warfare with agues, fevers, and physicians——the first brought my blood to so poor a state, that the physicians found it necessary to enrich it with strong bouillons, and strong bouillons and soups à santé threw me into fevers, and fevers brought on loss of blood, and loss of blood agues——so that as *war begets poverty, poverty peace*, etc. etc.——has this miserable constitution made all its revolutions; how many more it may sustain, before its last and great one, God knows—— like the rest of my species, I shall fence it off as long as I can. I am advised now to try the virtues of the waters of Banyars, and shall encamp like a patriarch with my whole household upon the side of the Pyreneans this summer and winter at Nice; from whence in spring I shall return home, never, I fear, to be of service, at least as a preacher. I have preached too much, my Lord, already; and was my age to be computed either by the number of sermons I have preached, or the infirmities they have brought upon me, I might be truly said to have the claim of a *miles emeritus*, and was there a Hôtel des Invalides for the reception of such established upon any salutary plain betwixt here and Arabia Felix, I would beg your Grace's interest to help me into it——as it is, I rest fully assured in my heart of your Grace's indulgence to me in my endeavours to add a few quiet years to this fragment of my life——and with my wishes for a long and happy one to your Grace, I am, from the truest veneration of your character,— Your most dutiful servant, L. Sterne."

The cause to which Sterne assigned his physical collapse cannot be taken at full value, though he had indeed innumerable sermons to his credit. He might surely have preached on for another decade but for *Tristram Shandy* and the indiscretions that followed in its wake. His letter, for what it said and for what it left unsaid, was most admirable as a request that he be released from all further parish duties. As he told his archbishop, he was going to Bagnères-de-Bigorre at the foot of the French Pyrenees to try the waters and a higher altitude. There was also another motive for the journey. *Tristram Shandy* could not continue much further on the lines it had been running. It had been Sterne's first design, according to John Croft, to travel Mr. Tristram Shandy over Europe, making under this disguise remarks and strictures on the different peoples and governments, and closing with an eulogium on England and her superior constitution. Sterne's mind now began to revert to the original design as modified by a sojourn abroad. From politics, his interest had shifted to men and manners, of which he would give a comic rendering. At Bagnères, he expected "much amusement from the concourse of adventurers from all corners of the earth"; and after exhausting Bagnères, it was his plan to cross the Pyrenees and spend a week in Spain, where he could collect in that time enough material "for a fertile brain to write a volume upon." At the end of the spa season in September, he was to return and winter somewhere in southern France or in Italy, perhaps at Nice or at Florence, almost anywhere except at Toulouse.

But the financial problem stared him in the face. Towards the end of March, he received from England a draft for £130, which he turned over to his Paris banker. At best, this remittance satisfied current debts and carried him through the spring at Toulouse. Eager to set out on his journey, he wrote to Foley on April 29, asking for a fortnight's credit and explaining his method of payment. His agent at York was to send up to London "a bill for four score guineas," with orders that it be paid into the hands of Foley's correspondent; and in the same way £20, presumably from Becket on the *Shandys*, was to be placed at his London account. All this would take time. "Therefore," said the request to the banker, "be so good as to give me credit for the money for a few posts or so, and send me either a rescription for the money, or a draught for it." Three weeks passed with no reply; and then, on May 21, Sterne sent a sharp note to Foley:

"It is some disappointment to me that you have taken no notice of my letter, especially as I told you we waited for the money before we set out for Bagnieres——and so little distrust had I that such a civility would be refused me, that we have actually had all our things pack'd up these eight days, in hourly expectation of receiving a letter.——Perhaps my good friend has waited till he heard the money was paid in London —but you might have trusted to my honour——that all the cash in your iron box (and all the bankers in Europe put together) could not have tempted me to say the thing *that is not.* . . . Mr. R[ay] of Montpellier, tho' I know him not, yet knows enough of me to have given me credit for a fortnight for ten times the sum. . . . After all, I heartily forgive you—for you have done me a signal service in mortifying me, and . . . I am determined to grow rich upon it. Adieu, and God send you wealth and happiness."

To this letter Foley duly responded with an enclosure for eighty or a hundred pounds. The real cause of the previous delay, the banker averred, was no distrust of Sterne, but merely distraction "with a multitude of business." Sterne accepted good-naturedly the excuse, and in turn apologized for his testy temper, saying that his grievance was mostly imaginary, as he had in his pocket Mr. Ray's letter of credit for £200, which he could use on a pinch. Three days after receiving Foley's remittance—on June 12,—the Sternes took chaise for Bagnères, in company with Mrs. M[eadows], who was going to another resort in the Pyrenees. The visit to Bagnères, so far as we have any record of it, is almost an intellectual blank in Sterne's life. Only one of his published letters bears the superscription of that place; and that is merely a request to Becket, dated July 15, 1763, to send him a bill on Foley for whatever *Shandys* may have been sold. The pleasures of Bagnères, he said, however, the next year, were not so "exalted" as those of Scarborough in the society of "Lord Granby and Co." The clue to his disappointment is given in an hitherto unpublished letter* from Montpellier later in the year to a Mr. Mills, merchant in Philpot Lane, London. From the moment he left Toulouse, Sterne never had a moment's respite from ill-health, and subsequently the "thin Pyranean air brought on continual breeches of vessels" in his lungs.

The journey into Spain was obviously abandoned, though we have no positive statement either way. His condition in nowise improved, Sterne left Bagnères with his family as early as the first of September—two weeks before the time set for departure—and began a course of travels through southern France in search of a comfortable place to camp in for the next winter. There were times when he "risked," according to the letter to Mills, "being taken up for a spy," so suspicious was the aspect he bore in the character of a wanderer, "now prying here, now there," as Pope would say. The patriarch first retraced his steps to Toulouse, where he was made happy by an order from Foley upon his correspondent to pay Mr. Sterne fifteen hundred livres, should the gentleman be in need of it. Sterne needed the sum and accepted it as a "friendly act of civility," prompted by the generous heart of his banker. A

* See letter XXIII in Chap. XXV of this biography.

filled purse sent the Sternes on to Montpellier, with stops and digressions all along the route. This town, which they had passed through before, must have pleased them for several reasons. Like Toulouse, it always had its English colony in the winter; and it was pleasantly situated on a slope whence were visible mountains and sea. We may wonder, too, whether it ever occurred to Sterne that Master Rabelais took his Baccalaureate degree in Medicine at the University of Montpellier and lectured there on Galen and Hippocrates. To Montpellier were found, however, two objections. Provisions there were "a third dearer than at Toulouse," and the place had "a bad character . . . as the grave of consumptive people." So the Sternes quickly broke camp for Aix and Marseilles, making the usual long detours. Aix, the capital of Provence, Sterne disliked because Toulouse had already given him a surfeit of parliaments. Marseilles, then a small town running about the old port, with wooded hills for background, was attractive enough; but house rent and cost of living were "enormous." "I could not take," said Sterne, "the most miserable apartments under nine or ten guineas a month," and everything else was "in proportion." Balancing the *pour* and the *contre* for each of the places which they had visited, Sterne decided upon Montpellier; and posted directly thither with his household. His purse was, of course, the determining factor in the account. As for life and death, he said, "I love to run hazards rather than die by inches."

The Sternes returned to Montpellier near the end of September. By taking apartments instead of a house—evidently their plan—they should have lived as cheaply, though not as luxuriously, as at Toulouse. Good lodgings on the hill, accommodating two or three persons, were obtainable for three guineas a month; and meals, without wine, cost a family of that number about ten livres a day. The local markets were "well supplied with fish, poultry, butcher's meat, and game, at reasonable rates." The ordinary wine of the district, if one wished to drink it, was exceedingly cheap; while the sweet wine of Frontignan, Yorick's favorite next to burgundy, was made near Cette, the seaport of Montpellier. The city was also famous for the distillation of pleasant drams or liqueurs of various sorts. Sterne, if he managed well, certainly had no cause for complaint.

A sojourn in Montpellier, though very like one at Toulouse, afforded greater variety of scene and character. "Four or five" English families stayed through the winter, taking houses or apartments near one another for free intercourse; but who they were we do not know, except that the Hewitts seem to have migrated hither so as to be with their friends. In the town resided also an English physician named Fitzmaurice, "a very worthy sensible" practitioner, and a "Mr. Ray, an English merchant and banker, . . . a gentleman of great probity and worth," who cashed the bills of his countrymen, looked after their letters, and helped them over all troubles. Sterne formed "a particular friendship," too, with a man who was buying up the wines of the present vintage to ship to London. Of his friend he wrote to the Earl of Fauconberg and offered to send over a couple of hogsheads as a present, provided his lordship would pay the duty thereon. The inhabitants of Montpellier were happy and prosperous, as a stranger might quickly see by a walk through the narrow streets on a pleasant evening; for he would observe all along his way "the better sort of both sexes" sitting out on the stone seats by their doors, "conversing with great mirth and familiarity," with here and there a group singing a roundelay accompanied by the violin.

To the east of the town, by the gate of the citadel, was a long esplanade, where people gathered every day to take the air, and to the west was the *Peyrou*, a still more agreeable promenade, whence one obtained a view of the Cévennes on the one side and of the Mediterranean on the other. The beautiful prospects and the pure elastic air attracted Sterne on first sight, for they would be, he thought, temptations to take him out of doors like the rest. At this time the town was garrisoned by two battalions, of which one was "the Irish regiment of Berwick, commanded by Lieutenant Colonel Tents," who treated the English with great politeness and hospitality. The social season opened with two concerts a week at the theatre,

called the *Comédie,* in the *place* of the same name; and these
entertainments were followed by a line of comedies, as at Toulouse, performed, it may be, by the identical company of
strollers. When Sterne berated Toulouse and Aix as parliament
towns which he could no longer endure, he seems to have forgotten that Montpellier was one also. As in the other provincial capitals, the season reached its height at Montpellier when
the states of Languedoc assembled at the Hôtel de Ville in
gorgeous processions and ceremonies, which Sterne called "a
fine raree-shew, with the usual accompanyments of fiddles,
bears, and puppet-shews." Then came, closing the winter, a
succession of dinners and receptions given by the governor and
óther high officials.

Now and then English tourists who were strolling through
southern France during the winter, stopped at Montpellier for
a week or so, staying at the Cheval Blanc or going into furnished lodgings. In November arrived Smollett the novelist,
all worked out and suffering from asthma, in company with
his wife and two other English ladies. Though on the way
from Paris to Nice, he made the long detour to lay the case of
his health before Dr. Antoine Fizès, "the Boerhaave of Montpellier," as he was called. Fearing the results of a personal encounter with the learned physician, who was reported arrogant
in deportment, Smollett consulted him by means of a long letter in Latin, and received in reply, to his disgust, a long letter
in French. The novelist proved the physician's diagnosis false,
turned with loathing from the usual prescription of bouillons
and ass's milk, and savagely denounced the "great lanthorn of
medicine" as a knave and arrant humbug. Unfortunately for
Montpellier, a week's rain set in a few days after Smollett's
arrival, "leaving the air so loaded with vapours that there was
no walking after sunset, without being wetted by the dew almost to the skin." There were, however, some bright days
during Smollett's visit, and he said many interesting things
about the city, its sociable inhabitants and their customs, upon
which we have based largely our account as a background to
Sterne's life there.

The novelist was especially pleased with his reception by the English residents, who made it a point to call upon all new-comers. Did Sterne, like the rest, pay his formal respects to the man whose *Review* had slashed his jerkin year after year? We have no direct information on that point; but neither Sterne nor Smollett could have let literary animosities inter-fere with the etiquette prescribed for gentlemen. The novelist, as he definitely stated, met and conversed with Mrs. Sterne,* who told him incidentally about a young consumptive among their friends, a Mr. Oswald of London, that came over for the treatment of the celebrated physician. After a month of it, Oswald said to the doctor one day: "I take your prescriptions punctually; but, instead of being the better for them, I have now not an hour's remission from the fever in the four-and-twenty.——I cannot conceive the meaning of it." The doctor replied that the reason should be plain, for "the air of Mont-pellier was too sharp for his lungs, which required a softer cli-mate." "Then you are a sordid villain," retorted the young man, "for allowing me to stay here till my constitution is irretrievable." A few months later Oswald died, it was said, in the neighborhood of Toulouse. On hearing this dismal story, Smollett, who feared consumption for himself, packed up and hastened to Nice.

The next month Sterne received a visit from a group of his most intimate friends, and missed the sight of others whom he would have been glad to see. In the previous summer, Tol-lot had taken the road with Thornhill and a younger brother, both of London, and a Mr. Garland, who will be remembered as one of the Demoniacs. From Paris they went into Belgium, where Garland left them at Brussels for home; while the others, after six weeks at Spa, journeyed leisurely through Lor-raine and Alsace into Switzerland, as far south as Geneva, to call upon their friend Rousseau; and thence they turned west to Lyons for a circular tour of southern France to Bordeaux and round to Paris again. At Lyons, they fell in with Hewitt

* Smollett, *Travels through France and Germany*, in *Works*, with an introductory essay by W. E. Henley, 128 (London, 1900).

and Charles Turner, a sporting Yorkshire squire of Kirk-leatham near Skelton, who was taking his wife to Aix for the winter. They all went south at the same time, some by chaise and others by boat. At Avignon the party divided, Hewitt for Montpellier and the rest for Aix. After being snowed in at Aix for a fortnight, Tollot and the Thornhills proceeded to Montpellier. They were delighted—Tollot is the spokesman in a letter to Hall-Stevenson—to see again the *"bon et agréable* Tristram,"* whom they found apparently enjoying himself to the full, just as at Paris two years before. But they pitied him for the persecutions of a wife who jealously followed him everywhere, causing him, they fancied, many unhappy moments, which he bore nevertheless with "the patience of an angel." In a word, the *bonne dame* was from their point of view *de trop.* On learning from Sterne that he was about to return to his "other wife," meaning thereby his church at Cox-wold, Tollot invited him to his own *hôtel* and table at Paris, and promised to conduct him safely back to England with his other friends.*

When the company broke up in anticipation of a joyous re-union at Paris, Sterne regarded himself in perfect health, de-spite the attack of rain, mists, and snows. But as ever, he was again deceived as to his real condition. On January 5, 1764, he began a letter to Foley, and, when half way through it, broke off to take a ride on the road towards Pézenas. His beast proved to be "as unmoveable as Don Quixote's wooden-horse"; no motion was to be got out of him at all except by continued lashings, which "half dislocated" Sterne's arm, until his head was turned homeward; and then he struck into a trot. The exertion on a chilly morning brought on a fever, which con-fined Sterne to his bed for more than a week. Not till the fif-teenth was he able to finish the letter to his banker, in which he said: "I have suffered in this scuffle with death terribly—but unless the spirit of prophecy deceive me—I shall not die but live—in the meantime, dear Foley, let us live as merrily but *as innocently* as we can———It has ever been as good, if not

* Cooper, *Seven Letters,* 5.

better, than a bishoprick to me—and I *desire no other*." During a month of convalescence, Sterne was put through the customary course of treatment, either under Dr. Fizès or under the local faculty who had acquired the art of medicine from his practice. "My physicians," he wrote on the first of February, "have almost poisoned me with what they call *bouillons refraichissants*—'tis a cock flayed alive and boiled with poppy seeds, then pounded in a mortar, afterwards pass'd through a sieve——There is to be one crawfish in it, and I was gravely told it must be a male one—a female would do me more hurt than good." At the end of the period, the physicians informed him, just as Dr. Fizès had informed young Oswald, that "the sharp air of Montpellier" would be fatal to him, if he remained longer. "And why, good people," Sterne replied, "were you not kind enough to tell me this sooner?" While still unable to be out, Sterne was particularly honored by a call from the Earl of Rochford, who was passing through Montpellier en route to assume his duties as English Ambassador to the Court of Spain. The two men who met here far from home and conversed of their common friends, must have been old acquaintances; for Lord Rochford, besides being an invariable subscriber to Yorick's books, was a lavish host in the political set among whom Sterne moved when in London.

One may readily see how events were driving Sterne back to England. Though his life may have been saved by his first hurried journey to Paris, his health, on the whole, had not been benefited by his long sojourn abroad. Indeed, it probably would have been better for him had he never gone to the south of France. From the first he fretted under his inability to proceed with *Shandy* and thus lay another tax—as he always expressed it—upon the public, so necessary to the support of his family. Hopeless on this score, he sent his books back to England the previous spring by way of Bordeaux, addressed in care of Becket his publisher. Not a chapter, so far as one knows, did he add to his work while staying at Montpellier. His financial as well as his physical condition had grown worse and worse. How he got through the winter would be a puzzle, did we not know Sterne as a skilful borrower. As early as November 24, 1763, he wrote to Mills, the London merchant, requesting that he might draw upon him to the extent of fifty pounds. As for surety, he said "the whole Shandean family" will stand bound for the capital; and as to immediate prospects, "you shall be paid the very first money God sends." He was doubtless helped out, as his letters would imply, by Foley, Ray, and other friends with whom he was living "as brothers." Really thrice a bankrupt, in purse, health, and intellect, Sterne wisely decided to manage henceforth as best he could in England, and to make another effort at *Tristram Shandy* in the quiet of Coxwold.

In carrying out this design, Mrs. Sterne strangely stood in the way. Whenever her husband suggested, as he had been doing for a year, a return to England, she pleaded her own welfare and her daughter's. Her rheumatism troubled her less in France than at home, and Lydia should stay on and complete her education. This opposition of wishes, though not "as sour as lemon," was not, in Sterne's phrase, "as sweet as sugar." Out of patience with her view of the situation, Sterne finally told his wife, after his last illness at Montpellier, that he was going back to Coxwold as soon as he should be able, but that she might remain on with Lydia for another two or three years, if she chose to do so. He clearly saw the financial and social difficulties of a separate maintenance, and agreed to it only with great reluctance when brought to his wit's end. His wife and daughter were to go to Montauban, north from Toulouse, for the present, and, if they wished, they might spend the summer at Bagnères. As first planned, he was to return by way of Geneva, for a visit doubtless with Rousseau and Voltaire, and "then fall down the Rhine to Holland," whence he could embark directly for Hull and avoid the temptations of Paris and London. But the generous offer of Tollot to share with him his apartments and table at Paris evidently determined him to retrace his steps by the old route. About the first of March, 1764, or as soon as he received his Christmas remittance from Coxwold, Sterne turned his face towards home "in high spirits . . . except for a tear at parting with my little slut," his affectionate name for Lydia. With his wife he left a hundred louis for pocket money, and promised her two hundred guineas a year.

Sterne traversed the road back to Paris without any incident he thought worth recording. On his arrival, in the second or third week of March, he went directly to the Hôtel d'Entragues, in the Rue Tournon near the Luxembourg, where were established Tollot and the Thornhills. With these "good and generous souls," though Tollot was continually out of sorts with the cold spring, Sterne lived "a most jolly nonsensical life" for two months and more. Across the Seine, in the Rue St. Nicaise, was their friend John Wilkes, who had recently been expelled from the House of Commons. Like many others, they regarded him as a martyr to free speech. Sterne and Wilkes often met, and on one occasion formed "an odd party"* with the "goddesses of the theatre," at the house of one Hope, whom the politician described as "a Dutchman metamorphosed into an Italian" by long residence in Rome and Venice. Much in their company, too, was Stephen Fox, "dissipating the ill-got fleeting wealth of his father." In the summer Lord Holland came abroad with his younger son, Charles James Fox; but that was too late for the humorist to fall in with them. Every day Sterne saw also Lawson Trotter, the Jacobite outlaw, who, despite exile, was "eternally joyous and jocundissimus." To complete the scene of Yorick's immediate society, he was "smitten with the tenderest passion that ever tender wight underwent." Once, twice, and thrice every day, when no other amusement was at hand, Sterne trudged off to this woman's *hôtel* for sentimental converse. Before the spring was over, she went to the south of France, and therewith ended the comedy.

It is to be presumed that Sterne renewed his intimacy with French society, revisiting the salons of d'Holbach, Suard, the

* Letter of Wilkes to Charles Churchill, dated Paris, April 10, 1764, in Wilkes's Correspondence with Churchill.—British Museum. Additional Manuscripts, 30878.

Comte de Bissy, and the Prince de Conti, where he had been so cordially received on his first coming to Paris. On this point, however, the meagre correspondence covering the period is silent. One misses greatly letters like those of two years before to Garrick, with whom he lost touch during a long absence. A letter to Garrick would doubtless have told us about "the uncommon applause" with which Voltaire's *Olympie* was greeted at the Comédie Française in March, and about the decorations, which were "allowed to be the most magnificent and striking that ever were exhibited on that stage."* The few letters that we have of these months relate to family affairs or to the English colony.

Two years before, there was hardly a score of English gentlemen in Paris and they were mostly birds of passage. Sterne, on account of his literary prestige, then easily became the lion of the season. In the meantime all was changed. Since the peace, says Horace Walpole, the way to Paris had become, "like the description of the grave, . . . the way of all flesh." To pay the expenses of the English who flocked thither, Foley was receiving every month out of England £30,000 in remittances.† An example for this display was set by the new Ambassador, the Earl of Hertford, a man of great wealth and generosity, who took for his residence the Hôtel de Lauragnais,‡ a large and luxurious mansion near the Louvre. With him was his son, Lord Beauchamp, an amiable young man whom everybody liked; and there still hovered about the embassy Lord Tavistock, son of the Duke of Bedford who had signed the articles of peace. Around these men centred the most fashionable English society. Every English gentleman, on coming to Paris, called at the embassy, and Lord Hertford returned the call, with invitations to dinners and receptions and to his Sunday chapel at the Hôtel de Lauragnais. No one was ostracized on account of political opinions. Lawson Trotter, who dared not step foot in England, might be seen almost

* *London Chronicle*, March 29-31, 1764.
† Walpole, *Letters*, edited by Toynbee, V, 345.
‡ *London Chronicle*, March 22-24, 1764.

any day at the embassy; and even Wilkes, convicted of libel against his Majesty's government, was tolerated, though with maimed rites. Sterne, who was an especial favorite, dined almost every week with the Ambassador or Lord Beauchamp or Lord Tavistock.

Lord Hertford brought over with him as his secretary, though the appointment was not quite official, Hume, the philosopher and historian. The choice seemed very odd to everybody who did not know Hume thoroughly. Hume was, if one likes to say it, "a coarse, clumsily built" Scotsman, halting and heavy in speech; and as to French, he sometimes could never get, if at all embarrassed, beyond *Eh bien! vous voilà.* And yet beneath this rough exterior was a man morally sound to the heart, of great and commanding intellect, and in disposition as genial and pliable as the author of *Tristram Shandy.* When Sterne reached Paris, Hume was feeding upon the same ambrosia of which he himself had grown sick two years before. "All the courtiers," wrote Hume to Adam Smith, "who surrounded me when I was introduced to Madame de Pompadour, assured me that she was never heard to say so much to any man."* A lady at court, it was rumored, fell into immemediate disgrace for asking who he was. With similar adulation Hume passed through all the great houses, where no reception was complete without him. Chamfort, being asked on one occasion what had become of the lion, replied: "I think he must be dead, for I have seen him only three times to-day." His presence was demanded at masquerades and tableaux and pantomimes; and at the theatre his big head "was usually seen between two pretty faces."

Paris could manage only one great sensation a season. In those days, it was either Sterne, Hume, Walpole, or Garrick, one at a time, never all together. This year Hume, who had the start of Sterne by several months, easily overshadowed him. A secondary rôle, nevertheless, had its honors, one of which

* *Life and Correspondence of David Hume,* II, 169 (Edinburgh, 1846).

Sterne particularly cherished. On a Saturday afternoon in March or April, while he was "playing a sober game of whist with the Thornhills," Lord Hertford's messenger appeared with a request that he preach, on the next morning, in the chapel at the new embassy in place of Dr. James Trail, the dull chaplain. Though Sterne had resolved never to preach more, this invitation could not be refused. He broke abruptly from his amusement, and set himself at once to the task of writing a sermon, on a text that came into his head at a flash without any consideration. The next morning the little chapel was filled with "a concourse of all nations and religions"— diplomats and officials from various embassies, Roman Catholics, Protestants, deists, and atheists. Hume was there, and, it is said, d'Holbach and Diderot. The text which Sterne chose on the spur of the moment was most amusingly inappropriate for anyone except a jester; and yet the preacher seemed unaware of the jest until all was over. His theme, based on 2 Kings xx. 15, was the rebuke that Isaiah administered to Hezekiah for exposing the treasures of the royal palace to the Babylonian ambassadors, and the subsequent prophecy that those treasures would some day be carried away to Babylon. "Nothing shall be left, saith the Lord."

The preacher related, with several fanciful enlargements, the story of Hezekiah's illness and of the miracle that was performed in his behalf. Instead of taking the Scriptures simply, which say that a prince of Babylon sent presents and messengers to Hezekiah to congratulate him upon his recovery, Sterne conjectured a hidden reason for this friendly act of courtesy. "As the Chaldeans," he said naïvely, "were great searchers into the secrets of nature, especially into the motions of the celestial bodies, in all probability they had taken notice, at that distance, of the strange appearance of the shadow's returning ten degrees backwards upon their dials; . . . so that this astronomical miracle . . . had been sufficient by itself to have led a curious people as far as Jerusalem, that they might see the man for whose sake the sun had forsook his course."

Sterne's honorarium was a dinner that Sunday evening at the English embassy, to which were invited the most distinguished of the congregation. It was presumably on this occasion that "a prompt French marquis," as related in the *Sentimental Journey*, mistook Hume for John Home, author of the once famous tragedy of *Douglas*, whose names were pronounced alike. Sitting beside the ambassador's secretary, the marquis turned to him and enquired whether he was Home the poet. "No, said Hume—mildly——*Tant pis*, replied the Marquis. It is Hume the historian, said another——*Tant mieux*, said the Marquis. And Mr. Hume, who is a man of excellent heart, return'd thanks for both."

This, however, was not the most amusing incident, if it occurred then, of the evening. The real merriment, in which all shared, started when Hume began to quiz Yorick slily on Hezekiah and the "astronomical miracle." Sterne, who—never a hypocrite—believed implicitly in miracles, accepted the challenge, while the other guests looked on and listened with delight to the droll combat. The story of the good-natured passage at arms, when it got out, was magnified into a hot dispute; and Sterne, troubled by the idle rumors, set matters right in one of his letters and no doubt in conversation. *"David,"* as he put it, "was disposed to make a little merry with the *parson*, and in return the parson was equally disposed to make a little mirth with the *infidel*; we laughed at one another, and the company laughed with us both." Not content with the mere statement of what occurred at Lord Hertford's table, Sterne took the occasion afforded by his letter to pay a most just tribute to the gentle temper of his friendly antagonist. "I should be most exceedingly surprized," he wrote, "to hear that David ever had an unpleasant contention with any man;—and if I should be made to believe that such an event had happened, nothing would persuade me that his opponent was not in the wrong; for in my life did I never meet with a being of a more placid and gentle nature; and it is this amiable turn of his character that has given more consequence and force to his scepticism than all the arguments of his sophistry."* The *amende honorable* was quite unnecessary.

Over-exertion resulted in another hemorrhage, which kept Sterne in Paris longer than he had intended to stay. As he turned his face once more towards England, for which he was passionately longing, his mind also reverted to his family in the south. On May 15, 1764, he wrote to Lydia, enumerating the presents that had been sent to her, and giving his final directions for her conduct in his absence:

"My dear Lydia . . . I acquiesed in your staying in France —likewise it was your mother's wish—but I must tell you both (that unless your health had not been a plea made use of) I should have wished you both to return with me.——I have sent you the Spectators, and other books, particularly Metastasio; but I beg my girl to read the former, and only make the latter her amusement.——I hope you have not forgot my last request, to make no friendships with the French women—not that I think ill of them all, but sometimes women of the best principles are the most *insinuating*——nay I am so jealous of you that I should be miserable were I to see you had the least grain of coquetry in your composition.——You have enough to do—for I have also sent you a guittar—and as you have no genius for drawing (tho' you never could be made to believe it) pray waste not your time about it.——Remember to write to me as to a friend——in short, whatever comes into your little head, and then it will be natural.——If your mother's rheumatism continues and she chooses to go to Bagnieres—tell her not to be stopped for want of money, for my purse shall be as open as my heart. . . . Kiss your mother from me, and believe me your affectionate L. Sterne."

* *Original Letters of the late Reverend Mr. Laurence Sterne*, 126-127 (London, 1788).

CHAP. XV.

Yorkshire and London. Tristram Shandy: Volumes VII and VIII. June, 1764—April, 1765

STERNE set out from Paris for home on Thursday, the twenty-fourth of May, in company with the Thornhills, and Tollot, who was going over to England. He should have reached London on the twenty-ninth; but there may have been delays, for the earliest notice of his return was an announcement in the postscript to *Lloyd's Evening Post* for June 2-4, that "The Rev. Mr. Sterne, the celebrated author of Tristram Shandy, is arrived from Paris, where he has long resided for his health." The news was taken up and repeated by other newspapers to an extent so unusual as to indicate that Sterne's presence in London at this time came as a surprise. During his long sojourn abroad, he had kept in correspondence with very few of his friends in town. Even Garrick, owing to a misunderstanding, had been dropped after the first weeks in Paris two years before. The coolness—if it may be called so—came about in this way. Sterne wrote to Garrick once or twice from southern France, but received no word in return. Garrick in fact duly replied, but his letters miscarried. Each supposed that he was "scalped" by the other, and so all letters between them ceased. Public interest in Sterne had flagged terribly. Becket sold few or no *Shandys* now, and other publishers were no longer putting out imitations. Indeed, the old rumor that Sterne was dead had never been quite laid, as one may see from an occasional letter to the newspapers through the year sixty-three. Somebody, for instance, attacked his memory in *St. James's Magazine*, a literary monthly conducted by Robert Lloyd; whereupon a correspondent, in the issue for July, 1763, vindicated Sterne's character by adapting Gray's famous elegy to "The Decease of Tristram Shandy," towards the close of which Sterne was conducted to the Elysian Fields and placed on an embowered seat near Rabelais, Lucian, and Cervantes.

The unexpected guest thus came upon London almost as
one returned from the dead. While in town he stayed, along
with Tollot, with the Thornhills, who had a house in John
Street near Berkeley Square. As it was the tag end of the
season, most of Sterne's old friends were away. Garrick, suffering, like Sterne, a temporary eclipse, was travelling with his
wife on the Continent. Foley, who was in London on business,
Sterne somehow missed, as if the two men were "two buckets
of a well," passing and drawing away from each other. Three
weeks were spent in London and the environs, during which
Sterne visited, though he gives few names, such friends as he
could find; among whom was Reynolds, who granted him a
sitting, as the painter's *Pocket-Book* shows, on Monday, the
eleventh of June. In this portrait the humorist was drawn at
half length on canvas measuring thirty by twenty-five inches.
Wearing his wig and gown, Sterne took his seat nearly facing
Sir Joshua and leaned his right elbow on a table, with the hand
supporting his tired head. It was a "very clever portrait . . .
in a less uniform tone" than was usual with Reynolds, though
lacking in that extraordinary insight into Sterne's character
displayed by the painter four years before.*

After his rest in London, Sterne went down to York alone,
where he arrived late in June.† As he intended never to preach
again, he passed the next two months idly in and about York.
The races in the third week of August, accompanied by balls
and concerts at the Assembly Rooms, to which he subscribed
this year, gave him an opportunity to see many of his old Yorkshire and more distant friends, including Hall-Stevenson, who
came in for the festivities. "Mr. Turner" and "Mr. Hall"
both entered horses and both lost. Tollot and Hewitt, who had
returned to England to look after his estates, were Sterne's

* This portrait was given by Sterne to Edward Stanley, who bequeathed it to his son-in-law, James Whatman of Venters, Maidstone.
It was engraved by Wivell and by Nagle.—Graves and Cronin, *A History of the Works of Sir Joshua Reynolds*, III, 935, IV, 1418.

† *York Courant*, June 26, 1764.

guests. And there were present, among his acquaintances of rank, the Marquis and Marchioness of Rockingham, Lord Fitzwilliam, and Lord Effingham of Surrey.*

As soon as the York races were over, Sterne went out to Coxwold to look after his "few poor sheep in the wilderness." Within a fortnight he grew uneasy of the quiet life, and decamped to Scarborough, whither were gathering people of quality for the spa season and the September races. Scarborough, at that time the most fashionable of the northern watering-places, is beautifully situated on a lofty cliff overlooking the German Ocean. The cliff, broken by a ravine, runs along in a curve so as to form an immense crescent enclosing a wide expanse of water. Down by the sea was the spa house, with a long line of the newly invented bathing machines, stretching out in either direction over smooth, hard sand, admirably adapted for promenading, driving, or racing. Thence rose an amphitheatre of streets and buildings, tier above tier, clustering on the north beneath the ruins of an old castle. At this romantic resort Sterne passed three weeks with the Earl of Shelburne and the Marquis of Granby, the politician and the soldier. He would have come away, he said, marvellously improved by the air and waters, had he not debilitated his strength as fast as it was gained, by "playing the good fellow" too much with his noble friends, whose pleasures were found rather exalted. His sojourn at Scarborough was marred only by the absence of Hall-Stevenson, who decided this year to drink the waters of Harrogate.

After these sacrifices to the god of laughter, Sterne settled down in his "philosophical hut" at Coxwold, where various matters of business awaited him. The Archbishop of York, not quite satisfied with James Kilner, the assistant curate of the parish, had delayed his ordination until Sterne's return from abroad. At the archbishop's request, Sterne enquired further into the conduct and character of his curate, and reported that "the man is well liked as a quiet and an honest man, and withal as a good reader and preacher." "I believe

* *York Courant*, August 28, 1764.

him," the humorist enlarged on his own part, "a good scholar also—I do not say a graceful one—for his bodily presence is mean; and were he to stand for ordination before a Popish Bishop, the poor fellow would be disabled by a Canon in a moment." At this time, too, Stephen Croft was taking the first steps towards enclosing and dividing Stillington Common and other waste lands, "containing in the whole, one thousand four hundred acres, or thereabouts." This project demanded Sterne's attention; for, as Vicar of Stillington, he was "entitled to the Tythes of Wool and Lamb, and to all the small Tythes and Vicarial Dues growing, arising, or renewing within the said Parish, and also to two Messuages or Cottages there, and to certain Lands within the said Fields and Ings."*

Presently a letter came from Mrs. Sterne, requesting fifty pounds immediately, and complaining of her treatment by Foley's correspondent at Montauban, who, in denying her credit for small amounts, hinted as the reason that she was separated from her husband for life. Sterne at once despatched a sharp letter to his Paris banker, in which he branded as false the ill-natured rumor in circulation at Montauban, and begged of him that Mrs. Sterne have credit up to two hundred guineas and more, should she ask for it. Sterne's heat was a bit Falstaffian, for he already owed his banker nearly a hundred guineas on his wife's account, and had to admit that a bill for fifty pounds could not be sent over just then, as his finances were falling short most unexpectedly. There was good reason for complaint on Sterne's part, though he kept silent, of the extravagance of his wife, who had already received a hundred pounds since his return. By good luck money became plentiful in a month or two, thanks to Becket's advances on the next *Shandys;* and Mrs. Sterne was put at her ease.

In the disposition Sterne made of his time, a scant six weeks, shortened by these interruptions, was allowed for completing *Tristram Shandy,* which had been commenced and broken off at Toulouse. It was about the first of October when he took up

* Stillington Enclosure Act, *Private Acts of Parliament,* 6 George III, c. 16.

in earnest, though he had dallied with it in the summer, the story of my uncle Toby and the widow Wadman, with the manifest intent of running it through the entire instalment of this year. But interest and fancy soon languished, notwithstanding hard cudgelling of his brains, so that by November he had arrived only at the end of one volume. Then he conceived the notion, it is a fair inference from his letters, of fitting into *Tristram Shandy* the comic version of his travels through France, already composed in whole or in part as a separate work or a loose continuation. Sterne now substituted Mr. Tristram Shandy for himself or Yorick as the name of the traveller, and let him recall while at Auxerre an earlier tour with the elder Shandys and Corporal Trim. This device for bringing the Shandy household over to the Continent has generally been regarded as very maladroit; but—besides the urgent call for something of the kind, if there were to be two volumes this year—Sterne saw a jest on the public, to whom he would give an opportunity, afforded by no other book, of pursuing two journeys through France at one and the same time. In order to lend a semblance of unity to the whole, my uncle Toby's courtship of the widow Wadman was put last, where it would give the final impression. The adjustment completed in this curious way about the middle of November, Sterne received a visit from a London friend recovering from a serious illness, with whom he went over to Skelton Castle for a week or ten days with Hall-Stevenson and his garrison, before leaving for London to try the public once more.

The seventh and eighth volumes of *The Life and Opinions of Tristram Shandy, Gentleman,* duly appeared from Becket's press on Tuesday, January 22, 1765. Each volume bore on its title-page a quotation from Pliny, likely through Burton: *Non enim excursus hic ejus, sed opus ipsum est,* meant as a sly apology for the inclusion of the travels; and at the top of the first numbered page of the seventh volume, the author placed his signature as a guarantee that the wit and humor were all his own. The price of the set was kept at four shillings.

As the instalment was much slighter than any hitherto put forth, Sterne had to accept a good deal of banter on the score that he was amusing himself at the cost of the public. Smollett's man on the *Critical Review** likened the two tiny volumes to "the invisible cock" which Corporal Trim paid his money to see within the showman's box, though he knew the thing invisible. And Suard, apropos of their appearance, retold the story of the man who advertised that he would put himself into a bottle before the eyes of his audience. On the appointed day, the theatre was thronged with a credulous multitude to behold the wonder; but the droll carried away their money and left the bottle as empty as the last two volumes of *Tristram Shandy*.†

The jest of the journey through France was not very well understood by the general public. As Sterne meant it, this part of his book was "a laughing good-tempered satire against travelling (as puppies travel)." To gain the desired effect, he let the thin narrative of his own journey, in which he professed to see nothing and to experience nothing beyond cross-accidents, run through all the customary details of the towns visited, such as the plan and history of Calais, the number of streets in Paris, and the wonders of Lyons—much as one might find them in the guide-books of Piganiol de la Force, which everybody thought indispensable to a trip abroad. All the scenes and objects which make travelling a delight, he playfully maintained, were not set down in the books; for none had told him that he would meet Janatone at Montreuil, Old Honesty at Lyons, or Nannette on the plains of Languedoc. However much these episodes might be admired for their charm and novelty, it was felt that the crude facts taken from histories and guide-books were mere padding to stuff out a six-penny pamphlet. And the story which Sterne foisted upon his travels—the story of the Abbess of Andoüillets and the little novice Margarita, who divide the syllables of two indecorous words between them to save a sin—brought out the

---

* January, 1765.
† Quoted in *London Chronicle*, April 16-18, 1765.

current charge of indecency, with a hint that the tale was "picked out of the common Parisian jest-books." In France, however, where the words were employed by every mule-driver, the episode was regarded as light and graceful ridicule of the formal morality which disfigured the cloisters. It far excelled, says Garat, Gresset's *Ver-Vert*, or the verse-tale of a parrot who came to an untimely end among the sisterhood at Nevers for repeating phrases caught on a journey down the Loire.*

The merriment against Sterne was long drawn out in the *Monthly Review* for February, 1765, through a score of pages in irony and burlesque. The reviewer represented himself as going in company with Mr. Shandy on the entire tour through France, and as quizzing him on the salient incidents by the way, and on the sequel describing my uncle Toby's assault, in military form, upon the heart of the widow Wadman. Much sport was made of Death, the long-striding scoundrel dogging their heels, of the adventure with Old Honesty at Lyons, and of the "Story of the King of Bohemia and his Seven Castles," which Trim and my uncle Toby lost somewhere between them. "Many choice wits," it was said of Sterne, "have excelled in telling a story, but none ever succeeded so well in *not* telling a story, as the British Rabelais hath done in this notable instance." The reviewer nevertheless appreciated in the main, as Suard and everybody else were doing, many "amazingly clever" anecdotes and episodes. After reading of Nannette and the vintage dance, he burst into a series of exclamations: "Give me thy hand, dear Shandy! Give me thy heart! What a delightful scene hast thou drawn! What good humour! What ease! What nature!" At length came the passage descriptive of the widow Wadman's lambent eye, which the critic could resist no more than could my uncle Toby:

* This poem had already appeared in English under the title of *Ver-Vert, or the Nunnery Parrot* (Dodsley, 1759), and must have been as well known to Sterne as to Hall-Stevenson, who imitated its style in *Crazy Tales*.

"It was not, Madam, a rolling eye——a romping or a wanton one——nor was it an eye sparkling——petulant or imperious——of high claims and terrifying exactions, which would have curdled at once that milk of human nature, of which my uncle *Toby* was made up——but 'twas an eye full of gentle salutations——and soft responses——speaking—— not like the trumpet stop of some ill-made organ, in which many an eye I talk to, holds coarse converse——but whispering soft——like the last low accent of an expiring saint—— 'How can you live comfortless, captain *Shandy*, and alone, without a bosom to lean your head on——or trust your cares to?' "

The humor of the new volumes was quite sufficient to reinstate Sterne in his former popularity. "Shandy sells well," he wrote from London in the middle of March, and "I have had a lucrative campaign here." As in the old time, social engagements, beginning moderately, thickened towards the end of the season until scarcely a moment could be stolen for letters to his family and best friends. His enjoyment during the first months was marred only by the absence of Garrick, who, in his long tour abroad, had swung round to Paris, where he was being overwhelmed with honors. But the actor's spirits were so blighted by "a terrible malignant fever" while in Germany, that it was uncertain whether he would ever return to the stage. As soon as Sterne found out that Garrick was in Paris, the old correspondence was renewed in full freedom. "I scalp you!——my dear Garrick! my dear friend!——foul befal the man who hurts a hair of your head!" So began one of Sterne's letters, which drifted off into the recurring burden: "Return, return to the few who love you and the thousands who admire you.——The moment you set your foot upon your stage—— mark! I tell it you——by some magic, irresisted power, every fibre about your heart will vibrate afresh, and as strong and feelingly as ever——Nature, with glory at her back, will light up the torch within you——and there is enough of it left, to heat and enlighten the world these many, many, many years." Frequently through the winter, Sterne occupied his box at Drury Lane, taking along with him the whole party where he dined, to see Powell, whom many thought the equal of Garrick, though that was not Sterne's opinion. "Powell! good Heaven!" he exclaimed, "give me some one with less smoke and more fire——There are who, like the Pharisees, still think they shall be heard for *much* speaking. Come—come away, my dear Garrick, and teach us another lesson." Nor did Sterne forget Mrs. Garrick, who had been likewise seriously ill. She had, it is said, "a real regard" for Mr. Sterne, though she often censured his indiscreet conduct. In recompense, Sterne addressed her as "the best and wisest of the daughters of Eve," and declared himself ready, after all the women he had seen, to "maintain her peerless" against any champion.

In one of these delightful letters, dated March 16, Sterne explained his plans for meeting the expense of another continental journey. "I am taxing the public," he told Garrick, "with two more volumes of sermons, which will more than double the gains of Shandy——It goes into the world with a prancing list *de toute la noblesse*—which will bring me in three hundred pounds, exclusive of the sale of the copy—— so that with all the contempt of money which *ma façon de penser* has ever impress'd on me, I shall be rich in spite of myself: but I scorn, you must know, in the high *ton* I take at present, to pocket all this trash——I set out to lay a portion of it in the service of the world, in a tour round Italy, where I shall spring game, or the deuce is in the dice.——In the beginning of September I quit England, that I may avail myself of the time of vintage, when all nature is joyous, and so saunter philosophically for a year or so, on the other side the Alps."

The labor of gathering in all the polite world for his *Sermons* Sterne took under his own direction and made it his sole business during the winter. Wherever he dined, one may imagine him requesting the honor of including the names of the guests; and he sent out, as we know, many letters asking for the aid of friends in obtaining subscriptions, that the great list might surpass all others in number and brilliancy. Very characteristic of the letters that have survived was one to Foley, concluding: "Pray present my most sincere compliments to Lady H——, whose name I hope to insert with many others. ——As so many men of genius furnish me with their names also, I will quarrel with Mr. Hume, and call him deist, and what not, unless I have his name too——My love to Lord W——. Your name, Foley, I have put in as a free-will offering of my labours——your list of subscribers you will send ——'tis but a crown for sixteen sermons——Dog cheap! but I am in quest of honour, not money.——Adieu, adieu."

The successful season in town was broken for a few weeks by illness, and towards the end of March Sterne sought the milder climate of Bath to recruit his strength. The fashionable city of the hills, where congregated people of all ranks from the nobility down to tradesmen and adventurers, afforded ample scope for light diversion——gossip and sentimental conversation in the pump-room looking out on the great Roman bath; strolls through the parks and along the parades, if one wished to take the air after drinking the waters; teas and chit-chat in the afternoon; and a concert or ball or theatre, much as one pleased, with which to end the day. Sterne was welcomed to Bath by Lord Cunningham of the Irish peerage, who invited him to his house and introduced him to a company of "his fair countrywomen," with whom the sentimentalist passed some of the happiest days in his life. In describing the household to a London friend, Sterne wrote: "There is the charming widow *Moor*, where, if I had not a piece of legal meadow of my own, I should rejoice to batten the rest of my days;——and the gentle, elegant *Gore*, with her fine form and Grecian face, and whose lot I trust it will be to make some man happy, who knows the value of a tender heart:——Nor shall I forget another widow, the interesting Mrs. Vesey, with her vocal and fifty other accomplishments."

Concerning the first two of these beautiful women over from Ireland to set Yorick's heart aflame, our narrative can say but little. Mrs. Gore must live, I fear, only for "her fine form and Grecian face." With Mrs. Moor, who had a house of her own at Bath, Sterne kept up a long correspondence, but none of their letters, if published, can now be surely identified through the dashes. Like Mrs. Vesey, she was doubtless a widow only in the sense that she came to Bath without her husband. Though perhaps not of this group, a certain merry widow—Mrs. F— was also drinking the waters. After he had left she wrote to a friend in London to ask whether Tristram Shandy was a married man or no; and Sterne, taking it upon himself to reply, told the "dear creature" that she must answer to her conscience for a question like that as he would answer to his for saying that nothing but mischief could come of the marriage of two wits—nothing but "satire and sarcasm— scoffing and flouting—rallying and reparteeing of it—thrusting and parrying in one dark corner or another."

There was still another house where Sterne was a most welcome visitor. For some time Mrs. Montagu's sister Sarah had been living at Bath, more or less, since the separation from her husband, George Lewis Scott, the mathematician. Mrs. Scott, who wrote novels and histories, was usually surrounded by a little group of sentimental admirers. As she was in ill health, she had a companion, a Miss Cutts, who seems to have acted as her secretary. When Sterne told Mrs. Montagu that he was going to Bath, she wrote to Mrs. Scott that she was sending to her Mr. Tristram Shandy, whom she liked better than his book. "He is full," she said, "of the milk of human kindness, harmless as a child, but often a naughty boy, and a little apt to dirty his *frock*. On the whole I recommend him to your acquaintance, and he has talents and qualities that will recommend him to your friendship." Much beyond Mrs. Montagu's expectations, her sister and friends enjoyed the conversation of Mr. Sterne, who did not dirty his frock when with them; and Miss Cutts averred that were she to quit her state of single blessedness it would be for him. Mrs. Montagu, who ought to have known her cousin better, took the light flirtation as a case of serious love and thought that it did Sterne great honor. "I am glad," she wrote to Mrs. Scott, "Tristram gave you some pleasure; I can never send you such another."*

While at Bath Sterne first met Gainsborough, then living in the newly-built Circus, a showy amphitheatre of residences on the hill. The painter, it was said by those acquainted with him, detested books, but read Sterne and wrote like him.† At the request of a friend, Sterne sat for his admirer. The portrait has never been quite identified; but a Gainsborough purporting to be of Sterne hangs in the Peel Park Museum at Salford. If really Sterne, it is a highly idealized portrait, such as might be painted at a few sittings without much study. The figure, drawn at half length, is scrupulously dressed, with short wig, and sleeves and front heavy with costly lace. The left hand is concealed, while in the right hand, almost buried in ruffles, a book lies open. A dreamy face tending to the oblong, with full eyes and full lips, gives the impression of soberness, almost of melancholy. The perplexing portrait may be Sterne's; for "Harlequin without his mask," as Thackeray once remarked, "is known to present a very sober countenance, and was himself, the story goes, the melancholy patient whom the Doctor advised to go and see Harlequin."‡

Returning to London before the end of April, Sterne "made a large company merry at Lady Lepell's table during a whole afternoon," by a comic version of his adventures with the Anglo-Irish at Bath. The Lady Lepell at whose table Sterne sat was a daughter of the effeminate John, Lord Hervey, so severely satirized by Pope as "that mere white curd of ass's milk." At the time of her marriage with Constantine Phipps, afterwards Baron Mulgrave of New Ross, Ireland, she was, says Walpole, "a fine black girl, but as masculine as her father should be." Her birth and her rank easily made her house the centre round which gyrated Anglo-Irish society.

* Blunt, *Mrs. Montagu*, I, 187-189.
† William Jackson, *The Four Ages*, 160 (London, 1798).
‡ The Gainsborough portrait is technically described by G. W. Fulcher, *Life of Gainsborough*, 219 (London, 1856). It was presented to the Museum at Salford by Mr. Thomas Agnew.

Under the excitement of the occasion, Sterne abandoned himself to his wit, apparently forgetting that Lord Cunningham and Mrs. Vesey belonged to the same set. Some umbrage was taken at his ridicule of their friends at Bath, especially by Lady Barrymore, who told the story. Disturbed by the incident, Sterne gracefully apologized for his sallies of wit, saying that he himself was born in Ireland and that he could never have intended ridicule of his "fair country-women." "I did," it was admitted, "talk of them, but as they would wish to be talked of,——with smiles on my countenance, praise on my tongue, hilarity in my heart, and the goblet in my hand."

Never more reckless in speech and conduct, Sterne closed the season with an indiscretion which has long lain heavily against him. The incident has been often related, but with a mistake in time and place, and with undue emphasis on the questionable character of the woman, slightly disguised in the printed correspondence as Lady P——. Among Sterne's acquaintances was Hugh Percy, eldest son of the first Duke of Northumberland, a young man twenty-three years old. He appears among the subscribers to Sterne's sermons as Lord Warkworth. After serving as an officer during the last years of the war with France, Percy was appointed colonel and aide-de-camp to George the Third, and subsequently fought bravely in the war with the American colonies, covering, for instance, the retreat of the British from Lexington and Concord. In the summer of 1764, he married Anne, daughter of the Earl of Bute who succeeded Pitt as Prime Minister. From the first, the marriage, which finally ended in divorce, did not prosper. Lady Percy quarrelled with her mother-in-law, the old Duchess of Northumberland, and insisted upon inviting her friends to call while Lord Warkworth was away. On one occasion, after Yorick's usual compliments, Lady Percy told Sterne that she would be glad to include him among her favored guests. Remembering the invitation on an April afternoon while on his way to dine in her neighborhood with Mr. Cowper of Wigmore Street, he entered the Mount Coffee-House, called for a sheet of gilt paper, and wrote off a nonsensical letter to Lady Percy, asking if she "would be alone at seven" and suffer him "to spend the evening with her." She was directed to send her reply to Wigmore Street by seven o'clock. "If I hear nothing by that time," said the billet-doux, "I shall conclude you are better disposed of——and shall take a sorry hack, and sorrily jogg on to the play——Curse on the word. I know nothing but sorrow—except this one thing, that I love you (perhaps foolishly, but) most sincerely." Though the conduct of Sterne and Lady Percy was severely criticised by Thackeray, it matters very little whether they passed the evening together or Sterne took a sorry hack to Covent Garden, where Miss Wilford, a beautiful dancer, was to make her début in the regular drama. Thus ended a series of flirtations that amused all concerned in them.*

* The letter to Lady Percy has become one of the most famous letters because of Thackeray's use of it in his lecture on "Sterne and Goldsmith" in the *English Humourists.* In editions of Sterne since 1780, this letter has usually appeared among those for the last part of April, 1767. Thackeray referred to it to show that Sterne was only shamming his passion for Mrs. Draper—the Eliza of a series of letters in the spring of 1767. But it is now known that Sterne was too ill at that time to visit Lady Percy or anyone else. In 1766 he was abroad. Hence the only year left for the letter is 1768 or 1765. If he cannot make an engagement with Lady Percy, Sterne says that he is going to Miss * * * * * * *'s benefit. No unmarried actress had a benefit on a Tuesday in the spring of 1768 before March 18, the date of Sterne's death. But on Tuesday, April 23, 1765, benefits were given to Miss Wright at Drury Lane, and to Miss Wilford at Covent Garden. The seven stars correspond to the letters in the name of Miss Wilford.—See Genest, *Some Account of the English Stage,* V, 69, 75.

CHAP. XVI.

Yorkshire and London Continued. Sermons: Volumes III and IV. May—October, 1765

IT was the twenty-third of April, as we may figure it out, when Sterne wished to pay a visit to Lady Percy, whose "eyes and lips," he said, "have turned a man into a fool, whom the rest of the town is courting as a wit." Two days later the Garricks arrived from Paris and went directly to their Hampton villa. Sterne at least saw them, hurried through his business in town, and hastened home earlier than usual, to prepare his sermons for the press in the ensuing September. At York he stayed some days with Hall-Stevenson, who left him "bleeding to death" of a vessel in his lungs. "The deuce take these bellows of mine!" Sterne wrote to the young Earl of Effingham, "I must get 'em stopped, or I shall never have to *persifler* Lord Effingham again." The hemorrhage which he thus dismissed carelessly, was nevertheless a warning that he must keep quieter than last summer, and be content to oscillate between York and Coxwold, with no thought of Scarborough or Harrogate.

When first seen in his retirement, he was sitting in the summer-house of Shandy Hall, "heart and head" full of his sermons. Near him lay a letter from Mr. Woodhouse to inform him that he was in love. To draw himself out of the pensive mood of the sermons, Sterne took up the letter for reply, beginning with the value of the passion to a man of his own temperament, an excellent commentary, in passing, on his infatuation for Lady Percy. "I am glad," said the man of large experience, "that you are in love—'twill cure you at least of the spleen, which has a bad effect on both man and woman —I myself must ever have some dulcinea in my head—it harmonises the soul—and in those cases I first endeavour to make the lady believe so, or rather I begin first to make myself believe that I am in love——but I carry on my affairs quite in the French way, sentimentally——'*l'amour*' (say they) '*n'est rien sans sentiment.*' "

Sterne had just received and replied to a formal proposal for the hand of his daughter from "a French gentleman of fortune in France." The marquis, if we may so call him, obtained Sterne's address from Foley's correspondent at Montauban, and, without the knowledge of Lydia, wrote to her father that he was deeply in love with her, as a brief prelude to the enquiry: "How much can you give her at present and how much at your death?" The substance of the parent's amusing reply, Sterne related for the benefit of his friend Woodhouse. "Sir," was Sterne's answer, "I will give her ten thousand pounds the day of marriage—my calculation is as follows ——she is not eighteen, you are sixty-two——there goes five thousand pounds——then, Sir, you at least think her not ugly —she has many accomplishments, speaks Italian, French, plays upon the guittar, and as I fear you play upon no instrument whatever, I think you will be happy to take her at my terms, for here finishes the account of the ten thousand pounds."

One day in August while Sterne was in the midst of parish business, "an affrighted messenger, on a breathless horse," arrived to acquaint him "that the parsonage house at Sutton was on fire . . . and burning like a bundle of faggots." By the time Sterne could reach Sutton, his house there was in ashes, though some of his furniture and books had been rescued from he flames. The fire was caused, he wrote to a friend, "by the carelessness of my curate, or his wife, or his maid, or some one within his gates." His loss he estimated variously from two hundred to three hundred and fifty pounds. It was not the loss, he said to another, that troubled him most, but "the strange unaccountable conduct of my poor unfortunate curate, not in *setting fire* to the house, for I do not accuse him of it, God knows, nor any one else; but in *setting off* the moment after it happened, and flying like *Paul* to *Tarsus,* through fear of a persecution from me." And again: "Heavens! how little did he know of me to suppose I was among the number of those wretches that heap misfortune upon misfortune—and when the load is almost insupportable, still to add to the weight! God, who reads my heart, knows it to be true—that I wish rather to share, than to encrease the burthen of the miserable—to dry up, instead of adding a single drop to the stream of sorrow.—As for the dirty trash of this world, I regard it not—the loss of it does not cost me a sigh, for after all, I may say with the Spanish Captain, that I am as good a gentleman as the king, only not quite so rich."

As always, so here Sterne's pity and humor, pen once in hand, helped him over the hardest rubs of fortune. The frightened curate, who decamped with his family the morning after the fire, was the Rev. Marmaduke Collier, who had been in charge of Sutton since 1760. Sterne soon persuaded him to come out of hiding, and took him in with wife and child at Coxwold, until a house could be provided for them elsewhere. The unlucky parson, after another year at Sutton, was replaced by Launcelot Colley, who was licensed to the cure on October 20, 1766. The recommendation was made by Sterne at an annual salary of £38.*

Soon after the fire, Sterne received a "kind epistle" from Mrs. Meadows, who had been a friend of the family at Toulouse, to enquire after Yorick's health and to inform him of her whereabouts since coming back to England. In reply Sterne invited her to Coxwold, and offered, if she were going abroad again, to escort her on the way. "Shall I expect you here," ran the alluring invitation, "this summer?——I much wish that you may make it convenient to gratify me in a visit for a few weeks——I will give you a roast fowl for your dinner, and a clean table-cloth every day—and tell you a story by way of desert—in the heat of the day we will sit in the shade—and in the evening the fairest of all the milk-maids who pass by my gate, shall weave a garland for you.——If I should not be so fortunate, contrive to meet me [in London] the beginning of October——I shall stay a fortnight after, and then seek a kindlier climate.——This plaguy cough of

* Institutions of the Diocese of York.

mine seems to gain ground, and will bring me to my grave in spight of me——but while I have strength to run away from it I will——I have been wrestling with it for these twenty years past——and what with laughter and good spirits, have prevented its giving me a fall——but my antagonist presses closer than ever upon me——and I have nothing left on my side but another journey abroad——A-propos——are you for a scheme of that sort? if not, perhaps you will accompany me as far as Dover, that we may laugh together on the beach, to put Neptune in a good humour before I embark——God bless you, my dear Madam,——and believe me ever your's."

Mrs. Meadows, I daresay, was unable to come to Shandy Hall this summer, or to go with Sterne farther than Dover Beach to see him off for France. But Sally Tuting, "a lady known and loved by the whole kingdom," wrote to him from London that she was setting out on a Continental pilgrimage in search of health, and received from Sterne advice on the mood she should cultivate in her travels: "No hard jostlings in your journey must disturb either body or mind one moment— if you have left a Philander—think not about him—You must smile upon inconveniences and impositions—upon bad inns and what will hurt you most of all because most contrary to your nature—upon unfeeling looks." Philander was destined to overtake "gentle Sally" in Rome or Naples.

As the time for Sterne's departure on his foreign tour was approaching, the recurrent trouble with his lungs took him frequently to York for change, and perhaps to consult Dr. Dealtry. "I am going to York," he again wrote to Woodhouse late in the summer, "not to walk by the side of the muddy Ouse, but to recruit myself of the most violent spitting of blood that ever mortal man experienced; because I had rather (in case 'tis ordained so) die there, than in a post-chaise on the road." Among his friends in the city whom envy still spared him, was Marmaduke Fothergill, to whom he used to go for advice in the Sutton period. One day Fothergill told him of a droll encounter with an apothecary in Coney Street; and Sterne, suppressing names, retold the story for the benefit of

Mr. Woodhouse: "A sensible friend of mine, with whom, not long ago, I spent some hours in conversation, met an apothecary (an acquaintance of ours)——the latter asked him how he did? Why, ill, very ill—I have been with Sterne, who has given me such a dose of *Attic salt* that I am in a fever—— Attic salt, Sir, Attic salt! I have Glauber salt——I have Epsom salt in my shop, &c.——Oh! I suppose 'tis some French salt——I wonder you would trust his report of the medicine, he cares not what he takes himself."

As usual, Sterne was in for the August races, expecting to meet by appointment Lord Effingham and Colonel John Blaquière, afterwards Chief Secretary for Ireland, both of whom were most congenial companions. With them doubtless he drove out to the race-course, where occurred an incident which connects him agreeably with Elizabeth Graeme, a romantic young woman from the colonies. Miss Graeme was a daughter of Thomas Graeme, physician and collector of customs at Philadelphia, and a granddaughter on her mother's side of Sir William Keith, a former governor of Pennsylvania. At the outbreak of the Revolution, she married a young Scotsman of Philadelphia named Ferguson, who accepted a commission in the British Army. It was she who bore Duché's famous letter to General Washington, urging that he persuade congress to rescind "the hasty and ill-advised" Declaration of Independence, and that, failing in the effort, he negotiate directly for his country at the head of the army. Back in 1765, when she went to England for her health, Miss Graeme was a clever young woman, twenty-five years old, fond of moralizing in verse and of entering into Platonic friendships. She figures as the "Laura fair" in the verses of Nathaniel Evans, the colonial poet. In her leisure, she translated *Télémaque* into English heroic verse, and transcribed, it is said, the entire Bible, that it might be impressed upon her memory. Of her visit abroad, she felt most honored by her gracious reception at Court and by an introduction to Laurence Sterne, which came about by chance. With a party of friends she attended the York races, where she took, it happened, a seat upon the same stage with Sterne. "While bets were making," says the narrative, "upon different horses, she selected a small horse that was in the rear of the courses as the subject of a trifling wager. Upon being asked the reason for doing so, she said, 'the race was not always to the swift, nor the battle to the strong.' Mr. Sterne, who stood near her, was struck with this reply, and turning hastily towards her, begged for the honour of an acquaintance. They soon became sociable, and a good deal of pleasant conversation took place between them, to the great entertainment of the surrounding company."*

All summer Sterne was busy, so far as he was able to work at all, with his sermons. He kept his face, as he phrased it, turned towards Jerusalem. During the revision he must have written many letters asking for subscriptions and acknowledging favors; of which two to Foley have long been known; and two others have come to light. One was to Lord Effingham to thank him, "as well as the *amiable comtesse votre chère mère,* for the honour of her name"; while the other, now in the library of Harvard University, was addressed to Thomas Hesselridge, Esq., of London, a gentleman in the service of Sir William Maynard, the fourth Baronet. It ran:—

"York, July 5.

"My dear dear Sir

"I made a thousand enquiries after you all this last winter and was told I should see you some part of it, in town——pray how do you do? and how do you go on, in this silly world? Have you seen my seven and eight graceless children? ——but I am doing penance for them, in begetting a couple of more ecclesiastick ones——which are to stand penance (again) in their turns——in Sheets about the middle of September——they will appear in the Shape of the third and fourth volumes of Yorick. These you must know are to keep up a kind of balance, in my Shandaic character, and are push'd into the world for that reason by my friends with as splendid

* M. Katherine Jackson, *Outlines of the Literary History of Pennsylvania,* 96-97 (Lancaster, Pa., 1906).

and numerous a List of Nobility &c—as ever pranced before a book, since subscriptions came into fashion——I should grieve not to have your name amongst those of my friends— and in so much good company as it has a right to be in——so tell me to set it down—and if you can—Lord Maynard's ——I have no design, my dear Hesselridge, upon your purse— 'tis but a crown—but I have a design upon the credit [of] Lord Maynard's name—and that of a person I love and esteem so much as I do you. If any occasions come in your way of adding three or four more to the list, your friendship for me, I know will do it.

"——N.B.——You must take their crowns—and keep them for me till fate does the courtesy to throw me in your way——This will not be, I fear, this year—for in September, I set out *Solus* for Italy—and shall winter at Rome and Naples. *L'hyvère à Londres ne vaut pas rien, pour les poumones—à cause d'humidité et la fume dont l'aire est chargée* ——Let me hear how you do soon——and believe me ever your devoted and affectionate friend and wellwisher

"L. Sterne"

If all the letters sent forth from Shandy Hall were as gay and courteous as this one, we may easily understand their success with the world of fashion. Very graphic was the metaphor of the prancing steed, which was also worked into letters to Garrick and Foley, and most likely into all the rest. The jest of saying that his sermons were to stand in sheets for *Tristram Shandy*, lay in the custom, still surviving at York in Sterne's day, of requiring one guilty of adultery to do penance by standing, with a sheet thrown over his head, on the steps of the cathedral. Mr. Hesselridge, almost needless to say, forwarded his subscription along with Sir William's. The splendid list, when completed, contained six hundred and ninety-three names, thus outnumbering the subscribers to the sermons of 1760 by a comfortable margin. Sterne's Yorkshire neighbors, even his old enemy, Philip Harland, were mostly there, as much as to say that they liked Yorick the preacher if not

Yorick the author of *Tristram Shandy;* and there, too, were hosts of friends among the nobility and gentry with whom Sterne had associated in London and at watering-places. To count the stars in the list would be but to enumerate all the great families of the kingdom; while France contributed to the roll of honor the names of Diderot, d'Holbach, Crébillon, and Voltaire.

Sterne was in London with his sermons the first week in October, somewhat later than he had at times expected. It was then arranged that he should set out at once on his journey, and leave their publication to Becket. This is the only instance, after the *Political Romance,* in which Sterne did not superintend in person his books through the press. But in this case, his presence in London was hardly necessary. The lights were all pricked in, and the array of subscribers assured the sale of a large edition. On the financial side, Becket was quite willing to make advances, so that, including royalties and the bills brought up from York, Sterne was able to leave with him £600, upon which Panchaud and Foley might draw at sight, according as Sterne or his wife should make it expedient. Everything was thus settled for a long absence. For good reasons Becket delayed publication until the opening of the London season. The two volumes, numbered three and four, as they appeared on Tuesday, January 21, 1766,* bore the old title for which Sterne had been censured: *The Sermons of Mr. Yorick,* which was followed by a table of contents, the old sub-title "Sermons by Laurence Sterne," etc., and "Subscribers Names." Sterne wrote a preface, but decided upon reflection that it would be better to let the sermons speak for themselves without apology. Along with their publication, a scribbler, who knew that no *Shandys* were intended by the author this year, favored the public with a spurious sequel to my uncle Toby's courtship, which the reviewers thought admirable, if not genuine.†

* The sermons were entered on this day at Stationers' Hall by Becket for himself and De Hondt.

† This is the spurious ninth volume of *The Life and Opinions of*

The new volumes contained only twelve sermons, instead of sixteen as planned in the summer. Among them were four that have been already described, to wit: the sermon at Coxwold on the coronation of George the Third, the charity sermon at the Foundling Hospital, the portrait of Hezekiah, and "The Abuses of Conscience," which had been published locally as a pamphlet and afterwards inserted in *Tristram Shandy*. To the last sermon, which closed the instalment, Sterne prefixed an advertisement asking pardon for its reappearance and for making the public "pay twice actually for the same thing."

"But it was judged," Sterne went on to say, "that some might better like it, and others better understand it just as it was preached, than with the breaks and interruptions given to the sense and argument as it stands there offered to the world.

"It was an Assize Sermon, preached in the Cathedral Church at York, and wrote by the same hand with the others in these four volumes, and as they are probably the last (except the sweepings of the Author's study after his death) that will be published, it was thought fit to add it to the collection,—where moreover it stands a chance of being read by many grave people with a much safer conscience.

"All the Editor wishes, is, That this may not after all, be one of those many abuses of it set forth in what he is now going to read."

Though a few more good sermons remained in manuscript at Shandy Hall, the twelve that Sterne picked for publication were in his opinion the best. Of the eight about whose history we know little or nothing, most were doubtless old sermons, recast or stretched out for the closet, while two or three, like "The Prodigal Son," may have been prepared solely for the press. Again Sterne pleased and edified his public as much as six years before. The reviewers took him up and ran through

Tristram Shandy, Gentleman, with facetious Latin quotations on the title-page, printed "for T. Durham, at Charing-Cross, and T. Caslon, in Pater-noster Row, 1766."

the volumes with long quotations; and for weeks an abridged
sermon by Parson Yorick held the place of honor in the newspapers. No longer was any indecorum discovered in his assumed name of the king's jester; and except for the mild censure of a flight of fancy here and there as too free for the
pulpit, everybody admired and spoke out in praise of the
gentle, generous heart of Yorick.

Strictly orthodox in those rare instances where he touched
upon points of doctrine, Sterne opened, as was his way, the
scroll of Biblical characters and adorned them with fresh reflections. His readers were treated to a history of religions, in
which were brought out the advantages of Christianity over
Greek paganism; they were warned against all manner of
pride—of birth, wealth, learning, and beauty—as unsocial
vices, and exhorted to practise the humility of their Master.
With the beautiful woman, proud of her loveliness, Sterne
was less severe than with the rest. "And yet," concluded the
moralist, "when the whole apology is read,——it will be
found at last, that Beauty, like Truth, never is so glorious
as when it goes the plainest.——Simplicity is the great friend
to nature, and if I would be proud of anything in this silly
world, it should be of this honest alliance." The old harangues
against the Church of Rome fell out of the new volumes, save
for survivals that were allowed to stand, such as the sermon
on conscience, and the definition of Popery, before quoted, as
"a pecuniary system, well contrived to operate upon men's
passions and weakness, whilst their pockets are o'picking." In
place of Roman Catholics, the Methodists came in for occasional censure on account of their spiritual pride—their professed illuminations and extraordinary experiences, which were
described as merely mechanical disturbances of disordered understandings. As in his first volumes, Sterne sometimes went
to Hall or to Tillotson for a start, but all was modernized to
the delectation of his audience.

It was just this power to depict as modern types striking
characters in Scripture, accompanied with the author's own
personal remarks and opinions, that makes Sterne's sermons

still readable. Take for instance his Shimei. It is related that
David, after his son Absalom rose against him, fled from Jerusalem for safety. While he was passing by Mount Olivet,
Shimei, of the house of Saul, came forth and cursed David;
"and threw stones and cast dust at him." When Absalom was
vanquished and David returned to Jerusalem in peace, Shimei
was the first man to greet him. Sterne, well knowing that nobody cared anything about the blood-feud existing between the
Benjamite and Israel, which explains in a clause the conduct
of Shimei, easily modified the story so as to make out of
David's railer a mean and abject time-server, such as he had
seen with his own eyes.

"O Shimei!" the preacher exclaimed after relating his history, "would to heaven when thou wast slain, that all thy
family had been slain with thee; and not one of thy resemblance left! but ye have multiplied exceedingly and replen-
ished the earth; and if I prophecy rightly—ye will in the
end *subdue* it.——There is not a character in the world
which has so bad an influence upon the affairs of it, as this of
Shimei: . . . Oh! it infests the court—the camp—the cabinet
—it infests the church——go where you will——in every
quarter, in every profession, you see a Shimei following the
wheels of the fortunate through thick mire and clay. . . .
Shimei is the barometer of every man's fortune; marks the
rise and fall of it, with all the variations from scorching hot
to freezing cold upon his countenance, that the smile will admit of.——Is a cloud upon thy affairs—see—it hangs over
Shimei's brow——Hast *thou been* spoken for to the king or
the captain of the host without success?——look not into the
court-kalendar—the vacancy is fill'd up in Shimei's face——
Art thou in debt?——tho' not to Shimei—no matter—the
worst officer of the law shall not be more insolent."

In a similar way Jacob became under Sterne's hand the
type of thousands who lament, when they see the end of life
approaching, that their days have been few and evil. Most
of the patriarch's misfortunes were shown, with much inge-
nuity, to have resulted from mistaken views on the manage-

ment of a family, from a "parental partiality or parental injustice," as common in England as it ever was in the East. There were several hard places in Jacob's career to slip over on this theory, but Sterne brushed away all obstacles. It is true, he admitted in a most difficult analogy, that no young man could be tricked nowadays into marrying a Leah, instead of a Rachel, in just the way that Laban tricked Jacob. "But the moral of it is still good; and the abuse with the same complaint of Jacob's upon it, will ever be repeated, so long as art and artifice are so busy as they are in these affairs. Listen, I pray you, to the stories of the disappointed in marriage:——collect all their complaints:——hear their mutual reproaches; upon what fatal hinge do the greatest part of them turn?——'They were mistaken in the person.'——Some disguise either of body or mind is seen through in the first domestic scuffle;——some fair ornament—perhaps the very one which won the heart—the *ornament of a meek and quiet spirit*, falls off;——*It is not the Rachel for whom I have served,*——*Why hast thou then beguiled me?* . . . When the night is passed, 'twill ever be the same story,——*And it came to pass, behold it was Leah.*"

For the ills that befell Jacob at his marriage and before and after it, Sterne expressed pity; but it was the pity he felt for all "splenetic and morose souls" who do not take life as they find it. "If there is any evil," he said, "in this world, 'tis sorrow and heaviness of heart.——The loss of goods,—of health,—of coronets and mitres, are only evil, as they occasion sorrow;——take that out—the rest is fancy, and dwelleth only in the head of man." And as for himself, though sickness and death pressed upon him, his prayer had ever been:

"Grant me, gracious God! to go chearfully on, the road which thou hast marked out;——I wish it neither more wide or more smooth:——continue the light of this dim taper thou hast put into my hands:——I will kneel upon the ground seven times a day, to seek the best track I can with it——and having done that, I will trust myself and the issue of my journey to thee, who art the fountain of joy,——and will sing songs of comfort as I go along."

Very curious was Sterne's analysis of the character of Felix, who, though convinced of Paul's innocence, would nevertheless not release him because disappointed of a bribe. Sterne quickly hit upon the Roman governor's ruling passion of avarice, but elaborated and explained it after an entirely new fashion. Paul's well-known saying that the love of money is the root of all evil, was flatly contradicted. Shifting the point of view, Sterne held that "the love of money is only a subordinate and ministerial passion, exercised for the support of some other vices; and 'tis generally found, when there is either ambition, prodigality, or lust, to be fed by it, that it then rages with the least mercy and discretion; in which cases, strictly speaking, it is not the root of other evils,——but other evils are the root of it." And so it was in Felix's case. Surprise was expressed by the preacher that none of the commentators had fully weighed the influence upon the Roman procurator of his mistress Drusilla, who "had left the Jew her husband, and without any pretence in their law to justify a divorce, had given herself up without ceremony to Felix, . . . a character, which might have figured very well even in our own times." Drusilla, Sterne would suggest, feeling her guilt, instigated Felix against Paul, so that it was well the Apostle suffered no more, since "two such violent enemies as lust and avarice were combined against him."

More curious still was the sermon on "The Levite and his Concubine," which the *Monthly Review* thought wore "too gay an aspect" for the pulpit. At the outset, Sterne was very careful to make clear that in the Jewish household the concubine was essentially a wife; that concubinage was practised by Solomon, who, however, rather abused his privileges under the law; and that, if the Levite needed any further justification for his one concubine, it should be remembered that there was no king in Israel at the time. So much, declared the preacher, might be said for the Levite, if one looked for explanations; but for himself he was content to rest the case with nature:

"For notwithstanding all we meet with in books, in many of which, no doubt, there are a good many handsome things said upon the sweets of retirement, &c. . . . yet still, *'it is not good for man to be alone.'* . . . In the midst of the loudest vauntings of philosophy, Nature will have her yearnings for society and friendship. . . . Let the torpid Monk seek heaven comfortless and alone——God speed him! For my own part, I fear, I should never so find the way: let me be wise and religious—but let me be MAN: wherever thy Providence places me, or whatever be the road I take to get to thee ——give me some companion in my journey, be it only to remark to, How our shadows lengthen as the sun goes down; to whom I may say, How fresh is the face of nature! How sweet the flowers of the field! How delicious are these fruits!"

With good taste, Sterne stopped short of the horrible catastrophe as related in Scripture, and in Bishop Hall, who was followed in places very closely; and pieced out his discourse with a few remarks on "the rash censurers of the world," who set up a "trade upon the broken stock of other people's failings, ——perhaps their misfortunes." "Certainly there is a difference," he told crabbed satirists finely with reference to his own art, "between *Bitterness* and *Saltness*,—that is,—between the malignity and the festivity of wit,——the one is a mere quickness of apprehension, void of humanity,—and is a talent of the devil; the other comes from the Father of spirits, so pure and abstracted from persons, that willingly it hurts no man: or if it touches upon an indecorum, 'tis with that dexterity of true genius, which enables him rather to give a new colour to the absurdity, and let it pass.——He may smile at the shape of the obelisk raised to another's fame,——but the malignant wit will level it at once with the ground, and build his own upon the ruins of it."

And finally we have Sterne where everybody should like to see him—in a sermon on the Prodigal Son, a theme which invited him to give loose rein to all the sentimental emotions in the train of pity and mercy, up to the climax where the preacher declared that the joy and riot of the kindly affections was but "another name for religion." Without restraint, Sterne let his fancy play with the parable, reviving, with all sorts of imaginary details, the remonstrance of the father against the rash enterprise of his son, the spendthrift's parting with his father and elder brother by the side of "camels and asses loaden with his substance," his varied life in many lands, until a mighty famine drove him back to his father's roof, and the fatted calf was killed, and the pavilion was lighted up for the dance and wild festivity. Of course, Sterne's graphic and pathetic pictures, flowing on in a well-ordered series, had little warrant in the brief narrative of St. Luke; but as literature the sermon was all the better for that. It was perhaps all the better, too, for his weakening, almost losing, the moral of the parable by the zest with which he related the prodigal's experiences at Nineveh and Babylon. The young man, his substance all wasted, has decided to return to his father and beg for forgiveness; and thereon says the preacher:

"Alas! How shall he tell his story? Ye who have trod this round, tell me in what words he shall give in to his father, the sad *Items* of his extravagance and folly?——The feasts and banquets which he gave to whole cities in the east,——the costs of Asiatick rarities,——and of Asiatick cooks to dress them ——the expences of singing men and singing women,——the flute, the harp, the sackbut, and of all kinds of musick——the dress of the Persian courts, how magnificent! their slaves, how numerous!——their chariots, their horses, their palaces, their furniture, what immense sums they had devoured!——what expectations from strangers of condition! what exactions! ——How shall the youth make his father comprehend, that he was cheated at Damascus by one of the best men in the world; ——that he had lent a part of his substance to a friend at Nineveh, who had fled off with it to the Ganges;——that a whore of Babylon had swallowed his best pearl, and anointed the whole city with his balm of Gilead;——that he had been sold by a man of honour for twenty shekels of silver, to a worker in graven images;——that the images he had purchased had profited him nothing;——that they could not be transported across the wilderness, and had been burnt with fire at Shusan;——that the apes and peacocks, which he had sent for from Tharsis, lay dead upon his hands; and that the mummies had not been dead long enough, which had been brought him out of Egypt:——that all had gone wrong since the day he forsook his father's house."

No one except Sterne could have imagined those romantic details of a spendthrift; or, had he done so, have put them into a sermon. But a greater surprise follows. Having brought the prodigal home and set the wine flowing, the man of the world proceeded to modernize the parable by offering "some reflections upon that fatal passion which led him,——and so many thousands after the example, *to gather all he had together, and take his journey into a far country*"—some observations, in short, upon the grand tour for which he himself was preparing. The desire for travelling on the Continent, the preacher held, was in no way bad, considered by itself. "Order it rightly, the advantages are worth the pursuit; the chief of which are—to learn the languages, the laws and customs, and understand the government and interest of other nations,——to acquire an urbanity and confidence of behaviour, and fit the mind more easily for conversation and discourse;——to take us out of the company of our aunts and grandmothers, and from the track of nursery mistakes; and by shewing us new objects, or old ones in new lights, to reform our judgments."

But few or none, said Sterne, of the young Englishmen who swarm the capitals of Europe bring back any part of this cargo. If they go out alone, "without *carte*,—without compass"—they escape well if they return only as naked as when they left home. If you place your son in charge of a scholar to act as bear-leader, "the upshot will be generally . . . that the unhappy youth will have the tutor to carry,—and not the tutor to carry him." You may choose for your son, not a scholar read in Greek and Latin, but a man "who knows the world, . . . who has been employed on such services, and thrice made the *tour of Europe, with success*,——that is, without breaking his own, or his pupil's neck." From such a guide, the young man "will learn the amount to a halfpenny, of every stage from Calais to Rome;——he will be carried to the best inns,——instructed where there is the best wine, and sup a livre cheaper, than if the youth had been left to make the tour and the bargain himself.——Look at our governor! I beseech you:——see, he is an inch taller as he relates the advantages.——And here endeth his pride——his knowledge, and his use."

Perhaps a fond father imagines that the stripling will be taken up everywhere he goes by distinguished natives of the country to whom he may carry letters of recommendation. Him Sterne would disillusion by observing that "company which is really good, is very rare——and very shy"; and as for letters to eminent men, they will obtain a courteous first reception but nothing more. "Conversation," it should be understood, "is a traffick; and if you enter into it, without some stock of knowledge, to balance the account perpetually betwixt you,——the trade drops at once. . . . There is nothing to be extracted from the conversation of young itinerants, worth the trouble of their bad language,——or the interruption of their visits." Cut off from his intellectual superiors, "the disappointed youth seeks an easier society; and as bad company is always ready, and ever lying in wait,——the career is soon finished; and the poor prodigal returns the same object of pity, with the prodigal in the Gospel."

So ended, by a violent reversal to the parable, the strangest of all Yorick's sermons, revised and redecorated just before his departure for Italy.

CHAP. XVII.

A Tour of Italy. October, 1765—May, 1766

WHEN the sermons came out, Sterne was in Rome, midway on the grand tour which has been immortalized in *A Sentimental Journey through France and Italy*. Considered as an actual record of the expedition, the famous book has, however, for the biographer very great perplexities, at first sight almost desperate, inasmuch as Yorick combined with the observations of this year characters and incidents of his first sojourn in France, and further mingled with both sets anecdotes heard and read by the way and elsewhere, as if they had really fallen within his own personal experience. Two distinct tours and some fiction were thus completely fused in one beautiful narrative. We may nevertheless eliminate much of the fiction and most of the first tour; and then, with the aid of various letters, retell the story of Sterne's last travels on the Continent. If the narrative, thus cut down and pieced out, loses much of its literary charm, there will emerge in its place a new biographical interest. Monsieur Dessein, La Fleur, and many names disguised under initials and stars will turn out to be real persons whom Sterne met and associated with on the journey, though no one should insist too far upon a literal interpretation of the incidents which fancy at times wove about them.*

Perhaps we should be reminded at the outset that the Yorick who made the tour of Italy was in all externals quite different from the Yorick whom we first saw as the rural parson cultivating his glebe and other lands. So careless and slovenly was he then in appearance as to attract the attention of boys when he came into York and shuffled through the streets. Referring

* In 1824 John Poole the dramatist went over the Sterne route from Calais to Paris, identifying Sterne's stopping-places and gathering up local traditions. See his two articles in the *London Magazine* for 1825, pp. 38-46 and 387-394.

to those days, he called himself "a lousy prebendary." Five years of London and Paris made out of him a Chesterfield. He grew scrupulous, though not extravagant, in dress; and no man of the age was more at ease in society—more courteous and more urbane. On his first coming to London, Reynolds painted him most fittingly in the clerical gown which he wore as Vicar of Sutton. In Carmontelle and Gainsborough he appeared in the costume of an aristocrat. And yet Yorick, possessing good taste, never assumed the fashionable colors of the period, but chose instead the equally fashionable complete black, with conspicuous white lace ruffles, neat and dignified, becoming a man of his age and profession as well as a man of the world. So, remembering what he once was, it is rather amusing to find Sterne writing to Foley from London on the seventh of October to request him to order from Madame Requière, against his reaching Paris in seven days, "une peruque à bourse, au mieux—c'est-à-dire—une la plus extraordinaire—la plus jolie —la plus gentille," for you know, he concluded, "j'ai l'honneur d'être grand critique—et bien difficile encore dans les affaires de peruques."

Sure of his Parisian wig, Sterne next packed "half a dozen shirts and a black pair of silk breeches" in his portmanteau, and took a place in the Dover stage, if his plans did not go wrong, on the morning of October 9, 1765. The following day he embarked on the nine o'clock packet for Calais, and five or six hours later he was refreshing himself at his inn on fricasseed chicken and burgundy. The inn where he rested after the voyage was not the old Lyon d'Argent—or the Silver Lion, as the English called it—where his wife and daughter once lodged a night, and whose master—Monsieur Grandsire— Sterne set down, after one experience with him, as "a Turk in grain"; it was the Hôtel d'Angleterre, recently established in "the principal street" of Calais by Monsieur Dessein. The host, it is said, had been a favorite waiter at the Silver Lion with the English passing through Calais, and had assumed his peculiar name from a compliment of one of them, who remarked: "Il a du dessein, ce gaillard là." This shrewd *garçon,* taking advantage of his master's unpopularity, opened a house of his own, to which most tourists, furious at Monsieur Grandsire's overcharges,* hastened to transfer their patronage. "No hotel in France," remarked Philip Thicknesse, the eccentric traveller, who spent a day there in 1767, "is equal to that from which I now write. Monsieur Dessein knows the *goût* of both nations and blends them with propriety; and he has the advantage of a palace as it were, to do it in."† Monsieur Dessein was rather odd in appearance—though Sterne scarcely noticed it,—as he had but one eye and wore a long wig with curls and tail, at a time when shorter wigs were the fashion. He was most civil and affable in bearing, though sharp in his charges and at a bargain. It was his custom to greet an innocent arrival from Dover with a bow and a side-look resembling the squint of a cock as he eyes a barley-corn, and then to ask Monsieur whether he had any English gold to exchange for French coin. These transactions were very profitable, for Monsieur Dessein knew how to make ten sous on every guinea.‡ But if he cheated his guests, it was done so pleasantly that they felt no resentment.

After Sterne's death, Dessein renovated his inn, adding a theatre, and fitted up a room in honor of his famous guest, hanging over the mantel a mezzotint of Reynolds's *Monsieur Sterne d'Yorick,* and painting on the outside of the door in large characters STERNE'S CHAMBER. There numberless Englishmen down to Thackeray slept, in the fancy that they were lying in the very place where Sterne once stretched his lean shanks. At the new inn Foote laid the scene of his *Trip to Calais,* containing a caricature of the master under the name of Monsieur Tromfort. There, too, stayed Frederic Reynolds,

* J. Wilkes to Humphrey Cotes, December 12, 1764: *Correspondence of Wilkes,* edited by J. Almon, II, 102-103 (London, 1805). It may be that Dessein first bought out Grandsire at the Silver Lion before setting up the Hôtel d'Angleterre.

† Letter dated August 10, 1767: Thicknesse, *Useful Hints to those who make the Tour of France,* 278-281 (London, 1768).

‡ Thicknesse, *A Year's Journey through France and Spain,* I, 9-30 (London, 1778).

another dramatist, for a day or two in 1782, while the merry host was still alive; and asking him whether he remembered Monsieur Sterne, received the interesting reply: " 'Your countryman, Monsieur Sterne, von great, von vary great man, and he carry me vid him to posterity. He gain moche money by his Journey of Sentiment—mais moi—I—make more through de means of dat, then he, by all his ouvrages reunies——Ha, ha!' Then, as if in imitation of Sterne, he laid his forefinger on my breast, and said in a voice lowered almost to a whisper, *'Qu'en pensez vous?'* "* To say truth, the mere mention of Monsieur Dessein in the *Sentimental Journey* made him "one of the richest men in Calais."

Sterne halted at Dessein's for no more than two or three hours, but time enough to set going a series of sweet and pleasurable emotions in himself and others, which was his premeditated aim in this tour. No churches, no monuments, no art galleries were to be visited, or even looked at if it could be helped; at least, they were nowhere to intrude upon a pleasant commerce with men and women, with strangers as well as with old friends whom he might chance to meet on the way to Italy. "I conceive," he said, in explaining the difference between his and all other journeys, "every fair being as a temple, and would rather enter in, and see the original drawings, and loose sketches hung up in it, than the transfiguration of Raphael itself." " 'Tis a quiet journey," he concluded exquisitely, "of the heart in pursuit of NATURE, and those affections which arise out of her, which make us love each other ——and the world, better than we do."

Sterne had not long to wait for his first emotional experience. Close by Dessein's was a convent of Franciscan friars— monks Sterne called them—one of whom was accustomed to attend all visitors at the inn and to do the duties of the *quête* for his order. Mrs. Thrale saw him in 1775, while at Calais with her husband and Dr. Johnson; and subsequently, when she had become Mrs. Piozzi, introduced him into her *Journey*

* *Life and Times of Frederic Reynolds, written by himself*, I, 179-181 (London, 1826).

through France as Father Felix, who, after a career in the army, had retired in old age to the convent for quiet and study. On hearing the story of his varied life, Dr. Johnson declared "that so complete a character could scarcely be found in romance." Sterne had drunk the last of his burgundy in a health to the King of France, and his arteries were all beating cheerily together under its influence, when Father Felix, or his earlier counterpart, entered and asked an alms for his convent. "It was one of those heads," Sterne saw at a glance, "which Guido has often painted—mild, pale—penetrating, free from all commonplace ideas of fat contented ignorance looking downwards upon the earth——it look'd forwards; but look'd, as if it look'd at something beyond this world."

Advancing into the room three paces, the thin and aged friar "stood still; and laying his left hand upon his breast (a slender white staff with which he journey'd being in his right)——when I got close up to him, he introduced himself with the little story of the wants of his convent, and the poverty of his order—and did it with so simple a grace—and such an air of deprecation was there in the whole cast of his look and figure—I was bewitch'd not to have been struck with it." Notwithstanding the supplicant's persuasive words and attitude, Sterne denied the alms for the effect of the denial upon his own and the friar's heart, as seen or felt in the blood coursing through their cheeks; and then for the same reason he begged the friar's pardon, and exchanged snuff-boxes with him, while watching "the stream of good feeling" gush from the mendicant's eyes. Never before had Sterne known, he averred, how sweet was a gentle contention ending in mutual good will.

With Monsieur Dessein, Sterne then strolled out to his *remise*, or magazine of chaises, to purchase one for the tour of Italy. As they walked along, each bent upon overreaching the other in the bargain, Sterne eyed his host askance, thinking him one moment a Jew and then a Turk; but while he was silently "wishing him to the devil," he encountered a beautiful woman, Madam de L * * *, who had just come in from Brussels on her way to Paris; and at once all the base and ungentle passions gave place to pity for the distress which he read in her look and bearing. "It was a face of about six and twenty —of a clear transparent brown, simply set off without rouge or powder——it was not critically handsome, but there was that in it, which, in the frame of mind I was in, attached me much more to it——it was interesting; I fancied it wore the characters of a widow'd look, and in that state of its declension, which had passed the two first paroxysms of sorrow, and was quietly beginning to reconcile itself to its loss——but a thousand other distresses might have traced the same lines." The fresh train of emotions, as Sterne took the hand of the unhappy Fleming by the door of the *remise* or sat with her alone in one of Monsieur Dessein's chaises, was broken off by the arrival of the count, her brother. What name was borne by the sentimental stranger who crossed Sterne's path at Calais matters little, but the curious filled out the stars into the Marquise de Lamberti. In bidding her adieu, Yorick was suffered to kiss her gloved hand twice; whereupon his heart so melted within him that he no longer recked of being cheated by Monsieur Dessein. With no word of protest, he paid the Turk twelve guineas for an old chaise, and ordered post-horses directly.

That evening Sterne probably went on to Boulogne; and thence to Montreuil in the rain, where he lay the next night at the old Hôtel de la Cour de France, kept by Monsieur Varennes. At this inn Sterne was again attended by Janatone, *la belle fille de chambre*, whom he had seen knitting her stocking on his first journey. In the interval she had grown more coquettish under the flatteries of English travellers, Sterne thought, to her harm. Was it Janatone, one wonders, or her successor, whom Mrs. Piozzi found the only interesting object at Montreuil? The girl, still handsome, complained to Mrs. Piozzi of the behavior of the lady's avant-courier. *"Il parle sur le haut ton, mademoiselle,"* apologized Mrs. Piozzi, *"mais il a le cœur bon." "Ouidà,"* retorted the smart *fille de chambre, "mais c'est le ton qui fait le chanson."**

* Hester Lynch Piozzi, *Observations and Reflections made in the Course of a Journey through France, Italy, and Germany* (London, 1779). For Calais and Montreuil, see I, 1-9.

On the road to Montreuil, Sterne came near losing his portmanteau, which fell off twice into the mud and took him out in the rain to tie it on. As a precaution against further mishaps, Monsieur Varennes advised him to take a valet, who would protect him against careless postillions, as well as shave him, dress his wig, and wait upon him at table. If the English gentleman wished such a servant, said the host, no one could suit him better than La Fleur, who was beloved by everybody in Montreuil. At that moment La Fleur, who had been standing at the door breathless with expectation, stepped into the room; and Sterne put him through an examination in the valet's art. La Fleur had been, he told his prospective master, a drummer-boy in the army; but finding that "the honour of beating a drum was likely to be its own reward, as it open'd no further track of glory," he retired *"à ses terres";* that is, with the varnish off, he had deserted and fled to Montreuil in disguise, where he was living as best he could, by performing small services for guests at the Hôtel de France. "He could make spatterdashes," it was brought out in the enquiry, "and play a little upon the fiddle"; while the host put in a word to say that the lad was trustworthy and even-tempered,—if he had a fault, it was that he was always in love with one girl or another. No further recommendation was necessary to the sentimental traveller, who immediately engaged La Fleur for the whole tour of Italy.

"He was," said Sterne in remembrance, "a faithful, affectionate, simple soul as ever trudged after the heels of a philosopher; and notwithstanding his talents of drum-beating and spatterdash-making, which, though very good in themselves, happened to be of no great service to me, yet was I hourly recompensed by the festivity of his temper——it supplied all defects——I had a constant resource in his looks, in all difficulties and distresses of my own——I was going to have added, of his too; but La Fleur was out of the reach of every thing; for whether it was hunger or thirst, or cold or nakedness, or watchings, or whatever stripes of ill luck La Fleur met with in our journeyings, there was no index in his physiognomy to point them out by——he was eternally the same."

That evening, as Sterne ate his supper, with his own valet behind his chair, he felt as happy as a monarch in his good fortune. The next morning La Fleur was placed in command of all details of the journey. He ordered his master's chaise, horses, and postillion to the door; and standing in his great jack-boots before the inn, took a tender leave of half a dozen girls, for all of whom he promised to bring pardons from Rome. Sterne passed out to his chaise through a long line of urbane beggars, among whom he distributed sous in return for their blessings; the postillion cracked his whip; La Fleur mounted a bidet and shot forward as avant-courier. Nothing happened until they were approaching Nampont, where La Fleur's horse shied at a dead ass in the road, cast his rider, and scampered back home. Whereupon Sterne took his valet into the chaise along with him, and they jogged on to Amiens for the night. There they overtook Madame de L * * * and her brother, who put up, however, at another inn. It may be that the lady, as says the *Sentimental Journey*, sent over to Sterne a letter of introduction to her friend Madame de R * * * of Paris;* and that he, perplexed in his French, repaid the courtesy by adapting one of La Fleur's old love letters to a suitable reply. In two days more, over which hangs silence, Sterne was again in Paris.

If the *Sentimental Journey* points true, Sterne took lodgings at the Hôtel de Modène, number 14 Rue Jacob,† then a pretty street, in the Faubourg St. Germain, with houses, as the imagination may still restore them, set back from the street and built around courts. On the second floor was his room, furnished with bureau and writing-table, and having bed and windows bright with crimson curtains. This dainty apartment Sterne chose for a scene with Madame de R * * *'s "fair *fille de chambre*," who came with an enquiry from her mistress; and for another scene with the grisette who sold him "a pair of ruffles" from her box of laces. It was there, too, that La Fleur appeared on a Sunday morning, dressed, to the sur-

* Probably Madame de Rambouillet.
† *Notes and Queries*, seventh series, IX, 366.

prise of his master, in a scarlet livery, which he had purchased
at a second-hand shop in the Rue de la Vieille Friperie for
four louis d'or, the first instalment of his wages; and there
Sterne sat the rest of the day translating a story for the *Sentimental Journey* out of the crabbed French of Rabelais's time.
In a long passage below, opening upon the courtyard, hung
the cage of an imprisoned starling, taught to cry with the plaintive voice of a child: "I can't get out——I can't get out."
Hearing the sad notes one day as he was going downstairs,
Sterne returned directly to his room, he says, and leaning his
head over the little table, imagined and wrote out the sketch
of the "pale and feverish" captive wasting away in a dungeon
of the Bastille.

The day after his arrival, if we may still go on with the
Sentimental Journey, Sterne procured his wig and dressed himself to call upon Madam de R * * *, to whom he bore a letter
from the brown lady he had exchanged gentle courtesies with
at Calais. It was but a short walk to her *hôtel* round the corner
in the handsome Rue des Saints Pères. But the day was so far
advanced before the barber and La Fleur had done with him,
that he changed his mind and decided to visit the Comédie
Italienne, popularly called the Opéra Comique, across the
river in the Rue Mauconseil. The old quarter of the city where
stood his hotel, was then, as it is now, a network of streets so
very perplexing that it was necessary for him to enquire his
way. Strolling along the Rue Jacob and its continuation in the
Rue du Colombier, "in search of a face not likely to be disordered by such an interruption," he saw, as he was about to
pass the door of a glove-shop, a grisette of uncommon beauty,
sitting in the rear and making a pair of ruffles. He stepped in
and purchased two pairs of gloves. During the transaction, his
fingers fell upon the grisette's wrist, that he might feel the
pulse of one of the fairest and best-tempered beings that he
had ever met with in his sentimental wanderings.

"I had counted twenty pulsations," as Sterne relates the
adventure, "and was going on fast towards the fortieth, when
her husband coming unexpected from a back parlour into the

shop, put me a little out of my reckoning.——'Twas nobody but her husband, she said——so I began a fresh score—— Monsieur is so good, quoth she, as he pass'd by us, as to give himself the trouble of feeling my pulse——The husband took off his hat, and making me a bow, said, I did him too much honour——and having said that, he put on his hat and walk'd out."

Poor Yorick was utterly overcome by the grisette's quick black eyes, which shot through long and silken eyelashes into his very heart and reins. He nevertheless went on, under the guidance of a lad from the glove-shop, to the Pont-Neuf, whence the route was clear to the Rue Mauconseil. At the play, his heart was disturbed by the selfishness of a "tall corpulent German near seven feet high," standing in the parterre, who persisted in keeping in front of a dwarf, and so shutting off for the little fellow all view of the stage. Sterne's plaudits were not for the actors, but for a sentinel who thrust the German back with his musket and placed the dwarf before him. "This is noble," exclaimed Sterne to a French officer in the same box with him, and clapped his hands together. After the play, he stopped a few minutes in the "long dark passage issuing out from the Opéra Comique into a narrow street," to watch the behavior of two tall and lean ladies, who, while waiting for their carriage, were wheedled out of two twelve-sous pieces by a beggar proficient in the art of that flattery which rules the world. On the way back to his hotel, he lost his way again, as well he might, after crossing the Pont-Neuf and reaching the Quai de Conti; but by chance he met Madame R * * *'s *fille de chambre*, who walked along with him to the Rue de Guénégaud, and bidding him adieu there, directed him to the Hôtel de Modène, where La Fleur was waiting to put his master to bed.

These incidents, related baldly without the author's embellishments, seem very trivial indeed; but they show Sterne clearly in lights which have hitherto only partially shone upon him. Human nature among all classes intensely interested him. He was as eager to learn what was going on in the heart and head of a grisette who kept her husband's shop, or of a dwarf in distress at the theatre, or tumbling into a gutter, as he was to divine the brilliant men and women who frequented the salons. If we could know, we should probably find that the evening at the Opéra Comique was but typical of many walks alone through the streets of Paris in quest of fresh emotions. But except in so far as we have cautiously employed it, the *Sentimental Journey* cannot be trusted as a guide for Sterne in Paris at this time. French gentlemen with whom he had previously associated and whom he brings upon the scene in his narrative, were mostly away on their estates in the country. The Court was still at Fontainebleau; and Hume, as *chargé d'affaires*, was there too. With the Court were likely also the Duc de Choiseul and the Comte de Bissy, whom Sterne represents himself as going out to see at Versailles. All this part of the *Sentimental Journey* was based upon Sterne's first reception in Paris three years before; while the hint of an excursion to Rennes to witness the Marquis d'E * * * * reclaim his sword before the assembled states of Brittany, is pure fiction. It was a touching story which Sterne heard or read of somewhere, and related because it fitted into his emotional scheme. Paris was this year only his stopping-place for not above ten days on the route to Italy. Arrangements had to be made with his bankers for remittances and for sending on his letters from home. In these transactions Foley, who was likely out of town, gave place to Panchaud, the other member of the firm, for whom and his unmarried sister Sterne expressed great esteem. By good luck Diderot and Baron d'Holbach were close by at Grandval, if not in the city; and they received Sterne into the old intimacy.

Amid the dearth of fashionable society, Sterne found amusement not only in sentimental pilgrimages among the tradespeople, but in the English colony which was beginning to gather for the winter. Wilkes, who had varied his exile by a visit to Italy, had just returned to Paris and settled near Sterne at the Hôtel de Saxe in the Rue du Colombier. With him or not far away was Foote the comedian, who was in

Paris for rest and recreation. The trio fell in with another
set of Englishmen, who hovered around John Craufurd of
Errol, "one of the gayest young gentlemen," wrote a cadet in
his service, "and the greatest gambler that ever belonged to
Scotland." The remark ought not to be taken as in the least
derogatory to Mr. Craufurd's character, as the world went
in those days; for he was one of the best known young men
in London and Parisian society. The season over at home, it
was Craufurd's custom to make a circular tour abroad which
should include Paris, where the blind and brilliant Madame
du Deffand took him under her protection. He put up usually
at the expensive Hôtel de Parc Royal, and had his dinners
served from the still more expensive Hôtel de Bourbon. As
befitted a young spark of wealth and leisure, he drove about
Paris in a French chariot, with a French coachman and a
French footman. In his company were the young Earl of
Upper Ossory, a man of finer grain, and Lord William Gordon, second son of the third Duke of Gordon. Horace Walpole was also in Paris, living, say his letters, most of the time
—when not with Madame du Deffand, or nursing the gout in
his lodgings—with Craufurd and Lord Ossory, the latter of
whom he classed among "the most amiable" men he had ever
known—"modest, manly, very sensible, and well bred."

Sterne must have known Craufurd beforehand, for he
wrote of him as "my friend"; and he now made the acquaintance of the rest in the group. Walpole, who had hitherto kept
out of Sterne's way, was at length trapped into his company,
either at Baron d'Holbach's or Craufurd's table, whence good
breeding would not let him escape. Wilkes and Foote were
present on the occasion. "You will think it odd," Walpole
wrote to Thomas Brand, on October 19, 1765, "that I should
want to laugh, when Wilkes, Sterne, and Foote are here; but
the first does not make me laugh, the second never could, and
for the third, I choose to pay five shillings when I have a mind
he should divert me."

Either then or at another time Craufurd related to the company the following strange adventure, which Sterne reworked

for "The Case of Delicacy" at the close of the *Sentimental Journey:*

On the way between Verviers and Aix-la-Chapelle, the young man once stopped at a crowded inn and engaged the only room left for the night. It was a large room with a closet containing another but smaller bed. Half an hour later, a Flemish lady, called Madame Blond in the story, arrived with her maid in a chaise, and asked for a night's lodging, with some perturbation of spirit when she saw that the inn was full. The landlady could not possibly accommodate her; but Madame Blond persisted in having a bed, saying that she would make any shift for one night. So it was finally arranged that she might take the closet of the English gentleman's apartment, if he would agree to it. Thereupon Madame Blond, sending her compliments in advance, came upstairs, and asked Mr. Craufurd, "with all the politeness in the world," if she might sit with him through the evening. With equal civility he made her welcome, and invited her to a game of cards while supper was preparing. When the evening had worn on to an end, Mr. Craufurd politely said: "If you like, Madame Blond, you may have the bed, as it will hold yourself and maid, and I will sleep in the closet." "By no means," replied the Flemish lady; "I am extremely obliged to you for the privilege of the little bed." "Come, madame," then rejoined Mr. Craufurd, "we will play at cards for the large bed." They accordingly played for it, and the lady lost. Madame Blond bade the English gentleman good-night, retired to her closet, and, as she did so, gave strict orders to her maid to bolt the door, though why was not quite clear to Mr. Craufurd, since the bolt was on the outside in his own room. The next morning Madame Blond went on to Spa, and Mr. Craufurd to Aix-la-Chapelle.*

Near the twenty-fourth of October, Sterne left Paris, taking La Fleur in his smart livery along with him, and pursued

---

* John Macdonald, a cadet of the family of Keppoch, *Travels in Various Parts of Europe, Asia and Africa* (London, 1790). The anecdote, preceded by an account of Craufurd, is given on pages 138-140.

his way southwards to Lyons—a week's journey by the long route which he chose through "the Bourbonnais, the sweetest part of France." It was "the hey-day of the vintage, when Nature is pouring her abundance into every one's lap, and every eye is lifted up—a journey through each step of which Music beats time to *Labour*, and all her children are rejoicing as they carry in their clusters." Amid "the joyous riot" of his affections, which flew out and kindled at every new scene, he was sobered, according to the *Sentimental Journey*, by the sight of a distracted peasant girl sitting by the roadside as his chaise drew near Moulins, the ancient seat of the Bourbons. Doubtless the account of the poor girl cannot be accepted precisely as Sterne rendered it; but it is quite certain that behind the adventure lay some emotional hint. Sterne related the story twice over, and a version subsequently got into current anecdotes, with the claim that it was derived from La Fleur. "When we came up to her," says the valet's version, "she was grovelling in the Road like an infant, and throwing the Dust upon her head——and yet few were more lovely! Upon Sterne's accosting her with tenderness, and raising her in his arms, she collected herself and resumed some composure—— told him her tale of misery and wept upon his breast——my master sobbed aloud. I saw her gently disengage herself from his arms, and she sung him the service to the Virgin; my poor master covered his face with his hands, and walked by her side to the Cottage where she lived."

If the narrative purporting to come from La Fleur cannot be proved authentic, it is at least a very good guess at what really occurred by the dusty roadside. Sterne himself, be it noted, really said no more than was attributed to his valet, nor quite so much as that, when he first told the story for the ninth volume of *Shandy*, though incident and emotion were graded by the most perfect art to a humorous conclusion:

"——They were the sweetest notes I ever heard; and I instantly let down the fore-glass to hear them more distinctly ——'Tis *Maria;* said the postillion, observing I was listening ——Poor *Maria*, continued he, (leaning his body on one side

to let me see her, for he was in a line betwixt us), is sitting
upon a bank playing her vespers upon her pipe, with her little
goat beside her. . . . It is but three years ago, that the sun did
not shine upon so fair, so quick-witted and amiable a maid;
and better fate did *Maria* deserve, than to have her Banns forbid, by the intrigues of the curate of the parish who published
them.——He was going on, when *Maria*, who had made a
short pause, put the pipe to her mouth, and began the air again
——they were the same notes;——yet were ten times sweeter.
It is the evening service to the Virgin, said the young man
——but who has taught her to play it——or how she came by
her pipe, no one knows.

"We had got up by this time almost to the bank where
Maria was sitting; she was in a thin white jacket, with her
hair, all but two tresses, drawn up into a silken net, with a
few olive leaves twisted a little fantastically on one side——
she was beautiful; and if ever I felt the full force of an
honest heart-ache, it was the moment I saw her——God help
her! poor damsel! above a hundred masses, said the postillion,
have been said in the several parish churches and convents
around, for her,——but without effect. . . . As the postillion
spoke this, Maria made a cadence so melancholy, so tender
and querulous, that I sprung out of the chaise to help her, and
found myself sitting betwixt her and her goat before I re-
lapsed from my enthusiasm.——Maria look'd wistfully for
some time at me, and then at her goat——and then at me——
and then at her goat again, and so on, alternately——Well,
Maria, said I softly——What resemblance do you find?"

A night at "an excellent inn," and Sterne went on into
the mountains of Lyonnais. As he was ascending Mount
Tarare in the evening, the thill-horse lost two shoes, making
it necessary, since the postillion had no nails, to stop at a little
farmhouse for repairs. On entering the house, Sterne found
a gray-haired peasant and his wife, with grown-up sons and
daughters and a numerous progeny out of them, "all sitting
down together to their lentil-soup; a large wheaten loaf was
in the middle of the table; and a flaggon·of wine at each end

of it, promised joy through the stages of the repast." The
peasant, rising up and stepping towards the stranger, cordially
invited him to join in the evening meal. "I sat down at once,"
says Sterne, who was as much at home with a French peasant
as with Baron d'Holbach, "like a son of the family; and to
invest myself in the character as speedily as I could, I instantly
borrowed the old man's knife, and taking up the loaf, cut myself a hearty luncheon." When supper was over, the sons and
daughters of labor all ran out on a little esplanade in front of
the house; and the peasant and his wife followed with their
guest, who sat down between them "upon a sopha of turf by
the door." The old man touched his *vielle*, and all the children
and grandchildren fell into the evening dance.

After watching the scene through a few dances, Sterne
pushed on to Tarare, a little town among the mountains,
where he engaged a voiturin with a couple of mules to conduct him in his own chaise down the descent to Lyons and on
through Savoy. At Lyons he spent a joyous week, "dining and
supping every day at the commandant's," in company with ten
or twelve other Englishmen who were accorded similar hospitality. Of them was a certain "Lord F. W.," and Horne
Tooke, the pugnacious parson who was about to turn political
agitator in favor of Wilkes. Mr. Horne, as he was then called,
was a young man under thirty who had not yet discovered his
true vocation. Some years before, he had "suffered," he told
Wilkes, "the infectious hand of a bishop to be waved over"
him, but he "was not ordained a hypocrite," and would go his
own way. On coming over to France as bear-leader to the son
of a Mr. Taylor of Brentford, he discarded his clerical dress,
and flaunted through Paris in scarlet and silver, alternating
with blue and silver. There were indeed no less than five varie-
gated suits in his wardrobe. After visiting Wilkes and offering
him his services, he started on the grand tour a day or two
before Sterne arrived in Paris. Although Sterne found him
an agreeable companion enough at Lyons, he was clearly bored
by his eulogies of the champion of British liberty. "Is there
any cause of coldness," Horne enquired in a letter to Wilkes,

"between you and Sterne? He speaks very handsomely of you, when it is absolutely necessary to speak at all; but not with that *warmth and enthusiasm*, that I expect from every one that knows you."* When the two men parted, Horne for Montpellier and Sterne for Italy, it was agreed that they should meet at Siena in the summer.

Sterne's route lay through the mountain passes of Savoy over Mont Cenis to Turin. A day's journey brought him to Pont-de-Beauvoisin, a small town almost surrounded by two branches of the Guiers-Vif, which takes its rise in the Alps. At this place Sterne was held prisoner for two or three days by the terrible autumn rains, which poured down upon him and his fellow travellers, as if heaven and earth were coming together. The petty rivulets swelled with the rains and the melting snow until they became impassable; and Sterne, hemmed in on all sides, could neither return to Lyons nor advance into the mountains. Setting forward at length on the eighth of November, with voiturin and mules, he was a full week in traversing Savoy, along precipices, up and down narrow valleys by the side of mountain torrents and cataracts, "which roll down great stones" from the summits. One evening, as he was hastening through a pouring rain from St. Michel to Modane, his mules came to a sudden halt before a huge fragment of rock which had fallen across the road. All day long the peasants had been trying to remove it; and for two hours more they labored on into the "wet and tempestuous night," while Sterne sat in his chaise, watching them through the window amid the flare of torches. When a narrow passage was finally cleared for him, it was too late to reach Modane, and so he stopped at a wayside inn, where he placed, in closing the *Sentimental Journey*, the delicate adventure with the Piedmontese lady and the maid of Lyonnais. To Sterne, who had none of the poet Gray's passion for the sublime, it had all been a perilous tour of "sudden turns and dangers"—"difficulties of getting up," and "horrors of getting down"—through a

* Alexander Stephens, *Memoirs of John Horne Tooke*, II, 76-77 (London, 1813).

province where nature lay in wild disorder, with little to give, except a sheltered habitation, to a "poor, patient, quiet, honest, people."

On the evening of November 14 Sterne entered Turin, the first Italian city he ever saw, through a *corso* of over-arching trees, ten miles in length and as straight as a line, leading to the spacious Piazza Castello, where stands the old royal palace, and near which Smollett a few months before had taken up his quarters. Sterne's agreeable emotions on entering a city of wide and regular avenues, like the Via di Po, flanked with colonnades against the sun, may perhaps be inferred from his remark about old Paris, whose streets, he said, were so narrow that a man could never tell on which side he was walking. It was his first intention to make Turin only a stopping-place on the way to Milan; but continual rains, which had laid the intervening country under water, rendered it impossible for him to proceed for a fortnight. It was "a joyous fortnight." Within twenty-four hours after his arrival he received invitations to "a dozen houses"; the following day he was presented to the King of Sardinia; and when that ceremony was over, he had his "hands full of engagements."

Only two other Englishmen were then in Turin—"Mr. Ogilby," who permitted Sterne to take down his name for five sets of the *Sentimental Journey* on imperial paper, and the young Sir James Macdonald of Skye, over whose death the Western Isles were soon to lament, as the Marcellus upon whom they had rested their hopes. Nothing else lets us into the charm of Sterne's personality quite so well as the ease with which he attached himself to young men, who choose their companions by a subtle instinct, which they never stop to explain, and could not explain if they tried. Between Sterne and Macdonald it was attraction at first sight. The young baronet, only twenty-four years old, united the best traditions of Eton and Oxford for scholarship with uncommonly fine manners, large talents for business, and "the patriarchal spirit," says Boswell, "of a great Highland chieftain." After sharing in "all kinds of honours" at Turin, the two men bade their friends adieu with regret, and started on November 28 for the south by a long detour, which included many of the towns of northern Italy. Macdonald was longing to see Rome; and Sterne, whose health again showed signs of breaking, thought it best to winter in Naples. Writing to Panchaud on business when they reached Florence, Sterne incidentally gave his delightful itinerary up to that point. "I have been a month," he said, "passing the plains of Lombardie——stopping in my way at Milan, Parma, Placenza, and Bologna——with weather as delicious as a kindly April in England, and have been three days in crossing a part of the Apenines cover'd with thick snow ——sad transition!"

At Milan Sterne was received by Count Firmian, the Austrian minister, at whose house he met Gian Carlo Passeroni, a gay priest, whom literature kept poor. In one of their conversations Passeroni understood Sterne to say that he took the design of *Tristram Shandy* from his *Il Cicerone*, a long facetious poem (the first part of which had appeared in 1755) unmasking the vices and follies of ancient Rome. The two ecclesiastics, of the same age, were indeed somewhat alike in style and temper. Both were whimsical and desultory. Still, I daresay, Sterne had never heard of Passeroni until he saw him. And so, if Yorick really made the remark attributed to him ("Mi chiamava suo duce e precettore"), it must have been due to excessive courtesy. On one occasion Sterne also met Alessandro Verri, a much younger man of letters, who was destined to become known beyond his own country for his vivid pictures of Roman life in the time of the Scipios. Sterne told Verri later that he intended to relate, without much attention to fact, his adventures in Milan (where he was evidently having a good time) for his *Viaggio Sentimentale d'Italia*. One of these adventures, it is well known, was actually tucked away in the *Sentimental Journey*.*

"I was going," as Sterne elaborated the story there, out of its place, "one evening to Martini's concert at Milan, and was just entering the door of the hall, when the Marquisina di

* Giovanni Rabizzani, *Sterne in Italia*, 29-37 (Roma, 1920).

F * * * was coming out in a sort of a hurry—she was almost upon me before I saw her; so I gave a spring to one side to let her pass——She had done the same, and on the same side too: so we ran our heads together: she instantly got to the other side to get out: I was just as fortunate as she had been; for I had sprung to that side, and opposed her passage again——We both flew together to the other side, and then back——and so on——it was ridiculous; we both blush'd intolerably; so I did at last the thing I should have done at first——I stood stock still, and the Marquisina had no more difficulty. I had no power to go into the room, till I had made her so much reparation as to wait and follow her with my eye to the end of the passage——She look'd back twice. . . . I ran and begg'd pardon for the embarrassment I had given her, saying it was my intention to have made her way. . . . I begg'd to hand her to her coach——so we went down the stairs, stopping at every third step to talk of the concert and the adventure—— Upon my word, Madame, said I, when I had handed her in, I made six different efforts to let you go out——And I made six efforts, replied she, to let you enter——I wish to heaven you would make a seventh, said I——With all my heart, said she, making room——Life is too short to be long about the forms of it——so I instantly stepp'd in, and she carried me home with her——And what became of the concert, St. Cecilia, who, I suppose, was at it, knows more than I. . . . The connection which arose out of the translation, gave me more pleasure than any one I had the honour to make in Italy."

The woman of this sentimental encounter was none other than the beautiful and cultivated Marchesa Fagniani, who became the friend of George Selwyn and the mother of Maria Fagniani, wife of the third Marquis of Hertford.

Sterne allowed only three days for Florence, or just time enough to exchange civilities with Sir Horace Mann, the English envoy to the Court of Tuscany. Since 1760 Mann had been reading the successive instalments of *Tristram Shandy*, which diverted him extremely, though he thought there was

some "humbugging" in the style; at least men did not talk
and write that way when he was last in England.* Macdonald
was also known to Mann through letters from their mutual
friend, Horace Walpole, who described him as "a very extraordinary young man for variety and learning, . . . rather too
wise for his age, and too fond of showing it," but likely to
"choose to know less" after seeing more of the world.† Sterne
and Macdonald were dined at the envoy's with two young men
of rank, whom they perhaps knew beforehand. One was Earl
Cowper, subsequently created a Prince of the Holy Roman
Empire, who was held bound to Florence by a sentimental
passion for a Tuscan lady; and the other was the Duke of
Portland, the future Prime Minister.

Tom Patch, the English engraver, was in Florence also as
Mann's friend. In burlesque of the Invocation to Death in
Tristram Shandy, Patch drew Sterne face to face with Death
the skeleton extending towards him an hour glass with the sand
all run down. The grim humor of the drawing lies in Sterne's
startled looks and Death's reluctance to accept a curt dismissal.
The "careless indifference" with which Sterne confronted
Death in his book gives way here to surprise and fear.

Before leaving Florence, Sterne of course visited the
Duomo, Santa Croce, and the Uffizi Gallery with his friends;
and yet the only positive evidence pointing that way is his
banter of Smollett in the *Sentimental Journey* for seeing "no
beauty in the features" of the Venus of Medici, and for thinking the attitude "awkward and out of character."

As the travellers drew near Rome, Sterne became impatient
for the morning when he might "tread the Vatican and be
introduced to all the saints of the Pantheon." Two weeks were
set aside for sight-seeing in the imperial city. There are vague
traditions that Sterne was several times received by the Pope,
and introduced to the noble families of Doria and Santa
Croce. Though all details of his reception are lacking, it is

---

* D. Doran, *Mann and Manners*, II, 71 (London, 1876).

† For Walpole on Macdonald, see especially *Letters*, edited by Toynbee, VI, 305-306, 313, 418, 423.

safe to say that Sterne could not have stayed in Rome a fortnight or more without his presence being widely known, nor
have forgone the humorous delight of an audience with the
head of the Church he had so abused in his sermons. The intimation in the *Sentimental Journey* that he encountered Smollett in "the grand portico of the Pantheon," and overheard
the satirist say, as he was leaving, that it was "nothing but a
huge cockpit," cannot be accepted literally; for Smollett was
then in England. If the two antipathies ever met face to face,
it was two years before at Montpellier.

At Rome Sterne and Macdonald overtook "a young gentleman of fortune" named Errington, a friend of three years'
standing, with whom they journeyed south to Naples, just in
time to witness a fresh outburst of Vesuvius.* By the middle
of January they were all established together in the same
house, said to have been the Casa di Mansel; and near them
were scattered a score of their countrymen, among whom was
"Mr. Symonds, a person of learning and character," who may
be identified with John Symonds, Professor of Modern History at Cambridge in succession to Gray. Sarah Tuting was in
Naples also. Sterne and his company had their own pastimes—
sight-seeing, games, and conversation over news from home
as it came in letters and in the *London Chronicle*—and invitations out with the most fashionable Neapolitan society.
"Many civilities and attentions" were shown them by Sir William Hamilton, then the British envoy at the Court of Naples.
"We have a jolly carnival of it," Sterne wrote to Hall-Stevenson in February, "nothing but operas—punchinelloes—fes-
tinos and masquerades—We (that is, *nous autres*) are all
dressing out for one this night at the Princess Francavivalla
[Francavilla], which is to be superb.—The English dine with
her (exclusive) and so much for small chat—except that I
saw a little comedy acted last week with more expression and
spirit, and true character, than I shall see one hastily again."

Neapolitan gaiety under a mild sun agreed perfectly with

* *St. James's Chronicle*, February 22-25, 1766.

Sterne's constitution. "I find myself infinitely better than I was," he wrote to his daughter Lydia, after three weeks at Naples, "and hope to have added at least ten years to my life by this journey to Italy——the climate is heavenly, and I find new principles of health in me, which I have been long a stranger to." Thus improving, even "growing fat, sleek, and well liking," Sterne stayed on into March; and then posted back to Rome with Macdonald, Errington, and Symonds, in time for the novel and impressive ceremonies of Holy Week. Of his journey he wrote amusingly to Sir William Hamilton on the seventeenth of March, two days after reaching Rome:

"My friend [probably Errington] and self had a voyage of it by Mount Cassino, full of cross accidents; but all was remedied along the road by sporting and laughter—We dined and supped and lay at the Monastery of Cassino where we were received and treated like Sovereign Princes—and on Saturday by eleven o'clock in the morning got here without bodily hurt except that a Dromedary of a beast fell upon me in full Gallop, and by rolling over me crushed me as flat as a Pankake —but I am growing round again."

While in Rome Sterne sat to Nollekens for a portrait bust in terra-cotta, which deservedly brought the sculptor "into great notice." The face, as one views it in profile, has none of the pinched Voltairean features of the Carmontelle portrait; it is large and full, indicative of renewed strength and vigor. "With this performance," says the sculptor's biographer, "Nollekens continued to be pleased even to his second childhood, and often mentioned a picture which Dance had made of him leaning upon Sterne's head."*

After Easter, Sterne's little company of travellers broke up. The first to leave was Symonds, who was going home through France. At his departure, Sterne gave him a note of introduction, as yet unpublished, to "Dr. Jemm† of Paris," which is

* J. T. Smith, *Nollekens and his Times*, edited by Gosse, 34 (London, 1895).

† Probably Dr. Richard Gem, then physician to the British Embassy at Paris. For an interesting account of Dr. Gem, see W. P. Courtney in *Notes and Queries*, eleventh series, II, 121-123 (August 13, 1910).

most interesting as Sterne's last word on the benefit and pleasure he had received from his sojourn in Italy. "I am much recover'd," he wrote on Easter Sunday, "by the Neapolitan Air ——I have been here in my return three Weeks, seeing over again what I saw first in my way to Naples. . . . We have pass'd a jolly laughing winter of it—and having changed the Scene for Rome; we are passing as merry a Spring as hearts could wish. I wish my friends no better fortune in this world, than to go at this rate——*hæc est Vita dissolutorum.*"

It was then Sterne's design to travel leisurely homewards through Germany, as companion to Errington. They were to start "in a few days" for Venice, where Sterne expected to meet "many worthy men" whom he esteemed, and proceed thence to Vienna, Dresden, Berlin, and Spa, and so on to England, either through Holland or by a loop which should give them a week or two in Paris. With this in mind while at Naples, Sterne requested Panchaud to draw him a small letter of credit upon Mr. Watson, his correspondent at Venice, and to forward all his letters thither by Ascension week in care of the banker. Hall-Stevenson was also commissioned to obtain for him a letter of introduction from Pitt or Lord Hertford to Lord Stormont, the English Ambassador at Vienna, "importing that I am not fallen from the clouds." At other times, opportunities of leading young men about Europe had come to Sterne, but he had let them all pass, expressing, as he did so, either a dislike of the gentleman in question or of a mode of travel which commonly made the tutor subservient to the whims of a mere boy. In this instance, however, the prospects were good for an enjoyable tour, which would cost him nothing beyond a little pocket money "in case of sickness and accidents." "As I know him," he wrote of Errington to Hall-Stevenson, "to be a good-hearted young gentleman, I have no doubt of making it answer both his views and mine ——at least I am persuaded we shall return home together, as we set out, with friendship and goodwill."

But for some reason Sterne changed his plans at the last moment, and decided to go home directly, either over the old

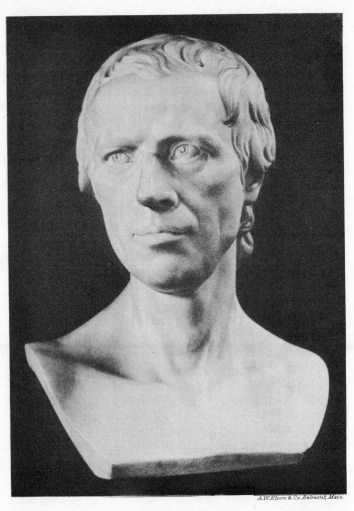

A.W.Elson & Co. Belmont, Mass.

Laurence Sterne
From a marble replica of the bust by Joseph Nollekens
in the National Portrait Gallery

route through Piedmont and Savoy, or more likely—after revisiting Siena and Florence—by boat from Leghorn to Marseilles, and thence to Paris and Calais. Was there a quarrel or a misunderstanding, such as Sterne had often seen, and feared for himself in these relationships? It may have been so. And yet what drew Sterne away from Errington into France was really, I think, a desire to visit his wife and daughter, and to persuade them to return with him to Coxwold. Such at least is the tenor of a letter to Lydia. He felt some anxiety, too, for their health. Mrs. Sterne was still troubled with rheumatism; and both herself and Lydia were trying to rid themselves of an ague which they had contracted at Tours during the winter.

Be the reason what it may, Sterne and Errington separated towards the end of April, leaving Macdonald behind them ill at Rome. The young Scot had been in miserable health all winter. While at Naples he came down with a malarial fever which assumed the deceitful complexion of rheumatism; but when spring approached he seemed to be recovering. Then came a relapse in Easter week at Rome. No one, however, felt any uneasiness as to the ultimate issue. His stomach, his physician told Macdonald, would soon regain its tone, and the palpitation of which he complained "must cease in time." But the palpitation ceased only with the beating of his heart on the twenty-sixth of July. To his memory his mother, Lady Margaret Macdonald, daughter of the Earl of Eglinton, erected a monument in the parish church of Sleat on the Isle of Skye, for which his friend George, Lord Lyttelton, wrote a long inscription, saying that at his death in Rome "such extraordinary honours were paid to his memory as had never graced that of any other British subject since the death of Sir Philip Sidney." Anyone who doubts the appropriateness of the comparison has only to read Macdonald's letters to his mother from Rome during his illness. "There is no circumstance of danger and pain," he wrote the night before his death, "of which I have not had the experience." But he kept his condition from his mother until the last moment, supporting his painful illness "with admirable patience and fortitude."

"Never was a parent more to be pitied," was the comment of Mrs. Montagu, when she heard that Sir James Macdonald was dying at Rome. "His country will lose its first ornament and his little Island relapse into barbarism and poverty from whence he was raising it."*

Near the first of May, Sterne entered France, ready to pay his respects to his wife; but he was uncertain where to look for her; for she had long since left Tours on a ramble with Lydia whither caprice might lead her. It was "a wild-goose chace" for the husband through "five or six different towns," until he discovered a trail which took him through Dijon, far off his route, into the old province of Franche Comté or Upper Burgundy. "Poor woman!" he wrote to Hall-Stevenson after he had found her, "she was very cordial, &c. and begs to stay another year or so——my Lydia pleases me much—— I found her greatly improved in everything I wish'd her—— I am most unaccountably well, and most unaccountably non-sensical——'tis at least a proof of good spirits, which is a sign and token given me in these latter days that I must take up again the pen——In faith I think I shall die with it in my hand, but I shall live these ten years, my Antony, notwithstanding the fears of my wife, whom I left most melancholy on that account."

Retracing his steps towards Dijon, he turned out of his road to "a delicious Chateau of the Countess of M——," an old Parisian friend, doubtless, who was at her country-seat with a house full of guests. There Sterne rested for a week, "patriarching it . . . with her ladyship and half a dozen of very handsome and agreeable ladies." It was "a delicious part of the world," and "most celestial weather," so that they could "lie all day, without damps, on the grass"; and twice a day

* On Macdonald see especially Boswell's "Journal of a Tour of the Hebrides" in *Life of Samuel Johnson*, edited by P. Fitzgerald, III, 297-299 (London, 1874). For his relations with Mrs. Montagu, see R. Blunt, *Mrs. Montagu, passim*. Though more than twenty years his senior, the Bluestocking was in love with Macdonald. The young Scot had heard of *Tristram Shandy*, but it is quite clear that he had never read the book, nor seen Sterne until they met in Turin.

conversation was "inspired . . . with the best Burgundy that grows upon the mountains." From this charming retreat, which reads like a scene out of Boccaccio, Sterne broke away on the twenty-sixth of May; and, to make up for lost time, posted night and day to Paris, "where"— he informed Hall-Stevenson—"I shall arrive in two days, and just wind myself up, when I am there, enough to roll on to Calais——so I hope to sup with you the king's birth day, according to a plan of sixteen days standing."

If Sterne kept the covenant to celebrate his Majesty's birthday with Hall-Stevenson, who was then in London, he had only three days for winding himself up in Paris. In passing through the city, he fell in with the Abbé Galiani, the Neapolitan envoy to France, a savant and wit near the first rank. Their conversation, which likely occurred over the dessert at Baron d'Holbach's, turned to Sterne's sojourn in Italy. Galiani, who looked upon the sentimental humorist as rather a bore, nevertheless set down one *bon mot* to his credit. Years afterwards, when recalled by the King of Naples, he wrote to Madame d'Epinay, saying, "The only good thing which that tiresome Monsieur Sterne ever uttered was his remark to me one day that it was far better to die in Paris than to live in Naples."* The influence of his Italian journey thus fading into the background, Sterne hastened home to catch the end of the London season. His valet, retaining the pretty name of La Fleur, which Sterne had given to him out of current French comedy, is said to have married one of the girls of Montreuil for whom he was to bring a pardon from Rome, and to have opened a public house in Calais for English sailors navigating packet boats across the Channel. Ill luck attended the enterprise after the outbreak of war between France and England, and La Fleur took up his career as valet again. The story may be mere fiction, and yet it seems probable enough to be true.†

* *Lettres de l'Abbé Galiani à Madame d'Epinay*, II, 137 (Paris, 1881). For the meeting between Galiani and Sterne see *Mémoires de l'Abbé Morellet*, I, 128 (Paris, 1821).

† An account of La Fleur and of Sterne's journey from the valet's

point of view appeared in the *European Magazine* in a long article running through September, October, and November, 1790. Parts of the narrative were reprinted by William Davis in his *Olio*, 25-32 (London, 1814). The story, although purporting to have come from the lips of La Fleur himself, is quite untrustworthy as a whole; but it has behind it a real La Fleur and vague traditions.

CHAP. XVIII.

The Last Volume of Tristram Shandy
June, 1766—March, 1767

MIDSUMMER saw Sterne once more in the "peaceful retreat" of his parish, meditating the maxim that "man's happiness depends upon himself," irrespective of where he may be, whether at Naples or at Coxwold. But with the best disposition in the world to be consoled by the shreds of philosophy, the moralist was ill at ease, moody, and inclined to keep close within his shell. This year we read of no visits to Skelton, Scarborough, or Harrogate, except as temptations of the devil to be resisted. Even invitations to Newburgh Priory, less than two miles away, were accepted only because they could not be declined, and with the complaint that these courtesies of his patron oppressed him to death. His visitations of Alne and Tollerton also, which he usually made in person when in Yorkshire, were performed this summer by his surrogate. And so nearly everything known about Sterne until he went up to London at Christmas points to the seclusion of Shandy Hall.

The reasons for his depressed spirits are quite obvious. Hemorrhages, from which he seems to have been free while abroad, set in again, and increased through the autumn until he had three in one month. Another source of trouble lay in his finances. If the cost of his sojourn in Italy had been lightened by the generosity of Errington and Macdonald, the gain thereby had been many times offset by the expenses of Mrs. Sterne, for whose mode of life the old allowance of two hundred guineas a year was proving inadequate. She was spending nearly double the sum. To balance his account to date, he directed Panchaud to draw upon Becket for a hundred and sixty pounds, that the banker's books might be clear for fresh credit —for fifty pounds, for thirty pounds, etc., just as Mrs. Sterne might need these sums. Sterne, perplexed though he was at his wife's extravagances, uttered no word of complaint. "You may rely," he wrote to Panchaud, "in case it ever happens that she should draw for fifty or a hundred pounds extraordinary, that it and every demand shall be punctually paid—and with proper thanks; and for this the whole Shandean family are ready to stand security." Mrs. Sterne's large expenditures, it is but just to add, were partly occasioned by ill health, which drove her from place to place, in hope of improvement by change of climate. One letter after another arrived at Shandy Hall from Lydia, describing her mother's alarming symptoms, and so wrought upon Sterne that he imagined his wife was "going the way of us all." She was so ill that at one time he began to make preparations to start for the south of France, in order to administer spiritual comfort in the last stages of the melancholy scene. But the journey proved to be unnecessary, for Mrs. Sterne recovered under the influence of liberal remittances.

Besides the affairs of his wife, urgent parish business, with which Sterne had fallen out of tune, entered Shandy Hall to disturb further his repose. The enclosure of Stillington Common and certain fields and meadows dispersed in the parish, which had been a question for some years, was now authorized by a private Act of Parliament, for which he had petitioned along with Stephen Croft and seven small landowners. Under the Act were appointed three commissioners to make the awards, with whom it was necessary for Sterne to meet, in order to safeguard his rights as vicar of the parish. In these affairs there were always disputes and differences over conflicting claims and minor questions of roads, hedges, and gates, all of which Sterne summed up in a letter to Hall-Stevenson, saying, "I'm tormented to death and the devil by my Stillington Inclosure."

But we should not draw too dark a picture of Sterne's distresses, for the pliability of his temper always saved him. In July, while he was sitting down "in good earnest" to *Tristram Shandy*, his vanity was flattered by a letter from the negro Ignatius Sancho, who felt constrained to tell the reverend author how much he had been benefited by books which are "universally read and universally admired." Sancho was a slave, born on a ship plying in the trade between Africa and the Spanish Main. Baptized at Carthagena under the name of Ignatius, he was brought to England when a boy; and subsequently the surname of Sancho was given to him, because of some fancied resemblance that his master saw between him and Don Quixote's squire. Of quick intelligence, he learned to read and write, and even attempted the rôles of Othello and Oroonoko on the stage. For many years he was in the service of George, the fourth Duke of Montagu, who gave him leisure to read and to cultivate his tastes in many ways. Like "millions" of others, he was in love with the "amiable" my uncle Toby; and as for Trim, he "would walk ten miles in the dog days, to shake hands with the honest Corporal"; but his heart had been touched and amended most by Yorick's sermons, especially by the discourse on the troubles of life as exemplified in Job's misfortunes, containing a sorrowful passage on the bitter draught of slavery which untold millions are compelled to drink to the dregs.

Can you not, Sancho besought Sterne, "give half an hour's attention to slavery as it is at this day undergone in the West Indies; that subject handled in your own manner, would ease the Yoke of many, perhaps occasion a reformation throughout our Islands——But should only *one* be the better for it—— gracious God! What a feast! very sure I am, that Yorick is an Epicurean in Charity. . . .——dear Sir, think in me you behold the uplifted hands of Millions of my moorish brethren ——Grief (you pathetically observe) is eloquent——figure to yourself their attitudes——hear their supplicatory address ——humanity must comply."* When Sancho's letter reached Shandy Hall, Sterne had just completed, by "a strange coincidence," "a tender tale of the sorrows of a friendless poor

* This letter, among the J. Pierpont Morgan Manuscripts, is in Sterne's own hand, and some of the phrasing is surely Sterne's, though there is no doubt that Sterne received from Sancho a letter which he dressed up in copying it.

negro girl"; and while his eyes were still smarting with it, he wrote back to say that he would weave the story, if it could be managed, into the next volume of *Shandy*, in the hope that it might help lift the "sad shade" which slavery was casting over the world.

A month after this affecting correspondence, the parson was called to York to give a dignified close to the great races. This year all classes, from the nobility down to adventurers, poured into the city, and all entertainments were on a grand scale, in honor of Sterne's friend, the young Duke of York, who condescended to be present throughout the entire gala week. The festivities began on Tuesday, the nineteenth of August, when the officials of the city in their formalities waited upon the duke, and congratulated him on his safe arrival. Then followed every day the races on the field of Knavesmire, with a play at the theatre and a ball at the Assembly Rooms in the evening, to say nothing of cock-fights, and noisy scenes of chance at the coffee-houses, where Yorkshire squires fell easy victims to professional sharpers down from London, or lost their purses while watching the game, nobody knew just how or just where.

On Saturday night ended a week such as no one could remember; and on the next morning everybody went in sober mood to the cathedral to listen to the moral of it all. As described in the newspapers of the day, it was an impressive scene in the great church. His Royal Highness, as the central figure, was escorted to the west door of the minster, "where he was received . . . by the residentiary and choir, the Lord Mayor, recorder, and aldermen, who ushered him up to the Archbishop's throne, where he heard an excellent discourse from the Rev. Mr. Sterne."* What the text was it is impossible to determine from the sermons of Sterne afterwards published, several of which, running upon a contrast between a godless and a Christian life, were appropriate enough to the occasion, though none contains the sure clue. It was Sterne's last sermon

---

* *St. James's Chronicle*, August 26-28, 1766.

in St. Peter's, where he won his laurels more than twenty years
before.

On Monday York reckoned up £10,000 as her gains from
the races; the duke set out for Scarborough with his retinue;
and Sterne, though he may have accompanied his royal friend
to the waters, returned, I daresay, to Coxwold to complete
Tristram Shandy. During his long absence abroad, Sterne had
lost interest in the work, which, however broadly its satire expanded at times under his hand, was essentially local in inspiration. His design now was to wind up my uncle Toby's amours
for the next winter, and then to proceed with an account of
his own travels on the Continent. Thus refreshed by a change
of theme, he thought that he might again take up the Shandy
household with greater zest.

Still, there was some fire left for Sterne in the old subject,
though it had narrowed down to my uncle Toby and the
widow Wadman. In nearly Sterne's best manner was the attack of the captain in military form on the heart of the self-
seeking widow, with their conversations over my uncle Toby's
wound in the groin, as they sat on the sofa in the parlor, while
the author stood by to translate into words what was going on
in Mrs. Wadman's fancy, as she blushed, turned pale, resumed
her natural color, or cast her look towards the door. And if
we must have a cock-and-bull story, it would be difficult to
match the one closing the book, reminiscent of the days when
Sterne was a farmer at Sutton-on-the-Forest. In the amusing
account the corporal gave of his brother Tom's courtship of
the Jew's widow who sold sausages at Lisbon, appeared, it may
be, the episode of the friendless negro girl which Sterne had
promised Sancho. Though not going very deeply into the question of slavery, it was a very "pretty picture," my uncle Toby
thought, as he imagined the poor girl in the sausage shop,
"with a bunch of white feathers slightly tied to the end of a
long cane, flapping away flies—not killing them." The narrative, scant as it was, satisfied Sancho and connected his name
with Sterne. The polite world, who soon knew why the Moorish girl got into *Shandy,* courted the sentimental negro, and

Gainsborough painted for them his portrait. In the years that followed, it became the fashion among the tender-hearted to rid themselves of flies, not by torturing or killing them, but by gently brushing them aside or spouting cold water upon them.

While Sterne was putting the last strokes of humor to his book, the troubled skies which had hung over him during the summer and autumn were fast clearing. The waste lands of Stillington were surveyed for a just division; and good news arrived from the south of France. Mrs. Sterne, said letters from Lydia asking for another hundred guineas, was now "out of danger"; and to complete the cure, Sterne sent her some of Huxham's Tincture of the Bark, the current remedy against agues. Wife and daughter, having ended their summer travels, rented a château near Avignon, in the picturesque valley of the Sorgue running down from the Fountain of Vaucluse, where they planned to settle for good, after a short visit to Marseilles for the Christmas carnival. They remained at Marseilles rather longer than they expected, owing, doubtless, to its large and agreeable English colony, composed this winter of "many young men of fortune," including the son and grandson of Lord Southwell, who were abroad with Edmond Malone,* the future editor of Shakespeare. Lydia's heart, however, was at Vaucluse, amid the romantic scenes where Petrarch lived, and wrote the sonnets to Laura. The pretty château which the genteel ladies chose, had "seven rooms of a floor—half furnished with tapestry, half with blue taffety,"—and carried, with an annual rental of sixteen guineas, permission to fish in the stream, and an allowance every week of partridges and other game.

Near them lived the Abbé de Sade, who had just written a book on Petrarch, mainly to prove that Laura was the wife of one of his ancestors. Calling almost every day for quiet talk, the Abbé overlooked Lydia's French as she was practising it on a translation of her father's sermons. There came to the château also a French marquis, who offered Lydia his heart and twenty thousand livres a year. One day he made a coarse

* James Prior, *Life of Edmond Malone*, 23-29 (London, 1860).

remark to the Abbé, apparently about Laura, which displeased
Lydia and brought the romance to a quick conclusion. Except
for the ill-breeding of the marquis, all these little details,
reaching Sterne post by post, delighted the fond father. Again
and again he pictured Lydia fishing by the Fountain of Vaucluse, translating his sermon on the House of Mourning, and
reading or listening to the story of Petrarch and Laura. Only
one element was wanting to the sentimental scene. Lydia broke
her guitar and could not replace it at Marseilles. As soon as
Sterne heard of the disaster, he besought Panchaud to make his
girl happy by sending one on from Paris. "It must be strung,"
were his precise directions in one of the few Italian sentences
surviving from his pen, "with cat-gut and of five cords——
si chiama in Italiano la chitera di cinque corde." Thereafter
Lydia might sit on the banks of the Sorgue, fishing or playing
her guitar at will.

In good spirits again, though greatly weakened by recent
illness, Sterne posted to London at the beginning of January,
through a heavy fall of snow, which blocked travel or made
it dangerous during half of the month. On reaching town, he
wrote to Lord Fauconberg: "I left York on Saturday in such
à terrible Hurrican of wind and snow, as no one but a Captain
of the *blues*, and a Parson of the *true blues*, would have ventured out in——'twas one continued storm all the way, and
many stages had we to plough through Snow up to the horses
bellies."

Unusual interest centres round the lodgings which he selected this winter, for in them he was to take his final rest a
year later. They were in the most fashionable part of the
town, over a wig-maker's shop, on the west side of Old Bond
Street, off Piccadilly. The building—it was then number 41*
—stood for more than a century much as it was in Sterne's
day, except that the wig-maker gave place, in the revolution
of society, to a cheesemonger, and the cheesemonger in turn
to a picture dealer. Finally, sixty years ago, all was swept

* *Notes and Queries*, fourth series, XII, 158-159. It is not quite certain that Sterne had not previously occupied these lodgings.

away for a modern picture gallery. From these apartments in
Bond Street, Sterne sent out many letters to his friends, which,
when read side by side with the newspapers of the time, will
enable us to see Yorick as he enters and treads through another
round of pleasure among new as well as old scenes and faces.
To help him out on the expense of it all, he was yet to receive
from Becket more than two hundred pounds on the last instalment of his sermons, which had sold well.

Sterne's first day in London left him melancholy, for he
was all tired out, and most of his friends were still in the
country for the holidays. Nobody, he complained, was at St.
James's Coffee-House, where he just stepped in, except Sir
Charles Danvers, and "Gilly" Williams, who was in flight
for Brighton. But a few days later all was changed; and the
new year opened gaily for him with theatres, dinners, and
assemblies. Garrick had just brought out at Drury Lane a
romantic drama called *Cymon*, supposed to have been his own
in collaboration with Master Arne, the musician. For a month
London ran mad over its songs, costumes, and spectacular setting. Sterne, who always had a box at his disposal for any
evening, was present on the great night of the eighth when the
king attended with his royal party. He also sometimes dropped
in at Covent Garden, where Shuter was playing Falstaff and
the Miser; but the house he found empty except for "citizens'
children and apprentices." Murphy's *School for Guardians*,
which he saw at the rival theatre on the tenth, the friend of
Garrick pronounced "a most miserable affair," which barely
survived a first performance, so completely had *Cymon* drawn
off the polite world, which filled Drury Lane "brim full every
night." In these latter days, the theatre was thus becoming for
Sterne more than ever a place to go to with the company where
he happened to be dining, to see, meet, and converse with
friends.

He dined on a Sunday at Lord Ossory's with "the old folks"
and "the young virgins," and went afterwards "not much to
my credit," he said, to the Duchess of Hamilton's, for "there
were no virgins there." The Lady Hamilton of whose drawing

room Sterne spoke so ungallantly, was one of those Miss Gun-
nings whom everybody declared, when the two lucky Irish
girls first came upon the town penniless, and quickly won their
coronets, "the handsomest women alive." The duchess was still
a beautiful woman, but beauty without wit had little attraction
for Yorick.

Sterne was present, we may be certain, at the Earl of Shelburne's levee on the twelfth; where or elsewhere he apparently
fell in with the Virginian Arthur Lee, the youngest of three
famous brothers, of whom the others were Richard Henry and
Francis Lightfoot. The young Virginian, barely twenty-six
years old, had been educated at Eton and had taken a degree
in medicine at Edinburgh. After the grand tour and a visit
home, he had returned to England "as special agent"* of the
Massachusetts Bay Colony. The Stamp Act repealed, he was
then negotiating with Shelburne on the fisheries. Boswell, who
had associated with him at Edinburgh, trapped Dr. Johnson
into a dinner with the "patriot" and Wilkes; and Sterne, in
return for the Virginian's interest in his books, introduced him
to his friends and acted as his adviser in sentimental attach-
ments. "The idol of your heart," he wrote to him recklessly,
before the year was over, "is one of ten thousand. The Duke
of —— has long sighed in vain——and can you suppose a
woman will listen to you, that is proof against titles, stars, and
red ribbands? . . . Take my advice, and pay your addresses
to Miss —— she esteems you, and time will wear off an attachment which has taken so deep a root in your heart.——I
pity you from my soul——but we are all born with passions
which ebb and flow (else they would play the devil with us)
to different objects." Franklin was also in London representing

* The Lee Manuscripts. (Harvard University Library.) Among
them is an undated letter from Shelburne, inviting Lee to Bath. See
also R. H. Lee, *Life of Arthur Lee*, I, 185-190 (Boston, 1829). Sterne's
"A. L—e, Esq.," as his name appears in the published correspondence
between the two friends, cannot be identified positively with this Arthur Lee; but the fact that both Sterne and the Virginian were associating intimately with Wilkes and Shelburne renders the identification very
probable.

the colony of Pennsylvania. Meeting Sterne somewhere, he gave in his name for Sterne's sermons promised in the autumn. Sterne put him down in his private book for two sets, and—indicative of Franklin's business methods—wrote after the entry the word *paid*.*

The first week or two Sterne was also much in the society of the Duke of York. His Royal Highness, who had been spending Christmas in the country with Lord Spencer at Althorp, returned to town two or three days after Sterne's arrival, and began a series of "grand entertainments" at his house in Pall Mall.† Of this young gentleman, Sterne liked to write familiarly, as if he were, as was likely true, a favorite guest. "The Duke of York," he casually remarked in a letter to Lord Fauconberg, "was to have had a play-house of his own, and had studied his part in the Fair Penitent, and made Garrick act it twice on purpose to profit by it; but the King, 'tis said, has desired the Duke to give up the part and the project with it." Though the duke indeed stopped work on his own play-house in the palace, Sterne nevertheless had an opportunity of seeing him play Lothario to Lady Stanhope's Calista at the private theatre of their friends the Delavals.‡ At the Duke of York's table the humorist met the Earl of March, better known in social annals by his subsequent title, the Duke of Queensberry, or "old Q," as he was called in his age, after fifty brilliant years in the service of pleasure. The earl was a small, keen-eyed man of hot temper, at that time one of the lords of his Majesty's bedchamber. With this nobleman and "a large company of the Duke of York's people," Sterne dined on the eighth, before going to the theatre to see the king; but the conversation seems to have fallen short of his expectations; for "I came away," said the guest, "just as wise as I went." The acquaintance with the Earl of March never led to any intimacy.

It was, however, in this set that Sterne discovered, soon

* *Whitefoord Papers*, 235.
† *Lloyd's Evening Post*, January 2-5 and 5-7, 1767.
‡ Walpole, *Letters*, edited by Toynbee, VII, 112.

after coming to London, Commodore James, a friend who will pass from these memoirs only with the death of the author. As a boy, William James had an adventurous career on the Spanish Main, which prepared him for one still more adventurous in the Bombay marine service. Under his command, the sea was swept of pirates which had long imperilled the trade of the East India Company. With reckless daring, says the historian Orme,* he pushed his ships into the very harbors of the pirate-chief Angria—first at Severndroog and then at Gheriah—and blew up fortifications which were supposed impregnable. And when news reached Bombay early in 1757 that the French had. declared war against England, he was chosen of all others to carry it on to Clive, then in the valley of the Hooghly. He made the voyage up the Bay of Bengal against the northeast monsoon in an incredibly short time, by discovering a passage which thereafter rendered winter navigation of the bay free from great danger. With a fortune won in prize-money, Commodore James returned to England in 1759, married a beautiful wife—Anne, daughter of Edmond Goddard of Hartham in Wiltshire—and purchased a villa at Eltham within easy reach of London. Orme's story of his exploits brought him into quick notice. He became chairman of the board of directors of the East India Company; and the king subsequently honored him with a baronetcy.

When Sterne fell in with him, the commodore was living for the winter in one of the large houses in Gerrard Street, Soho, suitable for the entertainments expected of him, and for the reception of visitors from India, who seem to have imposed upon his hospitality. His wife was a woman of fine manners and character, very fond of a pretty daughter who reminded Sterne of his own child as she had been in past years. Once admitted into the family circle, Sterne let no Sunday pass, unless ill health prevented, without dining with his dear friends in Gerrard Street. After one of these visits, he wrote

* *A History of the Military Transactions of the British Nation in India*, I, 411-414 (fourth edition, London, 1799). The first edition of the first volume appeared in 1763.

to Lydia: "I wish I had you with me—and I would introduce you to one of the most amiable and gentlest of beings, whom I have just been with, . . . a Mrs. James, the wife of as worthy a man as I ever met with——I esteem them both. He possesses every manly virtue——honour and bravery are his characteristicks, which have distinguished him nobly in several instances——I shall make you better acquainted with his character, by sending Orme's History, with the books you desired ——and it is well worth your reading; for Orme is an elegant writer, and a just one; he pays no man a compliment at the expense of truth.——Mrs. James is kind—and friendly—of a sentimental turn of mind—and so sweet a disposition, that she is too good for the world she lives in——Just God! if all were like her, what a life would this be!" Nothing ever occurred to disturb this friendship, which continued to the last dismal scene.

Dinners and social functions, so necessary to Sterne's enjoyment, were checked by the snows of January, which covered England two or three feet deep. "When we got up yesterday morning," he wrote to Lord Fauconberg on the ninth, "the streets were four inches deep in snow——it has set in now with the most intense cold. I could scarse lay in bed for it, and this morning more snow again." And at the end of a week, when wild rumors of accidents and sufferings had reached London: "There is a dead stagnation of everything, and scarse any talk but about the damages done over the Kingdom by this cruel storm. . . . We had reports yesterday that the York stage coach with fourteen people in and about it, were drown'd by mistaking a bridge—it was contradicted at night—as are half the morning reports in town." During the progress of the storm, while most people were content to remain indoors and wait for the inevitable thaw, Sterne ploughed through snow up to his knees, on an "intensely cold" Sunday morning, to the king's levee and afterwards on to church, where to his disappointment few were found in either place. At length a thaw set in, the streets became passable, though filled with slush, and everybody who could obtain a ticket turned out on the night of the fifteenth for Mrs. Cornelys's great assembly, the first of the year.

This was just then the most fashionable resort in London. "All the high and low demireps of the town," says Thackeray's Barry Lyndon, "gathered there, from his Grace of Ancaster down to my countryman, poor Mr. Oliver Goldsmith the poet, and from the Duchess of Kingston down to the Bird of Paradise." The woman who called herself Mrs. Theresa Cornelys had been long known under other names, as an operatic singer in London and Continental theatres. Abandoning the stage in 1760, she purchased Carlisle House in Soho, which she turned into an assembly for a "society of ladies and gentlemen" with herself as manager. Little noticed at first, the enterprise flourished beyond expectation, so that she was able to enlarge and redecorate the mansion, hanging the "vast" assembly room with blue satin and the rest of the suite with yellow. At appointed times, widely advertised in the newspapers, Mrs. Cornelys opened her house to "the nobility and gentry" for "a grand concert of vocal and instrumental music," to be followed by "a grand ball," before and after which were served "tea, coffee, chocolate, and other refreshments."

All details of these famous nights were planned and carried out under the personal direction of the hostess herself. "Those Ladies and Gentlemen," ran the usual advertisement on the day before an assembly, "who come in carriages . . . are requested to be very particular in ordering their coachmen to the door in Soho-square, and with their horses' heads towards Greek Street; chairs to the usual door.——The tickets (which are limited as to number) will be delivered out this day at Arthur's in St. James's Street, and at the office in Soho-square, at a guinea each, which will admit one gentleman or two ladies. . . . The house will be opened precisely at nine."* So great was the demand for tickets, though rather expensive, that they could hardly be obtained for love or money. But Sterne, who had means of finding one where others com-

* *Public Advertiser,* March 30, 1767.

plained of failure, made the acquaintance this year of Mrs. Cornelys, the professional entertainer of rank and royalty. The next morning he wrote to Lord Fauconberg briefly but enthusiastically of the occasion, adding a word relative to his patron's brother and family: "Last night it thaw'd; the concert at Soho top full——and was (this is for the ladies) the best assembly and the best concert I ever had the honour to be at. Lady Anne had the goodness to challenge me, or I had not known her, she was so prudently muffled up; Lord Bellasyse, I never saw him look so well; Lady Bellasyse recovers *à merveille*—and your little niece I believe grows like flax."

The literary event for people who frequented Carlisle House was the appearance of the ninth and last volume of *The Life and Opinions of Tristram Shandy, Gentleman*, on Friday, January 30, 1767.* "I miscarried of my tenth volume," he wrote on the sixth of January, "by the violence of a fever I have just got through." The two-shilling pamphlet, authenticated by the humorist's signature over the first chapter, had as motto a sentence which Burton attributed to Scaliger when beseeching Cardan not to censure him if his treatise seemed too light: "*Si quid urbaniusculè lusum a nobis, per Musas et Charitas et omnium poetarum Numina, Oro te, ne me malè capias.*"† As in the first instalment of his book, the author again linked his name with Pitt's, in "A Dedication to a Great Man," saying prettily, in allusion to the statesman's recent elevation to the peerage under the title of Earl of Chatham: "My opinion of Lord * * * * * * * is neither better nor worse, than it was of Mr. * * *. Honours, like impressions upon coin, may give an ideal and local value to a bit of base metal; but Gold and Silver will pass all the world over without any other recommendation than their own weight." A few chapters on, Sterne gave his parting thrust to Warburton, his old friend and enemy, by expressing the hope that *Tristram Shandy*, now completed, would "swim down the gutter of

* *St. James's Chronicle*, January 29-31, 1767.
† *Anatomy of Melancholy*, edited by Shilleto, III, 9.

time" along with *A Tale of a Tub* and *The Divine Legation of Moses.*

A fortnight after publication, Sterne informed Panchaud that the last volume of *Tristram Shandy* was liked the best of all by his friends, and requested him, giving thereby an index of brisk sale, to remit a hundred louis to his wife at Marseilles. The conclusion of my uncle Toby's amours, we can well understand, with its nice approaches to forbidden ground, though never quite reaching there, hit exactly the tone of society for which the book was written. To their heart's content, author and reader moved together in these pages, to use Coleridge's expression, through a sort of moral twilight, which is neither light nor darkness. But by the outside public, whose hearts had been corrected by Yorick's sermons and the death of Le Fever, Sterne was reprobated in no uncertain language, save for thankfulness that my uncle Toby had been brought through a severe ordeal, unharmed by the wiles of Mrs. Wadman. "Censor," for example, charged Sterne, in *Lloyd's Evening Post* for March 11-13, with exhausting the salacious wit of England, France, and Spain ("where he has been to recruit"), and with now ransacking "poor old antiquity" as the only storehouse left for him. "Surely," concluded Censor, "our spiritual rulers must frown at these things." Likewise appeared in the *Public Ledger* of March 30, a communication from "Davus," calling upon the Church to intervene. After reading the last article, a number of persons actually prepared and sent to the Archbishop of York a long letter leading up to a hint that Sterne be unfrocked. The anonymous letter, dated March 30, 1767, and signed by "several," began and closed as follows:

"Several well wishers to your Grace, and to religion and the cause of virtue, modesty, and decency, think it a duty incumbent on them, consistently with that regard they have for them, as well as order and right conduct, to refer your Grace to a letter, signed *Davus*, in the '*Public Ledger*' of this day, very justly, as they humbly think, animadverting on the scandal they have long taken and oftener conceived at the works of 'Tristram Shandy,' as written by a *clergyman* and a *dignified* one, uncensured by his superiors. They harbour no malice or private peek against him, having no personal knowledge of him or view by this; but are moved merely by indignation on seeing the above letter. . . . No conduct . . . surely more deserves a censure. But whether private or public, your Grace is best judge of. The former probably has been bestowed in vain, and the latter may have a bad effect, by increasing curiosity; yet, perhaps somewhat more than frowns or contempt should be done, that such scandal should no longer exist, or religion and the clergy will be no gainers by it."

The letter was duly received by Archbishop Drummond, who found nothing to censure, so far as we know, in the conduct of Sterne, always a most welcome visitor at the palace. The old charge of impropriety which was urged by the anonymous correspondents, had grown stale with the monthly critics, who were now inclined to accept Sterne in the character of Harlequin or the English Rabelais. "We wish," said the *Critical Review* of the last volume in February, "that it had been a little better accommodated to the ear of innocence, *virginibus puerisque;* but, perhaps, of all the authors who have existed since the days of Rabelais, none can with more justice than Tristram put his arms a-kimbo, strut through his room and say, 'None but myself can be my parallel.'" The pages which Sterne left blank were also thought diverting. The author had played with this jest before, but in a different manner. According to the earlier device, the reader was invited to fill in the blank pages with whatever he might wish in the way of narrative and comment; while in this case Sterne affected to be unable to compose, when he came to them, the most interesting parts of my uncle Toby's courtship; and so they were deferred until he should be in the mood for them. At length he returned to the missing chapters, and thus succeeded in the feat of writing a book backwards.

Exclusive of my uncle Toby, the volume contained two or three pieces of eloquence that arrested the attention of all who read. Jenny, who had appeared in the first instalment seven years before, as a slight and uncertain shadow of Miss Fourmantelle, re-appeared for an apostrophe to time, which brings all things to an end. Commonplace as the thought is, Sterne, who felt the nearness of death, lifted it into the realm of poetic beauty. "Every letter I trace tells me," he concluded, "with what rapidity Life follows my pen; the days and hours of it, more precious, my dear *Jenny!* than the rubies about thy neck, are flying over our heads like light clouds of a windy day, never to return more——every thing presses on ——whilst thou art twisting that lock,——see! it grows grey; and every time I kiss thy hand to bid adieu, and every absence which follows it, are preludes to that eternal separation which we are shortly to make.——Heaven have mercy upon us both!" Then there was that invocation, unsurpassed outside of Fielding, to the "Gentle Spirit of sweetest humour, who erst did sit upon the easy pen of my beloved Cervantes"; which glided into "They were the sweetest notes I ever heard," and the whole musical episode of the distressed maid of Moulins. These were the purple passages which went far and wide through magazines and newspapers.

The story of Maria, unconnected with all the rest, may be regarded, if we do not press the point too literally, as an advertisement of the *Sentimental Journey.* Though Sterne was in London for pleasure, he was there for business also. The *Sentimental Journey,* which had been in his mind the previous summer, was clearly delayed a year, that he might prepare the way for its publication by talk about it and a preliminary list of subscribers. Nothing could have served his purpose better, whether the act were premeditated or not, than his slipping into *Tristram Shandy* an episode of his forthcoming travels, in precisely the same manner as he gave the public a taste of Yorick's sermons years before, when he let Trim read one to Dr. Slop. It may take something from the dignity of literature to imagine Sterne availing himself of the Duke of York's entertainments or of Mrs. Cornelys's assemblies to recruit his purse, but such was an old custom not quite dead in the days of the third George. So successful was the author in his solicitations that he could write to Panchaud on the thirteenth of February: "I am going to publish a Sentimental Journey through France and Italy——the undertaking is protected and highly encouraged by all our noblesse—'tis subscribed for, at a great rate—'twill be an original—in large quarto—the subscription half a guinea——If you can procure me the honour of a few names of men of science, or fashion, I shall thank you——they will appear in good company, as all the nobility here almost have honoured me with their names." Before the winter was over, Sterne had a vision of a thousand guineas from his new book.

To judge from the list as it appeared the next year, few were approached who failed to permit Sterne to take down their names, though a letter to Sancho points to some labor over gathering in the scattered half-guineas. After thanking the negro for leaving at his lodgings several subscriptions of the Montagu family, Sterne reminded him that the transaction was only half completed: "You have something to add, Sancho, to what I owe your good-will also on this account, and that is to send me the subscription money, which I find a necessity of dunning my best friends for before I leave town ——to avoid the perplexities of both keeping pecuniary accounts (for which I have very slender talents), and collecting them (for which I have neither strength of body or mind) and so, good Sancho, dun the Duke of Montagu, the Duchess of Montagu, and Lord Montagu for their subscriptions, and lay the sin, and money with it too, at my door."

On a rainy day in January, while he was collecting in the guineas, Sterne received, at his lodgings in Old Bond Street, a visit from Alessandro Verri, whom he had seen on his passage through Italy. "He gave me some chocolate, and a thousand caresses," Verri wrote home to his brother Pietro; "he took off my coat wet with the rain and spread it over a chair; he embraced me, he pressed my hand and led me to the fire." Some days later the two men met at a public assembly, at Mrs. Cornelys's perhaps, where Sterne stepped up to Verri, embraced him, and began a delightful conversation, whispering, as was

Yorick's manner, in his friend's ear. According to his Italian admirer, Sterne went everywhere without pay, and was by everybody loved. Instead of his customary black, he was wearing that evening a gray coat and closely cut wig (*una parrucca tonda*). The conversation running over many things always drifted back to the *Sentimental Journey*, and to the thousand guineas that had been paid in before a word of the book was written.*

* Giovanni Rabizzani, *Sterne in Italia*, 34-35 (Roma, 1920).

The Journal to Eliza. March—October, 1767

I.

IN the Anglo-Indian society which gathered round the Jameses, Sterne met the Eliza of the *Sentimental Journey*, the one great passion of his life, shining through a decade of flirtations. At first sight, Eliza appeared to him as a rather plain young woman who affected the air and simper of fine ladies bent upon conquest; but the story of her misfortunes, as he heard it from Mrs. James, awakened his compassion; he began to study her face and eyes under more favorable conditions, much as my uncle Toby did the widow Wadman's; and then all was over with Yorick's poor, weak heart. "Not Swift," he was soon writing to her, "so loved his Stella, Scarron his Maintenon, or Waller his Sacharissa, as I will love and sing thee, my wife elect! All those names, eminent as they are, shall give place to thine, Eliza."

The woman whom Sterne placed among the famous presences that poets and men of letters have felt in their work was Elizabeth, wife of Daniel Draper, who since his youth had held various appointments in the service of the East India Company. She belonged to the Sclaters originally of Slaughter, in Gloucestershire, where they had been lords of the manor for three centuries.* From various branches of the family which took root in the neighboring shires and in northern England, came a line of Oxford and Cambridge men distinguished as scholars and divines. The head of the family is now Lord Basing of Hoddington, near Odiham in Hampshire, whose grandfather, George Sclater-Booth, the politician, was

* The story of Mrs. Draper's early life and of her family was originally based upon her letters and other unpublished material at Hoddington. These letters, with many family details, have since been published by A. Wright and W. L. Sclater in *Sterne's Eliza* (New York, 1923).

elevated to the peerage on his succession to the Hampshire
estates in 1887. Going back to the eighteenth century, Christopher Sclater, Rector of Loughton and Chingford by Epping
Forest, married Elizabeth, daughter of John May, Esq., of
Worting, Hants. Of their thirteen children, the fifth son,
May Sclater, born October 29, 1719, became the father of
Sterne's Eliza. When a young man, May Sclater went out to
India, where he married Judith, daughter of Charles Whitehill, who became Chief of the settlement at Anjengo. Of the
marriage were born three daughters while the family was living on the Malabar Coast, at Anjengo and other factories
of the East India Company,—Elizabeth, who gave as her
birthday April 5, 1744, and her younger sisters, Mary and
Louisa, all born within a year of one another. Their father
died in 1746 and their mother two years later. After growing
into girlhood among the Malabars, of whom Elizabeth became
very fond, the orphans were sent to England by their grandfather, Charles Whitehill, for their education. Elizabeth was
then about ten years old. While in England, she apparently
stayed much with her aunt Elizabeth, a prim woman, married
to Dr. Thomas Pickering, Vicar of St. Sepulchre's, a kindly
humorist, who appreciated the girl's smartness. But she liked
best her cousins Tom and Bess, the children of her uncle
Richard of Hoddington. Between her and Tom existed, so her
letters read, rather more than cousinly affection. "All my kin's
folk," she wrote to him after the mistake of her marriage,
"are in comparison of thee, as trifling . . . as my little finger
in comparison to my two bright eyes."

The girl, already vain, I fancy, of her bright eyes and
round face, was placed with her sisters in some school in or
near London for the "frivolous education" accorded to "girls
destined for India." "The generality of us," she said in sorrowful retrospect, ". . . were never instructed in the importance of any thing, but one worldly point, that of getting an
establishment of the lucrative kind, as soon as possible, a toler-
able complection, an easy manner, some degree of taste in the
adjustment of our ornaments, some little skill in dancing a

minuet, and singing an air." Having received no training in "useful employments," she returned, in the summer of 1757, to India, from which she had been away long enough to be struck by novel sights and customs. Her grandfather was then settled at Bombay, in the best house of the city, "where a great deal of company," she wrote, "comes every day after dinner." Among these guests was Daniel Draper, a promising official of the East India Company, to whom she was married on the twenty-eighth of the following July, when barely fourteen years old. Her husband, her elder by twenty years, was near akin, brother or cousin, to Sir William Draper, who captured Manila and otherwise distinguished himself in the East. The year after her marriage, Daniel Draper was appointed Secretary to the Government at Bombay, where he was stationed mostly, save for short intervals at Surat and Tellicherry, during the rest of his life in India. His faithful services were eventually rewarded by a seat in the Council and the post of Accountant General. If a somewhat heavy official, he was described by a friend and admirer as "a very mild and good-humoured man."*

There was nothing unusual about the Draper marriage, which now seems so ill-sorted in respect to age; and we may suppose that neither husband nor wife found it too uncomfortable. A son was born in 1759, and two years afterwards a daughter named for her mother—the Eliza or Betsy of several tender letters. In 1765, the Drapers brought their children to England that they might be given an English education. After travelling about for several months in visits to their relatives and to various watering-places as far north as Scarborough, Draper went back to Bombay, leaving his wife in England to see the children established in school and to recover her health, which had been weakened by child-bearing and the heats of India.

The children were fixed in school at Salt Hill with or near an aunt on her mother's side, while Mrs. Draper moved about

* David Price, *Memoirs . . . of a Field Officer of the Indian Army*, 61 (London, 1831).

pleasantly among the Sclaters and Whitehills, still having most regard for Tom, now Thomas Limbrey Sclater, heir to Hoddington. As the intimate friend of Mrs. James, she made a wide circle of friends, which included, besides the Anglo-Indians coming and going, families like the Nunehams of Nuneham Hall, Oxford, among whom she was known, because of her beauty and free attractive manners, as the *belle Indian*. Everybody in the intimacy of the James household— Lord Ossory as well as John Dillon, Esq.—seems to have liked and flattered her; one admirer telling her that she ought to go on the stage, and another that her forte was literature. To say truth, her conversation, if we may judge from her letters, readily caught the accent of sentimental society. Although a mere girl, she had read widely in the poets and essayists of the Queen Anne period, whom she was fond of quoting.

The first meeting between Sterne and Mrs. Draper took place soon after the author reached London in January, 1767; if we may imagine it so, at one of the Sunday dinners in Gerrard Street. Advances beyond casual acquaintance were made by Sterne a fortnight or so later, when he sent Mrs. Draper a full set of his works accompanied by the following letter:

"Eliza will receive my books with this——the Sermons came all hot from the heart——I wish that could give em any title, to be offer'd to Y^{rs}——the Others came from the head——I'm more indifferent ab^{t} their Reception——

"I know not how it comes in——but I'm half in love with You.——I ought to be *wholy so*——for I never valued, (or saw more good Qualities to value,)——or thought more of one of Y^{r} Sex than of You.——

So adieu—

Y^{rs} faithfully

if not aff^{tly},

L Sterne"*

* The letter is reproduced here, with Sterne's usual dashes, from a copy made by Mrs. Draper—in the collection of Lord Basing, at Hoddington.

Mrs. Draper, honored by the attentions of an author whom all the polite world was courting, met her admirer half way. In return for the familiar Eliza, she was soon referring to him as Yorick, "the mild, generous, and good," or calling him by a pretty fancy her Bramin, the source of all wisdom. The new title, lifting him into the spiritual caste of India, pleased Sterne, who repaid the compliment by addressing Eliza as his Bramine, or counterpart in the knowledge of the heart. With no thought of concealing their sentimental attachment as it grew apace, Mrs. Draper sent a copy of Sterne's letter to her cousin Tom, and Sterne wrote to his daughter Lydia of his "dear friend." They visited places of amusement together or with Mrs. James, dined *tête-à-tête* at Sterne's lodgings in Bond Street, and made excursions to Salt Hill and Enfield Wash to visit the Draper children. Every morning there passed between them letters arranging for the disposal of their day or announcing the peremptory call of other engagements. Wherever Sterne went to dine, Mrs. Draper was "the star that conducted and enliven'd the discourse." At Lord Bathurst's, says one of Sterne's letters, "I talked of thee an hour without intermission with so much pleasure and attention, that the good old Lord toasted your health three different times; and now he is in his eighty-fifth year, says he hopes to live long enough to be introduced as a friend to my fair Indian disciple, and to see her eclipse all other nabobesses as much in wealth, as she does already in exterior and (what is far better) in interior merit. ——I hope so too. This nobleman is an old friend of mine. ——You know he was always the protector of men of wit and genius; and has had those of the last century, Addison, Steele, Pope, Swift, Prior, &c. &c. always at his table."

On these occasions Sterne sometimes took along a letter or two of Eliza's, from which he read scraps to his more intimate friends, who, like himself, found the style "new" and the sentiments "very good and very elegantly expressed." "Who taught you," asked the flatterer, "the art of writing so sweetly, Eliza?——You have absolutely exalted it to a science!" For further inspiration, he gave Mrs. Draper his portrait, which she placed over her writing-desk; and in return she sat for him, it would seem, to Cosway, the famous miniaturist. The little portrait of Mrs. Draper, apparently a miniature, in which she appeared simply dressed as a vestal, without her usual adornments of "silks, pearls, and ermines," Sterne showed to half the town, and communed with it alone in the quiet of Bond Street, whence he wrote to Mrs. Draper on a morning when at the height of his infatuation: "Your eyes and the shape of your face (the latter the most perfect oval I ever saw) . . . are equal to any of God's works in a similar way, and finer than any I beheld in all my travels."*

While Sterne was thus cantering up and down deliciously with his passion, Mrs. Draper was suddenly prostrated by a letter from her husband asking for her immediate return to India. The news of her illness came as a shock to Sterne on a February morning when, on making his usual call, he was told by the house-maid that Mrs. Draper was not well enough to receive him. After passing a sleepless night, he despatched a note in remonstrance the next day, saying in part: "Remember, my dear, that a friend has the same right as a physician. The etiquettes of this town (you'll say) say otherwise.—— No matter! Delicacy and propriety do not always consist in observing their frigid doctrines." For six weeks thereafter, the frigid doctrines of the town were neglected while Sterne watched Mrs. Draper through her illness and convalescence, fearful at times of her death.

Mrs. Draper's other friends likewise sympathized keenly with the distress of a young woman who must leave her children and go back to a husband for whom she had no affection, and to a dull life which offered no scope for her talents.

* Sterne's portrait of Mrs. Draper has never been discovered. A portrait purporting to be hers forms the frontispiece to Wright and Sclater's *Sterne's Eliza*. It is described as a photograph from a stipple engraving by J. Kingsbury after a picture by J. Hoppner. There must be a mistake somewhere; for Hoppner was not born till 1758; and Mrs. Draper died in 1778. If Hoppner painted her, she was then eight or ten years older than when Sterne knew her.

In short, nothing but the duty of the wife to her husband under the law called her oversea to India. Neither her father nor her mother, as has been related, was living; her grandfather, Charles Whitehill, the rich man of Bombay, had retired and settled with a second wife at Worfield in Shropshire; and in the career of her favorite sister the unhappy woman read her own fate. Mary, or Polly, as the family called her, was, like Mrs. Draper, a girl of gay and lively spirits, who jested with her uncle Thomas while lighting his pipe for him in the seclusion of St. Sepulchre's. After the usual trivial education, she also returned to India, to become the child-wife of Rawson Hart Boddam of Bombay. For three years she bore up against the enervating climate and childbirth until she became a shadow of her former self, and then died, in her eighteenth year, under most melancholy circumstances. Of all Mrs. Draper's friends, none—except an unnamed family, perhaps the Pickerings—was disposed to criticise her reluctance to run the risks of India in her present condition; and yet none could quite venture the advice that she disobey her husband. At the last moment, however, when Mrs. Draper again fell ill, Sterne went so far as to say: "Put off all thoughts of returning to India this year.——Write to your husband—tell him the truth of your case.——If he is the generous, humane man you describe him to be, he cannot but applaud your conduct." If the expense of another year in England would be troublesome, he declared, in an exalted mood of generosity, that he stood ready to subscribe his whole subsistence, and then sequester his livings, if necessary, rather than see such "a creature . . . sacrificed for the paltry consideration of a few hundreds." Should Mrs. Draper wish it, his wife and daughter might be summoned over to take her with them to the south of France, where he himself could join them for a winter in Florence and Naples.

However sincere Sterne's proposals may have been, they were clearly impracticable. Though his attachment to Mrs. Draper may have caused, except in the case of one nameless family, no adverse comment among those who understood the

relation between them, it was yet quite impossible for Sterne
to take under the protection of his purse another man's wife.
Such a course would not have been tolerated by public opinion,
lenient as it was outside of a few strict conventions. So it was
settled that Mrs. Draper should sail for India on the *Earl of
Chatham,* which was expected to leave Deal, weather permit-
ting, early in April. In the meantime little presents passed between Mrs. Draper and her friends. For Mrs. James and the
Nunehams, as well as for Sterne, she had her portrait painted
in the dress and attitude each most admired. Besides the "sweet
sentimental picture" left with Sterne, she presented him with
"a gold stock buccle and buttons," which he rated above rubies,
because they had been fitted to him by the hand of friendship
and thereby consecrated forever. At last came the farewell
visit to the children, whom Mrs. Whitehill generously offered
to take under her personal charge at Worfield. "God preserve
the poor babies," wrote Mrs. Draper, "and may they live to
give satisfaction to their parents—and reflect honour on their
amiable protectress!"*

In order to make the necessary preparation for a long voyage, Mrs. Draper took post-chaise for Deal some ten days
in advance of the probable sailing, in company with Hester
Light, who was going out to Madras to marry George Stratton, a councillor of the East India Company. Sterne, as he
records the parting scene, handed Mrs. Draper into the chaise
and then turned away to his lodgings in anguish of spirit,
never to see his friend again, unless perchance he made a visit
to the seaport the next week with the Jameses. For a day or
two he lay ill of another hemorrhage, during the fever of
which he fancied that Mrs. Draper returned just as he was
dying, clasped him by the knees, and raising her "fine eyes,"
bade him be of comfort. None the less for his weakness, he
sent Mrs. Draper every morning a letter directing her movements as if present and arranging from a distance many little

* The son died at Worfield in 1769; the daughter married Thomas
Nevill in 1785 and became the mother of a son and three daughters.—
Wright and Sclater, *Sterne's Eliza,* 184.

details of her cabin. A pianoforte which she took along with her to Deal, proving to be, as soon as set up, out of tune, Sterne purchased for her a hammer and pliers, and told her to tune the instrument from her guitar that it might again vibrate sweet comfort to their hopes. "I have bought you," says the letter further, "ten handsome brass screws, to hang your necessaries upon: I purchased twelve; but stole a couple from you to put up in my own cabin, at Coxwould——I shall never hang, or take my hat off one of them, but I shall think of you. . . . I have written, also, to Mr. Abraham Walker, pilot at Deal, that I had dispatched these in a packet, directed to his care; which I desired he would seek after, the moment the Deal machine arrived. I have, moreover, given him directions, what sort of an armchair you would want, and have directed him to purchase the best that Deal could afford, and take it, with the parcel, in the first boat that went off. Would I could, Eliza, so supply all thy wants, and all thy wishes."

With these and similar tokens of friendship went much advice as to Mrs. Draper's conduct on shipboard, which, though variously phrased, was always pitched to the following key: "Be cautious . . . my dear, of intimacies. Good hearts are open, and fall naturally into them. Heaven inspire thine with fortitude, in this, and every deadly trial! Best of God's works, farewell! Love me, I beseech thee; and remember me for ever! . . . Adieu, adieu! and with my adieu——let me give thee one streight rule of conduct, that thou hast heard from my lips in a thousand forms—but I concenter it in one word, REVERENCE THYSELF. . . . Blessings, rest, and Hygeia go with thee! May'st thou soon return, in peace and affluence, to illumine my night! I am, and shall be, the last to deplore thy loss, and will be the first to congratulate and hail thy return."

The *Earl of Chatham*, with other outbound ships, set sail from Deal on Wednesday, April 3, 1767, under a brisk northeast wind which bore them quickly through the Channel.* At the point of departure, it was Mrs. Draper's hope that

* *Lloyd's Evening Post*, April 3-6.

her husband would soon retire from the service, or at least permit her to revisit her friends and children in the course of a year or two. There were times also when Sterne encouraged her imagination to play with more distant contingencies, as in a curious summary of their attachment which he wrote out for her a few weeks later anent references to their passion in the *Sentimental Journey:*

"I have brought," he said in a sketch which was to be submitted for her approval before it should be entrusted to posterity, "I have brought your name *Eliza!* and Picture into my work—where they will remain—when you and I are at rest forever——Some annotator or explainer of my works in this place will take occasion, to speak of the Friendship which subsisted so long and faithfully betwixt Yorick and the Lady he speaks of——Her Name he will tell the world was Draper—a Native of India—married there to a gentleman in the India Service of that Name—who brought her over to England for the recovery of her health in the year '65—where she continued to April the year 1767. It was about three months before her Return to India, That our Author's acquaintance and hers began. Mrs. Draper had a great thirst for knowledge—was handsome—genteel—engaging—and of such gentle dispositions and so enlighten'd an understanding,——That Yorick (whether he made much opposition is not known) from an acquaintance——soon became her Admirer——they caught fire, at each other at the same time——and they would often say, without reserve to the world, and without any Idea of saying wrong in it, That their affections for each other were *unbounded*——Mr. Draper dying in the year . . . this Lady return'd to England, and Yorick the year after becoming a Widower——they were married—and retiring to one of his Livings in Yorkshire, where was a most romantic Situation—they lived and died happily—and are spoke of with honour in the parish to this day."

II.

JUST before their separation, Sterne and Mrs. Draper spent a

Saturday evening together in London, when or at another time
it was agreed that each should keep an intimate journal in order
that they might have "mutual testimonies to deliver hereafter
to each other" on the glad day of their reunion. While Mrs.
Draper was at Deal making ready for her voyage to India,
Sterne sent her all that he had written; and on the thirteenth
of April he forwarded by a Mr. Watts, then departing for
Bombay, a second instalment of his record. These two sections
of Sterne's journal—and likewise all of Mrs. Draper's, for we
know that she kept one—have disappeared. The extant part
begins on the thirteenth of April, 1767, and comes down to
the fourth of August in the same year. The sudden break was
occasioned by the expected return of Mrs. Sterne from France,
the thought of whose presence, to say nothing of the reality of
it, the author felt as a restraint upon his fancy. A postscript
was added on the first of November announcing that Mrs.
Sterne and Lydia, after some weeks with him at Coxwold, had
just gone to York for the winter, while he himself was to
remain at Shandy Hall to complete the *Sentimental Journey*.
There were hints that the journal would be resumed as soon
as the author reached town in the following January. But
Sterne probably did not carry out his intention. At least nothing is known of a later effort.

And what we have of the journal lay for a century in
hidden places. Sterne doubtless took the manuscript, as he
thought of doing, with him to London in the winter of
1767-68, where it may have been discovered among his papers
after death and turned over to the Jameses, if indeed it had
not already been confided to their care by Sterne himself as
death was approaching. Favoring this conjecture is the fact that
when the journal came to light, it was in the company of two
letters from Sterne to these friends, an unfinished scrawl from
him to Eliza's husband, and a long "ship letter," amounting
almost to an autobiography, from Mrs. Draper to Mrs.
James. All these manuscripts drifted into the library of a
Mr. Gibbs of Bath, and upon his death, to a room set apart

by the family for waste papers, old letters, and old commonplace books regarded as of no documentary value whatever.
While playing in the room one day and looking about for
paper "to cut up into spills to light candles with," Mr. Gibbs's
son Tom, a boy of eleven, popped upon the names of Yorick
and Eliza, which he had seen before, and pulled out the
journal and letters as too good for candle lighters. Sterne's
letters may not be exactly adapted to the perusal of children,
but had not this boy—Thomas Washbourne Gibbs—known
of Sterne, the world would have lost a most illuminating
document. Hearing in May, 1851, that Thackeray was to
include Sterne among his *English Humourists*, the second
Mr. Gibbs sent the curious journal and other pieces to the
novelist for use in his famous portrait of Yorick. It is rather
strange that Thackeray, though he thanked Mr. Gibbs for
the courtesy, then made no reference to the journal in his
lecture on Sterne and Goldsmith, but reserved his private
information for a terrific assault upon Sterne in a *Roundabout* several years later. Except for Thackeray's mere mention of the journal which had been lent him by "a gentleman
of Bath" (the passage was afterwards suppressed*), nothing
was publicly known concerning the manuscripts until March,
1878, when Mr. Gibbs read before the Bath Literary Institution a paper on "Some Memorials of Laurence Sterne,"
the substance of which was printed in *The Athenæum* for
March 30, 1878. On the death of Mr. Gibbs in 1894, the
manuscripts passed under his bequest to the British Museum.†
The journal covers, besides an introductory note and a lone
entry at the end, seventy-six pages of writing with about
twenty-eight lines to the page, all in Sterne's own hand. The
leaves are folio in size, and, except in the case of the first and

* For the original passage, see "A Roundabout Journey: Notes of
a Week's Holiday" (*Cornhill Magazine*, November, 1860). Two letters
from Thackeray to Gibbs are preserved with the Gibbs MSS. at the
British Museum (Additional MSS., 34527).

† The journal was first published, under my editorship, in the *Life
and Works of Laurence Sterne*, 12 vols. (New York, 1904).

the last, both sides are written upon. As if designed for publication, the manuscript contains numerous blots and interlineations for better phrases, in addition to the introductory note, which was clearly framed to mystify the general reader, who in those days took pleasure in a preface like the following:

"This Journal wrote under the fictitious names of Yorick and Draper—and sometimes of the Bramin and Bramine—but 'tis a Diary of the miserable feelings of a person separated from a Lady for whose Society he languish'd——The real Names—are foreigne—and the account a copy from a French Manuscript,—in Mr. S——'s hands——but wrote as it is, to cast a Viel [sic] over them——There is a Counterpart—which is the Lady's account [of] what transactions dayly happened—and what Sentiments occupied her mind, during this Separation from her admirer——these are worth reading——the translator cannot say so much in favour of Yorick's which seem to have little merit beyond their honesty and truth."

To vary Sterne's phrasing, the *Journal to Eliza* (as we may style the document with Swift's *Journal to Stella* in memory) is a record of personal incidents accompanied by the sensations and fancies that arose out of them day by day, sometimes hour by hour, in a mind losing its poise under the subtle influences of passion and disease. It is the emotional history lying behind and thus explaining in a measure the style, tone, and mood of the *Sentimental Journey,* of which the author regarded Mrs. Draper as the main inspiration. "Were your husband in England," he wrote to her at Deal while gazing at her portrait, "I would freely give him five hundred pounds (if money could purchase the acquisition), to let you only sit by me two hours in a day, while I wrote my Sentimental Journey. I am sure the work would sell so much the better for it, that I should be reimbursed the sum more than seven times told." In order to keep her image before him through the next months, he purchased charts and maps whereby he might follow her ship every day, wondering where she was and what she was doing; and when tired of this, he fell to imagining that she was still by him, talking to him, and overlooking his work. "I have you more in my mind than ever," he wrote long weeks afterwards, "and in proportion as I am thus torn from your embraces——*I cling the closer to the Idea of you.* Your Figure is ever before my eyes—the sound of your voice vibrates with its sweetest tones the live long day in my ear—I can see and hear nothing but my Eliza."

The first pages of the journal are taken up with details of an illness which threatened to put an end to Sterne's life. Already "worn out both in body and mind" by a long stretch of dinners, Sterne completely broke down under the strain of Mrs. Draper's departure for India. "Poor sick-headed, sick-hearted Yorick!" he exclaims, "Eliza has made a shadow of thee! . . . how I shall rally my powers alarms me." Recovering sufficiently from his first hemorrhage to go about, he imprudently dined with Hall-Stevenson at the Brawn's Head on the twelfth of April and supped at the Demoniac's lodgings in the evening with "the whole Pandemonium assembled." For this indulgence he "paid a severe reckoning all the night," and "got up tottering and feeble" in the morning, resolved to dedicate the day (which was Sunday) "to abstinence and reflection." At night came on a fever which kept him in for two days more, during which he read over and over again Mrs. Draper's letters, filing them away; and dosed himself with Dr. James's Powder, a popular remedy of the period that was guaranteed to allay "any acute fever in a few hours though attended by convulsions." This nostrum, which Madame Pompadour took in her last illness and which was destined to kill Goldsmith a few years later, working differently upon Sterne, brought him to his feet for a day or two, so that he was able to set up his carriage in preparation for the journey home in a style suitable to his dignity.

It was, however, very dangerous, as Sterne discovered, to go out immediately after taking a concoction so strongly diaphoretic in its action as was the mysterious powder. While trying his horses in the park—described as an "exceeding good" pair when they were sold the next year—he caught a severe cold, which sent him to bed "in the most acute pain." To satisfy his friends, he summoned two able members of the faculty—a physician and a surgeon—with whom there was a lively contention when the sick man learned their diagnosis of his case and the kind of treatment that it involved:

"We will not reason about it, said the Physician, but you must undergo a course of Mercury.——I'll lose my life first, said I—and trust to Nature, to Time—or at the worst—to Death.——So I put an end with some Indignation to the Conference. . . . Now as the father of mischief would have it, who has no pleasure like that of dishonouring the righteous—it so fell out, That from the moment I dismiss'd my Doctors—my pains began to rage with a violence not to be express'd, or supported——every hour became more intollerable——I was got to bed—cried out and raved the whole night—and was got up so near dead, That my friends insisted upon my sending again for my Physician and Surgeon. ——I told them upon the word of a man of Strict honour, They were both mistaken as to my case——but tho' they had reason'd wrong—they might act right."

Thus brought to bay by sharp suffering, Sterne at once parted with twelve ounces of blood under the lancet of the eminent surgeon in order to quiet what was left in him. The next day the two gentleman re-appeared with a demand for more of Yorick's thin blood; and after their second visit his arm broke loose from their bandage, with the result that he nearly bled to death during the night before he was aware of the accident. All nourishment, including his four o'clock dish of tea, was denied him, with the exception of water-gruel, which he abhorred worse than the ass's milk he had drunk on former occasions. This lowering treatment, which, like the method practised by the famous Dr. Sangrado upon Spanish ecclesiastics, sought to displace the patient's blood with water, reduced Sterne to so great weakness that he momentarily feared that the breath which he was drawing would be the last for which he had strength. "I'm going," he wrote on a morning as he gasped out a farewell to Eliza, "I'm going———"; but he was able to add as the day wore on, "Am a little better———so shall not depart as I apprehended."

In spite of the prohibition, he managed to have, through the kindness of Molly the house-maid, his afternoon tea and soon his boiled fowl and "dish of macaruls," whereby he improved so rapidly that a week later "my Doctors," says the journal, "stroked their beards, and look'd ten per cent wiser upon feeling my pulse, and enquiring after my Symptoms." As their final prescription, they insisted upon thrusting down his throat Van Swieten's Corrosive Mercury, as if they were bent upon sublimating him to "an ethereal substance." His doctors finally dismissed, he experimented on his own account with a French tincture called *L'Extraite de Saturne*, and ordered his carriage for a drive about town.

In sickness as in health, Sterne was overwhelmed with attentions. Mrs. James, missing him at her Sunday dinner, sent her maid to enquire after his health and to bid him preserve a life so valuable to herself and to Eliza. The next day forty people of fashion came to his bedside; and thereafter his room was "allways full of friendly Visitors," and his "rapper eternally going with Cards and enquiries." "I should be glad," was his comment, "of the Testimonies——— without the Tax." As soon as he could be helped into his carriage, he visited Mrs. James to thank her for her daily messages and to weep with her over the loss of Mrs. Draper. It was a scene of woe which better than all else lets the reader into the morbid state of the emotions that gave birth to the story of poor Maria in the *Sentimental Journey:*

"Tears ran down her cheeks," Sterne wrote after the ordeal with Mrs. James was over, "when she saw how pale and wan I was———never gentle creature sympathized more tenderly———I beseech you, cried the good Soul, not to regard either difficulties or expences, but fly to Eliza directly———

I see you will dye without her——save yourself for her——
how shall I look her in the face? What can I say to her,
when on her return I have to tell her, That her Yorick is no
more!——Tell her my dear friend, said I, That I will meet
her in a better world——and that I have left this, because
I could not live without her; tell Eliza, my dear friend,
added I——That I died broken hearted—and that you were
a Witness to it.——As I said this, she burst into the most
pathetick flood of tears—that ever kindly Nature shed. You
never beheld so affecting a Scene——'twas too much for
Nature! Oh! she is good—I love her as my Sister!——and
could Eliza have been a witness, hers would have melted
down to Death and scarse have been brought back, an Extacy
so celestial and savouring of another world.——I had like to
have fainted, and to that Degree was my heart and soul
affected, it was with difficulty I could reach the street door;
I have got home, and shall lay all day upon my Sopha—
and to morrow morning my dear Girl write again to thee;
for I have not strength to drag my pen."

Three weeks were still necessary before Sterne felt strong
enough to venture on the journey homewards. During the
period of convalescence, with its frequent relapses from over-
exertion, he occasionally dined with a friend or sat for an
hour or two at Ranelagh, or drove on a morning through
Hyde Park, where he encountered one day, as amusingly related in the journal, a former passion who was taking the
air on horseback. In their flirtation, the unknown woman,
perhaps Lady Percy, whom Mrs. Draper had supplanted in
Yorick's affections, had figured fancifully as the Queen of
Sheba who once came to Jerusalem with camels, spices, and
gold, to prove the wisdom of Solomon. Of the modern Sheba
and Solomon, says the journal:

"Got out into the park to day——Sheba there on Horseback; pass'd twice by her without knowing her—she stop'd
the third time—to ask me how I did—I would not have ask'd
you, Solomon! said she, but your Looks affected me for you'r
half dead I fear——I thank'd Sheba very kindly, but with-

out any emotion but what sprung from gratitude——Love alas! was fled with thee Eliza!——I did not think Sheba could have changed so much in grace and beauty——Thou hadst shrunk poor Sheba away into Nothing, but a good natured girl, without powers or charms——I *fear* your wife is dead; quoth Sheba.——No, you don't *fear* it Sheba, said I. ——Upon my word Solomon! I would quarrel with you, was you not so ill——If you knew the cause of my Illness, Sheba, replied I, you would quarrel but the more with me ——You lie, Solomon! answered Sheba, for I know the Cause already—and am so little out of Charity with you upon it——That I give you leave to come and drink Tea with me before you leave Town, . . . and so canter'd away."

Whether Sheba and Solomon enjoyed a dish of tea together before the latter left town, our narrative does not say; but the visit is improbable, for Sterne's last week in London was occupied with formal leave-takings among other friends, old and new. To John Dillon, Esq., the "gentlest and best of souls," was sent a playful note congratulating him on his success with a "fair Indian"—was it some friend of Eliza's, or Eliza herself?—while himself must "go bootless home"; and to Mrs. Draper he wrote under the stimulant of the *Extraite de Saturne* a long letter, which was to go overland by way of Aleppo and Bussorah, that it might await her on her arrival in India. During his illness had come an anxious enquiry from the Earl of Shelburne, Secretary of State for the Colonies, who was recruiting at Bath after the labors and levees of a hard season. In return Sterne thanked him for "numberless and unmerited civilities," and recast for his lordship's entertainment the whimsical account given in the journal of his troubles with the doctors. Finally, he attended Court on his last Sunday in town, and accepted invitations for large dinner parties from "seven or eight grandees," among whom was Lord Spencer, who presented him on the evening before his departure with "a grand Ecritoire of forty guineas."

The last glimpse of Sterne in London this year occurs

under date of Friday morning, the twenty-second of May, as he sat in his lodgings hurriedly scrawling off replies to farewell messages which awaited him on his return from Lord Spencer's, while his chaise and horses stood outside ready to bear his "poor body to its legal settlement." "I am ill, very ill," he wrote at parting, "I languish most affectingly—— I am sick both soul and body." Owing to his extreme weakness, more than a week was required for a journey which travellers usually performed in two or three days. Completely exhausted by the time he drove into Newark on Saturday evening, he was compelled to remain over Sunday, whence was despatched, before setting forward, the following characteristic note to Hall-Stevenson, descriptive of his fatigues and his miserable condition on the road thus far:

"Newark, Monday, ten o'clock in the morn.

"My Dear Cousin,——I have got conveyed thus far like a bale of cadaverous goods consigned to Pluto and company ——lying in the bottom of my chaise most of the route, upon a large pillow which I had the *prevoyance* to purchase before I set out——I am worn out—but press on to Barnby Moor to night, and if possible to York the next.——I know not what is the matter with me—but some *derangement* presses hard upon this machine——still I think it will not be overset this bout.——My love to Gilbert. We shall all meet from the east, and from the south, and (as at the last) be happy together——My kind respects to a few.——I am, dear Hall, truly yours, L. Sterne."

Too ill to reach York on Tuesday, Sterne was forced to halt at Doncaster, where he passed two nights with the Archbishop of York, who was then staying at his house near the town. This was the first meeting between Sterne and Dr. Drummond since the anonymous letter from London asking that the profane parson be unfrocked. If any mention was made of the incident, it passed off in jest, for each was devoted to the other. "This good prelate," Sterne remarked in the journal, "who is one of our most refined Wits and the most of a gentleman of our order——oppresses me with his kindness——he shews in his treatment of me, what he told me upon taking my Leave—that he loves me, and has a high Value for me——his Chaplains tell me, he is perpetually talking of me and has such an opinion of my head and heart that he begs to stand Godfather for my next Literary production." Without any reserves, Sterne showed the archbishop, his lady, and sister the portrait of Eliza, and related the story of his friendship with the original. Becoming a little stronger by Thursday, he drove through to Coxwold that day and went directly to bed on Van Swieten's Corrosive Mercury. Only rest, temperance, and good hours, it proved, were needed to re-instate Sterne in his usual health and spirits. At the end of three weeks, he cast to the dogs the medicines which were tearing his frame to pieces, began to drink ass's milk, and concluded that he would not descend to Pluto for a year at least or, on a nearer reckoning as it turned out, until he had trailed his pen through the *Sentimental Journey*.

There were days when he felt as well as at any time since leaving the university and when he looked forward to a summons from Mrs. Draper to meet her in the Downs and bring her home as his wife. In the meantime, whether for one or for five years, he would enjoy himself to the full, accepting, with resignation, health and sickness like the periodical returns of light and darkness. It is altogether a delightful picture which we have of Sterne as he settled into this mood for his summer's task, varied by excursions with his friends. "I am in the Vale of Coxwould," he wrote in his journal to Eliza when summer was advancing, and similarly in a letter to his friend Arthur Lee, "and wish you saw in how princely a manner I live in it——'tis a Land of Plenty——I sit down alone to Venison, fish or wild foul—or a couple of fouls—with curds, and strawberrys and cream, (and all the simple clean plenty which a rich Valley can produce,——with a Bottle of wine on my right hand (as in Bond street) to drink your health——I have a hundred hens and chickens about my yard——and not a parishioner catches a hare, a rabbit or a

Trout—but he brings it as an offering——In short 'tis a golden Valley—and will be the golden Age when you govern the rural feast, my Bramine."

Anticipating the golden age, Sterne re-arranged and re-decorated Shandy Hall—more in fancy, perhaps, than in fact —that it might become a fit habitation for its mistress. "I have this week finished," records the journal only ten days after Sterne's arrival, "a sweet little apartment which all the time it was doing, I flatter'd the most delicious of Ideas, in thinking I was making it for you——'Tis a neat little simple elegant room, overlook'd only by the Sun—just big enough to hold a Sopha; for us—a Table, four Chairs, a Bureau, and a Book case.——They are to be all yours, Room and all— and there Eliza! shall I enter ten times a day to give thee Testimonies of my Devotion——Was't thou this moment sat down, it would be the sweetest of earthly Tabernacles." " 'Tis a little oblong room," the narrative goes on into further details, "with a large Sash at the end—a little elegant fireplace— with as much room to dine around it, as in Bond street—— But in sweetness and Simplicity, and silence beyond any thing. ——Oh my Eliza!—I shall see thee surely Goddesse of this Temple,——and the most sovereign one, of all I have—and of all the powers heaven has trusted me with."

Off from the temple—or sitting room, to write plainer English—were to be other rooms dedicated to Mrs. Draper, the journal adds later in the season: "I . . . am projecting a good Bed-chamber adjoining it, with a pretty dressing room for you, which connects them together—and when they are fin-ish'd, will be as sweet a set of romantic apartments, as you ever beheld——the Sleeping room will be very large—The dressing room, thro' which you pass into your Temple, will be little—but Big enough to hold a dressing Table—a couple of chairs, with room for your Nymph to stand at her ease both behind and on either side of you—with spare Room to hang a dozen petticoats—gowns, &c—and Shelves for as many Band-boxes."

Mrs. Draper's apartments were to be enriched with many

Shandy Hall

From a photograph taken in 1906

little gifts of Sterne's own devising, besides more costly presents from his friends, which would be placed in due time at her disposal. If she were a good girl, she might hang her cabinet with "six beautiful pictures" which he had just received from Rome of the "Sculptures upon poor Ovid's Tomb, who died in Exile, though he wrote so well upon the Art of Love"; and on her table might rest "a most elegant gold snuff box" valued at forty guineas, which a gentleman—Sir George Macartney—was having fabricated for Sterne at Paris. On the outside was to be an inscription in Sterne's honor, and within the cover a portrait of Eliza.

In like manner Sterne adorned his study with numerous trinkets given him by Mrs. Draper as pledges of affection, never forgetting to take her portrait from his neck or pocket and to place it upon the table before him, that he might look into "her gentle sweet face," as he wrote of the fair Fleming, the beautiful grisette, or the heart-broken Maria. There were indeed moments bordering upon hallucination, when Mrs. Draper seemed to enter his study without tapping and quietly take a chair by his side, to overlook his work and talk low to him in counsel for hours together. At length the hallucination would pass, and the figure of Mrs. Draper would fade into a melancholy cat sitting and purring at his side, and looking up gravely into his face as if she understood the situation. "How soothable," remarked Sterne on one of these occasions, "my heart is, Eliza, when such little things sooth it! for in some pathetic sinkings I feel even some support from this poor Cat——I attend to her purrings——and think they harmonize me——they are pianissimo at least, and do not disturb me. ——Poor Yorick! to be driven, with all his sensibilities, to these resources——all powerful Eliza, that had this Magical authority over him, to bend him thus to the dust!"

In one of his pathetic sinkings, Sterne so far lost self-control as to draft a letter (which was probably never sent) to Eliza's husband, hinting at better care of her health and explaining his interest in her. It was evidently a rather difficult exercise in composition, for Yorick begins a sentence, breaks it off, starts in anew, draws pen through word and phrase once more, and finally passes into chaos on arriving at the verge of a proposal that Mrs. Draper be permitted to return to England and live under his platonic protection. As well as can be made out, the curious letter was intended to run somewhat as follows:

"I own it, Sir, that the writing a Letter to a gentleman I have not the honour to be known to——a Letter likewise upon no kind [of] business (in the Ideas of the world) is a little out of the common course of Things——but I'm so myself ——and the Impulse which makes me take up my pen is out of the common way too—for [it] arises from the honest pain I should feel in avowing so great esteem and friendship as I do for Mrs. Draper, if I did not wish and hope to extend it to Mr. Draper also. I fell in Love with your Wife——but tis a Love, you would honour me for——for tis so like that I bear my own daughter, who is a good creature, that I scarse distinguish a difference betwixt it——that moment would have been the last of my acquaintance with my friend (all worthy as she is).

"I wish it had been in my power to have been of true use to Mrs. Draper at this Distance from her best Protector—— I have bestowed a great deal of pains (or rather I should [say] pleasure) upon her head——her heart needs none——and her head as little as any Daughter of Eve's, and indeed less than any it has been my fate to converse with for some years—— God preserve her.——I wish I could make myself of any service to Mrs. D. whilst she is in India——and I in the world——for worldly affairs I could be of none.

"I wish you, dear Sir, many years happiness.——Tis a part of my Litany to pray to heaven for her health and Life—— She is too good to be lost and I would out [of] pure zeal t[ake] a pilgrimage to Mecca to seek a Medicine."*

Partly breaking from the obsession of Mrs. Draper's image, Sterne made several excursions during the summer. He was

* This letter forms a part of the Gibbs Manuscripts. Facsimile reproduction in *The Journal to Eliza and Various Letters*, 153-154, in Sterne's *Works* (New York, 1904)

twice at Crazy Castle—a week near the end of June for re-
cuperation, and three or four days midway in July, on a special summons to come over for a large party of "the most
brilliant Wits of the Age," including, said the newspapers,
Garrick and Colman the dramatist. While at Skelton, he dined
with "Bombay-Lascelles," an old acquaintance of Mrs.
Draper as well as of himself, who, back from India, had taken
a house two miles away; and there was "dining and feasting
all day" with Mr. Charles Turner of Kirkleatham, than
whom none of the Yorkshire gentlemen entertained more
lavishly, and none was married to a more beautiful wife.
These visits mark the last time that Sterne and his friends were
to race chariots along the beach by Saltburn "with one wheel
in the sea and the other in the sand."

On taking final leave of Skelton, Hall-Stevenson accompanied him home to Shandy Hall for a few days' rest preliminary to several short trips together. They passed a whole day at
Bishopthorpe with the Archbishop of York, who honored
Sterne with a subscription to the *Sentimental Journey* on imperial paper; then they put off to Harrogate, where they drank
the waters through a week at the height of the season, and
thence they returned to York for the summer races. At York
was delivered to Sterne, two hours after his arrival, as if timed
to it, the first news from Mrs. Draper since she sailed from
Deal. It was the journal of her voyage, in two long letters,
as far as Santiago in the Cape Verde Islands and to some point
across the line, where a Dutch ship, returning from India, took
aboard the *Earl of Chatham's* mail. How Sterne's heart was
upset when he broke the "dear packets" alone in his lodgings,
may be left to his journal to relate:

"I cannot give vent to all the emotions I felt even before
I open'd them—for I knew thy hand—and my seal—which
was only in thy possession——O 'tis from my Eliza, said I.
——I instantly shut the door of my Bed-chamber, and ordered
myself to be denied——and spent the whole evening, and till
dinner the next day, in reading over and over again the most
interesting account—and the most endearing one that ever

tried the tenderness of man.——I read and wept—and wept and read till I was blind——then grew sick, and went to bed—and in an hour call'd again for the Candle. . . . O my Eliza! thou writest to me with an Angel's pen—and thou wouldst win me by thy Letters, had I never seen thy face or known thy heart."

All summer long, letters came in from friends to join them at Scarborough, but he waited until the full season, when he went over as the guest of Dr. Jemmet Brown, Bishop of Cork and Ross. Writing to Mr. and Mrs. James of the visit, Sterne said: "I was ten days at Scarborough in September, and hospitably entertained by one of the best of our Bishops; who, as he kept house there, press'd me to be with him——and his household consisted of a gentleman, and two ladies—which, with the good Bishop and myself, made so good a party that we kept much to ourselves." The gentleman was Richard Griffith, to whom Sterne showed the incomplete manuscript of the *Sentimental Journey.* The two ladies were Lady Anne Dawson and Sterne's old friend Mrs. Vesey, both of whom were at Scarborough for the restoration of their nerves. They amused themselves by standing on the cliff until they were giddy, as they watched "the poor Bishop floundering and sprawling" in the sea; and in the evening were tea-parties, and excursions in their chaises.*

Before the company broke up, the good bishop made Sterne "great offers" if he would settle in Ireland, and requested the honor of marrying him to Mrs. Draper as soon as all obstacles should be removed. With Dr. Brown's offer came another from a friend in the south, who would have Sterne exchange Sutton and Stillington for a parish in Surrey, only thirty miles from London and valued at three hundred and fifty pounds a year. Under the second arrangement, Sterne was to retain, as explained to Mrs. Draper, Coxwold and his prebend; but in his present weakened state of body and mind, he

* *Letters of Mrs. Elizabeth Carter,* edited by Montagu Pennington, III, 320 (London, 1809). See also J. M. S. Tompkins, *Triglyph and Tristram,* in the *Times Literary Supplement,* July 11, 1929.

was unable to go through the details of the transfer. "I could get up fast," he wrote for Mrs. Draper, "the hill of preferment, if I chose it—but without thee I feel Lifeless——and if a Mitre was offer'd me, I would not have it, till I could have thee too, to make it sit easy upon my brow."

Mrs. Draper was thus never long absent from Sterne's imagination. Wherever he went, he always took with him his journal, writing in it nearly every day, and Eliza's portrait, which was passed round the table at Skelton and Kirkleatham, while all the guests, even the ladies, "who hate grace in another," drank to the health of the original. Visits to his best friends were only distractions which drew him from the quiet of Coxwold, with which, as it was now haunted by Mrs. Draper's spirit, he was never so much in love. "O 'tis a delicious retreat," he exclaimed on returning from Skelton, "both from its beauty, and air of Solitude; and so sweetly does every thing about it invite your mind to rest from its Labours and be at peace with itself and the world——That 'tis the only place, Eliza, I could live in at this juncture.——I hope one day you will like it as much as your Bramin." Until that day should arrive, Mrs. Draper's apartments were to be his own.

Her likes and dislikes, so far as he remembered them from casual conversation, were consulted in purchasing a chaise for driving about the parish with her by his side in fancy. Her favorite walk, like his own, would likely be to a secluded "convent," as he called it, doubtless the romantic ruins of Byland Abbey under a spur of the Hambleton hills two miles away. Anticipating the morning when Mrs. Draper should visit the ruins with him, he plucked up one day the briars which grew by the edge of the pathway, that they might not scratch or incommode her when she should go swinging upon his arm to "these delicious Mansions of our long-lost Sisters," where he sometimes stayed far into the night dreaming of Eliza and the beautiful Cordelia who lay buried there. And before the summer was over, he built for his future companion a pavilion in a retired corner of his house-garden, where he was wont to stroll or sit in reverie during the heat of the day or in the evening twilight, waiting for a day's sleep whence he might awake and say: "Behold the Woman Thou hast given me for Wife."

III.

STERNE was destined, however, to behold on waking from his visions, not Mrs. Draper bending over him with her large languishing eyes, but the plain, everyday woman who had been given him for wife twenty-five years before. In short, Mrs. Sterne was hastening home post-chaise from France. The collapse of all his fancies Sterne took mainly in good part, commenting gaily, as he anticipated it, upon "the last Trial of conjugal Misery," which he wished to have begin "this moment that it might run its period the faster."

Mrs. Sterne, it will be recalled, was intending to stay in southern France for a year or two longer; but soon after hearing that her husband had fallen under the spell of a Mrs. Draper, she changed her mind. The news was brought to her early in February by an English traveller who crossed her path at Avignon on the road to Italy. Though she told the busybody "that she wished not to be informed and begged him to drop the subject," the rumor made her so uneasy that Lydia was forthwith directed to enquire about it of her father. Sterne's reply that he had indeed a friendship for Mrs. Draper, "but not to infatuation," could hardly be accepted, in the light of subsequent letters describing her as an "incomparable woman," "a drooping lily," etc.; for Mrs. Sterne had heard these very phrases before her marriage, and knew what they meant. Her suspicions were further aroused by the infrequency of her husband's letters and by delays in remittances from Panchaud and Foley, all of which in her opinion argued neglect. When called to account for his conduct, Sterne informed his wife through Lydia that she was getting ninepence out of his every shilling, and that the post, not himself, was responsible for the irregular arrival—and perhaps loss—of his letters. Amid these misunderstandings, Sterne was glad to receive a hint that they would all be cleared up by the return of his wife and daughter to Coxwold for the summer. "For God's sake persuade her," Sterne wrote to Lydia of his wife near the first of April, "to come and fix in England, for life is too short to waste in separation——and whilst she lives in one country, and I in another, many people suppose it proceeds from choice——besides, I want thee near me, thou child and darling of my heart."

But Sterne's attitude towards the return of his wife and daughter was reversed by subsequent letters from them outlining their plans. They were coming home, it was made clear to him, merely for a visit at his expense without the slightest intention of resuming their former life at York and Coxwold. After a few months with him, they would go back to France, where they were to leave behind them all their clothes, plate, and linen; and in order that they might never again be incommoded by the want of money, the demand was made upon Sterne that he should purchase for them an annuity of £200 in the French funds. This was certainly a proposition at which a country parson receiving a few hundred pounds a year from his books might well balk. All his friends commiserated with him, advising him to sell "my life dear and fight valiantly in defence both of my property and life."

Hall-Stevenson, outdoing the rest, made Yorick's conjugal tribulations the theme of "an affecting little poem" to circulate among the Demoniacs. Sterne, likewise falling into the jest of the situation, poured forth pages of self-pity over madame's approaching reconciliation with her husband. To Mrs. James he wrote: "I went five hundred miles the last Spring, out of my way, to pay my wife a week's visit——and she is at the expence of coming post a thousand miles to return it.—— What a happy pair!——however, en passant, she takes back sixteen hundred pounds into France with her—and will do me the honour likewise to strip me of every thing I have." And similar, but more amusing in its details, is the record of the journal for Mrs. Draper: "I shall be pillaged in a hundred small Item's by them—which I have a Spirit above saying, *no* ——to; as Provisions of all sorts of Linnens—for house use— Body use—printed Linnens for Gowns—Mazareens of Teas

—Plate, (all I have but six Silver Spoons)——In short I shall be pluck'd bare—all but of your Portrait and Snuff Box and your other dear Presents—and the neat furniture of my thatch'd Palace——and upon these I set up Stock again, Eliza."

Notwithstanding his humorous murmurings, Sterne acquiesced after a month or two in his wife's plan for a settlement, and awaited her arrival for the purpose more complacently perhaps than is implied by a literal reading of his journal. He was quite willing to be fleeced or to have his back flayed, provided he could escape with his life. All else Mrs. Sterne might gather up and decamp with, whither she list, on condition that she trouble him no more. His apparent indifference, which no one will take too seriously, did not prevent him from sending to his wife and daughter his customary directions for a safe and comfortable journey. Lydia was told to throw all her rouge pots into the Sorgue before setting out from Avignon, for no rouge should ever invade Shandy Hall; but she might bring along her lively French dog, though he was rather "devilish" the last time Sterne saw him, as a companion for the lonely house-cat purring by Yorick's side, if she would promise to guard against "a combustion" when the two animals met. On reaching Paris, the travellers were to go at once to Panchaud's, who would offer them every civility, fill their purses, and advise them about the proposed annuity. While in the city they were to make all necessary purchases of clothing; and as soon as they arrived in London, Mrs. Sterne was to take out a life insurance policy in favor of Lydia. Finally, they must inform him, several posts ahead, of their coming, that he might be in York to meet them with his chaise and long-tailed horses, neither of which had they ever seen. Though the chaise had already been given to Mrs. Draper in the fancies which he was weaving about her, he could yet say to his wife and daughter, "The moment you both have put your feet in it, call it hereafter yours."

Mrs. Sterne and Lydia arrived in York, where Sterne awaited them, on the last day of September; and the next

morning they enjoyed their first ride in the new chaise over
to Coxwold. Sterne was a little fearful that he might not find
grace with madame, but there occurred no untoward incident,
much less a scene. The greeting between Sterne and his daughter, now a young woman, was most cordial. "My Lydia,"
Sterne wrote immediately to his Parisian banker, "seems transported with the sight of me.——Nature, dear Panchaud,
breathes in all her composition; and except a little vivacity—
which is a fault in the world we live in—I am fully content
with her mother's care of her." He likewise intended it as a
compliment when a few days later he added in the postscript
of a letter to Mrs. James: "My girl has returned an elegant
accomplished little slut——my wife—but I hate to praise my
wife——'tis as much as decency will allow to praise my
daughter."

The united family apparently passed a pleasant month together, during which the details of Mrs. Sterne's plan were
discussed and worked out to a slightly different issue. A prospective purchaser was found for a part of their real estate,
which was to be turned into an annuity for Lydia; and Mrs.
Sterne was promised a liberal allowance. These financial arrangements and other stipulations, as finally agreed upon when
husband and wife decided to go apart after a marriage of
twenty-five years, are all summed up in a postscript to the
journal under the date of the first of November:

"All, my dearest Eliza, has turn'd out more favourable than
my hopes——Mrs. S.—— and my dear Girl have been two
Months [a slip for one month] with me and they have this day
left me to go to spend the Winter at York, after having settled
every thing to their heart's content——Mrs. Sterne retires into
France, whence she purposes not to stir, till her death,——and
never, has she vow'd, will give me another sorrowful or dis-
contented hour.——I have conquered her, as I would every
one else, by humanity and Generosity—and she leaves me,
more than half in Love with me.——She goes into the South
of France, her health being insupportable in England——and
her age, as she now confesses, ten Years more than I thought,

being on the edge of sixty*———so God bless—and make the remainder of her Life happy—in order to which I am to remit her three hundred guineas a year—and give my dear Girl two thousand pounds, which, with all Joy, I agree to,—but tis to be sunk into an annuity in the French Loans."

Behindhand a month with the *Sentimental Journey*, Sterne did not accompany his wife and daughter to York, but had them driven in by his man. None of the three wished the approaching separation to be regarded as quite final. The version of it which was to go to the world, Sterne gave out in a letter to Arthur Lee, descriptive of the affecting scene between himself and Lydia as the chaise stood by the door of Shandy Hall:

"Mrs. Sterne's health is insupportable in England.———She must return to France, and justice and humanity forbid me to oppose it.———I will allow her enough to live comfortably, until she can rejoin me.———My heart bleeds, Lee, when I think of parting with my child———'twill be like the separation of soul and body—and equal to nothing but what passes at that tremendous moment; and like it in one respect, for she will be in one kingdom, whilst I am in another.———You will laugh at my weakness—but I cannot help it—for she is a dear disinterested girl———As a proof of it—when she left Coxwould, and I bade her adieu, I pulled out my purse and offered her ten guineas for her private pleasures———her answer was pretty, and affected me too much: 'No, my dear papa, our expences of coming from France may have straiten'd you—I would rather put an hundred guineas into your pocket than take ten out of it.'———I burst into tears."

* She was but fifty-three.

CHAP. XX.

A Sentimental Journey. June, 1767—*February,* 1768

APART from its strict biographical details, the journal to Eliza has several interesting aspects. The chief of them no one can regard as literary, though the manuscript offers an opportunity here and there for studying Sterne's method of composition from the first hastily written sentence down to the smoothing out of phrase and clause with new words in a new order. The manuscript also casts a curious side-light on the psychology of Sterne's plagiarisms. In his *Sermons* and in *Shandy*, he stole, it is charged, from others; in the journal he stole from himself. A good passage or a good story, whether originally his own or somebody else's, he could not keep from re-working when occasion called for it, any more than could Charles Lamb.

A letter, for example, to Arthur Lee describing the golden age at Coxwold, was adjusted a month later to the journal; and in reverse order, the Shandean account of Sterne's illness, first recorded in the journal, was re-told in a letter to the Earl of Shelburne. The dear Eliza of the journal was frequently transformed into dear Lydia for letters to his daughter, each being "the sweet light burthen" which he hoped to bear in his arms up the "hill of preferment"; and, stranger still, long passages were taken from the stale letters to Miss Lumley, written as far back as 1740, and transferred to Mrs. Draper, as applicable, with few changes, to the new situation. It was hardly more than writing "Molly" for "Fanny," or "our faithful friend Mrs. James" for "the good Miss S———," and the old "sentimental repasts" with Miss Lumley in Little Alice Lane—house-maid, confidante, and all—could be served up anew for Mrs. Draper in Bond Street.

But the real significance of the journal to Eliza lies not in its literary artifice nor in its parallelisms, which would be disreputable were the process not so amusing; it lies in the fact that it completely reveals the pathological state of the emotions—long suspected but never quite known to a certainty—whence sprang the *Sentimental Journey*, during the composition of which Sterne was fast dying of consumption, barely keeping himself afoot much of the time with ass's milk; for when he ventured upon a more substantial diet, there stared him in the face the dreadful corrosive mercury.

Each work is the counterpart of the other. In the journal, we have the crude expression of the maudlin sentiment which often accompanies a wasting disease; in the *Sentimental Journey*, we have sentiment refined to an art so exquisite as to place the author among the first masters of English prose. In real life, Sterne bursts into a flood of tears while conversing with Mrs. James over their separation from Eliza—he almost faints, and with difficulty reaches the door; when he writes his book he weeps his handkerchief wet over the distracted maid of Moulins who has lost her lover. In the journal, he plucks up the briars along the path which Mrs. Draper will sometime tread by his side; in the *Sentimental Journey*, it is a nettle or two growing upon the grave of a poor Franciscan whose feelings he has wounded. In the one he communes with the house-cat as she lies purring by the fire; in the other with a travel-worn German peasant sitting on the stone bench of the inn by Nampont, and weeping at the death of the donkey which has been his faithful companion all the way to the shrine of St. James of Compostella and thus far on the long journey home to Franconia. Eliza, her miniature always opposite to him on his desk when he took pen in hand, sat for the slightly varied portraits of the brown lady, the grisette, and the *fille de chambre* of the *Sentimental Journey*, all of whom awaken precisely the same sexual emotions, never quite gross but sometimes suggestive of grossness. It is not the strong, healthy sexuality of Smollett or Fielding, but rather the sexuality of waste and enervation, such as inspired the harmless passion for Mrs. Draper, a feeble stir of the blood which Sterne felt as he held the hand of a beautiful woman, stooped to fasten her shoe-buckle, or slept in a room near her at a wayside inn. It is all quite innocent provided one takes it so.

A book of travels, we remember, had been in Sterne's mind ever since the winter at Toulouse, and in the succeeding instalment of *Tristram Shandy* he tried his hand, we also remember, at one based upon his journey from Calais to Paris and south to Avignon and across the plains of Languedoc. His design at that time was comedy running into farce and satire. He played with current guide books, whose *videnda* were eventually set aside in favor of ludicrous incidents by the way, accompanied with the claim, gravely expressed, that he loved better than all else dusty thoroughfares along which there was nothing to see, and so nothing to relate, beyond an occasional beggar, pilgrim, or fig-vender on the road to Beaucaire. The idea was well enough worked out in a narrative memorable for Old Honesty and the vintage dance; but with the plan as a whole, details neglected, there was nothing very novel or striking. It was in fact only a whimsical variant, however well carried through, of the comic adventures which everybody had read in Cervantes, Scarron, or Fielding. Clearly not satisfied with the outcome, Sterne made another tour abroad to gain, besides his health, fresh incidents for a second journey which should include Italy also.

In the meantime, Dr. Smollett, likewise sick and in fear of death, had gone over nearly the same route and brought out two volumes of *Travels through France and Italy*. Keen as was the novelist's intelligence, his irritable temper, accentuated by over-strained nerves, warped everything he saw. Crossing Smollett's path at Montpellier, Sterne introduced him into the *Sentimental Journey* as a type of the "splenetic traveller" under the appropriate name of "Smelfungus," and as a fit companion to "Mundungus," or "the proud traveller"—a thin disguise for Dr. Samuel Sharp, another sick surgeon who was publishing his impressions of the Continent.* "The learned Smelfungus," says Sterne, "travelled from Boulogne to Paris —from Paris to Rome—and so on—but he set out with the

* *Letters from Italy* (London, 1766).

spleen and jaundice, and every object he pass'd by was dis-
coloured or distorted——He wrote an account of them, but
'twas nothing but the account of his miserable feelings." The
inn at a seaport town near Genoa where the novelist took
up his night's lodging was kept, says Smollett's record, by a
butcher who "had very much the looks of an assassin. His wife
was a great masculine virago, who had all the air of having
frequented the slaughter-house. . . . We had a very bad
supper, miserably dressed, passed a very disagreeable night, and
paid a very extravagant bill in the morning. I was very glad
to get out of the house with my throat uncut."

The women of Italy Smollett found "the most haughty,
insolent, capricious, and revengeful females on the face of the
earth." The Tuscan speech, so often praised for its sweetness,
was to his ear harsh and disagreeable. "It sounds," he said, "as
if the speaker had lost his palate. I really imagined the first
man I heard speak in Pisa had met with that misfortune in the
course of his amours." While in Florence, he was attracted to
the Uffizi gallery by the fame of the Venus de Medici; but he
at once discovered, to quote again famous phrases, that there is
"no beauty in the features" of the marvellous statue, and that
"the attitude is awkward and out of character." When he
reached Rome, he was "much disappointed at the sight of the
Pantheon which looks," said the sick traveller, "like a huge
cockpit, open at the top. . . . Within side it has much the air
of a mausoleum. It was this appearance which, in all probability, suggested the thought to Boniface IV. to transport
hither eight-and-twenty cart-loads of old rotten bones, dug
from different burying-places, and then dedicate it as a church
to the blessed Virgin and all the holy martyrs."

The reaction of Sterne's mind upon Smollett's gave him
the point of view for which he had been long striving. Like
Smollett's, his travels were to deal with observation, personal
and direct, rather than with incident, comic or exciting; but
"my observations," he said, "shall be altogether of a different
cast than any of my forerunners," just as my temperment, he
might have added, differs from theirs. In distinction from

the jaundiced traveller, to whose eye all things, they say, look yellow, Sterne proclaimed himself the sentimental traveller, or one who, disregarding all the rest, seeks and finds, wherever chance takes him, only those objects and incidents which excite and keep going a series of pleasurable emotions. "Was I in a desert," he said, "I would find out wherewith in it to call forth my affections——If I could not do better, I would fasten them upon some sweet myrtle, or seek some melancholy cypress to connect myself to——I would court their shade, and greet them kindly for their protection——I would cut my name upon them, and swear they were the loveliest trees throughout the desert: if their leaves wither'd, I would teach myself to mourn, and when they rejoiced, I would rejoice along with them." His design in writing the *Sentimental Journey*, he told Mrs. James, "was to teach us to love the world and our fellow creatures better than we do——so it runs most upon those gentler passions and affections, which aid so much to it."

There was also a more personal aim hinted at here and there in Sterne's letters. Feeling the approach of death, he wished to leave the world with a different impression than had been made upon it by *Tristram Shandy*. Above his humor, which had led him into many indecorums of speech, he prized his sensibility, which had kept his heart right, as everybody might now see for himself. That side of his talent which the public had admired in the story of Le Fever was now to find expression on a larger scale. Incidentally the book was to be so chaste that it might lie upon any lady's table; or heaven have mercy upon her imagination.

Subdued to this mood by passion and disease, Sterne began the *Sentimental Journey* within a week of his arrival at Coxwold towards the end of May. Ten days were passed in sorting and arranging the miscellaneous notes and sketches of his travels, which had long lain by him, before he was ready to write the introductory chapter immortalizing the name of Eliza. At first, progress was slow because of extreme weakness and the intrusion of Mrs. Draper's image in and out of season. "Cannot write my Travels," was the pretty complaint on the third of June, "or give one half hour's close attention to them, upon thy Account, my dearest friend——Yet write I must, and what to do with you, whilst I write——I declare I know not——I want to have you ever before my Imagination—— and cannot keep you out of my heart or head. . . . Now I must shut you out sometimes——or meet you Eliza! with an empty purse upon the Beach." At length health mended; the journal to Eliza, which kept his heart bleeding, was closed up; and all his energies were bent upon the book that he must have ready for his subscribers by the next winter. "It is a subject," Sterne informed Mrs. James when well into it, "which works well, and suits the frame of mind I have been in for some time past." During the period of composition, the manuscript was submitted to the Demoniacs and other "Geniuses of the North," who declared it, Sterne assured Becket in September, "an Original work and likely to take in all Kinds of Readers"; but "the proof of the pudding," the author added, "is in the eating."

The even course of Sterne's pleasure at his task was broken by a week's illness in August "with a spitting of blood," and by the visit of his wife and daughter, to whose comfort and entertainment was devoted the entire month of October. To make up for lost time, Sterne spurred on his Pegasus violently through November, "determined not to draw bit," until his book should be completed. Utterly exhausted by this final spurt, he wrote to the Earl of Shelburne at the end of the month: "Yorick . . . has worn out both his spirits and body with the Sentimental Journey——'tis true that an author must feel himself, or his reader will not——but I have torn my whole frame into pieces by my feelings." Thereupon followed the inevitable collapse—a succession of hemorrhages with fever, which confined Sterne to his room for three weeks. As soon as the fever left him, his old buoyancy of spirit brought him to his feet again, and he set off for London in company with Hall-Stevenson, who was going up to see through the press a volume of facetious verse-tales called *Makarony Fables*. The journey was mere madness on Sterne's part, for nothing was left of him but a shadow. "I am weak," the Jameses were warned in advance while he was resting at York, "I am weak, my dear friends, both in body and mind——so God bless you ——you will see me enter like a ghost——so I tell you before-hand not to be frightened."

But besides having a book to publish, Sterne still believed that he might once more recruit mind and body, as had so often happened in past years, by a change of scene and faces. For months his friends had been calling him to London, all eager to hear him read from his sentimental travels amid the old intimacies. Lord Shelburne, he hoped, would be pleased with his book, and then his labor would not have been in vain. The earl must, it was urged, make the acquaintance of the Jameses before the winter was over. "You would esteem the husband, and honour the wife——she is the reverse of most of her sex——they have various pursuits—she but one—that of pleasing her husband." Sir George Macartney wrote to Yorick from St. Petersburg, where the diplomat was negotiating a commercial treaty with Russia; and after his return Sterne congratulated him upon the success of his mission, adding, "I shall have the honour of presenting to you a *couple of as clean brats* as ever chaste brain conceiv'd." Macartney, Craufurd, and Sterne were to renew their convivial friendship.

A certain "Sir W," perhaps Sir William Stanhope, brother to Chesterfield and one of the Delaval set, came north during September for a week at Scarborough, stopping at York, where he and Sterne met over their "barley water" at Bluitt's Inn in Lendal. This gentleman was to be convinced by the *Sentimental Journey* that sensibility has no kinship with sensuality. "I take heav'n to witness," Sterne replied to him on being rallied for the freedoms of *Tristram Shandy*, "after all this *badinage* my heart is innocent——and the sporting of my pen is equal, just equal, to what I did in my boyish days, when I got astride of a stick, and gallop'd away. . . . Praised be God for my sensibility! Though it has often made me wretched, yet I would not exchange it for all the pleasures the grossest sensualist ever felt." Among friends without rank were not forgotten honest Sancho, who must make his usual morning calls in Bond Street; and Arthur Lee, to whom Sterne was continuing to give expert counsel in matters of the heart.

Mrs. James was deeply chagrined when she heard a rumor that Yorick had paid a flying visit to London in the autumn without calling upon her. Sterne set the idle story at rest, explaining how it all may have come about, and remonstrating with his friend that she should even fancy him capable of so great incivility: "Good God! to think I could be in town, and not go the first step I made to Gerrard Street!——My mind and body must be at sad variance with each other, should it ever fall out that it is not both the first and last place also where I shall betake myself, were it only to say, 'God bless you.' . . . I . . . never more felt the want of a house I esteem so much, as I do now when I can hear tidings of it so seldom——and have nothing to recompense my desires of seeing its kind possessors, but the hopes before me of doing it by Christmas." Mrs. Ferguson, the witty widow, was waiting for January when she might obtain a peep at the *Sentimental Journey*. And there was another unknown woman, a certain Hannah, who, falling across Sterne's way last season, wished to be still kept in his memory. Hannah was a sprightly girl, whose chit-chat amused him and to whom he replied in kind, claiming, on the receipt of her first letter during the summer, that he could not exactly place her among the many Queens of Sheba who had honored him with visits. "It could not be," he replied, "the lady in Bond-street, or Grosvenor-street, or —— Square, or Pall Mall.——We shall make it out, Hannah, when we meet. . . . How do you do? Which parts of Tristram do you like best?——God bless you." With the help of another letter from Hannah, he was able to recall the "good dear girl" and her sister Fanny, whom the *Sentimental Journey*, Yorick predicted, would make "cry as much as ever it made me laugh, or I'll give up the business of sentimental writing."

Thus anticipating the pleasure of laying a new book at the feet of his friends, Sterne drove up to his old lodgings

in Bond Street on the first or second of January, 1768. It was
the worst sort of weather, cold, raw, and damp. Influenza
had set in and was carrying off poor people so fast that the
newspapers feared not enough laborers would be left to do the
work of the next summer. Everybody was warned against exposure to the inclemency of the season. "Their Majesties,"
said the newspapers, under date of Monday the fourth of
January, "did not attend service yesterday at the Chapel Royal
on account of the badness of the weather, but had private
service performed in their apartments at the Queen's palace."

On that Sunday, Sterne, becoming careful of his health for
the first time in his life, watched the rain from his window
all day, forgoing the pleasure of a call on the Jameses and of
dining with them and their friends in the evening. But mind-
ful of the engagement, he sent over to Gerrard Street the
compliments of the new year to all the household gathered
about the firesides—"Miss Ayscough the wise, Miss Pigot the
witty, your daughter the pretty, and so on"—with an enclosure
for Lord Ossory, should he be present. On Sterne's table lay
scattered cards, notes, and invitations out, enough to carry him
through a fortnight of dinners. Among them was an urgent
request from Mrs. James for aid in obtaining a ticket to Mrs.
Cornelys's forthcoming assembly. Never before had there been
so great a demand for tickets to this social function, which was
to assume added splendor this year. Mrs. James, at whose
table sat Lord Ossory, had pleaded with all her friends, and
had everywhere failed. Would Mr. Sterne use his influence?
Sterne wrote back that he was not a subscriber to Soho this
year, but that he might be depended upon to do his best for her.
So he began despatching notes round among his friends; and
as they all brought in unfavorable responses, he set out himself
the next morning to see what he could do by his presence. The
episode concluded pleasantly, if unsuccessfully, with the following letter to the Jameses, on Monday, January 4, 1768:

"My dear Friends,——I have never been a moment at rest
since I wrote yesterday about this Soho ticket——I have been
at a Secretary of State to get one—have been upon one knee

to my friend Sir George Macartney, Mr. Lascelles—and Mr. Fitzmaurice*—without mentioning five more——I believe I could as soon get you a place at court, for everybody is going ——but I will go out and try a new circle—and if you do not hear from me by a quarter after three, you may conclude I have been unfortunate in my supplications.——I send you this state of the affair, lest my silence should make you think I had neglected what I promised——but no—Mrs. James knows me better, and would never suppose it would be out of the head of one who is with so much truth her faithful friend."

Though Sterne felt unequal to a Soho assembly, he was drawn, so far as health would permit, rather reluctantly into the old life. If his friends could not have him always at their tables, they visited him in Bond Street, where was held every morning a sort of levee. "I am now tyed down," he complained to the Jameses in February, "neck and heels (twice over) by engagements every day this week, or most joyfully would have trod the old pleasing road from Bond to Gerrard street. . . . I am quite well, but exhausted with a room full of company every morning till dinner——How do I lament I cannot eat my morsel (which is always sweet) with such kind friends!"

As usual, his guests sent in little presents for remembrance, or enrolled themselves among his subscribers, in return for the pleasure of hearing the charming Yorick read from his sentimental travels in advance of publication. This year he was especially honored with a series of prints from "L. S——n Esq," as the heading to a letter has the blundering disguise, but really, I think, from George Selwyn, the grim wit and politician, who put his name down for the *Sentimental Journey*. On receiving the gift, accompanied by a note proffering friendship, Sterne replied in his most courteous manner, beginning: "Your commendations are very flattering. I know no one whose judgment I think more highly of, but your partiality for me is the only instance in which I can call it in question.

* Probably Edwin Lascelles, M.P. for Yorkshire; and Thomas Fitzmaurice, M.P. for Calne.

——Thanks, my good sir, for the prints—I am much your debtor for them——if I recover from my ill state of health and live to revisit Coxwould this summer, I will decorate my study with them, along with six beautiful pictures I have already of the sculptures on poor Ovid's tomb."

There came to Sterne also a much prized gift from overseas in the form of a curiously carved walking-stick, double handled and twisted into all sorts of shapes, which Dr. Eustace of North Carolina* sent over in company with a letter giving its history and uses. The colonial physician, after introducing himself as "a great admirer of Tristram Shandy" and "one of his most zealous defenders against the repeated assaults of prejudice and misapprehension," went on to explain whimsically why the walking-stick should belong to Sterne. "The only reason," he said, "that gave rise to this address to you, is my accidentally having met with a piece of true Shandean statuary, I mean according to vulgar opinion, for to such judges both appear equally destitute of regularity or design. ——It was made by a very ingenious gentleman of this province, and presented to the late Governor Dobbs, after his death Mrs. D. gave it me: its singularity made many desirous of procuring it, but I had resolved, at first, not to part with it, till, upon reflection, I thought it would be a very proper and probably not an unacceptable, compliment to my favourite author, and in his hands might prove as ample a field for meditation as a button-hole, or a broom-stick."

It was too late for the walking-stick of Governor Dobbs ever to go into *Tristram Shandy;* but Sterne sent back by the next ship a meditation, taking, as the physician wished, the singular gift as a symbol of his book for an attack upon all who had failed to appreciate its humor. Never quite sound in his judgment since the old days of his quarrel with his uncle

---

* Dr. John Eustace of Wilmington, N. C., described as a man "who united wit, and genius, and learning, and science." See G. J. McRee, *Life and Correspondence of James Iredell,* I, 27-28, 194 (New York, 1857).

Jaques, Sterne still imagined that he had been persecuted through his literary career by a conspiracy formed against him. Under date of February 9, 1768, Sterne wrote to Dr. Eustace:

"Sir,—I this moment received your obliging letter, and SHANDEAN piece of sculpture along with it; of both which testimonies of your regard I have the justest sense, and return you, dear sir, my best thanks and acknowledgments. Your walking stick is in no sense more SHANDAIC than in that of its having more handles than one—The parallel breaks only in this, that in using the stick, every one will take the handle which suits his convenience. In TRISTRAM SHANDY, the handle is taken which suits their passions, their ignorance or sensibility. There is so little true feeling in the HERD of the WORLD, that I wish I could have got an act of parliament, when the books first appear'd, 'that none but wise men should look into them.' It is too much to write books and find heads to understand them. The world, however, seems to come into a better temper about them, the people of genius here being, to a man, on its side, and the reception it has met with in France, Italy and Germany, hath engag'd one part of the world to give it a second reading, and the other part of it, in order to be on the strongest side, have at length agreed to speak well of it too. A few Hypocrites and Tartufe's, whose approbation could do it nothing but dishonor, remain unconverted.

"I am very proud, sir, to have had a man, like you, on my side from the beginning; but it is not in the power of any one to taste humor, however he may wish it—'tis the gift of God —and besides, a true feeler always brings half the entertainment along with him. His own ideas are only call'd forth by what he reads, and the vibrations within, so entirely correspond with those excited, 'tis like reading HIMSELF and not the BOOK.

"In a week's time, I shall be deliver'd of two volumes of the sentimental travels of MR. YORICK through France and Italy; but, alas! the ship sails three days too soon, and I have only to lament it deprives me of the pleasure of sending them

to you, being, dear sir, with great thanks for the honor you
have done me, and with true esteem,

"Your oblig'd and humble servant,

Lau. Sterne."

Having uttered his last word on *Tristram Shandy*, Sterne
was looking forward, as we see, to the *Sentimental Journey*,
which was to win over the poor remainder of his enemies.
The work had been passing through the press rather slowly,
owing to the author's numerous corrections in the text, apparently down to the moment of publication. To judge from the
extant part of the manuscript,* now in the British Museum,
and comprising the first volume as published, Sterne brought
up with him from Coxwold a fair copy in his own hand for
the printer, leaving blank pages enough for easy changes and
additions. There is a notion, warranted only by Yorick's jesting remarks, that Sterne was a careless writer who put down
and printed whatever came into his head without premeditation. How false this notion is I have shown in discussing *Tristram Shandy*, whose several instalments were playfully organized, we concluded, on Locke's theory of associated ideas,
while all details were studied with scrupulous concern for
humorous or pathetic effects. Much that was there half guessed
at may be seen in the manuscript of the *Sentimental Journey*
—a neat, underlying copy, which after six weeks of inter-
mittent labor was covered all over with deletions, and interlinear substitutions reaching out into margins and blank pages.
Sterne knew, artist as he was, that a point just missed may
sometimes be retrieved merely by a new word or a new phrase.

It is perhaps saying too much to imply that Sterne had any
occasion in the last stages of his book to retrieve himself from
real failure. Already complete was that wonderful series of
portraits, ebbing and flowing with the author's emotions, in
the order as we now have them, from the poor Franciscan, the
Flemish lady, and La Fleur, on to the dwarf and the beautiful
grisette from whom Yorick purchased the gloves. It is rather

* Egerton MSS., 1610.

that these portraits sometimes needed here and there just those touches which make for perfection. No scene in the *Sentimental Journey* struck the fancy of Europe more than the exchange of snuff-boxes between Yorick and Father Lorenzo after their amiable contention. It led in Germany to the formation of little coteries for the study of Sterne, the members of which presented one another with horn snuff-boxes, and promised to cultivate Yorick's gentleness, content with fortune, and pity and pardon for all human errors.* Before turning in his manuscript to the printer, Sterne hesitated between a bald relation of the incident and the details as the world now knows them. In its cancelled form the passage read: "The monk rubbed his horn box upon his sleeve and presented it to me with one hand, as he took mine from me in the other; and having kissed it, with a stream of good nature in his eyes he put it into his bosome—and took his leave." When printed, the passage ran: "The monk rubb'd his horn box upon the sleeve of his tunick; and as soon as it had acquired a little air of brightness by the friction—he made a low bow, and said, 'twas too late to say whether it was the weakness or goodness of our tempers which had involved us in this contest——But be it as it would ——he begg'd we might exchange boxes——In saying this, he presented his to me with one hand, as he took mine from me in the other; and having kissed it—with a stream of good nature in his eyes he put it into his bosom—and took his leave." How much the scene gains by the elaboration everyone must feel. The mendicant who had come to ask an alms, gave instead all that he had to Yorick, but not until he had heightened the value of his gift by "a little air of brightness."

In view of what Sterne did here, we wonder whether we should not regard as a happy afterthought the *bit of rust* which caught the eye of the Marquis of E * * * *, as he drew his sword from its scabbard before the assembled states at Rennes,

* For the queer story of these Lorenzo orders, see H. W. Thayer, *Laurence Sterne in Germany*, 84-89 (New York, 1905): and J. Longo, *Laurence Sterne and Johann Georg Jacobi*, 39-44 (Wien und Leipzig, 1898).

and, dropping a tear upon the place, remarked, "I shall find some *other way* to get it off."

The account of Monsieur Dessein's vamped-up chaise, for whose sorrowful adventures through the passes of Savoy and over Mont Cenis Yorick sought to awaken pity, was rather tame as Sterne originally had it; for he wrote at first: "Much indeed was not to be said for it—but something might—and when a few little words will set the poor chaise of an innocent traveller agoing, I hate the man who can be a churl of them." Subsequently a clause was crossed out and another written in its place, so as to make the whole read: "Much indeed was not to be said for it—but something might—and when a few words will rescue misery out of her distress, I hate the man who can be a churl of them." On this passage, Thackeray once put the rhetorical question: "Does anybody believe that this is a real Sentiment? that this luxury of generosity, this gallant rescue of Misery—out of an old cab, is genuine feeling." Whether Sterne or Thackeray was right, it is worth while to observe that the sentiment was fully premeditated.

The sketch of the beautiful Fleming whom Yorick on a sudden turn of his head met full in the face on his way to Monsieur Dessein's magazine of chaises, was likewise carefully re-worked. "Heaven forbid!" the strange lady exclaimed in the first version, "laying her hand upon her eyes." But as this is not the natural gesture in warding off a threatened blow, Sterne substituted "raising her hand up to her forehead." A moment later Yorick took the stranger's hand and led her towards the *remise* door in silence; whereof Sterne remarked that it was one of those situations "which can happen to a man but once in his life." In after-thought he struck out the comment, preferring to leave undetermined the rarity of the occurrence in real life.

The lament of the Franconian peasant over his dead ass by the roadside caused Sterne much trouble; for several of the sentences were begun, abandoned, and tried two or three times over before the sentiment could be rendered precisely as he wished it. Another perplexity was who should compose the merry kitchen at Amiens on the evening when La Fleur pulled out his fife and led off the dance. At the first trial Sterne was certain that the "*fille de chambre*, the *maître d'hôtel*, the cook, the scullion, etc." would be there; but it took two more humorous trials to unroll *etc.* into "all the household, dogs, and cats, besides an old monkey." There was some doubt, too, as to the sobriquet most fitting for Smollett, the author's archenemy. Sterne had him at first Smeldungus, but left him Smelfungus. In like manner was partially deodorized the anecdote told of Madame de Rambouliet, by merely substituting a French phrase for the plain, blunt English, originally writ large. Again, while counting the pulse of the grisette, Yorick lost his reckoning, it will be remembered, at the fortieth pulsation, owing to the unexpected entrance of the husband, who passed through the shop from the back parlor to the street. As a late addition came the grisette's remark—" 'Twas nobody but her husband,"—which put Yorick at his ease in running up a fresh score on the pretty wrist still extended towards him. On bidding adieu, Yorick gave the hand of the beautiful grisette, as it was first written, "something betwixt a shake and a squeeze." Had the vulgarity been permitted to stand, the scene would have been spoiled, so whimsically delicate is it in every other detail.

These are merely examples of Sterne's alterations, so numerous that no adequate notion could be given of them without photographing large parts of the manuscript. True, one turns many a clean folio, but substitutions such as have been described are the rule; words and phrases are also frequently transposed, and sentences are re-cast, curtailed, or added to,— all for exactness, clearness, and rhythm. Every change, however, relates to details, never to the general outline of a portrait or to the emotional transition from one to another, any difficulties with which, if they were encountered, are not revealed by a manuscript wherein we see the author only refining, sometimes to an amusing degree. For example. Yorick was not sure whether the packet which bore him across the Channel should reach port at one, two, or three o'clock in the afternoon. He first wrote *two*, then *one*, and finally drawing his pen through each, settled upon *three* o'clock as affording sufficient dramatic time for the Calais episode before the approach of evening. Neither was he sure whether he gave six or eight sous to "the sons and daughters of poverty" who surrounded him as he was leaving the inn at Montreuil; nor whether, on his return to Calais, he walked *a league* or *two leagues* to pluck "a nettle or two" growing over the grave of Father Lorenzo.

More important than attentions to time, place, and number, is the keen sense that Sterne everywhere displayed for the differences of meaning between synonyms, though the right word was often slow in making its appearance. Of the following list, he finally chose the second of each pair, crossing out the first and writing the second above it or on the margin: *insolence* and *triumph*, *literata* and *précieuse*, *quest* and *pursuit*, *withdrew* and *disengaged*, *hurt* and *mortified*, *motives* and *movements*, *consolation* and *comfort*, *donnoit* and *présentoit*, *un joli garçon* and *a clever young fellow*, and so on in a descent through scores of others to *ocean* and *sea*, *entered* and *came into*, where rhythm or the desire to escape repetition won the day. Throughout the process Sterne managed his French easily. At times it was not quite correct; accents were often forgotten; and occasionally were dropped off final vowels and consonants of words like *Londre* for *Londres* and *désobligeant* for *désobligeante;* but it was all clear enough to the eye. Beyond these and similar slips, the French translator of the *Sentimental Journey* found it necessary to make very few corrections in the many French phrases scattered through the book. For Sterne's *fille de chambre* was substituted the more usual *femme de chambre*, though both were in use; and *voilà un persiflage* of necessity became *voilà du persiflage;* while the *billet doux* which Yorick sent to Madame de L * * * was left intact except for *corporal*, which should have been *caporal*.

Here in the *Sentimental Journey* occurs Sterne's beautiful rendering of the French proverb: *A brebis tondue Dieu mesure le vent.* "God tempers the wind," said the unfortunate maid of Moulins, "to the shorn lamb."* Precisely how Sterne attained to the perfect phrasing along with the perfect rhythm, no one can ever know, for the manuscript does not extend thus far; but if inference be justifiable from analogies supported by the manuscript, moral epigrams did not come to him in full expression all at once and without effort. To cite an instance, Yorick was so disturbed while at the Opéra Comique by the boorish conduct of a German towards a dwarf standing in front of him in the parterre, that he was ready to leap out of his box and run to the aid of the poor fellow. Over Yorick's emotions, Sterne first remarked: "An injury sharpen'd by an insult is insufferable"; but not satisfied with the commonplace, he ran his pen through the last part of the sentence, and then re-worked the whole to "An injury sharpen'd by an insult, be it to whom it will, makes every man of sentiment a party." And so it likely was with the famous proverb, which seems easy enough to frame now that the feat has been accomplished. It was only throwing, one may say, the French sentence into the English order and translating *mesure* by *tempers*, and there you have Sterne. Yes: but George Herbert tried his hand at the French proverb in a slightly different form before *près* had dropped out between *brebis* and *tondue*, and gave us the awkward "To a close shorne sheep God gives wind by measure."† Sterne tried his hand and gave us "God tempers the

* In the *Fragment in the Manner of Rabelais*, written in the Shandy period, Sterne has a phrase about tears which "temper the wind" that was rising upon a discourse. And in *Original Letters of Laurence Sterne*, 154-159 (1788), there is a letter in which it is said of "the kind Being who made us all" that "*he even tempers the wind to the shorn lamb.*" This letter to an unnamed friend, bearing the superscription "Lyons, Nov. 15," relates to Sterne's impressions thus far on his journey through France into Italy in the autumn of 1765. Though the letter has been often quoted or referred to as genuine, it is probably a forgery, perpetrated after Sterne's death. On November 15, 1765, Sterne had reached Turin. The forger did not know that. There is, therefore, no real evidence that Sterne's famous proverb, in the form he gave it, occurs in any of his writings before the *Sentimental Journey*, though he was on the way to it in his *Fragment*.

† *Outlandish Proverbs*, No. 861 (London, 1640).

wind to the shorn lamb," thereby puzzling many a clergyman who has taken the proverb for a text and afterwards searched for it through the wisdom of Solomon, in vain.

Not since the first instalment of *Tristram Shandy* had Sterne taken so great pains with a book, the publication of which Becket was forced to delay until Wednesday or Thursday, the twenty-fourth or twenty-fifth of February, 1768,* a full month beyond the usual time for Sterne to make his annual literary entrance into society. The work, bearing the title *A Sentimental Journey through France and Italy*, appeared in two styles—in two small octavo volumes with pages measuring about six inches by three and three quarters, and in two larger octavo volumes on imperial paper with wide-margined pages measuring about seven inches by four. In the first style, the price of the set, pages sewed but unbound, was five shillings; in the second style, the price was apparently half a guinea. Except for one episode clearly out of place and for a few incidental references, the travels contained nothing about Italy; indeed, they were extended beyond Paris only by working over in a more sentimental mood the story of Maria and the scene of the vintage dance from *Tristram Shandy*, with the addition of an anecdote re-told after John Craufurd of Errol. But as an announcement that the public might expect an Italian tour in continuation, Sterne had a loose page printed and slipped into the copies for his subscribers. The loose page, rarely to be seen nowadays, read as follows:

"Advertisement.

THE Author begs leave to acknowledge to his Subscribers,
that they have a further claim upon
him for Two Volumes more than these
delivered to them now, and which
nothing but ill health could have
prevented him, from having ready
along with these.

* Registered at Stationers' Hall, February 27, 1768.

"The Work will be compleated
and delivered to the Subscribers early
the next Winter."*

There were two hundred and eighty-one subscribers, who took altogether, some entering their names for more than one copy, three hundred and thirty-four sets—one hundred and ninety-nine on ordinary paper, and one hundred and thirty-five on imperial paper. The result may seem disappointing when compared with the immense array that ushered in the *Sermons of Mr. Yorick* only two years before. Of all Sterne's publications, his sermons, it must be admitted, were the most immediately profitable; but their subsequent sale could not be counted upon; nor is a subscribers' list a sure index of a first sale, inasmuch as many a person who would hesitate to patronize a book which might prove another *Tristram Shandy*, would nevertheless purchase and read it. The new list of subscribers, though falling short of expectations, was a most notable advertisement, wherein were again marshalled troops of friends among the nobility, gentry, and distinguished commoners, including nearly everybody prominently connected with his Majesty's government, all the way down from the Duke of Grafton, the First Lord of the Treasury. And as an assurance that the book contained nothing to bring a blush to the most innocent cheek, one might read in the roll of ecclesiastical titles

* It has been asserted more than once (*Notes and Queries*, fifth series, IX, 223) that this advertisement was issued with only the large paper copies. This is an error, for the advertisement as given here is taken from a small paper copy.

There were to have been, it is clear, four volumes of the *Sentimental Journey*—two for France and two for Italy. Sterne's conversation with Alessandro Verri, as quoted in a previous chapter, shows that the author expected to have the work complete at this time; but was prevented by ill health. Subscribers were entitled to four volumes, but they now received only two, with the promise of two more which Sterne never lived to write. The result was that subscribers paid a guinea for two volumes on imperial paper and a half-guinea for copies on ordinary paper—or double the price at which the sets were sold to the outside public.

names like York and Peterborough. All who could afford imperial paper had the honor of a star after their names. Sir George Macartney was thus starred for five sets, and "the young rich Mr. Crewe" was starred for twenty sets, the largest single subscription except Panchaud's, who engaged the same number of small copies for Paris.

No subscribers' list was necessary to ensure the success of the *Sentimental Journey*, the first edition of which was exhausted within a month.* All who wrote of the book in newspapers, magazines, and letters were now ready to take off their hats to Mr. Sterne's genius. All, I should say, except one. Smelfungus, as the type of the splenetic traveller from "a well-known original," of course could not be passed by without a return thrust from Smollett's man on the *Critical Review*,† who lamented, on observing chapters which bore no number, that Yorick was again imposing upon the public "whim for sentiment and caprice for humour." As the reviewer waxed hot, poor Yorick was charged with "making the sufferings of others the objects of his mirth" and of rising "superior to every regard for taste, truth, observation, and reflection"; while La Fleur, "the least unmeaning" of all the sketches, the angry reviewer finally asserted without any attempt at proof, was "pieced out with shreds . . . barbarously cut out and unskilfully put together from other novels." On the other hand, Walpole, who could never get through three volumes of the "tiresome *Tristram Shandy*," thought the new book "very pleasing, though too much dilated," and recommended it for its "great good nature and strokes of delicacy."‡ Elizabeth Montagu, who used to lecture Sterne so severely on the free wit of *Tristram Shandy* that "he would shed penitent tears" approved of the *Sentimental Journey*, which, she said, "would not have misbecome a young ensign."

One by one the portraits, beginning with the monk and end-

* The second edition appeared on Tuesday, March 29.—*London Chronicle*, March 26-29, 1768.

† May, 1768.

‡ *Letters*, edited by Toynbee, VII, 175.

ing with the last scene at the Piedmont inn, were taken up for comment by the *Monthly Review* in a notice running through March and April. Quite naturally the reviewer was disposed to sport with his "good cousin Yorick," in memory of old days when each had slashed the other's jerkin; but it was all kindly banter. Why should "one of our first-rate pens," it was asked, write "a black pair of silk breeches" instead of the more accurate "a pair of black silk breeches"? or why should he descend to the vulgarism of *lay* for *lie,* as when he says "Maria should *lay* in my bosom," as if Maria were "the name of a favourite pullet"? But these blemishes were all "pitiful minutiæ," it was concluded, of no account in a series of travels abounding in "masterly" portraits, "affecting," "touching," "delicate," and so on through the list of epithets of praise.

Tristram Shandy had long ago made Sterne's name familiar through the greater part of literary Europe. Many read the book in France and in Germany; but few even among its friends at home, Sterne used to say, really understood its drift. Certainly none of those who were translating it had any adequate conception of its meaning. The *Sentimental Journey,* clear of any disorder in its art, could be more easily read. Everybody could feel its sentiment and pathos, though its lurking humor might escape them, just as it escaped Thackeray a century later. True, the *Sentimental Journey* does not cut so deeply into life as *Tristram Shandy* but for literary charm time has rightly given it the preference. The narrative—if it be narrative—moves through a series of dramatic portraits, which, like the emotions underlying them, rise bright out of one another, and, after glowing for a moment, fade away with consummate art. Literature has nothing like these little pictures of French life drawn with a fine brush. They have been aptly compared to the choicest pastels of Latour and Watteau, always delicate and yet always brilliant in their coloring. Unlike *Tristram Shandy,* there was nothing local about the *Sentimental Journey,* nothing provincial, nothing even racial. It at once assumed its place as a cosmopolitan classic by the side of *Robinson Crusoe.*

Translations appeared in French and German within a year, and thereafter in Italian, Spanish, Polish, and Russian. Bode, the German translator, when puzzled how to render the word *sentimental*, appealed for aid to his friend Lessing, who coined the adjective *empfindsam* after the analogy of *mühsam*, thus giving, through Sterne, a new word to the German language. It was in this translation, followed by *Tristram Shandy* in 1774, that Goethe and Heine mainly knew Sterne, of whom the former once said: "Yorick Sterne is the best type of wit that ever exerted an influence in literature. Whoever reads him feels himself lifted above the petty cares of the world. His humour is inimitable, and it is not every kind of humour that leaves the soul calm and serene."[*]

Frénais, the French translator, likewise troubled for an equivalent of *sentimental*, decided to take the word over into French, in the hope that it would prove useful for expressing a new idea. This mutilated version of the original, missing as often as hitting the point of Sterne's anecdotes, brought Yorick's name and strange personality back to the salons which had been captivated by his conversation. The book, said Madame Suard, amused and pleased many, while some few had for it the most profound contempt. The vivacious Mademoiselle de Sommery, for instance, was surprised that anyone should find interest in a dead ass, a lackey, or a mendicant who asks an alms. And she shook with laughter at Yorick's pleasure in holding the gloved hand of a beautiful woman or in counting her pulse beats with the tips of his fingers.

To this and similar ridicule Madame Suard replied finely in a letter to a mutual friend. "The chapters descriptive of these incidents," she said there, "certainly have little promise in them; but Sterne's merit, it seems to me, lies in his having attached an interest to details which in themselves have none whatsoever; in his having caught a thousand faint impressions, a thousand fleeting emotions which pass through the heart or the imagination of a sensitive man, and in having rendered them all in piquant phrase and image. He enlarges, so to speak,

[*] Thayer, *Laurence Sterne in Germany*, 105.

the human heart by portraying his own sensations, . . . and thereby adds to the stores of our enjoyment. . . . If you do not love Sterne, beware of telling me so, for I fear I should then love you less."*

To a later period belongs the impassioned tribute of Heine, who was as sensitive as Sterne to "the great black eyes" and "pale elegiac faces" which he saw in Italy. "Laurence Sterne," declared Heine in his enthusiasm, "is the born equal of William Shakespeare; and he, too, was nurtured by the Muses on Parnassus. But after the manner of women they quickly spoiled him with their caresses. He was the darling of the pale, tragic goddess. Once in an access of fierce tenderness, she kissed his young heart with such power, passion, and madness, that his heart began to bleed and suddenly understood all the sorrows of this world, and was filled with infinite compassion. Poor young poet heart! But the younger daughter of Mnemosyne, the rosy goddess of humor, quickly ran up to him, and took the suffering boy in her arms, and sought to cheer him with laughter and song; she gave him for playthings the comic mask and the jester's bells, and kissed his lips soothingly, kissing upon them all her levity and mirth, all her wit and mockery."†

* *Lettre d'une Femme sur le Voyage sentimental de Sterne*, in J. B. A. Suard's *Mélanges de Littérature*, III, 111-122 (Paris, 1803). Frénais states his troubles over the word *sentimental* in his *Avertissement* to the *Voyage Sentimental* (Amsterdam et Paris, 1769). Likewise Bode in his *Vorbericht* to *Yoricks Empfindsame Reise* (Hamburg und Bremen, 1768).

† *Die Romantische Schule.* Bk. III, ch. III.

CHAP. XXI.

Illness and Death. March, 1768

BUT Sterne never lived to enjoy to the full his final triumph. Reynolds was to paint the author of the *Sentimental Journey* as he had already twice painted the author of *Tristram Shandy*. Sittings were arranged for the twenty-second of February and the first of March.* The second appointment Sterne was probably unable to keep; and the portrait was left unfinished. The last time we see Sterne afoot is on a Sunday, late in February. He was to breakfast with Beauclerk, the friend of Dr. Johnson, and pass an hour afterwards with Lord Ossory. In the evening he was to dine along with Selwyn with their friends in Gerrard Street. Mrs. James, he had discovered, possessed a talent for drawing. "I presented her last year," he wrote to Selwyn ten days before, "with colours, and an apparatus for painting, and gave her several lessons before I left town.——I wish her to follow this art, to be a compleat mistress of it——and it is singular enough, but not more singular than true, that she does not know how to make a cow or a sheep, tho' she draws figures and landscapes perfectly well." All this was a pretty introduction to a request that Selwyn bring with him an Italian print or two from his collection of "cattle on colour'd paper" for Mrs. James to copy. The two men planned to go over to Gerrard Street half an hour before dinner to see a picture of Mrs. James just "executed by West, most admirably." "He has caught," said Sterne in concluding his letter to Selwyn, "the character of our friend——such goodness is painted in that face, that when one looks at it, let the soul be ever so much un-harmonized, it is impossible it should remain so.——I will send you a set of my books——they will take with the generality——the women will read this book in the parlour, and Tristram in the

* Reynolds, *Pocket Book* for 1768 (Manuscript at the Royal Academy of Arts).

bed-chamber.——Good night, dear sir——I am going to take my whey, and then to bed."

The Sunday evening at Mrs. James's was the last of the thousand dinners which had attended Yorick in his fame. The same week he came down with the winter's influenza, which he had thus far escaped, notwithstanding his weakened condition. At first he tried to maintain his old buoyancy of spirit. "I am ill—very ill," he wrote to Mrs. Montagu, "yet I feel my Existence strongly, and something like revelation along with it, which tells, I shall not dye——but live——and yet any other man would set his house in order." He began a comic "Romance," which he thought might be finished in the course of a week, should his illness continue so long as that. At worst he would brave evils, "Quand je serai mort, on mettra mon nom dans le liste de ces Héros, qui sont morts en plaisantant."* That is, with Scarron and Cervantes and the author of the *Moyen de Parvenir*, who was, like himself, "a poor Canonical." Of his "Romance" we hear no more. As the fever increased, he became less certain of his recovery, as may be seen from his last letter to his daughter near the beginning of March. Mrs. Sterne, who was still ailing, feared that she was going to die and leave Lydia in the hands of a father who would send her out to India as a companion to Mrs. Draper. On hearing from Lydia of his wife's delusion, Sterne wrote back that he never had such a design, that in case his daughter should lose her mother, Mrs. James would become her protector. The disrespectful reference to Mrs. Draper in the letter now to be quoted was doubtless edited in by Lydia, according to her custom as we know it from extant originals. Sterne's last pathetic letter to his daughter, in the form she printed it, ran as follows:

"My dearest Lydia,——My Sentimental Journey, you say, is admired in York by everyone——and 'tis not vanity in me to tell you that it is no less admired here——but what is the gratification of my feelings on this occasion?——the want of health bows me down, and vanity harbours not in thy father's

* R. Blunt, *Mrs. Montagu*, I, 192.

breast——this vile influenza——be not alarm'd I think I shall get the better of it——and shall be with you both the first of May, and if I escape, 'twill not be for a long period, my child—unless a quiet retreat and peace of mind can restore me.——The subject of thy letter has astonish'd me.——She could but know little of my feelings, to tell thee, that under the supposition I should survive thy mother, I should bequeath thee as a legacy to Mrs. Draper. No, my Lydia! 'tis a lady, whose virtues I wish thee to imitate, that I shall entrust my girl to——I mean that friend whom I have so often talk'd and wrote about——from her you will learn to be an affectionate wife, a tender mother, and a sincere friend——and you cannot be intimate with her, without her pouring some part of the milk of human kindness into your breast, which will serve to check the heat of your own temper, which you partake in a small degree of.——Nor will that amiable woman put my Lydia under the painful necessity to fly to India for protection, whilst it is in her power to grant her a more powerful one in England.——But I think, my Lydia, that thy mother will survive me——do not deject her spirits with thy apprehensions on my account.——I have sent you a necklace, buckles, and the same to your mother.——My girl cannot form a wish that is in the power of her father, that he will not gratify her in—and I cannot in justice be less kind to thy mother.——I am never alone——The kindness of my friends is ever the same——I wish tho' I had thee to nurse me —but I am deny'd that.——Write to me twice a week, at least.——God bless thee, my child, and believe me ever, ever thy affectionate father, L. S."

Influenza prepared the way for pleurisy, which set in during the second week of March; and despite all that could be done for him, the patient grew worse from day to day. On Tuesday, the fifteenth, feeling the approach of death, he took his farewell of the world in a noble and tender letter to Mrs. James, asking her to look to the welfare of Lydia and pleading for pardon for the many follies which had pained his best friends:

"Your poor friend is scarce able to write——he has been

at death's door this week with a pleurisy——I was bled three times on Thursday, and blister'd on Friday——The physician says I am better——God knows, for I feel myself sadly wrong, and shall, if I recover, be a long while of gaining strength.——Before I have gone thro' half this letter, I must stop to rest my weak hand above a dozen times.——Mr. James was so good to call upon me yesterday. I felt emotions not to be described at the sight of him, and he overjoy'd me by talking a great deal of you.——Do, dear Mrs. James, entreat him to come to-morrow, or next day, for perhaps I have not many days, or hours, to live——I want to ask a favour of him, if I find myself worse—that I shall beg of you, if in this wrestling I come off conqueror—my spirits are fled—— 'tis a bad omen—do not weep my dear Lady——your tears are too precious to shed for me—bottle them up, and may the cork never be drawn.——Dearest, kindest, gentlest, and best of women! may health, peace, and happiness prove your handmaids.——If I die, cherish the remembrance of me, and forget the follies which you so often condemn'd—which my heart, not my head, betray'd me into. Should my child, my Lydia want a mother, may I hope you will (if she is left parentless) take her to your bosom?——You are the only woman on earth I can depend upon for such a benevolent action.——I wrote to her a fortnight ago, and told her what I trust she will find in you.——Mr. James will be a father to her—he will protect her from every insult, for he wears a sword which he has served his country with, and which he would know how to draw out of the scabbard in defence of innocence——Commend me to him—as I now commend you to that Being who takes under his care the good and kind part of the world.——Adieu——all grateful thanks to you and Mr. James. Your poor affectionate friend, L. Sterne."

Sterne lingered on in the full possession of his faculties for three days more. Death came at four o'clock in the afternoon of Friday, March 18, 1768.*

* *St. James's Chronicle*, March 17-19.

Around the closing scenes in his Bond Street lodgings has grown up a legend, starting from a fact or two, to show that a life of pleasure, as in the case of the *Rake's Progress*, must end in lonely bitterness. "The celebrated writer Sterne," said Malone in repeating what he had heard in his youth, "after being the idol of this town, died in a mean lodging without a single friend who felt interest in his fate except Becket, his bookseller." A little while before his death, according to other parts of the story, Sterne complained like Falstaff of cold in his feet; whereupon one attendant chafed them while another plucked out his gold sleeve-buttons. The next day his landlady, to be sure of her rent, sold his body, Allan Cunningham heard, to dissectors.*

It is quite easy to dispose of most of the legend. The "mean lodging" was a suite of apartments in the most fashionable quarter of the town, where Sterne was accustomed to receive every morning men of the first rank. As his last illness was coming upon him, he wrote to Lydia in the letter already quoted: "I am never alone——the kindness of my friends is ever the same." This kindly anxiety, it is safe to infer, continued till the end. Mrs. Montagu sent him jellies and other delicacies. Commodore James, we know, called on Monday, the fourteenth, and apparently on the succeeding Thursday. If visitors dropped away during the week, it was only because Sterne was too ill to see them. On the first signs of pleurisy, a physician was summoned to bleed and blister in accordance with the usual practice, and a nurse was placed in watch over

* For stories concerning Sterne's death, see Prior, *Life of Malone*, 373-374 (London, 1860); Leslie and Taylor, *Life and Times of Sir Joshua Reynolds*, I, 293 (London, 1865); Cunningham, biographical sketch of Reynolds in *Lives of Eminent Painters*, edited by W. Sharpe (London, 1886); John Ferriar, *Illustrations of Sterne*, II, 42 (London, 1812); *Notes and Queries*, fifth series, VIII, 249. Cunningham has an amusing story. "The death of Sterne," he relates, "is said to have been hastened by the sarcastic raillery of a lady whom he encountered at the painter's [Reynolds's] table. He offended her by the grossness of his conversation, and, being in a declining state of health, suffered . . . so severely from her wit—that he went home and died."

the patient. That Molly the house-maid, a cherished servant, who packed and unpacked Sterne's luggage and served his meals through two seasons, robbed him of sleeve-buttons or other trinkets while death was creeping upon him, may be believed by readers who know nothing of the strong attachment that ever existed between Sterne and those who served him. "The poor girl," Sterne wrote in his journal the year before, "is bewitch'd with us." His landlady appears to have been brusque of speech, but there is no evidence that she was a ghoul. If Sterne was in arrears for his rent, we may be certain that Becket discharged the obligation out of the proceeds of the *Sentimental Journey*, which was fast advancing to a second edition. The sick man must have known when he came up to London that the chances were against his return to Coxwold. In his death was nearly fulfilled the wish which he had expressed in *Tristram Shandy*, that he might not die in his own house, but rather in "some decent inn" away from the concern of friends, where "the few cold offices" he should want might be "purchased with a few guineas and paid me with an undisturbed and punctual attention."

Without the aid of fictitious incident to point a moral, the contrast between the full life Sterne had lived and his last moments is sufficiently striking to the imagination. Had he been in his health that Friday afternoon, he would have been a guest at the table of John Craufurd of Errol. Returning from Paris in January, this old friend had established himself for the season, with a French cook and a retinue of other French servants, near Sterne in Clifford Street, in the house of Sir James Gray, who was going as ambassador to Spain. On that Friday afternoon his friends were gathering for a four o'clock dinner. There were present the Duke of Roxburgh, just appointed a lord of his Majesty's bed-chamber, the Earl of March, afterwards Duke of Queensberry, the Earl of Upper-Ossory, the Duke of Grafton, Mr. Garrick, Mr. Hume, and Mr. James. The conversation turned to the illness of Mr. Sterne, "a very great favourite," says the relater, "of the gentlemen's"; and on hearing how serious his illness was,

Craufurd immediately sent out John Macdonald, a cadet of a Highland family, then in his service, to enquire how Mr. Sterne was to-day. "I went to Mr. Sterne's lodgings," is the cadet's record from memory; "the mistress opened the door; I enquired how he did? She told me to go up to the nurse. I went into the room, and he was just a dying. I waited ten minutes; but in five he said, 'Now it is come.' He put up his hand, as if to stop a blow, and died in a minute. The gentlemen were all very sorry, and lamented him very much."*

The news of Sterne's death passed quickly on from his friends to the public. Lady Mary Coke, as noted in her journal, heard of it that evening while playing loo at Caroline Howe's. Of the party were Horace Walpole, the Earl of Ossory, and Lord Eglinton. Lord Ossory, on coming in from Craufurd's dinner, announced the death of "the famous Dr. Sterne." "He seemed," remarked Lady Mary, "to lament him very much. Lord Eglinton said (but not in a ludicrous manner) that he had taken his 'Sentimental Journey.' "†

Newspapers contained the usual death notice, some of them adding Hamlet's lament over the skull of "poor Yorick, . . . a fellow of infinite jest." And within a week or two, verses began to circulate in newspapers and magazines on Sterne's humor and pathos. Very sprightly was a poem in which a poetaster expressed doubt as to where Yorick might now be sojourning, whether in the Elysian Fields or in the darker realms of Pluto. Taking notice of this and other illiberal pens which were meanly endeavoring to injure the reputation of Mr. Sterne, the *London Magazine* for March felt sure that "if the accusing spirit flies up to heaven's chancery with his indiscretions, it will blush to give them in," or that "the recording angel in writing them down will drop a tear upon each and wash it away forever."

The report of Sterne's death, travelling abroad through the next month, reached Lessing at Hamburg. Though Lessing

* John Macdonald, *Travels*, 146-147 (London, 1790).
† *Letters and Journals of Lady Mary Coke*, II, 215-216 (Edinburgh, 1889).

never met Sterne, he had been reading *Tristram Shandy* since
1763, and recommending it for enlightenment. On being told
by Bode, the translator, that Yorick was dead, the great critic
and dramatist made a famous remark, afterwards variously
repeated to other friends. "I would have given ten years of
my own life," said Lessing, "if I had been able to lengthen
Sterne's by one year."* Like many other Germans, Lessing
wished Sterne to live on, that he might write more lives and
opinions, more sermons and more journeys, or no matter what.

Were the moralists of aftertimes to be trusted, Sterne's
funeral was "as friendless as his death-bed," though the very
little really known concerning it points to nothing out of the
usual course. Sterne was buried on Tuesday, the twenty-second
of March,† from his lodgings in Bond Street, then within the
parish of St. George's Church, Hanover Square. Whether few
or many mourners came for a last look at Yorick in his death
there is no record. The service was conducted, according to
John Croft, by the chaplain of the late Prince of Wales.‡ The
interment was, we may well believe, as was said twelve years
afterwards, "most private"; § for the burial-ground belonging
to the fashionable church in Hanover Square lay far out
Oxford Street on the Bayswater Road, over against the broad
expanse of Hyde Park. It was a new ground which had been
enclosed and consecrated only four years before, with a small
mortuary chapel at the entrance. Among the few "gentlemen"
who, tradition says, attended Sterne's body through the chapel,
named the Ascension, on to his grave by the west wall, were
certainly Becket and Commodore James. The record closes

---

* Bode, *Vorbericht* to his translation of the *Sentimental Journey;*
and Thayer, *Laurence Sterne in Germany*, 40 (New York, 1905).

† Paris Registry, St. George's, Hanover Square.

‡ *Whitefoord Papers*, 230. Croft goes on to say that the chaplain
took charge of Sterne's personal effects and burned his "loose papers."
Croft was mistaken. The clergyman who did this was Mrs. Sterne's
brother-in-law, John Botham, of Ealing, who probably read the funeral
service also.

§ *Memoirs* prefixed to the collected edition of Sterne's works (London, 1780).

with the entry which the sexton made in his book, that six-teen shillings and sixpence—a rather large sum—was paid for prayers at the chapel and for the candle kept burning previous to interment.

The appropriate resting place for Sterne's body would have been the beautiful church at Coxwold by Shandy Hall. But none of his Yorkshire friends, who might have borne the trouble and expense of removal, were in London at the time of his death. Hall-Stevenson had returned to Skelton, and Lord Fauconberg remained at his country-seat through the winter. The group of London gentlemen who took charge of his funeral knew little or nothing of his associations in the north. Since Sterne died in the parish of St. George's, the burial-ground attached to that church must have appeared to them the most natural place for his interment. And yet they should have considered the danger attending burial in the suburbs at a time when dissecting-tables were furnished, without any scruple on the part of anatomists, from remote grave-yards. They should have known, if they read the newspapers, that for some time before Sterne's death the resurrection men had been at work on the Bayswater Road and in the neighbor-ing parish of Marylebone. In the hope of putting an end to the sacrilege, the wardens of St. George's placed over their ground a watch with a large mastiff dog; but in spite of this precau-tion, a corpse was stolen on a Sunday in the preceding Novem-ber, while the watch was asleep; and the very dog was carried off with the burden.* It is charitable to suppose that this warn-ing in the newspapers had escaped the notice of those friends who bore Sterne's body to the grave.

However that may be, they were soon to hear, with "great concern and astonishment," that Sterne had gone to the dissecting-table. As the story was told to Hall-Stevenson when he came up to London the next winter, "the body of Mr. Sterne, who was buried near Mary[le]bone, was taken up some time after his interment, and is supposed to have been carried to Oxford, and anatomised by an eminent surgeon of

* *St. James's Chronicle*, November 24-26, 1767.

that city."* Besides the mistake in the place of burial, Hall-Stevenson seems also to have been misinformed as to the exact disposition of the body. For Oxford the more carefully elaborated story has Cambridge. To give all the gruesome details of the narrative then current, Sterne's body was stolen from his grave by resurrectionists on the night of Wednesday or Thursday following the interment, and carried the next day in a case to Cambridge, where it was sold to "the anatomical professor" of the university, since identified as Dr. Charles Collignon, "an ingenious, honest man," much skilled in his art. To mitigate the horror of the crime, it is said that none involved in the robbery knew that the body was Sterne's. The discovery came about by mere accident. The professor of anatomy invited two friends to view the dissection of a nameless corpse which had just arrived from London. The work was nearly over when one of them out of curiosity uncovered the face of the dead man and recognized the features of Sterne, whom he had known and associated with not long ago. The poor visitor fainted at the sight, and Professor Collignon, on learning what a famous man lay under his scalpel, took care to retain the skeleton, which "the Rev. Thomas Greene"— presumably the Dean of Salisbury—claimed to have seen at Cambridge a few years after. Since the opening of the nineteenth century, various attempts have been made to identify Sterne's skull in the collection at Cambridge, but they have all been fruitless. The tradition has nevertheless persisted among Dr. Collignon's successors down to Dr. Alexander Macalister† that Sterne's skull once reposed in the Anatomical Museum of the university. There is, moreover, an old manuscript note at the end of a copy of the first edition of the *Sentimental Journey*, wherein the writer says that the story was confirmed by

* Hall-Stevenson, Preface to *Yorick's Sentimental Journey Continued* (second edition, London, 1769). In a third edition, he said that there was no foundation for the story.

† Macalister, *History of the Study of Anatomy in Cambridge* (Cambridge, 1891). See also Willis's *Current Notes*, April, 1854, for a summary of the evidence.

Dr. Collignon. Certainly it was very generally believed in
after years that Sterne's sojourn was brief on the Bayswater
Road.

In consequence of this and other exhumations, it is said,
St. George's burial-ground fell into great ill-repute. Over-
grown with nettles and weeds, it was for a long time among
the most neglected grave-yards in all London; shunned by
everybody out of instinctive feelings of horror, it was a spot
where no one, if he could help it, ever permitted his friends to
be buried. And so it became a place where the poor might be
huddled into their graves. Since those days all has changed:
the metropolis has spread her protecting wings far beyond
Hyde Park; and the old abandoned cemetery by the great
Marble Arch, long since closed against the dead, appears as a
quiet spot in the midst of a throbbing life.* But as a fitting
symbol of the Gothic fears which it formerly inspired, lie
some distance from where Sterne was buried the bones of Ann
Radcliffe, the once popular romancer of crime and death.

As evidence of final and complete neglect, it has been many
times repeated that neither Sterne's friends nor his family
cared enough for his memory to mark his grave. The assertion
in this form is quite untrue, for none knew Sterne well but to
hold him at least in pleasant remembrance; and a stone was in
fact projected, for which Garrick wrote the brief epitaph—

"Shall Pride a heap of sculptur'd marble raise,
  Some worthless, unmourn'd titled fool to praise;
  And shall we not by one poor grave-stone learn
  Where Genius, Wit, and Humour, sleep with *Sterne?*"—

which Lydia, in the warmth of her heart, thought a "sweet"
tribute to her father from one who "loved the man" as well
as "admired his works." The project was abandoned, not
because of indifference nor of a desire to leave Sterne undis-

* Cecil Moore, *Brief History of St. George's Chapel* (London,
1883). Though one should not lightly set aside tradition, I rather think
that Sterne's body was never exhumed. The story may have started as a
jest.

tinguished among the dead, but very likely because, in the belief of many, and perhaps on positive assurance from Cambridge, his body no longer reposed in St. George's parish. In succeeding years the want of a memorial to an author whom scores of pens were lauding in verse and prose was not understood by men unacquainted with rumors no longer in active currency. So it happened that Sterne was finally indebted for a headstone, sometime near 1780, to two freemasons, who had read Sterne's books, but had never seen the man. Their inscription, summarizing Sterne's literary career and attributing to him all the virtues of freemasonry, though he did not belong to the order, read as follows:

Alas! Poor Yorick.
Near to this Place
Lyes the Body of
The Reverend Laurence Sterne, A.M.
Dyed September 13th, 1768,
Aged 53 Years.

[Design]

Ah! Molliter ossa quiescant!

If a sound Head, warm Heart, and Breast humane,
Unsullied Worth, and Soul without a Stain;
If mental Powers could ever justly claim
The well-won Tribute of immortal Fame,
STERNE WAS THE MAN, who with gigantic Stride,
Mowed down luxuriant Follies far and wide.
Yet what, though keenest Knowledge of Mankind
Unseal'd to him the Springs that move the Mind;
What did it boot him? ridicul'd, abus'd,
By Fools insulted, and by Prudes accus'd.
In his, mild Reader, view thy future Fate,
Like him despise, what 'twere a Sin to hate.

This monumental Stone was erected to the memory of the deceased, by two BROTHER MASONS: for although he did not live to be a Member of their SOCIETY, yet all his incomparable

Performances evidently prove him to have acted by Rule and Square: they rejoice in this opportunity of perpetuating his high and irreproachable character to after ages.

W & S

The monument was pronounced at the time "very unworthy" of Sterne's memory, and the strangers who erected it have since been described as "tippling masons." It is quite difficult to see in the inscription anything to suggest tippling, nor does it appear on what grounds the brotherhood of masons may be called tipplers, if that be the insinuation. Why not take things as they are? The memorial was a simple slab such as the two men could easily afford; and the inscription, reflecting the bad taste of the authors and their ignorance of Sterne, was yet a sincere encomium from humble admirers of *Tristram Shandy* and the *Sentimental Journey*. Sterne's grave remained for more than a century much as the brother masons left it; but thirty years ago the owner of his uncle Richard's seat near Halifax corrected the obvious mistakes in age and date of death on the headstone, and erected a footstone having the more appropriate inscription:

In
Memory of
The Revd Laurence Sterne, M.A.
Rector of Coxwould, Yorkshire,
Born November 24, 1713.
Died March 18, 1768.

The Celebrated Author
of
"Tristram Shandy"
and
"The Sentimental Journey"
Works unsurpassed in the English language,
For a Richness of Humour and a pathetic sympathy
Which will ever render the Name of their Author
Immortal.

"Requiescat in pace."
The Headstone to this grave
Was Cleaned and Restored, by the owner of the "Sterne"
Property,
At Woodhall, near Halifax, in the County of York,
Who also erected the foot and border stones
In the Year
1893.

As if Sterne's death had been expected in the north, his Yorkshire parishes and the prebendal stall which he held in St. Peter's, were immediately filled by men who were waiting for them. On March 25, or within three or four days after the news of Sterne's death could have reached York, the Rev. Andrew Cheap was collated to Sutton-on-the-Forest, and Dr. William Worthington to the canonry and prebend of North Newbald. Two weeks afterwards Lord Fauconberg nominated the Rev. Thomas Newton to Coxwold, and the Archbishop of York signed the license on the nineteenth of April.* Into these transactions one might read unusual haste, were it not that ecclesiastical business of this kind was always quickly despatched at York and elsewhere in the old days. None of Sterne's successors, family, or friends, as has been often remarked, placed a mural tablet to his memory at Coxwold or at Sutton. This neglect, at first sight rather strange, is sufficiently accounted for by the fact that he died out of his parishes. Where the body lies should be the monument, was then the rule.

Shandy Hall, by the roadside beyond the church at Coxwold, apparently never again used as the parsonage, was occupied for a time by a local surgeon, who let it fall into disrepair. After his death, its owner, Sir George Wombwell of Newburgh Priory, a descendant of Lord Fauconberg, turned the old rambling house into laborers' tenements, blocking up in the process inner passages and turning two of the lead-pane windows into

* Institutions of the Diocese of York, and *York Courant*, April 5, 1768.

outer doorways. Fortunately the desecrating hand barely touched Sterne's study with its great yawning fireplace; and in amends for the past, a bronze tablet has since been placed by the gateway, saying to all travellers:

> Shandy Hall
> Here dwelt Laurence Sterne
> Many Years incumbent
> of Coxwold.
> Here he wrote Tristram Shandy
> And the Sentimental Journey.
> Died in London in 1768
> Aged 55 Years

Thus little by little the author of *Tristram Shandy* has been accorded those slight emblems of fame which untoward circumstances rather than anything else denied him immediately after death. Once or twice Sterne expressed a wish that, should he die at home, his body might be laid by the side of his great-grandfather, the archbishop, in the cathedral at York. Although hardly hoping for this honor, he seems to have expected that a marble replica of the Nollekens bust would sometime be placed to his memory near the tomb of his most distinguished ancestor.*

* A marble replica was made for John Hall-Stevenson. It is now at Skelton Castle.

CHAP. XXII.

Lydia and her Mother. Posthumous Sermons and Letters

NO will was found among Sterne's papers. On the fourth of June following his death, letters for the administration of his goods were granted the widow in the Prerogative Court of York, which was still presided over by Francis Topham, the meddler whom Sterne had silenced in the *History of a Good Warm Watch-Coat*. Mrs. Sterne's sureties on the customary bond entered at the same time were two friends of the family, Arthur Ricord, father and son, attorneys at York. The document was signed and sealed in the presence of Robert Jubb the notary, another of their friends. As indicative of the valuation placed upon Sterne's effects, the sureties jointly bound themselves to the sum of £500. No inventory of goods was ever exhibited for comparison with this valuation, but the estimate was nearly correct. Indeed, Sterne's personal effects had already been sold, and all claims upon his estate had been called in by Mr. Ricard the senior, to whom Mrs. Sterne delegated the details of administration. Thus, without strict legal authority, an auction was held out at Shandy Hall, on April 14, for the sale of "all the household goods and furniture of the late Mr. Sterne, . . . with a cow, . . . a parcel of hay, a handsome post-chaise with a pair of exceeding good horses, and a compleat set of coloured table-china." To tempt purchasers, the china was placed on exhibition at a shop in York, and the horses at Bluitt's Inn in Lendal Street, whence the fastest post-chaises set out for London. Sterne's books, including the lot which he had purchased "dirt cheap" a few years before, were sold to Todd and Sotheran at the sign of the Golden Bible in Stonegate, in whose catalogue for 1768 they were advertised to the public. The books brought £80 as

John Hall-Stevenson
From a painting at Skelton Castle

against £60 for the horses and chaise. From the sale of Sterne's personal effects altogether was realized about £400.*

Against these assets were funeral expenses, and debts, Lydia wrote to Wilkes, amounting to £1100, which must have been the slow accumulation of several years. According to Sterne's account-book, which came under the eye of John Croft, the author received "£1500 of Dodsley at different times for his publications"; and Becket should have paid him quite as much more. The £3000 had all gone in visits to London, in foreign travel, and in the maintenance of wife and daughter abroad. Had the Sternes been good managers, their income from various sources might have proved adequate for their new mode of living, but they were all improvident. Ever since their first sojourn in France, the head of the family had been borrowing small sums from this or that acquaintance—ten, twenty, or fifty pounds here and there—and binding therefor the whole Shandy household until the appearance of a forthcoming instalment of his book. The *Sentimental Journey*, Sterne had hoped, would put him even with the world and enable him, after the sale of his real estate, to make permanent provision for his family.

In the midst of these expectations Sterne died, and the day of reckoning with his creditors was at hand for his widow. From all sides bills came flocking in—for shoes from London, twenty-five pounds for wine from a York merchant, and so on and so forth. Wishing to avoid the disgrace of insolvency, Mrs. Sterne "nobly engaged" to pay off little by little all of her husband's debts out of the rent of the lands at Sutton which had been purchased with the "fortune" she brought him at the time of their marriage, and which yielded forty or fifty pounds a year. At this juncture Hall-Stevenson, with the assistance of Miss A. Moritt of York, a friend of Mrs. Montagu's, came to the rescue of the family by raising a subscription at the

* The auction at Shandy Hall was advertised in the *York Courant*, April 12, 1768. Among Sterne's books which went to Todd and Sotheran were Béroalde's *Moyen de Parvenir*, Bouchet's *Serées*, and Bruscambille's *Pensées Facétieuses.*—See Willis's *Current Notes*, April, 1854.

York races in the following August, which amounted to more than eight hundred guineas. "Nothing less than five guineas" would be accepted from any one person. Lord Rockingham and Sir George Savile headed the list with fifty. Lord Scarborough put his name down for thirty-five, and the Archbishop of York for ten. It was understood that the handsome purse was for Lydia's benefit only, perhaps to be converted into an annuity; for Mrs. Sterne, Miss Moritt wrote to Mrs. Montagu, "was so little liked or esteemed, there would not have been a single guinea given if that condition had not been made." Later in the year, John Craufurd, out of "the sincere regard he had for Mr. Sterne," sent in upwards of a hundred guineas, which he collected from his friends, among whom were several of the gentlemen that were dining with him on the day of Sterne's death. There was also a gift from Lord Spencer. In addition to all this, Mrs. Montagu promised Lydia twenty pounds a year; and the Archbishop of York made application for a pension of six or eight pounds for Mrs. Sterne to be paid out of a fund established for the widows of clergymen.*

All of Sterne's personal debts seem to have been eventually paid with the exception of certain notes never presented by his most intimate friends. It proved to be unnecessary to sell any of Sterne's real estate, or to draw upon the subscription money. There was, however, one claim against Sterne's estate which the widow stoutly resisted on the advice of her attorney. The parsonage-house at Sutton, which burned to the ground three years before, still lay in ashes, though Sterne "had been frequently admonished and required to rebuild" it. As vicar of the parish, Sterne was liable for any impairment to the value of the living while he held it. But in this case were two extenuating circumstances which might be pleaded against strict en-

---

* For these and other details, see Lydia's letters to Wilkes and Hall-Stevenson in J. Almon, *The Correspondence of the late John Wilkes*, V, 7-20 (London, 1805). See also *Whitefoord Papers*, 230-231; *Memoirs* prefixed to Sterne's *Works* (Dublin, 1779); and especially R. Blunt, *Mrs. Montagu*, I, 195-213.

forcement of the law. The house had been set on fire while Sterne was not in residence—by a careless curate or by some member of his family, from whom it was impossible to recover damages. Again, the house in ashes was not much worse than the house in ruins, such as Sterne found it when he entered upon the living at an expense for repairs which staggered him. Certainly it was not quite just to ask him to build anew to the impoverishment of his estate. Arguing in this way, Sterne easily found means for evading what the Archbishop of York thought the performance of an obvious duty to his parish. At his death came the crisis. His successor, the Rev. Mr. Cheap, after vainly trying persuasion with Mrs. Sterne, brought suit against her for dilapidations; whereupon, in order to escape the payment of damages, she was compelled to pocket her pride and make an oath of insolvency. Thus in danger of recovering nothing, the Rev. Mr. Cheap accepted from Mrs. Sterne £60 in satisfaction for the claim. All this was afterwards recorded by the angry vicar in the parish registry of Sutton in company with his impressions of the Shandy household, and with the statement that the cost of the suit and of rebuilding reached the sum of £576. 13s. 5d.

Among Sterne's effects upon which an appraiser could have placed no certain value, were his manuscripts, consisting of copies or drafts of letters, fragments or passages cast aside in the final revision of *Tristram Shandy*, notes and suggestions for the continuation of the Sentimental Journey through Italy, and an odd lot of eighteen sermons, which the author had rejected in making up his previous volumes for publication. Of such manuscripts as have survived, the letters are particularly interesting. Clearly anticipating their publication after his death, Sterne copied out many of them which had passed between himself and friends into a letter-book, prefaced with the following information for his wife and daughter: "Fothergil I know has some good ones——Garrick some—— Berenger has one or two——Gov. Littleton's Lady (Miss Macartney) numbers——Countess of Edgecomb——Mrs. Moore of Bath——Mrs. Fenton, London——*cum multis* *aliis.*—These all, if collected with the large number of mine and friends in my possession would print and sell to good account. Hall has by him a great number, [which] with those in this book and in my Bureau——and those above——would make four vols. the size of Shandy——they would sell well—and produce 800 pds. at the least."*

There were other letters and papers also which Sterne had with him in London when he died. At the request of Mrs. Sterne, her brother-in-law, the Rev. John Botham, who then had a parish at Ealing, took charge of all "the loose papers" he could find in the Bond Street lodgings, along with Sterne's wearing-apparel and trinkets. Everything for which there was a ready purchaser was sold, except Sterne's gold snuff-box, which was given as a present to Hall-Stevenson. The manuscripts Mrs. Sterne directed should be sent down to her. This the Rev. Mr. Botham refused to do. He destroyed a part of them instead. How the evangelical clergyman behaved was told in a letter from Lydia to Mrs. Montagu: "He has read every paper of my poor Father's and has burnt what he did not think proper to communicate to us.—It was not Mama's intention that anyone shou'd read my Father's papers, well knowing that there was some amongst them which ought not to have been seen, no not even by his daughter, nor shou'd I have wished to see one of them. Mama is very much chagrin'd at this, for notwithstanding she can perhaps rely on Mr. Botham's secrecy yet it grieves that even he should be so well acquainted with certain anecdotes. But to burn any paper was very wrong. I hope he will cease so doing and leave that care to Mama."†

Did the comic "Romance" which Sterne was writing when the influenza attacked him go into the fire? Probably. But some of the letters (among them a few to Mrs. Draper) escaped the "pious holocaust," and eventually came into Mrs. Sterne's hands or were seen by her. All the manuscripts that

---

* Some leaves of this old letter-book form a part of the Sterne Manuscripts in the Pierpont Morgan Library. See chapter XXV.

† R. Blunt, *Mrs. Montagu.* I, 199.

could be brought together were carefully examined later by widow and daughter with a view to profit rather than to the enhancement of Sterne's fame. For the present it seemed best to hold the letters, which required editing, for further consideration and to publish as soon as possible the sermons, which might go to the world without much editorial supervision, under the patronage of Mrs. Montagu and Sterne's other friends.

Many local subscribers sent in their names through the winter; and then in the spring Mrs. Sterne and Lydia left York for London to complete the list on the way to France, where they had decided to settle in some quiet place. While in town, they lodged with a "Mr. Williams, paper-merchant,"* in Gerrard Street near the Jameses, who showed them every courtesy and kindness. Through the Jameses and Mrs. Montagu or on their own initiative, they met scores of Sterne's London acquaintances, to whom they told a melancholy story, and gained thereby the coveted subscriptions. In this business, Lydia, who figured as the type of beauty in distress, took the leading part. Adopting the style and manner of her father, she sat in' her lodgings despatching requests about town for aid in obtaining subscriptions, or for permission to visit her father's more influential friends in order to make a personal plea in the interest of her mother. "Mrs. and Miss Sterne's compliments," began a formal note in Lydia's hand to John Wilkes, just committed to the King's Bench prison, "wait on Mr. Wilkes. They intend doing themselves the pleasure of calling upon him, if not disagreeable; and would be obliged to him if he would appoint an hour when he will not be engaged. They would not intrude; yet should be happy to see a person whom they honour, and whom Mr. Sterne justly admired. They will, when they see Mr. Wilkes, entreat him to ask some of his friends to subscribe to three volumes of Mr. Sterne's Sermons, which they are now publishing. . . . The simple story of our situation will, I doubt not, engage Mr. Wilkes to do what he can." This and similar appeals brought

* The address is given in Wilkes's List of Addresses (British Museum, Additional MSS., 30892).

the number of subscribers up to seven hundred and twenty-nine, a larger, though not more distinguished, list than any that had appeared before Sterne's books during his life-time.

In negotiating with the publishers, Lydia came perilously near sharp practice. As first planned, the sermons were to go to Becket, who made a liberal offer for the copyright; but as the day of publication approached, he demanded a year's credit and otherwise assumed arbitrary airs, to the great annoyance of the widow and daughter, who stood in need of money to take them into France. Thereupon Lydia, resolving to sell the copyright to the highest bidder, sent Becket's final terms to William Strahan, a rival publisher in the Strand, along with the following letter:

"I enclose you Mr. Beckett's proposal—when he last offer'd £400 for the copyright he insisted on no such terms as these ——this affair of not offering them to anyone else must be managed with the greatest caution—for you see he says that he will not take them if offer'd elsewhere. He will be judge of the quantity and quality——and insists on a year's credit. All these points my mother and myself most earnestly desire you to consider.——Unless you could be pretty sure of getting us more than £400, the offering them might perhaps come to Becket's knowledge——yet believe me, Sir, we had rather anyone had them than Becket——he is a *dirty fellow*."

In the end was effected some sort of compromise, whereby Mrs. Sterne and Lydia may have received £400 in cash for the first edition and for the copyright, which was purchased by a small group of publishers formed by Strahan, Cadell, and Becket. Under their joint auspices appeared, near the first of June, 1769, "Sermons by the late Rev. Mr. Sterne," comprising volumes five, six, and seven of the complete issue. Subscribers' books, it was announced in the newspapers, would be delivered by Becket. The price of the set was 7s. 6d.

In fear of this posthumous collection of miscellaneous sermons, Sterne humorously described them three years before as "the sweepings of the Author's study after his death." This remark of Sterne's was one of the reasons why Becket hesitated to publish them. Lydia, lacking in the humorous imagination of her father, countered by saying that any one of her father's sermons was as good as another, that he always kept them in a bag and when he wanted one "shaked" it up and took the first one that came. Notwithstanding Lydia's remembrance, the extant manuscript* of the "Temporal Advantages of Religion," written all over with corrections, tells another story. It is certain that Sterne had considered the publication of sermons contained in these volumes, revising, curtailing, and adding to them; but rightly decided after a little thought that they had better be kept from the light, for they were mostly ordinary parish homilies, good enough for the nonce, but altogether too commonplace for an audience that should include the nobility and gentry of the kingdom. And beyond this, the sermons abounded in repetitions, not only of thought but of phrase and sentence, sometimes to the extent of a paragraph or more. Half of the sermon entitled the "Thirtieth of January," to cite an extreme instance, on the "great trespass" of our forefathers in putting to death Charles the First, was taken bodily over into "The Ingratitude of Israel." Among these sermons occurs, too, the most flagrant act of plagiarism that has ever been charged against Sterne. In 1697, Walter Leightonhouse, late Fellow of Lincoln College, Oxford, and then Prebendary of Lincoln, published twelve sermons which he had preached in his cathedral. It was a volume of rather mediocre sermons by a rather obscure clergyman, which Sterne freely appropriated on urgent occasions when a sermon must be prepared on short notice. How closely Sterne followed Leightonhouse the curious may see by comparing the two preachers on the text "Put thou thy trust in the Lord." Sterne did hardly more than paraphrase him.

The Prebendary of Lincoln, in closing, said:

"And although the Fig-tree should not blossom, neither should fruit be in the Vine; although the Labour of the Olive should fail, and the Fields should yield no Meat; although the Flock should be cut off from the Fold, and there should be no

* Formerly in the library of Mr. W. K. Bixby of St. Louis.

Herd in the Stall; yet let us rejoice in the Lord, let us joy in the God of our Salvation."

And the Prebendary of York, by this time aweary of his task, copied out his brother nearly word for word:

"Although the fig-tree shall not blossom, neither shall fruit be in the vines;——although the labour of the olive shall fail, and the fields shall yield no meat;——although the flock shall be cut off from the fold, and there shall be no herd in the stalls; yet we will rejoice in the Lord, and joy in the God of our salvation.——"*

These are but examples of the manner in which Sterne revamped old sermons, whether written by himself or by others, in the business of his parish. A sermon entitled "Evil," to pursue the subject further, closes with a passage from a sermon on the "Advantages of Christianity"; and across the manuscript of sermon forty-four, justifying the ways of Providence to man, Sterne wrote that it was mostly borrowed from Wollaston. Still other sermons, like "Penances" and "On Enthusiasm," whether original or not in their phrasing, merely reflect the violent hatred against the Church of Rome prevalent in '45, a phase of passion through which Sterne had long since passed. And it seems almost impossible that a sermon could ever have come from Yorick's pen so tame and lifeless as the one on the "Sanctity of the Apostles."

In compensation for these inanities, Sterne is still visible here and there at his very best. It is Sterne the humorist who, on rising into the pulpit, reads two texts for the sermon on "Evil"—one from St. Paul and one from Solomon—and then, looking over his congregation, says: "Take either as you like it, you will get nothing by the bargain." Again it is Sterne the eloquent preacher who draws a portrait of the young George the Third under the guise of Asa, the peaceful king, who received his sceptre from the warlike Abijah. "His experience told him," says the preacher weightily of the young king,

* For this comparison, see Sterne's thirty-fourth sermon, and Leightonhouse's twelfth sermon in *Twelve Sermons preached at the Cathedral Church of Lincoln* (London, 1697). See also *Habakkuk*, 3, 17-18.

"that the most successful wars, instead of invigorating, more generally drained away the vitals of government,—and, at the best, ended but in a brighter and more ostentatious kind of poverty and desolation:——therefore he laid aside his sword, and studied the arts of ruling Judah with peace.——Conscience would not suffer Asa to sacrifice his subjects to private views of ambition, and wisdom forbade he should suffer them to offer up themselves to the pretence of public ones;——since enlargement of empire, by the destruction of its people (the natural and only valuable source of strength and riches), was a dishonest and miserable exchange.——And however well the glory of a conquest might appear in the eyes of a common beholder, yet, when bought at that costly rate, a father to his country would behold the triumphs which attended it, and weep, as it passed by him."

Finally, monotonies over "the degeneracy of the times" or "the wickedness of the world" are relieved by Sterne's descriptions of high life as he had seen it, wherein religion has become "a standing jest to enliven discourse when conversation sickens," and wherein are admitted men however infamous their character, and women however abandoned, "to be courted, caressed, and flattered." These fashionable people were exhorted in another sermon to search the Scriptures, if not for moral improvement, at least for æsthetic enjoyment. "There are two sorts of eloquence," the preacher told them; "the one indeed scarce deserves the name of it, which consists chiefly in laboured and polished periods, an over-curious and artificial arrangement of figures, tinsell'd over with a gaudy embellishment of words, which glitter, but convey little or no light to the understanding. . . . The other sort of eloquence is quite the reverse to this, and which may be said to be the true characteristic of the holy Scriptures; where the excellence does not arise from a laboured and far-fetched elocution, but from a surprising mixture of simplicity and majesty, which is a double character, so difficult to be united, that it is seldom to be met with in compositions merely human." These two types of eloquence Sterne then proceeded to illustrate in a running

parallel between great passages in Greek and Hebrew literature. If in the end he did not exactly prove the superiority of
the Bible over the classical literatures, he most ably presented
and defended a thesis novel to his audience. It would indeed be
hard to find, as Cardinal Newman once pointed out, anything
better than Sterne's on the "simplicity and majesty" of the
Old Testament.*

While publishing the sermons, widow and daughter formed
other projects for turning Sterne's popularity into money; in
one of which they were anticipated by Hall-Stevenson. It is
doubtful whether they could have pieced together in any sort
of narrative the notes left by Sterne towards the concluding
volumes of the *Sentimental Journey*, which had been promised
to subscribers at this time. Still, they must have been surprised
when Eugenius appeared in London with the manuscript of
Yorick's Sentimental Journey completed in two volumes, to
which was prefixed a short memoir of Sterne, remarkable for
its inaccuracies and the advertisement that the work had been
based upon the "facts, events, and observations" of the last
part of Mr. Sterne's travels abroad, as related to the author in
the intimacy of friendship. Despite his claim, Hall-Stevenson
merely re-told the familiar incidents of the *Sentimental Journey*, everywhere vulgarizing them. It was the author's plan to
represent Yorick as re-visiting the old scenes and describing the
changes wrought by a year or two. The grisette of silken eyelashes was glad to see her old friend again and to sell him more
gloves. Hearing at Moulins that Maria had just died of a
broken heart, Yorick sought out her grave, that he might shed
a tear upon it as a last tribute to virtue. Of the tour through
Italy, for which all readers were expectant, there was no word.
And yet, without serious censure, this impudent fraud upon the
public easily passed current at home and on the Continent.

Another project was suggested to the Sternes by Wilkes on
one of their visits to his prison. He offered to write for their
benefit the authorized biography of Sterne, provided Hall-
Stevenson, who had just shown his biographical skill, could be

* Sterne's forty-second sermon and Newman's *Idea of a University*.

drawn into partnership with him. Widow and daughter thereupon broached the scheme to the master of Skelton, who readily consented to have his name associated with the man most talked of in England. As her part in the undertaking, Lydia was to collect and arrange her father's correspondence supplementary to the memoir, and to draw a frontispiece for each volume. At near the same time, a new edition of *Tristram Shandy* was also to be brought out in six volumes, with six illustrations—the two well-known ones by Hogarth (Trim's reading the sermon, and the baptism of Tristram), and four new ones by Lydia, of which she submitted three sentimental subjects to Wilkes for his approval: "Maria with the goat, with my father beside her"; "the sick-bed of poor Le Fevre . . . with Uncle Toby and Trim by his bedside"; and "Le Fevre's son with the picture of his mother in his hand, the cushion by his bed-side on which he has just prayed." In the meantime, Becket was to be browbeaten, on the threat of giving the work to another publisher, into promising £400 for the "Life of Mr. Sterne" written by "two men of such genius as Mr. Wilkes and Mr. Hall."

These expectations were doomed from the first to disappointment. Hall-Stevenson, though of the best intentions, was too indolent for the serious labors of a biographer; and Wilkes, just then the centre of the political universe, was too busy with his trial for outlawry, and with manifestoes and Middlesex elections, to employ his pen for others. Lydia had none of the talent necessary for editing her father's letters, and her amateurish drawings would have excited ridicule when brought into competition with Hogarth's masterpieces.

As yet not disillusioned, Mrs. Sterne and her daughter retired for an indefinite period to Angoulême in southern France, where they resumed the genteel life of other days. "Angoulême is a pretty town," Lydia wrote to Wilkes on July 22, 1769, not long after her arrival; "the country most delightful, and from the principal walk there is a very fine prospect; a serpentine river, which joins the Garonne at Bourdeaux, has a very good effect; trees in the middle of it, which form little islands, where the inhabitants go and take the *fresco:*———in short, 'tis a most pleasing prospect; and I know no greater pleasure than sitting by the side of the river, reading Milton or Shakespeare to my mother. Sometimes I take my guitar and sing to her. Thus do the hours slide away imperceptibly; with reading, writing, drawing, and music."

Already the girl had misgivings about the biography. "It is now time," the letter went on to say, "to remind Mr. Wilkes of his kind promise—to exhort him to fulfil it. If you knew, dear sir, how much we are straitened as to our income, you would not neglect it. We should be truly happy to be so much obliged to you that we may join, to our admiration of Mr. Wilkes in his public character, tears of gratitude whenever we hear his name mentioned, for the peculiar service he has rendered us. Much shall we owe to Mr. Hall for that and many other favours; but to you do we owe the kind intention which we beg you to put in practice. As I know Mr. Hall is somewhat lazy, as you were the promoter, write to him yourself: he will be more attentive to what you say." Lydia began to fear, too, that she would be unable to furnish the illustrations for the work without the assistance of a drawing-master. And the correspondence of her father, on further examination, was quite different from what she and her mother expected. *"Entre nous,"* she informed Wilkes, "we neither of us wish to publish those Letters; but if we cannot do otherwise, we will, and prefix the Life to them." A note was earnestly requested from Wilkes, which should be addressed to "Mademoiselle Sterne, demoiselle Angloise, chez Mons. Bologne, Rue Cordeliers," to advise her in her perplexities over the drawings and the letters, and to assure her that in any case Mr. Wilkes would perform his part in the undertaking.

Through the long summer into the autumn, Lydia looked every day for a reply from Wilkes which never came; while in the meantime ready money had disappeared, and all that had been placed with Panchaud was in danger of being lost by the banker's unexpected failure in July. In desperation, Lydia again wrote a pitiable letter to Wilkes, dated October

24, 1769, to remind him once more of his obligations and to hold him up to them if possible. "How long," she pleaded with him, "have I waited with impatience for a letter from Mr. Wilkes, in answer to that I wrote him above two months ago! I fear he is not well; I fear his own affairs have not allowed him time to answer me; in short, I am full of fears. Hope deferred makes the heart sick. Three lines, with a promise of writing Tristram's Life for the benefit of his widow and daughter, would make us happy.——A promise, did I say? that I already have: but a second *assurance*. Indeed, my dear sir, since I last wrote we stand more in need of such an act of kindness. Panchaud's failure has hurt us considerably: we have, I fear, lost more than, in our circumstances, we could afford to lose. Do not, I beseech you, disappoint us: let me have a single line from you, 'I will perform my promise,' and joy will take place of our sorrow. I trust you will write to Hall; in pity, do."

Near the same time, the distressed girl wrote to Hall-Stevenson in similar vein. Autumn passed and winter came on with no word from either of her father's biographers. Upon Wilkes she could intrude no further, but to Hall-Stevenson was sent a last letter, requesting the courtesy of a reply if nothing more:

"Angoulême, Feb. 13, 1770.

"Dear Sir,

" 'Tis at least six months since I wrote to you on an interesting subject to us; namely, to put you in mind of a kind promise you made me, of assisting Mr. Wilkes in the scheme he had formed for our benefit, of writing the Life of Mr. Sterne. I wrote also to him; but you have neither of you favoured me with an answer. If you ever felt what 'hope deferred' occasions, you would not have put us under that painful situation. From whom the neglect arises, I know not; but surely a line from you, dear sir, would not have cost you much trouble. Tax me not with boldness for using the word *neglect:* as you both promised, out of the benevolence of your hearts, to write my father's Life for the benefit of his widow and daughter; and as I myself look upon a promise as sacred, and I doubt not but you think as I do; in that case the word is not improper. In short, dear sir, I ask but this of you; to tell me by a very short letter, whether we may depend on yours and Mr. Wilkes's promise, or if we must renounce the pleasing expectation. But, dear sir, consider that the fulfilling of it may put £400 into our pockets; and that the declining it would be unkind, after having made us hope and depend upon that kindness. Let this plead my excuse.

"If you do not choose to take the trouble to wait on Mr. Wilkes, send him my letter, and let me know the *oui ou le non*. Still let me urge, press, and entreat Mr. Hall, to be as good as his word: if he will interest himself in our behalf, 'twill but be acting consistent with his character; 'twill prove that Eugenius was the friend of Yorick——nothing can prove it stronger than befriending his widow and daughter. Adieu, dear Sir! Believe me your most obliged, humble servant, L. Sterne."

This letter was turned over to Wilkes in accordance with Lydia's request; and therewith ended the project for a biography of Sterne, supplemented by his original letters and embellished with original drawings by his daughter. Throughout the transaction a reader's sympathy at this late date rests with Lydia and her mother, who were betrayed by two affable gentlemen who broke promises as readily as they made them. On the other hand, the conduct of widow and daughter, if not exactly censurable, had been lacking in good taste and respectful consideration for Sterne's memory. All along, their one aim had been to make the most out of his literary remains. They were always short of money. They were always complaining of delay in remittances from their attorney at York, from Becket, from Mrs. James, from Mrs. Montagu. And it was always costing them more to live than they expected. What had become of the thousand guineas on which they were silent? They were restless, ill at ease, in their paradise. They were superior to the people with whom they had to associate. They were shut out from the world with a mere pittance from Mr. Sterne's friends. They looked around everywhere for more money and at length they decided to try Mrs. Draper.

Mrs. Draper, after a long but pleasant voyage, our narrative should explain, had safely reached Bombay early in 1768, "once more restored to health and strength." Her husband she found "in possession of health and a good post," and her sister Louisa, a widow after an unfortunate marriage, now in course of becoming wife to Colonel Pemble, then in command of the military forces at Bombay. "I live intirely in the Country with my dear Louisa," she wrote from High Meadow in the suburbs to her aunt Elizabeth, "bathe in the Sea daily, drink Milk, and have commenced Horsewoman."

This agreeable life with a sister who had grown attractive in her widowhood, had to be given up in the autumn because of Draper's transference to Tellicherry, as chief of the factory at that station. But it so turned out that Mrs. Draper was never happier than during the first months in her new sphere, where, according to the exigencies of the occasion, she played in turn the parts of "wife of a Merchant, soldier and Innkeeper, for in such different capacities," she wrote pleasantly, "is the chief of Tellicherry destined to act." And when her husband lost his two clerks, she took charge for a time of all his correspondence. This temporary position in his office she liked because, she wrote home, "it gives me consequence, and him pleasure." "The Country," to go on further with her intimate letters, "is pleasant, and healthy (a second Montpelier); our house (A Fort and property of the Company), a Magnificent one furnish'd too at our Masters expence and the allowance for supporting it Creditably, what you would term genteely, tho' it does not defray the charges of our Liqours, which alone amount to 600 a year; and such a sum, vast as it seems, is not extravagant in our situation,—for we are obliged to keep a Public Table—and six months in the Year, have a full house of shipping Gentry—that resort to us for traffic and Intelligence, from all parts of India, China, and Asia."

In these new surroundings were resumed the recreations

begun with her sister at High Meadow. "I ride on Horseback daily," she informed her cousin Tom, "I bathe in the Sea, read Volumes, and fill Reams of Paper, writing scribble." To her life at Tellicherry came additional zest from the perilous situation of the settlement at this time, for Hyder Ali and the fierce Mahrattas then held in subjection the territory about the town, and were infesting the coast as far north as Bombay, interfering with traffic on the sea and rendering unsafe passage from one station to another without a convoy. Under these circumstances, Mrs. Draper was always attended in her rides to the beach and in the neighborhood by "a guard of six sepoys armed with drawn Sabres and loaded Pistols," while a faithful Malabar servant followed her everywhere like a shadow. In spite of these precautions for her safety, "I was within a hour once," she wrote of Hyder Ali, "of being his Prisoner——and cannot say, but I thought it a piece of good fortune to escape that honour—tho' he has promised to treat all English Ladies well, that chearfully submit to the Laws of his Seraglio." One letter speaks of sorrow for the death of "our poor little boy" left behind in England with his sister; and there were moments in this uncertain life when she longed for the flatteries of those who told her that she was born for the stage or the salon rather than for India; but as yet Mrs. Draper was content to reign as queen of the little settlement on the Malabar Coast.

Then news reached her out of England, from letters and from all she talked with in the Company's ships, that Mrs. Sterne was threatening to make a public scandal of her relations with Yorick by publishing their correspondence. There was really nothing in those sentimental relations, Mrs. Draper averred in a letter to her cousin Tom, which could not be justified, were truth and candor her judges; but an ungenerous world, she was equally aware, would read whatever it pleased into her letters should they be once published. Under the impending exposure, Mrs. Draper suffered for months keen torture, during which she denounced the whole Sterne family, not omitting Yorick himself, because he had flattered her into an indiscreet correspondence.

As soon, however, as she understood the reason for Mrs. Sterne's conduct, she gained her poise and acted accordingly. On receiving the news of Sterne's death, Mrs. Draper, supposing that Mrs. Sterne was also dead or "privately confined" as an insane person, had immediately sent an invitation to Lydia to come out to the East and share her own prospects as friend and companion. At this letter Mrs. Sterne became furious since it contained no reference to herself, as if she were a nonentity; and Lydia in a belated reply resented the gratuitous interference. In this mood, Lydia and her mother came up to London. Either then or before they obtained some of Mrs. Draper's letters to Sterne, which the Rev. Mr. Botham may have discovered in Sterne's lodgings after his death and for some reason had not burned. There were also in London copies of ten letters from Sterne to Mrs. Draper, which Mrs. Draper herself had thoughtlessly made for some curious friend, just as she had sent one of them to her cousin Tom. These likewise seem to have come into possession of the widow and daughter. A few letters from Mrs. Draper had probably remained at Coxwold along with the draft of a letter to "My dear Bramine."*

At any rate, all or the major part of the correspondence between Yorick and Eliza, it was rumored, would appear among the original letters accompanying the biography by Wilkes and Hall-Stevenson. The truth of this rumor was subsequently confirmed either through Mrs. James or directly by Lydia, who sought to excuse herself and her mother on the score of necessity. Money must be had and the letters were now the only available source. Quick to take the hint, Mrs. Draper wrote to Mrs. James on the impulse of the moment: "O my dear Friend, for God sake, pay them all the money of

---

* See the draft in this biography. It is doubtful whether widow and daughter ever knew of the *Journal to Eliza*. See Margaret R. B. Shaw on "Sterne's Letters to his Wife," in *The Times Literary Supplement*, July 21, 1927.

mine in your Hands——would it were twice as much! the
Ring too is much at Mrs. Sterne's service—as should be every
thing I have in the world, rather than I would freely owe the
shaddow of an obligation to her."

On the tacit if not formal understanding that her letters
should be deposited with Mrs. James, Mrs. Draper promised
to pay Becket whatever he might hope to profit by their publication should they be offered to him, and to make up a generous purse for the Sternes out of India. Fulfilling the essential
half of the promise, she began sending Mrs. James various
small bills for the benefit of Mrs. Sterne and Lydia, which in
the course of two or three years amounted to twelve hundred
rupees. Half of the sum came from the contributions of acquaintances immediately surrounding her; and half was collected at her urgent request by Colonel Donald Campbell of
Barbreck among his fellow officers at Bengal. As an inducement to his share in the work, Mrs. Draper drew a very flattering portrait of Lydia in one of her letters to Colonel Campbell, suggesting that he seek an introduction to Miss Sterne on
his next visit to England and bring her back as his wife. And
to prepare Lydia for his coming, she sent a similar portrait of
the colonel to Mrs. James, saying: "He is, I think, one of ten
thousand—sensible, sweet tempered, and Amiable, to a very
great degree—added to which, lively, comical and accomplished—Young, Handsome, rich, and a Soldier!——What
fine Girl would wish more?"*

For this happy sequel to a transaction which humiliated Mrs.
Draper as much as it discredited Mrs. Sterne, Colonel Campbell arrived in England a year or more too late. Sometime in
the summer of 1770, Mrs. Sterne and Lydia left Angoulême,
migrating south to Albi, a lovely brick-built town on the Tarn,
not far from their old friends at Toulouse. "The situation of
this Village," Lydia wrote to Mrs. Montagu, "is pretty, our
little house is agreeable, but there is little society, and the little

* Colonel Campbell was then twenty-two years old. There is an account of him in James Douglas, *Bombay and Western India*, I, 425-427
(London, 1893).

there is, is scarce worth the trouble of searching after.—Both my mother and myself prefer Books to stupid conversation. And in such a little provincial Town as this the men are ignorant, the women still more so, except in the affair of the Toilet. But in general the French are good natured and sometimes we go amongst them, and return with more pleasure to our Books—I remember my Father complain'd at Toulouse that by conversing much with the French his understanding diminish'd every day."

From Albi on March 23, 1772, Lydia informed Mrs. Montagu, as her godmother, that she had had an offer of marriage, which "tho' not advantageous, yet was far from disagreeable" to her. Her mother objected to the marriage while not absolutely opposing it, Lydia said. There was of course a difference in religion; but the young man, though a Catholic, was no bigot, for he had assured Lydia that she would have as his wife "full liberty" to practice her own religion. What most troubled the girl was that his father "insisted upon very hard terms," namely, that her mother "should give up her estate immediately" as the bride's dower. Mrs. Sterne was "willing almost to leave herself without bread for the advantage of Lydia"; but it made the daughter's heart bleed to think of her mother destitute of all the necessaries of life. At this point in her letter, Lydia fell upon her knees and prayed that Mrs. Montagu, whatever might happen, would not withdraw her bounty of former years. It was "a humble petition" that Mrs. Montagu support Mrs. Sterne so long as she might live.

Mrs. Montagu readily agreed to transfer Lydia's allowance of twenty pounds a year to Mrs. Sterne; but as Lydia's godmother she could not assent to "the momentous affair" of her marriage "with the same good will." About that the woman who knew the world wrote to Lydia: "What I shall say on this subject is not meant to offend the gentleman who you have a desire to marry. I am a perfect stranger to his character, his fortune, and even his name. You do not say anything of them, all you give your friends is that you are going to marry a man of a different religion, and to reduce your mother to almost beggary, both these things you confess. You seem at the same time to declare steadfastness in religion and filial piety to your parent. My dear cousin, the actions not the words are what shall decide the judgment of God and man. If your husband has any zeal or regard for his religion he will be earnest to make you embrace it from regard to you and reverence to God; if he is void of religion he will think such a mark of your complaisance a trifle, and the authority of the husband will interpose where faith stands neuter. Your children must of necessity be ———"

Lydia was unable to heed the advice. The rest of the story is told by the archives of Albi. On April 28, 1772, Lydia Sterne abjured the Protestant religion in the private chapel of the provost's house, and was thereupon admitted to the Roman Catholic Church in order to remove the last obstacle to her marriage on the same day and in the same place with Jean Baptiste Alexandre de Medalle, described as only twenty years old, while Lydia was in her twenty-fifth year. The young man belonged to a good family, being the son of a gentleman employed in the Customs at Albi under the title of *receveur des décimes*. "*Le mariage*," it stands written in the *Inventaire des Archives Communales d'Albi*, "*était forcé, urgent; car alors la loi autorisait la recherche de la paternité*."* Attempts have been made to explain away this extraordinary gloss on the marriage; but its meaning should be clear to all who read, as much as if it said in an Englishman's blunt French: "*Mademoiselle Sterne était déjà à l'époque de son mariage en chemin de devenir mère*." By one of the ironies of fate a letter was on its way from Mrs. Draper at the very time of the inauspicious marriage, recommending to Miss Sterne the favorable reception of Colonel Campbell.

Mrs. Sterne, who was then very ill, did not witness the

---

* For the record of Lydia's marriage, the birth of a son, and Mrs. Sterne's death, see *Athenæum*, June 18, 1870; and *Notes and Queries*, fourth series, VI, 153, and XII, 200. The search in the archives of Albi was originally made by Paul Stapfer. His account as published contains several inaccuracies which are here corrected.

scene in the provost's chapel. Since coming into France she had been relapsing into her old malady. The hallucinations of pre-Shandean days returned. One night she imagined that an ugly man was descending the chimney on a rope with the intent to kill her with a large knife; and thereafter all the chimneys of the house at Albi had to be kept grated. Epileptic fits followed. Sometime in January, 1773, within a year of her daughter's marriage, Mrs. Sterne died at Albi—at the house of a physician named Lionières, at No. 9 Rue St. Antoine, within sight of the noble towers of Sainte Cécile. So ended the life of the vivacious Miss Lumley of the York Assembly Rooms, whose unhappiness began with her husband's fame.

As a dramatic close to the career of Lydia, has grown up a story that she and her husband took an active part in the French Revolution and fell victims to the Reign of Terror. In place of this legend can be presented only a few disjointed facts, not half so striking as the conclusion to the old historical romances dealing with the French Revolution, and yet really quite as tragic as any of them. During the autumn after Mrs. Sterne's death, Mrs. Medalle and her husband disposed of all the real estate at Sutton-in-the-Forest, very likely with the aid of the squire of Stillington. The Tindall or Dawson farm and the lands purchased of Richard Harland were conveyed by herself and husband (described in the deed as "gentleman") to the mortgagees, Dean Fountayne and Stephen Croft. The dwellings and closes which came to Sterne under the Sutton Enclosure Act were purchased in part by Thomas Proud of Newburgh and in part by Robert Wright of Claxton. All the conveyances bore as witnesses to the signatures of the Medalles, it may be of interest to note, the names of Jean François Gardes and Guierre Limory of Albi, who, we may suppose, were friends of the family.* Of Lydia's youthful husband there is only one word more. He died a year and some months later, leaving with his widow a son born soon after the marriage.

* Three deeds comprising the transaction were registered at North-allerton, one on May 4, and the other two on May 30, 1774.

Mrs. Medalle now took up again her father's correspondence, the publication of which had been deferred rather than
abandoned on the withdrawal of Wilkes and Hall-Stevenson
from the undertaking. For performing the labor alone she
received much encouragement from the attitude of the public,
which was absorbing every year sentimental tales and journeys put out in imitation of the original, while an anecdote
of the humorist or a letter purporting to be his found ready
admittance to newspapers and magazines. The first number of
the *Lady's Magazine,* for example, which was started in 1770,
opened with "A Sentimental Journey by a Lady," and three
years later a periodical called the *Sentimental Magazine* was
launched for promoting the sentimental style and philosophy
of the "inimitable" Yorick. The eagerness of the public to
read something more of Sterne's, or to know more about him,
led to many forgeries, of which may be mentioned an imaginary autobiography, eked out by moral sayings, that appeared
in 1770, bearing the title of *The Posthumous Works of a late
Celebrated Genius,* since known as *The Koran,* under which
name the forgery has been several times published in editions
of Sterne's works aiming at completeness. Its author, it should
have been known, was Richard Griffith the elder, who betted
with a friend that he could write a book which "would pass
current on the world as a writing of Mr. Sterne"; and won
(as he said himself) the bet.* Not much, however, really
Sterne's, appeared between 1769 and 1773, when somebody
edited and published ten letters from Sterne to Mrs. Draper,
which served to float more forgeries, sometimes interspersed
with genuine scraps.

As if her arrival had been timed to profit most by this
awakened interest in Sterne, Mrs. Medalle came to London
in the spring of 1775, with a rare collection of letters, which
she and Mrs. Sterne had brought together before going into
France, and to which additions were still to be made through
the summer. The daughter of Sterne took genteel lodgings, sat

* See Griffith's anonymous *Something New,* II, 152 (second edition,
London, 1772).

for her portrait, and altogether displayed her father's skill in whetting the public appetite for a new book by talk about it long in advance of publication.

"*Speedily will be published,*" as she and Becket phrased the advertisement for the newspapers, "Embellished with an elegant engraving of Mrs. Medalle, from a picture by Mr. West, (with a dedication to Mr. GARRICK) SOME MEMOIRS of the LIFE and FAMILY of the late Mr. LAURENCE STERNE. Written by Himself. To which will be added, 1. Genuine Letters to his most intimate friends on various subjects, with those to his wife, before and after marriage; as also those written to his daughter. 2. A Fragment, in the manner of Rabelais. Now first published by his daughter (Mrs. Medalle) from the originals in her father's hand-writing.

"Printed for T. Becket, Adelphi, in the Strand.

"Mrs. Medalle begs leave to return her most grateful thanks to those Ladies and Gentlemen who have already favoured her with so many of her father's letters, and still intreats those who may have any by them, to send them to her Bookseller as above, (as speedily as possible) that they may be inserted in the edition now prepared for the press."

After repeated advertisements of this kind, the letters and miscellanies—three volumes in the whole—were at length published on October 25, 1775. The title was varied from the announcement to "LETTERS of the late Rev. Mr. LAURENCE STERNE, to his most intimate FRIENDS. With a FRAGMENT in the Manner of *Rabelais*. To which are prefix'd, MEMOIRS of His LIFE AND FAMILY. Written by HIMSELF. And Published by his Daughter, Mrs. MEDALLE." The portrait by West, which was engraved by Caldwall for a frontispiece, represented Lydia in the fashionable dress of the period bending over the bust of her father, with one hand resting on his laurelled head and the other holding a sheet of manuscript. In no better taste was the dedication to Garrick, which aimed helplessly at the whimsical style of Sterne. A brief preface, following Garrick's epitaph, assured the public that the authenticity of the letters might be depended upon. Some of them, said Mrs. Medalle, had been preserved by her mother, and others had been furnished by her father's friends, from whom she had "experienced much benevolence and generosity." Then followed two elegies, reprinted from the magazines, in one of which Sterne was ranked next to Shakespeare. After these introductory details, came the brief autobiography that Sterne wrote near his death to satisfy Lydia's curiosity, and one hundred and eighteen letters, if we count *An Impromptu* forming part of a letter which was sent to the publisher by a certain S. P., living at Exeter. The third volume concluded with *The Fragment in the Manner of Rabelais*, which appears to have been a discarded digression originally written for the fourth volume of *Tristram Shandy*.

The autobiography was a masterly piece of condensation, what the French call a *précis*, wherein one continuous paragraph, running over a few pages, sufficed the author for the story of his ancestry and of his life down to the first visit to France, to say nothing of whimsical comment and anecdote by the way. No wonder that the marvellous sketch, as the first authentic revelation of Sterne in the pre-Shandean period, was widely quoted in magazines and newspapers, where it was usually given the place of honor on the first page. And for Sterne in his intimacies were the sentimental outpourings of the young Prebendary of York in letters to Miss Lumley while she was away in the country; descriptions of his doings in London in the first flush of his fame, sent down to his friend Stephen Croft, the squire of Stillington; reckless impromptus to Hall-Stevenson and the London smart set; promises of amendment to Warburton; his first French triumph all written out for Garrick; and his last letter to Mrs. James as he lay dying. Surely no one could ask for more. Walpole of course intended a compliment when he wrote to Mason two days after publication: "I have run through a volume of Sterne's *Letters*, and have read more unentertaining stuff."

In view of the rich material that Mrs. Medalle thus presented to the public, perhaps one should not be too insistent on her shortcomings as an editor. Misprints, mistakes in French phrases, and misnumbering of letters may be set down, if one wishes, to the ignorance of the compositor. Neither should a reader complain overmuch because proper names were suppressed, or indicated by their first and last letters or by an initial before a dash or a line of stars, for such was the custom of the day. People then liked to guess that D——d G——k, Esq., meant David Garrick, Esq., and to count the eight stars of the Earl of S * * * * * * * into the Earl of Shelburne. The task of editing Sterne's letters, it must be admitted further, would have been difficult for anyone however skilled, since many of them bore no date. Still, Mrs. Medalle cannot be excused for making slight attempt to place them in chronological sequence, for throwing them together, as it were, helter-skelter, so that they tell no continuous story. She began by assigning the Croft letters of 1760 to the indefinite period before the appearance of *Tristram Shandy*, and, with some improvements here and there, she proceeded in this slip-shod path to the end. It would, indeed, be difficult to find in the entire range of literary biography a more shiftless piece of work.

To incompetency Mrs. Medalle added an amusing dishonesty wherever her mother or Mrs. Draper was concerned. The merry references to Mrs. Sterne were eliminated from all the correspondence except the Latin epistle to Hall-Stevenson, which Lydia evidently could not read, else she would never have permitted to stand: "*Nescio quid est materia cum me, sed sum fatagatus et ægrotus de meâ uxore plus quam unquam.*" And in all the sentimental passages on Eliza, her portrait, and her journal, the editor either substituted her own name or removed the warmth of phrase, leaving them quite cool and harmless. Just how she did this, it will be pleasant to see. To a letter from Coxwold to the Jameses in the summer of 1767, Sterne appended a long postscript from which we have already quoted:

"I have just received as a present from a right Honourable a most elegant gold snuff fabricated for me at Paris——I wish Eliza was here, I would lay it at her feet——however,

I will enrich my gold Box, with her picture,——and if the Donor does not approve of such an acquisition to his pledge of friendship—I will send him his Box again——

"May I presume to inclose you the Letter I write to Mrs. Draper——I know you will write yourself——and my Letter may have the honour to chaperon yours to India. Mrs. Sterne and my daughter are coming to stay a couple of months with [me], as far as from Avignion—and then return——Here's Complaisance for you——I went five hundred miles the last Spring, out of my way, to pay my wife a week's visit—and she is at the expence of coming post a thousand miles to return it— what a happy pair!——however, en passant, she takes back sixteen hundred pounds into France with her—and will do me the honour likewise to strip me of every thing I have—except Eliza's Picture. Adieu."

After passing through Lydia's hands, the postscript came out reduced to the following brief paragraph:

"I have just received, as a present from a man I shall ever love, a most elegant gold snuff box, fabricated for me at Paris ——'tis not the first pledge I have received of his friendship. ——May I presume to enclose you a letter of chit-chat which I shall write to Eliza? I know you will write yourself, and my letter may have the honour to *chaperon* yours to India——they will neither of them be the worse received for going together in company, but I fear they will get late in the year to their destined port, as they go first to Bengal."

The motives for most of these changes are apparent enough. But why "a right Honourable"—meaning, it would seem, Sir George Macartney—should be turned into "a man I shall ever love" is an enigma. Whether mutilations like this extend generally through the letters edited by Mrs. Medalle, there are no means of determining, for few of the originals have come to light. It would of course be unfair to infer from one or two instances that Lydia everywhere played fast and loose with the text; it is more likely that she was content, unless her mother and Mrs. Draper were involved, merely to improve her father's style by substituting here and there a commonplace expression for his piquant phrases.

Her mission to England over, Mrs. Medalle returned to Albi. The rest of her story may be told, so far as one knows it, in a single sentence. Her son was placed in the Benedictine school at Sorèze, where he died in 1783, his mother, it was expressly stated, being already dead. Asthmatic from childhood, Lydia, who wrote to Mrs. Montagu in 1771 that she was very thin and in very bad health, had doubtless succumbed to the same disease that her father so long struggled against only to be overcome in the end. The little boy, "not made to last long," any more than were Sterne's brothers and sisters, was the last descendant of the humorist.

CHAP. XXIII.

Mrs. Elizabeth Draper

MRS. DRAPER, too, was already dead after an eventful career since we last saw her as queen of Tellicherry, attended in her progresses by a guard of sepoys. In 1771, her husband was appointed chief of the factory at Surat, the most lucrative position he had yet held, whence she wrote on her birthday a long letter to her cousin Tom descriptive of a typical day with friends amid the new scenes.* Every morning she rose with the lark and ambled out on her palfrey eight or ten miles, after the fox sometimes, and at rarer intervals joining large parties in the hunt for antelopes with leopards. At night there was an occasional dance followed by supping on a cool terrace till daybreak. But despite exercise in the open air and an abstemious diet, consisting of "soupe and vegetables with sherbet and milk," her health, she complained, was breaking under the fierce heats of Surat; and scandal, do what she might, persisted in pursuing her, all because she liked the conversation of sensible men better than the unmeaning chit-chat of the women around her. Far from being the "gay, dissipated, agreeable woman" that she was accounted by "the worldly wise," she would have much preferred to the life she was living at Surat the quiet of a "thatched palace" in England, with her books and an appreciative husband v ho could moralize with her the rural scene.

The next year, Draper was removed from his position at Surat and recalled to Bombay, not because of any inefficiency on his part, but owing, it was said, to a cabal formed against him. "We are adventurers again," Mrs. Draper wrote home from Bombay, "and so much to seek for Wealth as we were

* The account of Mrs. Draper is based mostly upon manuscript letters, some of which have been published by Wright and Sclater in *Sterne's Eliza*. See also a chapter on Mrs. Draper and incidental references to her in James Douglas, *Bombay and Western India*.

the first Day of our landing here." Neither husband nor wife was able to withstand adversity, though but temporary. There were hot altercations between them, culminating in criminations and recriminations which need be touched on but lightly. The ostensible point of dispute, to begin with, was over Mrs. Draper's return to England. Her husband, she claimed, had distinctly promised her that she might be with her daughter on her twelfth birthday, occurring in October, 1773. A longer sojourn in India, she often repeated, would mean a ruined constitution and quick-coming death. Draper, who perhaps did not deny his promise, pleaded the expense of the journey and of a life apart. If his wife's health were declining, she might follow the advice of her physician and visit the neighboring hot springs, which were as good as any in England.

The troubles between husband and wife were reaching an acute stage in the spring of 1772, when Mrs. Draper described her unhappy situation in two letters home—one to her cousin Tom and one to Mrs. James, which, taken together, really constitute an autobiography covering more than a hundred pages of print. Now thoroughly disillusioned, Mrs. Draper passed in review her trivial education, the ill-starred marriage to a "cool, phlegmatic" official, who was accusing her of intrigues which she had no opportunity of forming were she disposed to them, the friendship with Sterne, the efforts to aid his widow and daughter, her literary aims and ambitions, and the sorrow that was fast settling close upon her. Of Sterne she said, "I was almost an Idolator of His Worth, while I fancied him the Mild, Generous, Good Yorick, we had so often thought him to be." But "his Death," she must add with words underscored, "gave me to know, that he was tainted with the Vices of Injustice, meanness and Folly."

Of herself and husband, she wrote to Mrs. James: "I cannot manage to acquire confirmed Health in this detested Country; and what is far worse, I cannot induce Mr. Draper to let me return to England; tho' he must be sensible, that both my Constitution and Mind, are suffering by the effects of a Warm Climate——I do, and must wonder that he will not, for what good Purpose my Residence here can promote, I am quite at a loss to imagine, as I am disposed to think favorably of Mr. D's Generosity and Principles. My dear James, it is evident to the whole of our Acquaintance, that our Minds are not pair'd, and therefore I will not scruple informing *you*—that I neither do, nor will any more, if I can help it live with him as a Wife ——my reasons for this are cogent; be assured they are;—or I would not have formed the Resolution——I explain them not to the World—tho' I could do it, and with credit to myself; but for that very cause I will persevere in my silence ——as I love not selfish Panegyricks.——How wretched must be that Woman's Fate, my dear James, who loving Home, and having a Taste for the Acquitments [*sic*], both useful and Agreable, can find nothing congenial in her Partner's Sentiments—nothing companionable, nothing engagingly domestic in his Manner, to endear his Presence, nor even any thing of that Great, or respectful sort, which creates Public Praise, and by such means, often lays the Foundation of Esteem, and Complacency at Home."

The sad record was relieved by many charming feminine traits of character and ennobled by the mother yearning to be with her daughter left behind in England.

One aspect of the self-drawn portrait has especial interest somewhat apart from the approaching crisis in her relations with her husband. Since her return to India, Mrs. Draper had developed into a Bluestocking. She probably had no personal acquaintance with Mrs. Elizabeth Montagu, whose assemblies of Bluestockings were then famous; but the *Essay on the Writings and Genius of Shakespear* duly reached India. After reading Mrs. Montagu's book, Mrs. Draper declared that she "would rather be an Attendant on her Person, than the first Peeress of the Realm." And so under this new inspiration Mrs. Draper resumed the scribbling to which she had been encouraged by Sterne. "A little piece or two" that she "discarded some years ago," were completed; they were "not perhaps unworthy of the press," but they were never printed. Though these efforts seem to be lost, Mrs. Draper took advantage of the occasion to weave into her letter to Mrs. James various little essays, which may be described in her phrase as "of the moral kind," because they have to do with practical conduct. Anxiety for the welfare of her daughter Betsey, who had been put to school at Kensington, leads to several pages on the boarding-school and the parlor-boarder, which are good enough to find a place in one of Mrs. Chapone's essays. A little way on, she relates the "story of a married pair, which," she says, "pleased me greatly, from the sensible singularity of it." The tale tells of a wealthy and indolent man in North India who married a smart young woman to "rouse his mind from its usual state of Inactivity"—and he succeeded. The wife, too, discarded her light airs, and became a most agreeable woman. It all reads like a character-sketch from Margaret, Duchess of Newcastle. There is also an experiment in the sentimental style, wherein is told the story of "a smart pretty French woman," who, shutting out all promiscuous loves and friendships, kept her heart for her dear husband alone and one "sweet woman" across the Alps. "The lovely Janatone," writes Mrs. Draper, "died three Years ago—after surviving her Husband about a Week and her Friend a twelvemonth." This constant couple, she said, were travelling in England when she was there, and Sterne introduced them to her. (Was the devoted wife who could live but a week without her husband the Janatone that Sterne twice met at Montreuil on his sentimental tours? I daresay she was.) And besides these, there are other sketches from life, and vivid descriptions of society at Bombay. If Eliza did not write exactly, as Sterne flattered her, "with an angel's pen," she knew how to ramble agreeably.

Crudities that appear in Mrs. Draper's written speech were not observable in her conversation, which charmed the circle of young civilians and travellers who gathered round her at Bombay. To her more intimate friendship was admitted a certain George Horsley, who used to sit and read poetry to her. Illness sent him back to England, with extravagant letters of recommendation from her to the Sclaters and the Jameses, as a young man possessing "one of the most active Minds and

Generous Hearts that ever I knew inhabit a human Frame."
To his care she entrusted diamond rings and other jewels
valued at £600, which he was to sell for her in England. She
gave her passport, too, to a Mr. Gambier, "a fine youth and
dear to me and all who know him on the score of his Worth,
strict Principles, and Admirable Manners." Much greater men
than these, typical of many, came under her spell. James
Forbes, author of *Oriental Memoirs*, knew her well when a
young man, and remembered to the end her "refined tastes and
accomplishments."* Likewise the Abbé Raynal, the historian
of the Indies, made her acquaintance at Bombay, and experienced at their first meeting a sensation which puzzled him. "It
was too warm," he said, "to be no more than friendship; it
was too pure to be love. Had it been a passion, Eliza would
have pitied me; she would have endeavoured to bring me back
to my reason, and I should have completely lost it." And of
the personality that awakened his admiration, the ecclesiastic
added: "Eliza's mind was cultivated, but the effects of this art
were never perceived. It had done nothing more than embel-
lish nature; it served in her case only to make the charm more
lasting. Every instant increased the delight she inspired; every
instant rendered her more interesting."†

Mrs. Draper's sentimental friendships with young men,
from whom she accepted costly presents, were quite sufficient
to occasion comment and arouse suspicions in her husband,
though there may have been, as she always averred, no harm
in her conduct beyond impropriety from the standpoint of
convention. On the other hand, to restate her side of the story,
her husband had been engaged, ever since her return to India,
in one coarse intrigue after another. During their last year
together—for it had come to that—the Drapers lived at Marine House, Mazagon, sometimes called Belvidere House,
commanding a fine prospect of Bombay and its harbor.
Through the year Mrs. Draper continued to insist on her hus-

* *Oriental Memoirs*, I, 338-339 (London, 1813).
† Raynal, *Histoire Philosophique et Politique*, . . . *des Européens
dans les deux Indes*, II, 88-89 (new edition, Avignon, 1786).

band's fulfilment of his promise with reference to the visit to England, and he continued to remain hopelessly immovable in his refusal. The long impending crisis came early in January, 1773, when the time for Mrs. Draper's sailing was at hand, were she to arrive in England by her daughter's birthday. On the evening of Monday, the eleventh of January, occurred an altercation between husband and wife in which each accused the other of misconduct, Mr. Draper naming Sir John Clark of the British navy, and Mrs. Draper retaliating with the name of Miss Leeds, one of her women in attendance, whom she claimed had fabricated the story against herself out of jealousy. Driven to desperation, Mrs. Draper fled from Marine House on the night of the following Thursday, and placed herself under the protection of her admirer, thus lending color to the suspicions of her husband. She escaped, it was said at the time, by letting herself down to the officer's ship by a rope from her window.*

Three letters are extant which Mrs. Draper wrote on the evening of her elopement. In the first of them, she gave "a faithful servant and friend," one Eliza Mihill, about to return to England, an order on George Horsley for all her jewels. "Accept it, my dear woman," wrote Mrs. Draper, "as the best token in my power, expressive of my good-will to you." To Mr. Horsley she addressed a brief, impassioned note explaining what she had done for Betty Mihill and what she was about to do for her own freedom. The third letter, which was left behind for Mr. Draper in justification of her conduct, was composed under great agitation of mind at the moment of the last perilous step, for which she took full responsibility. After beseeching that her husband temper justice with mercy if he believed her "all in fault," Mrs. Draper proceeded to plead her cause:

"I speak in the singular number, because I would not wound you by the mention of a name that I know must be displeasing to you; but, Draper, believe me for once, when I solemnly assure you, that it is you only who have driven me to serious

* David Price, *Memoirs . . . of a Field Officer*, 61 (1839).

Extremities. But from the conversation on Monday last he had nothing to hope, or you to fear. Lost to reputation, and all hopes of living with my dearest girl on peaceable or creditable terms, urged by a despair of gaining any one point with you, and resenting, strongly resenting, I own it your avowed preference of Leeds to myself, I MYSELF Proposed the scheme of leaving you thus abruptly. Forgive me, Draper, if its accomplishment has excited anguish; but if pride is only wounded by the measure, sacrifice that I beseech you to the sentiment of humanity, as indeed you may, and may be amply revenged in the compunction I shall feel to the hour of my death, for a conduct that will so utterly disgrace me with all I love, and do not let this confirm the prejudice imbibed by Leed's tale, as I swear to you THAT WAS FALSE, though my present mode of acting may rather seem the consequence of it than of a more recent event. Oh! that prejudice had not been deaf to the reasonable requests of a wounded spirit, or that you, Draper could have read my very soul, as undisguisedly, as sensibility and innocence must ever wish to be read!

"But this is too like recrimination which I would w:sh to avoid. I can only say in my justification, Draper, that if you imagine I plume myself on the Success of my scheme, you do me a great wrong. My heart bleeds for what I suppose may possibly be the sufferings of yours, though too surely had you loved, all this could never have been. My head is too much disturbed to write with any degree of connection. No matter, for if your own mind does not suggest palliatives, all I can say will be of little avail. I go, I know not whither, but I will never be a tax on you, Draper. Indeed, I will not, and do not suspect me of being capable of adding to my portion of infamy. I am not a hardened or depraved creature—I never will be so. The enclosed are the only bills owing that I know of, except about six rupees to Doojee, the shoemaker. I have never meant to load myself with many spoils to your prejudice, but a moderate provision of linen has obliged me to secure part of what was mine, to obviate some very mortifying difficulties. The pearls and silk cloathes are not in the least diminished.

Betty's picture, of all the ornaments, is the only one I have ventured to make mine.

"I presume not to recommend any of the persons to you who were immediately officiating about me; but this I conjure you to believe as strictly true, that not one of them or any living soul in the Marine House or Mazagon, was at all privy to my scheme, either directly or indirectly, nor do I believe that any one of them had the smallest suspicion of the matter; unless the two evident Concern occasioned by my present conflict induced them to think Something extraordinary was in agitation. O! Draper! a word, a look, sympathetick of regret on Tuesday or Wednesday would have saved me the perilous adventure, and such a portion of remorse as would be sufficient to fill up the longer life. I reiterate my request that vindictive measures may not be pursued. Leave me to my fate I conjure you, Draper, and in doing this you will leave me to misery inexpressible, for you are not to think, that I am either satisfied with myself or my prospects, though the latter are entirely my own seeking.

"God bless you, may health and prosperity be yours, and happiness too, as I doubt not but it will, if you suffer your resentments to be subdued by the aid of true and reasonable reflections. Do not let that false idea of my triumphing induce you to acts of vengeance I implore you, Draper, for indeed that can never be, nor am I capable of bearing you the least ill-will; or treating your name or memory with irreverence, now that I have released myself from your dominion. Suffer me but to be unmolested, and I will engage to steer through life with some degree of approbation, if not respect. Adieu! again Mr. Draper, and be assured I have told you nothing but the truth, however it may clash with yours and the general opinion."*

Mrs. Draper's elopement startled all civil and military India, for no woman was more widely known in the East.

* Mrs. Draper's three farewell letters were published in the *Times of India*, February 24, 1894; and in the overland weekly issue of March 3, 1894.

She became by this act the beautiful heroine of romance rescued by her lover from the tyranny of an ill-sorted or hateful marriage. In her flight she sought refuge with her rich uncle, John Whitehill, at Masulipatam—his "seat of empire," whence he superintended the fiscal administration of five northern provinces ceded to the East India Company at the close of the war with Hyder Ali. "His House, his Purse, Servants, Credit" were all placed at his niece's devotion. While under the protection of her powerful uncle, Mrs. Draper could safely view from a distance the fury of a husband who saw himself outwitted on all sides. From the mayor's court at Bombay a writ was obtained for the arrest of Sir John Clark, but the sheriff was unable to serve it, owing to the violent interference of Captain Benjamin Marlow. And when the enraged husband threatened an action for divorce, Mrs. Draper, with the aid of her uncle, collected against him evidence to be placed in the hands of his superior officers so damaging to his private character that his better judgment called a halt to the contemplated proceedings. He was made to see that he could not take further action against his wife without endangering all hope of remunerative service for the future.

On going to her uncle's, it had been Mrs. Draper's intention to remain with him for the rest of her life should he wish it, for her prospects of ever seeing England again were then very remote. In the autumn of 1773, she accompanied him to Rajahmundry, some eighty miles distant, where he pitched his tents for the winter and began negotiations with the zemindars, or petty princes of his provinces, over the land taxes of the next three years. The novelty of life in tents, joined with renewed health, put Mrs. Draper into spirits for a time; but she soon found Rajahmundry as uncongenial to her taste as was any other part of India. This restlessness crept into a confidential letter to her cousin Tom of Hoddington, dated January 20, 1774, written to inform him of her present situation. Her uncle, she told Tom, was an "extraordinary character," upright in all his dealings with the native princes, and generous to a degree she had never before witnessed in any man; and yet, though possessing all these good qualities, he was so passionate and jealous in his affections that he could not brook any preference for others. Some sign of preference, though sentimental, Mrs. Draper showed in an unguarded moment for her uncle's devoted assistant in the administration, "premier" she called him, a young man near her own age, named Sullivan, who knew how to address "the heart and judgement without misleading either." After that unguarded moment, life ran less smoothly at Rajamundry, though there is no indication of open breach between uncle and niece.

The letter to her cousin clearly foreshadowed Mrs. Draper's return to England towards the close of 1774. Henceforth her life was to be passed with her daughter among relatives and friends at home. While in London she occupied lodgings at "Mr. Woodhill's, Number 3 Queen Anne Street West, Cavendish Square,"* within comfortable reach of the Jameses and the Nunehams, among whom she could hardly have failed to meet Mrs. Medalle, unless precautions were taken against it. Eclat was given to her re-entrance into the old circles by the publication, two years before, of ten letters which she had received from Sterne at the height of his infatuation. Some mystery surrounds the appearance of the little volume bearing the title of *Letters from Yorick to Eliza*, printed for W. Johnston. It was ushered in with a dedication to Lord Apsley, then Lord High Chancellor, whose father, the old Lord Bathurst, once introduced himself to Sterne at the Princess of Wales's court and took him home to dine with him. A preface by an anonymous editor in the guise of publisher authenticated the letters, saying that they had been faithfully copied with Mrs. Draper's permission by a gentleman at Bombay. He told the public who Eliza was, and commented upon "the tender friendship" between her and Sterne. What he said of Mrs. Draper was, so far as it went, accurate; it was first-hand knowledge; and except in capitals and punctuation, the letters seem to have been in no way tampered with; at any rate

* Wilkes, List of Addresses, in the British Museum.

a comparison of the printed text with the copy of the first letter, still extant in Mrs. Draper's own hand, reveals no differences beyond these minor details. Whatever may be one's opinion as to the propriety of the publication during Mrs. Draper's life-time, it was an honest book; and Mrs. Draper, if she consented to its publication while she was still in India, may be commended for not including in the volume the later letters from Sterne reflecting upon the greed and violent temper of his wife, since dead.

As the Eliza of this remarkable series of letters (of which three editions were brought out by other publishers a few months after her return to England), Mrs. Draper received many attentions from Sterne's old friends, who were curious to see the woman to whom Yorick sent his sermons and *Tristram Shandy*, to whom he indited love epistles on going out to breakfast, on returning from Lord Bathurst's, or while waiting in Soho for Mr. James to dress. They wanted to see, too, her replies from which Sterne quoted a moral observation or two, expressing the opinion that her part of the correspondence should be published. "When I am in want of ready cash," he said, "and ill health will not permit my genius to exert itself, I shall print your letters, as finished essays, 'by an unfortunate Indian lady.' The style is new; and would almost be a sufficient recommendation for their selling well, without merit ——but their sense, natural ease, and spirit, is not to be equalled, I believe, in this section of the globe; nor, I will answer for it, by any of your countrywomen in yours." On the strength of this warm recommendation of Mrs. Draper's epistolary style, a publisher tried to flatter her into print as another Lady Mary Wortley Montagu; but "her modesty was invincible to all the publisher's endeavours." "Altho' Mr. Sterne was partial to every thing of her's," she invariably replied, good sense triumphing over vanity, "she could not hope that the world would be so too." Some letters had better be published posthumously; and to this class belonged Mrs. Draper's. In lieu of what she refused to give out to the public, the literary forger, as might be expected, offered his wares. In

April, 1775, appeared *Letters from Eliza to Yorick*, purporting to be correct copies of Mrs. Draper's letters to Sterne received "from a lady, not more dignified by her rank in life, than elevated by her understanding." The slight volume was entirely the work of an outsider.

Several well-known men were at once eager to win Mrs. Draper's friendship. Wilkes, after introducing her to his daughter, set out on Sterne's path to closer relations by sending her a present of books, accompanied by praise of her wit and conversation. In return, Mrs. Draper thanked him for the volumes, but deprecated the politician's flattery, the intent of which she could not have failed to understand. William Combe, the subsequent author of *Dr. Syntax*, was also ambitious of standing in her favor, and long afterwards foolishly boasted that she was more partial to him than she had ever been to Sterne. But the nearest successor to Sterne was the Abbé Raynal, who, since their meeting at Bombay, had been in correspondence with Mrs. Draper and now associated with her in England. Like Sterne, he extolled her beauty, her candor, and sensibility, and imagined her the inspirer of all his work. Losing self-control completely, the Abbé proposed that she leave her family and friends and take up her residence with him in France. "What joy did I not expect," he wrote, "from seeing her sought after by men of genius, and beloved by women of the most refined tastes." Mrs. Draper valued the distinguished friendship; but if she ever had any thought of quitting England for Paris, she was prevented by illness and death.

After 1775 Mrs. Draper sinks from view. It is probable that she lived in retirement with her daughter among relatives, despite the attempts to allure her into questionable friendships. She was surely a welcome visitor at Hoddington, the seat of her cousin Thomas Limbrey Sclater, who had been her confidential correspondent since childhood. And by some turn in her fortunes, over which one can only idly speculate, she seems to have been taken under the protection of Sir William Draper, kinsman and perhaps brother to her husband. This old warrior, who had fought with his regiment by the side of Clive in India and led a successful expedition against the Philippines, was then settled on the Clifton Downs near Bristol. At his seat, named Manilla Hall, after the city which he had captured, Mrs. Draper may have passed her last years. Such at least is the conjecture of local history.*

In any case, Mrs. Draper's residence at Clifton was brief. The young woman whose oval face and brilliant eyes had startled two ecclesiastics out of propriety, died on August 3, 1778, in the thirty-fifth year of her age. She was buried in the cathedral at Bristol, where a diamond in the north aisle of the choir marks her grave. Near-by in the north transept was erected, two years after her death, a mural monument by Bacon, the popular sculptor. The addition of a nave to the cathedral a century later made it necessary to take down all the monuments in the transepts. Mrs. Draper's was then removed to the beautiful cloisters. From a plain base rises a pointed arch of Sienna marble, under which stand, by the side of a pedestal supporting an urn, two draped female figures of white marble in *alto relievo;* of which the one, holding a torch in her right hand, is looking away and upward, while the eyes of the other are cast down towards a basket in her left hand containing a pelican feeding her young. Across and over the urn, above and between the two figures, lies an exquisitely carved wreath. An inscription, interpreting the allegory, says that in Mrs. Draper were united "Genius and Benevolence."†

The three men who had professed admiration for Mrs. Draper took notice of her death, each in his own characteristic way. Wilkes bluntly wrote the word *dead* after her name in his address-book, else he might forget it. Combe, the literary hack, traded upon her name by bringing out the next year two volumes of *Letters Supposed to have been Written by Yorick and Eliza.* The fictitious correspondence, cleverly enough framed, began with Mrs. Draper's return to India in 1767,

---

* George Pryce, *A Popular History of Bristol,* 119 (Bristol, 1861).

† J. Britton, *History of the Cathedral Church of Bristol,* 63 (London, 1830); Pryce, *A Popular History of Bristol,* as above.

and closed with a farewell letter from Sterne just as death was impending. Raynal opened his *History of the Indies,* which was then passing to a second edition, and inserted a mad eulogy upon Eliza, from which I have quoted the soberer passages. "Territory of Anjengo," he exclaimed, addressing the land of her birth, "in thyself thou art nothing! But thou hast given birth to Eliza. A day will come when the emporiums founded by Europeans upon Asiatic shores will exist no more. . . . The grass will cover them, or the Indian, avenged at last, will build upon their ruins. But if my works be destined to endure, the name of Anjengo will dwell in the memories of men. Those who read me, those whom the winds shall drive to these shores, will say, 'There was the birthplace of Eliza Draper.' " To the influence of the happy climate of Anjengo were attributed the personal charms of Mrs. Draper, which even the gloomy skies of England could not obscure. "A statuary," said the Abbé, "who would have wished to represent Voluptuousness, would have taken her for his model; and she would equally have served for him who might have had a figure of Modesty to portray. . . . In every thing that Eliza did, an irresistible charm was diffused around her. Desire, but of a timid and bashful cast, followed her steps in silence. Only a man of honour would have dared to love her, but he would not have dared to avow his passion. . . . In her last moments, Eliza's thoughts were fixed upon her friend; and I cannot write a line without having before me the memorial she has left me. Oh! that she could also have endowed my pen with her graces and her virtue!"* If these concluding sentences may be read literally, Raynal received a letter from Mrs. Draper just before her death. Not long after this he visited Bristol with Burke. It is just a surmise, if nothing more, that he placed in the cathedral the monument to Mrs. Draper's memory.

Anjengo was again apostrophized by James Forbes in his *Oriental Memoirs;* and to the various places where Mrs. Draper lived while in India, travellers long made pilgrim-

* For the complete eulogy, see the *Histoire Philosophique,* II, 85-89.

ages. Colonel James Welsh of the Madras infantry visited the house at Anjengo in which, it was said, she was born, and carried away from a broken window pieces of oyster-shell and mother-of-pearl as mementos. He took pains to write also in his *Reminiscences* that the house she lived in at Tellicherry was still standing in 1812. A tree on the estate of her uncle at Masulipatam was called, it is said, Eliza's tree, in memory of her sojourn there after the flight from her husband. But a more interesting as well as more accessible shrine was the scene of her elopement overlooking the harbor of Bombay. Sketches of Belvidere House were brought to England by J. B. Fraser, the traveller and explorer; and from them Robert Burford painted a panorama for public exhibition in London. Those who were unable to make the voyage to India might thus imagine the window from which Mrs. Draper descended to the ship of Sir John Clark, and hear the story that many a person had seen her ghost o' nights flitting about the corridors and verandahs of Belvidere in hoop and farthingale.*

At the same time Gothic fancy built up a pretty legend round the prebendal house where Sterne sometimes slept when in York. The humorist wrote, they used to say, *Tristram Shandy* in the parlor below, and slept above in a large "old fashioned room, with furniture coeval with its form, heavy and dark and calculated to excite every association favourable to the abode of spirits dark as Erebus." For a full quarter century after his death, Sterne's ghost had the habit of revisiting the old bedroom every night just as the bell in the great minster tolled twelve, and of tapping thrice the forehead of anyone who might be sleeping there. The actor Charles Mathews, who took the lodgings while playing at York, because they were cheap, found Sterne's visitations in no wise troublesome, and at length laid the perturbed spirit.†

* Douglas, *Bombay and Western India*, I, 177, 403, 418. A vignette of the view of Belvidere was made for the *Mirror of Literature, Amusement, and Instruction*, July 9, 1831.

† *Memoirs of Mathews*, I, 247-255.

CHAP. XXIV.

A Character of Sterne

A CENTURY and a half has rolled by since Sterne's ghost last walked his chambers in Stonegate; but even now one may feel the spell that Yorick once cast over his contemporaries, who were loth to let him die; who, long after he was dead and gone, imitated him in their books and correspondence, who sometimes forged his name to letters and whimsical impromptus such as they imagined he might have written, and kept on relating anecdotes of him, as if he were still living.

Few or none who knew Sterne well, from his valet to his archbishop and the men of fashion who crowded round him in his lodgings or at St. James's, and gave him the place of honor at their tables, ever broke friendship with him. Johnson, it is true, refused his company and thundered against "that man Sterne," but Johnson had really no acquaintance with him or with his books. If Warburton in a passion called Sterne "a scoundrel," it was after Sterne had told the Bishop of Gloucester that he could not accept him as guide and pattern in literature and conduct, without suppressing such talents as God had endowed him with. On the other hand, Lord Bathurst took Sterne under his protection as the wit that most reminded him of the glorious age of Queen Anne. Lord Spencer invited him to his country-seat, filled his purse with guineas, and was ever pressing him to delay his journey into Yorkshire. A box was always reserved for him and his company at both the theatres. Garrick took him home, dined him, and introduced him to "numbers of great people"; while Mrs. Garrick, delighted with the new guest, told him to regard their house as his own, to come and go whenever he pleased. Suard, though he associated with Sterne for only a few months, carried the image of him down to death. Whenever in after years Yorick's name was mentioned, Suard's eyes brightened, and he began to relate anecdotes about the Chevalier Sterne as he appeared in the salons, imitating, as he did so, his voice, manners, and gestures.

Lessing's famous remark that he stood ready to shorten his own life could he thereby prolong Yorick's, would seem to be not quite sincere, had it not been several times repeated by the dramatist; for the two men never met. But Sterne's contemporaries made no distinction between Mr. Tristram Shandy and the book bearing his name. "Know the one," they used to say, "and you know the other." It has been reserved mostly for professional critics of later times to take Sterne to task for his slovenly style, for slang and solecisms, and for a loose syntax which drifts into the chaos of stars and dashes. Such criticism rarely occurred to those who knew the man or could imagine him. Whether speaking or writing, Sterne might be heedless of conventional syntax; but he was always perfectly clear. His dashes and stars were not mere tricks to puzzle the reader; they stood for real pauses and suppressions in a narrative which aimed to reproduce the illusion of his natural speech, with all its easy flow, warmth, and color. To read Sterne was for those in the secret like listening to him. Lessing, who was able to divine the author from his books, paid him as fine a compliment as was ever paid to genius.

Sterne's personality, like a great actor's, loses perforce its brilliancy in the pale reflection of a biography, wherein traits of manner and character are obscured by numberless facts, dates, and minor details necessary to a true relation of the humorist's career, but requiring effort to carry in the memory and thereafter combine into a living portrait. No biographer, though the spell may be upon him, can hope to make it quite clear why Sterne captivated the world that came within his influence. His wit, humor, and pathos, which exactly hit the temper of his age, seem a little antiquated now as we derive these qualities second-hand from the books which he left behind him, and from the numerous anecdotes which were related after him, all re-wrought for literary effect. His unpremeditated letters, such as have not been tampered with by editors and biographers, still retain most of their pristine flavor. In these letters perhaps the man will live long after his books,

as must sometime happen, have been overtaken by oblivion.
We may look upon the wonderful portraits that were painted
of him by Reynolds and Gainsborough and Carmontelle, and
observe his dress, figure, features, and bright, eager eyes; but
we must add from our imagination the smile and the voice of
the king's jester.

Moreover, manners and morals have changed in so many
ways since Sterne's time, that one is in danger of misjudging
him. No ecclesiastic could now live the life that was lived by
Sterne. He and his compeers would be promptly unfrocked.
The scenes through which Sterne passed, the men and women
with whom he associated, and the jests over which they laughed,
have long since become less frequent in society. Thackeray,
who knew more of other men surrounding the Georges than he
knew specifically of Sterne, made his confession when he said,
after reading the letters of Selwyn and Walpole: "I am scared
as I look round at this society—at this King, at these courtiers,
at these politicians, at these bishops—at this flaunting vice and
levity; . . . wits and prodigals; some persevering in their bad
ways: some repentant, but relapsing; beautiful ladies, parasites,
humble chaplains, led captains." In more complaisant mood
Thackeray nevertheless felt the fascination of it all. "I should
like to have seen," he then confessed, "the Folly. It was a
splendid, embroidered, beruffled, snuff-boxed, red-heeled, impertinent Folly, and knew how to make itself respected." In
this old world of the Georges, where the cardinal virtues were
all forgotten, Sterne reigned as the supreme jester.

When Sterne first came to London in triumph, he was far
from being an awkward country parson, lean, lank, and pale,
such as later caricature has represented him. He was a man
hardly beyond the prime of life, of slight figure, near six feet
in height, of rather prominent nose, with cheeks and lips still
retaining traces of youthful color and fulness,—and eyes soft
and gentle as a woman's when they were in repose, but dark
and brilliant when his spirit was stirred by conversation and
repartee. In bearing he was from the first supple and courteous to an extraordinary degree. His oddities, which friends

watched and commented upon, but never quite described, seem to have consisted in a drollery of face and voice when he paid a compliment or related a jest, combined, if under the excitement of burgundy and good fellowship, with droll movements of head and arms extending to the whole body, not at all ungraceful, one may be sure, but odd and peculiar, like Corporal Trim's. Then it was that his wonderful eyes took on their wild gleam.

This is all as it should be, for Sterne was a gentleman who had always chosen his companions among gentlemen. He belonged to an old and honorable family, whose men, sometimes possessing solid attainments, were commonly hasty of temper; whose women were alert and vivacious. His father, "a little smart man," inheriting the characteristics of the Sternes and Rawdons, was withal "of a kindly, sweet disposition, void of all design." Out of pity for the sad state of a woman beneath him in rank, the poor ensign married her, said the son, quarrelled with a fellow officer over a goose, and was straightway run through the body; but survived after a fashion, and followed his flag to the West Indies and to death of a fever. In thus describing his father, Laurence described his own temperament. Like his father, he showed himself lacking in that prudence and good sense necessary for getting on with grave people. He quarrelled with the one man who could make or unmake him at will. If not literally run through the body like his father before him, he received his quietus for the moment.

But time has its revenges. Sterne wrote his book; and within three months Mr. Tristram Shandy was as widely known throughout England as the Prime Minister who accepted the dedication. Thenceforth Sterne lived in the glare of the world. Blinded at first by the excess of light, he despatched letters down to York every day, saying that no man had ever been so honored by the great. No less than ten noblemen called at his lodgings on a single morning. Garrick came; Hogarth came; Reynolds came. The bishops all sent in their compliments; Rockingham took him to Court; and Yorick was soon dining with the ladies of her Majesty's bed-chamber. The jests and anecdotes with which he everywhere set tables in a roar were passed on to the coffee-houses, and thence through news-mongers to the world at large. And wherever the tall man in black went—and no doors were closed against him,—he was as much at home as when in his country parish, driving his cattle afield or running down a goose for his friend Mr. Blake of York.

Such was Sterne's career in its abridgment. I have often thought, in following it, of a remark that George Eliot once made of Rousseau and her other wayward literary passions. "I wish you thoroughly to understand," she declared to a friend, "that the writers who have most profoundly influenced me . . . are not in the least oracles to me. It is just possible that I may not embrace one of their opinions,—that I may wish my life to be shaped quite differently from theirs." Still she read on and on in Rousseau and the rest, under the irre-sistible sway of emotions and perceptions novel to all her pre-vious experiences. So it is with Sterne. It seemed to his con-temporaries, as it seems to us, that no man ever possessed so keen a zest for living. You see this in his early life, in his preaching, in his reading, in his pastimes, and even in his farm-ing. Write to me, he entreated a correspondent after returning home from his first campaign in town, and your letter "will find me either pruning, or digging, or trenching, or weeding, or hacking up old roots, or wheeling away rubbish." You see this zest in its startling fulness after the Yorkshire parson had begun his long and steady tramp through the rounds of plea-sure in London, Bath, Paris, and Italy. When his course was finished, he had exhausted all pleasurable sensations, those of the peasant as well as those of the great world. If there were times when melancholy and despondency crept over him, he wisely kept within his lodgings or at Shandy Hall away from friends, and fought out single-handed the battle with evil spirits.

In the background of Sterne's character thus lay, as Bagehot once pointed out, a calm pagan philosophy. Although he well knew that he was sacrificing his life to pleasure, he never halted or swerved from the path on which he had set out; for he felt that he was but fulfilling his destiny. To the physicians who told him that he could not continue in his course another month, he replied that he had heard the same story for thirteen years. When the dreadful hemorrhages, so numerous that we cannot count them, fell upon him, he accepted them without murmur, as the darkness which nature interposes between periods of light. And when he saw the approach of the "all-composing" night from which he knew no dawn would appear, he merely remarked that he should like "another seven or eight months, . . . but be that as it pleases God." It was doubtless this cheerful readiness of Sterne to take all that nature gives, down to the last struggle, that Goethe had in mind when he said that Sterne was the finest type of wit whose presence had ever been felt in literature.

This man who accepted life as he found it was endowed with none of the grave virtues or contemptible vices described by moralists. If you run through the list of them as laid down by Aristotle or by Dante, you may stop a moment upon this or that virtue or upon this or that vice, but you quickly pass on to the end, with the perception that none pertains greatly to this man's character. Indeed, for certain of the practical virtues, Sterne expressed the most profound contempt, classing them with the deadliest of the seven deadly sins. Caution and Discretion, for example—the virtues of Samuel Richardson and his heroines—were to Sterne only the evil propensities of human nature, inasmuch as they are always intruding upon a man's conduct to prevent the free and spontaneous expression of his real selfhood. "They encompass," he often said in varying phrase, "the heart with adamant." Such virtues and such vices as Sterne possessed were simple and elemental.

Sterne could always be relied upon to perform with fidelity all ecclesiastical offices with which he was charged by his archbishop or by his dean and chapter. When absent from Sutton or Coxwold, he was careful to place over them capable curates, and to see to it that his surrogates made annual visitations to

those other parishes lying within the jurisdiction of his commissaryships. In all his engagements and appointments, he
strove to be punctual to the hour, whether they were for business or for relaxation; and if illness or other circumstance
intervened to keep him at home, he sent a note of apology so
courteous in its phrasing that the receiver placed it aside among
his treasures. So it was in the obscure days at Sutton and so it
was after Sterne had entered the world of fashion. It must
have been quite worth while for Lord Spencer to have presented him with a silver standish merely for the sake of the
acknowledgment wherein Sterne blessed him in the name of
himself, wife, and daughter, saying that "when the Fates, or
Follies of the Shandean family have melted down every ounce
of silver belonging to it, . . . this shall go last to the Mint."
If Sterne made any remark at dinner in the licence of his wit
which he thought might hurt the feelings of the host or of a
sensitive guest, he appeared the next morning with a graceful
apology, or sent a messenger with a note laying it all to the
burgundy and asking that no offence be taken where none was
intended. Sterne was generous to all who were dependent upon
him. His contracts with the poor and obscure men whom he
left in charge of his parishes show a consideration uncommon
in those days, when pluralists were accustomed to grind and
otherwise misuse their curates. Sometimes he gave a curate the
whole value of a living. The persisting opinion that he long
neglected his mother, we now know, is quite untrue. Further-
more, Sterne was always most attentive to the welfare of his
wife and daughter, for whose health and ease he provided to
the full extent of his purse. Six months before his death, he set
in order his letters and stray papers, that they might be published for their benefit; and his last thoughts, as he lay dying,
were upon Lydia.

Strangely enough, Sterne has been depicted as a hypocrite,
as a Joseph Surface, thoroughly corrupt in his heart, but posing
as a moralist or a man of fine sentiments. No portrait could be
further from the truth, for Sterne never pretended to be other
than he was. Such qualities as nature gave him—whether they

be called virtues or whether they be called vices—he wore upon his sleeve. If he felt no zeal for a cause, he never professed to have any. For a brief period he joined with his Church in denunciation of the Stuart Pretender and the Jesuits who were seeking restoration in England, but his passions soon cooled; he became disgusted with the part which he was playing, and resolved "that if ever the army of martyrs was to be augmented or a new one raised—I would have no hand in it, one way or t'other." Rather than be suffocated, "I would almost subscribe," he added, "to anything which does not choke me on the first passage." In all this Sterne was perfectly sincere. Moreover, he believed the gospel as he preached it. He accepted his Church and all that it taught without question, not because he had meditated profoundly upon its doctrines, but because it was the Church of his ancestors in which he had grown up from childhood. To him the Bible was the most eloquent of books because it was inspired; and for the same reason the men and women therein portrayed were types of men and women of all times. When he set up a defence of miracles, taking Hezekiah for his theme, before the Parisian philosophers gathered at the English embassy, it was because he actually believed that the shadow went back ten degrees on the dial of Ahaz, certainly not because he wished to appear odd and facetious. Any other inference would be to misunderstand completely the Yorkshire parson.

In contrast with intellects so highly cultivated as Holbach's or Diderot's, Sterne was ludicrously weak in the reasoning faculty and in that poise of character which comes from it. Locke was the only philosopher whom he could understand; all others were charlatans who poured forth words without meaning. His sermons, always graceful and sometimes entertaining, display no logic, with the possible exception of the one which Voltaire praised for its subtle analysis of conscience. And even in that sermon, Sterne's discernments concern not so much the intellect as the feelings which lead conscience astray. "Reason," Sterne once said, "is half of it sense," and he thereby described himself. For his was a most abnormal personality. Exceedingly sensitive to pleasure and to pain, he gave way to the emotions of the moment, receiving no guidance from reason, for he had none. Himself aware of this, he said variously, "I generally act from the first impulse" or "according as the fly stings."

Had Sterne's heart been bad, he would have been a menace to society; but his heart was not bad. I can discern in him nothing mean or cowardly beyond the general run of people with whom he associated—Thackeray to the contrary notwithstanding. "The extravagant applause that was at first given to his works," wrote Mrs. Montagu, "turn'd his head with vanity. He was received abroad with great distinction which made him still more vain, so that he really believes his book to be the finest thing the age has produced." When Cousin Elizabeth said this Sterne had not yet written the *Sentimental Journey*, which as "poor Tristram's last performance," she thought "the best." Successful authors are always vain, if that be the right word. Mrs. Montagu was made "very happy" by the praises that greeted her *Essay on the Writings and Genius of Shakespear*. Though Sterne may have had a large dose of vanity, that worries us no longer. His books, really quite as fine as anything his age produced, have weathered the storms of nearly two centuries and are still afloat with colors almost as gay as ever. Against his vanity, "the last infirmity of noble minds," may be set the fact that he was always courteous, generous, and unselfish. A young man from Milan, as I have told the story, once came to London to learn about English manners and customs and to see the men whose names had reached Italy. He called upon the author of *Tristram Shandy* on a rainy day. Sterne greeted the visitor with an embrace, took off his wet coat and placed it over a chair, then led him to the fire and began "a delicious conversation" over the chocolate. Most who came within Sterne's circle watched him, as we have watched him, amused rather than shocked, to see him, oblivious of all conventions, follow his momentary impulses into the wild follies and extravagances of high life.

Only the grave shook their heads. To all others Sterne was a delightful absurdity.

Sterne's impulsive nature was nowhere more conspicuous than in his relations with women. Feminine beauty simply overpowered him. First came Miss Lumley, whom he married because she was the first; and then followed in his later days Miss Fourmantelle, "my witty widow Mrs. Ferguson," Mrs. Vesey with her blue stockings, Lady Percy, and Mrs. Draper home from India without her husband, to mention a few of the unnumbered names. The women who awakened his admiration, Sterne divided into three classes, discovering their types in Venus, Minerva, and Juno. None of the three goddesses, however, quite satisfied his ideal; for Venus, lovely as she was, had no wit; Minerva had wit, but she was inclined to be a prude; and Juno, for all her beauty, was too imperial. Venus he liked to look at as she whipped up to his carriage in Hyde Park and invited him to her cabinet for a dish of tea. Minerva and Juno, whom he saw in Mrs. Garrick and Mrs. James, he adored with bent knee from a safe distance, whence incense might be cast upon their altars. But when Venus and Minerva appeared in one woman, at once beautiful, witty, and vivacious, his poor heart utterly collapsed.

About women of this last type Sterne liked to dawdle, exchanging, in antiquated phrase, "tender sentiments"; he liked, no doubt,—as we read in the *Sentimental Journey*—to touch the tips of their fingers and to count their pulse beats, all for the pleasurable sensations which he felt running along his nerves. In return, these sentimental women were enraptured; sometimes they came north during the summer to meet him at York and to be chaperoned by him, as he called it, to Scarborough for a week or a fortnight. The infatuation, except perhaps in the case of Mrs. Draper, was never a deep passion; it was only a transient emotional quiver, which quickly passed unless renewed by another sight of the charming face and figure. "We are all born," said Sterne as we have before quoted him, "with passions which ebb and flow (else they would play the devil with us) to new objects." The Anglican clergyman, remarked a Frenchman who observed his behavior in Paris, was in love with the whole sex, and thereby preserved his purity. That may be quite true. Certainly it would be unjust to charge Sterne with gross immoralities, for there was nothing of the beast about the sublimated Yorick. His sins may have been only those sins of the imagination which frequently accompany a wasting disease; for we should not forget that Sterne had the phthisical temperament. Perhaps Coleridge correctly divined him when he said that Sterne resembled a child who just touches a hot teapot with trembling fingers because it has been forbidden him. And yet who knows? He lived in a society where the seventh commandment was most inconvenient and where no discredit fell upon a man if he broke it.

Of course I am entering no defence in behalf of Sterne's conduct. I am merely correlating it with his volatile disposition. Nor would it serve any purpose to censure him for those follies and indiscretions over which he wept penitent tears as he held the hand of Mrs. Montagu. True, one is amazed at the freedoms of the old society—amazed even now in the licence of the twentieth century, which is a rather pale reflection of what once was. Were it not for Sterne's humor, the man and his books would have become long since intolerable. But the everlasting humor of the man saves him; it lifts him out of the world of moral conventions into a world of his own making. We must accept him as he was, else close the book. Everything about him was unique—his appearance, what he did, what he said, what he wrote. Acts for which you would reproach yourself or your nearest friends, you pass over in his case, for in them lurks some overmastering absurdity. "I am a queer dog," he wrote in reply to an unknown correspondent who conjectured that he must be one when over his cups, "I am a queer dog,——only you must not wait for my being so till supper, much less an hour after,——for I am so before I breakfast." No one could ever predict what Sterne would do under given circumstances. When in company, he sometimes sat the melancholy Jaques; at other times, he flashed forth a wild jest; and if it took well, then came another and another still wilder. There is the same wildness in *Tristram Shandy*, which opens with a jest, runs into buffoonery, and closes with a cock-and-bull story. But Sterne's humor was often, as in the *Sentimental Journey*, quiet and elusive. If a fly buzzed about his nose, he must catch it and safely carry it in his hand to the window and let it go free. If he saw a donkey munching an artichoke, he must give him a macaroon, just to watch the changes in the animal's countenance as he drops a bitter morsel for a sweet one. Governed by his whims in small and great things, Sterne was thoroughly unstable where the emotions were concerned.

As we view him in his books and in his life, Sterne had brief serious moods, but he quickly passed out of them into his humor. When he advised a brother of the cloth "to tell a lie to save a lie," he did not exactly mean it so, but he could not resist the humor of the absurd injunction. He must have been sorely troubled over his wife's insanity, but he could not tell his friends of her illness without awakening a smile as he said: "Madame fancies herself the Queen of Bohemia and I am indulging her in the notion. Every day I drive her through my stubble field, with bladders fastened to the wheels of her chaise to make a noise, and then I tell her this is the way they course in Bohemia."

Nothing, however sacred, was immune against Sterne's wit. He was, if one wishes to put it that way, indecent and profane. And yet indecency or profanity never appears in his letters and books by itself or for its own sake. His loosest jests not only have their humorous point, but they often cut rather deeply into human nature. He had, as we have said, very little of the animal in him; and perhaps for this very reason, in the opinion of the late Theodore Watts-Dunton, he was amused by certain physical instincts and natural functions of the body when contrasted with the higher nature to which all lay claim. His imagination was ever playing with these inconsistencies, and down they went without premeditation, as might be easily illustrated from the conversations at Shandy Hall. Queer analogies of all sorts were ever running in Sterne's head. If it were a hot day, he thought of Nebuchadnezzar's oven. If he took a text from Solomon, he could not help questioning its truth on rising into the pulpit, for the antithesis between the wise man of the Hebrews and a York prebendary was too good to lose. He has been charged with parodies of St. Paul's greetings to the Corinthians. Of this he was, indeed, guilty on several occasions, but only when writing to a company of wits who spent their leisure in reading Rabelais and literature of that kind. The contrast between the little church that St. Paul founded at Corinth and a group of jesters that met under the roof of Hall-Stevenson could not be resisted. It must be sent to the Demoniacs for their amusement.

Sterne is, I daresay, the most complete example in modern literature of a man whose other faculties are overpowered by a sense of humor. He feels, he imagines, and he at once perceives the incongruities of things as ordered by man or by nature; but he does not think, nor has he any appreciation of moral values. What to others seems serious or sacred is to him only an occasion for a sally of wit. In a measure all great humorists since Aristophanes and Lucian have resembled him, for unrestrained utterance is essential to humor. The humorist is a free lance recognizing no barriers to his wit. All that his race most prizes—its religion, its social ideals, its traditions, its history, and its heroes—is fair game for him, just as much as the most trivial act of everyday life. He is, as Yorick named himself, the king's jester, privileged to break in at all times upon the feast with his odd ridicule. But most humorists have had their moods of high seriousness, when they have turned from the gay to the grave aspects of things. In *Don Quixote* there is so much tragedy behind the farce that Charles Kingsley thought it the saddest book ever written. Likewise Molière's *Le Misanthrope*, comedy though it is, has its tragic moments. Shakespeare passed from Falstaff and the blackguards that supped at the Boar's Head to Hamlet, Lear, and Othello. Fielding, in the midst of his comedy, had a way of letting one into a deeper self, as in that great passage where he cuts short an exaggerated description of Sophia's charms with the remark

—"but most of all she resembled one whose image can never depart from my breast,"—in allusion to his wife just dead. To all these men there was something besides the humorist. There were in reserve for them great moral and intellectual forces. However far they may have been carried by their humor, there was at some point a quick recovery of the normal selfhood. Sterne had no such reserve powers, for he was compounded of sensations only. In his life and in his books, he added extravagance to extravagance, running the course to the end, for there was no force to check and turn him backward. He was a humorist pure and simple, and nothing else.

The modern world had not seen another much like him. The ancients—though I do not pretend to speak with authority —may have had such a humorist in Lucian. But there is a difference in the quality of their humor. Lucian was sharp and acidulous. Sterne rarely, perhaps nowhere except in the sketch of Dr. Slop, reached the border where humor passes into satire; for satire means a degree of seriousness unknown to him. With Swift, Sterne said *vive la bagatelle;* but he added—what Swift could never say—*vive la joie,* declaring the joy of life to be "the first of human possessions."

This buoyant temper, however, should not be confounded with anything so formal as that peculiar optimism of his day which said that "this is the best of all possible worlds." Sterne knew nothing of Leibnitz and he laughed at all *isms* as whimwhams of the imagination. He lived for the pleasure of living, just as his books have lived for the pleasure they give.

Never, I daresay, since the sensation caused by the publication of *Tristram Shandy* has Sterne been more alive than he is to-day. He survived the Victorian era, though he was hard hit by it. Thackeray and Dickens absorbed him. Bulwer-Lytton imitated him and stole from him. But Sterne the man was mostly condemned as if the man and his books were not one. That phase passing, Sterne now steps out into the twentieth century. We have looked him over. He would be amused to know that we see in him, with some differences, a man of our own times. His "psychology of impulse," though he could never have invented a phrase like that, is ours. His sentimentalism, in a measure, is ours, though his but played over the surface of the mind, while ours has crept into the depths of the subconscious. That is to say, Sterne took delight in misplaced or excessive emotion, knowing it to be such; while sentimentalism is now inwrought in contemporary drama and fiction without our being fully aware of it; and when we suspect its presence, we pretend that it is not there—which is hypocrisy. Sterne's freedom in manners and conduct is very modern also, only his was less defiant. And in his disregard of tradition, his style is especially ours. Perhaps the parallel runs no further. The new generation in this industrial age makes pleasure a sober business; whereas Sterne took what the world has to give, lightly, naturally, humorously. His sense of humor we have somewhere lost; and could Yorick now revisit the upper air, he would doubtless find us, as he found the French on his sentimental travels, "too serious" and hence not a little dull.

CHAP. XXV.

Sterne's Letter Book

IT was Sterne's custom to make and keep copies of such of his letters as particularly pleased him and, to some extent, of letters that he received from others. As early as 1761, in the "Memorandums" left with Elizabeth Montagu for his wife, when he feared that death was impending, he mentioned several places where "bundles" and "piles" of his letters might be found, if it were decided to publish them—in his bureau at Coxwold, in the garrets of his house at York, and with John Hall-Stevenson. These bundles must have been broken up and afterwards drawn upon by his daughter, Mrs. Medalle, when she brought out a collection of her father's letters in 1775. But for some reason she made no use of a Commonplace or Letter Book containing drafts and copies of Sterne's own letters along with copies of a few letters from his friends and admirers. Mrs. Medalle did indeed publish two letters found in the Letter Book, but her versions show that she obtained them from a different source. The Letter Book, which Mrs. Medalle overlooked or forgot about, was acquired in 1897 by the late J. Pierpont Morgan, and it now forms a part of the rare Collection of Sterne manuscripts in the Library bearing his name. By permission of the present J. Pierpont Morgan, the original Letter Book is here published for the first time.

This Letter Book, evidently incomplete* as we have it, consists of 35 leaves, measuring 7¾ x 6⅜ inches and written usually but not invariably on both sides. Only ten pages are blank. *It is all in Sterne's own hand.* Owing to a shifting of the leaves at some time, perhaps the fault of the binder, the letters do not always appear in chronological order, and I have taken the liberty of re-arranging them here and there. The spelling, abbreviations, and punctuation of the manuscripts

* For a reference to another page of the Letter Book, see this biography, p. 629.

Reduced facsimile of the first page of Sterne's Letter Book
From the manuscript in the Pierpont Morgan Library

have been carefully retained; but I could not, of course, reproduce in print the many interlinear alterations or the curious deletions that Sterne made by running his thumb or forefinger through a word or phrase he disliked as the quickest way of getting rid of it when something better came suddenly to mind. As his goose-quill (plucked from one of the birds running about the garden) moved along rapidly, he would place a period or draw a short line, if he had time for either, under the raised letters of common abbreviations like M^{rs}, y^{rs}, w^{ch}, and w^d. Otherwise he let them hang loose in the air. It would be refining too much to distinguish in print between a period and an embryonic dash; so it is all periods here if there was any mark in the manuscript beneath superior letters. Sterne paid no attention to the rule that the first word of an independent sentence had better begin with a capital letter nor that a word, especially if it be the name of a friend whom you are addressing, should not be spelled in too many ways. "You," however, he often wrote most courteously with an initial capital. Occasionally the end of a parenthesis or the end of a quotation is not indicated; and sometimes a word or a letter within a word is lost or repeated by a fast-moving quill. These slips I have let stand; and I have tried to retain Sterne's peculiar dash, which, having different meanings according to its length, the humorist lifted into the realm of art. This dash survives in the less flexible three dots . . . of Mr. H. G. Wells and his brother novelists, just as his "That is another story" has survived in the tales of Mr. Rudyard Kipling.

In several instances, it has been difficult, if not impossible, to determine whether a particular letter is a draft of a letter or a copy of a letter as it was actually sent, or a letter with some re-phrasing made with a view to publication. This threefold question I have taken up in my comment upon each of the letters.

The Letter Book, it will be quickly seen, is the most interesting group of Sterne manuscripts that has come to light since the publication, twenty-five years ago, of *The Journal to Eliza*. Some of the letters exhibit Sterne in his gayest moods, where little or no sentiment intrudes. In others he is playing upon the emotions of sentimental women who have written to him or enquired about him. And occasionally, as in his letter to the Bramine (which is pitched to the key of *The Journal to Eliza*), he gives free rein to his own sentimental imagination. A few of the letters, it should be said in conclusion, have already been published, but from other sources. In these instances, a comparison between the letters as given here and as they have appeared elsewhere, will show how ingrained was Sterne's sense for style.

The Letter Book ends, in my re-arrangement of it, with the letter to the Bramine, numbered XVIII. But I have added several other autograph letters from manuscripts in the Pierpont Morgan Collection. These letters differ from most of the preceding in that no one of them is a draft or a copy: they are a group of Sterne's letters in their final form. With one exception, they have all been published somewhere, but usually with a number of misreadings of the manuscripts, or with an editor's attempt to improve upon Sterne's style by substituting commonplace for piquant phrases. The reader will not fail to see how Sterne, in two letters from York, paved a way over the length of England to Garrick's friendship, nor to compare his draft of a letter to Berenger, in the Letter Book, with the letter after Sterne's imagination has had a chance to play about his first humorous conception.

To this little group of letters, I have appended, also from the Pierpont Morgan Collection, the "Memorandums," a sort of advisory testament, which Sterne wrote out when confronted with the sudden apparition of Death.

I.

THIS is the surviving part of the wrapper which contained the letters in the Letter Book. It is a memorandum which Sterne evidently wrote down and left at Coxwold for his wife and daughter just before he set out on his last trip to London. Near the beginning is a deleted passage which in part reads as follows: "Hall has rec^d hundreds, they have been wrote most of 'em in too careless a way, besides he is careless."

Sterne's life-long friend, Marmaduke Fothergill, a gentleman of York, was the son of the Rev. Marmaduke Fothergill, D.D. He died, August 13, 1778. (See *Gentleman's Magazine* for 1778, page 392.) Mr. Hall is John Hall-Stevenson. Berenger and Miss Macartney are identified in letters that follow. The "Countess of Edgecomb" is Emma Gilbert, only daughter of John Gilbert, Archbishop of York. She married, August 6, 1761, George, third Baron Mount-Edgcumbe (afterwards Earl of Mount-Edgcumbe). None of the letters that passed between Sterne and Miss Gilbert have ever been published, though he several times mentions her in letters to others. She took his side in the controversy over the indecorums of *Tristram Shandy*. Mrs. Moore is "the charming widow" he met at Bath in April, 1765. Nothing is known of Mrs. Fenton, though some of Sterne's letters addressed to "Mrs. F——" may have been to her rather than to Mrs. Ferguson.

Fothergil I know has some good ones—Garrick some.—Berenger has one or two—Govr Littletons Lady. (Miss Macartney) numbers—Countess of Edgecomb—Mrs Moore of Bath —Mrs Fenton London—cum multis aliis—These all if collected with the large number of mine & friends in my possession would print & sell to good acc^t – – – –

Hall has by him a great number wth those in this book & in my Bureau—& those above w^d make 4 Vol^s the size of Shandy ————they would sell well———& produce 800 p^{ds} at the least—

II.

This is a careful copy of a draft of a letter which first appeared, without date and with many inaccuracies, in *The Westminster Magazine* for August, 1779, and was included as Letter CXXI in Sterne's *Works* (London, 1780). It has since been many times reprinted. In *The Archivist* for September, 1894 (vol. VII, No. 27, p. 40) the letter was printed from the manuscript then in the collection of Mr. E. Barker of West Kensington. The text of 1779-80 shows, in addition to misreadings, how the first editor played fast and loose with Sterne's phrases. The text of 1894 gives the letter correctly in its final form. The letter as it appears in the Letter Book is printed here for the first time. It varies greatly from the other two versions.

It is not known to whom the letter was addressed. Apparently he was a York friend acquainted with Marmaduke Fothergill.

York . Jan. 1. 1760

Dear Sir.

I have rec^d y^r Letter of Counsil which contrary to my natural humour, has set me half a day upon looking a little gravely and upon thinking a little gravely too. sometimes I concluded you had not spoke out, but had stronger grounds for some discourageing Hints upon Tristram Shandy, than what your good nature knew well how to tell me————particularly with regard to the point of prudence as a Divine &c————and that you really thought in your heart the vein of humour too light for the colour of my Cassock————a Meditation upon the four last things had suited it better—I own—but then it must not have been wrote by me.

My friend Mr Fothergil whom I regard in the class I do you, as my best of criticks and well wishers,—preaches every day to me upon this Text of yours————get your preferment, Lory, first he says and then write and welcome—but my dear gentlemen, suppose this self same preferment is long o' coming (& for aught I know I may not be prefer'd till the resurrection of the Just)—& I continue all that time in hard Labour— how shall I manage my pains?—You both fright me with *after pains*, like good philosophers, knowing that one passion is best to be combatted by another.

————I deny it————I have not gone as far as Swift—He keeps due distance from Rabelais————& I from him. Swift sais 500 things, I dare not say,————unless I was Dean of Saint Patricks.

As for the ambitiosa Ornamenta you hint at,—Upon revising my book, I will shrift my conscience as I go along upon that sin—and whatever ornaments it confesses to, of that kind, shall be defaced without mercy—they are vices of my constitution more than a Love of finery & Parade when I fall into them—and tho' I have a terrible dread of writing like a dutch Commentator—yet these luxuriant Shoots, as far as I am a Judge, shall be pruned, if not entirely cut away for the tree's good.

As for Slop's fall——'tis most circumstantialy related, & the affair most trifling—& perhaps you may be right in saying 'tis overloaded——but not, dear S^r because of the slightness of the incident—that very thing should constitute the humour, which consists in treating the most insignificant Things with such *Ornamenta ambitiosa,* as would make one sick in another place.

I know not whether I am entirely free from the fault Ovid is so justly censured for—of being *Nimium ingenij sui amator.* the hint however is right—to sport too much with a Man's own wit is surfeiting: like toying with a man's mistress, it may be delightful enough to the Inamorato but of little or no entertainment to By-standers. in general I have ever endeavour'd to avoid it, by leaving off as soon as possible whenever a point of humour or Wit was started, for fear of saying too much; and tother day a gentleman found fault with me upon that very score—but yours and my friend Fothergils Judgment upon this head, I hold to be more truely nice and critical—and on that side, it is the safest to err.

After all, I fear Tristram Shandy must go into the world with a hundred faults——if he is so happy as to have some striking beauties, merciful & good Judges will spare it as God did Sodom for the ten Righteous that are therein.

I am, Sir

Y^rs L. Sterne

III.

Unpublished. This is the draft of a letter that Sterne sent, on a Saturday in March, 1760, to Richard Berenger, Gentleman of the Horse to George the Third. The letter as afterwards elaborated was first published by Percy Fitzgerald in his *Life of Laurence Sterne,* Vol. 1, 160-161 (revised edition, London, 1896). For the letter as it passed through the post, see No. XXI.

My dear Berenger.

You bid me tell you all my wants――what the duce can the man want now? what would I not give to have but ten strokes of Howgarth's witty chissel at the front of my next Edition of Tristram Shandy [the Vanity of a pretty woman in the hey-day of her Triumphs, is a fool to the vanity of a successful author――*Orna me*, sigh'd Swift to Pope,—unite something of yours to mine to wind us together in one sheet down to posterity――I will, I will; said Pope――but you don't do it enough said Swift――

Now the loosest Sketch in nature of Trim's reading the sermon to my father & my uncle Toby will content me――

I would hold out my lank purse――I would shut my eyes— & you should put your hand into it, & take out what [you] liked for it――Blockhead! This gift is not bought with money—perish thee, & thy gold with thee.

What shall we do? I would not propose a disagreeable thing to one I so much admire, for the whole world:――You are a hard faced, impudent honest dog――prithee stop, & *sans menagement*, begin thus.

"Mr Hogarth, my friend Shandy――but go on your own way――as I shall do mine, all my Life.

So adieu.

IV.

UNPUBLISHED. The letter from William Warburton (the Bishop of Gloucester) to which Sterne refers, was written from Prior-Park, June 15, 1760. Sterne's reply is dated "Coxwould, June 19" [1760]. The letter to Miss Macartney thus appears to have been written at Coxwold late in June, 1760.

Mary Macartney, whom Sterne met in London the previous winter, was the daughter of James Macartney of Longford, Ireland. On June 2, 1761, she married William Henry Lyttelton (afterwards Lord Lyttelton, Third Baron of Frankley), who was at the time Governor of South Carolina. The next year her husband was transferred to Jamaica, where she died May 28, 1765.

To Miss M. Macartny

An urn of cold water in the driest stage of the driest Desert in Arabia, pour'd out by an angel's hand to a thirsty Pilgrim, could not have been more gratefully received than Miss Macartny's Letter————pray is that Simile too warm? or conceived too orientally? if it is; I could easily mend it, by saying with the dull phlegm of an unfeeling John Trot, (*suivant les ordinances*) That Y^{rs} of the 8th Inst. *"came safe to hand."*

————Lord defend me from all literary commerce with those, who indite epistles as Attornys do Bonds, by filling up blanks, and who in lieu of sending me what I sat expecting— a Letter————surprize me with an Essay cut & clip'd at all corners. to me inconsiderate Soul that I am, who never yet knew what it was to speak or write one premeditated word, such an intercourse would be an abomination; & I would as soon go and commit fornication wth the Moabites, as have a hand in any thing of this kind unless written in that careless irregularity of a good and an easy heart————& now tis time & justly critical too to thank you for y^{rs} and tell you twas just such a one as my soul delights in.

Yes————You was extreamly good in writing to Tristram at all————but in writing to him so soon, you was infinitely so: nor can all y^r wit talk me out of the belief: tis the 40th article of my faith & I adore you for it: but is there any need in thus apotheosizing Miss Macartney to make a Devil of myself———— no; fair Angel (for now I have got you into heaven, I will keep you there as long as I chuse)—I was not six weeks in deliberating whether I should worship you, or no————nor how ————nor with what insense, or with what ceremonies————but the cares and dissipations of this world had got in betwixt me and my devotion—as they do to many other good people———— till Conscience awoke and would no longer be trifled with it.

I admire your Simile of conjugal squabbles ending in very pleasant harmony and if I durst would write you a Sermon upon this Text of yours—but I am upon my good behaviour; god bless you however, for what you say upon *Discretion* (or Reflection I forget w^cb—but I verily believe you take a delight in recommending these two prudent old gentlewomen to me, merely because you know they are not entirely to my taste—I'm sure with regard to Discretion, tho' I have no great communications with her—I had always a regard for her at the bottome—She is a very honest Woman; & I should be a brute to use her ill————only I insist upon it, she must not spoil good company.

"God forgive me, for the Volumes of Ribaldry I've been the cause of"—now I say, god forgive them————and tis the pray'r I constantly put up for those who use me most unhandsomely—the Bishop of Glocester, who (to be sure) bears evils of this kind—so as no man ever bore 'em, has wrote me a congratulatory Letter thereupon—the Summ total of all w^cb is— That we bear the Sufferings of other people with great Philosophy—I only wish one could bear the excellencies of some people with the same Indifference————

           & that I was not so much, as I
           am, Y^rs

                    L. Sterne

V.

UNPUBLISHED. Mr. Brown was a clergyman living in Geneva, where Hall-Stevenson became acquainted with him. On receiving the enquiry about the author of *Tristram Shandy*, the master of Skelton sent the letter over to Coxwold. Sterne made a copy of it and doubtless returned the original to Hall-Stevenson.

From Mr Brown to J. Hall Esqre

                  Geneva, July 25 . 1760

————Tristram Shandy has at last made his way here. never did I read any thing with more delectation. What a comical Fellow the author must be! & I may add also what a Connoisseur in Mankind! Perhaps if the Book has any fault at all, it is, that some of his touches are too refined to be perceived in their full force & extent by every Reader. We have been told here he is a Brother of the cloath; pray is it really so? or in what part of the Vineyard does he labour? I'd ride fifty miles to smoak a pipe with him, for I could lay any wager that so much humour has not been hatch'd or concocted in his pericrainium without the genial fumes of celestial Tobacco: but perhaps like one of the same Trade, tho' his Letters be strong and powerful, his speech is mean and his bodily presence contemptible—

—Yet I can hardly think it. He must be a queer dog, if not sooner, at least after supper; I would lay too, that he is no stranger to Montaigne; nay that he is full as well acquainted with him, as with the book of common prayer, or the Bishop of London's pastoral Letters; tho at the same time I would be far from insinuating, either on one hand, that his Reverence is not as good a Tradesman in his way as any of his neighbours, —or on the other, That this celebrated Performance of his, is not perfectly an Original. The Character of Uncle Toby, his conversations with his Brother, who is also a very drole and excellent personage, & I protest such Characters I have known —his Acc^{ts} of the Campaign &c &c are inimitable. I have been much diverted wth some people here who have read it. they torture their brains to find out some hidden meaning in it, & will per force have all the Starts—Digressions—& Ecarts which the Author runs out into, & which are surely the Excellencies of his Piece, to be the constituent Members of a close connected Story. is it not provoking to meet with such wise acres who, tho' there be no trace of any consistent plan in the whole of their insipid Life, & tho their Conversation if continued for half a quarter of an hour has neither head or tail, yet will pretend to seek for connection in a Work of this Nature.

Adieu . Dear Sir
&c &c—

VI.

UNPUBLISHED. This letter, a reply to the foregoing, appears to be *not* a draft, but a copy of the letter as sent to Mr. Brown. In neither of the two letters are there any of Sterne's usual attempts at deletion of phrases that did not quite satisfy him.

To Mr Brown at Geneva

York. Sep^t 9 . 1760

Sir

My good friend Mr Hall knowing how happy it would make me, to hear that Tristram Shandy had found his way to Geneva, and had met with so kind a reception from a person of your Character, was so obliging as to send me y^r letter to him. I return you Sir, all due thanks and desire you will suffer me to place the many civilities done to this ungracious whelp of mine, to my own account, and accept of my best acknowledgements thereupon.

You are absolutely right in most of your conjectures about me (unless what are excessively panygerical)—1st That I am "a queer dog"—, only that you must not wait for my being so, till supper, much less till an hour after—for I am so before I breakfast. 2^d "for my conning Montaigne as much as my pray'r book"—there you are right again,—but mark, a 2^d time, I have not said I admire him as much;—tho' had he been alive, I would certainly have gone twice as far to have smoakd a pipe with him, as with Arch-Bishop Laud or his Chaplains, (tho' one of 'em by the bye, was my grandfather). As for the meaness of my speech, and contemptibility of my bodily presence,—I'm the worst Judge in the world of 'em—Hall is ten times better acquainted with those particulars of me, & will write you word. In y^r Conjecture of smoaking Tobacco—— there you are sadly out—not that the conjecture was bad but that my brain is so—it will not bear Tobacco, inasmuch as the fumes thereof do concoct my conceits too fast so that they would be all done to rags before they could be well served up—the heat however at 2^d hand, does very well with them, so that you may rely upon it, that for every mile you go to meet me for this end, I will go twain; and tho I can not smoak wth you, yet to shew you, I am in full harmony with you, I'll fiddle you a grave movement whilst you pipe it in your way & Hall shall dance a Saraband to us with a pair of bellows & Tongs, in which accompanyment You must know, he has done wonders since he left Geneva.

The Wise heads I see on the continent are made up of the same materials, & cast in the same Moulds, with the Wise heads of this Island,—they philosophize upon Tristram Shandy alike to a T——they all look to high—tis ever the fate of low minds.

Be assured I am an unworthy Labourer in the Vineyard— and I verily believe some of the Lords of it, wish me out— being under terrible alarms that I may one day or other do more harm than good in it.——

If you honour me wth a Letter directed to me Prebendary of York, it will find me either pruneing, or digging or trench- ing, or weeding, or hacking up old roots, or wheeling away Rubbish——Whatever I am about, depend upon it, Y^r Letter will find me much Y^{rs} for I am with the greatest esteem

for Y^r Character & self

S^r Y^r most Obliged &c . L. Sterne

VII.

FIRST published in *Sterne's Letters to his Friends on Various Occa- sions* (London, 1775). It is Letter IX in that collection. This is Sterne's first letter to Mrs. Elizabeth Vesey, the Bluestocking, known as "The Sylph" among her intimate friends. As we find Sterne go- ing to Ranelagh with Mrs. Vesey the next winter, the June of this letter is 1761.

Until recently this letter has been regarded as spurious. Here, however, we have it in Sterne's own hand as he copied it for his Letter Book. A comparison between the copy and the printed version shows some inaccuracies and re-phrasing by the editor of the volume in which it first appeared.

To Mʳˢ Vesey.

London
June 20.

of the two bad cassocs, fair Lady which I am worth in the world, I would this moment freely give the better of 'em to find out by what irresistable force of magic it is, that I am influenced to write a Letter to you upon so short an Acquaintance—*short*, did I say—I unsay it again: I have had the happiness to be acquainted with Mʳˢ Vesey almost time immemorial—surely the most penetrating of her sex need not be told that intercourses of this kind are not to be dated by hours, days or months, but by the slow or rapid progress of our intimacies which can be measured only by the degrees of penetration by wᶜʰ we discover Characters at first sight, or by the openess and frankness of heart wᶜʰ lets the by-stander into it, without the pains of reflection; either of these spares us, what a short life can ill afford and that is, that long and unconscionable time in forming Connections, which had much better be spent in tasting the fruits of them—now, I maintain that of this frame & contexture is the fair Mʳˢ Vesey—her character is to be read at once; I saw it before I had walk'd ten paces besides her.—I believe in my Conscience, dear Lady, that you have absolutely no inside at all.——

That you are graceful, & elegant & most desirable &c &c. every common beholder, who only stares at You as a dutch Boore does at the Queen of Sheba in a puppit Show can readily find out; But that You are sensible, and gentle and tender—& from end to the other of you full of the sweetest tones & modulations, requires a Connoisseur of more taste & feeling— in honest truth You are a System of harmonic Vibrations— You are the sweetest and best tuned, of all Instruments—O Lord! I would give away my other Cassoc to touch you— but in giving this last rag of my Priesthood for this pleasure you perceive I should be left naked—nay if not quite dis-*ordered:*—so divine a hand as yʳˢ would presently get me into order again—but if You suppose, this would leave me, as You found me—believe me dear Lady, You are mistaken.

all this which being weigh'd and put together, let me ask
you my dearest Mrs V. what business you had to come here
from Ireland—or rather, what business have You to go back
again—the deuce take you wth your musical and other powers
—could nothing serve you but you must turn T. Shandys head,
as if it was not turn'd enough already: as for turning my
heart; I forgive You, as you have been so good as to turn it
towards so excellent & heavenly an Object——

now, dear Mrs Vesey, if You can help it, dont think of
Y^{r}self. but believe me wth great Esteem for y^{r} Character &
self. Y^{rs} L— S—

VIII.

UNPUBLISHED. Copy with minor alterations. This letter should be
read in connection with Letter IV in *Original Letters of the Late
Reverend Mr. Laurence Sterne* (London, 1788), having the superscription, "Coxwould, near Easingwould, August 8, 1764." The
Telemachus in both letters, to whom Sterne plays the part of
Mentor in dealings with "Calypso and her Nymphs," was probably
William Combe, who had met Sterne in France and subsequently
visited Sterne at Coxwold and Hall-Stevenson at Skelton. After
running through a small fortune, Combe, it is said, tried the army
for a time. Hence the reference to him as "my Militia Captain."
The Calypso from whom the two men ran away was some unknown
lady (possibly the Countess of Edgcumbe), by whom they were entertained in London in June, 1764, when Sterne stopped there for
three weeks on his way home from France. The girl who at parting
gave Sterne "a golden-headed pencil and pinchbeck ruler" is most
courteously disguised under the name of the beautiful Princess of
Micomicon, somewhere in Guinea—whom Sancho Panza wanted to
marry.

The letter was written just after Sterne reached York at the end
of June, 1764.

York.

Do You think, dear Lady,—shandy-headed as I am, that I
could be served with a Letter de Cachet, without instantly

obeying the summons, or sending some lawful excuse by the return of the Courier?

—fugitive as I am—I have not run away from my loyalty —I fled with a Militia captain: it was not from Principles of rebellion,—but of virtue, that we made our escapes: The Goddess of Prudence and Self-denial bears witness to our Motives—We ran headlong like a Telemachus and a Mentor from a Calypso & her Nymphs, hastening as fast as our members would let us, from the ensnaring favours of an enchanting Court, the delights of which, we forefelt in the end, must have un-*captain'd* the Captain—& dis-*order'd* the Priest. We beseech You, to think of both of us, as we are—nothing extenuate, or set down aught in malice.

To begin, (in good manners) with myself. think not, dear xxxx, when I fled,—think not, that I could run away from the remembrance of past kindnesses, or the expectation of future ones—Good God! Is it possible I could forget my red leather pocket-book with silver clasps?—my two sticks of seal wax—my Scissars, (which by the bye want grinding) & my pen-knife. Unhappy man! wander where I may, have I not the *trioptick* hibernian pair of Spectacles, wch xxx gave me, ever upon my nose, magnifying every crooked step I take? do I not carry about me the golden headed pencil & pinchbeck Ruler which the truely virtuous & open hearted Princess Micomicon, put into my hands at parting—hallowed & mystick Gifts convey'd by a heavenly hand, to mark & measure down my back-slidings and my fore-slidings—*les egarments de mon coeur, & mon esprit pendent mon exile!*

As for my Militia-Captain, my thrice worthy fellow wanderer, and the kind contriver & coadjutor of my escape——Let not my pen—but let his own Atchievements write his elogy. This moment that I am writing is he preparing to plunge himself into dangers, to forget himself—his friends—& think only of his country—now does the drum beat—& the shril Fife shriek in his ears—his pulse quickens—mark how he girds on his sword—for heaven's sake! where will this end?

he is going, with his whole Batallion to Leeds—to Leeds?—

yes, M^{dm} he is going to root out the manufactures—to give the spinsters & Weavers no elbow room—to compliment Industry with a Jubilee—by all that is good! He will do the State some service; & they shall know it.

I am
&c &c—
L. S.

IX.

UNPUBLISHED. Apparently a copy, with some re-phrasing, of a letter to Miss Sarah Tuting, about to leave for Italy. Sterne overtook her at Naples. In a letter to Mr. Foley, his banker in Paris, dated August 6, 1764, Sterne described her as "a lady known and loved by the whole kingdom."

To Miss T———

Coxwould Augst
27. 1764

———Well! once more adieu!——farewell! God be with you! in this long journey may no thorn grow near the path you tread; and when you lie down, may your pillow, gentle Sally, be soft as your own breast; and every dream be tinged with pleasures which hearts like yours are only destined to inherit— so get well, dear Lady, merely not to lose y^r birth right *here*— & do not die to enter upon it too soon hereafter.

This is mere Selfishness; and yet I thought I was writing the most sentimental Letter that ever the hand of true gallantry traced out—and o' my conscience I still believe I am— but I wait to be accused before I justify.

Now is it possible I can give you any advice in wch your good sence & philosophy has not got the start of me in regard to your health? so far as it depends upon your mind. for here I must take the Liberty to inform You, that it is oweing to that great & good sensibility of Y^{rs}, that any hint upon that upon that [*upon that* repeated] score, can be made excusable: for if you hunger and thirst like a kindly Soul with too warm an impatience after those You have left behind—You will languish away the little fragment which is left of you to a shadow: The heart must be chearful and free from desires during all this Pilgrimage in search of health—no hard jostlings in your journey must disturb either body or mind one moment—if you have left a Philander—think not about him —You must smile upon inconveniences and impositions—upon bad inns—& what will hurt you most of all because most contrary to y^r nature—upon unfeeling looks.

The gentle Sally T———— is made up of too fine a texture for the rough wearing of the world—some gentle Brother, or some one who sticks closer than a Brother, should now take her by the hand, and lead her tenderly along her way—pick carefully out the smoothest tracks for her—scatter roses on them— & when the tax'd and weary fibre tells him she is weary—take her up in his arms————————

I despise Mankind, that not one of the race does this for her————You know what I have to say further ————but adieu.

Y^{rs} faithfully
L. S

X.

UNPUBLISHED. Copy with some dressing-up for publication. This nonsensical letter, in which Sterne for obvious reasons refers to himself as but forty-four years old, though he was really in his fifty-second year, was probably written soon after his return to London from a visit to Bath in the spring of 1765. The Mrs. F——— to whom the letter is addressed has not been identified. She could not have been Mrs. Ferguson, for Sterne had been acquainted with that "witty widow" for many years. She was another "witty widow." Was she Mrs. Fenton? and did Sterne first meet her at Bath? The questions may be asked but not answered.

To M^{rs} F———

—and pray what occasion, (either real or ideal) have You Madam, to write a Letter from Bath to Town, to enquire whether Tristram Shandy is a married Man or no?—and You may ask in Your turn, if you please, What occasion has Tristram Shandy gentleman to sit down and answer it?

for the first, dear Lady (for we are beginning to be a little acquainted) You must answer to your own conscience—as I shall the 2ᵈ, to mine; for from an honest attention to my internal workings in that part where the Conscience of a gallant man resides, I perceive plainly, that such fair advances from so fair a Princess—(freer & freer still) are not to be withstood by one of Tristram Shandy's make and complexion—Why my dear Creature (—we shall soon be got up to the very climax of familiarity)—If T. Shandy had but one single spark of galanty-fire 'in any one apartment of his whole Tenement, so kind a tap at the dore would have call'd it all forth to have enquired What gentle Dame it was that stood without—good God! is it You Mʳˢ F – – – –! What a fire have you lighted up! tis enough to set the whole house in a flame

"If Tristram Shandy was a single Man"—(o dear!)—"from the Attacks of Jack Dick and Peter I am quite secure—(this by the by Madam, requires proof)—But my dear Tristram! *If* thou wast a single man—bless me, Madᵐ, this is downright wishing for I swear it is in the *optative Mood* & no other—well! but my dear T. Shandy wast thou a single Man, I should not know what to say—& may I be Tristram'd to death, if I should know what to do——

do You know my dear Angle (for you may feel I am creeping still closer to you and before I get to the end of my letter I forsee the freedome betwixt us will be kept within no decent bounds)—do You know I say to what a devil of a shadow of a tantalizing Help mate you must have fallen a victim on that supposision—why my most adorable! except that I am tolerably strait made, and near six feet high, and that my Nose, (whatever as an historian I say to the contrary), is an inch at least longer than most of my neighbours—except that —That I am a two footted animal without one Lineament of Hair of the beast upon me, totally spiritualized out of all form for conubial purposes——let me whisper, I am now 44—and shall this time twelve-month be 45——That I am moreover of of a thin, dry, hectic, unperspirable habit of Body—so sub-limated and rarified in all my parts That a Lady of y^r Wit would not give a brass farthing for a dozen such: next May when I am at my best, You shall try me—tho I tell You before hand I have not an ounce & a half of carnality about me —& what is that for so long a journey?

In such a Land of scarsity, I well know, That Wit profiteth nothing—all I have to say is, That as I sh^d have little else to give, what I had, should be most plenteously shed upon you.— but then, the devil an' all is, You are a Wit Y^{r}self, and tho' there might be abundance of peace so long as the *Moon* endured—Yet when that luscious period was run out, I fear we sh^d never agree one day to an end; there would be such Satyre & sarcasm—scoffing & flouting—rallying & reparteeing of it, —thrusting & parrying in one dark corner or another, There w^d be nothing but mischief—but then—as we sh^d be two people of excellent Sense, we sh^d make up matters as fast as they went wrong—What tender reconciliations!—by heaven! it would be a Land of promise—milk & Honey!

—Honey! aye there's the rub—

—I once got a surfeit of it

I have the honour to be with the utmost regard

Mad^m Y^r most obed^t humble Servt

T. Shandy.

XI.

UNPUBLISHED. Copy. The jest of this letter was suggested by two passages in the fourth instalment of *Tristram Shandy*, which was published January 22, 1765. (See Book VII, Ch. XIII; and Book VIII, Ch. V.) Like the Pythagoreans, Jenny had a way of "getting out of the world, in order to think well." Some unknown reader at Bath saw a chance for a jest and sent it in, some time in the spring or summer of 1765. Sterne thought it worth copying into his Letter Book.

Sir

Poor Mr Shandy's Sister Jennny [*sic*] going down into the cellar (tho' I am not very sure with which foot she took the first step, but believe it was the left) to draw beer, surrounded with a cloud of philosophical thoughts, observed the beer run in a constant stream into the black utensil—the noise immediately calling to her remembrance that which she had heard so often, she naturally look'd down, but saw no water———

The Shandy-family desire this may be the 2^d chapter of y^r next book, and that this original Letter be preserved with the same care, & in the same Cabinet with the Bishop of Glocester's Letter .

from Sir
y^r humble Servant
Jenny Shandy

Bath

XII.

Unpublished. Apparently a copy, with one alteration, of a letter to John, Lord Spencer (created Viscount Spencer of Althorp in 1761, and Earl in 1765), thanking him for a silver standish. An account of the friendship between Sterne and Lord Spencer is given in this biography.

Coxwould Oct. 1. 1765

My Lord

I wish I knew how to thank you properly for your obliging present; for to do it with all the sense I have of your goodness to me, would offend You; and to do it with less—would offend myself. I can only say to Lord Spencer *"That I thank him"* and promise him at the same time what I know will be more acceptable, That I will make his kind Wish in the Inscription* as prophetic as the singularity of so odd a composition as I am made up of, will let me.

I will trouble your Lordship with nothing more upon this subject—but this—That when the Fates—or Follies of the Shandean family have melted down every ounce of silver belonging to it—

—That this shall go last to the Mint,—but I blush at the thought; for in the worst wreck that can happen, I hereby ordain and decree, That the rest of the Shandeans retire philo-

sophically into some corner of the world with this Testimony
of Lord Spencer's Kindness to their Ancestor.

> I have, my Lord, the
> honour to be, with the
> truest regard

* Laurentio Sterne A. M:
Joannes Comes Spencer
Musas, charitasque omnes
propitias precatur.

> Y^r Lord^{ps}
> faithful Servant
> L. Sterne

XIII.

UNPUBLISHED. A fair copy made by Sterne from an unpublished
letter by Hall-Stevenson on the attacks upon him in the London
magazines. These attacks were especially violent on the appearance
of *Two Lyric Epistles* in April, 1760. On the part played by William Warburton, the Bishop of Gloucester, in the controversy over
these facetious poems, see Warburton's letter to Sterne, June 15,
1760, and Sterne's reply, June 19, 1760.

> Crasy Castle
> July 13 – 1766

From J. Hall Esqre

You see, my dear Cosin, the Reviewers have have [*sic*] had
a stroke at me, and in good truth not without cause—and so I
am very contrite for my bestiality with the Bishop of G——
but there is no help for it; so lend me some assistance to set
me well again with myself. it was against my own feelings—
but for the sake of a Joke many a wiser man has done as
beastly a thing.

> Adio.
> Antonio.

XIV.

UNPUBLISHED. Draft or copy (with some re-phrasing) of Sterne's
reply to the foregoing letter. In his reply Sterne alludes to his letter
to Dr. * * * * * * *, dated January 30, 1760, concerning Dr.
Kunastrokius and to a passage in the first instalment of *Tristram
Shandy* (Book I, Ch. VII).

This and the preceding letter, though clearly dated 1766, probably belong to the summer of 1760. That is, in making copies of them, Sterne inadvertently wrote 1766 for 1760. There are instances of similar mistakes in Sterne's correspondence.

Coxwould

July 15 . 1766

To J. Hall Esqre

Thou has so tender a conscience my dear Cosin Antonio, and takest on so sadly for thy sins, that thou wast certainly meant and intended to have gone to heaven—if ever Wit went there—but of that, I have some slight mistrusts, inasmuch as we have all of us (accounting myself, thou seest, as one) had, if not our good things, at least our good sayings in this life; & the Devil thou knowest, who is made up of spight, will not let them pass for nothing: and now I am persuaded in my mind, that it was by suggestions of Satan, which, I trust my dear Antonio, we shall live finally to beat down under our feet, That thou gavest heed unto these Reviewers, & didst not rather chuse to cut them, as Jehudi did the role, with a penknife, than vex and pucker thy conscience at the rate thou doest. Heaven forgive me! for I said twice as much both of Kunastrokius and Solomon too—but every footman and chamber maid in town knew both their stories before hand—& so there was an end of the matter.

These poor Devils, as well as thou and I, will have *their Say*"—or else they cannot have their supper; & the best way I trow is to let them stop their own mouths—

A thousand nothings, or worse than nothings, have been every day snatching my pen out of my hands since I parted with you; I take it up today in good earnest & shall not let it go till York races—unless the devil should tempt you in y^r contritions to Scarborough—If you would profit by y^r misfortunes, & laugh away misery there for a week—ecco lo il vero Punchinello! I am your man, only send me Letter of *Ifs*, and *hows*, and *whens*" for you know I have reformed my Cavalry—B – – – has left me his post chaise, & when I say my Lord's prayer, I always think of it—to understand w^cb it will put thee Antony, to runing over thy *Pater noster* w^cb I fear thou hast not done these many years.

> May god give you grace
> & believe me, dear Cosin
> most Aff^ly Y^rs
>
> L. S.

XV.

PUBLISHED, from another manuscript, by Sterne's daughter, Mrs. Medalle, in *Letters of the late Rev. Mr. Laurence Sterne*, Vol. III, 22-26 (London, 1775). This letter could not have been written just as it is by Sancho. Not only is it in Sterne's own hand but it is mostly in Sterne's style. As I surmise, the original letter that Sterne received from Sancho was elaborated for the Letter Book. It is a fair copy ready for the printer.

At this time Sancho, as the letter shows, was in the service of Charles, Lord Cadogan, a colonel in the Horse Guards and a trustee of the British Museum.

The sermon from which Sancho's quotation was taken is the one entitled *Job's Account of the Shortness and Troubles of Life, Considered*.

Reverend Sir—

It would be an insult, (or perhaps look like one), on your Humanity, to apologise for the Liberty of this address—*unknowning* and *unknown* . I am one of those people whom the illiberal and vulgar call a Nee—gur—: the early part of my Life was rather unlucky; as I was placed in a family who judged that Ignorance was the best Security for obedience: a little Reading and writing, I got by unwearied application— the latter part of my life has been more fortunate; having spent it in the honourable service of one of the best families in the kingdome; my chief pleasure has been books; philanthropy I adore—how much do I owe you good Sir, for that soul pleasing Character of your amiable uncle Toby! I declare

I would walk ten miles in the dog days, to shake hands with the honest Corporal—Your Sermons good Sir, are a cordial: but to the point, the reason of this address. in your 10th Discourse—p.78 Vol.2^d. is this truely affecting passage. "Consider how great a part of our species in all ages down to this, have been trod under the feet of cruel and capricious Tyrants who would neither hear their cries, nor pity their distresses—Consider Slavery—what it is,—how bitter a draught! and how many millions have been made to drink of it——

of all my favourite writers, not one do I remember, that has had a tear to spare for the distresses of my poor moorish brethren, Yourself, and the truely humane auther of Sr George Ellison excepted: I think Sir, you will forgive, perhaps applaud me for zealously intreating you to give half an hours attention to slavery (as it is at this day undergone in the West Indies; that subject handled in your own manner, would ease the Yoke of many, perhaps occasion a reformation throughout our Islands—But should only *one* be the better for it—gracious God! what a feast! very sure I am, that Yorick is an Epicurean in Charity—universally read & universally admired —you could not fail. dear Sir think in me, you behold the uplifted hands of Millions of my moorish brethren—Grief (you pathetically observe), is eloquent—figure to yourselves their attitudes—hear their supplicatory address—humanity must comply

in which humble hope permit me to subscribe myself Revd Sir, your most humble and Obedient Servant

Ignatius Sancho .

July 21. 1766

(Lord Cadogan's White hall)—

XVI.

PUBLISHED, from a somewhat different copy, by Mrs. Medalle, in *Letters of the late Rev. Mr. Laurence Sterne*, Vol. III, 27-30. This and the preceding letter, taken together, form a sentimental discourse on slavery.

Coxwould

July 27. 1766

There is a strange coincidence, Sancho, in the little events, as well as the great ones of this world; for I had been writing a tender tale of the sorrows of a friendless poor negro girl, and my eyes had scarse done smarting, when your Letter of recommendation in behalf of so many of her brethren and Sisters came to me—by why, *her brethren?*—or yours? Sancho,—any more than mine: it is by the finest tints and most insensible gradations that nature descends from the fairest face about St James's, to the sootyest complexion in Africa: at which tint of these, is it, Sancho, that the ties of blood & nature cease? and how many tones must we descend lower still in the scale, 'ere Mercy is to vanish with them? but tis no uncommon thing my good Sancho, for one half of the world to use the other half of it, like brutes, and then endeavour to make 'em so.

for my own part, I never look westward, (when I am in a pensive mood at least) but I think of the burdens which our brethren are there carrying; and could I take one ounce from the Shoulders of a few of 'em who are the heaviest loaden'd, I would go a Pilgrimage to Mecca for their Sakes—which by the by, exceeds your Walk, Sancho, of ten miles to see the honest Corporal, in about the same proportion that a Visit of Humanity should one, of mere form—if you meant the Corporal more he is your Debtor

If I can weave the Tale I have wrote, into what I am about, tis at the service of the afflicted; and a much greater matter: for in honest truth, it casts, a great Shade upon the world, that so great a part of it, are, and have been so long bound down in chains of darkness & in chains of misery; and I cannot but both honour and felicitate you, That by so much laudable diligence you have freed yourself from one—and that, by falling into the hands of so good & merciful a family, Providence has rescued you from the other—and so, good hearted Sancho, adieu! & be assured I will not forget y^r Letter.

L. Sterne——

XVII.

Unpublished. Copy, with alterations, of an unpublished letter to some young man (perhaps William Combe) who had suddenly gone over to Paris.

To —— ——

London Bond street

Jan – 6 – 1767

I arrived here but yesterday, where, (after a terrible journey in most inhospitable weather) I was met agreeably with your Letter from Paris—I first sympathize for the unkind greeting upon french-ground which you met with by your over throw—may it be the last shock you receive in this world!— this reflection, costs me a deep Sigh—& alas! my friend! I dread it will let you go off no cheaper—I fear something has gone wrong with you; if so; why would not you make me a partner? I am a dab at giving advice,—& I esteemd and loved you—& you knew it.

If I am wrong, my friendship has only been too quick sighted and perhaps too easily alarm'd by false appearances; only there were some little mysterious turns & windings in the manner of your leaving England, which mark'd the steps of an entangled man. is it some nasty scrape of gallantry?—or a more cleanly one of simple Love? If it is the latter, I'll put off my Cassoc & turn Knight Errant for you, & say the kindest things of you to Dulcinea that Dulcinea ever heard—if she has a Champion—and words will not atchieve it—Ill enter the Lists with him, and break a spear in your behalf; tho by the by, mine is half rusty, and should be hung up in the old family hall amongst Pistols without Cocks, and Helmets which have lost their Vizards—

I miscarried of my tenth Volume by the violence of a fever, I have just got thro'—I have however gone on to my reckoning with the ninth, of wch I am all this week in Labour pains; & if to Days Advertiser is to be depended upon shall be safely deliver'd by tuesday.

adieu. I heartily wish your happiness—seek it where you will, my dear Sir, You will find it no where, but in Company with Virtue and Honour .

I am &c ——

L–S–

XVIII.

UNPUBLISHED. This, I infer from the erasures, is a draft rather than a copy of a letter to the Bramine, i.e., Mrs. Elizabeth Draper, then on the way to India. The superscription, which Sterne tried to blot out with his pen is "Coxwould, June 18." The year, not given, must be 1767. Towards the close of the letter, Sterne asks the Bramine why she has not yet written to him. Her first letter awaited him when he came to York on July 27. (See *The Journal to Eliza*, under that date.) Cordelia, over whose grave Sterne sentimentalizes, was one of the "long-lost sisters" who lie buried in the ruins of Byland Abbey, two miles from Coxwold.

My dear Bramine

I have some time forboded I should think of you too much; and behold it is come to pass; for there is not a day in which I have not of late, detected myself a dozen times at least in the fact of thinking and reflecting some way or other with pleasure upon you; but in no time or place, do I call your figure so strongly up to my imagination and enjoy so much of of y^r good heart and sweet converse as when I am in company with my Nuns: tis for this reason, since I have got down to this all-peaceful and romantick retreat, that my Love and my Devotion are ever taking me and leading me gently by the hand to these delicious Mansions of our long-lost Sisters: I am just now return'd from one of my nightly visits; & tho' tis late, for I was detain'd there an hour longer than I was aware of, by the sad silence and breathlessness of the night, and the delusive subject (for it was yourself) which took up the conversation—yet late as it is, I cannot go to bed without writing to you & telling you how much, and how many kind things we have been talking about you these two hours—Cordelia! said I as I lay half reclined upon her grave—long—long, has thy spirit triumphed over these infirmities, and all the

contentions to wch the human hearts are subject—alas! thou
hast had thy share—for she look'd, I thought, down upon me
with such a pleasurable sweetness—so like a delegated Angel
whose breast glow'd with fire, that Cordelia could not have
been a stranger to the passion on earth—poor, hapless Maid!
cried I—Cordelia gently waved her head—it was enough—I
turn'd the discourse to the object of my own disquietudes—I
talk'd to her of my Bramine—I told her, how kindly nature
had formd you—how gentle—how wise—how good—Cordelia, (me thought) was touchd with my description, and
glow'd insensibly, as sympathetic Spirits do, as I went on—
This Sisterly kind Being with whose Idea I have inflamed
your Love, Cordelia! has promised, that she will one night or
other come in person, and in this sacred Asylum pay your
Shade a sentimental Visit along with me—when? when? said
she, animated with desire—God knows, said I pulling out my
handkerchief & droping tears faster than I could wipe them
off—when God knows! said I, crying bitterly as I repeated
the words—God knows! but I feel something like prophetic
conviction within me, which says, that this gentlest of her Sex
will some time take sanctuary from the cares and treachery of
the world and come peacefully & live amongst You——and
why not sleep amongst us too?—O heaven! said I, laying my
hand upon my heart—and will not you, Yorick, mix your ashes
with us too?—for ever my Cordelia! and some kind hearted
Swain shall come and weed our graves, as I have weeded
thine, and when he has done, shall sit down at our feet and
tell us the Stories of his passions and his disappointments.

My dear Bramine, tell me honestly, if you do not wish from
your soul to have been of this party—aye! but then as it was
dark and lonely, I must have been taken by the hand & led
home by you to your retired Cottage—and what then? But I
stop here—& leave you to furnish the answer.—*a propos*—
pray when you first made a conquest of T. Shandy did it ever
enter your head what a visionary, romantic, kind of a Being
you had got hold of? When the Bramine suffered so careless
and laughing a Creature to enter her [roof?], did she dream
of a man of Sentiments, and that She was opening the door to

such a one, to make him prisoner for Life—O Woman! to
what purpose hast thou exercised this power over me? or, to
answer what end in nature, was I led by so mysterious a path
to know you—to love you—and fruitlessly to lament and sigh
that I can only send my spirit after you, as I have done this
night to my Cordelia—poor! spotless Shade! the world at least
is so merciful as not to be jealous of our Intercourse—I can
paint thee blessed Spirit all-generous and kind as hers I write
to—I can lie besides thy grave, and drop tears of tenderness
upon the Turf wch covers thee, and not one passenger turn his
head aside to remark or envy one—But for thee, dear Bramine, (for alas! alas! what a world do we live in)—it tells
me, I must not approach your Shrine, even were it to worship
you with with [*with* repeated] the most unspotted Sacrifise—
at this distance, it will give me leave to offer it up upon y^r
altar—and at present I must be content with that Licence—
then Let me, my dear Goddesse, accept it kindly—let me
swear before her Altar That She never had heard a prayer
from a warmer heart; or rec^d Insense from a more honest
Votary—Let me tell her once more I love her; and as a good
Christian is taught to love his maker—that is, for his own sake
and the excellencies of his Nature.

now in answer to all this, why have I never rec^d one gracious nod, conveyed thro' from You? why do you not write to
me? is writing painful? or is it only so, to me? dear Lady
write anything, and write it any how, so it but comes from y^r
heart, twil be better than the best Letter that ever came from
Pope's head—In short, write y^r Nonsense, if you have any—
write y^r Chit Chat—your pleasures, your pains, y^r present hu-
mours and present feelings (would to God I had just now hold
of y^r hand).—I want to hear you are well—I want to hear
You say, you have something more than cold esteem for me—
in short I know not what I want I want [*sic*]—

       I have the honour to be, dear Bramine——
              &c &c &c——
                The Bramin

XIX.

THIS is the very autograph letter that Sterne wrote out and sent to Miss Fourmantelle for her to copy and send to Garrick as if it were her own. Here we have Sterne's comment upon himself and *Tristram Shandy*. Published in *Unpublished Letters of Laurence Sterne*, pp. 8-9, in *Miscellanies of the Philobiblon Society*, Vol. II (London, 1855-1856).

York Jan. 1 [1760]

S^r

I dare say You will wonder to receive an Epistle from me, and the Subject of it will surprise You still more, because it is to tell You something about Books.

There are two Volumes just published here which have made a great noise, & have had a prodigious Run; for in 2 Days after they came out, the Bookseller sold two hundred— & continues selling them very fast. It is, The Life & Opinions of Tristram Shandy, which the Author told me last night at our Concert, he had sent up to London, so perhaps you have seen it; if you have not seen it, pray get it & read it, because it has a great Character as a witty smart Book, and if You think it is so, your good word in Town will do the Author, I am sure great Service; You must understand, He is a kind & generous friend of mine whom Providence has attach'd to me in this part of the world where I came a stranger—& I could not think how I could make a better return than by endeavouring to make you a friend to him & his Performance.—this is all my Excuse for this Liberty, which I hope you will excuse. His name is Sterne, a gentleman of great Preferment & a Prebendary of the Church of York, & has a great Character in these Parts as a man of Learning & wit,—the Graver People however say, tis not fit for young Ladies to read his Book. so perhaps you'l think it not fit for a young Lady to recommend it. however the Nobility, & great Folks stand up mightily for it, & say tis a good Book tho' a little tawdry in some places,—

I am dear Sir

Y^r most Obd^t &

humble Servant

XX.

Original letter to David Garrick. Removed in 1922 from the Autograph Album of the Duke of Sussex. First published in *The Archivist*, September, 1894 (Vol. VII, No. 27, p. 140-141). This letter may be regarded as "a follow-up" of the preceding. Dr. Goddard, to whom there is a reference, was probably the Harry Goddard who first informed Mrs. Montagu's brother, Matthew Robinson, of Sterne's marriage. See E. J. Climenson, *Elizabeth Montagu*, Vol. I, 73-74.

York Jan 27. 1760

Sir

I had a strong Propensity when I did myself the pleasure of sending You the two Vol^s, to have accompanied them with a Letter to You:——I took up my Pen twice——hang it!——I shall write a vile insinuating Letter, the english of which will be,——to beg Mr Garrick's good word for my Book, whether the Book deserves it [or] no——I will not,——the Book shall go to the Devil first.   But being told yesterday by Doct^r Goddard, That You had actually spoke well of my Book, that Scruple is got over, and I feel myself at Liberty to attend to the Movements of Gratitude (& perhaps of Vanity) to return You my Thanks, Sir, which I heartily do, for the great Service & Honour, your good Word has done me. I know not what it was (tho' I lye abominably, because I know very well) which inclined me more to wish for your Approbation, than any Other's——but my first Impulse, was to send it to You, to have had your Critique upon it, before it went to the Press——it fell out otherwise, and has therefore gone forth into the world, hot as it came from my Brain, without one Correction:——tis however a picture of myself, & so far may bid the fairer for being an Original.

I sometimes think of a Cervantic Comedy upon these & the Materials of ye 3^d & 4th Vol^s which will be still more dramatick,——tho I as often distrust its Successe, unless at the Universities.

Half a word of Encouragement would be enough to make

I know very well) which inclined me more to
wish for your Approbation, than any Other's — but
my first Impulse, was to send it to you, to have
had your Critique upon it, before it went to the
Press — it fell out otherwise, and has therefore gone forth
into the world, hot as it came from my Brain,
without one Correction: — 'tis however a picture
of myself, & so far may bid the fairer for being
an Original.

I sometimes think of a Cervantic Comedy
upon these & the materials of yᵉ 3ᵈ & 4ᵗʰ Vdˢ which
will be still more dramatick, — tho' I often distrust
its Success, unless at the Universities.

Half a word of Encouragement would
be enough to make me conceive & bring forth
something for the Stage (how good, or how bad,
is another Story).

I am Sir
with the most sincere Esteem for
yᵉ great Talents
yᵉ most obliged & humble servant
Laurence Sterne.

Reduced facsimile of a page from a letter to Garrick
From the manuscript in the Pierpont Morgan Library

me conceive, & bring forth something for the Stage (how
good, or how bad, is another Story).

I am
    Sir
with the most sincere Esteem for
    Y^r great Talents
        Y^r most obliged & humble Servant
                    Laurence Sterne.

XXI.

THE letter to Richard Berenger as it was sent. See No. III for the
draft and comment.

Saturday

My dear Berenger .

You bid me tell You all my Wants——What the Devil in
Hell can the fellow want now?——By the Father of the Sciences (you know his Name) I would give both my Ears (If I
was not to loose my Credit by it) for no more than ten Strokes
of *Howgarth's* witty Chissel, to clap at the Front of my next
Edition of *Shandy* .——The Vanity of pretty Girl in the Hey
day of her Roses & Lillies, is a fool to that of Author of my
Stamp——Oft did Swift sigh to Pope in these Words——Orna
me——Unite something of Yours to mine, to transmit us down
together hand in hand to futurity. The loosest Sketch in Nature, of Trim's reading the Sermon to my Father &c; w^d do
the Business——& it w^d mutually illustrate his System & mine
——But my dear Shandy with what face——I would hold out
my lank Purse—I would Shut my Eyes—, & You should put
in your hand, & take out what you liked for it—*Ignoramus!*
Fool! Blockhead! Symoniack!—This Grace is not to be
bought with money—perish thee & thy Gold with thee!

What Shall we do? I have the worst face in the world to
ask a favour with—& besides I would not propose a disagreeable thing to one I so much admire for the whole world—but
you can say any thing—You are an impudent honest Dog &
can'st set a face upon a bad Matter—prithee sally out to

Leicester fields, and when You have knockd at the door (for you must knock first) and art got in—begin thus "—Mr Hogarth, I have been with my friend Shandy this morning"— but go on y^r own Way—as I shall do mine I esteem You & am my dear Mentor

Y^rs most Shandaically
L Sterne

XXII.

ORIGINAL letter written by Sterne, when in London, to Mrs. Elizabeth Montagu. First published, with a few mistakes in reading the manuscript, by Emily J. Climenson, in *Elizabeth Montagu*, Vol. II, 175-176 (London, 1906). On the quarrels in the Church of York, see the fourth and seventh chapters of this biography. Dr. William Herring, the Chancellor, apparently tried to stir up trouble between Sterne and Dean Fountayne after the publication of *A Political Romance* in 1759. The letter that Sterne "wrote last month to the Dean" is also mentioned in the "Memorandums," dated December, 28, 1761. The correspondence probably belongs to the spring of 1761. Samuel Torriano, a young man in Mrs. Montagu's set, was then secretary to John Gilbert, Archbishop of York (who died at his house at Twickenham, August 9, 1761).

Madam .

I never was so much at a loss, as I find myself at this instant that I am going to answer the letter I have had the honour & happiness to receive from you by Mr Torriano; being ten times more oppress'd with the excesse of your candour & goodness than I was before with the subject of my complaint: It was entirely oweing to the Idea I had, in common with all the world, of Mrs Montague, that I felt sorrow at all—or communicated what I felt to my friend; wch last step I should not have taken but from the great reliance I had upon the excellency of y^r Character: I wanted mercy—but not sacrifise; and am obliged in my turn, to beg pardon of You, which I do from my Soul, for putting You to the pain of excuseing, what in fact was more a misfortune, than a fault; & but a necessary consequence of a train of Impressions given to my disadvantage; The Chancellor of York Dr Herring, was I suppose the person, who interested himself in the honour of the Dean of York, & requested that act of friendship to be done the Dean, by bringing about a Separation betwixt the Dean & myself— the poor Gentleman has been labouring this point many Years —but not out of Zeal for the Dean's Character, but to secure the next Residentiaryship to the Dean of St Asaph his Son; he has outwitted himself at last, & has now all the foul play to settle with his Conscience, without gaining, or being ever likely to gain his purpose:—I take the Liberty of incloseing a Letter, I wrote last month to the Dean, which will give some light into my hard measure—& shew You, that I was as much a protection to the Dean of York—as he to me: The Answer to this has made me easy with regard to my Views in the Church of York; & as it has cemented anew the Dean & myself beyond the power of any future breach, I thought it would give you Satisfaction to see how my Interests stand—& how much & undeserved I have been abused: when You have read it—It shall never be read more, for reasons your penetration will see at once.

I return You thanks for the Interest You took in my wife— & there is not an honest Man, who will not do me the Justice to say, I have ever given her the Character of as moral & virtuous a woman as ever God made—What Occasion'd Discontent ever betwixt us, is now no more—we have settled Acc^{ts} to each others Satisfaction & honour—& I am persuaded shall end our days with out one word of reproach or even incivility:

Mr Torriano made me happy in acquainting me that I was to dine with You on Friday: it shall be my Care as well as my Principle ever to behave so, That You may have no cause to repent of y^r goodness to me . I am Madam

with the truest Gratitude
y^r most obliged & aff^{te}
Kinsman Lau^r Sterne

XXIII.

UNPUBLISHED. Original letter, formerly in the Huth Library, addressed to Mr. Mills, a merchant in Philpot Lane, London. Mr. Oswald, mentioned in the letter, was a young man (presumably in the employ of Mr. Mills), with whom Sterne became acquainted at Montpellier. See chapter XIV of this biography.

Montpellier Nov.24.1763

My dear Sir, will you be so kind to me as to lend me fifty pounds till I get to England or rather give me leave to draw upon You to the extent of that Summ, in case I should find it needful upon winding up my bottoms on leaving this Country: now it seems a little paradoxical, when I have so many friends and well wishers I live with as Brothers, I should rather take this Liberty with a friend whose face I never yet saw—but the truth, upon running the List over in my mind, I found not one, I could take such a Liberty with, wth less pain of heart— which is all the apology I will make.

ever Since I had last the pleasure of writing to You before my going to Bagniers, till six Weeks ago, that I settled here, I have never had one moments respit from ill health—the Thiness of the pyrenean Air brought on continual breaches of Vessels in my Lungs, & with them all the Tribe of evils insident to a pulmonary Consumption—there seem'd nothing left but gentle change of place & air; & accordingly, I put myself into motion, & with a cheary heart, having traversed the South of France so often that I ran a risk of being taken up for a Spy, I jogg'd myself out of all other dangers—& hope in 9 or 10 Weeks to bekiss y^r hands in perfect (i.e. in relative health. You may be assured dear Sir, my first Visit will be to Philpot Lane, to bring along wth me, (at least) the Interest in ten thousand thanks—& for the Capital, the whole Shandean family will stand bound—You shall be paid the very first Money God sends—May he send You my dear friend its Blessings. wch in my Computation, are comprehended in Health & peace of Mind—present my Resp^{ts} with my kindest Wishes to Mr Oswald—& believe me most truely Y^{rs}

L . Sterne

XXIV.

LETTER to M. Foley, Sterne's banker in Paris. First published, altered and mutilated, by Mrs. Medalle, in *Letters of the late Rev. Mr. Laurence Sterne.* Printed from the manuscript by W. H. Arnold in *Ventures in Book Collecting,* 170-172. Address on the back.

The portrait that Sterne wishes to have copied was probably the water-color by Carmontelle. M. Pelletiere (Etienne Michel Le Pelletier de Saint-Fargeau), Avocat Général in the action against the Jesuits which led to their expulsion from France. See index for Holbach and Selwin.

York. Nov:11 · 1764

My dear friend

I sent ten days a go a bank bill of thirty pounds to Mr Becket and have this day sent him a Bill payable upon sight for fifty two pounds ten Shillings;—When I get to London wch will be in 5 weeks, you will rec^{ve} what shall always keep you in bank for Mrs Sterne—In the mean time, I have desired Becket to remit you this 82 p^{ds}—& if Mrs Sterne, before I get to London, sh^d have Occasion for 50 Louis—be so kind as to honour her draught upon You; but I believe I shall have paid the Money I purpose into Beckets hands by the time She will want—but if otherwise a week or fortnight, I know, will break no squares with a good & worthy friend. I will contrive to send you these 2 new Vol^s of Tristram, as soon as ever I get them from the press—You will read as odd a Tour thro' france, as ever was projected or executed by traveller or travell Writer, since the world began—

—tis a laughing good temperd Satyr against Traveling (as puppies travel)—Panchaud will enjoy it—I am quite civil to the parisians—et *per Cosa*—You know—tis likely I may see 'em again—& possibly this Spring . ——is it possible for you to get me over a Copy of my picture anyhow?—If so—I would write to Mlle Navarre to make as good a Copy from it as She possibly could—with a view to do her Service here—& I w^d remit her 5 Louis—I really believe, twil be the parent of a dozen portraits to her—if she executes it with the spirit of the Original in y^r hands—for it will be seen by half London

—and as my Phyz is as remarkable as myself——if she preserves the character of both, 'twil do her honour & service too——

write me a Line ab^t this—& tel me you are well, & happy &c—

will you present my most grateful resp^ts to the worthy Baron D'Holbach——I want to send him one of the best Impressions of my Picture from Reynolds, & another to Mon^s Pelletiere——

My kind respects to Mr Selwin——tell Panchaude I greet him kindly

& for y^rself, believe me dear Foley

most faithfully & warmly

Y^rs L – Sterne

XXV.

ORIGINAL letter with original cover, addressed to "Messieurs Foley & Panchaude Banquiers Rue St Sauveur a Paris." First published, without postscript, by Mrs. Medalle in *Letters of the late Rev. Mr. Laurence Sterne.*

Turin . Nov:15-1765

Dear Sir

After many difficulties I have got safe & sound—tho eight days in passing the Mountain's of Savoy. I am stop'd here for ten days by the whole Country betwixt here & Milan [being laid] under Water by continual rains—but I am very happy—and have found my Way into a dozen houses already—to morrow I am to be presented, to the King—and when that Ceremony is over, have my hands full of Engagements—no english here but Sr James Macdonald, who meets with much respect.—and Mr Ogilby—we are all together; and shall depart in peace together. my kind Services to all—& be so good as to forward the inclosed—

Y^rs most truely. L. Sterne

PS.

My Comp^s to Miss Panchaude——

XXVI.

THESE "Memorandums" (two leaves measuring 12½ x 7⅞ inches), which Sterne left with Mrs. Elizabeth Montagu for his wife in case he should die abroad, were never delivered. They formed a part of the immense body of manuscript letters preserved by Mrs. Montagu, and were first published, with many mistakes, by her great-great-niece, Mrs. Emily J. Climenson in *Elizabeth Montagu*, Vol. II, 270-272. Subsequently the manuscript was acquired by the late William Harris Arnold, who reprinted it, with fewer mistakes, in *Ventures in Book Collecting*, 163-166. The manuscript was purchased by Mr. Morgan in November, 1924. Two round yellow stains on the manuscript are supposed to have come from tears that Sterne let fall when he saw near at hand his departure from the world. One tear he let fall over the name of Lydia; the other upon the open space just after he had written for his wife "we shall meet again." The manuscript is endorsed, in another hand, "Sternes letters."

Sterne is not quite accurate when he says that his *Political Romance* "was never published." It was published, but suppressed. A few copies have been discovered. His *Conscio* (i.e. *Concio*) *ad Clerum* and his "long, pathetic letter" to Dean Fountayne have never come to light. "The Pictures of the Mountebank and his Macaroni" (i.e. Thomas Bridges and Laurence Sterne) have often been reproduced. It is not known who was the lady in the case. A guess would be the Countess of Edgcumbe.

Dec : 28. 1761 Memorandums left with Mrs Montagu, In Case I should die abroad.

L. Sterne

my Sermons in a Trunk at my friend Mr Halls St John Street.——2 Vols, to be picked out of them—NB. There are enough for 3 Vol^s.—

My Letters, in my Bureau at Coxwould & a Bundle in the Trunk with my Sermons—

Note. The large piles of Letters in the Garrets at York, to be sifted over, in search for some either of Wit, or Humor— or what is better than both—of Humanity & good nature— these will make a couple of Vol^s more.—and as not one of 'em was ever wrote, like Popes or Voitures to be printed, they are more likely to be read—if there wants aught to serve the Completion of a 3ᵈ Volume,—the Political Romance I wrote, wᶜʰ was never publish'd—may be added to the fag end of the Volˢ . . . Tho I have 2 Reasons why I wish it may not be wanted—first, an undeserved Compliment to One, whom I have since found to be a very corrupt man—I knew him weak & ignorant—but thought him honest.   The other reason is I have hung up Dʳ Topham, in the romance—in a ridiculous light—wᶜʰ; upon my Soul I now doubt, whether he deserves it—so let the Romance go to sleep, not by itself—for twil have Company.

My *Conscio ad Clerum* . in Latin wᶜʰ I made for Fountayne, to preach before the University, to enable him to take his Doctor's Degree—you will find, 2 Copies of it, with my sermons—

—He got Honour by it—what Got I?—nothing in my Life time. then Let me not (I charge you Mʳˢ Sterne) be robb'd of it after my death. That long pathetic Letter to him of the hard measure I have rcᵈ—I charge you, to let it be printed——Tis equitable, You should derive that good from my Sufferings at least.

I have made my Will—but I leave all I have to You & my Lydia—You will not Quarrel abᵗ it—but I advise You to sell my Estate, wᶜʰ will bring 1800 pᵈˢ (or more after the war)— & what you can raise from my Works—& the Sale of the last Copy-right of yᵉ 5 & 6 Volˢ of Tristram—& the produce of this last work, all wᶜʰ I have left (except 50 pᵈˢ) in my Bookseller Beckets hands, & wᶜʰ Mʳ Garrick will receive and lay out in Stocks for me—all these together, I wᵈ advise You to collect together—wᵗʰ the Sale of my Library &c &c—& lay it out in Goverment Securitys—If my Lydia shᵈ Marry—I charge you,—I charge you over again, (that you may remember it yᵉ more and ballance it more)—That upon no Delusive prospect, or promise from any one, You leave Yʳself DEPENDENT; reserve enough for yʳ comfort—or let her wait yʳ Death.

I leave this in the hands of Our Cosin Mrs Montague—not because She is our Cosin—but because, I am sure she has a good heart.

we shall meet again .

Mem^dun Whenever I die—tis most probable, I shall have ab^t 200ll due to me from my Livings—If Lydia sh^d dye before You: Leave my Sister, something worthy of y^rself—in Case you do not think it meet to purchase an annuity for your greater Comfort: if You chuse that—do it in God's name—
—The 2 Pictures of the Mountebank & his Macaroni—is in a Lady's hands, who upon seeing 'em—most cavallierly declared She would never part with them—And from an excesse of Civility—or rather Weakness, I could not summon up severity, to demand them:—If I dye. her Name &c is inclose[d] in a billet seald up & given with this—& then you must demand them—If refused—you have nothing to do, but send a 2^d Message importing—'tis not for her Interest to keep them.—

Laurence Sterne

Memorandums
left by
Mr Sterne in
Mrs Montagu's hands
before he left England

BIBLIOGRAPHY

I.

Published Works

THIS division of the bibliography has two purposes—perhaps of equal importance, though they are quite different.

One purpose is to describe the first editions of Sterne's separate works, and occasionally a second or a third edition if it has peculiar interest. The measurements, which vary in different copies, are by inches, height being given first. The abbreviation, p.l., stands for preliminary leaf or leaves. When obtainable, the exact date of publication is given for first editions; and where it appears necessary, there is added a certain amount of comment supplementary to the more general information which may be found in the biography itself. An attempt has been made, the comment will show, to settle several bibliographical questions long in controversy.

The other purpose is rather an aim towards a complete record of Sterne's writings, major and minor, that have ever been published. With this end in view, the contents of the first critical edition of Sterne's *Works* (1780) are given; and all of Sterne's writings that have since been discovered and published are listed in the order of their first appearance—whether in subsequent editions of his *Works*, in collections of his letters, in biographies of the humorist, in periodicals, or elsewhere.

The record is doubtless incomplete; and were it complete now it might not be complete a year hence, for there must be in existence many of Sterne's letters that have not yet come out into the light. There must be also several minor pieces hidden away in obscure places. Where, for instance, is the *Concio ad Clerum* that Sterne wrote for Dean Fountayne? And where is

the *Comic Romance* with which he was amusing himself a
fortnight before death?

1741

Query upon Query; / Being an / Answer to J.S's / Letter / Printed
in the *York-Courant Octo-* / *ber* 20, relating to the present / contested Election. / — / Μεγà Βίβλιον, Μεγà Καχòν / — / York: /
Printed in the Year 1741.

8 pages, octavo, Dated "York, Oct. 22. 1741."

Reprinted and described, with reproduction of title page, by L. P.
Curtis, *The Politicks of Laurence Sterne*, 47-58 (London, 1929).

Other political articles contributed to *The York Courant* and to *The
York Gazetteer* in 1741-42 have been identified and reprinted by Mr.
Curtis. Apparently several of these articles, with alterations, circulated
as pamphlets, though no other has yet been discovered.

1743

The Unknown World. / Verses occasioned by hearing a Pass-Bell. /
By the Rev. Mr. St—n. / But what's beyond Death? —Who shall
draw that / Veil? Hughes Siege of Damascus.

In *The Gentleman's Magazine*, XIII, 376, July, 1743. Reprinted in
The Scots Magazine, V, 318, July, 1743; *The Ladies Magazine*, II, xx,
312, July 27-August 10, 1751.

This poem probably first appeared in a York or London newspaper,
and was reprinted in these and other magazines. The curious symbols
and abbreviations were first given by Thomas Gill, who published the
poem from manuscript in his *Vallis Eboracensis*, pp. 199-200 (London,
Easingwold, 1852), with the title: "The Unknown ⊙ / Verses occasion'd by hearing a Pass-Bell, / Bye ye Revd Mr St—n."

Reprinted by Fitzgerald (1864), Cross (1909), and Melville
(1912), in their biographies of Sterne. First included in Sterne's *Works*
(New York, 1904). Sterne's authorship hitherto regarded as doubtful.

1745-1753

The York Journal, or the Protestant Courant.

Sterne probably wrote for this and other newspapers during the
Jacobite insurrection and at times later. No copy of *The York Journal*
earlier than May 13, 1746, known to exist. Sterne's special interest in
this newspaper, however, is shown by the fact that he kept a file from
the beginning down to March 8, 1748. See Curtis as cited above, xi.

1747

The Case of Elijah and the Widow / of Zerephath, consider'd: /

— / A / Charity-Sermon, / Preach'd on / Good-Friday, April 17, 1747. / In the Parish Church of / St. Michael-le-Belfrey, / Before / The Right Honourable the Lord-Mayor, / Aldermen, Sheriffs and Commoners of / the City of York, at the Annual / Collection for the Support of Two / Charity-Schools. / — / By Laurence Sterne, M.A. / Prebendary of York. / = / York: / Printed for J. Hildyard Bookseller in Stonegate: / And Sold by Mess. Knapton, in St. Paul's / Church-Yard; Mess. Longman and Shewell, / and M. Cooper, in Pater-noster-Row, London. / M.DCC.XLVII. / (Price Six-Pence.)

1 p.l. (Title); [iii]-iv (Dedication: "To the / Very Reverend / Richard Osbaldeston, D.D. / Dean of York."); 32 pp. (Printer's ornaments at head of Dedication, p. iii, and text, p. 1.) 7½ x 4⅝.

Published in July, 1747 (Gent. Mag., July, 1747, p. 348). Included in The Sermons of Mr. Yorick (1760), and in The Practical Preacher (London, 1762).

1750

The Abuses of Conscience: / — / set forth in a / Sermon, / preached in the / Cathedral Church / of / St. Peter's, York, / at the / Summer Assizes, / before the / Hon. Mr. Baron Clive, / and the / Hon. Mr. Baron Smythe, / on Sunday, July 29, 1750. / — / By Laurence Sterne, A.M. / Prebendary of the said Church. / — / Published at the Request of the High Sheriff and Grand Jury. / — / York: / Printed by Cæsar Ward: / For John Hildyard, in Stonegate, 1750. / [Price Six-pence.]

1 p.l. (Title); [i]-iii (Dedication: "To Sir William Pennyman, Bart High Sheriff of the County of York," and to others); 26 pp. (Printer's ornaments at head of Dedication and text. On p. 26, Advertisement: "By the same Author, The Case of Elijah and the Widow of Zerephath, consider'd: A Charity Sermon, Preach'd on Good-Friday, April 17, 1747. For the Support of Two Charity-Schools in York. Printed for John Hildyard. Price 6d.") 7⅝ x 4¼.

Some copies differ in punctuation of title.

Published August 7, 1750 (York Courant, August 7, 1750). In Tristram Shandy, Book II (1760), and in The Sermons of Mr. Yorick (1766).

1759

A / Political Romance, / Addressed / To —— ——, Esq; / of / York. / To which is subjoined a / Key. / — / Ridiculum acri /

Fortius et melius magnas plerumque secat Res. / — / [small ornament] / = / York: / Printed in the Year MDCCLIX. / [Price One Shilling.]

1 p.l. (Title); [1]-24 (A Political Romance &c., printer's ornament at head of caption title, tailpiece p. 24); 25-30 (Postscript, followed by printer's ornament, p. 30); 31-47 (The Key, followed by printer's ornament, p. 47); 49-52 (Letter "To —— ——, Esq; of York.", signed Laurence Sterne); 53-60 (Letter "To Dr. Topham.", signed Lawrence Sterne). 7¹¹⁄₁₆ x 4½.

Published *circa* February 1, 1759 (The two letters forming a part of the pamphlet are dated "Sutton on the Forest, Jan. 20, 1759.").

Of this rare pamphlet, supposed to have been suppressed, four copies are known to exist: one in the Library of the Dean and Chapter of York; one in the Public Library at York; one in the Library of Trinity College, Cambridge, England; one in the collection of Mr. Harold Murdock, Cambridge, Mass. Mr. Murdock's copy ends with page 47.

Reprinted, October, 1914, from the copy in the Library of the Dean and Chapter of York, by Mr. Bruce Rogers, with an introduction by W. L. Cross, for The Club of Odd Volumes, Boston, Mass.

A Political Romance brought to a ludicrous close a hot controversy, in which three other pamphlets appeared. The first was by Dr. Francis Topham of the Prerogative Court of York; the second by Dr. John Fountayne, the Dean of York; and the third by Dr. Topham. Published anonymously, their titles ran:

A Letter Address'd to the Reverend the Dean of York; in which is given a full Detail of some very extraordinary Behaviour of his, in relation to his Denial of a Promise made by him to Dr. Topham. York: Printed in the Year MDCCLVIII. [Price Six-Pence]

An Answer to a Letter address'd to the Dean of York, in the Name of Dr. Topham. York: sold by Thomas Atkinson, Bookseller in the Minster-Yard. MDCCLVIII.

A Reply to the Answer to a Letter lately addressed to the Dean of York. York: printed in the Year MDCCLIX. [Price Six-Pence.]

The first of the three pamphlets is dated York, December 11, 1758; to the second is appended an attestation dated York, December 24, 1758; and to the third an attestation dated December 26, 1758. Sterne thus wrote his Romance during the first three weeks of January, 1759.

It was intimated by Dr. Topham that Sterne bore a hand in the second pamphlet (the one by Dean Fountayne). He probably helped the Dean put it together; his style is visible here and there; and an attestation, dated "York, Dec. 22, 1758," is signed by "Laurence Sterne" along with "Wm. Herring" and "Will. Berdmore." See Chapter VII of this biography.

1760

The / Life / and / Opinions / of / Tristram Shandy, / Gentleman. / [Greek quotation, two lines] / Vol. I. [II] / 1760.

Vol. I: 1 p.l. (Title); 179 pp. Vol. II: 1 p.l. (Title); 182 pp. 6⅜ x 3⅞.

Published in London, January 1, 1760 (*London Chronicle*, December 29-January 1, 1760). Copies were placed on sale at York a week or two earlier by John Hinxman, the bookseller; and by that time a few copies were in the hands of London book reviewers. The statement, often made, that there was an earlier edition than the one described here is quite erroneous. On questions concerning the first edition, see Chapter VIII of this biography.

The / Life / and / Opinions / of / Tristram Shandy, / Gentleman. / [Greek quotation, two lines] / Vol. I. [II] / The Second Edition. / London: / Printed for R. and J. Dodsley in Pall-Mall. / M.DCC.LX.

Vol. I: Frontispiece (Trim reading the Sermon, Ravenet after Hogarth); 3 p.l. (Title, Dedication: "To the Right Honourable / Mr. Pitt."); 179 pp. Vol. II: 1 p.l. (Title); 182 pp. 6⅛ x 3¾.

Published April 3, 1760 (*London Chronicle*, April 1-3, 1760). In paper, type, and pagination (except for preliminary pages of Vol. I.) nearly identical with the first edition.

Twice re-issued by Dodsley in 1760 as The Third Edition and The Fourth Edition, and in 1761 as The Fifth Edition. The Sixth Edition appeared in 1767.

Some copies of The Second Edition (though not so named) have the imprint: "London Printed for D. Lynch, / MDCCLX." In the Pierpont Morgan Library and in the British Museum. Except for title-page the Morgan copy is identical in type, paper, and pagination with The Second Edition published by Dodsley; whereas "the Grenville copy" in the British Museum, bearing Sterne's signature, is a reset of The Second Edition. Lynch seems to have purchased a number of copies of The Second Edition from Dodsley on the understanding that he might put his own name on the title-page, and, when these copies were sold, to have been permitted, as Sterne's signature in the Grenville copy indicates, to reset the work on some royalty agreement. See H. Sellers in *The Times Literary Supplement*, Oct. 21, 1926.

The / Sermons / of / Mr. Yorick. / Vol. I. [II] / [Printer's ornament] / London: / Printed for R. and J. Dodsley in / Pall-Mall.

Vol. I: Frontispiece (Bust portrait of Sterne by Ravenet after Rey-

THE

LIFE

AND

OPINIONS

OF

TRISTRAM SHANDY,

GENTLEMAN.

Ταράσσει τὲς Ἀνθρώπες ἐ τὰ Πράγμαῖα,
ἀλλὰ τὰ περὶ τῶν Πραγμάτων, Δόγμάτα.

VOL. I.

The SECOND EDITION.

LONDON:

Printed for R. and J. DODSLEY in Pall-Mall.
M.DCC.LX.

*Facsimile of Title Page to the Second Edition of
"Tristram Shandy"*

nolds); 1 p.l. (Title); [v]-xi (Preface); 14 leaves (Subscribers 24 pp., Half title: "Sermons / by / Laurence Sterne, / A.M. Prebendary of York, and / Vicar of Sutton on the Forest, and / of Stillington near York. / Vol. I." Special title: "Sermon I. / Inquiry after Happiness."); 176 [i.e., 178] pp. Each Sermon has special half title, verso of p. 23, and half title of Sermon II omitted in paging. [107] (Advertisement); [109-111] (Dedication: "To the Very Reverend Richard Osbaldeston, D.D. Dean of York"). Vol. II: 2 p.l. (Title, Half title, on verso: Half title of Sermon VII); 238 pp. 6 x 3¾.

No date on title-page. Published May 22, 1760 (*London Chronicle*, May 20-22, 1760). Four London Editions within a year. Fifth Edition, 1763. Ninth Edition, 1768. Eleventh Edition, 1769. First Dublin Edition, 1761.

Sermons X and XI, "Job's account of the shortness and troubles of life considered," Job xiv, 1, 2; "Of evil speaking," Jas. i, 26, appeared also in *The Practical Preacher*, Vols. IV and II (London, 1762). Sermons VII and XIII, "Vindication of human nature," Rom. xiv, 7; "Duty of setting bounds to our desires," 2 Kings iv, 13, appeared also in *The English Preacher*, Vol. VIII (London, 1773).

Dialogue. / Sung by Mr. Beard and Miss Fromantel.

In *A / Collection of new / Songs / Sung by / Mr. Beard, Miss Stevenson & Miss Fromantel / at Ranelagh / Composed by / Mr Joseph Baildon / = / London Printed for John Johnson opposite Bow Church in Cheapside. / Of whom may be had / [three column list of 21 song books].* [1760?], pp. 21-23.

Also in *The Laurel, A Collection of English Songs, composed by Mr. Joseph Baildon, for the Voice, Harpsichord, and Violin. Book II. London, Printed for Harrison and Co., No. 18, Pater noster Row.* [1780?], 11-12.

On Sterne's authorship of this Dialogue, see Chapter VIII of this biography, and Sterne's letter to "My Witty Widow, Mrs. F., Coxwould, August 3, 1760."

1761

The / Life / and / Opinions / of / Tristram Shandy, / Gentleman. / Multitudinis imperitæ non formido judicia; meis / tamen, rogo, parcant opusculis—in quibus / fuit propositi semper, a jocis ad seria, a seriis / vicissim ad jocos transire. / Joan. Saresberiensis, / Episcopus Lugdun. / Vol. III. [IV] / London: / Printed for R. and J. Dodsley in Pall-Mall, / M.DCC.LXI.

Vol. III: Frontispiece (The Christening, Ravenet after Hogarth); 1 p.l. (Title); [5]-202 pp. Vol. IV: 2 p.l. (Half title, Title); [2]-220 [i.e. 211] pp. (pp. 147-155 omitted in numbering). 5¹⁵⁄₁₆ x 3¾.

In the copy owned by the late Beverly Chew, the frontispiece is by J. Ryland after Hogarth.

Published January 28, 1761 (*London Chronicle*, January 27-29, 1761). Probably a Second Edition, May 21, 1761 (*London Chronicle*, May 19-21, 1761).

1762

The / Life / and / Opinions / of / Tristram Shandy, / Gentleman. / Dixero si quid fortè jocosius, hoc mihi juris / Cum venia dabis.—Hor. / —Si quis calumnietur levius esse quam decet theo- / logum, aut mordacius quam deceat Christia- / num—non Ego, sed Democritus dixit.— / Erasmus. / Vol. V. [VI] / London: / Printed for T. Becket and P. A. Dehondt, / in the Strand. M DCC LXII.

Vol. V: 3 p.l. (Half title, Title, Dedication: "To the Right Honourable / John, / Lord Viscount Spencer."); 150 pp. Vol. VI: 2 p.l. (Half title, Title. Line divisions differ in quotation from Vol. V, and date is printed MDCCLXII); 155 pp. 5$\frac{15}{16}$ x 3$\frac{5}{8}$.

Sterne's signature usually appears at the head of the first chapter of volume V.

Published December 21, 1761 (*London Chronicle*, December 19-22, 1761).

1765

The / Life / and / Opinions / of / Tristram Shandy, / Gentleman. / Non enim excursus hic ejus, sed opus ipsum est. / Plin. Lib. quintus Epistola sexta. / Vol. VII. [VIII] / London: / Printed for T. Becket and P. A. Dehont, / in the Strand. M DCC LXV.

Vol. VII: 1 p.l. (Title, Errata on verso); 160 pp. Vol. VIII: 1 p.l. (Title); 156 pp. 6 x 3$\frac{3}{4}$.

There was a second issue without the Errata, the errors being corrected in the text.

Sterne's signature usually appears at the head of the first chapter of volume VII.

Published January 22, 1765 (*London Chronicle*, January 21-23, 1765).

1766

The / Sermons / of / Mr. Yorick. / Vol. III. [IV] / [Printer's ornament] / = / London: / Printed for T. Becket and P. A. De Hondt, / near Surry-Street, in the Strand. / M DCC LXVI.

Vol. III: 17 p.l. (Title; Contents of the Third Volume, 2 pp.; Contents of the Fourth Volume, 2 pp.; Half title; Subscribers, 24 pp.; Special title: "Sermon I. / The Character of / Shimei."); [3]-192 pp. Vol. IV: 3 p.l. (Title, Half title, Special title: "Sermon VII. / The History of Jacob, / considered."); [3]-207 pp.; [4] pp. (Books printed for T. Becket). 6 x 3⅝.

Published January 22, 1766 (*London Chronicle*, January 22-23, 1766).

1767

The / Life / and / Opinions / of / Tristram Shandy, / Gentleman. / Si quid urbaniusculè lusum a nobis, per Musas et Cha- / ritas et omnium poetarum Numina, Oro te, ne me / malè capias. / Vol. IX. / London: / Printed for T. Becket and P. A. Dehondt, / in the Strand. MDCCLXVII.

4 p.l. (Half title, Title, Dedication: "A / Dedication / to a / Great Man."); 145 pp. 6 x 3¾.

Sterne's signature usually appears at the head of the first chapter.

Published January 30, 1767 (*London Chronicle*, January 29-31, 1767).

German translation of *Tristram Shandy*, complete, by Bode (Hamburg and Bremen, 1774); French translation, first two vols., by Frénais (Paris, 1776), complete by Frénais and De Bonnay (Paris, 1784-1785); Italian translation, consisting of selections (1829).

Illustrations by Thomas Stothard (London, 1781); by Thomas Rowlandson from original drawings by Newton (*Beauties of Sterne*, London, 1809); by Cruikshank (London, 1832); and by many others.

1768

A / Sentimental Journey / through / France and Italy. / By / Mr. Yorick. / — / Vol. I. [II] / ═ / London: / Printed for T. Becket and P. A. De Hondt, / in the Strand. MDCCLXVIII.

Vol. I: 2 p.l. (Half title: "A / Sentimental Journey, / &c. &c. / Vol. I.," Title); [v]-xx (Subscribers); 203 pp. Vol. II: 2 p.l. (Half title: "A / Sentimental Journey, / &c. &c. / Vol. II.," Title); 208 pp.

In two styles: ordinary paper, 6¼ x 3¾; and "imperial paper" with wide margins, 7 x 4¼. Printed 2500 copies on ordinary paper; 135 copies on "fine" or imperial paper (Printer's memorandum on manuscript in British Museum).

Published February 24 or 25, 1768 (*Lloyd's Evening Post*, February 24-26, 1768).

Subscribers for copies on imperial paper have a star after their names. In some copies appears an Advertisement promising that the work will be completed the next year. Being originally a loose sheet, to be inserted in copies of either of the two styles, this Advertisement was rarely preserved. See Chapter XX of this biography.

Facsimile reprint by the De Vinne Press, 1885. Edition limited to 100 copies. Frontispiece, reproduction of Sterne's portrait from London edition of *Works* (1780). Copy in the Pierpont Morgan Library has original water-color drawings by Henriot, Paris, 1889.

A / Sentimental Journey / through / France and Italy. / By / Mr. Yorick. / — / Vol. I. [II] / — / The Second Edition. / = / London: / Printed for T. Becket and P. A. De Hondt, / in the Strand. MDCCLXVIII.

Vol. I: 1 p.l. (Title); [v]-xx (Subscribers); 203 pp. Vol. II: 1 p.l. (Title); 208 pp. 6 1/16 x 3 5/8.

Published March 29, 1768 (*London Chronicle*, March 26-29, 1768). The Second Edition was followed in the same year by "A New Edition," having the same collation with the omission of the Subscribers, and by an unauthorized cheap edition without publisher's or printer's name in the title. Published the next year in four volumes with *Yorick's Sentimental Journey Continued by Eugenius* (i.e. John Hall-Stevenson) and the first part of *A Political Romance*.

Two Dublin editions, 1768. German translation by Bode (Hamburg and Bremen, 1768); French translation by Frénais (Amsterdam and Paris, 1769); Italian translation by Foscolo (Pisa, 1813); Polish translation (Warsaw, 1817); Spanish translation (Madrid, 1821); Russian translation (Lipsk, 1845).

Edition with engravings by Thomas Stothard (London, 1792); with caricatures by Thomas Rowlandson (London, 1809); with sketches from designs by Maurice Leloir (New York, 1884); and by many others.

1769

Sermons / by / The late Rev. Mr. Sterne. / Vol. V. [VI, VII] / [Printer's ornament] / = / London: / Printed for W. Strahan; T. Cadell, / Successor to Mr. Millar; and T. / Beckett and Co. in the Strand. / M DCC LXIX.

Vol. V: 15 p.l. (Title; Contents of the Fifth Volume, 2 pp.; Subscribers, 24 pp.; Special title: "Sermon I. / Temporal Advantages of Religion."); [3]-172 pp. Vol. VI: 3 p.l. (Title; Contents of the Sixth Volume, 2 pp.; Special Title: "Sermon VII. / Trust in God."); [3]-174 pp. Vol. VII: 3 p.l. (Title; Contents of the Seventh Volume, 2 pp.; Special title: "Sermon XIII. / Asa: a Thanksgiving Sermon."); [3]-160 pp. 6 1/16 x 3 3/4.

Published June 10, 1769 (*London Chronicle*, June 10-13, 1769). Thereafter published in many editions with the earlier volumes.

German translation of Sterne's sermons began in 1766. There were several collections in German during the next ten years. French translation (Paris, 1786); Italian translation, selections (Milan, 1831).

A / Political / Romance, / Addressed / To —— —— Esq. / of / York. / London / Printed, and sold by J. Murdoch, bookseller, / opposite the New Exchange Coffe-house / in the Strand. / MDCCLXIX.

1 p.l. (Title); [iv]-ix [i.e., viii, vii omitted in numbering] (Advertisement); 1 leaf (List of characters, verso blank); [1]-35 pp.; [37]-47 (Postscript). 7⅟₁₆ x 4.

Published *circa* July, 1769.

This is a reprint, with numerous textual alterations, of the first half of *A Political Romance* as it appeared in 1759. The Key and the appended letters of the first edition are lacking. The Advertisement is mainly a re-working of a paragraph in the Preface to John Hall-Stevenson's *Yorick's Sentimental Journey Continued*, which had recently been published. The mutilated reprint was probably made from a copy of the 1759 edition which Sterne gave to Hall-Stevenson.

Reprinted with the title, *History of a Watch Coat*, in *Sterne's Letters to his Friends on Various Occasions* (London, 1775). Thence it passed into the edition of Sterne's *Works* (London, 1780), and into all subsequent editions of his *Works* claiming to be complete.

1773

Letters / from / Yorick to Eliza. / — / [Printer's ornament] / = / London: / Printed for W. Johnston, Nº. 16, / Ludgate-Street. / — / MDCCLXXIII.

3 p.l. (Title, Dedication: "To the Right Honourable / Lord Apsley, / Lord high Chancellor of England."); i-xviii (Preface); 64 pp. 6½ x 4.

Ten letters from Sterne to Mrs. Draper. Unnumbered.

Exact date of publication not determined. So far as observed, the volume was not advertised in the newspapers or given to the magazines for review. It appears to have been a semi-private publication. Letters III and IX reprinted with some editing in *The Matrimonial Magazine*, February, 1775.

The editor (who calls himself "the publisher" also) says of the letters that "with Eliza's permission" he "faithfully copied them at Bombay." That they were published from copies of the manuscript letters, with slight editing, is evident; for they show in a marked degree Sterne's peculiarities in style, spelling, abbreviation, and punctuation. It is equally evident, however, that numerous mistakes were made in reading the manuscripts and that corrections in the proofs were left to the printer. For example, the first letter has *summons* for *sermons;* and in the eighth letter, *y*ᵉ, Sterne's manner of writing *the* is printed *ye*. Still, the transcriber intended to be faithful to the manuscripts. Who he was is unknown. Three of Mrs. Draper's intimate friends had recently returned to England—Col. Donald Campbell, Mr. George Horsley, and a certain Mr. Gambier. For them see this biography. They had all, I daresay, "perused" the original letters.

Letters / from / Yorick to Eliza. / ═ / [Printer's ornament] / ═ / London, Printed: / Philadelphia, Re-printed, by John Dunlap, / in Market-street. / — / M, DCC, LXXIII.

1 p.l. (Title); [3]-4 (Dedication: "To the Right Honourable / Lord Apsley, / Lord High Chancellor of England."); 5-17 (Preface); 18-66 (Letters); 67-71 ("Mr. Sterne's acquaintance with Mrs. / Draper, is mentioned by him in the / following manner. Vide the 7th Vol. of / his works, page 113. / The Female Confucius."). 6¾ x 4¹⁄₁₆. Letters unnumbered.

A reprint of the London edition of the same year with the addition of *The Female Confucius* from *The Posthumous Works of a Late Celebrated Genius*, better known by its second title, *The Koran* (London, 1770), a forgery by Richard Griffith, so clever as to deceive even Goethe. See Chapter XXXIX of *The Koran.*

1774

A Letter written by the late Reverend Mr. Sterne. / Never before printed.

No date or place given.

In *The London Magazine*, XLIII, 136-137, March, 1774. Reprinted, as Letter V, "To * * * * * * * * * *," in *Sterne's Letters to his Friends* (1775); and probably from the manuscript, by Mrs. Medalle, as Letter LVIII, in *Letters of the late Rev. Mr. Laurence Sterne* (1775). Mrs. Medalle turns the ten stars into "To Mrs. M—d—s." [i.e., Meadows] and adds "Coxwould, July 21, 1765." Here and there the daughter corrected her father's idiomatic English.

An interesting letter concerning the loss of Sterne's house at Sutton by fire. Its authenticity, however, has been questioned. It appears to me to be in substance genuine, though the phrasing may have been considerably altered.

1775

Letters / from / Yorick to Eliza. / — / [Printer's ornament] / — / London: / Printed for T. Evans, / Near York-Buildings, Strand / MDCCLXXV.

LETTERS

FROM

YORICK TO ELIZA.

LONDON:

Printed for W. JOHNSTON, Nº. 16,
LUDGATE-STREET.

MDCCLXXIII.

Facsimile of Title Page to the First Edition of
"Letters from Yorick to Eliza"

1 p.l. (Title); [i]-ii (Dedication: "To the Right Honourable Lord Apsley, Lord High Chancellor of England"); iii-xix (Preface); 21-80 pp. 6⅛ x 3⅞.

Second London edition, though not so named. Ten letters. Unnumbered. With minor variations, text follows the first edition (London, 1773). Published March, 1775 (*Gent. Mag.*, XLV, 141, March, 1775).

Letters / from / Yorick to Eliza. / — / [Printer's ornament] / — / London, / Printed for G. Kearsly, at No. 46, in / Fleet-street; and T. Evans, near York- / Buildings, Strand. 1775.

1 p.l. (Title); [v]-vi (Dedication: "To the Right Honourable Lord Apsley, Lord High Chancellor of England,"); vii-xxiii (Preface); 80 pp. 5⅞ x 3¾.

Third edition, though not so named. Published April, 1775 (*London Magazine*, XLIV, 201, April, 1775).

Ten letters, numbered in this and later editions. Dedication and Preface of the preceding edition reprinted with a few corrections and alterations in the Preface. Seventh and eighth letters of the first and second editions arranged in reverse order. Text of letters varies from that of earlier editions in many details. The letters for this edition were probably set from another copy of the originals, perhaps supplied by Mrs. Draper. Though there is about the same number of obvious misreadings of the manuscripts in this edition, they are not always the same as in the two earlier London editions. Some changes in phrasing were made in the interest of a conventional style.

Letters / from / Yorick to Eliza. / A New Edition. / — / [Printer's ornament] / — / London, / Printed for G. Kearsly, at No. 46, in / Fleet-street; and T. Evans, near York- / Buildings, Strand. 1775.

2 p.l. (Half title: "Letters / from / Yorick to Eliza." Title); [v]-vi (Dedication: "To the Right Honourable Lord Apsley, Lord High Chancellor of England,"); 7-23 (Preface); [25]-104 pp. 6³⁄₁₆ x 3¹³⁄₁₆.

Fourth edition, though not so named. Preceding edition reset. This edition is described here because it has often been regarded as the first edition to appear in 1775. Dublin edition (1776). German translation by Bode (Hamburg, 1775); French translation by Frénais (Paris, 1776); Italian translation by Zambelli (Udine, 1836).

Sterne's Letters / to / His Friends / on / Various Occasions. / To which is added, his / History / of a / Watch Coat, / with / Explanatory Notes. / London, / Printed for G. Kearsly, at No. 46, opposite Fetter- / Lane, Fleet-Street; and J. Johnson, in / St. Paul's Church Yard. 1775.

1 p.l. (Title); [i]-vi (Introduction); 176 [i.e., 120] pp. (pp. 113-120 wrongly numbered 169-176). 6⅛ x 3¾.

Published July 12, 1775 (*London Chronicle*, July 11-13, 1775).

Thirteen letters, if we count the *Watch Coat* (a reprint of the abridged *Political Romance*), which is treated as a letter. Letters I-III comprise one of Sterne's letters to Garrick, Dr. John Eustace's letter to Sterne and Sterne's reply. Letters IV-V have generally been regarded as spurious, but they are, without much doubt, genuine. Letter V, which had appeared in *The London Magazine* for March, 1774, was to be published later in 1775 by Sterne's daughter from the original or a copy. Letter IX exists in Sterne's own hand; it is the letter to Mrs. Vesey dated "London June 20" in the Pierpont Morgan Library. (See this biography, Ch. XXV.) Letter X, in which Sterne refers to rumors of his death, may be accepted. So, too, Letter XII, on his library and books. There may be some doubt about Letters VI, VII, VIII, and XI, but they are, I think, genuine, though they must have been printed from imperfect copies or tampered with. The editor was probably William Combe.

Dr. Eustace kept a copy of his letter to Sterne, and the original of Sterne's reply; of which the latter is given in this biography (Ch. XX) as printed by G. J. McRee in *The Life and Correspondence of James Iredell*, I, 28 (New York, 1857).

Sterne's Letters / to / His Friends / on Various Occasions. / To which is added, / His History / of a / Watch Coat, / with / Explanatory Notes. / A New Edition. / London: / Printed for G. Kearsly, at No. 46, opposite / Fetter-Lane, Fleet-Street; / J. Johnson, in St. Paul's Church-Yard; / And T. Evans, in the Strand. / M DCC LXXV.

This is the first edition, with a new title-page. German translation by Bode (Hamburg, 1775); French translation by La Baume (Paris, 1788).

Letters / of the late / Rev. Mr. Laurence Sterne, / To his most intimate Friends. / With a / Fragment in the Manner of Rabelais. / To which are prefix'd, / Memoirs of his Life and Family. / Written by Himself. / And Published by his Daughter, Mrs. Medalle. / — / In Three Volumes. / — / Vol. I. [II, III] / — / London: / Printed for T. Becket, the Corner of the Adelphi, / in the Strand. 1775.

Vol. I: Frontispiece (Portrait of Lydia Sterne de Medalle engraved by Caldwall from a painting by West); 1 p.l. (Title); v-ix (Dedication: "To David Garrick, Esq."); xi (Epitaph); xiii-xiv (Preface);

xv-xvi ("In Memory of Mr. Sterne, author of / The Sentimental Journey."); xvii-xx ("A Character, and Eulogium of Sterne, / and his Writings; in a familiar Epistle / from a Gentleman in Ireland to his / Friend.—Written in the Year 1769."); [1]-25 ("Memoirs / of the / Life and Family / of the late / Rev. Mr. Laurence Sterne."); [27]-175 pp.; [1] p. (Advertisement). Vol. II: 1 p.l. (Title, the same as Vol. I, with the exception of the word "Prefixed" and a double rule after "Vol. II"); 192 pp. Vol. III: 1 p.l. (Title, same as Vol. II); [1]-163 pp.; [165]-179 (The Fragment). 6⅞₂ x 3¾.

Two letters are numbered XIV; a second letter appears as LXXVII with a star. All letters following LXXVII are misnumbered.

Published October 25, 1775 (*London Chronicle*, October 24-26, 1775). Preface dated "June 1775." At the same time Becket placed on sale a bronze bust of Sterne, "an exceeding good likeness."

This is the largest and best single collection of Sterne's letters as originally published. Of the 115 letters by Sterne brought together here, two (Nos. LVIII and LXXVI) had just been published from poor copies in *Sterne's Letters to his Friends*; but all the rest were new. Here also first appeared Sterne's brief *Memoirs of his Life and Family, An Impromptu*, and *The Fragment in the Manner of Rabelais*.

Reissued by Becket in 1776, without the frontispiece and with minor alterations and corrections.

Reprinted in Dublin, 1776, with the other collections of Sterne's letters of 1775. German translation (Leipzig, 1776); French translation (Paris, 1788).

1779

Genuine Letter of the late Rev. Mr. L. Sterne.

No date or place given. To whom written uncertain.

In *The Westminster Magazine*, VII, 400, August, 1779. Reprinted as Letter *CXXI* in Sterne's *Works* (1780). The manuscript has the superscription "York, Jan. 1. 1760." See Letter II in Chapter XXV of this biography.

1780

The / Works / of / Laurence Sterne. / In Ten Volumes Complete. / Containing, / I. The Life and Opinions of Tristram / Shandy, Gent. / II. A Sentimental Journey through / France and Italy. / III. Sermons.—IV. Letters. / With / A Life of the Author, / Written by Himself, / — / Volume the First. [-Tenth] / — / London: / Printed for W. Strahan, J. Rivington / and Sons, J. Dodsley, G. Kearsley, / T. Lowndes, G. Robinson, T. Cadell, / J. Murray, T. Becket, R. Baldwin, / and T. Evans. / M DCC LXXX.

Vol. I. The Life and Opinions of Tristram Shandy, Gentleman. Frontispiece (Portrait of Sterne engraved by I. K. Sherwin); 1 p.l. (Title); [iii]-vi (Advertisement); [vii]-xx (Memoirs); [4], 296 pp. Illustration.

Vol. II. The Life and Opinions of Tristram Shandy, Gentleman. 2 p.l. (Title, Half title); 307 pp. 2 illustrations.

Vol. III. The Life and Opinions of Tristram Shandy, Gentleman. 3 p.l. (Title, Half title, Dedication); 288 pp. Illustration.

Vol. IV. The Life and Opinions of Tristram Shandy, Gentleman. 4 p.l. (Title, Half title, Dedication); 264 pp. 2 illustrations.

Vol. V. A Sentimental Journey through France and Italy. Frontispiece (Portrait of Lydia Sterne de Medalle, engraved by Caldwell after West); 3 p.l. (Title, Half title); 242 pp. 2 illustrations.

Vol. VI. The Sermons of Mr. Yorick. [I-XIV]. 7 p.l. (Title, Half title, Preface, Contents, Half title); [3]-284 pp.

Vol. VII. Sermons by Laurence Sterne [XV-XXIX]. 4 p.l. (Title, Half title, Contents); 276 pp.

Vol. VIII. Sermons by Laurence Sterne [XXX-XLV] 4 p.l. (Title, Half title, Contents); 280 pp.

Vol. IX. Letters of the late Laurence Sterne to his most intimate Friends. 2 p.l. (Title, Half title); [v]-vii (Dedication); [ix]-x (Preface); [xi]-xii (In Memory of Mr. Sterne); [xiii]-xv (A Character and Eulogium of Sterne); [xvii]-xx (Contents); 209 pp.

Vol. X. Letters of the late Laurence Sterne: with a Fragment, in the manner of Rabelais; and The History of a Watch-Coat. 2 p.l. (Title, Half title); [v]-vii (Contents); 147 pp. [149]-159 (The Fragment); [161]-191 (History of a Watch-Coat); 192-198 (Postscript). 6¹¹⁄₁₆ x 4⅛.

Though there had been several so-called editions of Sterne's *Works* (in London, Dublin, and on the Continent), this is the first attempt at a critical edition, under the auspices of a group of London publishers including those who held the copyrights on the author's different publications. The portrait is a new engraving after Reynolds. In the Advertisement, the anonymous editor states the sound principles on which he proceeded. The Memoirs and the letters are briefly annotated, the letters are partially re-arranged and in some cases are given dates with other details that were absent in all earlier editions. The editor properly excluded *Yorick's Sentimental Journey Continued* (1769), which Hall-Stevenson claimed to have elaborated from Sterne's notes; *The Koran* (1770), a forgery by Richard Griffith; *Letters from Eliza to Yorick* (1775) and *Letters Supposed to have been Written by Yorick and Eliza* (1779), both of which were probably forgeries by William Combe. Of the 118 letters (115 by Sterne) in Mrs. Medalle's collection, the editor took 117, omitting, perhaps by mistake, Letter LVIII, to Mrs. Meadows. He took the ten letters of Yorick to Eliza, four other letters from the

anonymous *Sterne's Letters to his Friends on Various Occasions* (Nos.
II, III, XI, and XII in that collection), and from an unknown source
Letter CXXXI, which Sterne wrote on January 1, 1760, on the indecorums of *Tristram Shandy*. Altogether the editor assembled 132 letters,
of which only two are at all doubtful.

For translations of Sterne's works, genuine and spurious, into French,
see F. B. Barton, *Etude sur l'Influence de Laurence Sterne en France*
(Paris, 1911); into German, H. W. Thayer, *Laurence Sterne in Germany* (New York, 1905); into Italian, Giovanni Rabizzani, *Sterne in
Italia* (Rome, 1920).

1788

Original Letters / of / The late Reverend / Mr. Laurence Sterne; /
Never before published. / — / London: / Printed at the Logo-
graphic Press, / and sold by / T. Longman, Pater-Noster Row;
J. Robson, / and W. Clarke, New Bond Street; and / W. Richardson, under the Royal / Exchange. / 1788.

2 p.l. (Half title, Title); 216 pp. 7⅜ x 4½.

Thirty-nine letters from Sterne to various friends, of which thirty
had appeared in *The European Magazine* (February, 1787-February,
1788) and two in *The County Magazine*, Salisbury (December, 1787,
and January, 1788). Some of the letters are of doubtful authenticity,
and others have certainly been tampered with; but several of them are in
substance genuine beyond reasonable doubt. The persons to whom they
were addressed have been only partially identified. "Mrs. V——" is
Mrs. Vesey; "Lady C—H" is Lady Caroline Hervey; and "W.C.Esq."
is probably William Combe, Esq., who appears to have been responsible
for the publication.

Three of these letters Combe revamped for his periodical called *The
Pic Nic* (February 19, March 5 and 26, 1803); and several of them
have been reprinted by Lewis Melville in *The Life and Letters of
Laurence Sterne* (London, 1911). French trans. (The Hague, 1789).

1793

The so-called Hay letter.

In *The Gentleman's Magazine*, LXIII, Pt. II, 587-588, July, 1793.
Reprinted in Sterne's *Works, Letters and Miscellanies*, I, 124-126 (New
York, 1904), and in Lewis Melville's *The Life and Letters of Laurence
Sterne*, I, 92-93 (London, 1911). Supposed to have been addressed "to
a neighboring clergyman soon after the publication of the early volumes
of *Tristram Shandy*."

1806

Letter to Mr. Whatley [At Mr. Stratton's in Lothbury,] March 25,
1761.

In *The Monthly Repository of Theology and General Literature*, I, 406-407, August, 1806. Reprinted in *Life and Times of Laurence Sterne*, 255 (New York, 1909), and again in Chapter X of this edition.

1835

Facsimile of a letter to Garrick (January, 1762) with a view of the "Parsonage House Coxwold, Yorkshire. The Residence of Revd Laurence Sterne." (C. J. Smith, London, 1835.)

In Sterne's *Works, Letters and Miscellanies*, I, 208 (New York, 1904). Often reprinted. Reproduced in Walter Sichel's *Sterne, A Study* (London, 1910), and elsewhere.

1836

Letter to [Robert] Dodsley [October, 1759].

Concerning the publication of *Tristram Shandy*.

In T. F. Dibdin's *Reminiscences*, Pt. I, 207-208, note (London, 1836). Reprinted in Sterne's *Works, Letters and Miscellanies*, I, 127-129 (New York, 1904), and elsewhere, and again apparently from the original manuscript in Ralph Straus's *Robert Dodsley*, 261-263 (London, 1910).

1838

Letter to Mr. Pitt, "Friday, Mr. Dodsley's, Pall-Mall." [i.e., probably Friday, March 28, 1760].

In *Correspondence of William Pitt, Earl of Chatham*, II, 12 (London, 1838).

1841

Letter to William Warburton, Bishop of Gloucester, dated "Coxwould, June 19, 1760."

In Francis Kilvert's *A Selection from Unpublished Papers of the Right Reverend William Warburton*, 242-245 (London, 1841), with Warburton's reply dated Prior Park, June 26, 1760, 245-246. Reprinted by John Selby Watson in *The Life of William Warburton*, 504-506, 506-507 (London, 1863).

1844

Seven / Letters / Written by / Sterne and His Friends, / Hitherto Unpublished. / — / Edited by / W. Durrant Cooper, F. S. A. / — / London: / Printed for Private Circulation, / By T. Richards, 100, St. Martin's Lane. / — / 1844.

1 p.l. (Title); [iii]-v (Dedication: "To John Thomas Wharton, Esq. of Skelton Castle."); [1] p. (Contents, verso blank); [1]-20 (Letters, etc.); [21]-23 (Notes). 7⅜ x 4⁹⁄₁₆.

Only two of the letters are by Sterne—to Hall-Stevenson. They are dated "Paris, May 19, 1764," and "Coxwould, Dec. 17, 1766."

1852

Letter to Mrs. Sterne at York, dated "Paris, March 15, 1762."

In *Notes and Queries,* first series, V, 254, March 13, 1852. Contributed by H.A.B. Reprinted in Sterne's *Works, Letters and Miscellanies,* I, 214-217 (New York, 1904), and Lewis Melville's *The Life and Letters of Laurence Sterne,* I, 301-304.

1856

Unpublished Letters of / Laurence Sterne. [In *Miscellanies of the Philobiblon Society*, Vol. II. London, Printed for Charles Whittingham, 1855-56.]

[1] (Half title); [3]-7 (Introduction signed John Murray); 7-20 (XIII Letters). 8¼ x 6⅛.

Thirteen letters—twelve from Sterne to Catherine de Fourmantelle, and one which he wrote for her to copy and send to Garrick. The Introduction by John Murray, the publisher (1808-1892), gives the history of the manuscripts so far as he knew it. Five of the letters had previously appeared in an article on Sterne by Isaac D'Israeli in his *Miscellanies of Literature* (London, 1840).

1857

Letter to Mr. Becket, "Coxwould, Sept. 3, '67."

In *Notes and Queries,* second series, IV, 126, August 15, 1857. Contributed by Edward Foss.

1864

The Life / of / Laurence Sterne. / By / Percy Fitzgerald, M.A., M.R.I.A. / With Illustrations from Drawings by the Author / and Others. / In Two Volumes / Vol. I. [II] / London: / Chapman & Hall, 193, Piccadilly. / 1864.

Includes from manuscript three letters (with parts of others) from Sterne to the Rev. John Blake (I, 318-325); three letters to Archbishop Drummond, Paris, May 10, 1762, Toulouse, May 7, 1763, Coxwould, October 30, 1764 (II, 192-194, 217-219, 239-241); and two letters to Lord Fauconberg, January, 1767 (II, 330-331).

1870

Fragment inédit / — / To Mr. Cook

In Paul Stapfer's *Laurence Sterne—Sa Personne et ses Ouvrages—Étude précédée d'un Fragment inédit de Sterne,* [xv]-xlix (Paris, 1870). (English and French on opposite pages.)

Reprinted as "The Dream, To Mr. Cook," in Sterne's *Works, Letters and Miscellanies,* II, 268-281 (New York, 1904).

1873

The / Works / of / Laurence Sterne, / In Four Volumes, / with / A Life of the Author, / Written by Himself. / — / A New Edition, with Appendix, Containing Several Unpublished / Letters, &c. / — / Edited by / James P. Browne, M.D. / Vol. I [II, III, IV] / London: / Bickers and Son, 1, Leicester Square, W. C. / H. Sotheran and Co., 136, Strand. / — / 1873.

Some of the editions of Sterne's *Works* between 1780 and 1873 are interesting for a variety of engravings after the portrait by Reynolds or for many illustrations—notably by Stothard and Cruikshank. But none of these intervening editions contains any of the new material published after 1780. Dr. Browne, however, adds in an Appendix to his fourth volume the following: Sterne's letter to Warburton, Coxwould, June 19, 1760; Warburton's reply, June 26, 1760; the two letters from Sterne to Hall-Stevenson from Cooper's *Seven Letters;* the letters to Miss Fourmantelle; the three Blake letters from Fitzgerald; and the Fragment addressed to Mr. Cook from Stapfer.

Letter to Becket, dated "Paris, Oct. 19, 1765."

In *Notes and Queries,* fourth series, XII, 244-245, September 27, 1873. Reprinted in Sterne's *Works, Letters and Miscellanies,* II, 96 (New York, 1904).

1892

Three letters of Sterne: To Mr. Becket, Toulouse, March 12, 1763; To Mr. Becket, Paris, March 20, 1764; and To M. Panchaud, Florence, December 18, 1765.

Catalogue of the Collection of Autograph Letters and Historical Documents formed between 1865 and 1882 by Alfred Morrison, VI, 182, & plate 153 (London, Printed for private circulation, 1892).

The second letter is reproduced in facsimile, plate 153.

Reprinted in Sterne's *Works, Letters and Miscellanies,* II, 21-22, 49, 100 (New York, 1904). The first and third also reprinted in Lewis Melville's *Life and Letters of Sterne,* II, 22-23, 95-96.

1894

"Two Unpublished Letters of Laurence Sterne."

In *The Archivist*, VII, No. 27, 40-41, September, 1894. Contributed by E. Barker.

The first is the letter published, in a mutilated form, in Sterne's *Works*, X, 138-141 (London, 1780). The second, To David Garrick, dated York, January 27, 1760, reprinted in Lewis Melville's *Life and Letters of Laurence Sterne*, I, 212-213.

1896

The Life / of / Laurence Sterne / by / Percy Fitzgerald / Author of 'The Life of Garrick,' / 'The Lives of the Kembles,' 'Bozland,' etc. / With a Portrait / In Two Volumes / Vol. I. [II] / Downey & Co. / 21 York St., Covent Garden, London / 1896

Adds quotations from Sterne's copy book used at school (I, 9-10); two letters to Archdeacon Blackburne, Sutton, November 3 and November 12, 1750, the second letter not quite complete (I, 59-66); letter to Jaques Sterne, April 5, 1751, incomplete (I, 68-79); eight more letters to Blake (I, 82-94); letter to a York chemist, probably his friend Henry Jubb (I, 95); letter to Mr. Berenger, March, 1760 (I, 160-161); extracts from the *Journal to Eliza* (II, 138-142, 207-210); and draft of a letter to Daniel Draper (II, 144-145). A part of this new material Fitzgerald had incorporated in an anonymous article entitled "Sterne at Home," which he contributed to *The Cornhill Magazine* (New Series, XIX, 482-492, November, 1892).

1903

Four letters to Earl Fauconberg: Paris, April 10, 1762; Montpelier, September 30, 1763; London, [January 9?, 1767]; Bond Street, January 16, 1767.

In Historical Manuscripts Commission. *Report on Manuscripts in Various Collections*, II, 189-192 (London, 1903). Reprinted in Sterne's *Works, Letters and Miscellanies*, I, 225-228; II, 37-40, 132-133, 134-135 (New York, 1904).

1904

The / Works and Life / of / Laurence Sterne. [With an Introduction by Wilbur L. Cross. J. F. Taylor & Company, New York, 1904.]

"York Edition. The Sutton Issue of the Life and Works of Laurence Sterne, printed at The Westminster Press, New York, is limited to Seven Hundred and Fifty Sets." ["The Stonegate Edition," limited to 150 sets.]

[V. 1-4] The Life and Opinions of Tristram Shandy, Gentleman. In four volumes.

[V. 5-6] The Sermons of Mr. Yorick. [I-XLV] In two volumes.

[V. 7] A Sentimental Journey through France and Italy.

[V. 8-9] Letters and Miscellanies, I-II: Anecdotes; Letters of the Late Rev. Mr. Laurence Sterne to his Most Intimate Friends; Unpublished Letters; Miscellanies: The History of a Good Warm Watch-Coat, The Fragment; An Impromptu, A Dream, The Unknown World—Verses occasioned by hearing a Pass-Bell.

[V. 10] The Journal to Eliza and Various Letters taken from the Gibbs Manuscripts and other Sources, mostly published now for the first time.

[V. 11-12] The Life of Laurence Sterne by Percy Fitzgerald. [Revised by the Editor.] In two volumes.

Illustrations.

Re-issued in six volumes by "The Clonmel Society." New York and London. Edition limited to One Thousand sets.

Major and minor collections of Sterne's letters broken up and all letters placed, as nearly as could be determined, in chronological order. A few individual letters overlooked; and no letters taken from the volume of 1788, then believed to be wholly spurious. Contains also, from the Gibbs Manuscripts in the British Museum, various letters of Mrs. Draper and *The Journal to Eliza* complete.

Two years later I found three of the four copies of the first edition of *A Political Romance* now known to exist, which, with a considerable body of unpublished letters, became available for *The Life and Times of Laurence Sterne* (1909). Still other letters appear for the first time in subsequent editions of this biography.

Since 1904, better texts of many letters have become available. Nor do I now stand by several statements I then made.

1906

Letter to Mrs. Elizabeth Montagu.

Undated, probably written in the spring of 1761.

In *Elizabeth Montagu, the Queen of the Blue-Stockings*, by Emily J. Climenson, II, 175-176 (London, 1906). Reprinted in Lewis Melville's *Life and Letters of Laurence Sterne*, I, 282-283; also from the manuscript in Chapter XXV of this biography.

"Memorandums left with Mrs. Montagu in case I should die abroad. December 28, 1761."

In *Elizabeth Montagu, the Queen of the Blue-Stockings*, by Emily J. Climenson, II, 270-272.

Reprinted by Melville, I, 289-291, by William H. Arnold in *Ventures in Book Collecting*, 163-166 (New York, 1923), and from the manuscript in Chapter XXV of this biography.

1909

Letter to Mr. Hesselridge of London, dated "York, July 5," [1765].

In *The Life and Times of Laurence Sterne*, by Wilbur L. Cross, 349 (New York, 1909).

1914

A Political Romance / By / Laurence Sterne / [1759] / An Exact Reprint of the First Edition / With an Introduction by / Wilbur L. Cross / Author of "The Life and Times of Laurence Sterne" / [Printer's mark] / = / Boston / The Club of Odd Volumes / 1914 /

2 p.l. (Half title: A Political Romance &c., Title); [i]-xv (Introduction); 1 leaf (Title); [1]-24 (A Political Romance, &c.); 25-30 (Postscript); 31-47 (Key); [48] (blank); 49-52 (Letter "To ―― ――, Esq; of York."); 53-60 (Letter "To Dr. Topham."). 8⅜ x 5. On leaf at end: "One hundred and twenty-five copies printed for The Club of Odd Volumes, Boston, in the month of October, 1914. Bruce Rogers."
Printer's ornaments reproduced.

1915

Laurence Sterne's / Letter / to the / Rev. Mr. Blake / [Printer's ornament] / Privately printed from / original in possession of / William K. Bixby / St. Louis, Mo. / MCMXV

2 p.l. (1st: "Laurence Sterne," verso blank; Title, verso: "Two hundred copies of this edition were printed, of which this is number ――." At bottom, right: The Torch Press Cedar Rapids, Iowa.); 5-6 (Letter with introductory paragraph); Folded leaf (Photographic reproduction). 9 x 6½.
This letter to Blake had never before been published entire.

1923

Three letters to Mrs. Elizabeth Montagu.

Undated, but assigned by Blunt to May, 1767, February, 1768, and March, 1768. "May, 1767" should probably be June, 1764 or 1765.
In *Mrs. Montagu, "Queen of the Blues." Her Letters and Friendships*

from 1762 to 1800, edited by Reginald Blunt, I, 190-193 (London, 1923).

Letter to Sir William Hamilton, dated Rome, March 17, 1766.

In William H. Arnold's *Ventures in Book Collecting*, 173-174 (New York, 1923).

II.

Manuscripts

IN this part of the bibliography the aim is to give a list of the existing Sterne manuscripts, so far as they are known to the writer, with the addition of other manuscripts which, though they may no longer exist, have been mentioned in various places since the beginning of the nineteenth century. Such a summary catalogue for 1929, though necessarily incomplete, should be welcome to all who are interested in the literary fortunes of Laurence Sterne. As time goes on, the miscellaneous manuscripts (which have a speculative value) will pass from one collector to another, and eventually, it is to be hoped, find a resting place in the great libraries of England and the United States. But that is a far-off event, and in the meantime it is well to know where the scattered manuscripts uneasily repose in this year of grace.

An exact description of the manuscripts has not been regarded as so important as a list of them. Still, some bibliographical details, where easily obtainable, are given. All measurements—height and width of leaves—are by inches. The leaves of the Letter Book in the Pierpont Morgan Library, to which frequent reference is made, measure 7¾ x 6⅜ inches.

Unless otherwise expressly stated, the manuscripts are in Sterne's own hand.

1725-1728

Synopsis Communium Locorum ex Poetis Latinis Collecta.

A book Sterne used at the Halifax Grammar School, "scrawled over with writing, sketches, repetitions of his own name and those of his fellows."—Fitzgerald, *Life of Laurence Sterne*, I, 9-10 (London, 1896). Present ownership unknown.

1739-1747

The Parish Registry at Sutton-in-the-Forest.

A long narrow book, containing on inside of one cover and elsewhere a list of Sterne's ecclesiastical appointments, comment on the expense of making over the parsonage house, etc. Most of the entries of baptisms, marriages, and burials are in the hand of Sterne's curates. Those in Sterne's hand begin with Easter Tuesday, 1739, and close with the birth and baptism of his daughter Lydia, December 1, 1747. See Chapter II of this biography.

1743

Reply to a *questionnaire* concerning the affairs of his parish at Sutton-in-the-Forest, sent out by Archbishop Herring in May, 1743.

Among the manuscripts of the Archbishop of York at Bishopsthorpe. For a résumé of the contents see S. L. Ollard, "Sterne as a Young Parish Priest," in *The Times Literary Supplement*, March 18, 1926, and Chapter II of this biography.

The Unknown ☉.

See Chapter VI of this biography. Present ownership unknown.

A Receipt, dated December 31, 1743.

Formerly in the collection of the late John Boyd Thacher, of Albany, New York. Sold at the Anderson Galleries, January 10, 1916. Present ownership unknown.

Circa 1743

A letter to Mr. Cook.

Describing a dream. Manuscript owned by a lady at York in 1868. Fate of the manuscript unknown. See Chapter VI of this biography.

1750

Penances. Sermon XXXVII in the printed collections.

Thirty leaves, versos usually blank except for corrections and additions. $7\frac{1}{2}$ x $4\frac{1}{2}$, except last leaf, which measures $7\frac{1}{2}$ x $3\frac{1}{4}$.

Near the end is the endorsement: "Preached April 8th 1750. Present Dr. Herring, Dr. Wanly, Mr. Berdmore." In the Pierpont Morgan Library.

Our Conversation in Heaven. Sermon XXIX in the printed collections.

Near the end is the endorsement: "Made for All Saints and preached on that Day 1750 for the Dean.——Present: 1 Bellows Blower, 3 Singing men, 1 Vicar & 1 Residentiary.—Memorandum: Dined with Duke Humphrey." Once seen by Isaac Reed (1742-1807). Present ownership unknown.

Letter to Francis Blackburne, Archdeacon of Cleveland.

Dated Sutton, November 3, 1750. Two leaves, address on back. 12⅜ x 8⅛. In British Museum (Egerton MSS. 2325, f.1).

Immediately following this letter in the Egerton MSS. is a letter of Dr. Jaques Sterne to Archbishop Blackburne, dated York, December 6, 1750. Two leaves. 9¼ x 7¼. It has in another hand the interlinear description: "Mr Jaques Sterne—reprobation of his nephew Yorick— & mention of the Papist nunnery at York.—" First published in *Letters and Miscellanies*, I, 85-88, in Sterne's *Works* (New York, 1904).

Letter, Sutton, November 12, 1750.

Two leaves, versos blank. No address, but written to the Rev. Francis Blackburne, Archdeacon of Cleveland. 8¾ x 7¼.

First published, in part, by Percy Fitzgerald in *Life of Laurence Sterne*, I, 64-66 (London, 1896). Never published entire. In the collection of Mr. R. B. Adam, Buffalo, N. Y.

1751

Letter to Dr. Jaques Sterne.

Dated April 5, 1751. Written at Sutton. Six leaves. 12½ x 8¼. In the British Museum (Additional MSS. 25479, f.12).

This letter, which is not in Sterne's hand, is accompanied by the following note: "Copied by permission of Mr. Rob. Cole of Upper Norton Street from a copy carefully made by some person for Mr. Godfrey Bosvile formerly of Gunthwaite and bought by Mr. Cole with many other papers of the Bosviles, July 25, 1851."

The copy made for Mr. Godfrey Bosville (as he spelled his name) has recently come to light. It is owned by Mr. Lewis Perry Curtis, of New Haven, Conn., who purchased it of a York dealer. The copy, which forms a part of Mr. Bosville's Commonplace Book, was made towards the end of the eighteenth century. The fate of the original autograph letter is unknown.

1758

Letters to the Rev. John Blake, Master of the Grammar School at York.

Several written on foolscap, pages measuring 12⅛ x 7¼. Others on smaller paper. One measuring only 7⅜ x 6⅛ inches. Formerly belonged to Mr. A. H. Hudson of York, who received them from his father. Endorsed: "1756. Original Letters from the Revd L. Sterne to the Revd J. Blake. 16 in number." One of the letters is dated 1758; and most of them appear to have been written in that year. Broken up and sold for two pounds apiece, *circa* 1872.

Three in the Pierpont Morgan Library. One in the collection of Mr. R. B. Adam, Buffalo; one in the collection of H. H. Raphael (Sichel, 68); and one, long in the collection of Mr. W. K. Bixby of St. Louis, recently purchased by the Brick Row Book Shop, New York. One formerly owned by Mr. A. H. Joline, New York; one by George T. Maxwell, New York; and another by Charles Scribner's Sons. One formerly in the Alfred Morrison Collection. Twelve published by Fitzgerald (1896) and Cross (1904), and one by Bixby (1915).

1759

Letter to Robert Dodsley.

Undated. Written *circa* October, 1759. Manuscript apparently used by Ralph Straus in his *Robert Dodsley*, 261 (London, 1910). Present ownership unknown.

1759-1760

Letters to Miss Catherine de Fourmantelle.

Twelve letters addressed to Miss Fourmantelle. Twenty-two leaves, varying in size. And one letter placed in her hands to copy and send to Garrick—one leaf written on both sides, 7¼ x 6⅛. In the Pierpont Morgan Library.

A receipt shows that John Murray paid thirteen pounds and thirteen shillings for the copyright of these letters, March 16, 1818.

Ante 1760

Temporal Advantages of Religion. Sermon XXVIII in the printed collections.

Twenty-six leaves. Twenty-six pages written in full, the remainder for the most part consisting either of text references or interpolations, made with a view to publication. Formerly in the collection of the late Frederick Locker-Lampson, and later in that of Mr. W. K. Bixby. It is enclosed in a wrapper addressed to Rev. Dr. Clarke and bearing the autograph of Henry Fauntleroy, the banker and forger. Present ownership unknown.

The Ways of Providence Justified to Man. Sermon XLIV in the printed collections.

A perfunctory sermon, like the preceding, clearly belonging to the Sutton period, though its date cannot be precisely determined. Once seen by Isaac Reed (1742-1807). Present ownership unknown.

Letter to a York Chemist.

Dated "Sutton, Wednesday". Probably addressed to Sterne's friend, Henry Jubb, a York apothecary. The manuscript of this letter, clearly belonging to the pre-Shandean period, was formerly in the possession of Percy Fitzgerald.—*Life of Laurence Sterne*, I, 95 (London, 1896). Present ownership unknown.

1760

Sterne's copy of a draft of a letter to some unknown person who had warned him against the indecorums of Tristram Shandy.

Dated "York, Jan. 1, 1760". Five pages of the Letter Book. The manuscript of this letter as it passed through the post was formerly in the collection of Mr. E. Barker, 41 Gunterstone Road, West Kensington, by whom it was published in *The Archivist*, September, 1894 (Vol. VII, No. 27, p. 40). Present ownership unknown.

Letter to David Garrick.

Dated "York, Jan. 27, 1760". Two leaves, second leaf blank. 9⅛ x 7⅜. In the Pierpont Morgan Library.

Agreement with James Dodsley for the sale of the copyright of *Tristram Shandy*, Vols. I-IV, to the publisher.

Written by Sterne. "Dated Mar. 8, 1760". Signed: "L. Sterne, Ja⁸ Dodsley," and "Rich⁴ Berenger" as witness. One irregular sheet. *Circa* 6⅞ x 7¾. In the collection of Mr. A. S. W. Rosenbach.

Letter to Richard Berenger.

Dated "Saturday". Written in March, 1760. Two leaves. Address on back: "To Mʳ Berenger Suffolk Street". 8⅞ x 7⅜. Also Sterne's draft of this letter. Two pages of the Letter Book. Both in the Pierpont Morgan Library.

Letter to William Pitt, enclosing for the statesman's information (his approval being taken for granted) the Dedication of the Second Edition of the first instalment of Tristram Shandy: "To the Right Hon. Mr. Pitt".

Dated "Friday" [i.e., Friday, March 28, 1760]. Published from the manuscripts preserved by Pitt, in *Correspondence of William Pitt, Earl of Chatham*, edited by Taylor and Pringle, II, 12-13 (London, 1838). Fate of these manuscripts unknown.

Letter to Bishop Warburton.

Dated Coxwould, June 19, 1760. Printed from the manuscript by Francis Kilvert in *A Selection from the Unpublished Papers of William Warburton*, 242-245 (London, 1841). This letter was afterwards cut into transverse strips, one of which is now owned by Dean Maxcy of Williams College. Width of MS. 7⅜ inches. The last part of this letter was sold by Sotheby, December 21, 1928.

Sterne's copy of a letter to Miss Mary Macartney.

Undated. Written at Coxwold in June, 1760. Four pages of the Letter Book.

Sterne's copy of a letter from "Mr Brown to J. Hall Esqre".

Dated Geneva, July 25, 1760. Three pages of the Letter Book.

Letter to "My Witty Widow," Mrs. F——.

Dated Coxwould, August 13, 1760. Supposed to have been addressed to Mrs. Ferguson. Two leaves. Last page blank. Sold by Sotheby, London, June 21, 1922. Present ownership unknown.

Sterne's copy of a letter to "Mr Brown of Geneva".

Dated "York Sept. 9, 1760". Four pages of the Letter Book.

Tristram Shandy. Book IV.

A copy of the first seventeen chapters was in the family of Turner of Kirkleatham, Yorkshire, in 1859. W. Durrant Cooper, who saw the manuscript, thought that it was not as a whole an autograph copy. The concluding sentences of the seventh and fifteenth chapters, however, were, in his opinion, in the hand of Sterne himself by way of corrections. Charles Turner, to whom the manuscript was given, is mentioned in this biography as one of Sterne's friends. See W. Durrant Cooper in *Notes and Queries*, January, 1859 (second series, VII, 15). The fate of this manuscript (which may be an autograph) is unknown. Its date should be October or November, 1760.

The Fragment in the Manner of Rabelais.

Twenty-five leaves, apparently the leaves of a book. First and last leaves blank. Written on one side except for minor alterations on two versos. 7⅝ x 4¾.

Manuscript differs considerably from the text as published by Mrs. Medalle in 1775 and all subsequent editors. In the Pierpont Morgan Library.

The Fragment, as originally written, was a mad piece of ribaldry, probably intended for the fourth book of *Tristram Shandy*, and discarded on the protest of Stephen Croft, who thought Sterne was going too far in this instalment of his book. See Sterne's letter to Croft from London on Christmas day, 1760, and compare *The Fragment* with the anecdote about Phutatorius in the fourth book of *Tristram Shandy*. The manuscript may be tentatively assigned to the autumn of 1760.

1761

Letter to George Whatley, Treasurer of the Foundling Hospital.

Dated London, March 25, 1761. Found among Whatley's papers and published by J. T. Rutt (*The Monthly Repository of Theology and General Literature*, I, 406, August, 1806; and III, 9, January, 1808). Fate of this letter unknown.

Letter to Mrs. Elizabeth Montagu.

Undated. Probably written in the spring of 1761. Two leaves. Verso of second leaf blank. 9⅛ x 7⅜. Formerly a part of the Montagu MSS. In the Pierpont Morgan Library.

Sterne's copy of a letter to Mrs. Elizabeth Vesey.

Dated "London, June 20". Probably written in June, 1761. Three pages of the Letter Book.

An Agreement to pay the Rev. Marmaduke Collier sixteen pounds a year as curate of Sutton-in-the-Forest.

Dated September 6, 1761. In the Library of the Dean and Chapter at York.—Sir Sidney Lee, article on Sterne in *Dict. Natl. Biog.* (LIV, 209).

Tristram Shandy. Book V.

Walter Shandy's address to Health, in the first paragraph of the thirty-third chapter. Clearly not a part of the original manuscript as it went to the printer, but a copy which Sterne made and signed Sterne, for some friend. Underneath his name is written in another hand, "died 1768." The earliest date for the fragment is the autumn of 1761. In the collection of A. Edward Newton.

Tristram Shandy. Book VI.

The story of Le Fever down to "As this letter came to hand" in the seventeenth chapter was long preserved at Spencer House, St. James's Place, London. Over the manuscript Lord Spencer wrote: "The Story of Le Fever, sent to me by Sterne before it was published."—*Appendix to Second Report of the Historical Manuscripts Commission*, p. 20 (London, 1871). Apparently Sterne completed the Story of Le Fever by October, 1761. Manuscript, presumably an autograph, was sold *circa* 1898. Present ownership unknown.

Memorandums left with Mrs. Montagu.

Dated December 28, 1761. Two leaves. 12⅝ x 7⅞. Formerly a part of the Montagu MSS. In the Pierpont Morgan Library.

1762

Letter to David Garrick, requesting the loan of twenty pounds.

Undated. Written in London early in January, 1762. One leaf, written on one side. 4⅜ x 6¼. This "historic missive" was acquired many years ago by the late Adrian H. Joline, and after his death by the late William H. Arnold. Sold at the Anderson Galleries, February, 1926.

Letter to Mrs. Sterne at York.

Dated Paris, March 15, 1762. Contributed by H. A. B. [i.e., Henry Arthur Bright?] to *Notes and Queries*, March 13, 1852 (first series, V, 254). Present ownership unknown.

Letter to the Earl of Fauconberg.

Dated Paris, April 10, 1762. In the library of Sir Henry Herbert Wombwell, Newburgh Priory, Yorkshire.

Letter to Becket.

Dated "Paris, 12, 1762". The month is April. Two leaves. 8¾ x 7. In the British Museum (Egerton MSS. 1662, f.5).

Letter to Mr. Foley at Paris.

Dated Toulouse, Wednesday, December 8, 1762. In the Forster collection in the South Kensington Museum.

1763

Letter to Becket.

Dated Toulouse, March 12, 1763. The letter is endorsed: "Mr. Sterne Ansd April 7th. 1763. The state of Shandy, viz: Sold 182, Remnant 991, Accd for before 2827, No printed 4000". Formerly in the Alfred Morrison Collection. Present owner, W. G. Pegg, Rothley, England.

Letter to Mr. Foley, Paris.

Dated Toulouse, March 29, 1763. Two leaves. Written on first leaf only. Address on back. Seal torn away. Formerly in the library of Mr. Robert Hoe, New York. Sold at the Anderson Galleries, January 22, 1929.

Letter to Becket.

Dated "Bagneres [i.e., Bagnères] de Bigorre, Gascoigne en France,

July 15, 1763". Two leaves. Written on two pages. Address on back. Seal. 8¾ x 6⅞. In British Museum (Additional MSS. 21508, f.47).

Letter to the Earl of Fauconberg.

Dated Montpellier, September 30, 1763. In the library of Sir Henry Herbert Wombwell, Newburgh Priory, Yorkshire.

Letter to Becket.

Dated Montpellier, October 18, 1763. Two leaves. Address on back. 9 x 7⅛. The letter is endorsed: "Mr. Sterne Ans^d Novr 22^d 13 16." It is an enquiry concerning the number of sets of *Tristram Shandy* sold since April 7, and the balance due on account—£13, 16s. In the collection of Mr. Frank B. Bemis.

Letter to "Mr. Mills, Merchant, Philpot Lane, London, Angleterre".

Dated "Montpellier Nov.24.1763". Two leaves. Written on two inside pages only. Address on back. 8⅞ x 7. Formerly in the Huth Library. In the Pierpont Morgan Library.

1764

Letter to Becket.

Dated Paris, March 20, 1764. One leaf. Formerly in the Alfred Morrison Collection. Present owner, W. Marchbank, Newcastle-on-Tyne.

Letter to John Hall-Stevenson.

Dated Paris, May 19, 1764. In 1844 the original was at Skelton Castle.—W. D. Cooper, *Seven Letters written by Sterne and his Friends.* Present ownership unknown.

Letter to Mrs. Elizabeth Montagu.

No superscription. Endorsed in another hand "Aug 1765." Probable date, June, 1764, or *circa* June 1, 1765. Written on journey from London to York. Four leaves. Written on three pages. 8⅞ x 7. Elizabeth Montagu manuscripts. In the Huntington Library.

Sterne's copy of a Letter to "Calypso."

Superscription, "York". No date. Probable date, June, 1764. "Calypso" may be a disguise for the Countess of Edgcumbe, daughter of John Gilbert, Archbishop of York. Four pages of the Letter Book.

Letter to Mr. Foley.

Dated York, August 26, 1764. Formerly in the collection of A. H. Joline. Sold at the Anderson Galleries, February, 1927.

Sterne's copy of a letter to Miss Sarah Tuting.

Dated Coxwould, August 27, 1764. Four pages of the Letter Book.

Letter to Mr. Foley.

Dated York, November 11, 1764. Two leaves. Written on three pages. Address on back: "A Monsr Foley Banquier rue St Saveur a Paris". 9¼ x 7½. Formerly in the collection of the late W. H. Arnold. In the Pierpont Morgan Library.

1765

Sterne's copy of a letter to Mrs. F——.

No place or date in the superscription. Probably written in London, *circa* May 1, 1765, and addressed to a lady Sterne had recently met at Bath—perhaps a Mrs. Fenton. Six pages of the Letter Book.

Sterne's copy of a letter signed Jenny Shandy, Bath.

No date. Author was some unknown admirer at Bath. The letter appears to belong to the late spring or summer of 1765. One page of the Letter Book.

Letter to "—— Hesselridge Esqre at Lord Maynards".

Dated "York, July 5" [1765]. Two leaves. Fourth page blank. 9¼ x 7⅜. For Thomas Hesselridge and this letter, see index of this biography. Formerly owned by Samuel Rogers, the poet. In the Widener Collection, Harvard University Library.

Letter or Letters to Lord Effingham.

Written in the summer of 1765 to Thomas Howard, third Earl of Effingham, then a young man in his nineteenth year. Quoted by Fitzgerald, *Life of Laurence Sterne*, II, 72-73 (London, 1896). Present ownership unknown.

Sterne's copy of a letter to Lord Spencer.

Dated "Coxwould Oct. 1. 1765". Two pages of the Letter Book.

Letter to Becket.

Dated Paris, October 19, 1765. Contributed anonymously to *Notes and Queries*, September 27, 1873 (fourth series, XII, 244-245). Formerly (1904) owned by Percy Fitzgerald and later (1906) by Robson & Co., London. Present ownership unknown.

Letter to Mr. Foley.

Dated "Turin Nov: 15, 1765". Two leaves. Written on first page only. Address on back: "Messieurs Foley and Panchaude Banquiers Rue S⸍ Saveur a Paris". 8⅞ x 7¼. In the Pierpont Morgan Library.

Letter to Mr. Panchaud.

Dated "Florence, Dec 18, 1765". One leaf. Seal. Formerly in the Alfred Morrison Collection. Sold by Quaritch in 1924.

1766

Letter to Sir William Hamilton, British Envoy at Naples.

Dated "Rome March 17, 1766". Two leaves. Address on fourth page. 9⅛ x 7⅜. Formerly in the collection of the late W. H. Arnold. Sold at the Anderson Galleries, November 11, 1924. Present owner, Miss Maud Motley, Rochester, New York.

Letter to Dr. Jemm [i.e., Dr. Richard Gem] at Paris.

Written in Rome and dated "Easter Sunday" [March 30, 1766]. Two leaves. Address on back and "N.B. To be given to Mr. Symonds when he pass'd by Rome". 9⅛ x 7⅜. Formerly in the Great Album of Frederick Locker-Lampson. Present ownership unknown.

Sterne's copy of a letter from John Hall-Stevenson.

Dated "Crasy Castle July 13 – 1766". One page of the Letter Book.

Sterne's copy of his reply to the preceding letter.

Dated "Coxwould July 15. 1766". Three pages of the Letter Book.

Sterne's copy of a letter from Ignatius Sancho.

Dated "July 21. 1766". Four pages of the Letter Book.
Sterne's copy of his reply to the preceding letter.

Dated "Coxwould July 27 – 1766". Three pages of the Letter Book.

Letter to John Hall-Stevenson.

Dated "Coxwould, Dec. 17, 1766". In 1844 original at Skelton Castle.—W. D. Cooper, *Seven Letters*. Present ownership unknown.

1767

Sterne's Copy of a letter to —— ———.

Dated "London Bond Street Jan – 6 – 1767". Evidently addressed to some young man, who may have been William Combe. Three pages of the Letter Book.

Letter [to the Earl of Fauconberg].

Dated "London Jan 6 1767 Bond Street." Two leaves. Second leaf blank. 9 x 7½. In the collection of Mr. A. S. W. Rosenbach.

Letter to the Earl of Fauconberg.

Dated "Friday [Jan. 9], 1767". In the library of Sir Henry Herbert Wombwell, Newburgh Priory, Yorkshire.

Letter to the Earl of Fauconberg.

Dated "Bond Street [London], Jan. 16, 1767". In the library of Sir Henry Herbert Wombwell, Newburgh Priory, Yorkshire.

A Receipt, in Sterne's hand, dated "January 21, 1767," for two hundred and five pounds, seventeen shillings, paid him by "Becket and Co" as the balance of the account due him "to this day."

One leaf. 3¾ x 6⅝. In the collection of Mr. Harold Murdock.

The first letter from Yorick to Eliza.

Copy in Mrs. Draper's hand. No date; but January, 1767. Printed from copy in this biography, Ch. XIX. In the collection of Lord Basing at Hoddington, Odiham, Hants.

Letter to Mr. Panchaud.

Dated, "London Feb. 27" [1767]. Two leaves. Written on first page only. Address on the back. Endorsed. 9 x 7⅜. In British Museum (Additional MSS. 33964, f.381).

Letter from Yorick to Eliza.

One sheet. Undated; but February or March, 1767. Inserted in a copy of *The Matrimonial Magazine* (1775).

Draft in Sterne's hand, from his Letter Book, of one of his letters to Mrs. Draper. 17 lines in ink and 12 lines in pencil. Manuscript varies from printed version. Memorandum on the back: "This page from Sterne's Letter-Book was given me by Miss Heard, the Gr. Grand Daughter of Mrs. Draper, who possessed the duplicate letter, with many others of the eccentric author, whose sentiment it appears was of that plodding character, that he wrote his love letters first in a book, and having bequeathed his papers to Eliza, her family possess both the copies and originals of all their correspondence." Sold by Robson & Co., London, *circa* 1906. Present ownership unknown.

Continuation of the Bramines Journal; i.e., The Journal to Eliza.

April 13, 1767—November 1, 1767. Forty leaves: 1-15, 13 x 7⅞; 16-40, 12½ x 7⅞.

The Journal to Eliza forms a part of the MSS. that came to the

British Museum in 1894 under the bequest of Thomas Washbourne Gibbs, of Bath (Additional MSS. 34527, ff.1-40). For further details, see Chapter XIX of this biography.

An Agreement, dated May 30, 1767, in Sterne's hand, between Sterne and the Rev. Mr. Walker, whereby the latter consents to act as curate at Stillington for forty pounds a year and the use of the vicarage house there.—*Appendix to the Sixth Report of the Hist. MSS. Commission,* 474 (London, 1877).

Sterne's draft or copy of a letter to Mrs. Draper.

Dated "Coxwould June 18". The year is 1767. Seven pages of the Letter Book.

Letter to Mr. and Mrs. James.

Dated Coxwould. "August 10, 1767". Text differs much from the letter as published by Mrs. Medalle. Addressed to "Mrs. James in Gerard Street, Soho, London". Lord Fauconberg's frank. Two leaves, 9 x 7⅜. Among the Gibbs MSS. in the British Museum (Additional MSS. 34527, ff.41-42).

Draft of a letter to Daniel Draper.

Undated. Probably written in the summer of 1767. Two leaves. 11⅛ x 8. Among the Gibbs MSS. in the British Museum (Additional MSS. 34527, ff.45-46).

This letter is followed in the Gibbs MSS. by a long letter from Mrs. Draper to "Mrs. Anne James," written on rice paper. Dated "Bombay 15th April, 1772," and signed "E. Draper". Twenty-three leaves. 11⅜ x 7½.

Letter to Becket.

Dated "Coxwould, Sept. 3, 1767". Published from manuscript in possession of Edward Foss in *Notes and Queries,* August 15, 1857. In the collection of Mr. A. S. W. Rosenbach.

Letter to Hannah.

This is the last part of the letter to "Mrs. H." as edited by Mrs. Medalle, with the superscription, "Coxwould, October 12, 1767." See *Letters of the Late Rev. Mr. Laurence Sterne* (London, 1775). One leaf, 5 x 7. In the collection of Mr. Harold Murdock.

Letter to Hannah.

No date, no address. But in a mutilated version as printed by Mrs. Medalle, there is the superscription: "Coxwould, November 15, 1767".

See letter LXXXIX in *Letters of the late Rev. Mr. Laurence Sterne* (London, 1775). One leaf. 8¾ x 7. In the collection of A. Edward Newton.

A Sentimental Journey &c – – – &c – – –

Manuscript of the first volume, with numerous alterations as Sterne prepared it for the press, *circa* November or December, 1767. A clear copy in Sterne's hand. 174 leaves. 8 x 6. Versos blank except for corrections. Printer's memorandum at top of first leaf: "13 sheets, N⁰ 2500, 150 fine". A letter with the manuscript gives its history from Sterne's own time. In the British Museum (Egerton MSS. 1610).

A Sentimental Journey &c – – – &c – – –

Manuscript covering both volumes. Partly in Sterne's hand, but mainly in two other hands, perhaps his wife's and daughter's. Bound in two volumes. Vol. I: 1 p.l. (Title); 174 leaves. Vol. II: 1 p.l. (Title); 184 leaves. 8 x 6¼. Versos blank. In addition each volume has two blank leaves—one before the title, and one after the text. Bookplate of "The Hon! Martha Agnew of Lochnaw." "M. Agnew" written at head of text of each volume. Text of first volume varies in places from text of the manuscript in the British Museum. Text of second volume, hence of both volumes, varies from text of first edition. Copy in part or as a whole made in the autumn of 1767, and probably presented to a member of the family of Sir Andrew Agnew (1687-1771). Apparently the Martha Agnew, into whose possession the manuscript came, was the Hon. Martha de Courcy, who married in 1792 Andrew Agnew, grandson of Sir Andrew. In the Pierpont Morgan Library.

Letter dated "York, Tuesday".

Two leaves. Written on first and third pages. No address. Endorsed. This unpublished letter gives directions about sending subscription copies of the *Sentimental Journey* out to India in care of Mr. George Stratton at Fort St. George. Probably written in December, 1767, the week before Sterne set out for London, where he arrived on the third of January. Letter must have been addressed to Becket (or his agent Mr. Edmunds). In the library of Mr. R. B. Adam, Buffalo, N. Y.

Letter to Mr. or Mrs. James.

Dated "December 28, 1767". Passages deleted by Mrs. Medalle in printed version. Two leaves. 8⅞ x 7¼. Original cover, with address "To Mr. or Mrs. James, Gerrard Street, Soho, London". Among the Gibbs MSS. in the British Museum (Additional MSS. 34527, ff.43-44).

1768

Letter of Dr. John Eustace to Sterne, and Sterne's reply, February 9, 1768.

A copy of Dr. Eustace's letter and the original of Sterne's reply discovered among the papers of James Iredell, Associate Justice of the U. S. Supreme Court. The two letters were published by G. J. McRee in *Life and Correspondence of James Iredell*, I, 27-28 (New York, 1857). Sterne's letter reprinted from McRee in Chapter XX of this biography. Fate of these manuscripts unknown.

Letter to Mrs. Elizabeth Montagu.

Probable date, February, 1768. In the collection of Mr. A. M. Broadley—Melville, II, 310.

Letter to Mrs. Elizabeth Montagu.

No superscription. Written in London, *circa* February 15, 1768. Two leaves. Written on first page only. Address on back. 9 x 7¼. Elizabeth Montagu manuscripts. In the Huntington Library.

Letter to Mrs. Elizabeth Montagu.

No superscription. Written during Sterne's last illness, probably in the first week of March, 1768. Two leaves. Written on three pages. Address on back. Seal. 9 x 7¼. Elizabeth Montagu manuscripts. In the Huntington Library.

Sterne's Accompt Book, covering the Sutton and Coxwold periods, showing what he received from his publishers, etc.—*The Whitefoord Papers*, edited by W. A. S. Hewins, 230 (Oxford, 1898). Fate of this book unknown.

Letters to the Rev. Daniel Watson.

According to Nichols (*Literary Anecdotes*, VIII, 343) there were extant in 1814 unpublished letters between Sterne and Daniel Watson, Vicar of Leake near Coxwold. Nothing has since been heard about them.

INDEX